CHINESE AMERICA
HISTORY AND PERSPECTIVES
2007

SPECIAL 20TH ANNIVERSARY ISSUE

Branching Out the Banyan Tree:
A Changing Chinese America
Conference Proceedings

榕華風貌

美國華人發展研討會論文集

CHINESE HISTORICAL SOCIETY OF AMERICA

Proceedings Sponsors

Dr. Kenneth Fong, California State University
Board of Trustees

Him Mark and Laura Lai

Lawrence Choy Lowe Memorial Fund

Chao Suet Foundation

Poon Foundation

San Francisco State University
   College of Ethnic Studies, Dean's Office,
   Dr. Kenneth P. Monteiro
   President's Office, Dr. Robert A. Corrigan

Chinese Community Health Care Association

Chinese Community Health Plan

H&P Editorial Committee

Colleen Fong, PhD, Committee Chair

Lorraine Dong, PhD, Proceedings Coordinator

Marlon K. Hom, PhD

Russell Jeung, PhD

Him Mark Lai

Laurene Wu McClain, JD

Ruthanne Lum McCunn

Ivy Wong, Proceedings Assistant

© 2007 by Chinese Historical Society of America
Conference Logo and Design: Vivian Young
Proceedings Design and Layout: Mark Stuart Ong,
Side By Side Studios
Copy Editing: Elisabeth Beller
Printed in USA by Thomson-Shore, Inc.

ISBN 1-885864-30-2

Contributors to *Chinese America: History and Perspectives 2007* express their own opinions, which may not necessarily be the views of the publisher.

Articles appearing in this journal are abstracted and indexed in *Historical Abstracts and America: History and Life*.

Publisher
Chinese Historical Society of America
965 Clay Street
San Francisco, CA 94108.
www.chsa.org

Sponsor
Asian American Studies Department
College of Ethnic Studies
San Francisco State University
1600 Holloway Avenue
San Francisco, CA 94132
www.sfsu.edu/~aas

Dedicated to Conference Honorees
Philip P. Choy and Him Mark Lai

Contents

Twenty Years of *Chinese America: History and Perspectives*

Him Mark Lai

In 1985, the Chinese Historical Society of America (CHSA) appointed Him Mark Lai, Fayette Taylor, and Judy Yung to serve on an editorial board assisting *CHSA Bulletin* editor Annie Soo. During a meeting of the group, Taylor raised the point that the *Bulletin's* format was too restrictive. It was awkward to publish longer historical essays because they would have to be printed in several installments. He suggested that CHSA start a new publication tentatively named *Occasional Papers* to provide a platform for such writings. His motion was passed unanimously and subsequently approved by the CHSA board under President Vyolet Chu. The board appointed Lai and Yung to be the editors of the intended publication, and in October 1985, an announcement was placed in the *Bulletin* calling for the submittal of papers.

In anticipation of the reviewing and editing tasks to prepare this intended annual collection of essays on Chinese American history and society, the editors invited author Ruthanne Lum McCunn to join them on an Editorial Committee. When the Committee met to decide upon a name for the publication, Lai suggested *Chinese America: History and Perspectives*. All present agreed on the title and the first issue was made available at the annual CHSA dinner held in early 1987, when Ted Wong was president.

CHSA volunteers did the typing and proofreading for the first two volumes, which was funded by donations from members and friends. Russell Leong of *Amerasia Journal* gave valuable advice. Don McCunn of Design Enterprise did the necessary production work to prepare the volume for publication. (Design Enterprise closed down after the second issue.) The committee then struck an agreement in 1989 with Asian American Studies (AAS) Department in San Francisco State University (SFSU), wherein CHSA was the publisher and the latter became a sponsor of the publication. Marlon K. Hom joined the Editorial Committee as the SFSU-AAS representative while Ted Wong was added on the CHSA side. George K. Woo, AAS chair at the time, and Michael C.M. Hornbuckle became respectively, production manager and assistant, to do the necessary computer production work. However, that arrangement was found to be too cumbersome for efficient production and AAS sponsorship was dropped beginning with the 1993 issue, although Hom remained on the editorial board.

Based on the experience gained in publishing the previous issues, it was decided to use professional help for the copy-editing, proofreading, and computer production work, a procedure that has been followed to the present time. In 1996, Hom was elected AAS chair and SFSU-AAS again became a sponsor of the journal beginning with the 1997 issue. The next year, increasing costs led to a decision to change the journal size from 6 x 9 to the current and a more cost-effective 8½ x 11 format.

For the early issues up to and including the 1993 issue, Catherine Brady did the copy-editing and the following volunteers did the remaining production work:

Typing: Annie Soo, Lillian Louie, Lorraine Dong, Marlon K. Hom

Proofreading: Daniel Chu, Betty and Bob Schwendinger, Edmund Jung, Annie Soo, Lillian Louie, Ted Wong, Laurette Lau, Suzanne Lo, Laurene Wu McClain, Haw Chan Jung, Emily Zukerberg

Fundraising: Vyolet Chu, Edmund Jung

The following have generously donated and supported the publication over the years up to and including the 2006 issue:

Fong Brothers Printing Inc., Grants for the Arts of the San Francisco Hotel Tax Fund, Lawrence Choy Lowe Memorial Fund, Candelaria Fund, Imperial Palace Restaurant, Tom Memorial Fund, Vallejo-Napa Chinese Club, Mr. and Mrs. Ernest Chann, Bruce Chin, Mr. and Mrs. Kenneth W. Chinn, Sr., Mr. and Mrs. Thomas W. Chinn. Philip and Sarah Choy, Vyolet L. and Daniel Chu, Herbert H. Gee, Yuji Ichioka and Emma Gee, Mr. and Mrs. Edmund D. Jung, Jeannette and William Kim, Him Mark and Laura Lai, Jennie L. Lee, Mrs. Moon Lim and Carole Lee, Pauline Lee, Robert Lee, Madeleine Leong, Russell Leong, Enid Lim Ng, Mr. and Mrs. David K. Low, Eve Armentrout Ma, James G. and Annie Soo, Vincent Tai, Dr. George S. and Florence Sue Wong, Mrs. H.K. Wong, and Ted. S. Wong.

The current special edition is funded by:

Kenneth Fong, Him Mark and Laura Lai, Lawrence Choy Lowe Memorial Fund, Chao Suet Foundation, Poon

Foundation, SFSU College of Ethnic Studies Dean's Office, SFSU President's Office, Chinese Community Health Care Association, and Chinese Community Health Plan.

Over the years the following have served on the Editorial Committee for *Chinese America: History and Perspectives*:

Him Mark Lai (1985-present)

Judy Yung (1985-1994, 1995-1996)

Ruthanne Lum McCunn (1985- present)

Marlon K. Hom (1988-present)

Ted S. Wong (1988)

Laurene Wu McClain (1990-present)

Colleen Fong (1992, 2000-present)

Lillian Louie (1993-2000)

Vitus Leung (1996-2000)

Madeline Hsu (1997-2005)

Beth Wilson (2001-2003)

Russell Jeung (2006-present)

Lorraine Dong (2006-present)

Going into its twenty-first year *Chinese America: History and Perspectives* remains a community-based journal that makes the research of lay and academic researchers available to the general public as well as the scholarly community. It has published more than 150 articles on aspects of Chinese American history and society in its twenty issues. The journal not only published original research papers on Chinese American history and society, but frequently also included primary source documents and oral histories. Another unique feature is that the journal coverage is not limited to papers written in English, but also selected essays and documents translated from Chinese language literature in the field, a treasure trove that has barely been tapped in the United States. It should be noted that although *Chinese America: History and Perspectives* is currently the oldest continuously published scholarly journal on Chinese American history and society, it was not the earliest. That honor belongs to *Annals of the Chinese Historical Society of the Pacific Northwest*, the first volume of which was published under the editorship of Douglas Lee in 1983; the *Annals* ceased publication with a third issue in 1985-1986.

Branching Out the Banyan Tree:
A Changing Chinese America
Conference Proceedings
Introduction
Lorraine Dong, PhD

The 2007 issue of *Chinese America: History and Perspectives* celebrates two milestones. First, it marks the 20th anniversary of the journal. Second, it contains the proceedings of the Chinese American town and gown conference, "Branching Out the Banyan Tree: A Changing Chinese America," that was held October 6 to 9, 2005, at the Radisson Miyako Hotel in San Francisco. It was thirty years ago that the Chinese Historical Society of America sponsored the first Chinese American conference in the nation. The 2005 conference is the 7th in the series of Chinese American conferences that CHSA initiated.

From July 10 to 12, 1975, the first Chinese American conference entitled, "The Life, Influence and the Role of the Chinese in the United States, 1776-1960," was held at the University of San Francisco with an attendance of 350-400. CHSA planned it in observance of America's bicentennial and it was endorsed by the American Revolution Bicentennial Administration and the San Francisco Twin Bicentennial, Inc. A proceedings was published with approximately 35 papers.

At the time of CHSA's founding in 1963, the academic disciplines of Asian American Studies and Ethnic Studies did not exist, and CHSA was the only institution established and dedicated to the study of Chinese American history. As Asian American Studies and Ethnic Studies began to take their place in the academe in the fall of 1969, additional Chinese American historical societies, museums, and organizations began to emerge throughout the country. In 1980, the Chinese Culture Foundation of San Francisco held a conference in conjunction with the opening of its "Chinese of America" exhibit, and invited CHSA to be a cosponsor. Its proceedings was entitled, "The Chinese American Experience: Papers from the Second National Conference of Chinese American Studies." It took another twelve years for the third Chinese American Studies conference to occur in 1992, when the Chinese Historical Society of Southern California in Los Angeles became the next sponsor. At this point, Stanley Mu of CHSSA initiated and pushed the concept of conferences to be hosted in turn by various Chinese American historical societies. Three more conferences resulted, sponsored by the Hawaii Chinese History Center in Honolulu in 1994, the Museum of Chinese in the Americas in New York in 1997, and the Chinese Historical Society of Greater San Diego and Baja California in San Diego, California in 1999.

Much has happened to the study of Chinese American history since 1975. Instead of only one organization devoted to Chinese American history, we had 18 historical societies, museums, and organizations dedicated to Chinese American history that attended the 2005 conference. They came from around the country, including Canada and Australia, and met together for the first time as a caucus on October 8 (see "Special Sessions"). And, instead of only community organizations interested in researching their own history, we now have Asian American Studies and Ethnic Studies in the academe acknowledging and researching Chinese American history, hence the union of CHSA and the Asian American Studies Department at San Francisco State University as lead cosponsors of the conference.

The mission and vision of the conference, as reflected in the town and gown union of CHSA and AAS at SFSU, were to open a multidimensional Chinese America for all to share. The conference had an attendance of 800-plus, 350 of whom were high school and university students learning side by side with people from both the community and academe. Over 250 participants from the community and academe presented their research and thoughts. Of these, 58% came from the community, 30% came from the academe, and 12% were students from high school and college. About 4 high schools and 60 colleges/universities were represented. There were also 13 panels sponsored by community organizations. In addition, members from 18 Chinese American historical societies and organizations presented papers and/or represented their organizations at the caucus. Attendees and presenters came from all over the United States as well as internationally from Canada, Australia, China, and Taiwan.

In accordance with the multi- and interdisciplinary nature of Chinese American Studies, the conference had 8 diverse tracks: gender and family; health; immigration and settlement; political activism; regional history; religion; representation: media, literature, and the arts; transnational perspectives; and youth and education. Among the 76 sessions, 11 were new book talks, 9 were documentaries or sneak peeks, and 4 were bilingual or Chinese language panels (see "Special

Sessions"). This was also the first time for CHSA and in the conference's thirty-year history that a Chinese-language track of four sessions and a track of two sessions comprised of high school student panelists were included as an integral part of the conference.

In addition, San Francisco State University's President's Office sponsored a special one-day high school program at the conference for 50 high school students. And, on the last day of the conference, participants went on four field trips: (1) China Camp and the shrimp junk *Grace Quan* with John Muir of the San Francisco Maritime National Historical Park, (2) the town of Locke with the assistance of the Locke Management Association, (3) the National Archives and Records Administration Regional Facility in San Bruno with Archives Director Daniel Nealand, and (4) San Francisco Chinatown with historian Philip Choy.

Highlighting the conference were three keynote speakers and two honorees. The opening luncheon, entitled "Town and Gown: A Mutual Commitment," featured two distinguished individuals who represented town and gown respectively: community activist and former California Department of Education Deputy Superintendent Henry Der, and California State University Chancellor Charles B. Reed. Both focused on education as their main topic (see "Luncheon Keynote Speeches"). The conference banquet keynote speaker was former Washington State Governor Gary Locke, the first Chinese American elected to be governor in U.S. history. The two conference honorees were Philip P. Choy, who celebrated his 79th birthday in December and Him Mark Lai, who celebrated his 80th birthday in November. Both men received their UC Berkeley undergraduate degrees in architecture and mechanical engineering, respectively, and both researched and studied Chinese America as a "hobby" before the existence of CHSA or Ethnic Studies. Together they taught the nation's first Chinese American history course at San Francisco State University in fall of 1969. Choy and Lai were dubbed the Grand Historians of Chinese America, and before an audience of 500-plus, their birthdays were celebrated with a memorable tribute at the conference banquet event entitled "Making History" (see "Banquet Tribute").

The Third World Student Strike in the fall of 1968 at San Francisco State University involved students and faculty from the academe as well as the community. One of its goals was to make the academe and community accountable to each other. It was in this spirit that the title of "Branching Out the Banyan Tree" was conceived. The banyan tree was chosen as the conference symbol because it is one of nature's most noble and respected creations. For the Chinese, especially those from the Pearl River Delta, the banyan tree is the core of the village, representing family, home, community, and communication. It is under this banner that the 2005 Chinese American Studies conference was held to unite community and academe.

The diversity of the town and gown conference is reflected in the 2007 special issue of *Chinese America: History and Perspectives*. The 56 conference papers and summaries presented here are written in both English and Chinese, and by individuals from a variety of backgrounds: professors with PhD degrees, educators, high school and college students, doctors, health professionals, community activists, artists, writers, filmmakers, and average citizens whose pastime is just to learn about Chinese America in general. Topics of research and interest are no longer simply about immigrant, first generation Chinese Americans from China. They now include Chinese people coming to America from all parts of the world, Chinese Americans who are 4th and 5th generation, and Chinese Americans of mixed heritage as well as LGBT (lesbian, gay, bisexual, and transgender) Chinese Americans. Chinese American Studies has expanded from being regional to being global and transnational, not only geographically but also culturally and conceptually.

All conference presenters were given the opportunity to submit their papers or summaries of their presentations. Shorter summaries for those who did not wish to submit anything can be found in the sections entitled "Conference Sessions" and "Special Sessions." The longer summaries and papers are grouped thematically, based on the eight conference tracks. Articles within each track are arranged numerically according to their original conference session number. All materials in the proceedings are published in their original form as tendered by the presenters. The affiliations and status of the conference participants also have not been changed from what they were at the time of the conference. Copy editing corrected only grammatical points, and submissions have not been scrutinized for their content. Note that the papers and summaries reflect the opinions and views of the respective authors, and not that of the Chinese Historical Society of America or the AAS Department at San Francisco State University.

Planning for the conference took over three years. The Chinese Historical Society of America and the Asian American Studies Department at San Francisco State University are deeply appreciative of everyone who have supported the conference and its proceedings. It took many sponsors and volunteers to make it possible for town and gown to unite and gather under the banyan tree, where everyone learned mutually from each other about Chinese America's new and unfinished history in the 21st century.

Conference Planning Committee

Lorraine Dong, PhD,	Russell Jeung, PhD
Alexander Lock, and	Him Mark Lai
Jeannie Woo, co-chairs	Sue Lee
Donald Chan	Marisa Louie
Colleen Fong, PhD	Russell Ow
Marlon K. Hom, PhD	Leonard Shek
Madeline Y. Hsu, PhD	Ivy Wong

Making History

Conference Banquet Tribute to
Philip P. Choy and Him Mark Lai

Marlon K. Hom, PhD

Professor, Asian American Studies Department, San Francisco State University
Resident Director, California State University International Programs in Beijing

Editor's Note: Philip P. Choy and Him Mark Lai, renown Chinese American pioneer historians, were the "Branching Out the Banyan Tree" conference honorees. At "Making Waves," the October 7, 2005 conference banquet, CHSA hosted a birthday celebration in honor of Chinese America's two "Grand Historians." Choy and Lai requested Marlon K. Hom to be the emcee and introduce them. Preceding the introduction was a ten-minute DVD presentation of their lives, entitled "America's Most Wanted."

Good Evening Friends,

As shown on the screen, these two gentlemen are "most wanted"—but not by the FBI. They are most wanted in the field of Chinese American history. They are our elders, in both age and knowledge. They are Chinese America's venerable pioneers, not vulnerable pensioners. They are armed with wisdom, not weapon; they are generous, not dangerous. They have dedicated themselves to research, preserve, advocate, and disseminate Chinese American history. They are Philip P. Choy and Him Mark Lai, lifetime members and leaders of the Chinese Historical Society of America and Adjunct Professors in the Asian American Studies Department at San Francisco State University.

When Chinese American Studies began at San Francisco State after the 1968 Third World Student Strike, it was a time of desperation to find support to build and develop this new academic program in higher education. However, most of the Chinese scholars in American university campuses would not touch, let alone lend their professional support to this new discipline because of the societal perception of it being a short-lived, radicalized, political movement which would eventually disappear in no time. Yet, Phil and Him Mark were there, offering themselves to teach the first Chinese American history class in the country. With that beginning, Chinese American history began its existence and has become a pivotal course in the Asian American Studies curriculum.

Their class syllabus became a 1971 publication entitled, *Outlines: History of the Chinese in America*. This publication, with its yellow cover, didn't make them rich—no tenure, no promotion. But ever since its publication, *Outlines* has defined the direction on how to study Chinese American his-

tory. As of today, teachers and scholars still follow the framework of *Outlines* for their lectures and research. As I see it, Mao Zedong had his little "Red Book" for China's Cultural Revolution. Phil and Him Mark have their "Yellow Book" for our Chinese American history restoration. By the way, both books were extremely popular during the 1970s in Asian American Studies.

Phil and Him Mark are role models for Chinese American Studies' paradigm of community service and involvement. Many younger scholars in the Asian American Studies arena know about their research, but they hardly know that both men have been active in the community since the 1950s. As a leader of the Mun Ching Club in San Francisco Chinatown, Him Mark helped young Chinese immigrants to adjust to their new life in America. He stubbornly resisted governmental surveillance and harassment during the dark era of McCarthyism and rendered his support to the Mun Ching Club members who were constantly victimized because of their immigration status. Some years later, he also wrote columns on Chinese American history for progressive community newspapers, and produced a community radio hour called *Hon Sing* to highlight Chinese culture and community news.

Phil volunteered his services in many community organizations and involved himself in historical landmark preservation. Most significant, in 1969, at the Transcontinental Railroad Centennial at Promontory Point, Utah, Phil was there, standing up and standing tall. He challenged the centennial organizers and America for overlooking the Chinese Americans, and ignoring the contributions and sacrifices of the Chinese railroad workers, thousands of whom died building the railroad in the 1860s. In the 1869 Promontory Point celebration of the completion of the transcontinental railroad, the Chinese workers were ignored, despite the fact that they laid the most tracks in one day and saved millions of dollars for the Central Pacific Railroad Company. One hundred years later at the centennial, there was still no public acknowledgement of the Chinese workers. It was Phil who took a CHSA commemorative plaque to be mounted onsite at Promontory Point, reclaiming, finally, after one hundred years, our ancestors' contributions and sacrifices in this nation-building project.

Together with Him Mark as historical consultants, Phil participated in and narrated *Gam Saan Haak* 金山客, the first extensive documentary on Chinese American history. Both men worked behind the camera to bring Chinese American history to the audience. To me, *Gam Saan Haak* is still more historically enriching than the recent big-budget million-plus dollar PBS production; and *Gum San Haak* was made more than twenty years ago with a pitiful budget and limited resources.

Phil and Him Mark are known to travel extensively to many old and contemporary Chinese American communities. They are also known for restaurant hopping in search of good food. Imagine, Him Mark and Laura in their big Buick, and Phil and Sarah in their little sport car—first the Plymouth Barracuda, and more recently, a Toyota MR2 and a Celica GTS—cruising around like the Chinese Bonnie and Clyde, all over North America, up and down California, not to rob banks but to check out various restaurants and Chinatowns and urban redevelopment sites where old Chinatowns were once located. They are, in a way, conducting original field survey with lots of fun. And what Chinese American scholar would think of doing such a thing except Phil and Him Mark?

As pioneers, Phil and Him Mark have always been, and still are, doing things that no one would think of doing. In the early 1970s, American-born scholars in Chinese American Studies would not deal with our ancestral connection in China, across the Pacific Ocean. That was a Chinese American insecurity and internalized response to institutional racism that contributed to Chinese American Studies being perceived by a racist and ignorant mainstream America as a foreign area study. Him Mark was among the very first few who, in the late 1970s, broke that self-imposed barrier. Like the late Yuji Ichioka, Him Mark differs from most people by advocating the importance of Asian language materials as being imperative to Chinese American Studies. He published two Chinese language reference catalogues, one on newspapers and one on books, to point out that Chinese language materials on the Chinese in America, published in both America and China, are necessary for a full understanding of the Chinese American experience. Ever since then, research on the emigrant regions of southern China, from where most of the pre-1965 Chinese Americans originated, began to appear, making Chinese American Studies more comprehensive and inclusive. Also of note is that Him Mark took a Chinese American history pictorial exhibit to Mainland China to educate the Chinese about the Chinese American experience. (However, Him Mark didn't bring the massive exhibit back. Too heavy, he said. I think it is because the content of this exhibit is so valuable that it became a state secret. As we all know: state secrets in China remain in China and it is a crime to take any state secret out of the country.)

Then in the 1990s, Him Mark started the In Search for Roots Program for young Chinese Americans to visit their ancestral homes in the Pearl River Delta. And, he was instrumental in the publication of our society's annual journal: *Chinese America: History and Perspectives*, the only journal dedicated to Chinese American Studies. All of Him Mark's activities were pioneering and led to many similar activities.

Meanwhile, Phil reveals another pioneering dimension in Chinese American Studies. His onsite research of big and small towns and ghost towns, illustrates that hands-on field studies will yield invaluable historical information beyond what armchair researchers can provide. Phil's field work on the old and forgotten sites of early Chinese American settlements in the foothills of the Mother Lode to the civic centers of Sacramento, San Francisco, and other California cities, shows that early Chinese Americans were everywhere in the building of America's West. Phil provides the best evidentiary testimony to reclaim our legacy and its deserved recognition in American history.

As far as I am concerned, Phil and Him Mark are the *yin* and *yang* of Chinese American history. Each holds his own and together, they are a dynamic unity. Their latest collaborative effort is the permanent Chinese American history exhibit at our CHSA Museum and Learning Center: *The Chinese of America: Towards a More Perfect Union*. Yes, this exhibit's message is crystal clear: we are the Chinese OF America, not just IN America. And yes, we do need a MORE perfect union and we are working towards that goal. Lorraine and I were also in this project, hence some people have called us the CHSA "gang of four"; but we are not the same as the Gang of Four of China. We do not destroy past history. We work together to preserve, not purge, our Chinese American experience. Besides, Lorraine and I were constantly trying to catch up and learn from their vast knowledge, putting together their wisdom for the exhibit. For over two years, we met every week and worked together to meet the deadline to inaugurate the grand opening of the CHSA Museum and Learning Center at 965 Clay Street. Specialists of Overseas Chinese Studies from China have told me that the CHSA permanent exhibit is the best they have ever seen in North America—accurate historical information, precise text, rich message, and elegant presentation.

These two elders, Phil and Him Mark, are still enjoying their work on Chinese American history. Are they doing it alone? Not at all. Whenever I am with them, I'll see Sarah and Laura by their side: Yes, Sarah and Phil, Laura and Him Mark. These names actually have a rhyme scheme. In the Cantonese vernacular, these two couples are the classic case of the "糖藕豆." In our American vernacular, they stick to each other like glue!

This year is the 80th birthday for Him Mark and the 79th birthday for Phil. Together they are older than the California Gold Rush 156 years ago. Indeed, they are the gold standard of Chinese American history. It is my fortune and honor that you have both asked me to introduce you tonight. To Phil and Him Mark: Happy Birthday!

*On October 9, 2005, Phil and Him Mark received two surprise presents: They were the first to receive emeritus board status created that year by the Chinese Historical Society of America Board of Directors. Choy and Lai were also awarded the San Francisco State University President's Medal in recognition of their contributions to the development and scholarship of Chinese American Studies. This is the highest honor that a California State University president can bestow upon an individual.

美國華人歷史的兩位太史令----
為麥禮謙先生胡垣坤先生祝壽

譚雅倫 撰

諸位所在銀幕看到的照片裏的兩個人，並不是美國聯邦調查局要通緝的罪大惡極的逃犯。他們是美國華人歷史領域裏，最受歡迎，最爲人敬仰的人物。他們也不是一般的領養老金過日子的退休老人，而是我們社區的德高望重的博學前輩。他們身懷絕技，但是懷的不是殺人絕招，而是驚人學識。他們兩位，獻身爲研究，保存，發揚美國華人歷史而努力。他兩位就是美國華人歷史學會的元老，美國華人歷史研究的前輩與今日美國華人歷史的權威，舊金山州立大學亞裔研究系的兼職教授一麥禮謙和胡垣坤兩位老先生。

1968年的第三世界學生運動推動之下，舊金山州立大學成功地創辦了全國首個美國華裔研究項目。當年這個革新的大學課程極需要大學裏的華裔學者支持；但大學裏許多華裔學者怕事而保持距離，不願意出面支持這個從美國民權運動意識冒出來的新的大學課程。他們覺得這只是一個極端左派分子的玩意，是充滿政治氣味的短期性質的社會運動，不久便要消失，不會長久立足於美國大學學術領域裏。當時，麥禮謙和胡垣坤兩位美國華人歷史學會的領袖，挺身而出，爲該新學系首次開辦美國華人史的課目。兩人合作編寫講義兼教授課程。自此以後，美國華人歷史的課程，一直沒有中斷過，更成爲舊金山州立大學亞裔研究係的主要課目。

在這裏值得一提的是他們兩位1971爲了授課而編寫了《美國華人歷史提綱》；在美國華人研究領域裏的影響遠大。這本黃色封面的提綱的出版，並沒有給他們兩位帶來了終身教授的職稱；他們也沒有收到任何版權稅而發財。可是，在三十多年后的今天，差不多每一位講授美國華人歷史課程的老師學者，都仍然引用他們編寫的《提綱》的内容爲他們的講課和研究的架構和藍本。所以，我認爲他倆人所編著的《提綱》是研究美國華人歷史的首次合作的寫作，也是經典之作。也可以這樣說：在中國當年的文化大革命年代，有毛澤東的"小紅書"導航；在我們美國華人

歷史研究領域裏，也有麥胡兩人的"黃皮書"指導我們一個正確探討華人歷史的方向。在亞裔研究的剛開始的當年，這兩本書都非常流行。

當然，麥禮謙胡垣坤兩位是我們華裔研究規範的典型人物。他們在五十年代起已經活躍於華埠，爲華人社區服務。他們這方面的生活，今日一般學院派的晚輩華裔學者，鮮爲知曉。當年年輕的麥禮謙是華埠〈民青〉組織的領袖，中堅分子。他協助華埠新移民青年會員融入美國華人社區，更勇敢的對抗當年美國美國政府，在麥加錫時期對冒籍來美的華人移民的〈民青〉會員的政治壓害。後來，他又參與華埠報業傳媒工作，寫專欄介紹美國華人的歷史。他也是華語〈漢聲〉廣播電臺的主腦，提供資料在華埠社區報道時事新聞與傳播中國文化。

胡垣坤當年也活躍于華埠社區，更投入歷史建築物保護的工作。1968年是美國越洲鐵路的一百周年，在猶他州普爾門托瑞點有盛大的百年紀念慶祝會。美國華人歷史學會派了代表團出席慶典，但受到主辦單位冷淡待遇。胡垣坤挺身而出，指責百年前華工的功勞沒有得到應有的承認，百年後的紀念慶祝會上，仍然漠視美國華工在當年建築鐵路的巨大犧牲和史無前例的偉大貢獻。在他的挑戰和堅持下，一個由美國華人歷史學會撰寫製造，確實一百年前華工參與建築越洲鐵路工程的紀念丰碑，獲得永久安放在普爾門托瑞點的鐵路站博物館與鐵路路軌旁邊。百年前的華工在橫貫美國大陸的鐵路工作上的巨大犧牲與貢獻，百年后在胡垣坤鍥而不捨的堅持下，正式獲得承認和表揚。

在麥禮謙的幕後支持下，胡垣坤製作了一套《金山客》，是第一部介紹美國華人歷史的錄像帶，在舊金山灣區的商業電視臺播出，推廣社會人士對美國華人歷史的認識。我個人認爲，他們當年製作的《金山客》在財力及資源缺乏的環境下，仍然之製造作出一套内容充實，有分量的

紀錄片，比早兩年用數百萬美元製作，在全國公眾電視網播放的華人專輯還好。

無可否認，麥胡兩人在美國華人歷史研究方面不是隨波逐流而是步伐先人，他們總是比其他人快，早做了他人還想不到要做的事。當他們有空閒時間，麥禮謙和夫人坐他們的別克大房車，胡桓坤和夫人坐他們的丰田小跑車，像兩對年輕的小子，各自分別在加州的大小公路奔馳，由南至北，從西到東，足跡踏遍各地大城小鎮，到處尋找鮮為人知曉的先輩華人居留的部落遺跡。見到好的餐館就停下，享受吃飯。既好吃又好玩，又有華人歷史考察價值。當年他們這種活動，也就是我們學術界所稱的實地調查或是田野研究，但是比不上他們方法輕鬆，有意義。更不用説口福服享受了。這是我們所羨慕的。

此外，麥禮謙先生早在七十年代已經和日裔歷史權威市岡雄二教授，積極呼籲亞裔研究的學者，在研究領域上關注太平洋彼岸的祖籍家鄉和有關亞裔的中日文字的資料。不過當時大多數的華裔研究工作者，認為美國華裔研究本身是美國本土研究的範疇；他們擔心如果研究題材涉及亞洲，此美國本土種族研究會被誤解為外國地域研究。因此他們由此顧慮而怯步不前。大多數華裔學者當年都不肯涉及在中國的僑鄉的研究，也因為語言障礙而無法引用中文文件檔案資料。這個自閉自封的形象，被麥禮謙一手打破。他出版了兩本華裔研究的中文資料參考書，一本是美國華人社區的中文報紙資料，一本是美國各大圖書館所藏有關美國華人的書籍文獻。他這方面的工作，指出了中文資料，可以提供華裔研究進入更完整的學術領域。自此，也引發了華裔研究的學者對廣東珠三角僑鄉研究的方向範圍。麥禮謙本人，也啟動了華裔在珠三角尋根的研究活動。他也把美國華人歷史的圖片展覽，帶到中國各地巡迴展覽，向中國本土人士介紹美國華人歷史。他本人寫的有關華人社區與中國僑鄉的文章，不斷刊登在他鼎力支持的美國華人歷史學會學報《華美：歷史與觀點》。他的專業精神，影響了不少晚輩，他們也開始在這方面跨越太平洋的華裔研究。

在另一邊，胡桓坤把其精力集中在探討調查加州各地淘金時代的大城小鎮的華人聚居部落。他的實地調查的成果，證實了早期美國華人散佈在美國西部各地，是開發西部社會和經濟的積極成員，胡桓坤提供給我們華人歷史研究工作者寶貴的原始資料，讓我們能夠重估華人先輩在開發美國西岸地區所佔的重要角色與地位。

其實，麥禮謙與胡桓坤就是中國道教意識之所謂的陰陽兩極。他們自己各有獨立研究興趣與方向，他們個別的華人歷史研究工作成果各有專長，互相輝映；他們聯合起來的華人歷史工作卻又是完滿和諧，天衣無縫，無懈可擊。他們最近的合作成果，是我們美國華人歷史學會博物館的華人歷史展覽曰《美國歲月：邁向大同》。該展覽設在學會總部會址。顧名思義，展覽主題是以美國華人歷史，爭取華裔在正統主流地位和認同。曾露凌和我也參與了此工作項目，兩年的時間我們差不多每一個星期都聚會，計劃商討展覽的內容的各樣相關事情。有人看見我們經常在一起，也就笑說我們是歷史學會的〈四人幫〉。不過我們並不是計謀破壞歷史粉碎文化的四人幫，而是共同計劃，互相討論如何運用最佳效果宣揚美國華人歷史地位與認同。我們成功在歷史學會總部正式啟用之日同時為陳列展覽的開幕日。其實，坦白說，曾露凌與我是從這個項目中趁機會向他們兩位前輩繼續學習；在展覽籌備策劃工作裏把他們的美國華人歷史知識與智慧公之於世。好些從中國來的華僑研究學者，參觀了我們歷史學會的《美華歲月》，他們的觀後感是非常肯定；說是他們在北美所參觀的最好的一個美國華人歷史展覽：歷史資料恰當，內容充實而不擠逼，解說文字簡潔而意義深長，陳列方式也非常高雅而不庸俗。

麥禮謙，胡桓坤兩位老先生，他們的美國華人歷史研究工作，數十年如一日。不過，他們並不是單槍匹馬，孤獨工作。我每一次見到他們時，也見到他們的另一半，他們的夫人，永遠都在他們身旁，也是數十年如一日，陪伴他們，協助他們的工作，是廣東人所形容的"糖黐豆" 天生兩對，真的是令人妒忌和羨慕極了。

今天我們一起慶祝麥禮謙先生的八十歲和胡桓坤先生的七十九歲壽辰。兩位壽星公的年紀加起來，比我們美國加州發現金礦的一百五十六年歷史還要長久。不錯，他們兩位土生土長的美國加州華人就是我們美國華人歷史研究的金礦，也是衡量我們華裔研究工作成果的金質標準。

我感激您們兩位指定我今天晚上發言介紹您們。謹祝您們兩位生辰快樂! 老當益壯!

Conference Honorees:
Chinese America's Grand Historians*

PHILIP P. CHOY 胡垣坤

Born in San Francisco Chinatown on December 17, 1926, Philip P. Choy grew up in a family of five children. His father, a paper son, was part owner of a meat market on the north end of Grant Avenue; his mother, American-born though having grown up in China, worked in a sewing factory.

After attending San Francisco public schools and Nam Kue Chinese School, Choy enlisted in the Army Air Corps during World War II. While in basic training in Biloxi, Mississippi, Choy witnessed segregation in its extremity, which was to motivate his activities in later years. Upon his return, Choy attended the University of California at Berkeley on the GI Bill. Graduating with a degree in architecture, he would continue to work in residential and commercial design for fifty years.

As president of the Chinese Historical Society of America (CHSA) during the Civil Rights era, Choy sensed a growing interest and demand for Chinese American history to be taught in schools and universities. His opportunity came in September 1969, when he and fellow CHSA member Him Mark Lai co-taught the first college-level Chinese American history course in the nation at San Francisco State University (SFSU), known then as San Francisco State College. Although no longer actively teaching, Choy holds the title of Adjunct Professor of Asian American Studies at SFSU.

Given his background in architecture, Choy has had a strong presence in historic preservation, serving on the San Francisco Landmark Advisory Board and the California State Historical Resources Commission, and conducting the extensive 1978 historical/cultural survey of San Francisco Chinatown. He was also an early advocate for the preservation of Angel Island Immigration Station, sitting on their Historical Advisory Committee and writing the case report to nominate the site to the National Registry of Historic Places. Choy then devoted much of his time to the Chinatown YWCA, helping them to secure landmark status for their Julia Morgan-designed brick building. His work would come full circle, as he would later support CHSA's acquisition of the building.

Honored by countless organizations for his work in the community, Choy is also co-author of *A History of the Chinese in California: A Syllabus; Outlines: History of the Chinese in America;* and *The Coming Man: 19th Century American Perceptions of the Chinese.* He has served as consultant and advisor for many projects, exhibitions, and media presentations on the Chinese American experience. Choy's particular favorites are the lifesize diorama of Chinese railroad workers at the Sacramento Railroad Museum and the "Chinese Pioneers" exhibit at the Federal Courthouse.

Choy and his wife of 53 years, Sarah, have three children and five grandchildren. He continues to serve on the board of the Chinese Historical Society of America and is co-curator of CHSA Museum's main exhibit. His most recent exhibit is "Pandering to Sinophobia: The Chinese Question in Political Cartoons," currently housed in the Philip P. Choy Gallery that was named and dedicated by CHSA in recognition and honor of his continuous community volunteerism and dedication to the preservation of Chinese American history.

HIM MARK LAI 麥禮謙

Born in San Francisco Chinatown on November 1, 1925, Him Mark Lai grew up in a family of five children. The son of immigrant garment workers, Lai attended San Francisco public schools and Nam Kue Chinese School. Graduating from the University of California, Berkeley in 1947 with a degree in engineering, he would work for thirty-one years as a mechanical engineer for Bechtel Corporation.

Lai's involvement in the Chinese American community began after graduation. During the 1950s, he was president of the Mun Ching Youth Club, which was active in promoting a better understanding of the People's Republic of China. In 1960, after having taken Stanford Lyman's pioneering Asian

American Studies course through UC Berkeley Extension, Lai began his journey as a scholar in Chinese American history.

When the Civil Rights movement in the 1960s led to rising activism and ethnic awareness among Chinese Americans, Lai joined CHSA and began writing articles on Chinese American history in the bilingual weekly *East-West*. In 1969, Lai co-authored *A History of the Chinese in California: A Syllabus* which was followed by co-teaching the first Chinese American history course in the nation with Philip Choy at San Francisco State College (now University). Subsequently, as a member of the state legislature advisory committee to preserve Angel Island Immigration Station, Lai would go on to co-author *Island: Poetry and History of Chinese Immigrants on Angel Island, 1910-1940*. In addition to writing numerous articles, Lai helped CHSA to initiate the publication of its annual journal, *Chinese America: History and Perspectives*, serving on the editorial committee ever since its first issue in 1987.

Lai's pioneering work is unparalleled because of his advocacy and use of both Chinese language and English language sources. Towards this end, he has published the bibliographies *Chinese Newspapers Published in North America, 1854-1975* and *A History Reclaimed: An Annotated Bibliography of Chinese Language Materials on the Chinese of America*, as well as *Cong Huaqiao dao Huaren: Ershi shiji Meiguo Huaren shehui fazhan shi* [From Chinese overseas to Chinese American: A history of the development of Chinese American society during the twentieth century].

Stepping outside the boundaries of the United States, Lai was involved in the 1979 joint study of Taishan emigrant villages by University of California in Los Angeles and Zhongshan University in Guangzhou. Subsequent participation in international conferences enabled him (with Albert Cheng) to initiate the In Search of Roots program at the Chinese Culture Center.

Lai and his constant companion and wife of 52 years, Laura, live in San Francisco. He continues to serve on the board of CHSA and is Adjunct Professor of Asian American Studies at SFSU. His more recent activities include co-curating CHSA Museum's main exhibit and publishing *Becoming Chinese American: A History of Communities and Institutions*. Lai was also the subject of Evan Leong's 2004 documentary, *Him Mark Lai: A People's Historian*. Dubbed informally by the world as the "godfather" or "dean" of Chinese American history, Him Mark Lai is crowned in a *Chronicle of Higher Education* article as "the scholar who legitimized the study of Chinese America."

---

*Grand historians (太史令 *taishiling*) in imperial China had the official responsibility of recording the country's history. The most famous of all grand historians is Sima Qian (149?-90? BC).

"Town and Gown: A Mutual Commitment"

October 7, 2005

Conference Luncheon Keynote Address

Charles B. Reed, EdD
Chancellor, California State University

Thank you very much for this opportunity to speak. I am honored to be a part of this event and to meet so many distinguished guests.

I'd like to start by sharing a few words from a good friend of mine, a successful businessman and former California State University trustee, Stanley Wang. Stanley gave our system an amazing gift a few years back. He and his wife Franny donated $1 million to be used over ten years to recognize outstanding faculty and administrators. When he made this gift, he told us that he wanted to do so because he believed in the power of education. He told us, "In our shrinking world, the interdependence of the global economy requires greater knowledge and understanding between the West and the East." He said he was confident that helping to strengthen education and build partnerships would lead to great success for California students in the global economy. I know that Stanley was right. And when we step back and look at our university system and its role in the state and global economy, I remember Stanley and his wisdom about the importance of making connections and building bridges.

Most people, when they think of the California State University, think of their local campus, like San Francisco State. In fact, the California State University system is the country's largest four-year university system with approximately 400,000 students. It is the most diverse, with minority enrollment at over 53%, and it is one of the most affordable, with some of the lowest student fees in the country.

CSU graduates 82,000 students each year into California's workforce. We graduate 58% of California's Hispanic graduates, 52% of California's African American graduates, 53% of California's Native American graduates, and 39% of California's Asian Pacific Islander graduates. I should note here that Asian Americans are the second largest ethnic population at CSU–making up 17% of our students. Altogether we have more than 17,000 Chinese students.

From an economic perspective, CSU's impact is enormous. CSU-related expenditures create over $13 billion in economic impact and support over 207,000 jobs in California. All told, California reaps more than a fourfold benefit from every dollar the state invests in CSU. Given our critical role in California, we see ourselves as bridge-builders–building continuity across the spectrum from education...to the economy and workforce...to community.

We are proud to support your efforts in Chinese American Studies as we continue to build bridges between academia and our communities.

HIGH SCHOOL OUTREACH

Our bridge-building begins with high school outreach. We have a number of outstanding high school students with us today. Will they stand so we can recognize them?

I had a chance to talk with them briefly about some of CSU's efforts to make sure they are on the path for college success. One of the most important tools we have to reach high school students is the Early Assessment Program, or EAP. We developed this test, along with the California Department of Education and the State Board of Education, to help 11th grade students to get a "snapshot" of their mathematics and English/Language Arts proficiency. The test incorporates CSU's placement standards into the California Standards Tests for English and math. If the EAP test shows that a student needs more work, they can make the most of their 12th grade experience by using that time to brush up on the skills they need for college. We have also designed programs for both teachers and students to help them make the most of the final high school years. Plus we created websites called *www.csuenglishsuccess.org* and *www.csumathsuccess.org* to help students make sure that they are ready for CSU math and English placement tests.

Another effort is our support for adopting what we call the A through G curriculum, the curriculum required for admission to CSU or University of California, for all students. In May, we joined with the Alliance for a Better Community to support their effort to establish the A-G curriculum as a requirement for graduation at LAUSD. We will continue to be outspoken public supporters of this effort as we work with ABC and others to help more students become eligible for a four-year university.

A third major project is our "How to Get to College" poster. For the last six years, we have distributed copies of this poster in English and Spanish to middle and high schools throughout California. Last year, we started printing copies in Chinese, Korean, and Vietnamese. I hope all of our high school students read and study the poster so they can make sure they stay on track to go to college and succeed.

AT CSU

At the university level, our work continues with a diverse population of students who reflect what California really looks like. We offer our students opportunities to understand and engage with their culture and community. Thirteen CSU campuses have Asian and Asian American Studies programs and we offer Ethnic Studies opportunities across the CSU system.

I'm sure many of you know from Professor Lorraine Dong that San Francisco State houses the first and only College of Ethnic Studies in the country. Also, the Chancellor's Office has recognized San Francisco State's Asian American Studies Department as an "exemplary program." Some other programs worth noting:

- Cal State East Bay has been offering business management and public administration programs to Chinese since 1993, and has executive MBA programs in Beijing, Hong Kong, Vienna, Moscow, and Singapore.
- Cal State Northridge houses a $38 million collection of Chinese antiquities, donated by entrepreneur Roland Tseng. He said he chose Cal State Northridge because of the university's longstanding connections with China, and because the university is a place where the antiquities can be publicly shown and studied in many different disciplines.
- San Jose State's Asian American Center offers events and opportunities for students and community members to learn about Asian American history and culture.

Another important systemwide program is the Wang Scholarship, established by our friends Stanley and Franny Wang. These scholarships provide students and faculty an opportunity to study and teach in China and Taiwan. While Stanley was a trustee, I had the opportunity to travel with him on trips to universities in China and Taiwan. What impressed me the most on these trips was the willingness of those administrators and faculty to enter into partnerships and work collaboratively with CSU. That kind of collaborative spirit is essential to success in the 21st century. I know that the students who study there will do well in today's partnership-driven, global economy.

AFTER GRADUATION

When our students complete their studies at the CSU, we help them make the transition into fields that are needed in California. In 2003–04, we granted 3,562 degrees to Chinese and Chinese American students. Some of our outstanding alums include:

- From San Francisco State—Fred Lau, San Francisco's first Asian American police chief.

- Leland Yee, the first Asian American to rise to Speaker Pro Tem of the California State Assembly.
- From Fresno State—Faye Woo Lee, Commissioner, City and County of San Francisco Human Rights Commission.
- From San Jose State—International bestselling author Amy Tan.

And there are many, many others who are leading companies, heading research projects, designing buildings, teaching in classrooms, and working in communities.

We are proud of what we do for California and for all of its people. That is why we continue to reach out to the community, especially at events like this one. I know that the partnership between San Francisco State and the Chinese Historical Society of America is considered to be a model of town-and-gown cooperation. I thank you for all that you do to help us stay connected and informed about community and cultural issues, and as always, I welcome your feedback on how we can serve your communities better.

Thank you again for the opportunity to speak.

CHARLES B. REED, EdD 葦察理

Dr. Charles B. Reed has served since March 1998 as Chancellor of the California State University, the largest four-year university system in the United States. As the system's chief executive officer, he oversees more than 42,000 faculty and staff, and nearly 400,000 students on 23 campuses.

The CSU currently offers approximately 1,100 bachelor's degree programs, 700 master's programs, and 17 joint doctoral programs in 240 areas. It also prepares the majority of the state's new public school teachers and 10% of the nation's K-12 instructors. Reed is dedicated to the mission of the CSU, which is to provide California's students with access to a high-quality, affordable college education. His priority issues include improving access to the CSU, building excellence in academic programs, strengthening teacher preparation, creating stronger partnerships with K-12 schools, and preparing students for the workforce of the future.

Reed also works with many national organizations and advisory boards to build collaborative efforts between higher education and other segments of the community. He currently serves on several national boards, including ACT, the National Center for Educational Accountability, and the National Business-Higher Education Forum.

Reed received his BS in Health and Physical Education from George Washington University in 1963 and continued to receive his EdD from the same university in 1970. Before joining the CSU, he served for 13 years as Chancellor of the State University System of Florida. Prior to that, Reed served as Chief of Staff to the Governor of Florida.

"Town and Gown: A Mutual Commitment"

October 7, 2005

Conference Luncheon Keynote Address

Henry Der
Former Deputy Superintendent of Public Instruction
California Department of Education

In my comments this afternoon, I would like to talk about the state testing program, the federal No Child Left Behind accountability system, and their effects on Chinese and other racial minority students.

The California Postsecondary Education Commission has documented over the years the high percentage of Asian high school graduates eligible for admission to University of California (UC) and California State University (CSU). The eligibility rate of Asian students for UC freshman admission is double that of white students. The eligibility rate of Asian students for CSU freshman admission is one-third higher than that of white students. Asian college graduates have pursued successful careers from the sciences and medicine to business. Unlike their predecessors, today's Asian students have plenty of role models and many believe everything and anything are achievable.

What have we learned from our collective experience in public education? What responsibilities do we, as Chinese Americans, have to public education, an institution that has helped immensely Chinese and other Asians achieve greater socioeconomic status?

In comparison to performance by all students, Chinese and Asian students in general have performed well on statewide standardized tests. Chinese Americans are in a unique position to challenge the state's testing program and to probe what can be done to assist those who do not perform well on required tests, due to their language background and/or economic status.

Has the state burdened students with too many tests, especially immigrant, English language learners?

Take for example, the tests that a 10th grade English Language Learner has to take, not counting classroom quizzes, mid-terms, and end-of-the semester exams:

- English Language Development Test
- California Standard Test (ELA, Math, Science, and History)
- SAT 9—for national comparison purposes
- High School Exit Exam
- Physical Education Test

For high school juniors, the burden of testing increases, as these students, including more English language learn-ers and racial minorities, take the SAT I, II, and Advanced Placement.

In the case of my third child who was a high school junior when the statewide testing program was rolled out, as a parent and not in my role as deputy superintendent at the California Department of Education, I exercised the waiver for her not to take the STAR test. I asked myself how many more tests does she have to take in order to assess her readiness and eligibility for college admission? Not many more, without creating undue pressure and imposing time constraints to participate in the state testing program.

Well before the high school exit exam was constructed and implemented, some of us at the California Department of Education knew certain populations of students, such as English language learners and low-income students, would not do as well as their English speaking, middle-income counterparts. Today's high school exit exam results bear out our initial fears. Two in three English language learners are not passing the English portion of the high school exit exam in San Francisco, as well as throughout California. One in two low-income students is passing the English portion of the HSEE, in comparison to four in five non-low income students. Not enough attention has been paid to improve teaching strategies and classroom support for these and others students to pass the high school exit exam and other tests. I'm not sure schools have done a sufficient job of connecting at-risk students to learning, learning that will sustain a student's interest and skills in learning, thereby improving test performance.

We need to be mindful that testing is not teaching. An increasing number of teachers, especially at the elementary grade levels, are saying all they do everyday in the classroom is to teach to the test. While student test scores are generally rising in school districts throughout California, we need to ask, do teachers have time to teach social studies, in particular the history of the Chinese American experience and that of other minority groups who have experienced discrimination and unequal treatment? Sadly the answer is no.

Why does it take a catastrophe like Hurricane Katrina to open the eyes of our students that poverty and racism exist in America, rooted in history and public policies? In the movement to improve K-12 student academic performance, the educational system has lost sight of addressing the needs of students to be aware of their own culture and history, as well as that of others.

As students graduate from high school and matriculate to college, it is vital for our colleges and universities to prepare our students to be leaders in a multiracial society, with the competency to understand and do something about poverty and racism in America. Just as there can never be enough UCs, CSUs, or community colleges to provide educational opportunities, our students deserve access to Ethnic Studies so they'll be prepared to be leaders, shakers, and doers in a multicultural society.

The state testing and federal No Child Left Behind accountability system expose a particular dilemma and challenge for Chinese students and their families, especially in San Francisco's public schools.

.Under the state testing system, schools are ranked, based on student test results. There are high performing schools and low-performing ones. Federal law provides if a poor school doesn't improve test scores, the school district must provide the opportunity for students to leave their low-performing school.

At the most personal level, parents of all racial backgrounds want to secure a well performing school for their children. Amidst the dysfunctional relationship between the San Francisco school board and superintendent, certain officials have been quick to tout San Francisco as the best performing urban school district in California. Such a proclamation hides the deep achievement gap that exists between racial groups in our public schools. For example, in 5th grade, one in five African American students is performing at grade level in English language arts, in contrast to two of three Chinese students. Compared to African American students in other large urban school districts in California, African American students in San Francisco schools rank the lowest in academic performance.

Among Chinese families, there is intense desire and competition to enroll their children in high-performing schools, many of which are located in the west side of San Francisco. There has been great disappointment and anger among some Chinese families whose children are not assigned to one of these high-performing schools. Some Chinese Americans have called for a return to "neighborhood schools" to remedy the situation. They also claim that Chinese American students are being "excluded" from some of the "best" schools in San Francisco. A close examination of student enrollment at these schools indicates that Chinese and Asian American representation is as high as 70% of total student body. Seventy percent representation is hardly what one could call "exclusion." It's in the interest of the Chinese community to support efforts to close the achievement gap among identified racial groups.

Greater numbers of African American and Latino students performing at a higher academic level will increase the number of schools that are deemed to be high-performing, thereby improving school choices for Chinese families and their students. At a time when there's heightened political interest in student test scores and solutions to poor student academic performance, Chinese Americans and their allies should demand more public resources and support for successful teaching and learning strategies that raise academic performance for all students. We are in a unique position to make this demand very publicly and loudly.

Thank you.

HENRY DER 謝國器

Henry Der is Senior Program Officer at the Evelyn & Walter Haas, Jr. Fund, a philanthropic organization serving the San Francisco Bay Area. He has programmatic responsibility for the Fund's Immigrant Rights and Reform Initiative. The Initiative supports non-profit, tax-exempt groups to protect the civil liberties of immigrants, promote the civic engagement and integration of immigrants, and support the legalization of undocumented persons and reunification of family members.

Prior to joining the Haas, Jr. Fund in November 2003, Der served as the State Administrator of the Emery Unified School District for two years. Appointed by the State Superintendent of Public Instruction, he led Emery Unified out of fiscal bankruptcy by initiating steps to achieve financial recovery through controlling expenses and securing new sources of revenues to support educational programs for district students. From 1996 to 2001, Der served as a Deputy Superintendent of Public Instruction at the California Department of Education. And, from 1993 to 1995, he was appointed by the Assembly Speaker to serve two six-year terms on the California Postsecondary Education Commission (CPEC) and was commission chairperson for three years.

Prior to his work in state education administration, Der served as Executive Director of Chinese for Affirmative Action (CAA) from 1974-1996, where he led coalition efforts to promote equal opportunities in employment, education, and voting rights for Asian Americans and other racial minorities. Before that, he taught English as a Second Language to adult immigrants at the San Francisco Community College District from 1971 to 1973. He also served as a Peace Corps Volunteer in Machakos, Kenya, working with agricultural youth clubs from 1968 to 1970. Der is a native San Franciscan and a 1968 graduate of Stanford University.

Banquet Keynote Speaker

GARY LOCKE, JD 駱家輝

Born in 1950 in Seattle, Washington to a family of five children, Gary Locke is a third-generation Chinese American with ancestral roots in Hong Kong and in Taishan, Guangdong Province. After graduating from Yale University in 1972 in Political Science, Locke went on to receive his JD from Boston University in 1975.

In 1982, Locke's South Seattle district elected him to the Washington House of Representatives, where he served as chairman of the Appropriations Committee. Eleven years later, in 1993, he made history by becoming the first Asian American elected as King County Executive, defeating the incumbent candidate. In 1996, Locke was elected as Washington's 21st governor, making him the first Asian American governor in the history of the mainland United States. On November 7, 2000, he was re-elected by an overwhelming majority.

As governor, Locke worked to make Washington a better place to live, work, and raise a family by dramatically raising academic achievement in the public schools, strengthening the state's economy, improving transportation, expanding health care for vulnerable children and adults, and making state government more publicly accessible. On the national stage, Locke was also recognized as a rising political star, and was chosen to give the Democratic Party's response to President George W. Bush's 2003 State of the Union address. In July 2003, Locke announced he would not seek a third term because of his duties as a father and husband.

Since leaving office, Locke has become partner in the Seattle office of international law firm, Davis Wright Tremaine LLP, working in their China and governmental relations practice groups. He married Mona Lee in 1994. Lee, whose parents are from Shanghai and Hubei, China, has extensive experience in journalism and is a television reporter with KIRO/7 in Seattle. They currently live in Washington with their children Emily, Dylan, and Madeline.

CONFERENCE PAPERS
AND SUMMARIES

Similarities in Given Names of Chinese and Anglo-Saxon Origins

Emma Woo Louie

Studies of personal names show that history, language, and social attitudes are some of the information encoded in all names, which include family names or surnames and given names. The term "given name" is used in this paper instead of "first name" for describing the name or names we are given at birth, or which we give ourselves. I believe it is a more appropriate and inclusive term because the family name in many countries comes first in a name.

Names of Chinese origin in America have close ties with the history and language of Chinese America. For example, Cantonese-sounding surnames, many with Americanized spellings, dominated its first one hundred years. The removal of restrictions on immigration from Asian countries in 1968 and the end of the Vietnam War in 1975 brought about tremendous new immigration that resulted in the proliferation of different dialect-sounding names. Mandarin-sounding names now predominate, and, due to immigration from the People's Republic of China since 1980, Pinyin spelling is replacing Wade-Giles romanization in popularity. Also, since 1980, the foreign-born constitutes the majority in Chinese America.

Social attitudes can be detected in the use of given names. Since the change in demographics, Chinese given names are more frequently seen today; sometimes combined with a Western given name. Native-born Chinese Americans, whose legal names usually consist solely of one or two Western given names, are also likely to possess a Chinese given name, except that it is written in Chinese only. It seems natural to have one to go with a surname of Chinese origin. While Chinese Americans as an ethnic group do not share the same collective memory of Chinese America, they have a common legacy of Han Chinese name traditions (*Han Chinese* refers to the vast majority of the people of China).

CHINESE GIVEN NAMES

Chinese given names consist of either one or two characters. A name of two characters is simply *one* name even though each character is written as a separate word. It is composed of two words that have been selected to form one name. Historically, one-character and two-character given names fluctuated in usage. The two-character name tended to decline in times of political turmoil, but usage always rose again in times of prosperity and political calm. This occurred because the two-character given name usually consists of a *generation name* that identifies individuals by family, a naming custom that will be described later on. Although there has never been a law requiring it to be used, over 80 percent of Han Chinese, by 1900, had a two-character name.[1] In a study of names in Qingdao, Shandong province, the figure rose to 95 percent for females and to over 90 percent for males by 1940.[2] The two-character given name is considered the quintessential Chinese name.

COMPARING ORANGES AND APPLES

Unfortunately, recent writings about the two-character given name would have us believe it consists of two separate names. One writer calls the first character the "middle name" and the second character, the "first name."[3] A Southeast Asian writer calls the first character of the two-character name the "first name" and the second character, the "middle name."[4] Still another Southeast Asian writer refers to the second given name character as a "last name."[5] These terms "first name," "middle name," and "last name" have specific meanings in the English language so that using these terms to describe a Chinese two-character given name is misleading and confusing. It is like comparing oranges and apples.

Although the Chinese also have one-character and two-character family names, there has never been any confusion about the two-character surname being one name. Each character may be transcribed into English as two separate words, as in "Soo Hoo," yet you would never hear anyone say that the first character is the first surname and the second is the second surname.

ANGLO-SAXON NAMES

A far better comparison for the Chinese two-character given name is the two-worded Anglo-Saxon name, a name such as Edith or Robert. Anglo-Saxons, a people of English and Germanic stock, also had names that consisted of either one or two words. The Chinese and the Anglo-Saxons of England had, remarkably, very similar naming practices.

The Anglo-Saxon period occurred from about 500 to 1066 CE. That was a time when Chinese name customs were still being honed and perfected. Anglo-Saxons, however, identified themselves by one name only; they did not have surnames.[6] By comparison, the Chinese had family names early on. These were required of all households at the onset of the Qin dynasty—255–209 BCE. However, family names had existed several hundred years earlier among the aristocratic clans, which were abolished by the first Qin emperor.[7]

Nonetheless, describing Anglo-Saxon naming customs is also to describe Chinese name traditions. Anglo-Saxons did not have "ready-made" names; names were composed from words selected from the language they spoke. And the majority of words selected for names were ordinary nouns and adjectives. Their names consisted mostly of one word only but by the ninth century, names of two words became standard form. To the Anglo-Saxons, a name composed of two words was simply one name that was created by placing two words together.[8] For example, *Edith* consists of the words "rich" and "war"; *Robert* is composed of the words "fame" and "bright."[9]

The Chinese still have manufactured given names. There are no books listing Chinese ready-made names as there are in the English language. There are, however, books today that suggest Chinese given names that have a positive meaning or are based on the sound of a Western given name. For example, *Anna* may be phoneticized into Chinese by the characters for "peace" and "graceful." Because of the countless possible combinations of two words, it is unusual to find two persons in a roomful of Chinese people who have the same two-character given name.

When citing the meaning for an Anglo-Saxon name—which includes Old English and Germanic names—name experts point out that the correct way is to state the meaning of each word without embellishment.[10] *Robert* therefore does not mean "bright in fame." This applies as well to the Chinese two-character name. For instance, the given name of the late author Lin Yutang means "language, hall." It does not mean "hall of language."

Other Anglo-Saxon name practices also describe Chinese name traditions:[11]

- A child was not named after relatives.
- Every child was given a unique name, completely different from any other in the same village.
- Words for names were often selected to inspire the child in the growing-up years.
- Even though words selected for names did not have to make a meaningful combination, they often did.
- Since new names for individuals were continually created, the list of given names was enormous in number.
- There was no clear way to distinguish between the names of men and women.

There is an exception for the Chinese, however, to the third and last name traditions: in the great desire for sons, parents have been known to give an unwanted daughter a name that would forever remind her and everyone else of her despised status. Names could express such thoughts as "Don't want" or "Hope for brother."[12]

DITHEMIC OR TWO-THEME NAMES

The two-worded Anglo-Saxon name is variously described as a *dithemic* name and a *two-theme* name because each of the two words could be combined with other words to create other names. Each new word, in turn, could be paired with other words to create still more names. Each repeated word is therefore like a *theme*. Some theme-words had to be placed first in a name while others formed the second word. Most words could be in either position.[13]

For example, the word "bright" (originally spelled *beorht*) was a favorite word in Anglo-Saxon names. It could be either the first or second theme-word. *Bertha* means "bright." *Bertram* means "bright, raven." *Albert* means "noble, bright."[14] The Chinese also like *bright* or *Ming* in names. *Ming* can be a one-character given name; it can be the first or second word in a two-character given name. It is also a surname.

FAMILY RELATIONSHIP IN NAMES

In addition to wanting individualistic names, both Anglo-Saxons and Chinese also wanted names to indicate family relationship. Anglo-Saxon parents did so by selecting words that began with the same letter or the same initial sound.[15] In the tenth century, Eadweard of Wessex (an old Germanic kingdom in England) repeated the theme-word *Ead,* meaning "rich" or "prosperity," of his name, in the names of his sons and daughters. His sons were Eadred and Eadmund and his three daughters, Eadburg, Eadgifu, and Eadgyth.[16]

The Chinese also used different ways to indicate family relationship in names, and, toward the end of the fifth century, it became common practice to use a full character instead of part of a character for repeating in the names of siblings.[17] The repeated character is called the *generation name*. The Chinese, as a rule, would never repeat the same theme-word in the names of members of different generations. The whole idea of showing family relationship in names was to distinguish members of one generation from those of previous and succeeding ones.

Traditionally, sons and daughters had different generation names. For example, the famous Soong sisters, whose lives were closely tied to events in modern Chinese history, were named E-ling, Ching-ling, and Mei-ling. Their brothers were Tse-vung, Tse-liang, and Tse-an. Their generation names "ling" and "tse" show that the generation name could be either the first or second word in the two-character name. In traditional China, men received another generation name when they married and adopted a *marriage* or *adult* name. Beginning with the Northern Song dynasty (960–1126), a poem, in which no word was repeated, was used by many clans for predetermining in advance the generation name for the marriage name. In this way men knew their place in the genealogy of their clan and their ranking in relationship to one another.[18]

Since the early 1900s, the traditional generation-name system has been modified. The custom of men having a marriage name is no longer followed. Modern-thinking parents began giving the same generation name to their sons and daughters. For example, the Chinese given names for the son and two daughters of Chang-lin Tien, the late Chancellor of the University of California at Berkeley, are Chihan, Chih-ping, and Chihyih. Immigrants from Taiwan and Hong Kong brought this naming practice to America in recent decades. In comparison, the generation-name custom may not be observed in mainland China since Han Chinese families have had to abide by the one-child-per-family law that was enacted in 1979.[19]

Perhaps the Anglo-Saxons might have developed the generation-name practice had it not been for the Norman Conquest of 1066. Their name customs came to an almost abrupt end after William, Duke of Normandy, invaded and conquered England. The Normans looked down on the Anglo-Saxons and their name practices, and within two to three generations, the old Anglo-Saxon names practically all disappeared. Only a few survived. A main feature of Norman French name customs, which the English began adopting, was to repeat the same given name over and over, from one generation to the next, in the same family. Due to the scarcity of Norman given names, especially for women, it became popular to use biblical names. The scarcity of given names also led to the use of surnames in England.[20]

Actually, many Norman names that were taken to England, such as William, Richard, Roger, and Henry, were of Saxon or Germanic origin.[21] The dithemic Anglo-Saxon names that survived the Conquest were respelled as the English written language evolved. For example, *Eadweard* became *Edward* and *Ael-fraed* changed into *Alfred*. The Norman Conquest completely changed English name customs.

Although Chinese name traditions have undergone modifications, these can be found in every country in which the Chinese settled. Some immigrant parents even adapt the generation-name custom when choosing Western given names for their children. For example, the three sons of a Mu family in Los Angeles were named Stanley, Stanton, and Stanford. In San Francisco, three brothers received names that ended in the same sound: Raymond, Edmund, and Gilman. The daughters of a Wing family in Evanston, Wyoming, were bestowed names that began with the letters "Li": Lily, Lilac, Lillian, and Lilia. In Paris, the older siblings of a Chuan family

were named Victor and Victoria. To be sure, immigrant parents may misunderstand Euro-American name customs. In a Sacramento, California, family, for instance, two brothers were named Bill and Billy. In a San Francisco family, two brothers were named Ed and Eddie.

NAME STYLES

On the other hand, descendants of the immigrant generation may not understand Chinese name customs and may assume the two-character given name is composed of separate names since each word or syllable is written as a separate character in the Chinese writing system. Perhaps the custom of having a generation name makes it seem to be a separate name. Or perhaps certain name styles contribute to the difficulty of understanding that the two-character given name is one name.

For example, the name style used by the eminent linguist Yuen Ren Chao was to write his two-character given name as separate words. This is still a popular name style in use today. The late Professor Chao always placed his surname last, as in Western practice. The name style used by I. M. Pei—may also give the impression that the two-character name is composed of two different names. In comparison, in the Wade-Giles romanization method for Mandarin, a hyphen is placed between the two words—as in "Yo-Yo Ma"—to indicate their connection. In Pinyin romanization, the two-character name is written as one name, as in Lin Yutang's name. He may have been the first Chinese to advocate treating the two-character name as a polysyllabic name and writing it as one name.[22]

Unfortunately, computers may not recognize a given name composed of two separate words as being one name. This came to my attention during plans for a Louie family reunion. In our attempt to eliminate recording middle names so as to save space on a family tree banner, the relatives with the same generation name and who transcribe their Chinese given names as separate words all ended up with the same "first name." Fortunately, the hyphenated name was accepted in that single space.

There is one great advantage to using the hyphenated name style. When the first word of a two-character name ends in a vowel and the second word begins with a vowel, the hyphen is an aid to pronunciation. For example, my Chinese given name is pronounced in Cantonese as *yauh oi*, meaning "friend, love." If transcribed as one word, as in *Yauhoi*, it looks as though it should be pronounced "yau hoi." If transliterated into Mandarin Pinyin as *Youai*, it may sound like the protest of a cat.

CORRECTNESS IN NAME SPELLING

Nonetheless, it should be pointed out that, in America, the correct way to spell a person's name is according to its owner and family members. The choice of spelling and use of name style is the prerogative of the owner of a name. There have never been naming laws that require American citizens or residents to spell their names according to dictionary or official listings. Mandarin may be China's national language and Pinyin its official spelling system, but a name of Chinese origin in this country is an American name. Moreover, as Patrick Hanks, editor of *Dictionary of American Family Names*, pointed out, "...origin must not be confused with correctness" in the spelling of personal names.[23]

CONCLUSION

In conclusion, citing certain two-worded names of Old English and Germanic origins helps to explain how the Chinese two-character given name is one name composed of two words. Anglo-Saxon names such as William and Willard, Edward and Edwin, Robert, Gilbert and Hubert, which were originally composed of two separate words to form one name, are also excellent examples to explain the Chinese generation-name system. Equating the two-character given name as being like a "first name" and "middle name" or a "last name" is to compare oranges and apples. But it points out the importance of using terminology that will carry the same meaning to people who speak different languages and observe essentially different customs in order for it to be meaningful.

Until the Chinese themselves realize that certain name styles make it seem that the two-character given name is composed of two separate names, misunderstanding will continue to occur. At the same time, it is important to recognize that the diversity in spelling and name styles is part of the history, language, and social attitudes that pertain to particular times in Chinese America.

NOTES

1. Wolfgang Bauer, "Der Chinesische Personenname" [Chinese personal names], *Asiatische Forschungen* 4 (1959): 66–73; Emma Woo Louie, *Chinese American Names: Tradition and Transition* (Jefferson, NC: McFarland & Co., 1998), 47–48.
2. Li Zhonghua, "Given Names in China: One-character or Two-character Given Names" (paper presented at the American Name Society Annual Meeting, Oakland, California, January 6–8, 2005). To be published in *Onomastica Canadiana*.
3. Thomas W. Chinn, "Genealogical Sources of Chinese Immigrants to the United States," in *Studies in Asian Genealogy*, ed.

4. Spencer J. Palmer (Provo, UT: Brigham Young University Press, 1972), 224.
4. Evelyn Lip, *Choosing Auspicious Chinese Names* (Singapore: Times Editions, 1988; Torrance, CA: Heian International, 1997).
5. John B. Kwee, "The Many Implications of Name Change for Indonesian-born Chinese," in *The Chinese Diaspora, Selected Essays*, vol. 2, ed. Wang Ling-chi and Wang Gungwu (Singapore: Times Academic Press, 1998): 51.
6. C. M. Matthews, *English Surnames* (New York: Charles Scribner's Sons, 1966), 17–18.
7. Louie, *Chinese American Names*, 16, 20.
8. Matthews, *English Surnames*, 19, 20.
9. George R. Stewart, *American Given Names* (Oxford: Oxford University Press, 1979), 104, 252; Leslie Dunkling and William Gosling, *The New American Dictionary of Baby Names* (New York: Signet/Penguin Books, 1985), 115, 359.
10. Elsdon C. Smith, *Treasury of Name Lore* (New York: Harper & Row, 1967), 165.
11. Matthews, *English Surnames*, 19–21; Stewart, *American Given Names*, 4; J. R. Dolan, *English Ancestral Names: The Evolution of the Surname from Medieval Occupations* (New York: Clarkson N. Potter, 1972), 2–3; Teresa Norman, *Names through the Ages: Includes Thousands of Names from the Dark Ages to Contemporary Times* (New York: Berkley Books, 1999), 9; Elsdon C. Smith, *New Dictionary of American Family Names* (New York: Harper & Row, 1973), xix.
12. Louie, *Chinese American Names*, 46.
13. Stewart, *American Given Names*, 3; Matthews, *English Surnames*, 19.
14. Stewart, *American Given Names*, 50, 68.
15. Smith, *Treasury of Name Lore*, 165; Norman, *Names through the Ages*, 9.
16. Smith, *Treasury of Name Lore*, 166.
17. Louie, *Chinese American Names*, 52–53.
18. Louie, *Chinese American Names*, 53–54, 56.
19. Lu Zhongti and Celia Millward. "Chinese Given Names Since the Cultural Revolution," *Names* 37 (1989): 275–76; Li, "Given Names in China," indicated that the two-character given name dropped in usage from 1965 to 1989 due to new social policies, the Cultural Revolution (ca. 1966–1976), and declined use of generation names. But since 1990, usage began to recover, and since the year 2000, the two-character name reached its former maximum of 90% of all given names.
20. Matthews, *English Surnames*, 29; Stewart, *American Given Names*, 5; Leslie Alan Dunkling, *First Names First: New Ideas, Information and Anecdotes about the First Names of the English-speaking World* (New York: Universe Books, 1977), 51.
21. Patrick Hanks, ed., *Dictionary of American Family Names* (New York: Oxford University Press, 2003), xv; Norman, *Names through the Ages*, 18.
22. Lin Yutang, *My Country and My People* (New York: Halcyon House, 1938), 366.
23. Hanks, *Dictionary*, xi.

Black Chinese
History, Hybridity, and Home
(Original Title: Black Chinese: Historical Intersections,
Hybridity, and the Creation of Home)
Wendy Marie Thompson

In entering into the twenty-first century, one might affirm that the face of Chinese America has changed, or has it? Chineseness has been constantly conceptualized through the measure of phenotype, the quantity of blood, the preservation of language, or the possession of surname. But what happens when African American bodies and other nonwhite cultural sites are introduced into dialogue with Chineseness and Chinese American history in order to create a different story?

It is true that due to cultural, linguistic, and perceived citizenship differences, the historical extent of nineteenth-century interaction between Chinese immigrants and African American residents was somewhat limited, but in geographically mapping Chinese and African American communities in large metropolitan cities, one will find that many Chinese quarters across the United States were situated next to or on the fringes of black neighborhoods. And too, in the realm of labor, many employers whose staff was predominately African American would occasionally hire Chinese or "Oriental" men as strikebreakers and cheaper labor replacements in the transportation industry, as in on trains as porters or as field workers on agricultural estates.

That said, my primary focus in looking at situations of African American and Chinese overlap is on what came from it: the creation of hybrid spaces between people. In this paper I use four key visual images to uncover the sporadic sexual, working, and living relationships that culminated between Chinese and African Americans during the late nineteenth century and into the twenty-first.

My choice in using visual images is rooted in my personal belief that an image—photography, video, portrait, postcard, comic book—serves as a multidimensional tool that preserves and contests: it preserves a particular social, political, cultural moment in time while contesting other narratives that stand as the singular strand, the prevailing story.

But when there is a lack of a visual record (or a written one for that matter), there arises a condition that leads people to assume that such events—social, political, cultural, racial, communal, tribal—did not exist. With the following images, I am both bringing forth and attesting to a mixed race communal existence and using these artifacts as a lens that will help us visualize a different kind of Chinese America.

However, I would like to begin this paper at the crux of the late-twentieth century and the sudden boom of chic black/Asian mixed-race representations in popular culture as seen through a contemporary American gaze. The physical embodiment of African American and Asian American intersections were for the first time made widely accessible through figures on television or in the entertainment industry, represented in part through part Thai and part African American (or more popularly stated "Cablinasian") golfer and consumer endorsement icon, Tiger Woods; native Floridian and African American Filipina, Melissa Howard, who starred on MTV's the *Real World: New Orleans;* and African American Korean R&B singer Amerie Rogers.

Additionally, the American public became versed in films and visual landscapes which featured the mesh of humor, culture, and the absurd in such parallel worlds of Chinatown/Hong Kong and urban working-class urban black America with the films *Rush Hour* and *Romeo Must Die.* Concurrently, the commercial hip hop scene was graced with the lyrical spitting of Chinese American rapper Jin the Emcee who was able to utilize a particular racialized urban vernacular on the Black Entertainment Television program *Freestyle Fridays* to win rap battles against black opponents seven consecutive times in a row before going on to be signed with Ruff Ryder Records.

From these cultural scenes, a seeming cultural fusion was on the verge of happening between blacks and Asians in the United States after a rough period of conflict (the zenith arrived with the intense rioting and civil clashes between Korean small-business owners and urban black residents in Los Angeles, California). But to look at the underlying landscape between black and Asian or to even make the bare assumption that there is a common landscape is where we must begin to posit these two seemingly oppositional identities outside of popular culture.

In terms of the physical realities of mixed race Afro-Asian bodies, there exists some form of historical context following the children born of Asian and African American parentage drawn primarily from the U.S. militarization and occupation narrative: the children of war, the children of camp-town women, the children of bar hostesses, and the children of American imperialism in a postcolonial Asia-Pacific.

But when talking about Chineseness and Chinese America and the larger-scale historical, political, social, or lived intersections with African Americans, we are left without much context: there was no pretext of war that gave way to the occupied presence of African American troops in China or Taiwan or Hong Kong, and where scholars have studied African American and Chinese American histories, what has been left as an aside are the richest parts found in the slippage of a footnote.

In the art world, two Caribbean artists who have maintain their creative posts on the vertebrae of cultural location and national identity—and who both now make their home in the United States—have both used their artistic works to reveal their own questions regarding the presence of both an African and Chinese lineage. Albert Chong, who works in photography and mixed media, introduces decorated portraitures—something like mini *altares*—of various members of a mixed Afro-Chinese Jamaican family.

Performance artist, poet, and Jamaican national Stacey-ann Chin has also addressed the issue of origin and (mixed) race in her most recent performance *Border/Clash: A Litany of Desires*, which ran in New York City in 2005. Her performance, in part, set out to re/claim roots in Jamaica where her parents first fell into a relationship and where her black Jamaican mother became pregnant with her. Her Chinese father who worked at a furniture store, never acknowledged Chin as his own child although he would eventually live with another black Jamaican woman as well as the children produced from that union.[1]

Still, even with these valuable narratives, I am forced to ask myself: are these our only stories of desire, of family, of the self?

This absence that bleeds into invisibility is dangerous. So after moving from California to the East Coast to attend graduate school, I quickly decided to dedicate much of my time to combing through archival documents, printed sources and published articles, monographs, and other texts to see if I could find what was out there, to see what other documents or accounts I could uncover.

JOE GOW NUE STORE AND THE CHINESE IN THE AMERICAN SOUTH

This first photo I found in the Farm Security Administration—Office of War Information Collection at the Library of Congress is of Joe Gow Nue and Co. Grocery and Meat Market, which was taken in Leland, Mississippi, in the 1930s and relates somewhat indirectly to the life of Arlee Hen and her father Wong On (whose name upon immigration to the United States was noted as Charlie Sing). But before I go into their family history, I would like to give historical context to the following image through describing a very different landscape of the American South.

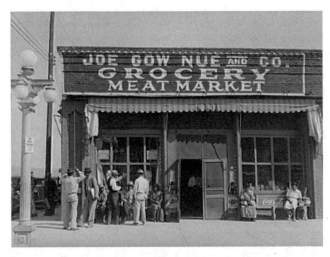

Figure 1. Library of Congress, Prints and Photographs Division, FSA-OWI Collection [LC-USF34-052450-D DLC]

It was during the latter half of the nineteenth century that the labor of recently emancipated black slaves became so difficult to regulate that it was believed Chinese labor would be beneficial and a more productive source of maintaining the southern plantation system. Planters thought the Chinese to be a good replacement considering them less likely to practice open resistance or random desertion when faced by low wages or abusive treatment by employers.

A conference held in Nashville, Tennessee, found that most agreed that the Chinese should be imported into the Mississippi Delta region as agricultural laborers who would tend to the cotton, sugar, rice, and tobacco fields in Mississippi, Arkansas, and Louisiana. Consequently, a call was put out, and the small population of Chinese men who answered had previous credentials as "coolies," some having been previously indentured in the West Indies and others arriving from California, the midwest region, or directly from Hong Kong.[2]

As first expected, the Chinese proved to be a godsend in replacing emancipated slaves. However, things quickly took a spiraling turn as some of the Chinese employed under contract began protesting exploitative working conditions that sometimes included open-handed threats and assaults from employers. In even more explosive cases, some of the employed Chinese would fight back, taking up arms and battling their overseers.[3] Additionally, running away was a common solution to breaking a contract, and it was likely that Chinese laborers could find jobs elsewhere as cooks, servants, noncontract sharecroppers, or hired hands.

Eventually, the entire proposition fell apart when Chinese labor was found to cost more than the planters had first planned. It was also decided from multiple firsthand plantation accounts of disputes, strikes, uprisings, and runaways that the Chinese were no more dependable than black labor. Finally, as the economic and social landscape of the South moved into a mechanized industrial one, slave labor and the plantation system were eventually rendered obsolete.

Of the few Chinese who remained in the South (where most had migrated elsewhere at the beginning of the twentieth century), the majority went into the small grocery business where they sold goods to black customers who were refused service by larger white-owned and serviced emporiums and markets. This created a racial stratification system in the South which placed the Chinese in a middle space where they were considered neither white nor necessarily "colored" (Negro).

Regarding sexual relations, with the ban on immigration and entry of Chinese women into the country, Chinese men were encouraged to seek out arrangements with local women but with a catch. Stringent antimiscegenation laws made this endeavor a severely limited one due to restrictions that made involvement with white women illegal. And so if not with white women, Chinese men took up freely with Spanish, indigenous, and African American women.[4] In terms of relationships built around the institution of the small Chinese store, it was found common for the owner to shack up with hired African American women who assisted around the store, many of these relationships having moved organically from employer-employee to that of live-in partner.

This added benefit of having an African American woman around the store begged to legitimize the Chinese store owner's place within a black community where he made his business. It also opened up the opportunity for the Chinese owner to start a family where immigration blockage inhibited reentry or fatherhood within a Chinese family context. For most, it was a matter of a long gap in time until they returned to China, if they returned at all. Also of benefit was the African American female partner whose marriage promised small social accommodations, such as courtesy from whites when they learned of her last name, class, status, and relation.

Returning to the image of Joe Gow Nue and Co., it is unknown to me if this market hired black employees or what the marital or sexual status of the owner(s) were. What I do know about this image is that the name Joe Gow Nue referred to a man who had been one of a cohort who traveled by boat south—one of the cohort being Wong On—and who had settled in the Greenville, Mississippi, area. At some point, Joe Gow Nue bought a grocery store which was located on Washington Avenue near a levee around 1910.

A white missionary named Ted Shepherd remembered visiting this Washington Avenue store as a young boy and looking at the "Chinese articles they had for sale: tea pots, chop sticks, beaded sandals, etc."[5] And contrary to the caption taken from the original negative print held in the Library of Congress, Shepherd insists there was never a Joe Gow Nue store in Leland, Mississippi. There was however a Joe Gow Nue No. 2, which was opened up by a family named Chow.

How this store relates to black Chinese history and the personal family history of Arlee Hen are found among the links between them: Arlee was a daughter born to one of Joe Gow Nue's traveling partners, Wong On, a man who had made the trip down to Greenville and married a "Negro" woman by the name of Emma Clay. As a teen, Arlee Hen had worked at a store owned by her father in Stoneyville before transferring as a clerk to the original Joe Gow Nue store. At one point, Arlee's father had attempted to send her and her sister Edlee away to acquire an education in China. This was prevented in part by their mother's strong refusal to part with her daughters and the unfortunate incident in which Arlee was struck by a bout of typhoid fever.[6]

In 1929, Arlee married a Chinese man by the name of Joe Suen Heung, and with the help of her father, Arlee and Joe Suen Heung (who later either changed his surname or had it changed by city officials to Hen) opened up their own store, J. S. Hen and Company. After years of serving both white and black customers from behind the counter, with abacus in hand, Arlee and Joe Suen Heung's store was sold in 1964. They never left Greenville. They had no children.[7]

It was not until the end of Arlee's life that the ugliness of antiblack racism and the puritanical obsession of the Chinese community of Greenville, Mississippi, for community race purity came to confront Arlee Hen. When her husband died on March 5, 1980, his body was prepared to be buried in the local Chinese cemetery, but six policemen were hired as pallbearers for—as I read it—it would have been a humiliation to have asked any of the Chinese men in the community to carry the body of one of their kinsmen who had married a Chinese woman of African descent.[8] Arlee Hen Joe was not offered the same invitation in death and was even denied burial at the same Chinese cemetery.

My desire to make known the biography of Arlee Hen and the story of the Chinese grocer in the American South, is to reveal the ways race and racism work for and against Chinese Americans in their choices to dis/identify with African Americans—or in Arlee Hen's case—mixed-race African American Chinese people.

This history of the Chinese in the South roughly between 1880 and the mid-1940s stands to show a complex shifting case of race and economics, social class and ethnic identity status, and marital negotiations due to laws barring entry and certain sexual barriers.[9] And inlaid within this history are even smaller histories, of families constructed out of proximity or opportunity, of children who were sent between black relatives in southern regional sites and extended in-laws in China, of communities bound by shop, marriage, and connection to place.

EARLY TWENTIETH-CENTURY CHINESE LAUNDRIES AS SITES OF LABOR, RELATIONS

This next image taken in 1942, shows an African American woman ironing laundry on a Monday morning inside

Johnnie Lew's Chinese laundry in the District of Columbia. The institution of the laundry remains an unusual site for exploring the racial overlap between Chinese men and black women since the profession had previously been dominated by emancipated African American women who—slapped by the backhand of Jim Crow race politics—were limited to few avenues of employment outside of domestic help.

After 1865, a good number of black women took up work as "cooks, maids, and child-nurses" with a few women finding employment "in local hotels."[10] Yet laundering provided many with access to their own families, which other types of employment prevented. Historian Tera W. Hunter writes that in one town, a common sight for many of the residents was that of "tall, straight negro girls marching through the street carrying enormous bundles of soiled clothes upon their heads" to wash and return to clients the next week.[11]

But as the national demand for Chinese labor on contracted regional, county, and state transportation and irrigation projects declined, Chinese men found themselves having to push into business enterprises with relatives and kinsmen, running laundries and grocery stores and owning Chinese restaurants.

The earliest record of Chinese and African American overlap in the hand washing business took place in San Francisco, California, around the 1850s when a journalist described a scene at Washerwoman's Lagoon, noting that among the black laundresses who convened by the water to work, was "a Chinese man walking along and singing 'Carry me back to old Virginy.'"[12] It was not uncommon to see recorded reports of violence between the two groups, one such occurring during the summer of 1877 in Galveston, Texas.

It was following an effort by black male laborers to protest wage cuts that a handful of independent black laundresses—in an act of public demonstration—stormed J. N. Harding's steam laundry and attempted to board up the front

Figure 2. Library of Congress, Prints and Photographs Division, FSA-OWI Collection [LC-USF34-013506-C DLC]

windows and door before making their way on to another local competitor: the Chinese laundry. The laundresses made demands in the paper directed to "Sam Lee, Slam Sling, Wu Loong and the rest" stating that the Chinese launderers had better close up shop and leave Galveston within fifteen days or they would be forcibly driven out."[13] Eventually the strike was resolved.

However, as the Chinese laundry, particularly east of California, became a more established entity in the twentieth century—with machines rendering hand washing obsolete—many owners sought out help and made it common practice to hire local black women to assist around the shop. In Chinese laundries throughout the District of Columbia, black women were hired to do the washing.[14] During the 1930s and 1940s, graduate student Paul C. P. Siu conducted a sociological study of Chinese laundrymen in Chicago, Illinois, where he found that it was not uncommon for the girls to "learn to eat Chinese food." And while there was some consensus from the launderers that "Negro women…[were] not reliable…if the day is too hot and there is too much work to do, [the women] do not show up as expected," in most cases the women were found to be indispensable with one laundry employing a woman who was able to "mark the laundry ticket, writing Chinese characters on it."[15]

Further gathered from Siu's sociological observations of the everyday lives of immigrant Chicago Chinese launderers are stories regarding sexual solicitation and consensual interracial affairs with black and mulatto women. Taken from his published dissertation, Siu documented scenes in which many of the laundry workers (his informants) talked openly about either paid visitations to prostitutes or casual lovers they kept—choosing not to repress their sexual desires or finding masturbation insufficient. Other times, Siu himself would observe particular women visiting the laundry to flirt with the employees and solicit sex or money.

In one example, Siu had been sitting with some men in a laundry and informally asked a launderer about his sexual practices. This was his response:

> There are some night clubs in the "Black-Devil's Nest" [Negro area] at Fifty-fifth and State Streets. There are two around the neighborhood. One is better than the other. I have been in both of them many times. Sometimes I just pick up black girls on the street corner. They are walking back and forth on the street, looking for a man. I would rather starve than not see a girl and have a good time.[16]

Another example was one in which Siu sat inside a laundry, recording the happenings. A launderer named Lum had a mulatto woman in her twenties named Dotty come by to call on him one afternoon at four. Siu recorded the dialogue between them, which can be found in its entirety in *The Chinese Laundryman: A Study of Social Isolation*. But to summarize, Dotty enters the laundry looking for Lum. A partner who works in the laundry asks Dotty if she has come to sleep with him. She ignores him and proceeds to ask Lum for five dollars to buy some stockings and a handbag. Lum insists he does not have five dollars and then accuses Dotty of asking for money without giving sex in exchange. He offers her three dollars but only if she will perform oral sex on him to which she asserts, "You bad boy! What do you think I am. I'm not that kind of a girl. I'm no street walker."[17] Still, Dotty and Lum continue with their seemingly playful banter over money until Lum gives Dotty three dollars and Dotty leaves the laundry. She returns shortly with a pair of boxed stockings and retreats into the back room with Lum where they are alone for about half an hour.

Another illustration of constructed intimacy and accommodating relationships ran on October 7, 1927, in an article in the *New York Times* in which the effort of a Jersey City Chinese laundryman to legally adopt an eight-year-old African American boy named Firman Smith was reported. Lemon Lee Sing who had cared for Firman since the boy was a one-year-old went to Judge Thomas F. Meaney on matters regarding a reimbursement of a ten dollar payment Sing had made in 1920 for a bond of the Irish Republic.

In articulating Sing's desire to adopt the boy, the newspaper reported that Sing "lost no face" as Firman Smith turned out to be one of the brightest students at Public School 30. Additionally, it was stated that according to the favor of Sing's joss, the launderer planned to have Firman continue on to college after completing high school. Sing himself was sixty-one and from Canton with "no relatives either in the Celestial Kingdom" or the United States.[18] Furthermore, the article stated that the boy had been abandoned by his mother and that Sing had found him.

However in an accompanying article in the *Pittsburgh Courier,* Firman Smith was the son of a fourteen-year-old girl who had worked three months in Lemon Lee Sing's laundry before giving birth. Sing paid for the young girl's medical fees and when a sore developed on baby Firman's neck, Sing called for his own doctor to treat the boy. Later on when Firman's mother fell ill, she had the boy sent along with his clothes to Sing's laundry at 111 Ocean Avenue to be cared for. The *Courier* made mention that "so far as anybody could prove [Firman Smith]…never had a father."

After a long spell, Firman's mother recovered and soon after married, leaving Firman with Sing due to the boy's having become so attached to the man. It was after that point that Sing set out to gain legal custody to prevent Firman's mother from coming back to claim the boy, and to secure the laundry's savings and a $2,000 insurance policy taken out on behalf of Firman. Regarding the possibility of separation, Sing was quoted as saying, "If I miss him, I would drop—I couldn't stand."

At one point, Sing had become angered over the racial teasing of Firman by neighborhood boys—they found it funny that a black child would live with a Chinese parent—and went straight to Judge Thomas F. Meany to handle the situation, an obvious gesture of parental concern over one's child. In a comment that further marginalized the launderer and his adopted son, the newspaper called Sing and Firman a "strangely assorted pair."[19]

Strange or not, it was the invention of the automatic washing machine after the Second World War that pushed nearly all Chinese launderers into other professions and ended the occupational relationship between black women and Chinese men. A popular consumer product has given way to future racial estrangements.

OF BLACK CHINESE DESCENT: CONFIGURATIONS OF CHINESENESS AT THE END OF THE TWENTIETH CENTURY

This last image that I would like you to consider is of me and my mother taken when she had come out to visit me on the East Coast where I was attending graduate school at the time. This image is one that I would like to leave you with, in case you have never before seen an African American Chinese person or never really articulated blackness as being remotely related to Chineseness, especially in the physiobiological form. This last image functions more as artifact, as a historical record of the existence of black Chinese intermarriage (however uncommon) and black Chinese people (however superficially invisible).

It was always a longstanding, almost obsessive concern with me to attempt to build an existence outside of the world of racism, animosity, and rejection that I felt, separated from other Chinese people. I was told I was not Chinese by both relatives and unrelated people alike and believed that I wasn't because of it. Never did I question the validity of these statements that cut me off from my mother, from Chineseness, nor did I feel much at home in my blackness alone. And so I lived with this sense of tension inside me, a tension built on popular belief that blackness as a race, as a color was

Figure 3. Carmela Chi Hwee Song with her daughter Wendy Marie Thompson in Silver Spring, Maryland, June 29, 2005.

capable of canceling out anything lighter than itself, erasing all other parts of culture, enveloping a person in darkness. But I refused to see the eclipse, to believe my experience, my identity inherited maternally through blood and culture was false.

This is were my own personal investment in this topic comes from as it is not likely obvious from my name or in photographs where my mother is absent; it is that I am an African American Chinese living in the center of two cultural imaginations.

My birth occurred in January 1981 to a Burmese Chinese woman and her African American husband in the California Bay Area exactly fifteen years after antimiscegenation laws meant to prevent black-white sexual relations and intermarriage in the United States were struck down by a Supreme Court ruling in the case of *Loving v. the Commonwealth of Virginia*.

I was born the eldest of three girls who all hold a different skin tone, phenotype, hair texture, and relationship to race and cultural identity. However, what we share is an individual relationship to Chineseness, a personal quarrel with having to prove that we owned a biracial space outside of a generalized assumption of what we were and where we should stay because of it. Since childhood, we tended to identify culturally with our mother—who we spent most of our time with, who we felt comforted by, who we loved dearly, and who conversely saw her offspring as Chinese Americans.

It was in this way that I knew myself to be a different kind of Chinese, a different kind of race on the cusp of both immigrant and American, transplant and native. Where outsiders claimed they knew what I was for me, there lived a counter-narrative within my self. I had my own knowledge of my language, my foodways, my genealogy, what customs became familiar to me without question. Still I knew that the home I grew up in was a culturally hybrid home, different from that of other Chinese folk my mother would on the odd occasion take me with her to visit.

I had a mother who was born in Rangoon, Burma (now Yangon, Myanmar), in the mid-1950s and grew up in the wrap of *longyis*, pagodas, and Burmese nursemaids. Her father had sent her and two brothers away to Taiwan to "learn Chinese," and I now assume it was not only the language he was talking about but had to do more with his ambivalence about his nine children running barefoot, eating by fingers, and speaking Burmese. She was nine when she was sent away to "become Chinese." Her life would be full of transitions.

At twenty-three my mother became a bride, and in the duration of a long, difficult marriage, frowned upon by her family because of (my father's) race, she became American. But always caught in the periphery, this woman who went from being Burmese to Chinese to American learned what she could in wifehood—red beans and rice, ham hocks, cornbread, and collared greens—by watching her African American mother-in-law, her in-laws having themselves migrated from Louisiana to the San Francisco Bay Area in the late 1940s during the Second World War to work in the defense and shipbuilding industries.

Early on in this household, we lived in a language of shame where my sisters and I did not attend Chinese language school, were raised roughly bilingual being that our mother, who arrived in the United States in 1974, found it easier to navigate every so often in Chinese. It would be in second grade that I would charge home and tell her to stop speaking to me in Chinese because in "America we speak English."

Decades before, my mother as an adolescent was told by her China-born father that she and her siblings should stop speaking Burmese because they were Chinese and Chinese people should speak Chinese.

This shame that was born with language twisted until it branched beneath the skin. It would be shared by my mother's family, their prejudice that drove them to disown her, even before the birth of any children or word of any marriage. And it would go on like this even after her children were born, a continued slip of embarrassment under the tongue in the things matter-of-factly stated or left unsaid. But still, we were family even for the lack of any open apologies after we had all grown up.

The way I see race now, I feel that there is a way socially, among disparate Chinese and Chinese American communities and peoples, that blackness gets interpreted as a flat generalization, as a contrast for understanding the self—*all* black people are *x*, but *we* are Chinese and we are *y*. I want to know where this places those of us who don't "fit" into categories, into racial interpretations of others, of the self. And I want to know how it is that these set categories and separate demarcations benefit us when we ourselves and our communities are partitioned by differing citizenship categories, nationalities, age groups, queered and sexed bodies, dialects, and economic class statuses, which all of us are constantly navigating on a daily basis.

To borrow a theoretical expression here, I want to know if we can imagine otherwise, if we can imagine Chineseness otherwise, as a space where intersections with blackness or other nonwhite local indigenous identities is legitimate, possible.

In becoming comfortable with the varied ways we eat, dress, speak, live, learn, and die, we will be more apt to expand and interrogate these identities we all dis/claim if we ask ourselves and each other: What determines Chinese and Chinese American communities? What are the reasons for the absence of blackness, black histories, and black people when talking about Chinese American spaces, families, and geographies? What does it mean to be Chinese in the diaspora? What prevents us from imagining Chineseness in other bodies, with other phenotypes?

What does it mean to be Chinese?

NOTES

1. Felicia R. Lee, "A Def Poetry Jam of Her Very Own," *The New York Times,* July 17, 2005.

2. James W. Loewen, *The Mississippi Chinese: Between Black and White* (Cambridge: Harvard University Press, 1971), 25, 28; Robert Seto Quan, *Lotus among the Magnolias: The Mississippi Chinese* (Jackson: U niversity Press of Mississippi, 1982), 4–6; Lucy M. Cohen, *Chinese in the Post-Civil War South: A People without a History* (Baton Rouge: Lousiana State University Press, 1984), 85, 107.

3. Cohen, 99–100, 111–112.

4. While the general assertion of Chinese laborers tends to mark the predominately male immigrant community as bachelors, many of these men were actually married and had wives and children in China who were barred from entering the country due to various exclusion acts targeted toward restricting unskilled Chinese labor. With those marriages that occurred with noncitizens or persons of color who were not considered American citizens by the government and the white-dominant citizen population, many were common law, performed outside of religious institutions, and not always recorded in city, county, or state documentation.

5. Ted Shepherd, *The Chinese of Greenville, Mississippi* (Greenville, MI: Burford Brothers Printing Company, 1999), 5.

6. Ruthanne Lum McCunn, *Chinese American Portraits: Personal Histories, 1828-1988* (San Francisco: Chronicle Books, 1988), 81–83.

7. Interview with Judy Yung, Greenville, Mississippi, May, 31, 1982.

8. Shepherd, 5.

9. I use the decade of the 1940s to demarcate detachment in social and sexual relations between African Americans and Chinese due to shifting communities and racial consciousness among Chinese Americans who saw the arrival of Chinese women—wives from China and new Chinese brides—after the Second World War. This composition changed the physical and social meaning of Chineseness, perhaps reinforced a monolithic type of Chinese identity rooted in part in phenotype, which forced many of the black Chinese families to disband or leave various Chinese communities who at this time worked to change their status (from "colored" or lower-class laborers to middle-class Chinese entrepreneurs) economically, socially, culturally, and politically in the United States.

10. Tera W. Hunter, *To 'Joy My Freedom: Southern Black Women's Lives and Labors After the Civil War* (Cambridge, MA: Harvard University Press, 1997), 26.

11. Hunter, 57.

12. Rudolph Lapp, *Blacks in Gold Rush California* (New Haven: Yale University Press, 1977), 104.

13. Hunter, 77–78.

14. Esther Ngan-ling Chow, "From Pennsylvania Avenue to H Street, NW: The Transformation of Washington's Chinatown," in *Washington Odyssey: A Multicultural History of the Nation's Capital*, ed. Francine Curro Cary (Washington: Smithsonian Books, 1996), 194.

15. Paul C. P. Siu, *The Chinese Laundryman: A Study of Social Isolation* (New York: New York University Press, 1987), 84, 263.

16. Siu, 267.

17. Siu, 267–268.

18. "Judge to Help Chinese Adopt a Negro Boy," *The New York Times,* October 7, 1927, 20.

19. Grace Robinson, "Chinese Would Adopt Race Boy," *Pittsburgh Courier,* October 22, 1927, 6.

"My Race, Too, Is Queer"[1]
Queer Mixed Heritage Chinese Americans Fight for Marriage Equality[2]
(Original Title: My Race, Too, Is Queer: Chinese Hapa People
Fight Anti-Miscegenation and Anti-Gay Marriage)

Wei Ming Dariotis, PhD

BROAD OVERVIEW

This essay grew out of a presentation at the Seventh Chinese American Studies conference, "Branching Out the Banyan Tree: A Changing Chinese America," on October 8, 2005. It has been revised to integrate my analysis with a narrative of the panel, "Queer Chinese Hapa People and Marriage Rights: Intersections between Same Sex Marriage and Interracial Marriage," which consisted of myself and Queer Mixed Heritage Chinese American community activists Stuart Gaffney and Willy Wilkinson on the subject of the interconnections between the struggle for the right to marry across racialized boundaries and the fight for same sex marriage equality.[3] Just as our parents' generation struggled against antimiscegenation[4] laws, so today are we struggling for the right of same-sex marriage.

Both Stuart Gaffney and Willy Wilkinson have one European American parent and one Chinese American parent who at the time of their marriages (in the early 1950s) were affected by California's antimiscegenation laws (my white father and Chinese mother were married in Hawai'i in 1968). California's antimiscegenation laws had been struck down in 1948, but until 1967, the year of the landmark Supreme Court case, *Loving v. Virginia*, marriage between whites and "nonwhites" was still illegal in seventeen states. Gaffney and Wilkinson married their long-time same-gender partners when San Francisco Mayor Gavin Newsom made this possible in early 2004. They are now fighting to reinstate the legality of their marriages after the California courts declared them null and void on August 12, 2004.

Because of the history of the Chinese Exclusion Acts and other legislation and customs that limited the immigration of Chinese women, some Chinese American men were involved with the struggle against antimiscegenation laws, or to put it another way, they fought for the right to marry whomever they wanted, including white women. It is perhaps not a coincidence that Chinese Americans are now also intimately involved in the struggle for same sex marriage equality[5] in California. By positioning both the panel and this essay as a space in which to specifically address the intersections of mixed heritage Chinese American and queer identities, I argue that negotiations over the transgressions of race and gender in the realm of marriage rights are a critical juncture for investigating the ontological hermeneutics[6] of Chineseness and also provide a useful space for renegotiating the boundaries of Chinese America.

TERMINOLOGY

For the purposes of this essay, I use "queer people" as a reclaimed, nonderogatory term to include bisexual, lesbian, gay, and transgender people. I use the term "same sex marriage equality" rather than the commonly used term "gay marriage" because "gay" is not inclusive.

"Antimiscegenation" is used without a hyphen, to emphasize that there is no such thing as "miscegenation"—a racist term that denotes the degradation of whiteness through intermixing with people of color. On similar grounds, I use the term "mixed heritage" rather than "mixed race" to avoid reinscribing the notion that there are separate "races" (that by the same definition should not be mixed).

"Chinese American" is a complex category that has shifted meaning over time and is now inclusive of first-generation immigrants, like my mother, who were not born in America but expect to live and die here; of mixed heritage people like myself and fellow panelists; and of people adopted from China and raised by United States citizens of any heritage. *Chinese American* refers not only to a personal identity but also to an affiliation with a community. My use of the term "Chinese American" thus acknowledges that we have community members who have not one drop of Chinese "blood."[7]

CHANGING CHINESE

I was asked to organize this panel, and another panel on mixed heritage Chinese American media artists, by the conference co-chair, Lorraine Dong. Lorraine asked me to organize as many mixed heritage panels as I could—she stressed that these were important because the focus of the conference was "Branching Out" Chinese America—and specifically looking at "A Changing Chinese America," and she wanted to recognize the significance of mixed heritage people in that reconceptualized community. Even more significantly, she was the one who stressed the need for a panel recognizing the relationship between the historical struggle against anti-miscegenation laws and the current fight for same sex marriage equality.

Our presence at the conference means that there is recognition that Chinese America is indeed changing, but how? Is Chinese America branching out the banyan tree to embrace those previously left outside its protection? Or should we be thinking about the shifts in Chinese America in some other way? Insofar as Chinese America is at least partially a self-defined state—and we are now being recognized as part of that "self"—we Queer Mixed Heritage Chinese Americans have in a Derridean sense "always already" been in a process of redefining Chineseness and by extension Chinese America. Queer Mixed Heritage Chinese Americans make us question: What does Chineseness mean when it is not bound by appearance or phenotype? When it is not bound by so-called "traditional" gender roles? When it is not bound by a mandate to reproduce itself in a recognizable fashion? In *The Location of Culture*, Homi Bhabha writes of the "ambivalence of the 'nation' as a narrative strategy"[8] and we can understand from this that the story of ethnic identity, of culture, is always moving between two points (ambi-valent)—the constructed center and its other—leaving the margins between self and other ragged, both torn and unformed.

What is the relationship between Chineseness and Americanness? Are they inverse constructions of identity, where the term "American" is constructed as a catchall, the melting pot, the ultimate Baudrillardian simulacra—infinite copies with no original? And is Chineseness, oppositionally, the *ultimate* original, the point of origin from which emanates global diaspora? Bhabha critiques the metaphor of nation building, "*the many as one,*"[9] which has been in America constructed, *E pluribus unum,* as though outside of a center, which may be why it is so difficult for America to see itself as an empire. While all roads lead to Rome, America is the land of immigrants, meaning there is, at least in theory, or in popular metaphor, no *original* American identity. Given these two oppositionally constructed identities, Chinese and American, the question of what it means to be a Chinese American must necessarily include a ragged edge. All Chinese Americans, whether first generation or fifth, gay, straight, or transgender, must live in this liminal space. But even heterosexual, mono-ethnic Han Chinese people *in China* are also implicated in this question of authentic identity, or *originary* identity, because, as Bhabha writes, *culture* is always changing. There is no such thing as static culture. Thus, there is no such thing as authentic "Chineseness." Chineseness is always already changing. One might say that Chineseness *is* change, but in a different way than Americanness *is* change. Where do Queer Mixed Heritage Chinese Americans fit within this dynamic view of Chi-

neseness? By virtue of always moving along multiple axes of identity, do Queer Mixed Heritage Chinese Americans bring something important to this town meeting under the banyan tree—a new way of looking at it, perhaps; or a different way of being it? Or both?

Cultural critic Ien Ang, in her book, *On Not Speaking Chinese*, underscores what she calls the "straightjacket" effect of identity; Ang writes, "'who I am' or 'who we are' is never a matter of free choice."[10] A straightjacket is not merely a restraint like any other—rather, Ang's choice of this specific term evokes insanity, mental disturbance, and schizophrenia. It is a common stereotype that mixed heritage people are by definition schizophrenic, and, in this "compassionate" day and age, the question still commonly asked of interracial couples, "What about the children?" resonates with the potential for "schizophrenic-like" identity crises of being "torn between two worlds." While mixed heritage was never formally recognized by the American Psychological Association as an identity equivalent to a mental illness the way queer sexualities have been pathologized, numerous studies by psychologists and sociologists, and a "common-sense" reading of mixed heritage identity, have reified the notion that *to be mixed* is to be *mixed up*. The pseudoscientific construction of queer people and of mixed heritage people as mentally ill is deeply rooted in the history of eugenics, a pseudoscience dedicated to "perfecting" humanity through the culling of those perceived as deviating from the ideal—the straight, white, wealthy ideal. Acting both directly and indirectly in conjunction with structures of misogyny, heterosexism, racism, Christian-centrism, classism, and nativism, U.S. eugenicists advocated the sterilization and institutionalization of women, people deemed mentally ill (for example, gays and lesbians), people classified as sexual deviants, people of color, non-Christians (including Jews and Catholics), the poor, and (non-Western European) immigrants.[11]

QUEER MIXED HERITAGE CHINESE AMERICANS AND MARRIAGE RIGHTS

For Queer Chinese Americans of mixed heritage, particularly for those born before the landmark 1967 Supreme Court case, *Loving v. Virginia,* which abolished antimiscegenation laws, the social and legal conflicts over their right to marriage equality reflect their parents' legal and social struggles to love and marry across the boundary of "white purity."[12] Comparisons of the current struggle over same sex marriage equality with the fight for the right to marry interracially reveal important intersections between social and legal processes of constructing race, gender, and sexuality. Mixed Heritage Studies scholar Maria P. P. Root, in her "Bill of Rights for People of Mixed Heritage" (1993, 1994), proclaims the right "to freely choose whom [to] befriend and love." This declaration, the last and by that situation perhaps the most important of the twelve rights Root asserts, is a subtle inter-section of queer and mixed heritage identities. Her "Bill of Rights for People of Mixed Heritage" does not overtly address queer issues, focusing instead on race; however, her subse-quent "Multiracial Oath of Social Responsibility" (2004) ends with the statements, "I must fight all forms of oppression as the oppression of one is the oppression of all" and under this the commitment, "I recognize that my life interconnects with all other lives." Though Root does not explicitly mention homophobia as a form of oppression, it is clear that her work around mixed heritage issues encompasses other dynamics of oppression, including those around sexuality and gender. Root's recognition of this complexity is no surprise, given that mixed heritage activists and queer activists alike are finding common cause in the fight for marriage equality.

In his experimental documentary video, *Transgressions* (2000), in which Gaffney borrows footage from the 1993 David Cronenberg film version of David Henry Hwang's play, *M. Butterfly*, Gaffney tells the story of his parents' interracial relationship and his own mixed heritage and queer identity. At one point, Gaffney says, "I don't look or love like my par-ents." With this simple statement Gaffney encapsulates the complex situation of queer, mixed-heritage people—our identities are different from those of our parents on at least two of the most important identity axes—that of racializa-tion and/or ethnic identity and that of sexuality. And yet Gaffney himself recognizes that his "queer love" *is* similar to his parents' interracial love—it is, similarly, transgressive. In fact he wonders whether his parents' "transgressive love" had somehow given rise to a "transgressive love in [him]." He *equates* the "transgression" of interracial love with the trans-gression of same-gender love, aligning both as what could be called "queer" in the way he says his "*race*, too, is queer." To be transgressive *is to be* "queer" in a binarily oppositional world that sees only perfection and nonperfection, white and nonwhite, straight and nonstraight. In the same way, then, that his parents' love was not wrong, Gaffney argues that his own love is just as worthy of legal and social recognition. At a critical moment in *Transgressions*, Gaffney declares, "From now on I will say my sexuality is queer and my race, too, is queer." This moment is a critical turning point in Gaffney's film, which up to this point has been occupied with ques-tions about identity; this statement is one of the few places Gaffney suggests an answer to those questions. This line, "my race, too, is queer," raises the question: What can be learned from examining the "queering" of race not only in terms of looking at queer people of color at the experiential level, but from—additionally—looking at the social and legal under-pinnings of these connected systems of oppression? Critical Mixed Heritage Legal Studies and Critical Queer Legal Stud-ies would best serve their purpose if they would work hand in hand to challenge the oppressive proposal to *change the U.S. Constitution* to redefine marriage, at a national level, as a union between a man and a woman.

Wilkinson, in her special article to the *Chronicle*, "Family Values: Lesbian Newlywed Breaks Barriers Just as Her Parents Did More Than 50 Years Ago," writes,

> Today in 2004, as interracial marriages flourish and mixed-race people abound, these stories seem archaic, mean-spirited and representative of an era of ignorance left in the past. But are they? Opponents of interracial marriages considered the unions to be "immoral" and "unnatural." Sound familiar?…
>
> Call it what you want—codifying and controlling the rights of marriage for heterosexuals only, insisting that heterosexuals are uniquely qualified to love each other and raise families within the institution of marriage, or just plain asserting that heterosex-uals know best—it all piles up to unequal treatment under the law, and that spells discrimination.[13]

Wilkinson equates the abhorrent sounding rhetoric of histori-cal interracial marriage opponents, with that of current oppo-nents of same sex marriage. By making this analogy, Wilkin-son's rhetorical strategy suggests that the same, currently socially unacceptable intolerance evident in antimiscegena-tion logic is at play in the opposition to same sex marriage. This also means that the same application of constitutional rights that applied in *Loving v. Virginia* should apply in the case of same sex marriage. In *Loving v. Virginia*, Virginia's anti-miscegenation laws were held to violate the Equal Protection and Due Process Clauses of the Fourteenth Amendment. In other words, *Loving v. Virginia* forms the logical legal basis for same sex marriage equality.

The video Gaffney showed at the conference, his 2004 *MUNI to the Marriage,* primarily consists of footage he shot as a reenactment of riding MUNI to meet his partner John Lewis at City Hall to get married. As with Gaffney's other films, the hypnotic effect of visual footage overlaid with voiceover is experimental in that the video does not always directly depict the actions described in Gaffney's voiceover. This disjunction between image and narration forces viewers to attempt to fit the visual and aural elements together in some way to create meaning. In *MUNI to the Marriage*, Gaffney's journey on the MUNI can be read as symbolic of the liminal space of being between identities and even of being between states of being. This liminal state, like a doorway, is not just a space between other, more clearly defined spaces (dining and living room, white and Chinese); rather, it is more like a hallway—a space which is a room one can be in as well as a space through which one is moving. In this case, Gaffney is on a trajectory toward one thing and away from another: moving toward being married and away from being barred from marriage. The voiceover narration by Gaffney manifests the fragility of that certain trajectory. Gaffney describes the fear he and Lewis had over having the marriage license ripped from their hands before they could actually be married. Viewing the film at the conference, the audience already knew what Gaffney did not know when the video was made—that the marriages would eventually be declared illegal. The fixed track of the MUNI thus represents a space in which one can move both forward and back again, just as Gaffney and Lewis moved from being barred from marriage to being married, then again having the right to marriage, and legality of their marriage, stripped away from them.[14]

In an op-ed piece, Gaffney and his husband John Lewis describe their feelings when they became newlyweds, and, for the first time, "[their] government recognized [their] love as worthy of the highest respect under the law and treated [them] as fully equal human beings."[15] They realized that they had until the moment of their marriage been denied a fundamental human right. Yes, they could live together, yes, they could love each other, but they could not have that love recognized by fundamental institutions in our society. What does it feel like to be told, "Your marriage is null and void"? The people who best understand this feeling turn out to be Gaffney's own parents, who had had their own marriage challenged by social mores of the time. The support of his and Lewis' parents is perhaps even more deeply meaningful to them because of the history of Gaffney's parents' interracial marriage.[16] In fact, Gaffney has said[17] that his struggle for same sex marriage equality has brought him closer to his parents because they have found *kinship* in what they view as a shared struggle for the right, in the words of Maria P. P. Root, "to freely choose whom [to] befriend and love"[18]—and then to marry.

CHINESE AMERICANS AND ANTIMISCEGENATION

In *Interracial Intimacy: The Regulation of Race and Romance*, Rachel Moran describes the history of the social and, eventually, legal processes by which Chinese were added to the antimiscegenation laws that had already been imposed on African Americans and American Indians. Moran describes how Chinese were analogized to blacks and Native Americans, and that with this analogy came the recommendation that the Chinese be removed to reservations. Moran cites "[a] California magazine [which] confirmed the depravity of Chinese women noting that their physical appearance was 'but a slight removal from the African race.'"[19] Further, "These racial images in turn were linked to a degraded sexuality."[20] Ultimately, the result of this campaign was the 1878 California state constitutional amendment to restrict interracial marriage of Chinese with whites and a 1901 criminalization of Chinese-white intermarriage, reinstituted after a legislative correction in 1905.[21] Moran argues that "California's 1905 antimiscegenation law reflected fears of both racial difference and sexual deviance."[22] The sexual deviance rumored of Chinese men was, like that rumored of African American men, a predilection for white women. Chinese women were presumed to all be prostitutes and thus morally lax. In the sense of being *outside of normative sexuality*, the sexuality of Chinese was deemed "queer"—specifically because of their

race. Thus being able to determine or define someone's "race" is the foundation of the power of the state to prevent racially "queer" or "transgressive" sexuality.

FINAL THOUGHTS ON [QUEER, MIXED HERITAGE] CHINESENESS

In her chapter, "Can One Say No to Chineseness?" cultural critic Ien Ang, to use her subtitle, "push[es] the limits of the diasporic paradigm" and discusses the paradox of minority identity in the context of a worldwide Chinese diaspora.[23] The "indeterminate signifier"[24] that *is* Chineseness intersects intriguingly with identity nodes for Queer Mixed Heritage Chinese people to create a kind of biofeedback loop through which Chineseness itself can be usefully reconceived. Mixed Heritage Studies theorist, George Kitahara Kich, proclaims,

> If the ambiguity that comes from the struggle can be tolerated and there is generosity towards reconnection, then the marginalized can reflect back, as an archaeological returning or re-membering to the "monopeoples" of the world, their own shadowed, buried, altered, and disowned projections.[25]

Chinese identity can seem so fixed, so definite—perhaps because of the vast number of people in the world who identify as "Chinese," perhaps because of the longevity of Chinese history and the dominance of Chinese culture and language, but in the words of Wayne Wang's film, *Chan Is Missing*, the question, "What kind of Chinese Chinese are you?" can generate millions of responses—varying not only from individual to individual, but also over the lifetime of one individual as they change—like my mother who has shifted from Shanghainese to Chinese immigrant to Chinese American. Being open to these shifts and variations may be partially a function of being "generous toward reconnection" on all sides of the margin, and I like to think of the image of the banyan tree—roots and limbs connecting midair—as a symbol of the process by which Queer Mixed Heritage Chinese Americans participate in reconceiving the notion of Chineseness. Being Chinese in the postdiaspora, transnational age is complicated but not impossible. Perhaps the answer to Ang's question, then, is not that one can "Say No to Chineseness" but rather that one can say "no" to exclusionary definitions of Chineseness, or of any category. It requires being free from the idea of a point of origin—whether that is China or Chinatown, and yet continuing to recognize that place as a continued point of reference. To use airline terminology, we are moving away from a hub system dependent on always returning to a particular home base,[26] toward a point-to-point system in which each point is a home, a place to go back to, or a place to travel to in the future. Each point is equally relevant, rather than a system in which the point of origin is the most authentic, and those circles radiating outward, like ripples in the water, become only weaker.

ENDNOTE

After the panelists made their presentations, an audience member who identified herself as Chinese American came up to us and thanked us for speaking; she also commended Lorraine Dong for being brave enough to encourage such a panel at this Chinese American community event. The woman intimated that the subject matter of the panel was still challenging for Chinese Americans generally, even to a group like that gathered around the Chinese Historical Society of America, who were largely community scholars. Notably, there was a large attendance for our panel (over twenty-five people) and we received only positive, supportive comments from an audience that consisted mostly of community members in their forties to sixties as well as a large group of college students. I thank everyone involved for participating in this community discussion of Queer Mixed Heritage Chinese American identities and issues.

NOTES

1. Stuart Gaffney, *Transgressions*, 2000, videotape.
2. I wish to thank both Willy Wilkinson and Stuart Gaffney for a lively exchange of ideas as well as the careful attention they each gave to this essay. That being said, however, any and all mistakes are mine, and this essay should not be taken as a representation of them or their ideas, only as my interpretation. This essay has been revised to present a narrative of the panel, while portions of my analysis of Gaffney's video, *Transgressions*, have been reconstructed into another essay: "'I'm Not Bisexual, But I should Be': Bisexuality and Biraciality in *Transgressions* by Stuart Gaffney." The two essays can be read as companion pieces.
3. The term "sex" is fraught with misuse. In this specific case of legal definition, the term is used to mean biological sex assigned at birth. In contrast, gender is about personal identity. Thus, according to Willy Wilkinson, "No one is talking about same-gender marriage because the legal battle is for marriage recognition based on legal sex, not gender identity." (Personal correspondence, December 2005.)
4. I write *antimiscegenation* without a hyphen because I disagree with the racist concept of "miscegenation"—that is, the fundamental illegality of marriage between people of different racialized groupings. By writing *antimiscegenation* without a hyphen, I wish to delegitimize the legal and social structures that coined the term "miscegenation" in the first place.
5. Though I do not discuss it, it is important to note that the lead plaintiffs in the California same-sex marriage equality lawsuit, *Woo vs. Lockyer*, include Chinese Americans Cristy Chung and Lancy Woo.
6. *Ontology*, originally based in religious arguments about the existence of God, has come to be a system by which logical arguments are made regarding the existence of ideals. *Hermeneutic,* meaning *interpretive,* has roots in religious, philosophical, and literary interpretation of texts. By using the phrase "ontological hermeneutics of Chineseness," I am trying to suggest the idea of Chineseness as a kind of text or ideal that is communicated between people, where relative levels of "authenticity" are measured in relation to transgressions of race, gender, and sexuality.
7. And I make the blatantly biological reference to blood deliberately to invoke the tension between biology and self-identity that runs throughout this essay.
8. Homi Bhabha, *The Location of Culture* (New York: Routledge, 1994), 140
9. Bhabha, *Location,*142; italics in original.
10. Ien Ang, *On Not Speaking Chinese: Living Between Asia and the West* (New York: Routledge, 2001), vii.
11. Please note, I wrote these words several days before former Secretary of Education William Bennett's remarks to the effect that crime would be greatly reduced if all black babies were aborted. Eugenics, it seems, is not merely a theory from the past (September 28, 2005).
12. Antimiscegenation laws were always about maintaining the presumed "purity" of whiteness; they were always designed to prevent intermarriage between those deemed white and those deemed nonwhite. That there were never laws preventing intermarriages between groups of people of color implies that the principle of preventing "race mixing" across the board was never the issue; the only concern was "white purity."
13. Willy Wilkinson, "Family Values: Lesbian Newlywed Breaks Barriers Just as Her Parents Did More Than 50 Years Ago," *San Francisco Chronicle*, March 5, 2004, *http://www.sfgate. com/cgi-bin/article.cgi?file=/chronicle/archive/2004/03/05/WBG-GC58DQQ1.DTL.*
14. I am tempted here to liken this to being moved by BART from the suburban outreaches of the Bay Area into the city center of San Francisco and then having to go back again.
15. OPINION | Open Forum by Stuart Gaffney and John Lewis, September 13, 2004, *PlanetOut.com* (accessed October 1, 2005).
16. John Lewis and Stuart Gaffney, "September 2004 JUST MARRIED: John & Stuart, 'Newlyweds' After 17 Years Together," *San Fancisco Spectrum* (accessed October 1, 2005).
17. Stuart Gaffney, phone interview, October 6, 2005.
18. Maria P. P. Root, "Bill of Rights for People of Mixed Heritage," *http://www.drmariaroot.com/.*
19. Rachel F. Moran, *Interracial Intimacy: The Regulation of Race and Romance* (Chicago: University of Chicago Press, 2001), 31.
20. Moran, *Interracial Intimacy*, 30.
21. Moran, *Interracial Intimacy,* 16.
22. Moran, *Interracial Intimacy*, 32.
23. Ang, *On Not Speaking Chinese,* 37.
24. Ang, *On Not Speaking Chinese,* 38.
25. George Kitahara Kich, "In the Margins of Sex and Race: Difference, Marginality, and Flexibility," in *The Multiracial Experience: Racial Borders as the New Frontier*, ed. Maria P. P. Root (Thousand Oaks, CA, London, and New Delhi: Sage Publications, 1996), 276.
26. This is a reference to Shawn Wong's 1979 novel—irresistible, given that I also moderated for the conference, the sneak peek at Mixed Heritage Chinese American filmmaker Eric Byler's film version of Wong's novel, *American Knees.* Byler's film is titled *Americanese.*

Marriage Rights in the Media

Stuart Gaffney

My mother, who is Chinese American, was only able to marry my father, who is white, because of the California Supreme Court's 1948 *Perez* decision overturning California's anti-miscegenation law. Without that decision, my family might not exist. Similarly, I was only able to marry my partner of nineteen years, John Lewis, because San Francisco Mayor Gavin Newsom enforced the California Constitution's guarantees of equality under the law in 2004.

In "Marriage Rights in the Media," I discuss the contrast between directing marriage-themed films and videos and then having the camera turned on me as my husband and I became the subjects of media coverage. I presented two of my own video works—*Muni to the Marriage,* which explores the parallels between my parents' marriage and my own, and *Secret Sounds*, which tells the story of my discovery that my grandfather had two wives. I then presented news clips from television coverage of our 2004 San Francisco Chinese New Year Parade wedding float featuring same-sex couples married in San Francisco City Hall. In addition, panelist Willy Wilkinson and I each told our personal stories of getting married in San Francisco City Hall and experiencing our city government recognizing our relationships as fully deserving of equality under the law.

In the proud tradition of Chinese Americans and Asian Pacific Islander people standing up for equal marriage rights, John and I became plaintiffs with Cristy Chung and Lancy Woo in *Woo v. Lockyer,* the California lawsuit seeking to declare California's ban on marriage for same-sex couples unconstitutional. I closed my presentation by quoting from California Assemblymember Judy Chu's remarks before the California Legislature when she rose in support of AB 849, Assemblymember Mark Leno's marriage equality bill. She stated:

> I rise in support of AB 849….125 years ago, on this very floor of the California State Legislature, a law was passed to specifically prohibit marriage between Chinese and whites. It was the result of a California Constitutional Convention to look at what they called the "Chinese problem." A multitude of Chinese laborers were brought into California, and there was a hysterical backlash against them. In a debate on the floor that was probably just like this one, a state delegate named John Miller stood up to say, "Were the Chinese to amalgamate at all with our people…the result of that amalgamation would be…a mongrel of the most detestable that has ever afflicted the earth." And so, the California Legislature passed the bill….So here I am, serving in the same California legislature that for 68 years would have prohibited me from marrying a white person….I know that I do not want that same kind of marriage hysteria to be leveled against other human beings in the state of California. I know that if I expect full and equal treatment to be given to me, then it is my responsibility to ensure that there is full and equal treatment for others. That is why I support AB 849. I urge you to not repeat what this California legislature did 125 years ago to legalize marital discrimination. Let's come out of the dark ages where hysteria and prejudice rule. Let us make today the day that will ensure true marriage equality in California.

Subsequently, I have been interviewed by the Chinese Historical Society of America as part of the Spring 2006 exhibit on the history of the San Francisco Chinese New Year Parade. Our marriages are part of San Francisco history, and now they are part of the history of the San Francisco Chinese New Year Parade.

The Emergence of Chinese American Women

(Original Title: The Emergence of Chinese Women)

Loni Ding, Jennie Chin Hansen, Daphne Kwok, and Doreen Yang

ALICE LOWE, MODERATOR

The Square and Circle Club, the oldest Chinese American women's community service organization in America, was founded on June 15, 1924, by seven teenaged girls in San Francisco Chinatown, who wanted to help flood and famine victims in China. These girls—Alice Fong (Yu), Daisy K. Wong, Ivy Lee (Mah), Anne Lee (Leong), Daisy Wong (Chinn), Bessie Wong (Shum), and Jennie Lee—adopted an old Chinese saying as their motto: "In Deeds Be Square, In Knowledge Be All-Round." They drew a square enclosed within a circle for their club insignia. For over eighty years, members have proudly adhered to the club's tradition by raising funds and providing service to numerous Chinese organizations and individuals in both the San Francisco Bay Area and abroad. They have also encouraged Chinese women to develop their full potential and achieve their life goals.

A presentation of photos and press clippings was followed by a panel discussion on "The Emergence of Chinese American Women" and featured Chinese American women who have succeeded in various nontraditional careers. Included were Jennie Chin Hansen, former executive director of On Lok Senior Health Services and now board member of AARP and Chair of its Foundation; Loni Ding, pioneer Chinese American woman television producer; Daphne Kwok, executive director of Angel Island Immigration Station Foundation and civil rights activist; and Doreen Yang, president of Square and Circle Club and an early Chinese American pharmacist. The moderator was Alice Lowe, the first Asian chair of the Asian Art Museum, the largest museum in America devoted exclusively to Asian art. The consensus was that role models such as the above and others are inspiring Chinese American women to emerge from their traditional roles of meekness and subservience to that of individual and community leadership. The discussion ended on a positive note, namely that there is greater acceptance now of women in broader fields and levels of responsibility and that women themselves have become more assertive and more confident of their own abilities. Much more remains to be done but much has also been accomplished.

Contested Childhoods

The Pacific Society for the Suppression of Vice vs. the WHMS Methodist Oriental Home, 1900–1903

Jeffrey L. Staley, PhD

INTRODUCTION

Historical investigations of Protestant child rescuers in San Francisco Chinatown are not new, but surprisingly there are no studies of the Methodist women's work in the Chinese quarter, even though it actually predates by four years the well known Presbyterian Occidental Mission.[1] The purpose of this essay is therefore to investigate Methodist women's rescue work in Chinatown, specifically looking at two rescues undertaken by Deaconess Margarita Lake of the Methodist Episcopal Church's Oriental Home, showing how the politics of child rescue in early twentieth-century Chinatown were often complex—more complex than has generally been acknowledged by other analyses that have focused only upon the rescues of her contemporary, Donaldina Cameron of the Presbyterian Chinese Mission Home.[2]

The two cases discussed below are particularly interesting and unusual because two Caucasian child-rescuing groups are pitted against each other—The Pacific Society for the Suppression of Vice/Pacific Society for the Prevention of Cruelty to Children and Animals, and the Methodist Oriental Bureau, which ran the Oriental Home. Both groups were involved in a two-year struggle for the guardianship of two Chinese girls, "Sau Chun" and "Ah Ying," and in the process of court battles, their differing views of child-rearing become evident. The Pacific Society for the Suppression of Vice was Roman Catholic in origin, and men filled all its leadership roles. William P. Sullivan, San Francisco Chief of Police who died in November 1901, was a former director of the Society. The Oriental Bureau, on the other hand, was a Protestant organization run entirely by women. The Pacific Society preferred "placing out" as a solution to raising neglected, delinquent, or orphaned children; the Oriental Bureau preferred the more controlled environment of an asylum for its rescued children.

The two cases discussed below are made all the richer by the variety of sources open to critical analysis: newspaper articles, annual reports of the two child-saving societies, Methodist women's magazines, and unpublished documents preserved by descendants of Margarita Lake.[3]

ORIGINS OF THE ORIENTAL HOME

The Methodist Episcopal Church's Oriental Home in San Francisco Chinatown had its origins in 1868, when the Reverend Otis Gibson, with his wife Eliza Chamberlain, was asked to establish a Chinese Domestic Mission in California. The Gibsons had been missionaries in Foochow, China, for ten years prior to moving to California and had been forced to return to the United States because of Eliza's poor health. A few months before the December 25, 1870 opening of their new Chinese Mission building at 916 Washington Street, the Gibsons and a small group of Methodist women met and formed the Woman's Missionary Society of the Pacific Coast to evangelize the Chinese women in Chinatown. Its central purpose was "to elevate and save heathen women, especially on these shores, and to raise funds for this work."[4] As a result of that meeting a rescue asylum was set aside on the top floor of the new Methodist Mission house, and within a year the Methodist women had their first "inmate."

The WMSPC functioned under the auspices of the MEC General Missionary Society for many years, sheltering trafficked Asian (Chinese and occasionally Japanese) women and girls, teaching them English and other cultural survival skills, and marrying them off to responsible Asian men. But in 1893, the WMSPC joined the ten-year-old MEC Woman's Home Missionary Society as its new "Oriental Bureau," and eight years later the Oriental Bureau built its own "Oriental Home for Chinese Women and Girls" at 912 Washington Street, just across Trenton Street from the original mission house. Both buildings were destroyed in the 1906 earthquake and fire, and the women and children of the Oriental Home were forced to take up temporary residence in Berkeley and Oakland until a new building opened in 1912 in San Francisco, at 940 Washington Street, on the site of Reverend Gibson's original Chinese Domestic Mission.

DEACONESS MARGARITA J. LAKE

In 1896, the WHMS Oriental Bureau hired twenty-three-year-old Margarita J. Lake as missionary, and her widowed

RANCISCO. WEDNESDAY MORNING, APRIL 3, 1901.

STATE'S ATTORNEYS MOVE TO CLOSE THE SLAVE PENS

MISS MARGARITA LAKE

MISS DONALDINA CAMERON.

Margarita Lake, an ordained Methodist deaconess, wearing her deaconess collar and hat. (Unidentified newspaper clipping, Kate B. Lake Scrapbook 2, p. 51, David W. Garton Collection)

mother, Kate Burton Lake, as matron of their Rescue Asylum. Margarita was a recent graduate of the two-year Methodist Deaconess Training School in Chicago, and her mother had taught in public and private schools for nearly twenty years. Margarita took the position with the Oriental Bureau thinking that it would be good training for her intended goal—which was to go to China as a missionary. However, neither she nor her mother would ever get that far. Instead, they would work for seven years in Chinatown, becoming outspoken crusaders for immigrant Chinese women's and children's rights, and indefatigable rescuers of trafficked persons.

CALIFORNIA AGE OF CONSENT LAWS AND CHILD-SAVING STRATEGIES

Prior to 1889, the legal age of (sexual) consent in the state of California was ten years old.[5] And although atypical, common-law marriages were recognized for children as young as seven years of age.[6] In 1889, the age of consent was raised to fourteen, and eight years later, in 1897, it was raised to sixteen. Finally, in 1913, the age of consent was raised to eighteen, and prostitution itself was curbed significantly with the "Red Light Abatement Act."[7]

In traditional Chinese culture, children were considered to be a year old at birth and they turned a year older during the Chinese New Year festival, which falls between January and February. So it was entirely possible for Chinatown brothel keepers trying to comply with California law to honestly consider their girls legally "of age," when by Western reckoning they were nearly two years *under* the age of consent (that is, girls barely twelve by Western reckoning could be "fourteen"

by Chinese accounts, and girls fourteen could be "sixteen" by Chinese accounts). Thus, it is not surprising to find that in 1897, when the age of consent in California was raised to sixteen, San Francisco newspapers ran numerous articles about Protestant missionaries rescuing twelve- to fourteen-year-old girls from Chinatown brothels. Yet, the women of the Methodist Rescue Asylum did not rescue sex workers in brothels without having some evidence that girls were clearly underage or wished to escape "the life," as they euphemistically called prostitution. Girls in brothels would often pass written messages (in English or Chinese) to the Protestant women doing "home visitation," or to members of the Chinese Society of English Education. Often a Chinese man who wished to marry a girl from a brothel would take a plea for rescue to one of the missions, and that would set the rescuers to work.

Children below the age of consent could legally be in brothels, saloons, or dance halls if accompanied by a parent or guardian. However,

> any child apparently under the age of sixteen…found wandering, and not having any settled place or abode, or proper guardianship, or visible means of subsistence …[who] frequent[ed] the company of reputed thieves or prostitutes or houses of prostitution or dance houses, concert saloons,…without parent or guardian [could] be arrested and brought before a court or magistrate.[8]

Thus, under these legal provisions, Methodist women and other religious and reform-minded organizations felt a moral responsibility to rescue Chinese children "found wandering" or "frequenting" immoral places—without seeking the consent of the parties involved.

RESCUING THE CHILDREN— AH CHUN AND AH YING

In December 1900, Deaconess Margarita J. Lake asked the Pacific Society for the Suppression of Vice to assist her in the rescue of a five-year-old Chinese girl called "Ah Chun" whom Margarita apparently had seen in the brothels of Spofford Alley and who had been befriended by the Salvation Army. Francis J. Kane, the Secretary of the Pacific Society for the Suppression of Vice, had been deputized as a "Special" by the San Francisco police department[9] and on a number of earlier occasions he had helped rescue girls for Donaldina Cameron of the Presbyterian Chinese Mission Home.[10] But this would be his first rescue attempt for the Methodist women.

Margarita had tried to secure the aid of the Eureka Society for the Prevention of Cruelty to Children in Ah Chun's rescue a year and a half earlier, and although the Society had promised to help on that occasion, for some reason it had not.[11] But Margarita persisted, and over the next few months she continued to watch little Ah Chun. Finally, on October 30, 1899, she was able to enlist the help of "officer McMurray" from the Children's Protective Society for a rescue attempt.[12] Together with a doctor, they took the sick child from her supposed mother, Kim Yook, a brothel keeper at 11 Spofford Alley.[13] Ah Chun was then placed under the temporary care of "Mary," a Chinese "Salvation Army lassie," who lived across the alley from the brothel, and there she stayed for a number of months until the brothel keeper reclaimed her.[14] A little over a year later, in the late morning of December 11, 1900, Frank Kane took Ah Chun from Kim Yook again—this time bringing her back to Margarita Lake at the Oriental Home.

A week and a half after Ah Chun's successful rescue, Kane found himself again helping Margarita Lake. Three days before Christmas seven-year-old Ah Ying was taken from a brothel at 829 Washington Street, where the mother was working. Although no one at the Methodist Oriental Home had contacted Kane about participating in the rescue, apparently he happened to be at the Mission house as the team was about to depart. Margarita Lake would later claim that Kane had never investigated Ah Ying's home or surroundings before they left to attempt the rescue.[15] But Kane could have argued that he knew the building well, having made a number of raids on a Japanese brothel next door.[16] Margarita Lake assumed from Ah Ying's clothing that Ying was a boy, but when she took the child back to the Mission house for a bath, she discovered that the child was a girl, dressed in boy's clothing.[17]

Apparently both of these rescues went smoothly, for neither one was mentioned in the following days' San Francisco newspapers. However, seemingly without Margarita Lake's knowledge or explicit consent, Kane went to Superior Court and named himself as temporary guardian of the two Chinese children. It is not entirely clear why he did this,[18] since there is no evidence suggesting that he had followed a similar procedure when he undertook rescues for Donaldina Cameron and the Presbyterian mission. But since these were the first two times he had worked with Margarita Lake and the Methodists, he may not have fully trusted their intentions nor been completely happy with the living arrangements on the third floor of the Mission house, where former prostitutes would be living in close proximity to the little girls.[19] Whatever his reasons for initiating the guardianship papers for Ah Ying and Ah Chun, over the next two years Kane's politics of rescue and guardianship would clash sharply with those of the Methodist women. In the end, neither group could claim complete legal victory over the two children. Kane and Lake would each "win" one child, with Ah Ying returning to her mother, and the girl known as "Ah Chun" growing up in the Oriental Home to become my wife's grandmother.

FRANCIS ("FRANK") J. KANE AND THE SOCIETY FOR THE SUPPRESSION OF VICE

Very little is known about Francis J. Kane apart from his work with at-risk children. At the time of the 1900 census, Kane was living in San Rafael; he listed his occupation as "secretary," and his age as forty-two years old. His parents were both born in Ireland, and he was born in California. He was married and had two children living at home. Mr. Kane was still living in San Rafael three years later, but his name does not appear in any subsequent California census records.[20]

Kane had been deputized and authorized by the San Francisco police department to wear a "Special's star" in 1888, most likely in conjunction with his position as Superintendent of the Youths' Directory on Howard Street, San Francisco.[21] According to James Flamant, the Youths' Directory was a Catholic charity connected with St. Vincent's Asylum (for boys) in San Rafael,[22] and as a lay organization, it raised funds through its quarterly publication, *St. Joseph's Union*.[23] The Directory, founded in 1886, "intended especially to provide a temporary home and employment for all those homeless and neglected boys that [did] not properly come under the care of the orphan asylums, nor receive State appropriation."[24] Because of the Youths' Directory's Roman Catholic connections, it is reasonable to assume that Kane was also Roman Catholic. He was still working for the organization in 1894, when a writ of habeas corpus was filed against him on behalf of the children of Henry and Annie Hunt, children for whom Kane sought guardianship.[25]

Apparently when possible, the Youths' Directory tried to place orphaned or neglected children with Catholic families,[26] for out of the 112 children the Directory helped in 1887, slightly fewer than half were turned over to orphan asylums.[27] But in 1898 and 1899, when Frank Kane was Secretary of the Pacific Society for the Suppression of Vice, nearly three-fourths of the 459 children rescued by that society were placed in "public institutions" instead of with families.[28] Milicent Shinn had argued as early as 1880 that there was a "necessary antagonism between the advocates of orphan asylums and the advocates of aid societies,"[29] noting that the

> Massachusetts State Board of Charities inveighed against "institutional life" for children, and urged that nature herself pointed to the home as the only place for them. The friends of asylums and reform schools reasoned that really proper homes, where people were willing to take stray children, often vicious ones, were too rare to be counted on; that in the asylum wise and experienced managers, experts in dealing with neglected children, could be had, and would be much better for them than miscellaneous strangers all over the country; that no really close guard could be kept over children so scattered.[30]

As secretary of two different "aid" societies, Kane's stance on this controversial child welfare issue must have been reasonably clear: when possible, "place out" neglected or orphan children with families in rural settings. Moreover, one might surmise that the former superintendent of a lay Roman Catholic charitable organization whose job included "seizures of obscene literature and pictures" would have his own personal, moral reasons for taking out temporary guardianship papers for two little brothel-dwelling Chinese girls and then resist turning them over permanently to a Protestant asylum for rescued prostitutes.

Kane had been a member of The Pacific Society for the Suppression of Vice since 1896[31]—a group founded in 1883 whose mission was, in part, to confiscate and destroy pornographic materials, pills and powders used by abortionists, lottery tickets, and gambling coupons.[32] By 1897—if not earlier—Kane became the secretary of the Pacific Society for the Suppression of Vice/Pacific Society for the Prevention of Cruelty to Children. That same year San Francisco newspapers wrote that he was arrested for battery while taking a little girl from a Mrs. Holstrom.[33] A few months later he was charged with contempt of court for "allegedly kidnapping" Katie Brown, "a minor given to its mother's custody by the court." In that case the prosecution contended that Kane had become the "catspaw of a certain Private Detective Dillon, who lay claim to [her deceased father's] property in some way."[34]

Over the next few years Kane's often confrontative and combative rescue strategies (both verbally and physically abusive) were occasionally and unfortunately coupled with financial transactions that raised the suspicions of the judges who granted guardianships.[35] Kane's financial transactions gave the appearance that clandestine payoffs were being made in the context of domestic disputes. The unfortunate result for him was that irrespective of his moral crusading, serious questions were being raised about the motives behind his child rescuing activities.

Kane did not renew his "Special's star" after July 1, 1896, and it was apparently revoked in 1897, perhaps as a result of his arrest and contempt of court ruling that year.[36] However, Kane never turned in the star to the police department. Apparently thinking it was lost, the police department issued a duplicate and reassigned it to someone else. Kane, meanwhile, continued to wear his original star when going about his rescue work, since its "authority" allowed him to gain entrance into homes and businesses where he had no search warrant and where other rescuers were refused admittance.[37] When Kane's Special's star was finally confiscated in 1903, it bore the initials "B.H." and belonged to a man in the Potrero named "James Flaherty."[38]

Apparently neither Donaldina Cameron nor Margarita Lake knew of Kane's ambiguous status in the police department when they first solicited his help for their Chinatown rescues. Or if they did know of his checkered past, perhaps the women considered his brushes with the law as regrettable but understandable side effects of child rescuing. After all, the two Lake women had been arrested on at least one occasion,[39] and they could probably be easily convinced that Kane held the moral high ground in a city where graft and financial payoffs were blatant and often went unchecked. Kane could argue—and did argue—that the suspicions raised with regard to his past rescues resulted from the dealings of shady lawyers and unscrupulous judges.[40]

So it was under these somewhat clouded circumstances that the Roman Catholic Kane assisted Protestants Lake and Cameron in a number of rescues between January and March 1901.[41] But it may have been a bungled rescue attempt on March 21, 1901—the second failed raid at 710½ Jackson Street in less than two weeks—that forced Margarita Lake to reconsider her relationship with Kane.

Margarita Lake's journal entry for March 21, 1901, reads: "Tried to rescue a girl from 710½ Jackson St. and was put out by watchman and police."[42] But the next morning's newspapers filled in the details, reporting that Kane's men had cursed and thrown punches and furniture at city police. Perhaps their unbecoming responses, splashed across the pages of San Francisco newspapers, brought Lake's association with Kane under the close scrutiny of Protestant supporters of the mission. Although her mother and Mission Home matron, Mrs. Kate Lake, defended the rescue attempt by arguing that Kane was an officer of the law and stated that the police who broke up the rescue attempt also knew Kane was an officer, a cursory police investigation revealed that Kane was not an officer, despite the fact that he wore a Special's star.

The upshot of the March 21 fiasco was that Kane was accused of impersonating an officer and trespassing without a search warrant.[43] But Kane (and the Lakes) claimed that he did not need a search warrant to take underage children from brothels.[44] And although he was not actually arrested, Kane agreed not to use the star again. Without Kane's authoritative star leading Chinatown's anti-trafficking crusade, and with the stain of his cursing accomplices besmirching the high moral ground of Methodist mission rescues, the Lakes may have thought it wise to quietly drop the Society for the Suppression of Vice from their list of partners-in-rescue. There is no evidence that he was involved with the Methodists (or the Presbyterians) in any subsequent rescue attempts.

MARGARITA LAKE AND THE ORIENTAL HOME VERSUS FRANK KANE AND THE SOCIETY FOR THE SUPPRESSION OF VICE: ROUND ONE

In December 1900, Kane took out temporary guardianship papers for (Ah) Sau Chun and Ah Ying, the first two girls he had helped Margarita Lake rescue.[45] A little over a month later, the two girls appeared in court—apparently with Kane and Lake standing beside them. Sau Chun's initial court hearing was held January 16, 1901, and with the help of the Chinatown Corps Salvation Army "lassies," Margarita Lake easily convinced Superior Court Judge Coffey that little Chun was probably not Kim Yook's child and would be better off in the Methodist Rescue Home than in a Spofford Alley brothel.[46] Ah Ying's hearing was five days later, on January 21, 1901, and would prove to be a bit more complicated.[47] Although Ah Ying's mother opposed Kane being named as guardian of her child, her protests were of no avail.[48] In both cases Kane was awarded custody of the girl in question, without any hint that the Methodists objected to his guardianship status. However, the children were left in the rescue home with the Lake women.[49]

Evidence collected in Ah Ying's guardianship dispute revealed that her mother, Hing Sam, was a widow and worked as a general cleaning woman in a brothel at 829 Washington Street. Because of her long hours (usually from ten in the morning to about midnight) and because of the leftover food available in the brothel, Hing Sam often brought Ah Ying to her workplace. Occasionally she would leave Ying with a neighbor woman who did not keep her very clean, for when Ying was rescued she was filthy and covered with vermin.[50] Moreover, Ying was dressed as a boy and called herself a boy when she first entered the Mission Home.

Perhaps because Ah Ying had been taken from her biological mother without the mother's consent, the case was viewed as "an important test...and the courtroom was thronged with spectators, white and yellow,"[51] including "about a dozen prominent church women...who [were] interested in mission work among the Chinese."[52] A week after the hearing, Margarita Lake wrote in her journal that on January 28, she had seen Ah Wing's [sic] mother go into the house at 829 Washington Street,[53] and a week after that she described a visit to the Mission Home of Ah Ying's mother:

> Ah Ying's[54] mother and sister called to see her at half-past two, and a man. Suie and Grace were in the room. When the child was taken into the room she would not go up to speak to them. Acted as though she was afraid. I had to speak to her two or three times. They asked her if she did not want to go out. They would take her to the theater. Asked this two or three times. The mother cried. I told her not to cry, and that I could not see why she cried over this daughter. And I asked if she cried over her daughter that she had sold. They brought some candy.[55]

Perhaps it was not the only time the family visited Ah Ying, for Mrs. Lake wrote in a December 9, 1901, court statement, "The mother and the brothers and sisters have never been denied the right to see her at any time."[56]

From January 1901, when Kane was appointed guardian of the two girls, to August 3, 1901, when he petitioned for writs of habeas corpus for them, there were no articles about the cases in the San Francisco newspapers. But on July 17, Kane appeared on the steps of the new Oriental Home, ironically on the day of its grand opening, and served the Lakes with a letter demanding that they turn the two children over to him. The letter stated that Mr. Kane wished to place Ah Ying with Mrs. Sitton, the wife of a Cumberland Presbyterian pastor on Clay Street, who ran the little Chambers Memorial Mission,[57] while (Ah) Sau Chun was to be placed with the family of Chan Wing Chun, a Chinese merchant.[58] To add weight to his demands, Kane argued that he had been "importuned" by the Chinese Consul General Ho You "to make the proposed disposition."[59] However, Margarita Lake had evidence refuting Kane's claim, for the consul general had assured her that he had made no

Ah Ying and Sau Chun with Margarita Lake at their habeas corpus hearing, August 2, 1901. (San Francisco Examiner, Sunday, August 4, 1901, p. 29)

such request. Moreover, Margarita Lake claimed that she herself had been offered a large sum of money to turn over the girls to a Chinese guardian who had "excellent papers," but whose emissary came from one of the brothels where the girls had formerly lived.[60] Kane then wrote a second letter and gave it to the Lakes. But when it, too, was ignored, he sued out the writs of habeas corpus for the girls. And so Margarita Lake was forced to appear in court on August 2, holding Ah Ying and Sau Chun by the hand.

On August 17, the San Francisco Superior Court denied Kane the writs of habeas corpus, and both children were "remanded to the custody of Miss Margarita Lake."[61] But the guardianship dispute was far from over. Two days later Margarita Lake wrote in her journal that her lawyer

> Mr. Henderson telephoned in the afternoon about little Ah Chun and Ah Ying (or John). [He] said he did not get up to court on Saturday[62] until 11 o'clock, and that he thought we had better not [be] making [a] move for a week or so and see what Mr. Kane would do. He said if we took the initiative we would have a very hard fight as the parents would come up again and try to take them again.[63]

Some months later, Mr. Kane made his move. He was able to secure a citation from the Superior Court that ordered Oriental Home matron Mrs. Kate Lake to produce Ah Ying in court. But on December 9, Mrs. Lake appeared without the girl, requesting instead that the court appoint a new guardian. Since Margarita Lake was on an extended trip to the East Coast, the judge granted a postponement of the hearing until January 6—much to Kane's chagrin.[64] Nevertheless, Kane made the most of the hearing, bringing fresh arguments to the bench. First, on a positive note, he said Ah Ying's mother was presently employed as a domestic with a Christian family and was thus "capable of raising her offspring in a fitting manner."[65] Second, and on the negative side, he stated that in the months since he had been appointed guardian, "adult Chinese women, who were taken from houses of ill repute, had been received into the [Oriental H]ome,...and [thus he] did not think it a fit place for a girl nine years old, as these women might have a bad influence on her."[66] However, Judge Troutt was not persuaded by Kane's arguments, and concluded the day's hearing by suggesting that Kane "produce evidence that the girl would be better off by going to the place that Kane had chosen than by remaining at the [H]ome."[67]

Within a few days of Judge Troutt's refusal to hand over Ah Ying to Kane, posters appeared in Chinatown that were probably intended to raise doubts in the Chinese community about the Methodist women's reasons for conducting their rescues.[68] The David W. Garton Collection has preserved a notice that the Oriental Home put up around Chinatown in response to those placards. The undated Methodist document begins by alluding to "the unwarranted publication of a notice concerning the recent rescue of a Chinese child Ah Ying from a Chinese brothel," and ends with the warning: "Neglect your children, allow them to enter dens of vice and iniquity and you wil [sic] have us as well as the Law arrayed against you. Be kind to your children, keep them pure and clean and the Law will befriend you and you will have our aid and support."[69]

It is impossible to determine whether the placards exacerbated the natural suspicions that many Chinese immigrants already had toward the Oriental Home or whether the placards were generally ignored. But the Methodist notice would do little to assuage nascent Chinatown fears. First, there is no evidence to suggest that it was translated into Chinese. Second, it failed to recognize the complicated socioeconomic issues related to being a member of a despised immigrant community, and a single mother trying to raise a girl in Chinatown. For example, dressing the child as a boy and calling her a boy could be construed as an act of motherly protection in a community where girls were bought and sold on the open market. By disguising her child as a boy, Sam Hing might have been protecting her daughter from being kidnapped and sold. But Margarita Lake believed that the disguise was merely to "throw the Mission workers off their guard."[70] Third, keeping her daughter with her at work in the brothel could just as easily be construed as an act of concern and care as an act of negligence. Because Sam Hing was

a widow, she was forced to work long hours in order to survive. By keeping her daughter with her, she could ensure the child's welfare and safety. Finally, cleanliness was simply not easily maintained in poverty-stricken neighborhoods of San Francisco, which much of Chinatown was.

The fact that Sam Hing began working as a domestic in a Caucasian home soon after her child was taken from her would seem to prove Kane's point: The mother had taken advantage of the economic opportunity afforded her, and thereby had shown herself to be a fit mother. But regardless of the Chinese community's response to the poster war, the placards provoked members of the Oriental Home Board to more aggressive action.

On December 30, 1901, and in preparation for the January 6 continuance, Mrs. L. P. Williams, secretary of the WHMS Oriental Bureau filed a petition for letters of guardianship over Ah Ying.[71] Taking a proactive stance, she charged Kane with "being derelict in the performance of his duties as guardian...[and] abus[ing] his trust."[72] And she further "allege[d] that Kane's claim that he intended placing the child under the care of Miss Seton [sic] [wa]s without foundation" and "that the society of which Kane is secretary is absolutely under his control and that upon his failure to secure the child, a systematic effort to injure the [H]ome was made in Chinatown by means of placards in which the orders of the court were grossly misrepresented."[73]

Although the Lake scrapbooks contain no newspaper clippings of the January 6, 1902, continuance, the scrapbooks do contain two newspaper accounts from later in the month that mention Kane. Both deal with an eleven-year-old girl whose mother and stepfather had lost her to Kane, and the stepfather makes the claim that a family acquaintance had once remarked that he would "give $500 to get possession of the girl."[74] There are no subsequent newspaper clippings suggesting that Kane received payment for taking the eleven-year-old girl from her mother, whom he claimed was "not a fit woman to be in charge of any child."[75] But no doubt the Lakes kept the newspaper articles because these gave the impression that Kane might be "rescuing" children for profit. Margarita Lake hinted at this in Ah Ying's final hearing on March 10, when she "charged Kane with being subsidized by the Chinese who had before sought to get possession of the child."[76]

Despite Judge Troutt's decision against Margarita Lake, which argued that "the mother was the natural guardian for the child and that she now appeared to have a respectable home,"[77] Margarita Lake had the final parting shot. She was "determined to watch the woman and her child, and if the infant is not well cared for [I] will probably come into court again with a claim for its custody."[78] The Oriental Home finally closed its books on the Ah Ying case with a terse and poignant note in its March 1902 monthly report: "March 6th we lost Ah Ying little Jean."[79]

But what did Margarita Lake and the Oriental Home lose? They had lost Ying's body: "Habeas corpus. You (Mr. Kane,

WON THE JUDGE WHEN SHE SANG

Jan 17th 1901

LITTLE SOW JUN, WHO SANG A SALVATION ARMY HYMN IN JUDGE COFFEY'S COURT YESTERDAY.

Sau Chun's first guardianship hearing, January 1901. (Unidentified newspaper clipping, Kate Lake Scrapbook 2, p. 7, David W. Garton Collection)

Sam Hing) now have her body." Perhaps, too, they had lost her educational and spiritual potential. Newspaper accounts emphasize that Ah Ying was learning to read English and Chinese.[80] But if Ying survived childhood, if the mother was able to keep her new job and provide for her child, then in the end surely all concerned parties had won.

MARGARITA LAKE AND THE ORIENTAL HOME VERSUS FRANK KANE AND THE SOCIETY FOR THE SUPPRESSION OF VICE: ROUND TWO

On Tuesday, December 11, 1900, Margarita Lake wrote in her journal:

> Mr. Kane got little Ah Chun from a house on Spofford Alley, and brought the mother and the child up to 916 Washington St. about 1 o'clock.
>
> We questioned the mother for about an hour, and at last Mr. Kane told the woman that she must go and leave the child.
>
> She said, "No," and that the child was too timid to have her in the Home. So [Kane] allowed her to take her to the door.

Then he separated them. I carried the baby upstairs and put the old woman out.

> God's Regular Army came up to see about the child, and a Chinese doctor called a number of times to see her. Dr. Wong.[81]

If the "God's Regular Army" member who came to "see about the child" was May Thomas, then she may have given Margarita Lake a phone number to get in touch with the Brewers, who had worked in Chinatown with the Salvation Army "Junior Corps" a few years earlier. For in less than a week after (Ah) Sau Chun's rescue, Margarita Lake received a letter from Mrs. Harry Brewer, Jr., who had worked with the Salvation Army Chinese Corps from November 1896 until June 1900.[82] Edith aka Mrs. Harry Brewer claimed Ah Chun had been sold to Kim Yook for about $100, and that the parents lived in Fresno.[83] Additional sleuthing would reveal that (Ah) Sau Chun had been sold for $101 when she was about two years old (1897).[84] It was thus fairly clear early on that Sau Chun was not Kim Yook's natural child. In Chinese terms, Sau Chun was a *mui tsai* (a debt slave),[85] and since she had no blood relationship to her *kwai po* (owner), California state law could be more easily enforced in her case than in Ah Ying's guardianship dispute.[86] Thus, whereas Ah Ying's guardianship case ultimately rested on the moral character of her natural mother (was she negligent?), Sau Chun's case would have to be resolved on the twin issues of race and social formation: What type of home would be better for the Chinese girl? A Caucasian institution (the Oriental Home), a Caucasian family (Kane's family),[87] or a Chinese merchant family? The solution to this guardianship dispute was not self-evident, and both sides would have a more difficult time playing the moral purity card in their attempts to win Sau Chun.

In August 1901, the court had rejected rather quickly a direct transfer of Sau Chun to Kane's Chinese merchant family, when Margarita Lake had been able to show that Mr. Chung already had children, and that adding a daughter to the family would be viewed as an economic liability (unless the girl functioned as a *mui tsai* or was subsequently sold).[88] After his request for a writ of habeas corpus for Sau Chun was denied, Kane seems to have forgotten about her guardianship. He would not act on her behalf until months after the court had restored Ah Ying to her natural mother. An unidentified note in the David W. Garton Collection confirms this: "From November 1901 till October 1902 Mr. Kane never inquired about Sau Chün."[89]

But much to the consternation of the Oriental Home, in November 1902, Kane began a second habeas corpus proceeding to take Sau Chun out of the Home.[90] As he had argued the year before in Ah Ying's case, Kane believed that Sau Chun's "mind and morals [were] in danger of corruption in the Home,"[91] since the Home gave asylum to prostitutes and was a "bargain counter for Chinese females rescued from brothels at the request of Chinamen who wished them taken to the home so that ultimately they would fall into their hands."[92] But Mrs. L. P. Williams, secretary of the WHMS

Oriental Bureau, mounted a strong counterattack to Kane's charges, claiming that the merchant with whom Kane wished to place Sau Chun was in fact a "saloon keeper, and the consort of the woman from whom the child had been taken."[93] The conclusion of the Methodists was that Kane was acting as "the representative of the Chinese who claim[ed] slave ownership of the little Mei Chun."[94] Finally, Mrs. Williams impugned Kane's character, arguing that he was "irascible and quick-tempered and unfit as guardian."[95]

When the case came up in Superior Court on January 10–11, 1903, Mr. Monroe, the Oriental Home attorney, was able to draw a plausible connection between a recent financial transaction and a transfer of guardianship that raised questions about Kane's methods of work. In the case cited, Kane had been asked to take guardianship of a sixteen-year-old girl named Lillian Young, and the foster mother had made a payment of $21 to Kane's assistant for the legal fees in transferring her foster daughter's guardianship. Kane then filed an affidavit stating that Mrs. Young was too poor to pay the amount and had the court remit all but one dollar of the fee. However, neither Kane nor his assistant ever returned Mrs. Young's $20. The attorney for the Oriental Home was thus able to argue that Kane's interest in Sau Chun's guardianship might likewise have more to do with collecting "legal fees" from a third party, than with his concern for the girl's welfare.[96]

But if the newspaper accounts are to be trusted, it may have been little seven-year-old Sau (Maud Mei) Chun herself who ultimately won over the Superior Court judge to the side of the Methodist women, rather than either contestant's legal arguments.

> "Let's hear what the little girl says," suggested the Judge. "Come here little one," he called, and the child was brought forward.
>
> "Do you want to go home with Mr. Kane, my child," he said.
>
> "No," wailed little Sow Jun.
>
> "He has a nice home in San Rafael, and he has some nice little boys and girls of his own. Wouldn't you like to play with them?"
>
> Sow Jun's tiny brown hand clasped the white one of the Judge and she forced her elfin self under his arm till she rested her head in his lap. Then with her eyes filled with tears and her red lips quivering the little girl begged not to be sent to Mr. Kane's.
>
> "Do you want to stay with me?" asked Coffey gently.
>
> "Oh, I want to go home," cried the little girl. "I want to go home."[97]

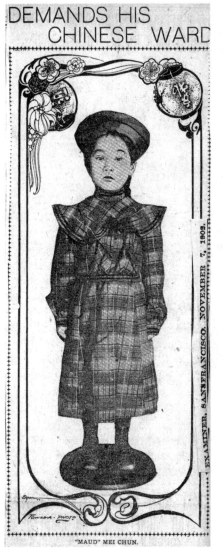

DEMANDS HIS CHINESE WARD

"MAUD" MEI CHUN.

Sau Chun's (Maud's) fourth courtroom appearance. (Kate Lake Scrapbook 2, p. 111, David W. Garton Collection)

Although the judge decided in favor of the Oriental Home, Mrs. L. P. William's order to remove Kane as guardian was dismissed, and Kane kept the title. But as he was walking out the courtroom door, Kane was arrested for impersonating an officer of the law.[98] However, within a few days the charges against him were dropped,[99] and three weeks later Kane was reelected secretary and treasurer of the Pacific Society for the Suppression of Vice. The Society went so far as to pass a resolution supporting Kane "in his action in the case of the little Chinese girl Lou [sic] Jun,"[100] and it authorized him "to take any steps he saw fit to remove the stigma that had been placed upon the society by the court's order taking the custody of Sow Jun, a minor Chinese girl, out of their hands."[101] Encouraged by the Society's public affirmation of his action in the case, Kane appealed to the California State Supreme Court, hoping that it would grant him an alternate writ of habeas corpus for the girl.[102] However, the Supreme Court refused his petition, and within a few months Mrs. L. P. Williams was granted full custody and guardianship of Sau Chun.[103]

For all intents and purposes, Kane and the two Lake women dropped out of the San Francisco newspapers at the conclusion of the Sau Chun guardianship dispute. And although there were other internal issues at the Oriental Home that led to the Lakes' abrupt dismissal at the end of January 1903, no doubt Kane's persistent agitation to wrest Ah Ying and Sau Chun from the Methodist women's control had worn down all concerned parties, both physically and emotionally. In June 1903, Mrs. L. P. Williams resigned from her position as Secretary of the Oriental Bureau for "health reasons,"[104] but it is entirely possible that her health problems were simply a cover for an ongoing power struggle in the Oriental Home. It may be that the Kane guardianship debacle led to her forced resignation. By the end of 1903, Margarita Lake had taken a new position within the Oriental Bureau, becoming the missionary in the WHMS Ellen Stark Japanese Home for Women and Girls, a position that would occupy her time and energy until her marriage in 1910. There is no clear evidence that she ever again had contact with Ah Ying or Sau Chun after she left her position in the Oriental Home.

Not insignificantly, the Oriental Home and Conduct Committee was restructured within a few months of the Lakes' dismissal and Mrs. L. P. Williams' resignation. And a new set of rules was established to keep order in the Home. Among the list of twelve rules—a list that no doubt was posted in the building—was Rule 5, which stated: "No two girls must enter the bathroom or take bath at the same time."[105] It is highly likely that this was adopted in response to one of Kane's concerns: the morality of having preadolescent girls sharing living space with former prostitutes.

CONCLUSION

Thanks to the recent discovery of unpublished Oriental Home records and the Lake women's turn-of-the-century collection of newspaper clippings—together with WHMS magazine articles, Oriental Bureau annual reports, and annual reports of the Pacific Society for the Suppression of Vice, the guardianship disputes of Ah Ying and Sau Chun deepen our understanding of the complexity of child-rescue strategies in turn-of-the-century San Francisco. While this essay has focused exclusively upon the strategies of two Caucasian child-rescuing societies struggling for the control of two Chinese children, it has done so precisely because such struggles were so rare. As Milicent Shinn argued in 1890, "the [Caucasian] community...is by no means convinced that it is a matter of any importance to save Chinese children from abuse,"[106] and as a result the Protestant missions generally found themselves in legal battles with lawyers representing Chinese clients, not in contests with other Caucasian child-saving organizations.

The Chinese community itself may seem to play only a minor role in these two guardianship disputes, but it should be noted that "Old Mary," the Chinese Salvation Army "lassie" who sheltered Sau Chun for a number of months before the little girl was taken to the Methodist Rescue Asylum, committed suicide in June 1903 as a result of her continued involvement in rescues for the Methodist women.[107] Neither is there any clear evidence that previously rescued teenage girls of the Oriental Home such as Grace Wong and Caroline Lee (Yuk Ying) worked as translators and guides on the two rescues highlighted in this essay. However, those girls were involved in numerous other rescues in 1900 and 1901.[108]

The guardianship disputes of Sau Chun and Ah Ying deserve further investigation, particularly because of the religious issues involved (Protestant versus Catholic; differing views of sin and perfection); the competing theories of child-rearing and differing conceptions of childhood (where is the best place to raise an orphan/neglected child—with a family or in an institution?); and gender politics (male rescue organization versus female rescue organization)—not to mention the ever-present issues of race and class. Yet within this complexity is the strong voice of the Chinese child, Sau Chun—who, if newspaper accounts are to be trusted, claimed her own authority and won for herself a future far different from that of a *mui tsai* in a nameless brothel on Spofford Alley in San Francisco's Chinatown.

NOTES

1. The most important studies of the Presbyterian Chinese Mission Home are Carol Green Wilson, *Chinatown Quest: One Hundred Years of Donaldina Cameron House*, rev. ed. (San Francisco: California Historical Society, 1974); Laurene Wu McClain, "Donaldina Cameron: A Reappraisal," *Pacific Historian* 27 (1983): 24–35; Mildred Crowl Martin, *Chinatown's Angry Angel: The Story of Donaldina Cameron* (Palo Alto, CA: Pacific Books, 1986); Peggy Pascoe, *Relations of Rescue: The Search for Female Moral Authority in the American West, 1874-1939* (New York: Oxford University Press, 1990). See also Lucie Cheng Hirata, "Free, Indentured, Enslaved: Chinese Prostitutes in Nineteenth-Century America," in *History of Women in the United States: Historical Articles on Women's Lives and Activities*, vol. 9 of *Prostitution*, ed. Nancy F. Cott (New Providence, NJ: K. G. Saur, 1993), 123–149; and Benson Tong, *Unsubmissive Women: Chinese Prostitutes in Nineteenth-Century San Francisco* (Norman, OK: University of Oklahoma Press, 1994).
2. Pascoe's *Relations of Rescue* is the best at analyzing the politics of rescue, but does not deal with the differences between the Methodist and Presbyterian missions or with cases where two different rescue organizations fight for the same girls (Pascoe, *Relations of Rescue,* 86, 93–100).
3. The latter is a collection consisting of two scrapbooks of newspaper articles and other ephemera related to the Lakes' six years of work in Chinatown, and over 200 additional internal documents related to the work of the Oriental Home, 1896–1903. These materials, loaned to me by Margarita's grandson, have been labeled "David W. Garton Collection."
4. Author unknown, *History of the Mission of the Methodist Episcopal Church to the Chinese in California* (San Francisco: B. F. Sterett, 1877), 10.
5. This was part of the general rape law (*California State Assembly Statutes and Amendments to the Codes*, 1855 [105]; 1889 [223]; 1897 [201]).
6. "Age of Consent: Marriage and issuance of a license without approval of parents," *California Law Review* 7 (1919): 279. Perhaps the law is rooted in Spanish California betrothal traditions.
7. Patricia O'Flinn, "The Elimination of Prostitution? Moral Purity Campaigns, Middle-Class Clubwomen, and the California Red Light Abatement Act," *http://userwww.sfsu.edu/~epf/1996/redlight.html*.
8. "Statutory Laws," *Annual Report of the Pacific Society for the Suppression of Vice [and] Prevention of Cruelty to Children and Animals* (1900), 45. These California laws were enacted in 1878 (Milicent W. Shinn, "Charities for Children in San Francisco," *Overland Monthly and Out West Magazine* [January 1890], 89), and Shinn correctly notes that they were the legal basis for the Chinese mission rescues (91). See also Frances Cahn and Valeska Bary, *Welfare Activities of Federal, State, and Local Governments in California, 1850-1934* (Berkeley: University of California Press, 1936), 75.
9. Cahn and Bary, *Welfare Activities,* 51.
10. *Annual Report of the Society for the Suppression of Vice [and] Prevention of Cruelty to Children and Animals* (1898–1899), 27–31.

11. Margarita had written in her journal for Monday, May 29, 1899: "Called at the ~~Urica~~ Society twice to get them to do some[thing] for the little girl Ah Chun. They promised to do something that night, but did not" ("Journal of Margarita Lake," David W. Garton Collection)."Urica" appears to be Margarita Lake's misspelling of the word "Eureka," which she had crossed out.

    San Francisco newspapers are notoriously inexact in naming the child protective societies involved in rescues. For example, sometimes the Eureka Society is called the "Eureka Society for the Prevention of Cruelty to Children," and at other times the same group is apparently called the "California Society for the Prevention of Cruelty to Children" (cf. "Lie Wan, the Beautiful, Breaks Her Bonds and Escapes to China," unidentified newspaper clipping, April 5, 1899 [Lake Scrapbook 1, 70]; "Does Not Want to Be Rescued," unidentified newspaper clipping, July 15, 1899 [Lake Scrapbook 1, 83]); and "My Work Is among the Chinese Women and Girls" [David W. Garton Collection, file 17b]).In two 1897 newspaper articles, Mr. Holbrook is called the secretary of the "Eureka Society for the Protection of Children," whereas a few years earlier he had been designated the secretary of the "California Society for the Prevention of Cruelty to Children" ("Torturing Helpless Children," unidentified newspaper clipping, July 18, 1897 [Lake Scrapbook 1, 19]; "Taken out of a Den of Slaves," unidentified newspaper clipping, July 26, 1897 [Lake Scrapbook 1, 22]; cf. James Flamant, "Child-Saving Charities in This Big Town," *The Call,* May 28, 1893, 18, *http://www.sfgenealogy.com/sf/history/hgcsc.htm#list*).

    Finally, to confuse matters just a little more, in a letter to editor of the *San Francisco Examiner,* July 31, 1899, the attorney for the Methodist mission, Henry E. Monroe, stated that the "Society for the Suppression of Vice" had helped to rescue a girl that an earlier newspaper article had credited to the "Eureka Society for the Prevention of Cruelty to Children" ("Why Kim Oy Went Back to Chinatown," *The Examiner,* July 31, 1899 [Lake Scrapbook 1, 86–87], "Does not Want to be Rescued," unidentified newspaper clipping, July 15, 1899 [Lake Scrapbook 1, 83]).

12. In an interview in March 1899, Margarita Lake told a reporter that "In the last two years Mr. McMurray of the Children's Protective Society has located many a young girl for us by going around as a tourist. The keepers, however, now know him by sight, and our tactics must be changed every day." ("How We are Fighting to Free Girl Slaves in Chinatown," *The Examiner,* March 2, 1899 [Lake Scrapbook 1, 76–77]). It is not entirely clear whether this society is different from the Eureka Society or the California Society mentioned above.

13. According to one 1901 newspaper report, the lessee of the brothel property at 11 Spofford Alley was "Suey Sin" ("Will Fight to Suppress Slave Trade in Chinatown," *Evening Post,* February 18, 1901 [Lake Scrapbook 2, 28–31]).

14. Margarita's journal entry for November 17, 1899 reads: "Called early this morning on a Salvation lassie about Ah Chun.…Went out between 12 and 1 to see [the] doctor about Ah Chun." It is unclear from this entry whether the "Salvation lassie" is a Chinese woman, but other records indicate that "Chun" was placed in the care of "Mary, Salvation Chinese woman" (unpublished note, David W. Garton Collection), and according to the Salvation Army newspaper, "Sister Mary [is] our only Chinese lassie" ("Celestial Clean-ups," *The War Cry: An Official Gazette of the Salvation Army Pacific Coast Region,* no. 568 [October 15, 1898], 8).In his history of the Salvation Army in Chinatown, Check-Hung Yee writes, "Sister Mary…was dressed in full uniform with a hallelujah bonnet, and stepped into the ring in a

community where it was customary that no lady be seen in the company of men" (*For My Kinsmen's Sake: A Salvation Army Officer's Quarter Century of Service in San Francisco Chinatown* [Rancho Palos Verdes, CA: Salvation Army Western Territory, 1986], 61).

15. Unpublished note, David W. Garton Collection. Ah Quai, an "inmate" of the 829 Washington Street brothel, had previously spent some months at the Methodist mission and would manage to escape to the mission in late March ("Chinatown Slave Girl's Thrilling Dash for Liberty," *The Examiner,* March 30, 1901, 1). She would tell a story that implicated the Chief of Police, William P. Sullivan, in the Chinatown sex trafficking scandal ([Lake Scrapbook 2, 49]; cf. *The Star,* May 4, 1901 [Lake Scrapbook 2, 153]).

    An article in the *Japan Tribune,* probably from early May 1901, states, "When Sullivan was the President of the Pacific Society for the Suppression of Vice, he was regarded as an honorable man, and had the respect of the community, as a conscientious and zealous worker in the humane endeavors of that worthy organization.…" ("The Captain Wittman Plague," n.d. [Lake Scrapbook 2, 26]). Biggy, who was also in the running for chief of police when Sullivan was chosen for the position, was vice president of the Society "while Frank J. Kane was doing excellent work under them" (ibid.).

    William P. Sullivan died November 11, 1901. He was Roman Catholic, and must have known Frank Kane well.

16. *Pacific Society for the Suppression of Vice Annual Report* (1900), 51.

17. Mrs. L. P. Williams, "Two New Little Girls," *Children's Home Missions,* 6 (1901): 39–40. It is perhaps not too far off to suggest that Edith Maud Eaton's (Sui Sin Far) short story "A Chinese Boy Girl" (*Century Illustrated Magazine,* April 1904) might have been based upon the story of Ah Ying, since Eaton did live in San Francisco from 1898 to 1900.The story is set in Los Angeles and focuses on a troublesome Chinese "girl" who is learning English at Miss Mason's school. Miss Mason is able to procure the help of the president of the "Society for the Prevention of Cruelty" to try and rescue the child from "her" father and send "her" to a home for Chinese girls in San Francisco. But the "girl" cannot be found, and Miss Mason eventually discovers that the child she thought was a girl was in fact a boy dressed as a girl to keep demons from finding and killing him. Although Eaton was living in Seattle by the time of Ah Ying's rescue, it is possible that she could have read about Ah Ying's guardianship dispute in newspaper articles sent to her or in letters from her friends in San Francisco.

18. A later newspaper account states: "When the Methodist Rescue Home made Frank J. Kane guardian of little Maud Mei Chun two years ago, the proceeding was so much a matter of form that the possibility of his ever claiming the child was an idea too remote for consideration. Officers who had assisted in the rescue of Chinese slave girls had figured sometimes, as a matter of convenience, in guardianship papers, but always with the understanding that the child in question was the ward of the home. This was the case when Kane was appointed the legal protector of Mei Chun" (*The Examiner,* November 7, 1902 [Lake Scrapbook 2, 110–111]).

19. "Chinese Mission Opposes Kane," unidentified newspaper clipping (Lake Scrapbook 2, 79); "Kane's Methods Inquired Into," *The Call,* January 10, 1903, 5.

20. "Think They Can Identify White Child Rescued from its Chinatown Captors," *The Examiner,* January 10, 1903, 2.

21. San Francisco city directories for 1889 and 1890 list Frank Kane as "Superintendent" of the Youths' Directory (W. H. L. Corran, *Langley's San Francisco Directory* [San Francisco: Fran-

cis, Valentine and Co., 1889]; *Langley's San Francisco Directory* [San Francisco: Painter and Co., 1890]; and *St. Joseph's Union* lists him still as "Superintendent" in 1892 (6, no. 3 [1892]: 7). But the 1893 Youths' Directory lists him as "Secretary" (*Langley's San Francisco Directory* [San Francisco: Crocker and Langley, 1893]).

22. Flamant, "Child-Saving Charities in This Big Town."

23. Milicent W. Shinn, "Poverty and Charity in San Francisco, II," *Overland Monthly and Out West Magazine* (December 1889): 592.

24. Shinn, "Charities for Children in San Francisco," 81.

25. "In re Minor Children of Henry Hunt, on Habeas Corpus," No. 21143, Supreme Court of California, July 3, 1894. Kane filed what was perhaps his last quarterly report for the Directory in December 1895 ("Report of Frank J. Kane," *The Call*, December 16, 1895, 12).

26. Shinn, "Charities for Children in San Francisco," 81. Cahn and Bary state that the Youths' Directory had been founded "primarily to assist in placing city children in homes in the country" (Cahn and Bary, *Welfare Activities,* 23).

27. Shinn, "Charities for Children in San Francisco," 81; Cahn and Bary, *Welfare Activities*, 23. In one three-month period of 1892, 43 of 71 children placed in orphanages were placed in St. Vincent's Orphan Asylum, and 54 of 128 children were placed with families (*St. Joseph's Union* [1892], 7).

28. *Pacific Society for the Suppression of Vice/Prevention of Cruelty to Children and Animals Annual Report* (1898–1899), 5. Economic depression may account for this statistical change.

29. Ibid., 85.

30. Ibid. See also E. Wayne Carp, "Two Cheers for Orphanages," *Reviews in American History* 24 (1996): 277–284.

31. "Mrs. Lang's Children," *The Call*, July 24, 1896, 7; "Transcript of the Evidence Taken and Proceeding Had before the Assembly Committee of the Legislature of the State of California, Sitting in San Francisco, California, Commencing Tuesday, Feb. 6, 1901," California State Archives, Sacramento, CA, 543.

32. *California Society for the Suppression of Vice*, Abstract, 9th Annual Report, 5.

33. "Secretary Kane Arrested," *The Call*, February 9, 1897, 7. The California Society for the Suppression of Vice and the California Society for the Prevention of Cruelty to Children had joined to form one "society" by 1898, when Kane is listed as secretary (*Pacific Society for the Suppression of Vice Annual Report* [1898–1899]).

34. "Kane's Contempt Case," *The Call*, June 13, 1897, 6.

35. "Man and Wife Want the Child," *The Chronicle*, January 23, 1902 (Lake Scrapbook 2, 71); "Father Demands His Daughter," unidentified newspaper clipping (Lake Scrapbook, 2, 71).

36. "Judge Conlan Still Demands the Truth," *The Call*, July 24, 1900, 9; "Kane Not Entitled to Wear a Special's Star," *The Call*, March 28, 1901, 9; "Arrest Kane at Court Door," *The Chronicle*, January 11, 1903, 28; "Charge against Kane Dismissed," *The Call*, January 15, 1903, 7.

37. "Transcript of the Evidence," 543. Dennis Smith states that a "Special's" uniform and patch were "virtually indistinguishable—to all but careful inspection—from those of standard police issue. The regular police [in 1906] wore a seven-point star on their jacket and breast, but a special police officer wore a six-point star" (*San Francisco Is Burning: The Untold Story of the 1906 Earthquake and Fires* [New York: Viking, 2005], 159–160).

38. "Kane Is in More Trouble," *The Bulletin*, January 11, 1903, 36; "Showed a Star He Had No Right to Wear," *The Examiner*, January 11, 1903, 27. Smith notes that a Special's six-point star had "two or three letters in the center rather than a number" like

a regular police officer's badge, and that "the first time a particular badge was assigned, the letters represented the wearer's initials, but when it was returned, it was usually reissued to someone whose initials did not match" (*San Francisco Is Burning*, 160).

39. "Legal Obstacles in Their Way," unidentified newspaper clipping, September 6, 1897 (Lake Scrapbook 1, 41).

40. "Specimen Cases," *Pacific Society for the Suppression of Vice Annual Report* (1898–1899), 27–28; "An Unfair Judge," *Pacific Society for the Suppression of Vice Annual Report* (1900), 50–57.

41. For example, "Rescue of a Child Slave Girl from Chinese Den Frustrated by White Watchman," *The Examiner*, March 2, 1901 (Lake Scrapbook 2, 71); "Raided a Slave Den," unidentified newspaper article (Lake Scrapbook 2, 70). In February 1901, Kane states that he made seven or eight rescues in the past two months, and that he had been out in Chinatown just the night before with Miss Lake ("Transcript of the Evidence," 543–544).

42. "Journal of Margarita Lake (Dragon Exercise Book)," David W. Garton Collection, unpublished.

43. "Secretary Kane and Special Police Fight," *The Call*, March 22, 1901, 7; "Rescue of a Slave Balked by Strong Force of the Police," *The Examiner*, March 22, 1901, 3; "His Star Set Long Ago," *The Examiner*, March 28, 1901, 2; "Charge That Patrolmen Stopped Rescue of Slave Girl," unidentified newspaper clipping (Lake Scrapbook 2, 46).

44. See note 44; "The Grand Jury's Report," *The Star*, May 4, 1901, 4.

45. *Pacific Society for the Suppression of Vice Annual Report* (1900), 35.

46. "Won the Judge When She Sang," unidentified newspaper clipping, January 17, 1901 (Lake Scrapbook 2, 7). The date "Jan 17, 1901" is handwritten on the clipping. However a search of the San Francisco *Examiner*, *Call*, *Evening Bulletin*, and *Chronicle* for January 16–18, 1901, has not uncovered this source.

47. "Girl in Boy's Attire," unidentified newspaper clipping, January 22, 1901 (Lake Scrapbook 2, 8).

48. Mrs. Lake's later court deposition used the words "opposed by the relatives," when in fact one of the "relatives" opposing the guardianship was the child's own mother ("Chinese Mission Opposes Kane," unidentified newspaper clipping [Lake Scrapbook 2, 79]; "Girl in Boy's Attire").

49. "Won the Judge When She Sang."

50. "Churchwomen Interested," unidentified newspaper clipping, January 22, 1901 (Lake Scrapbook 2, 8); "Owing to the Possible Misconception of the Objects of the Chinese Mission Work," David W. Garton Collection, unpublished document, n.d. The brothel at 829 Washington Street was next door to the "Yoshiwara House" at 843 Washington Street, a Japanese brothel where three prostitutes would die of bubonic plague, July 8–11, 1901 (Marilyn Chase, *The Barbary Plague: The Black Death in Victorian San Francisco* [New York: Random House, 2003], 96–98).

51. "Girl in Boy's Attire."

52. "Churchwomen Interested."

53. "Journal of Margarita Lake."

54. Ibid. The text in ink reads "Ah Wing," but in pencil it has been corrected to "Ah Ying."

55. Ibid. Margarita Lake's charge that Hing Sam had sold a daughter is not mentioned in any other records.

56. "Chinese Mission Opposes Kane."

57. "Contest for Possession of Little Chinese Maiden," *The Evening Post*, December 9, 1901 (Lake Scrapbook 2, 73); "To Apply for the Guardianship for Ah Lin," *The Examiner*, January 11, 1903, 28.

58. The Chung family lived at 754 Washington Street ("Chinese Maiden Causes a Fight," unidentified newspaper clipping, August 3, 1901 [Lake Scrapbook 2, 70])

59. "Kane Suspected of Treachery," *The Chronicle*, August 3, 1901 (Lake Scrapbook 2, 70).

60. Ibid.

61. "Secretary Kane Defeated in Court," *The Evening Post*, August 17, 1901 (Lake Scrapbook 2, 70).

62. That is, August 17.

63. "Journal of Margarita Lake."

64. "Chinese Mission Opposes Kane," unidentified newspaper clipping (Lake Scrapbook 2, 79); "Frank Kane and Mrs. Lake Battle for Child," *The Call*, December 10, 1901, 10.

65. "Frank Kane and Mrs. Lake Battle."

66. "Chinese Mission Opposes Kane."

67. Ibid.

68. Mrs. L. P. Williams' courtroom accusation obliquely mentioned "...a systematic effort to injure the home was made in Chinatown by means of placards in which the orders of the court were grossly misrepresented" ("Claims Kane Abuses Trust," *The Call*, December 31, 1901, 5). The Oriental Home response to the placards focuses on *where* Ah Ying was found and what she *looked* like when rescued ("Owing to the Possible Misconception").

69. "Owing to the Possible Misconception."

70. "Will Investigate Slave Traffic," *The Evening Post*, February 25, 1901 (Lake Scrapbook 2, 35). Ms. Lake's argument seems to make little sense, since it was illegal for *any* underage child—boy *or* girl—to be in a brothel without the presence of a parent.

71. "Claims Kane Abuses Trust."

72. Ibid.

73. Ibid.

74. "Father Demands His Daughter," unidentified newspaper clipping (Lake Scrapbook 2, 71); "Man and Wife Want the Child," *The Chronicle*, January 23, 1902 (Lake Scrapbook 2, 71).

75. "Man and Wife Want the Child."

76. "Child Awarded to Its Mother," unidentified newspaper clipping, March 10, 1902 (Lake Scrapbook 2, 71). A document in the David W. Garton Collection simply states, "in Feb. 1902 the Ah Ying case came up," and "the case was decided March 10" ("Sau Chūn: Rescued for the First Time Oct. 30-1899," David W. Garton Collection, unpublished document, n.d.).

77. "Child Awarded to Its Mother."

78. Ibid.

79. "March 1st There Were 17 Girls in the Home," David W. Garton Collection, unpublished document, n.d.

80. "Chinese Mission Opposes Kane."

81. "Journal of Margarita Lake," 29–30.

82. Known as Lieutenant Edith Graham when she first arrived in Chinatown, she became Captain of the Chinese Corps in October 1898 and held that position until she and her husband moved to Monterey (Check-Hung Yee, *For My Kinsmen's Sake*, 275; 1900 Federal Census, California, Monterey County). Margarita Lake's association with the Salvation Army may go back to about 1892 when she probably attended a Salvation Army camp meeting at Elim Grove, Cazadeoro, California (Letter to "My Dearest Margie," September 14, 1894, David W. Garton Collection).

83. This was, in fact, correct. Ah Chun's father, Lai Foon, was a partner in an opium joint at 71 China Alley in Fresno, and the name of Chun's older brother, Seu Ho, can be found along with the rest of the Lai family living at 1145 G Street, Fresno, in 1900 (U.S. Federal Census). Maud Mei Chun Lai would be a witness at her brother Seu Ho's reentry to the United States

on August 19, 1919, and she would keep his Alien Identity records until her death.

84. Some early newspaper accounts say that she was sold when "only fifteen days old" ("Will Investigate Slave Traffic," *Evening Post*, February 25, 1901 [Lake Scrapbook 2, 35]), but Margarita Lake states under oath that the fifteen-day-old child in her care was sold for three hundred dollars ("Transcript of the Evidence," 495), and later newspaper articles will say Ah Chun was two years old when sold (see, for example, "Chinese Maiden Causes a Fight").

85. See especially, Maria Jaschok, *Concubines and Bondservants: The Social History of a Chinese Custom* (London: Zed, 1988); and Maria Jaschok and Suzanne Miers, *Women and Chinese Patriarchy: Submission, Servitude and Escape* (Hong Kong: Zed, 1994).

86. "Statutory Laws," 45.

87. "Arrest Kane at Court Door."

88. "Chinese Maiden Causes a Fight."

89. "Sau Chūn Rescued for the First Time," 2.

90. "Demands His Chinese Ward."

91. Ibid.

92. "Kane's Methods Inquired Into," *The Call*, January 10, 1903, 5.

93. "Mrs. Laura P. Williams Scores Secretary Kane," unidentified newspaper clipping (Lake Scrapbook 2, 111); "They Don't Want Kane as Guardian," *The Examiner*, November 13, 1902, 9.

94. "Demands His Chinese Ward," *The Examiner*, November 7, 1902 (Lake Scrapbook 2, 110).

95. "Mrs. Laura P. Williams Scores."

96. "Kane's Methods Inquired Into"; "Kane Is Appointed on Payment of Money," unidentified newspaper clipping (Lake Scrapbook 2, 99); "Kane Attempts a Vindication," unidentified newspaper clipping (Lake Scrapbook 2, 99).

97. "Arrest Kane at Court Door," *The Chronicle*, January 11, 1903, 28.

98. Ibid.

99. "Kane Gets Change of Venue," *The Call*, January 13, 1903, 4; "Charge Against Kane Dismissed," *The Call*, January 15, 1903, 7.

100. "Humane Society Upholds Secretary," *The Bulletin*, February 5, 1903, 5.

101. "Pacific Humane Society," *Bulletin*, February 5, 1903, 3.

102. "Kane Gets Another Setback," *The Call*, February 14, 1903, 14.

103. On October 22, 1926, Mrs. L. P. Williams signed a deposition stating that she had been appointed guardian of May Chun Lai in 1902 ("In re the American Nativity of May Chun Lai," [personal collection]). Although the guardianship year is clearly in error, Mrs. Williams must have become Ah Chun's guardian shortly after the Lakes' dismissal from the Oriental Home in late January or early February 1903, but before Mrs. Williams resigned from her position as secretary of the Oriental Bureau in July 1903.

104. *Fourteenth Year of the California Conference of the Woman's Home Missionary Society Annual Report* (1903), 21.

105. "Rules of Inmates of Home," David W. Garton Collection.

106. "Charities for Children in San Francisco," 91.

107. Carrie Davis, "Record of Work in Oriental Home From Feb. 1903" (Gum Moon Women's Residence), 2; "Threatened Woman of China Takes Her Life," *The Examiner*, June 7, 1903, 25.

108. "Risks Her Life to Rescue Other Slaves in Chinatown," *The Examiner*, April 5, 1901, 7; "Exodus of Slaves from Chinatown," *The Examiner*, April 9, 1901, 9.

Oral History Workshop

Judy Yung, PhD

Drawing from thirty years of experience as a practitioner and teacher of oral history, Judy Yung provided the nuts and bolts of conducting an oral history interview with a Chinese American. As she said, of utmost importance is preparation—having a sense of purpose and specific objectives for the interview, doing the necessary background research on the person and topic, preparing a list of questions beforehand, and making sure equipment to be used is in good working order.

It is best to interview people in their homes and alone, to show good manners by bringing a gift or some refreshment to the interview, and to ask permission to tape the interview. Some basic tips on conducting the interview include:

- Establish trust and rapport by being pleasant, attentive, and respectful.
- Ask open-ended and clear questions one at a time, be flexible with your line of questioning, and be on your toes to ask follow-up questions.
- Do not dominate the conversation; give the person time to respond.
- Jot down notes in regard to dates, names, places, and questions you want to pursue later.
- Plan on a two-hour interview, but end the interview whenever the person appears tired. Then arrange for a second interview if necessary.
- Use photos, artifacts, and hearsay to spark memories.
- Have the person sign a consent form at the end of the interview if you intend to publish or share the interview with the public.

Soon after the interview, listen to the tape with follow-up questions in mind, and transcribe the interview according to guidelines provided in oral-history manuals. Provide the interviewee with an opportunity to review and correct the transcript. Consider depositing the transcript in an oral history archive for the use of other researchers. Jot down your impressions of the interview situation and key revelations from the interview.

In conclusion, keep the following ethical issues and cautions in mind:

- An oral history is not a snapshot of the past but an interpretation of it. Like any other historical source, an individual account needs to be critiqued and cross-checked for accuracy.
- Oral history is the result of the interaction between two people. Be aware of your effect as the interviewer on the outcome of the interview, and be sensitive to the culture, emotions, and rights of the interviewee.
- Do not take quotes out of context or misuse an interview for personal gain, do not betray the trust of your informant, and be sure that no one is hurt by the final product.
- Give back to the interviewee or the community you are studying in the form of financial returns or a copy of the final product.

For further reading, consult Valerie Yow, *Recording Oral History: A Practical Guide for Social Scientists* and Judy Yung, "Giving Voice to Chinese American Women: Oral History Methodology," in *Unbound Voices: A Documentary History of Chinese Women in San Francisco*.

The Chinese Health Agenda

Proposed Strategies for Improving Chinese American Health and Wellness

(Original Title: The Chinese Health Agenda—Proposed Strategies for Improving Chinese American Community Health and Wellness)

Layla R. Hall, MPH, and Kent Woo, MSW

INTRODUCTION

The purpose of this report presented by Kent Woo, Executive Director of the NICOS Chinese Health Coalition, is to share with a wider audience the wealth of valuable information and innovation that was generated during the first Chinese Community Health Summit. It contains a brief summary of the Summit, documentation of the Summit sessions, and an analysis of key themes that emerged from the day's proceedings.

The first Chinese Community Health Summit, held on May 26, 2004, was born out of NICOS Chinese Health Coalition's mission to enhance the health and well-being of the San Francisco Chinese community. The Summit was a component of the San Francisco Chinese Community Health Agenda Project, a three-year endeavor funded by the California Endowment to address the health care access and preventive care needs of the city's underserved Chinese Americans.

On the day of the event, there were more than thirty presenters, fifteen informational booths, and more than 250 people in attendance. The Summit brought together panelists and participants with a range of expertise in serving the Chinese community. Present were health and human service providers, advocates, public officials, policy-makers, community professionals, and consumers. Simultaneous translation was available for non-English speaking Summit participants.

The Summit was designed to serve as a vehicle to report on and explore issues affecting the health and well-being of Chinese Americans as well as to develop and ultimately implement strategies to improve the population's overall health. Plenary speakers at the Summit provided participants with both quantitative and qualitative data on the health and wellness of the San Francisco Chinese community. During the eight breakout sessions that followed, a variety of issues were explored. Four of the sessions were primarily topical in nature, with expert panelists presenting on their areas of expertise. The other four sessions were focused on strategy development. Panelists shared their experiences, but Summit participants were expected to actively participate in the generation of new strategies for improving the well-being of the Chinese community. During the last session of the day, spokespersons from the strategy-building sessions shared their ideas with the entire Summit and elicited feedback from a panel of professionals invested in working to improve the health of the Chinese community.

SUMMIT GOALS AND OBJECTIVES

The overarching goal of the Summit was to create a shared vision and mission to improve the health and well-being of the Chinese community, particularly those members who are economically and/or socially disadvantaged.

The Summit objectives were:

- To inform participants of up-to-date data findings on the health status and health care access, usage, and needs of San Francisco's Chinese community.
- To develop effective collaborative strategies to address specific community health issues.
- To build participants' skills and knowledge, enabling them to address key community health concerns.
- To provide participants the opportunity to network with others engaged in ensuring the health of the community.

PLENARY SESSION: DATA REPORT FINDINGS

During the plenary session, Dr. Edward A. Chow, president of the San Francisco Health Commission, presented current quantitative data on the demographic and health characteristics of the San Francisco Chinese population, adopting the World Health Organization's view of health as a state of physical, mental, and social well-being. Data sources for his presentation included the 1997 Chinese Community Health Study, the 2000 Census, the 2001 California Health Interview Survey (CHIS), and the San Francisco Department of Public Health.

According to the 2000 Census, 20 percent of San Francisco's population is Chinese. Of this 20 percent, 108,000 are foreign born, many of whom have difficulty with English. Furthermore, San Francisco's Chinese population faces disparities in income and education when compared with the city's white population. Elderly Chinese are particularly at risk for low educational attainment and limited English skills, while the noncitizen population is particularly prone to income below the poverty level.

The Chinese population faces difficulties accessing and utilizing health care. CHIS data indicates that the impoverished and the uninsured often lack a usual source of health care. Furthermore, the Chinese Community Health Study found that lack of preventive care is common among San Francisco's Chinese Americans. According to CHIS, disparities exist in utilization of dental visits, routine checkups, mammograms, pap smears, bone-density tests, colonoscopies, and PSA tests for prostate cancer.

The Chinese population experiences many common health problems: high blood pressure, asthma, heart disease, and diabetes. Of particular concern among immigrant Chinese is tuberculosis. The city has, however, had success controlling TB by implementing a targeted testing program and providing medication at local health centers throughout the city.

Dr. Chow concluded his presentation by emphasizing the need for cultural competency when planning programs and providing services for the Chinese community.

PLENARY SESSION:
FOCUS GROUP FINDINGS

Also during the plenary session, Kent Woo, executive director of NICOS Chinese Health Coalition, conducted a presentation on his agency's recent focus group study, entitled "Chinese American Voices on Health." He provided a qualitative complement to the data presented by Dr. Chow.

The study took place between November 2003 and January 2004 and included over 100 San Francisco Chinese American residents. In total, there were nine focus groups— seven among healthcare consumers and two among providers. The consumer groups were divided into the following categories: the uninsured, newcomers, seniors, women, clinic consumers, the privately insured, and Mandarin speakers (all other consumer groups were held in Cantonese). The focus groups were designed to uncover thoughts, perceptions, and attitudes toward the following: health issues, healthcare access, preventive care, traditional Chinese medicine, mental health, health knowledge and sources of health information, and quality of care.

Economic concerns including housing costs, lack of affordable insurance, and high unemployment were raised in all nine groups. Additionally, the lack of bilingual services outside of Chinatown and the Sunset and Richmond districts, was often raised as a concern. Further barriers to care included long wait times at providers' offices, limited hours at health clinics, lack of transportation, and lack of interpreters.

Focus group participants named a variety of ways to live a healthy lifestyle, including both Chinese and Western concepts; however, they felt that poverty and long work hours often prevented them from putting these things into practice. The providers' group expressed concern about the low use of routine examinations.

Traditional Chinese medicine was a major topic of discussion. Most focus group participants used a combination of Eastern and Western medicine and saw the two as complementary. They typically perceived traditional Chinese doctors as preferable to Western-style doctors in their manner of relating to and caring for patients, yet they sought care with Western-trained physicians first.

In discussions of mental health, many participants equated mental illness with being insane and did not believe that it could be organic in nature. Consequently, many didn't believe in seeking help for mental health concerns. The providers group felt there was a lack of bilingual/bicultural mental health professionals and a lack of coordination between these professionals and primary care physicians.

Regarding sources of health information, participants reported the following as the most trusted: (1) healthcare professionals, (2) the Chinese media, and (3) community-based health educators. Participants were generally satisfied with the quality of care they received but had the following recommendations: spend more time with patients and have greater respect and concern for patients.

SUMMARY OF BREAKOUT SESSIONS

This table provides a brief illustration of the key issues and suggested solutions generated during the Summit's eight breakout sessions.

Areas	Key Issues	Suggested Strategies
Health care access: bilingual/bicultural services	• Limited bilingual healthcare workforce • Limited bilingual/bicultural services • Need for more interpretation and cultural-competence training materials • Lack of communication between community programs	• Train bilingual/bicultural staff in competency and interpretation. • Advertise and share training materials between organizations. • Recruit international health professionals, bilingual volunteers, and bilingual staff. • Engage and interest youth in health professions. • Advocate aggressively for funding and to protect existing services. • Use NICOS to facilitate communication between organizations.
Health disparities	• Lack of a community resource infrastructure to address disparities in a long-term, systematic manner • Lack of funding for programs and services that address health disparities • Underutilization of preventive services in minority communities • Lack of collaboration among sectors	• Develop policy-level intervention at all public levels: city/county, state, and federal. • Monitor programs to ensure efficacy. • Lobby for services and funding. • Encourage employers to provide healthcare for employees. • Identify ethnic-specific best methods of delivering health messages. • Increase partnership between CBOs and government agencies to disseminate health education information.
Communicating health messages	• Underutilization of the media in distribution of health information • Need for health messages founded on research	• Develop relationships with individuals in the Chinese media. • Use personal stories; give stories an angle that is relevant to the community at the time. • Conduct research on the target population: age; level of acculturation; source of health information; health beliefs and practices; barriers to care. • Target messages to specific groups; incorporate a call to action in the message. • Use a multifaceted approach to message dissemination.
Meeting of medicines: East and West	• Utilization of traditional Chinese medicine (TCM) common among San Francisco Chinese Americans, with both negative and positive effects on health. • Need for physicians to be aware of patients' use of TCM and respond appropriately • Need for integration of TCM with Western-style medicine	• Educate Western-trained doctors to understand the potential toxicity of some Chinese medicines, as well as the potential for drug interactions. • Educate consumers on safe herbal medicine use. • Encourage Western-trained doctors to respect patients' use of TCM and educate themselves about TCM. • Embrace the positive elements of TCM and educate the community on these elements.
Mental health	• Existence in the Chinese community of a mental health stigma • Need for integration of mental health services with other health and social services • Need for partnership between mental health providers and other community organizations • Lack of appropriate mental health services for the Chinese community	• Use the media to educate the public about mental health. • Integrate mental health lessons into high school health education classes. • Educate the professional community—teachers, religious leaders, community leaders, and physicians—to identify mental health problems and refer people for care. • Provide mental health services in natural settings—doctor's offices, schools, churches, and so on. • Advocate for funding for new and existing mental health programs; inform policy makers and legislators of the Chinese community's needs.

Continues on next page

Areas	Key Issues	Suggested Strategies
Health awareness and prevention	• Lack of awareness of healthy preventive practices in many segments of the Chinese population • Lack of Chinese-specific research on best practices for raising health awareness • Need for organizations to collaborate and focus efforts • Growing obesity epidemic in the Chinese population	• Develop a NICOS plan for organizing health promotion work in the Chinese community, ensuring that messages are delivered with power and efficiency. • Conduct culturally specific research on how to best deliver health messages to the Chinese population. • Provide health education where the people are— schools, churches, workplaces, and so on. • Take a comprehensive approach to combating obesity: advocate for funding; educate politicians, physicians, and the general community on the problem; promote policies that encourage healthy eating and physical activity.
Social issues	• Existence of domestic violence in the Chinese community and lack of knowledge and services to address it • Widespread problem gambling in the Chinese community • Lack of affordable housing for Chinese families, leading to residence in single resident occupancy hotels	• Conduct ethnic-specific research on domestic violence. • Expand domestic violence services to include the following: transitional housing for monolingual victims; domestic violence assistance for male victims; counseling for monolingual batterers; and parenting classes for single mothers who are battered. • Raise awareness of problem gambling in the community. • Include questions on problem gambling in social worker- and counselor-client intake protocols; refer for services. • Work with Chinatown Community Development Center to conduct outreach to SRO families.
Creating change	• Need for community organizing as an advocacy tool • Disproportionate under-representation of Chinese Americans in government • Need to form relationships with elected officials	• Organize client base to speak out on behalf of the Chinese community; register them to vote and educate them on political issues. • Engage youth in politics: provide Asian political role models; involve youth in advocacy activities; create political internships for young people. • Get to know local elected officials; inform them of issues; make them understand that clients are constituents who are registered to vote.

ANALYSIS OF SUMMIT

The Chinese Community Health Summit covered a wide range of topics related to the health and well being of San Francisco's Chinese community. While these topics were quite specific in nature, a number of shared themes and concerns emerged from both the plenary speeches and the breakout sessions. Likewise, many of the solutions and strategies proposed by speakers and Summit participants were echoed across the various topical areas.

The most commonly observed themes throughout the Summit were the following:

1. Advocacy is an essential tool in improving the health of the San Francisco Chinese community.
2. There is a need for more Chinese-specific research on health and social problems, and their solutions.
3. Outreach efforts to the Chinese community must be both thorough and varied.
4. Funding constraints pose a significant problem in both the private and public sectors.
5. The media, both Chinese and English, is a valuable instrument for promoting health and well-being in the Chinese population.
6. There is a need for greater communication and collaboration between organizations and individual providers.
7. There is a lack of bilingual and bicultural professionals, which impacts the availability of bilingual and culturally competent services.

1. Advocacy. The need for strong advocacy was repeated in many Summit discussions. Advocacy was seen as essential to making the needs of the Chinese community understood by those with the power to influence policy and funding.

Specifically, advocacy efforts should target the media, policy-makers, and legislators.

Advocacy efforts that involved the clients as partners were seen as very effective. It is important to provide people from the Chinese community with a forum in which they can voice their concerns and be heard. One key component to this is the need to increase the volume by building a large base of clients who are willing to speak out and tell their personal stories. These personal stories go to the heart of the listener in a way that is often more powerful than data and statistics.

One aspect of such community organizing includes educating clients on political issues and turning them out to vote. This provides elected officials with the incentive to work on behalf of the Chinese community.

2. *Research.* Both of the plenary speakers talked about the value of conducting research on the San Francisco Chinese population. Such research generates data that can be used to inform program development as well as support advocacy efforts.

In the breakout sessions of the Summit, participants expressed the need to conduct more research on the most productive methods of reaching the Chinese population with health messages. This includes identifying the best channels for health education as well as the most effective messages for raising awareness and changing health behavior. Furthermore, community-based organizations should conduct more rigorous evaluation on their programs, not only to ensure that organizational funds are being well spent, but also to more powerfully make the case for continued program funding.

3. *Outreach.* Across topics, the need for active outreach to the Chinese community was considered essential to improving access to and utilization of health and social services. San Francisco has a large and steadily increasing population of foreign-born Chinese with varying levels of English proficiency and acculturation. This population faces a variety of challenges as well as a certain degree of isolation.

In many sessions, Summit participants spoke of the need to provide bilingual and bicultural services not only in Chinatown, but also in other communities throughout the city. Furthermore, it is important to conduct health education and outreach activities where the people are, not just in clinics and community based organizations. This means taking education to workplaces, schools, churches, SROs, and so on.

In addition to using a variety of physical venues, the Chinese media was considered an excellent way of reaching the Chinese population with health messages.

Finally, it should be noted that outreach to the provider community is also needed. Health care providers must be educated on a variety of issues, including use of traditional Chinese medicine, mental health issues, and the growing obesity epidemic in the Chinese population.

4. *Funding.* Most Summit participants viewed limited funding as a serious constraint to providing quality service to the Chinese community. Budgetary constraints have limited interpretive services, staff positions, and even entire programs.

In light of the poor economic climate, advocacy is especially important. Organizations must fight hard to maintain programs and services. It is also essential to use existing resources within the community innovatively and efficiently. This includes recruitment and training of bilingual volunteers and staff members in interpretation, as well as increased cooperation between organizations in the provision of services.

5. *Media.* Utilization of the English and Chinese media was raised repeatedly throughout the Summit. The role of the media is twofold: (1) it provides a vehicle for advocacy messages to reach the greater community and (2) it is an excellent way to reach the Chinese population with health messages.

News stories with a personal face or voice get the attention of both politicians and the general public, and health is a topic that always attracts interest. As mentioned previously, personal stories reach the heart and can galvanize others to take action. The print media also enables concerned individuals to write op-ed pieces that raise awareness on important issues.

Many, if not most, San Francisco Chinese listen to Chinese radio, read Chinese newspapers, and watch Chinese television. Furthermore, focus group participants in NICOS' Chinese American Voices on Health study reported that the Chinese media was second only to healthcare professionals as their most trusted source of health information. Many Summit participants confirmed the value of the Chinese media in health education and awareness by telling their organizations' stories of successful media usage.

6. *Communication and Collaboration.* Across the board, the need for increased partnership was considered essential to providing the best possible service to the Chinese community. It was proposed that NICOS could play an important role in facilitating and organizing collaboration between organizations. Collaboration should take place on many levels—among CBOs; between CBOs and government organizations; and at the local, state, and federal levels of government.

Collaboration and partnership can lead to a more efficient use of resources. Organizations can share education and training materials, and they can form work groups to focus their efforts on priority issues and avoid duplication of services.

Increased communication between professionals, especially in the area of mental health, was also considered important. If doctors, teachers, religious leaders, and other community professionals are trained to recognize mental health problems, they can refer people for care.

7. Bilingual and Bicultural Professionals and Services. In many topical areas, the lack of bilingual and bicultural professionals was raised as a serious concern. This includes both a lack of Chinese American health and social service providers and a lack of Chinese American elected officials. The lack of professionals was seen as a contributing factor in the difficulty of providing culturally and linguistically competent services to the Chinese community.

Speakers in several breakout sessions felt that it was important to conduct outreach to youth, getting them involved and interested in health and politics from an early age. Active recruitment and retention of bilingual and bicultural staff and volunteers could also offset the lack of health and social service professionals.

CONCLUSION

Coordinated by NICOS Chinese Health Coalition, the Chinese Community Health Summit was an ambitious, collaborative effort to address the many and varied health and wellness issues faced by the Chinese community of San Francisco. The event helped to define the most pressing issues of beginning to explore solutions and even helped to create a Chinese Health Agenda with strategies to improve community health.

Accommodating Care of Type 2 Diabetes for the Chinese American Family

Christine M. L. Kwan, PhD, Kevin M. Chun, PhD,
and Catherine A. Chesla, RN, DNSc, FAAN

Type 2 diabetes is an illness that affects the Chinese American population disproportionally. Although Chinese American diabetic patients have reported the importance of the family in adequate diabetes care, little is known about how Chinese American families go about supporting or negotiating the care of diabetes. This constitutes the impetus for the current study.

With a subsample from a larger study on couple and family relations in diabetes care, repeated, narrative group interviews with sixteen Chinese American immigrant families were conducted to understand the culturally specific responses to type 2 diabetes. Three culturally specific considerations emerged from the narratives. First, patients and spouses conceptualized diabetes in terms of an imbalance of an internal "hot" and "cold" dynamic, and they ingested "hot" and "cold" food or herbs as a counterbalancing measure to help diabetes care. Second, rather than viewing food as simply a form of sustenance, patients and spouses viewed food as essential to quality of life and quality of social relationships. Third, families accommodated as a way to provide care. Patients and spouses enacted various practices and concerns to balance quality of life and care for the family on one hand with diabetes management in their daily lives on the other.

These findings have useful implications. Specifically, it might be helpful for healthcare providers to elicit and understand patients' and families' conceptualizations of diabetes and its management, thereby enhancing patient-provider relationship and patients' adherence to treatment recommendations. Also, to address the cultural significance of food, it would be important for healthcare providers to offer additional and culturally receptive efforts to help patients and families negotiate the challenge of dietary restrictions. Lastly, to address the key role of family, healthcare providers might consider creating opportunities to engage patient-selected family members in diabetes care.

This paper was presented by Christine M. L. Kwan, PhD, Department of Family Health Care Nursing, University of California, San Francisco. She coauthored the paper with Kevin M. Chun, PhD, Department of Psychology, University of San Francisco, and Catherine A. Chesla, RN, DNSc, FAAN, Department of Family Health Care Nursing, University of California, San Francisco.

The Use of Complementary and Alternative Medicine among Chinese Women with Breast Cancer

(Original Title: Chinese Women, Immigration, and Breast Cancer)

Evaon Wong-Kim, PhD, MPH, MSW

INTRODUCTION

Breast cancer is the number one cause of cancer-related mortality for Asian American and Pacific Islander (AAPI) women, who have the lowest rate of both screening and early detection compared to all other ethnic groups.[1] The incidence of breast cancer is rising rapidly among the fast-growing demographic groups of AAPIs; in a recent ten-year period, incident cases of breast cancer in Los Angeles County doubled for AAPIs overall, and among women of Chinese descent specifically.[2] The incidence rate for AAPI breast cancer in the San Francisco Bay area, where our study was conducted, is approximately 50 percent higher than in Los Angeles County.[3] Among Asian American females in San Francisco, the annual age-adjusted incidence rate is 83.2 per 100,000 for invasive breast cancer and 24.6 per 100,000 for in-situ breast cancer. Between 1995 and 1999, a total of 774 Asian American women were diagnosed with breast cancer in San Francisco.[4] Of these women, 599 had invasive breast cancer and 175 had in-situ disease. According to the national Surveillance, Epidemiology, and End Results data from 1988–1992, the breast cancer rate among Chinese women was 55.0 per 100,000.[5]

According to the Year 2000 Census, Chinese make up the largest Asian group in the United States, constituting 23.8 percent of the nation's total Asian American population. Of the fifty states, California has the largest population of Asian Americans, and Chinese outnumber other Asian groups in the state, at 980,642 or 2.9 percent of the state's total population.[6] Foreign-born Asian women generally have a lower breast cancer rate when compared with U.S.-born Asian women;[7] however, Chinese immigrants are at a higher risk of being diagnosed with breast cancer than their peers living in China, and being diagnosed at a more advanced stage.[8]

Research on cancer-related beliefs indicates that some Chinese people believe cancer is contagious,[9] and that breast cancer is due to tragic luck.[10] These beliefs, combined with a low compliance with breast cancer screening,[11] may compromise the survival rate and quality of life of Chinese women. Further, little is known about the perceptions of *complimentary and alternative therapy* (CAM) among Chinese breast cancer survivors who are recent immigrants as well as CAM use among breast cancer survivors who were born and raised in

the United States. Studies conducted in the area of CAM indicated the use of CAM includes herbs and vitamins, spiritual healing, relaxation, massage, acupuncture, energy healing, hypnosis, therapeutic spas, lifestyle diets, audio or videotapes, medication wraps, and osteopathic, homeopathic, and chiropractic treatment.[12] According to Correa-Velez, Clavarino, and Eastwood (2005),[13] most participants self-treated with CAM and perceived CAM modalities as complementary rather than alternative to conventional cancer treatments. Within this context, CAM is used to prolong survival, palliate symptoms, or alleviate the side effects of conventional cancer treatments, detoxify their bodies, boost immunity, and enhance their overall quality of life. In another study conducted by Yates and colleagues (2005),[14] 91 percent in their study sample reported using at least one form of CAM. The most widely used forms of CAM were prayer, relaxation, and exercise. In this study, CAM users tended to be women chemotherapy patients with at least a high school education. The most frequent CAM modalities discussed with at least one physician were diets, massage, and herbal medicine. Although more and more studies as well as clinical trials are conducted on CAM and the effectiveness of CAM, little is known about the attitude and utilization of CAM among Chinese diagnosed with cancer.

In this pilot study we utilized the qualitative method to ascertain attitudes toward CAM among breast cancer survivors and compared those who were born and raised in the United States to those who came from China, Hong Kong, or Taiwan. We speculate Chinese breast cancer survivors utilize CAM to alleviate pain and chemotherapy side effects. However, due to the limited research in this area, much information needs to be obtained to describe CAM use among Chinese breast cancer survivors. Besides attitudes toward CAM and what form of CAM they used, we were also interested to find out what were the factors that might influence these women to utilize CAM on a regular basis.

METHOD

Research Design. A qualitative design was used to explore cancer-related beliefs and quality of life among Chinese women with breast cancer. In-depth, semistructured face-to-face interviews were conducted with fifteen foreign-born and fifteen U.S.-born Chinese women (N = 30).

Sample. The sample was comprised of Chinese women whose primary language was English, Mandarin, or Cantonese, who were diagnosed with breast cancer at any stage within twenty-four months of study initiation, and who were no longer on active treatment such as chemotherapy, surgery, or radiation therapy. Women taking Tamoxifen were included in this study because it is considered a noninvasive treatment. To ensure that the foreign-born participants reflected Chinese cultural beliefs, eligibility was limited to those who resided in the United States for fewer than fifteen years. U.S.-born Chinese women were used as a comparison group so that acculturation and the effect of immigration can be studied.

The sample was recruited from oncologists serving the Chinese community in the San Francisco Bay Area. Each oncologist compiled a list of their Chinese patients who satisfied the study's inclusion criteria and who did not have a mental health condition that would affect their participation. Women on the list were sent a standardized letter in her preferred language explaining the purpose of the study and indicating that a member of the study team would call to invite her participation in a face-to-face interview. This letter encouraged the women to review an enclosed copy of the informed consent document and to contact the researchers if they had questions. It also indicated that their decision to participate in or decline this study would not affect their right or access to medical treatment.

A research assistant fluent in English, Mandarin, and Cantonese contacted each woman who was sent an introductory letter by the oncologist within two weeks in order to answer questions about the study and determine her interest in participation. If she was interested, the research assistant administered a brief screening interview to verify the woman's ethnicity, place of birth, immigrant status, and the length of time she has lived in the United States. An interview appointment was arranged for women who were eligible for the study and who agreed to participate. This process was followed until a sample size of fifteen U.S.-born and fifteen foreign-born Chinese patients was reached.

Interview Guide. A semistructured interview guide was used to guide the participants in a discussion about the follow topics: (1) knowledge of CAM, (2) the effectiveness of CAM, and (3) barriers to using CAM. Probes were used to obtain additional information and get specific examples from the participants.

Procedure. Bilingual interviewers were recruited and trained in interviewing techniques and study procedures. Once a participant was screened for eligibility and had verbally consented to the interview, a face-to-face interview appointment was arranged by phone. Patients were interviewed for approximately ninety minutes at their residence or in a mutually convenient location. At the start of this appointment, the interviewer introduced herself, briefly repeated the study purpose, reviewed the elements of informed consent, and asked the patient to sign an informed consent document.

Each interviewer followed a standardized protocol to ensure that all the interviews were conducted in a similar manner and that an identical set of questions was discussed. Interviewers took handwritten notes and audiotaped the interview. Also, they rated the quality of the interview on a scale of 1 (poor) to 5 (excellent), and recorded information about any factors that might have affected the information provided, for example, the presence of another family member. The author reviewed the notes and audiotape for each interview immediately after it was completed, and talked with the interviewer to clarify any ambiguous notes or interview segments on the audiotape.

Data Analysis. To facilitate data analysis, verbatim transcriptions of interviews were prepared. Because the author is fluent in Chinese, the interviews conducted in Chinese were transcribed and analyzed in Chinese to preserve linguistic meanings and enhance the trustworthiness of the data. The narratives from these transcripts were analyzed using a constant comparative approach[15] to identify concepts and develop categories that provide a structured framework for organizing the data.

Results. Table 1 summarizes the demographic profile of the study sample. Although both groups are comprised of Chinese women, the foreign-born women reported a lower level of education than the U.S.-born sample and they earned much less than their U.S.-born peers. In this study, foreign-born and U.S.-born Chinese women described the types of CAM they used and what some of the barriers were for using CAM.

Types of CAM Being Used. Most U.S.-born breast cancer survivors define CAM in broader terms. While foreign-born Chinese women identified herbal medicine and acupuncture as CAM, U.S.-born survivors consider yoga and meditation to be CAM:

> *U.S.-born:* I started meditation during the holidays in December because I felt that after all this treatment and then all I have is Tamoxifen and this little pill is going to prevent cancer, you know, I thought oh, my God, what am I going to do? You know, 'cause I think I'm pretty stressed out thinking about it. So I thought I'll try meditation and that's something that I can take with me....And I just thought this would be a good thing. I didn't know exactly what meditation was all about but I'm beginning to understand it and the benefits.

> *U.S.-born:* I did have a massage and that felt really good. But with touch therapy I learn to relax with the touch of a hand. And at some points you could be so relaxed that you fall asleep, which is a good thing, you know. And then sometimes right after touch therapy I would go into meditation class and boy, I could just get into meditation.

U.S.-born: You know, I've been taking this Chinese tea, but I don't know the name of the Chinese tea. It's supposed to clean…cleanse your body—whatever that is like toxic stuff, it will clean the body, so I've been taking that.

U.S.-born: Sometimes I do breathing exercises. That's 'cause I've been attending classes; even before, I go to yoga classes. I'm not practicing real strict yoga. I do it for the exercise.

TABLE 1: SAMPLE DEMOGRAPHICS

	U.S.-born N = 15	Foreign-born N = 15
Age (Mean)	57	51
Marital status		
Single	5	2
Married	10	13
Education		
Sixth grade or below	0	3
Elementary school	0	1
Middle school	0	4
High school graduate	1	6
Some college	3	0
College graduate	7	0
Graduate school	4	1
Annual household income		
$10,000 or less	0	6
$10,001–$20,000	3	3
$20,001–$35,000	2	2
$30,001–$50,000	2	2
$50,001–$60,000	5	2
$60,001 or more	3	0
Health insurance		
Medicaid	0	6
Private insurance	15	9
Number of visits with Western medical doctor in past 6 mos.		
Less than 10	9	11
10 or more	6	4
Number of visits with Chinese medical doctor in past 6 mos.		
Less than 10	13	6
10 or more	2	9
Type of treatment received (duplicated)		
Radiation therapy	12	7
Chemotherapy	8	7
Lumpectomy	11	5
Mastectomy	4	8

U.S.-born: I'm trying to do the mindful meditation. Some meditation, you know, doing yoga….Yoga meditation, trying to relax more, but I haven't done any acupuncture or I don't take any Chinese herbs.

Foreign-born: Western medicine is the primary. I do take Chinese herbal tea, but the point is I don't totally rely on it. When I feel somewhat "hot," I would brew some [herbal tea] to drink. Like now, there is SARS [in Hong Kong], and some people suggest some herbal drinks, I will have some. I will brew some and drink it. Or when other people brew it, I will drink it too. When others ask if I am afraid to drink, I will look at it and say: "No, I am not afraid. These are common Chinese herbal 'cooling' tea; I am not afraid to take it." I still have one concoction here that I have not prepared yet.

Attitude toward CAM Effectiveness. Most participants in our study found CAM to be effective to alleviate aches and pains but did not consider it to be a substitute for medical interventions such as chemotherapy or radiation therapy:

U.S.-born: I do think that [CAM] does help to relieve some pressure from whatever joint or pain. I think that not only Western but Eastern medicine's very good too. So I think sometimes if you know what specifically the problem is you can try CAM. Now I don't think it will work with cancer. Acupuncturists are good with pains and aches in the joints and things like that. Back pain I think an acupuncturist can help.

U.S.-born: [I] know that [CAM] doesn't help too much except for aches and pains of some joint or some sort. [CAM] relieves the pressure. I recommend people go to acupuncturists. I would recommend if you have arthritis to try acupuncture. Because I have no aches and I don't have joint problem [therefore I don't use CAM]. I would not go [for CAM] for this cancer.

U.S.-born: You know, I'd gone the route of this chemotherapy, very strong medicines and radiation and all of that. I was hesitant to try or I wouldn't recommend alternative medicine until all of that has run its course 'cause you wouldn't want to counteract anything.

U.S.-born: I really haven't investigated alternative medication, or herbs or whatever, yet. And, it takes a whole lot….For me, it takes…ah, time…to accept something. I have to thoroughly understand it and understand the outcome, before throwing it in my body.

U.S.-born: I just felt that I wanted to treat [breast cancer] aggressively, and I wanted to remove it out of my system, I'm very confident in American/Western medicine. I just thought we could get it out, and I do believe in Eastern medicine, but I don't know a whole lot about it, and I haven't tried it a lot….

Foreign-born: Yes, I do. I go to the Chinese doctor every now and then. I had never gone to a Chinese doctor before. Not Chinese or Western doctors because I was very healthy. When I went through chemotherapy, I felt pain all over my body. A friend at the Support Group told me that acupuncture would help reduce the pain. So I decided to give it a try. The first time it seemed to help, the pain went away. So I decided to test if it happened by chance. I tolerated for a few days to see if the pain would go away on its own or because of the acupuncture. After a few days, I went for acupuncture and the pain went away. I then believed in it. I started going for acupuncture once a week or sometimes one or two times every other week.

Foreign-born: I'd rather take medication for my pain, which is the fastest to stop the pain. I think herbs and other Eastern medicine takes too long and I can't stand waiting for it to work. Acupuncture and herbal medicine are just too troublesome to get and take too long to work.

Foreign-born:

有時啲針灸睇吓你係乜嘢啦。有時好好㗎。好似啲人胃痛呀，或者月經痛呀，頭痛呀，腰痛。但係腰痛你要針後面。即係嗰啲穴位有好多係後邊。咁你自己針唔到。咁我又曾經係呢度睇過一個跌打。睇過一次。不過佢話你呢啲咁耐啲嘅腰骨痛咗咁耐都好乜用。同我求其敷啲藥收咗我二十文。咁我再無去睇。

(Sometimes it is good to use acupuncture depending on the problem. Sometimes it's good. Such as stomachache, or pain caused by menstrual cycle, headache, back pain. But you need acupuncture on your back if you have back pain. There are many nerves and focal points on the back. So you can't do it yourself even if you know acupuncture. So I did see an acupressure practitioner, only once but he said my back pain had been there for so long that there was nothing he could do. He charged me twenty dollars for doing nothing so I didn't go again.)

Foreign-born:

針灸中醫嗰啲呢，如果有啲係叻嘅呢，我就好信。如果唔叻嗰啲我就唔係好信。因為我發現好多係中國嚟嘅中醫，你都唔知佢邊個好邊個唔好。如果佢真係咁好俾我睇到咁好，我就會嘗試。

(In terms of acupuncture and herbal medicine, if the practitioner is good I can really trust it to be effective. But those who are not good I don't believe in their effectiveness. You just don't know who's good and who's not among those practitioners from China. If I can find someone who is good then I will try using acupuncture.)

Barriers to CAM utilization. U.S.-born and foreign-born Chinese women experienced different types of barriers to using CAM. While foreign-born Chinese women considered cost and interaction with Western medicine as major barriers to CAM use, for U.S.-born women, limited Chinese language skills, as well as the lack of regulation in practicing CAM were considered to be major barriers to using CAM.

U.S.-born: And then lots of the alternative medicines such as herbs. I know a lot of people take mushroom tablets and all of this and that, right? But they have no regulation over the production of lots of the herbs. So it troubles me to ingest something that hadn't been prepared or produced in a manner where safeguards are taken. You know, you don't want other things growing inside of you because standards are so poor. There's no regulation.

U.S.-born: I might consider it, you know, if I really have to, but I think that, you know, being born here I would, you know, I would probably tend towards the Western but I wouldn't mind trying, you know, the Asian medicine 'cause I know that there are some Asian medicines that are pretty good or the herbal stuff that you drink is pretty good. So I don't mind trying.

U.S.-born: I wouldn't know how to use it. The only time I know how to use it is when I put, you know, herbs in a soup, or something….

U.S.-born: Once I did: drinking the herbs and stuff….But, I just find it's really hard to go into the herb stores, and usually the person there is only Chinese-speaking, I mean…I don't know…. I think you have to go to a Chinese doctor, and they give you the prescription [laughter] for the Chinese herb….Yeah…and I just, you know…haven't gone that route, yet.

Foreign-born:

因為我自己理解咁囉，因為食一種西藥係唔可以同一種中藥黐埋食。咁我諗住化療呢種藥都幾勁囉，唔知啱唔啱呢同夾埋食唔知啱唔啱。所以我就無去睇中醫。但講中醫我以前都會去睇嘅。譬如有感冒咁樣，我都會走去睇嘅。但因為呢啲藥太勁我就唔知啱唔啱，所以即使係寄咗啲藥俾我食呢，係化療期間我都唔會食。即係嗰個星期之內我唔會食囉。即係寧願，我理解等到啲藥清得七七八八時我先至食。

(Because I don't understand the interaction [between Western medicine and CAM]. Because you are not supposed to mix Western and Chinese medicine. I think the chemotherapy drugs are really strong and I don't know if it will go with Chinese herbs. So I haven't been to the herbalist for quite a while. Before I was diagnosed I used to see the Chinese herbalist. Like when I have a cold, I used to get seen by an herbalist. But the chemo drugs are just too strong and I don't know if I should be taking other stuff at the same time. During the time I was getting chemo, I didn't use CAM. I will wait until the chemo drug is about 70 to 80 percent absorbed before I start on herbs again.)

Foreign-born:

無呀，嗰啲一嚟需要私人出錢，邊度有錢呀？ 唔使錢就會喎。可以調劑下。呢一層係好過喎。

(No, [I have not used CAM], those treatments require self payments; where do I find money? If it doesn't cost money, then I will use it to supplement my treatment. That will be a good thing.)

CONCLUSION

The findings from this study clearly indicated the value of using CAM for breast cancer survivors. There are marked differences between the two groups in terms of definition of CAM, impression of CAM effectiveness, and barriers to using CAM. However, affordability and quality assurance are important issues that need to be addressed. Although research indicated an increasing number of cancer patients are using CAM in the United States, oncology and CAM are two totally separate disciplines. There is no communication or coordination between these two, and patients often get trapped in the middle. Although patients feel that there may be some benefit to using CAM to alleviate the side effects of chemotherapy and radiation therapy, they are also afraid that the two types of medication may have negative interactions and cause harm to their body or minimize the effectiveness of the treatment. A more friendly relationship between oncologists and CAM practitioners will ensure breast cancer survivors have greater access to treatment in order to fully utilize the two different approaches to pain management and treatment side effects from cancer regiments such as surgery, chemotherapy and radiation therapy. Future medical research should look at the possibility of a more comprehensive approach to cancer treatment that includes a combination of Western medicine and CAM. A more holistic approach to cancer care will hopefully be offered someday that will maximize treatment benefits to all cancer patients.

ACKNOWLEDGMENT

This study was supported by a grant from Asian American Network for Cancer Awareness, Research, and Training (AANCART). Special thanks go to the following individuals for their contribution to the development of the study: Angela Sun, MPH; Sarah Stearmam, MPH; Betsy Woo RN; and Cecilia Pang.

NOTES

1. M. Kagawa-Singer and N. Puorat, "Asian American and Pacific Islander Breast and Cervical Carcinoma Screening Rates and Healthy People 2000 Objectives," *Cancer* 89, no. 3 (2000): 696–705; D. Deapen, L. Liu, C. Perkins, L. Bernstein, and R. K. Ross, "Rapidly Rising Breast Cancer Incidence Rates among Asian-American women," *International Journal of Cancer* 99, no. 5 (2002): 747–750.

2. Deapen, et al., "Rapidly Rising Breast Cancer."

3. E. S. Yu, K. K. Kim, E. H. Chen, and R. A. Brintnall, "Breast and Cervical Cancer Screening among Chinese American Women," *Cancer Practice* 9, no. 2 (2001): 81–90.

4, Greater Bay Area Cancer Registry, *Annual Incidence and Mortality Reports: 1988-1999, Region 8* (n.p.: Northern California Cancer Center, 2002).

5. Deapen, et al., "Rapidly Rising Breast Cancer."

6. Yu, et al., "Breast and Cervical Cancer Screening."

7. Kagawa-Singer and Puorat, "Healthy People 2000 Objectives."

8. K. Ganz, R. T. Croyle, V. Y. Cholette, and V. W. Pinn, "Cancer-related Health Disparities in Women," *Research and Practice* 93 (2003): 292–298; W. Luo, N. J. Birkett, A. M. Ugnat, and Y. Mao, "Cancer Incidence Patterns among Chinese Immigrant Populations in Alberta," *Journal of Immigrant Health* 6 (2004): 41–48; T. S. Tang, L. J. Solomon, and L. M. McCracken, "Cultural Barriers to Mammography, Clinical Breast Exam, and Breast Self-exam among Chinese-American Women 60 and Older," *Preventive Medicine* 31 (2000): 575–583.

9. E. C. Wong-Kim, A. Sun, and M. C. DeMattos, "Assessing Cancer Attitude in a Chinese Immigrant Community," *Cancer Control* 10 (2003): 22–28.

10. K. T. Ashing-Giwa, G. Padilla, J. Tejero, J. Kraemer, K. Wright, A. Coscarelli, S. Clayton, I. Williams, and D. Hills, "Understanding the Breast Cancer Experience of Women: A Qualitative Study of African American, Asian American, Latina and Caucasian Cancer Survivors," *Psycho-Oncology* 13 (2004): 408–428; H. S. Juon, Y. Choi, and M. T. Kim, "Cancer Screening Behaviors among Korean-American Women, *Cancer Detection and Prevention* 24, no. 6 (2000): 589–601.

11. C. J. Bradley, C. W. Given, and C. Roberts, "Race, Socioeconomic Status, and Breast Cancer Treatment and Survival," *Journal National Cancer Institute* 94 (2002): 490–496; S. J. McPhee, J. A. Bird, T. Davis, N. T. Ha, C. N. H. Jenkins, and B. Le, "Barriers to Breast and Cervical Screening among Vietnamese-American Women," *American Journal of Preventive Medicine* 13 (1997): 205–213.

12. J. M. Fouladbakhsh, M. Stommel, B. A. Given, and C. W. Given, "Predictors of Use of Complementary and Alternative Therapies among Patients with *Cancer*" *Oncology Nursing Forum* 32, no. 6 (2005): 1115–1122.

13. I. Correa-Velez, A. Clavarino, and H. Eastwood, "Surviving, Relieving, Repairing, and Boosting Up: Reasons for Using Complementary/Alternative Medicine among Patients with Advanced *Cancer*: A Thematic Analysis," *Journal of Palliative Medicine* 8, no. 5 (2005): 953–961.

14. J. S. Yates, K. M. Mustian, G. R. Morrow, L. J. Gillies, D. Padmanaban, J. N. Atkins, B. Issell, J. J. Kirshner, and L. K. Colman, "Prevalence of Complementary and Alternative Medicine Use in *Cancer* Patients during Treatment," *Supportive Care in Cancer: Official Journal of the Multinational Association of Supportive Care in Cancer* 13, no. 10 (2005): 806–811 (electronic publication, February 15, 2005).

15. A. Strauss, and J. Corbin, *Basics of Qualitative Research: Grounded Theory Procedures and Techniques* (Newbury Park, CA: Sage, 1990).

The Development of a Community-Based Integrated Health Care System for the San Francisco Chinese Community

(Original Title: Accessing Culturally Competent Health Care in the 21st Century)

Edward A. Chow, MD, Bernard Lau, L. Eric Leung, MD, Richard Loos, and Brenda Yee, MSN

Much has been written about the experience of the Chinese in America. However, there has been little consideration given to how the Chinese obtained health care. The early immigrants came with their own Eastern traditions, but how the Chinese were able to gain access to Western medical care in the largest Chinese settlement in America is an important part of the history of the Chinese. The history of Chinese medicine goes back centuries, perhaps millennia.[1] How those who were raised in one medical system would accept another medical system, and how they would gain access to Western medicine in an environment of discrimination are exemplified in the development of the Chinese Hospital and its integrated medical system.

Of the approximately 12 million Asians and Asian Americans living in the United States, the Chinese comprise the largest ethnic group (2.4 million), with heavy concentrations in large metropolitan areas such as New York, Los Angeles, and the San Francisco Bay Area. The city of San Francisco is home to approximately 152,000 people of Chinese descent, approximately 20 percent of the city's population.[2] The characteristics of San Francisco's Chinese population differ from the city as a whole. Significant segments of the local Chinese population in San Francisco struggle financially and educationally due in part to San Francisco often being the first port of entry for immigrants and a comfortable enclave for the elderly. On average, the Chinese of San Francisco tend to be less educated, have a larger proportion of elderly and youth, and have lower average family incomes than the general population. Over 108,000 of San Francisco's Chinese are foreign-born, with about 50 percent of this group having limited English proficiency. Among the Chinese aged sixty-five years or older, nearly 70 percent speak English poorly or not at all. Many struggle financially, with 20 percent of Chinese households having an annual income of less than $15,000. Chinese households are also less likely to have an annual income greater than $75,000. Additionally, the average Chinese household is larger than that of whites, so that the financial resources are spread more thinly within their households. In comparison to the general San Francisco population, more Chinese lack a high school diploma and fewer attain a bachelor's degree or higher level of education; in fact, 25 percent of the adult population have less than a ninth grade education. This is largely due in part to the disproportionate number of older Chinese who are less educated than their younger counterparts. These conditions affect their ability to gain access to the Western health care system.[3]

While the history of the Chinese in California, specifically San Francisco, is relatively well known, the history of their access to health care is not as often discussed. Chinese immigrants were systematically excluded from participating in social and political institutions in San Francisco and California. A variety of taxes were unfairly levied upon the Chinese, ranging from discriminatory mining and laundry taxes to taxes funding public education despite institutional denial of access to public education.[4] Chinese immigrants were also denied the opportunity to obtain American citizenship and therefore the right to vote and influence policy as well as the right to testify in courts. Chinese immigrants were required to pay a hospital tax upon entry into San Francisco. Despite their monetary contributions, they were denied access to San Francisco City and County Hospital. Yang recounts several examples of Chinese individuals being refused admission to the City and County Hospital even with seemingly medically severe conditions, for example, pulmonary tuberculosis. Between the years of 1870 and 1897, there were never more than thirty-four Chinese admitted to San Francisco City and County Hospital in any given year, even though the city's Chinese population exceeded 8,600.[5] While the Chinese comprised 5 to 10 percent of the population of San Francisco, Chinese patients made up less than 0.1 percent of total admissions to the hospital.

Exclusionary practices of the hospital and the San Francisco Board of Health only partially explain the low admission rates of Chinese during this period. The distance from Chinatown made it inconvenient for Chinese to seek care from the hospital; additionally, travel to the hospital made individuals susceptible to violence such as rock throwing, assault, or mob violence, which were not uncommon during the period. Additionally, linguistic barriers made communication and the clinical encounter difficult to navigate.[6]

Chinese physicians and their traditional practices were often the preferred sources of care for Chinese immigrants. Chinese medicine offered diagnoses and treatment regimens familiar to them, when compared to Western medicine, thus creating more comfortable clinical encounters compared to a Western clinic or hospital.

By the late nineteenth century, Western medicine gained greater overall acceptance and advances in technology and the understanding of medical science led to modernization of hospitals, transitioning from asylums and almshouses to modern scientific institutions that would be judged by their level of cleanliness, efficiency, and expertise. In 1872, the new City and County Hospital was opened; it contained all of the medical technologies of the time and, like most new hospitals at the time, was designed in a manner that promoted hygiene and circulation of clean air.[7] However, due to its continued exclusionary practices, the Chinese community was deprived of the advances in clinical sciences that the new hospital offered. During this period, different religious and ethnic groups in the City established hospitals to serve their communities. Although several new hospitals were being opened, such as those for the French, German, and Jewish communities, these new hospitals also did not offer care for the Chinese. Chinese community leaders also wanted to create a Chinese hospital to serve the Chinese population in San Francisco. The community submitted a petition in 1892 but was denied by the Board of Health because such an institution was seen as a nuisance and a danger to the surrounding neighborhood.[8] Finally, the Board of Supervisors gave permission for a dispensary to be opened in Chinatown.

Through fundraising, in the form of collecting donations from Chinese merchants, the Chinese Six Companies[9] raised $26,000 and in 1899 opened the Tung Wah Dispensary, located at 828 Sacramento Street. The two-story building measured 25 feet by 60 feet and housed twenty-five beds. The Tung Wah Dispensary offered both Western and Chinese medicine and represented a significant improvement to the access to medical care for the Chinese. The American physicians were volunteers from surrounding hospitals, assisted by in-house interpreters, and traditional Chinese physicians came from the surrounding community. The dispensary, through continued fundraising by the Six Companies on its behalf, provided care, advice, and medicine free of charge to patients. The Tung Wah Dispensary represents the first organized institution dedicated to providing culturally competent health care for the Chinese community.

As a result of the 1906 earthquake, the Tung Wah Dispensary was destroyed and rebuilt on 14 Trenton Street. While it continued to provide free care to the Chinese, it was recognized that the need for and usage of services from the facility would outgrow its ability to meet these demands. In 1918, the Chinese Six Companies began fundraising to expand and remodel the dispensary. In collaboration with the prominent community groups of the day, including family and district associations, the Chinese Chamber of Commerce, Chinese Democratic Constitutionalist Party, Chinese American Citizens Alliance, Chinese Nationalist Party (Kuomingtong) in

America, Chinese Christian Union, and the Chinese YMCA, the Chinese Six Companies raised funds and developed a plan for a modern hospital. The hospital project was approved by the Board of Supervisors in 1923 and construction of the Chinese Hospital (Tung Wah Hospital, in Chinese) was completed in 1925. The governance of the hospital would be under a board of directors with one representative from each of the fifteen major participating community organizations. The hospital opened on April 18, 1925, at 835 Jackson Street and provided approximately sixty beds. Although the hospital was created to care for the Chinese, the hospital would be Western medicine–based and would also have white physicians, as there were few Chinese physicians trained in Western medicine. The hospital had four Western-trained Chinese physicians on the medical staff, and thirty-two white physicians from surrounding hospitals and medical schools also provided their assistance.[10] Over time, with greater acceptance of Western medicine by the Chinese population, and continued fundraising, the hospital became financially stable; Chinese Hospital established itself as a major center of service for the Chinese community in San Francisco.

In the 1970s, discussions about expanding the hospital were initiated, as more space was needed for modern technology such as radiology and laboratory. However, Hill-Burton funds were only available for outpatient facilities.[11] In 1975, the hospital Board signed a $5.4 million agreement to utilize Hill-Burton funding along with fundraising from the community to build a new outpatient clinic.[12] When the 1925 hospital building was determined not to meet fire code standards, the federal authorities felt the hospital should consider merging with another facility. However, with significant community support from business, family and district associations, and the general public, permission was granted to convert the outpatient clinic facility into the new Chinese Hospital which opened on September 29, 1979. The new hospital, situated adjacent to the old hospital, houses fifty-four acute care beds and offers medical, surgical, and specialty programs previously unavailable at the old hospital. In 2005, there were over 265 physicians on the medical staff, with forty-three categories of subspecialists. Seven percent of the medical staff were born at Chinese Hospital. Offering twenty-four-hour emergency room services, the hospital includes intensive care and coronary care units, same-day surgery, and significant outpatient services, including endoscopy, pharmacy, and ophthalmology and urological procedures.

In the late 1970s and early 1980s, managed care became a major trend in the delivery of care in California. These offerings were popular because indemnity type insurance programs were increasingly and prohibitively expensive for employers and individuals. Health maintenance organization (HMO) health plans were organizing physician groups and hospitals to participate in the managed-care business. Enrollees were required to access care from physicians and hospitals selected by the plans. Due to business considerations by the mainstream health plans who did not feel a need to include Chinese physicians or the Chinese Hospital, enrollees were deprived of access to culturally competent health care. Organized by the Chinese Hospital's medical staff, fifty-four physicians formed the Chinese Community Health Care Association (CCHCA) to deliver managed-care products as a nonprofit, mutual benefit association in 1982. The formation of CCHCA was necessary so as to obtain contracts from health plans to be able to offer culturally-appropriate care to the Chinese population.

In 1982, CCHCA partnered with Chinese Hospital and worked with Blue Shield of California to offer an exclusive provider plan (known as an Exclusive Provider Organization or EPO under the Department of Insurance) to the Chinese community. In 1985, working with the Children's Hospital Health Plan of San Francisco, CCHCA and Chinese Hospital became a site of service for the Children's Hospital Health Plan thus making available to seniors and employees language-appropriate, culturally competent care. Today, over 174 physicians in more than thirty specialties serve over 26,000 enrollees in five plans, including Chinese Community Health Plan, Blue Cross California Care HMO, Health Net commercial, PacifiCare Commercial, and San Francisco Health Plan MediCal and Healthy Kids.

The Chinese Community Health Care Association's status as a nonprofit, mutual benefit association is unique among physician groups. In contrast to most physician groups, CCHCA sets itself apart in that it was founded with the intention to serve the Chinese community, and form what would be similar to a family association. Unlike other independent practice associations (IPA), CCHCA physicians do not share ownership of the organization and therefore do not receive dividends. Its by-laws have been established to promote the organization's participation in and support of the community. There is an advisory committee composed of prominent civic and community leaders, two of whom also sit on the board. Compensation schedules for its physicians are determined by a nonphysician majority of the Compensation Committee. CCHCA was instrumental in the establishment of the Asian American Pacific Islander American Health Forum (APIAHF), acknowledged to be the leading advocate for health services for Asian Americans and Pacific Islanders at the federal level. CCHCA has participated in the National Cancer Institute's special populations project, as the only nonuniversity affiliated site of investigation for the Asian American Network for Cancer Awareness, Research, and Training (AANCART). In the first five years of the grant, the AANCART Chinese site, also known as the AANCART Chinese Council, worked as a community collaborative to highlight Hepatitis B awareness in the community. It developed educational programs and a set of guidelines for the recognition and follow-up for those who had active Hepatitis B or are Hepatitis B carriers. CCHCA was also a founding partner of the NICOS Chinese Health Coalition for San Francisco, a collaborative of public, private,

and community health and service organizations working to enhance and promote the health and well-being of the Chinese community of San Francisco. In 2004, CCHCA provided support for NICOS' Chinese Community Health Summit, as part of the organization's San Francisco Chinese Community Health Agenda Project to update the health needs of the Chinese community. As part of its commitment to health service, education, and programs in the community, CCHCA has provided over $3,000,000 in funding for the Chinese Community Health Resource Center, Chinese Hospital Emergency Treatment Room, and grants for health-related community projects.

In the early 1980s, Blue Shield of California partnered with Chinese Hospital and the physicians as a community benefit project to create a managed-care plan. In 1984, Blue Shield introduced the Chinese Community Health Plan, an exclusive physician organization plan under the Department of Insurance, which functioned much like an HMO. In 1985, with the continued support and assistance of Blue Shield, Chinese Hospital obtained a license from the state of California, under the Knox-Keene Act, to develop their own community-based health plan. In 1987, the proposed HMO was determined to be viable by the regulatory agency (the Department of Corporations), and Blue Shield transferred the title of the Chinese Community Health Plan to the new entity. CCHP is a wholly-owned subsidiary of Chinese Hospital and was established to provide affordable health plans for the Chinese community, many of whom were culturally and linguistically isolated and therefore in need of language-appropriate and culturally sensitive and affordable care. CCHP also targeted small business, which many Chinese-owned businesses were. With an affordable premium and a set of physicians able to deliver culturally appropriate care, CCHP began enrolling members in October 1987.

Almost simultaneous to the development of CCHP, French and Children's Hospitals in San Francisco were providing Medicare managed-care programs for the elderly. As a result, many seniors in the community who were with limited English proficiency joined these programs. Unfortunately, these enrollees were now unable to utilize their physicians in the community. Children's Hospital Health Plan requested that Chinese Hospital identify physicians who could help care for this population. In 1985, after mutually productive discussions, Chinese Hospital and its physicians in CCHCA became providers and a site of service for the Children's Hospital Health Plan. This was the beginning of a partnership of physicians and the hospital to deliver managed-care products in the mainstream community leading to contracts with larger plans such as Blue Cross and PacifiCare. It also offered the opportunity, when Medicaid mandated a managed-care program for the AFDC population, to have patients stay with their doctors and hospital.[13]

The Chinese Community Health Plan had obtained permission from Health Care Financing Administration (HCFA) to host its own Medicare managed-care program. However, because of the success of the Children's Hospital Health Plan Senior program, which ultimately became a part of Health Net of California, the activation of this program was deferred until 1994 because Health Net perceived inadequate capitation from HCFA and increased the monthly premium. This was a significant hardship on the Chinese community, and in 1996, the CCHP Senior program for members with Medicare Part A and Part B was offered at a minimal monthly premium. This CCHP Medicare program proved to be very beneficial to a large number of people. In early 2005, when the Centers for Medicare and Medicaid Services (CMS), the successor of HCFA, offered special-needs programs, CCHP qualified for a program to serve the dual-eligible population.[14] The response to this important program was overwhelming. By the end of 2005, CCHP held 6.4 percent of the total market share (percentage of enrollees out of all insured individuals) of the Chinese in San Francisco, including 17.1 percent market share of the Chinese over sixty-five years of age. As of 2005, the combined managed programs of Chinese Hospital, Chinese Community Health Plan, and Chinese Community Health Care Association serve nearly 18 percent of San Francisco Chinese and an estimated 27 percent of those with limited English capability. The hospital and physicians also provide the same culturally sensitive care for additional thousands on a fee-for-service basis.

The virtually integrated health delivery system uses CCHP as the third-party administrator for the Chinese Hospital and CCHCA, supporting their participation in mainstream health plans and the San Francisco Health Plan, which provides access for the Medicaid and healthy families population of San Francisco. This allows the system to function seamlessly as one, for patients, practitioners, and facilities. Today, the system serves the entire city of San Francisco, with enrollment of CCHP and the other plans evenly distributed in all quadrants of the city. Chinese Hospital has created two outpatient facilities to serve this population, and private physicians are opening offices throughout San Francisco.

Recognizing the importance of educating the community on the benefits of Western medicine in a culturally sensitive manner, Chinese Hospital, CCHCA, and CCHP created Chinese Community Health Resource Center (CCHRC), a nationally recognized, bilingual educational and research organization based at Chinese Hospital.[15]

The Chinese community in San Francisco from the earliest days recognized the need to have health care available to its population and sought access to care in spite of discrimination, historic exclusionary practices, and more recently due to the constraints of managed care. This is complicated by a dual medical system of Eastern traditional and Western medicine, and by language access. They met this need with the establishment of the only community-owned Chinese Hospital in San Francisco in the early twentieth century. Responding to the challenges of access in the late twentieth century with the development of its own managed-care plan (CCHP) and the establishment of a nonprofit mutual association of physicians (CCHCA), these unique efforts are a nongovernmental model of responding to a community's need for culturally competent health care.

NOTES

1. Ilza Veith, *The Yellow Emperor's Classic of Internal Medicine* (Berkeley: University of California Press, 1972), 5; Edward A. Chow, "Chinese American Health Care Needs," *Asian American and Pacific Islander Journal of Health*, 4, no. 1–3 (Winter–Summer, 1996): 137–141.

2. U.S. Census Bureau, *The Asian Population: 2000*, *http://www.census.gov/prod/2002pubs/c2kbr01-16.pdf* (2002); NICOS Chinese Health Coalition, *The Chinese Community Health Summit Report* (2004).

3. Ibid.

4. Chalsa M. Loo, *Chinatown: Most Time, Hard Time* (New York: Praeger, 1991); Joshua Shu Yang, "A Model to Increase Access to Care for Immigrants: Charting the Development of San Francisco Chinatown's Ethnic-Specific Health Care System" (Ph.D. diss., University of California, Los Angeles, 2005), 115.

5. Yang, *A Model to Increase Access*, 115–116; Joan B. Trauner, "The Chinese as Medical Scapegoats in San Francisco, 1870-1906," *California History* 57, no. 1 (1978): 70–87.

6. Yang, *A Model to Increase Access*, 116.

7. Ibid., 123–124.

8. Ibid., 126; Chinese Hospital Association, *The Chinese Hospital of San Francisco* (Oakland: Carruth & Carruth, 1899); Trauner, "The Chinese as Medical Scapegoats."

9. The Chinese Six Companies, also known as the Chinese Consolidated Benevolent Association, served as the unofficial leadership of San Francisco Chinatown. It is formed of various district associations in San Francisco. Victor G. Nee and Brett de Bary Nee, *Longtime Californ': A Documentary Study of an American Chinatown* (New York: Pantheon, 1972).

10. Collin Quock, *Chinese Hospital Medical Staff Archives, 1978-1981* (San Francisco: Chinese Hospital Medical Staff, 1982).

11. The Hill-Burton Act, also known as the Hospital Survey and Construction Act, was originally passed by Congress in 1946 to provide federal funding to improve the physical plant of the U.S. hospital system. In 1975, the Hill-Burton Act was amended and became Title XVI of the Public Health Security Act. United States Department of Health and Human Services, *http://www.hhs.gov/ocr/hburton.html* (2000); USDHHS, *http://www.hrsa.gov/osp/dfcr/about/aboutdiv.htm* (2005).

12. Chinese Hospital, *Chinese Hospital, 70th Anniversary* (San Francisco: Chinese Hospital, 1995).

13. AFDC refers to Aid to Families with Dependent Children. USDHHS, *http://www.acf.dhhs.gov/programs/afdc/* (2000).

14. The term *dual-eligible* refers to those who are eligible for Medicare and Medicaid, typically someone who is both elderly and indigent.

15. Angela Sun, Sarah Stearman, and Edward A. Chow, "Accessing Cultural Competent Health Education Programs in the 21st Century," manuscript submitted to *Chinese America: History and Perspectives*, 2005.

Accessing Cultural Competent Health Education Programs in the Twenty-first Century

(Original Title: Accessing Culturally Competent Health Care in the 21st Century)

Angela Sun, MPH, Sarah Stearman, MPH, RD, and Edward A. Chow, MD

Chinese Community Health Resource Center

INTRODUCTION

According to the 2000 census, there were approximately 2.4 million Chinese in the United States, and about 152,000 of them resided in San Francisco. The 2000 census also revealed that about 39 percent (versus 23 percent nationwide) of the residents in the San Francisco Chinatown area who spoke Asian and Pacific Island languages spoke English "not well" or "not at all."[1] A recent study by Goel stated that there are disproportionately more foreign-born within the Asian American and Pacific Islanders group than non-Hispanic white Americans. Moreover, foreign-born individuals are at a greater risk for receiving poor quality health care due to lower participation in preventive services, lack of a regular health care provider, lack of lower rates of insurance coverage, cultural and language barriers, and lack of acculturation.[2] Even if Chinese-speaking patients have access to a Chinese-speaking physician, the limited time during the office visit is not sufficient to answer all of their health questions. As the trend of preventive health care gains momentum in the United States, the health care professionals' responsibility is to make health information accessible to community members in a linguistically and culturally sensitive manner.

Better access to reliable bilingual health information is especially important in San Francisco. According to the 2004 Chinese Community Health Report (data drawn from U.S. Census 2000), which is published by the NICOS Chinese Health Coalition, "70 percent of the Chinese population in San Francisco is foreign born, [and] in 44 percent of Chinese households, no one aged fourteen and over is able to speak English without difficulty."[3] Other Chinese, although bilingual, are more comfortable receiving information in their own language and cultural setting. In a 1999 survey of cancer beliefs and attitudes among Chinese in San Francisco, 66 percent of the respondents said they preferred reading or watching television in Chinese.[4] Moreover, a report of the 2005 Men's Health Day (a biennial health fair conducted by CCHRC) showed that 92 percent of the Chinese participants preferred to receive health information in Chinese.[5]

ESTABLISHMENT OF CCHRC

The Chinese Community Health Resource Center (CCHRC) is a nonprofit organization whose mission is to promote a healthier lifestyle through bilingual health education, programs, and services and to participate in community-based research related to health care. CCHRC is funded by Chinese Hospital, Chinese Community Health Care Association (CCHCA), Chinese Community Health Plan (CCHP), and grants. Prior to the establishment of CCHRC, there were limited culturally competent health education programs available for the Chinese immigrant community. The three local community healthcare leaders—Chinese Hospital, CCHCA, and CCHP—recognized this need and shared the vision and financial commitment to create a health education unit specially tailored for the community. Since its founding in 1989, CCHRC has worked closely with physicians and national organizations such as the American Cancer Society and the Susan G. Komen Breast Cancer Foundation to provide the San Francisco Bay Area Chinese community with a multitude of programs and services.

Among CCHRC's many programs and services are health seminars and forums, disease management, individual nutrition counseling, cancer-related information and support, a bilingual wellness library, a bilingual website (*www.cchrchealth.org*), a friendly patient navigation program, and annual health day events. In recent years, CCHRC has also conducted and participated in several research projects related to the Chinese community. For example, over the past six years, CCHRC has been a partner of the AANCART special project of the National Cancer Institute, conducting education and research in cancer-related topics appropriate to the community. As part of the AANCART Chinese Council, CCHRC played a leading role in the education of physicians on the new diagnosis and treatment for Hepatitis B, awareness programs for Hepatitis B in collaboration with NICOS Chinese Coalition, and in the development of local guidelines for follow up for Hepatitis B carriers and their families with CCHCA. This year, it will be the lead organization to recommend Chinese materials on cancer for the public

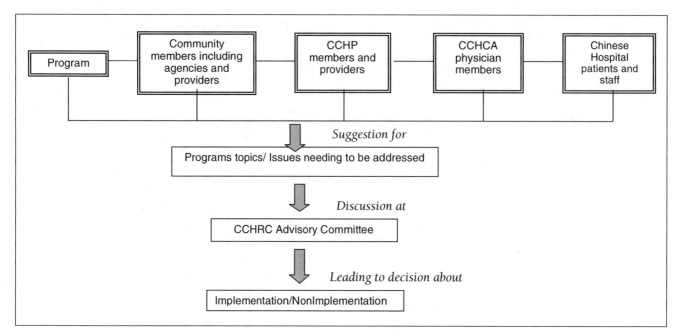

Figure 1. Education Program Implementation Process

website of AANCART and the American Cancer Society (*www.aancart.org*).

In designing and implementing programs and services, CCHRC seeks to include a wide range of suggestions. The topic selection process is an interactive one that brings together the input of community members, program participants, Chinese Community Health Plan, Chinese Community Health Care Association's physician members, and Chinese Hospital patients and staff. Suggestions are reviewed and program topics are identified at the advisory committee level, leading to implementation of programs (see Figure 1).

CCHRC provides approximately 15,000 services annually; 90 percent of the recipients are monolingual, over 65 percent are female, 30 percent are Medicaid (Medi-Cal in California) recipients, and approximately 15 percent have no insurance coverage.

Modes of program delivery include seminars and forums, individual nutrition counseling, our annual community health day (women's and men's), health screenings, printed material, our bilingual website, patient navigation program, and collaboration with local and national organizations.

MODES OF PROGRAM DELIVERY

Health Seminars. CCHRC's bilingual health seminars are open to the public and cover an array of topics in several categories, including general health, geriatric health, women's health, and perinatal health. Our most popular seminars cover diabetes management, cancer awareness, heart failure, cholesterol and heart health, injury prevention among the elderly,

and healthy eating. In 2004, close to two thousand community members from the San Francisco Bay Area attended our health seminars. Seventy-six percent of the seminar participants were aged fifty or older, and almost 20 percent traveled from outside the city of San Francisco to take advantage of the opportunity to learn about health in their own language and culture.

Individual Nutrition Counseling. As a service to Chinese Community Health Plan members and clients whose health insurance medical group is the Chinese Community Health Care Association, CCHRC offers free individual nutrition counseling with a registered dietitian. In 2004, 37 percent of those who took advantage of this service had diabetes, 26 percent had hyperlipidemia, 24 percent had multiple diseases, and the remaining 13 percent had other ailments. Twenty-eight percent of all contacts were Medi-Cal recipients.

Patient Navigation Program. Many Chinese (particularly recent immigrants) face numerous challenges when it comes to navigating the oftentimes already complicated health care system even if they have family members who can translate for them. These "translators" are usually their children/grandchildren or nephews/nieces who are minors and may not be familiar with the health care system. In addition to linguistic barriers, the monolingual Chinese population must contend with cultural differences, lack of health insurance coverage, and a lack of financial means for basic living expenses. Of the few services that are available in the Chinese language or culture, many Chinese are not aware of them. According to CCHRC's service statistics, approximately 30 percent of the referrals are for clients who are unfamiliar with public or private health/ social services in the San Francisco Bay Area. Some common issues of these clients include domestic violence, mental health issues, and health insurance options. Moreover, even for clients who are insured, some are unable to take advantage of the services that are available (e.g., second opinion), because they do not know the ins and outs of the health care system. They need someone to guide them along the sometimes confusing health care web and point them in the right direction. CCHRC's navigation program seeks to help the community circumvent these barriers through several channels, including making referrals to relevant public health agencies.

Bilingual Health Library. Knowledge is power. CCHRC's bilingual health library first opened its doors in 2003 and continues to empower community members by offering reliable bilingual health information through books, newsletters, booklets/pamphlets, and audio/video tapes on an array of topics, including tuberculosis, Hepatitis B, cancer, diabetes, and heart disease. To maintain the highest quality of health information, CCHRC carefully reviews the wellness library collection to ensure that the contents are accurate and current. CCHRC staff consults Chinese healthcare professionals in the United States for recommendations on health-related printed and/or audio/visual titles. Titles are not limited to publishers and producers in the United States. All titles from overseas (e.g., China and Taiwan) are reviewed to verify that health information is consistent with U.S. guidelines. In addition to housing hundreds of bilingual titles, which are available for leisure reading/viewing on site or as loans, the library also houses the American Cancer Society–endorsed Chinese Community Cancer Information Center (CCCIC). Chinese Cancer patients and/or their caretakers come to the CCHRC library for up-to-date bilingual cancer-related information as well as referrals to community resources/services such as cancer support groups and financial assistance. The library's knowledgeable and friendly staff assists clients in Cantonese, Mandarin, and English to obtain community referrals and resources and search for up-to-date health information on the World Wide Web. Usage of the library is free of charge to all community members who made approximately 4,700 visits to the library in 2004 alone. The CCHRC health library is a place for local Chinese with limited English skills to access a wealth of health information and to obtain assistance on navigating the complicated healthcare system.

Educational Material Development Process. When planning and developing health education materials, CCHRC adopts a comprehensive, inclusive method, taking into consideration suggestions from several fronts, including those from our health seminar participants and requests from healthcare providers. The process also incorporates health trends and local needs based on health statistics. Recommendation for educational material topics are discussed and determined at the advisory committee level. Then CCHRC health education staff develops and translates the educational materials based on current literature. Focus groups and lay people are involved in field-testing the materials, and providers' feedback is always solicited for clinical accuracy before finalization (see Figure 2).

Bilingual Health Education Literature. CCHRC makes available to the community a vast array of printed bilingual health education materials covering a multitude of topics, including allergy, breast health, back health, cancer education, diabetic care, eye care, gastrointestinal care, heart health, hypertension, injury prevention, lead poisoning, medication, nutrition, perinatal education, respiratory health, tuberculosis, weight control, wellness, and women's health. CCHRC also publishes a quarterly bilingual newsletter, which addresses community health topics and has an average circulation of 18,000 copies. These materials are prescreened, updated regularly, and free to the public.

www.cchrchealth.org. In May 2004, CCHRC launched its comprehensive bilingual health website, allowing around-the-clock access to health information with bilingual articles on various health topics and direct links to over forty websites, some of which contain Chinese health education materials. This website enables healthcare providers and caretakers who are illiterate in Chinese to search for health information for monolingual Chinese individuals in English and print the Chinese version without taking too much time to seek out reliable sources of bilingual materials. Moreover, Chinese Americans with limited English proficiency and basic Internet navigation skills can visit this website with ease and confidence. The website allows users the option of downloading the desired materials in PDF format, free of charge. The CCHRC bilingual website increases access to health information by providing Chinese-language education materials online to healthcare providers and the public. The website receives an average of 12,000 visits annually.

Women's Health Day. The Women's Health Day project is a collaborative project involving the Chinese Community Health Resource Center (CCHRC), Chinese faith communities, grassroots community agencies, and sponsors such as the Chinese Community Health Plan, the Susan G. Komen Breast Cancer Foundation, Chinese Hospital, Chinese Community Health Care Association, and pharmaceutical companies. The purpose of the project is to provide health education opportunities to monolingual Chinese-speaking women, who cannot benefit from health education opportunities offered in English and to provide free preventive health screenings, especially for the uninsured participants. The Women's Health Day emphasizes wellness, prevention, and health promotion and is free to all participants. The format of the event is a

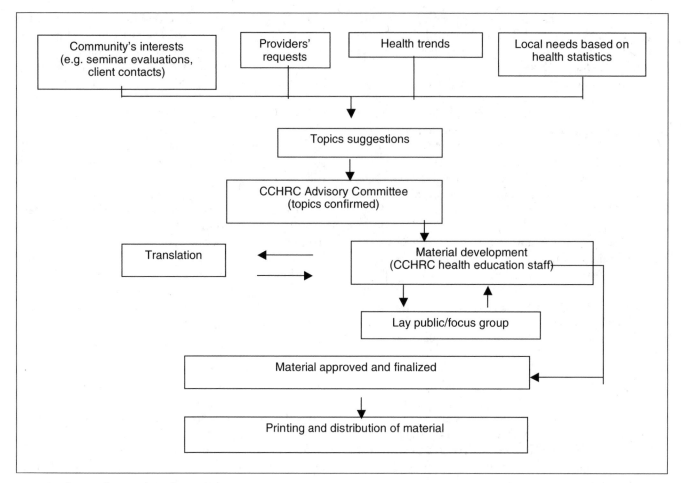

Figure 2. Educational Material Development Process

combination of seminars on topics such as diabetes, meno-pause/sexuality, common gynecological issues, mental health, neck and lower back pain, heart health and stroke prevention, and osteoporosis, and offree health screenings such as blood sugar, blood pressure, cholesterol, Hepatitis B, bone density, body fat analysis, fecal occult blood test, and clinical breast exam. There are also free clinical breast examinations and assistance with enrollment into various free mammography programs since approximately 30 percent of the targeted women have no health insurance coverage and 42 percent have household income below $20,000.

The project was launched in 1999 and is in its fifth year of offering, drawing a total of over 3,600 women in the San Francisco Bay Area. Participants were asked to complete a program evaluation prior to leaving the facility. An average of 59 percent of the participants completed the evaluation; 66 percent rated the Health Day as above average. Twenty-five percent had never had a mammogram, 15 percent had never had a clinical breast examination, and 36 percent did not perform breast self-examinations regularly. During the past three Women's Health Days, over 170 clinical breast examinations were performed and mammograms were ordered for those

who have no health insurance and have not had a mammogram within a year. Five patients were identified with possible breast cancer, of which all cases were diagnosed at an earlier stage (Stages I and II) and followed up by oncology clinicians.

Men's Health Day. There are dramatic racial and ethnic differences among Californians receiving potentially life-saving health screening. According to the California Health Investigation Study 2001, 79.1 percent of Chinese males have never heard of a PSA test compared to white males at 51.5 percent; and 69.9 percent have not had a colorectal exam compared to Caucasian males at 52.1 percent. Some contributing factors are the stigma associated with cancer, language and cultural barriers, lack of insurance, and poverty. Because male Chinese immigrants are less likely to utilize cancer screening and detection services than females, the Chinese Community Health Resource Center (CCHRC) created a Men's Health Day in 2003.

Similar to Women's Health Day, Men's Day seeks to disseminate information on issues related to men's health, including cancer education to the monolingual Chinese community. Because monolingual Chinese men are less likely than women to be informed on health issues, Men's Health Day offers seminars on health issues including prostate health, sexual dynamics after forty, neck and lower back pain, heart health and stroke prevention, mental health issues, and colorectal and liver cancer. Average attendance over the past two men's health days was approximately 800, with about 70 percent male participation. In addition to the seminars, free screenings, including PSA, blood sugar, blood pressure, cholesterol, Hepatitis B, waist circumference, body fat analysis, and fecal occult blood tests were offered. Out of 165 participants screened for hepatitis, 10 tested positive. Thirty-three out of 207 males tested for PSA had an elevated PSA level. In addition, approximately 90 percent of the respondents indicated that the event was the only opportunity for them to receive health information and screenings in their language and culture. The Men's Health Day reached an underserved population that has limited access to preventive health services such as cancer screening.

RESEARCH PROJECTS

Research papers from the CCHRC include *Cancer Attitudes* (1999), *Breast Health Media Campaign* (2000), *Perception of Domestic Violence in the Chinese Community* (2003), and *Quality of Life among Chinese Breast Cancer Patients* (2003–2004). Participants at CCHRC's annual Health Day are surveyed about the frequency of their health screenings, their knowledge about various health topics, income, and insurance status. Results help CCHRC assess the relevance and effectiveness of our current programs and assist us in developing new programs better tailored to the Chinese community.

RESEARCH ITEMS

Cancer Beliefs among Chinese Immigrant Community (1999). Although many studies have focused on cancer-screening utilization and attitudes, CCHRC's cancer belief survey was the first to examine community beliefs toward a cancer diagnosis and some of the beliefs about cancer and cancer patients. While certain types of cancer have been decreasing in the Caucasian population, minority populations are more likely to be diagnosed in a later stage and die of cancer. Stigmas caused by a cancer diagnosis and the disease itself may be a contributing factor in late detection and increased mortality.

CCHRC conducted a telephone survey of 798 Chinese immigrants living in San Francisco. Participants were asked several questions with established responses regarding their beliefs about cancer. One quarter of the 798 participants still believed cancer is contagious, and as many as 9 percent of them thought cancer was punishment as a result of ancestor's conduct. A logistic regression model indicated that women who were at a low-income level and resided in the United States for an extended period of time were more likely to believe cancer is contagious. It is suspected that the lack of exposure to educational materials or information may have contributed to long-held beliefs and attitudes regarding cancer. The length of time spent in the United States without exposure to other acculturation variables may solidify long-held beliefs, and it appears that this represented a gap group that has not had access to the wealth of information about cancer and its various treatments and potential positive prognosis. This study was published in the September/October 2003 issue of *Cancer Control*.

Breast Health Media Campaign (2000). To increase the awareness and practice of breast health guidelines, a media-based education campaign on breast health was launched among monolingual Chinese-speaking communities in San Francisco. The media campaign included airing two public service announcements (PSAs) on Chinese television and radio stations and publishing the same message in Chinese newspapers during 2000. Seven hundred and ten face-to-face interviews were conducted with women who were recruited from various settings in the city of San Francisco to evaluate the impact of the campaign. Survey participants were asked to describe the content of the PSAs. Having viewed the PSA was significantly associated with the ability of identifying all four guidelines: knowing how to perform a breast self-examination (BSE), having performed BSE within the past month, and having a clinical breast examination and mammogram in the past year. Study findings supported that a media campaign utilizing PSAs was effective in improving knowledge of breast health guidelines, teaching Chinese women how to perform breast self-examination, and increasing breast health practices.

Quality of Life among Chinese Breast Cancer Patients (2003–2004). Several studies have reported on the impact breast cancer and its treatments have on the physical, emotional, psychological, financial, and spiritual aspects of multiethnic breast cancer survivors' lives.[6,7] Nonetheless, it is unclear if quality of life (QOL) changes among Chinese women who recently immigrated to the United States. To the researchers' knowledge, at the onset of the QOL project in 2003, no study had been conducted to examine how breast cancer may jeopardize the QOL of this population. Observations in working with Chinese immigrant women, however, suggested that a breast cancer diagnosis might be more detrimental to their well-being than for Chinese women who are born and raised in the United States. This may be due to the lower socioeconomic status and limited English proficiency of immigrants. Their lack of educational and financial resources and understanding of the Western medical system often impose more hardships on this population.

This qualitative pilot study sought to increase understanding of the relationship between cultural beliefs and QOL among immigrant Chinese breast cancer patients in San Francisco. Specific aims were (1) to identify these patients' beliefs regarding cancer, life expectancy, and discussion of advance directives, (2) to explore how these beliefs relate to patient QOL, and (3) to generate hypotheses for further study. The purpose of the pilot study was to investigate questions central to this issue, including what defines QOL for immigrant women. To determine whether Chinese immigrants and American-born Chinese women differ in their cancer-related beliefs and QOL, in-depth, face-to-face interviews were conducted with fifteen breast cancer patients from each group. Chinese women diagnosed with breast cancer within the past twenty-four months and no longer under active treatment for this disease were eligible for the study.

A written transcript of each interview was prepared in the language of the interview. Emerging issues were written into memos and reanalyzed to discover new themes, categories, or hypotheses to be studied in future research. Data analyses suggested that there are important differences between American-born and foreign-born Chinese women in their beliefs about, perceptions of, and experiences with breast cancer, which may have important implications for cancer support services and survivorship. Both groups of women described their breast cancer diagnosis as a wake-up call to remind them to take better care of themselves. Both identified cancer support groups as a way of helping them to cope with cancer. However, both groups identified a need for additional supportive services, especially in-home support services. This study was published in the December 2005 issue of *Cancer Control*.

Perception of Domestic Violence in the Chinese Community (2003). Family violence is a global problem, which exists in all communities. In the Chinese society, historically, family violence, wife beating, or child beating has been culturally and institutionally legitimized. Family violence includes physical, sexual, verbal, emotional, and financial abuse. To combat family violence in the Chinese community, the community's perception and attitude toward family violence must first be assessed and programs developed accordingly. In the last two decades, researchers and advocates have collected data on family violence in the Asian Pacific Islander (API) population; however, most data collected are aggregated under the API population as opposed to separated by sub-ethnic groups. This aggregated data collection method contributed to the scarcity of data on family violence in the Chinese community.

To assess the community's current perception and attitude on family violence, CCHRC, in collaboration with the Alliance against Asian Domestic Violence, conducted 588 self-administered questionnaires in 2003. The questionnaire was finalized based on feedback from focus groups. Out of all surveyed, 10.7 percent had experienced family violence and 6.6 percent did not know or were unsure if they had experienced family violence. Overwhelmingly, the study participants considered physically based acts to be acts of family violence. Only participants with self-reports of personal experiences of family violence considered emotionally-based acts, such as blaming, put-downs, and name-calling, to be acts of family violence, which means 82.7 percent of the study participants did not consider emotionally-based acts to be acts of violence. The study findings indicate a need to educate the Chinese community that verbal abuse is a form of violence.

CONCLUSION

To meet the health educational needs of a monolingual Chinese population, the Chinese Community Health Resource Center was established by Chinese Hospital, CCHCA, and CCHP, and involved the community in identifying pertinent issues. CCHRC is committed to provide effective and innovative health education programs and to bring the value of research to the community, thus providing education and resources to improve the health of our community.

NOTES

1. U.S. Census Bureau (2000), *Statistical Abstract of the United States, http://www.census.gov/prod/2001pubs/statab/sec01.pdf.*
2. M. S. Goel, "Breast-saving Surgery Underused by Some," 2005, *http://www.northwestern.edu/.*
3. NICOS Chinese Health Coalition, *2004 Chinese Community Health Report.*
4. E. Wong-Kim, A. Sun, and M. C. DeMattos, "Assessing Cancer Beliefs in a Chinese Immigrant Community," *Cancer Control* 10, no. 5 (September/October 2003): 22–28.
5. CCHRC, 2005 Men's Health Day Report.
6. K. T. Ashing-Giwa, et al., "Understanding the Breast Cancer Experience of Women: A Qualitative Study of African American, Asian American, Latina and Caucasian Cancer Survivors," *Psycho-Oncology*, 13 (2004): 408–428.
7. M. Kagawa-Singer, D. Wellisch, and R. Durvasula, "Impact of Breast Cancer on Asian American and Anglo American Women," *Culture, Medicine, and Psychiatry* 21 (1997): 449–480.

Overview and Examples of NARA San Francisco Historical Resources Then and Now, 1975–2005

Daniel Nealand

In 1975, the National Archives Pacific Region–San Francisco published its very first *Reference Information Paper*, *Chinese Studies in Federal Records*. First discussed were case files of U.S. District and Circuit Courts in San Francisco, from 1850 to the 1970s. Besides famous cases, the publication includes unexplored nineteenth- to early twentieth-century case files. Indexed RG 21 habeas corpus files, 1882–1883, predate our renowned INS immigration files collection and are in essence the earliest surviving Chinese Exclusion Act case files. Also covered was RG 36, U.S. Bureau of Customs–San Francisco. Of special interest is *Correspondence for the Collector of Customs* dated 1882–1900. The San Francisco Customs Bureau initially developed and enforced Chinese Exclusion Act procedures.

In 1976, NARA received records of RG 90, the U.S. Public Health Service Quarantine Station at Angel Island, 1892–1948. NARA's 250,000 RG 85 Immigration and Naturalization investigative case files, 1884–1950s, were received, beginning in 1987, and included all those available for Angel Island Immigration Station. Post-World War II San Francisco "General Immigration" or "1300" case files, dated 1945–1955, document investigations of post-CEA Chinese, Latin American, European, and other Asian immigrants. NARA also has Honolulu District Office immigration case files dated c.1903–1950.

Other resources include RG 276 Ninth Circuit Court of Appeals case files, 1891 to the1970s, which cover appeals from U.S. District Courts in nine Western states including famous Chinese American–related cases. RG 527 Records of the U.S. Marshal–San Francisco, 1874–1919, contain largely unexplored correspondence about Chinese immigration. New Finding Aids include the 2004 *Guide to Records of Asian Americans and Pacific Islanders at NARA Pacific Region–San Francisco*. Our in-progress index to immigration files is now online at U.C. Berkeley's Haas Business School website. Finally, NARA hopes soon to begin accessioning modern RG 85 USCIS-INS Alien Registration or "A Files"—a system established in 1940 that contains many "uploaded" older documents.

NARA is grateful to have served thousands of researchers in Chinese American history, and we hope to assist many thousands more.

Beyond Black and White
Race, Class, and Chinese Americans in Multiracial Chicago
Shanshan Lan

In both the academic and popular imagination, Asian Americans have long been considered to occupy an in-between position in a Black and white racial framework. This bipolar view of U.S. race relations not only fails to describe the quickly changing U.S. racial landscape, but also reinforces an essentialized Asian American identity as homogeneous. Based on sustained ethnographic fieldwork in Chicago, this research examines how class differentiation among Chinese Americans mediates their understanding of racialized differences in a multiracial neighborhood in Chicago. In his study of racial knowledge in Cuba, Frank Guridy[1] conceptualizes race not merely as an identity or as a marker of social inequality, but as a form of social knowledge. He understands racial knowledge as a meaning system and an interpretive framework that is constructed out of interrelated social, economic, cultural, and political processes yet has been naturalized as a social fact. Following Guridy's efforts to denaturalize racial knowledge as a social fact, this article explores the unevenness in Chinese American's learning of racial knowledge in a multiracial urban center. By identifying class/social mobility as one of the major factors contributing to the differential racialization of distinct groups of Chinese Americans, I want to draw attention to the intersection of race and class in shaping the daily life experiences of Chinese Americans in a multiracial Chicago.

Bridgeport was, until recently, a white working-class neighborhood known for its history of resistance against housing desegregation and substantial anti-Black racial violence.[2] The neighborhood has been home to different waves of European immigrants: Irish, German, Lithuanian, Czechoslovakian, Polish, Ukrainian, and Italian. Today African Americans constitute only 1.05 percent of Bridgeport's population, but they play an important role in the neighborhood's racial imagination. For example, in 1997, a thirteen-year-old African American youth, Lenard Clark, was beaten into a coma by two white youths in a park near Bridgeport. The two offenders later bragged to their friends that they had kept Bridgeport white.[3] Starting from the 1980s and throughout the 1990s, an influx of immigrants from Asia and Latin America has transformed Bridgeport into a multiracial community. Currently, the population is 26 percent Asian American, 30 percent Latino, and 41 percent white.[4] Although the neighborhood is demographically multiracial, its political identity remains strongly white. Five of Chicago's mayors hailed from Bridgeport, including the current Mayor Richard Dailey. The expansion of Chinese Americans from Chinatown to Bridgeport is largely shaped by the intricate power relations in Bridgeport. Chinese Americans, mostly working-class immigrants from Hong Kong and Canton, are allowed to move in as a buffer group to prevent the integration of African Americans and to check the growing political power of Latinos. In reality, Chinese American immigrants are caught in a complicated network of overlapping racializations: they are often racialized together with Latinos as "foreigners" who are taking over the nation,[5] as people of color side by side with African Americans, and as the model minority in opposition to both Latinos and African Americans.[6]

In their study of residential patterns of immigrant minorities in the United States, Richard Alba and Nancy Denton note a discrepancy between the increasing heterogeneity of urban populations and the reification of racial differences, "At the broadest level, we argue that the trend for immigrants and for the racial hierarchy has been toward greater heterogeneity and toward a loosening of once more rigid structures, while for places of residence, despite greater diversity at the neighborhood level, there has been a hardening of the urban residential structure."[7] The same thing can be said of Bridgeport, where racial integration was achieved mainly in the physical and geographical sense. There are still gaps and ruptures in the neighborhood's daily life that point to the hierarchical power relations inscribed in its hidden racial landscape. In general, Chinese social life in Bridgeport is heavily confined to public places such as schools, parks, and libraries. There are many hardcore white ethnic spaces such as private social clubs, pubs, ethnic churches, and family parties that continue to exclude Chinese Americans. Many Chinese Americans in Bridgeport expressed feelings of alienation during my interviews with them. One Chinese American community activist told me, "I happen to live in a place called Bridgeport, but all my friends are in Chinatown."

In his study of New York's Chinatown in the 1970s and 1980s, Peter Kwong noted the polarization of Chinese American population by distinguishing between the "Uptown Chinese" and "Downtown Chinese."[8] The former are usually middle-class professionals with college degrees who live out-side Chinatown, while the latter are mainly new, working-class immigrants who barely speak English and who are working at the lowest tier of the service industry in Chinatown. The same bifurcation exists in Chicago's Chinese American community today, and it takes on a new racial twist with the multiracial transformation of urban U.S. population. Besides the expansion of Chinese population from Chinatown to its neighboring Bridgeport, there is also a constant flow of Chinese Americans between the city and the suburbs. Some new immigrants live in Bridgeport but work in suburban restaurants (rides are provided by restaurant owners so that the workers do not need to learn how to drive). For this group of working-class Chinese immigrants, life is still very much focused on Chinatown, since they need the Chinese language infrastructure in the city to survive. However, there is another small group of Chinese Americans who live in the suburbs and own businesses in Bridgeport and Chinatown, such as law firms, real-estate companies, medical clinics, insurance companies, and so on, which target new immigrants as major clients. Mostly educated in the United States, these middle-class Chinese Americans also function as community leaders and cultural brokers between working-class immigrants and mainstream white society. In reality, there is often an exploitative relation between new Chinese immigrants and middle-class Chinese Americans due to the latter's monopoly of the ethnic market. New immigrants usually have to pay an exorbitant fee to get the service they need due to their inability to speak the English language and their unfamiliarity with the American system. It is not uncommon that certain ethnic businesses shield information from new immigrants in order to maximize profits. There is actually a vicious circle within the immigrant community: the more money new immigrants pay to ethnic brokers, the harder and longer they have to work in the lowest tier of the American economy. In this sense, some middle-class Chinese Americans virtually help in perpetuating and reproducing the cheap immigrant labor market much needed by postindustrial U.S. capital. Ironically, the economic wealth generated from new immigrants ends up facilitating middle-class Chinese Americans' differential racialization from working-class immigrants.

I first met Mr. Moy during my preliminary fieldwork in Chicago in the summer of 2003. Mr. Moy came to the United States in 1963 and got his college degree on the north side of Chicago. He speaks fluent English, Cantonese, and Mandarin. His real-estate company is one of the earliest ones that opened the Bridgeport housing market to new Chinese immigrants. As a shrewd businessman who knows the neighborhood well, Mr. Moy is very careful in his choice of words and his way of talking. When asked which part of the city is safe to live in, he replied promptly, "[T]hat's a police question. I think you should go to the police department for help." Mr. Moy then told me a story. Once a realtor's Chinese agent designed an advertisement, in which he mentioned that the place is located in a white neighborhood and is desirable in every way as a perfect residential area. Someone reported this to the police as racial discrimination. As a result, the realtor's license was suspended for six months. "It's a very sensitive topic," said Mr. Moy, "It's not even right to speak of German town, Italian town nowadays. Anything with ethnic labels can be accused of racial prejudice."

The story serves as a context to explain why Mr. Moy refused to answer my question: he had learned to be color-blind from the downfall of one of his colleagues. Looking back at his career as a real-estate businessman, Mr. Moy told me, "My customers consist of two types: buyers and sellers. Twenty years ago, 100 percent of the sellers are non-Chinese and 99 percent of the buyers are Chinese. Now 15–20 percent of the sellers are Chinese, but the demand is larger than supply. Eighty percent of my clients are Chinese now." Although carefully phrased and presented as a social fact, Mr. Moy's statistics bear witness to one of the crucial moments of the multiracial transformation of the United States: while post-1965 immigration and deindustrialization have drastically reorganized the socioeconomic and racial landscape of urban America, many whites are moving to the suburbs with preferential policies by the federal government, leaving new immigrants and minorities of color to the confines of the inner city.[9] Mr. Moy's reluctance to talk about race and his calculated performance of race-blindness paradoxically underscores his thorough knowledge of the intricate racial landscape in Bridgeport. Commenting on the expansion of Chinese population to Bridgeport, Mr. Moy said,

> There is a saying that "whenever a Chinese family moves into a neighborhood, the neighborhood will improve." The reverse will happen if *a certain ethnic group* moves in. You know what I mean? It's the fear of crime, of undesirable elements in the neighborhood. It's like a domino effect. When *that group* moves in, the whole neighborhood will decline quickly.

Mr. Moy's depiction of African Americans echoes the majority of whites' fear of racial desegregation. As a real-estate businessman, he knows well the anti-Black history of Bridgeport and also learns well whites' negative attitude toward African Americans through his long-time business transactions with white sellers. While sharing with most whites the fear of being labeled a racist (the use of "that group" as euphemism for "African Americans"), Mr. Moy is very conscious in drawing the boundaries between Chinese and African Americans, and his portrayal of the two groups fits exactly the white stereotype of the model minority versus the urban underclass.[10] While Mr. Moy's negative portrayal of African Americans can be easily interpreted as evidence for his internalization of white racism, there is also an economic side of the story. Because of Bridgeport's history of white racism against Blacks, many white residents are more willing to sell to Chinese: at least they are not Black. In this context, the success of Asian American real-estate businesses in the neighborhood largely depends on how skillfully the realtors manipulate the color line.[11] Mr. Moy's business prospers because he knows how to take advantage of negative white racial attitude toward African Americans to achieve maximum economic profit for his Asian American business. In this sense, posing the model minority against the urban underclass becomes part of Mr. Moy's marketing strategy, which eventually facilitates his upward mobility in this country.

On the other hand, social mobility achieved through virtual compliance with white racism against African Americans consequently fosters a strategic alliance between whites and a segment of Asian Americans.[12] When asked about his opinion on racism against African Americans in Bridgeport, Mr. Moy remarked,

> Some people may be deep-seated racist, *but statistics won't lie.* For example, a white people is walking on the street, if a Chinese passes by, he or she will not feel any threat because he/she knows the statistics for a Chinese to be a criminal is very low. But if a Black passes by, the white people may feel threatened because he knows he may be attacked since that ethnic group has a higher rate of crime according to statistics. This kind of prejudice is justified because it is a human instinct for survival, for self-preservation.

Here Mr. Moy's identification with majority white attitudes toward African Americans is marked by his faith in statistics generated by a white racist structure. While trying to neutralize racism against African Americans by highlighting the credibility of government statistics and the universal human nature of self-preservation, Mr. Moy fails to note (or chooses not to note) that statistics are collected by human beings who are not always absolved of prejudice. What gets erased from these apparently objective statistics are Bridgeport's specific history of white racial violence against African Americans and the multiple levels of complexity in daily human experiences. In this case, Mr. Moy's racial learning about African Americans is not based on his daily life encounters with the latter, but on his accommodation (or internalization) of a white racist structure, which is reconfigured in the name of multiculturalism and colorblindness.[13]

It would be too simplistic to assume that middle-class Chinese Americans like Mr. Moy totally embrace a white racist structure. In fact, Mr. Moy displayed great enthusiasm for Asian American politics during my interview with him: he has a thorough knowledge of Asian American history in the United States, he knows the names of many outstanding Asians, and he talks about the killing of Vincent Chin in Detroit in 1986. Reflecting on his own career path, Mr. Moy said, "When one gets to top management position, it's very hard for Asians to get promoted, to get admitted by the Old Boys' Club. I am not one of them, so I started my own business." Explaining why he is interested in Asian American activism, Mr. Moy said, "My root is now in America. I want to struggle to see my rights get protected in this country." Mr. Moy's encounter with the glass ceiling and his feelings of marginalization in the U.S. society speaks to the limitations of Asian American mobility in a racially hierarchical society.[14] However, they do not prevent him from taking pride in the

model-minority myth. He informed me that he was writing a book, *Born in China, Made in the United States.* "I plan to develop it into a book series. I want the success stories of self-made Asians being told to the American public," he said ambitiously. In a sense, Mr. Moy's pride in the model-minority myth is indispensable from his ethnic pride of being Chinese. It can be interpreted, on the one hand, as his defensive response to the marginalization of Asian Americans in mainstream white society; on the other hand, his choice of ethnicity over race betrays the limitation of middle-class Chinese American social activism. As noted by Mary Waters, "the more socially mobile the individual, the more he or she clings to ethnic identity as a hedge against racial identity."[15] Mr. Moy's celebration of his Chinese ethnicity functions not so much as a protest against white racism, but as a tactical manipulation of the Black and white color line in the name of multiculturalism and colorblindness. After all, his American dream is not based on hardworking and personal struggles alone, but on collusion with the white status quo. In this way, Mr. Moy's antiracism is kept safe within the boundary of an essentialized notion of Chinese ethnicity.[16]

In contrast to Mr. Moy's colorblind talk, working-class Chinese American youth present to me a highly color-conscious picture, which is a detailed map of how space gets racialized in Bridgeport. Paul, a twenty-year-old college student who grew up in Bridgeport told me:

> As long as you know some rules here, you will be fine. Rule one, never go out after dark; rule two, when someone say stupid things to you like "Ching Ching Chong Chong," ignore them and walk away; rule three, don't stare at people; rule four, always look back when you are walking alone and make sure no one is after you; rule five, don't appear threatening to them; rule six, always choose a busy street whether driving or walking. Never go into a dark street.

Paul went on to educate me on which part of the neighborhood is safe and which part is not, "I know some areas where those kids hang out and I try to avoid going to those places. One is 31st and Halsted, there are gangs there. Another place is Shields and 30th Street. There is an Italian club there. Once my cousin drove there, they threw baseball bat at her car window." It is important to note that the place where Paul's cousin was harassed is quite close to the place where the African American youth Lenard Clark was beaten into a coma by two white youths in 1997. Paul himself is aware of this, and he had no problem naming that site of white racial violence against African Americans, "Yes, we tried to avoid going to that place, Armour Park."

For working-class youths like Paul, racial learning at the street level becomes one of their primary strategies for survival in a multiracial Bridgeport, where the racialization of working-class Chinese Americans is mediated by the neighborhood's sedimented history of white racial violence against Blacks. This accumulation of racial knowledge is often marked with psychological traumas and feelings of hurt, which cannot be captured and represented in mainstream statistics. Talking about his growing-up experience in Bridgeport, another Chinese American college student Steve told me, "I have this sense of inferiority to white people, and even today when I go back to Bridgeport, I still feel this way—inferior and insecure. It's like they can smell fear in you. When you look scared, they pick you up and harass you more." Steve's parents have a Chinese takeout restaurant at 65th Street. It's a Black neighborhood, but Steve said he felt safer there than in Bridgeport, "because down there everybody knows I'm my mom's son. When my parents originally opened their business there, they got robbed and things like that. But they've been there so many years that they've been accepted by the neighborhood. My mom has lots of Black friends down there." The fact that Steve—a working-class Chinese American youth—finds his sense of belonging in a Black neighborhood rather than in Bridgeport speaks volumes about the social isolation he and his parents experienced in the racially changing Bridgeport. In contrast to Mr. Moy's embracing of a colorblind white racial ideology, most of the working class youths I interviewed strongly identify with their racialized identity as Asian Americans. Moreover, the racial attitude of many working-class Chinese American youths toward African Americans is not based on the antipodal image of the model minority versus the urban underclass, but on shared racialization experiences with African Americans. Steve told me that he felt threatened after the beating of Lenard Clark in 1997, "I know I will never be like whites because of the way I look. I feel more affinity toward African Americans. At least we are both minorities."

I present stories of Mr. Moy and the youth here not to establish a binary opposition, but to point out that there are alternative understandings of the racialized experience of Asian Americans that go beyond the model-minority myth. In fact, among working-class Chinese Americans themselves, there are fine distinctions between first-generation Chinese American immigrants and second- (or 1.5-) generation Chinese Americans in their racial attitudes toward African Americans. My interview with Mr. Leung, a retired restaurant worker in his sixties, illustrates the mixed feelings of first-generation Chinese immigrants toward African Americans. Mr. Leung was born in China. His family moved to Hong Kong when he was young. He later went to work in Taiwan and eventually immigrated to the United States in the 1980s. As a diasporic Chinese, Mr. Leung has a keen awareness of his marginalized status in all three places he had stayed, "I am an outsider in Hong Kong, an outsider in Taiwan, and an outsider in the United States too." During my interview with him, I mentioned the American stereotype of Chinatown as a crime-ridden place. Mr. Leung said,

> No, many Americans have good impression of Chinese. They didn't want to come to Chinatown because they are afraid of Blacks. Like New York's Chinatown, it was Mexicans and Blacks who made the place dangerous. In the past, Chinese restaurants depended on Black clients because Blacks love Chinese food. We should really thank Blacks because they gave us business. In the past, Chinese restaurants mainly served American customers.

> Blacks brought a lot of wealth to Chinese. Those Blacks who rob and steal are bad people, but not all Blacks are bad. It was some of the bad Blacks who ruined the reputation of Blacks among Chinese. Those bad Blacks, they not only bother Chinese, they bother the whole society. I heard that even within the Black community, they kill each other.

Although Mr. Leung's depiction of African Americans bears traces of the model-minority and the urban underclass stereotypes, he is quite straightforward in identifying the mutual dependence of Chinese Americans and African Americans in the urban U.S. economy. Moreover, Mr. Leung has a nuanced understanding of the heterogeneity within the African American community. By distinguishing between "good Blacks" and "bad Blacks," by posing "bad Blacks" not only against Chinese, but against the whole society and against the larger African American society, Mr. Leung proves himself to be more forward looking and sophisticated thinking than many of the American scholars who still focus their attention on the Asian-Black conflict model. In their study of how early Irish immigrants acted as hosts in the racial learning of new immigrants from Eastern Europe in the late nineteenth and early twentieth centuries, David Roediger and James Barrett comment that "the development of racial knowledge by recent immigrants to the United States is equally layered and complex."[17] This is largely true with Chinese immigrants in Chicago. Generally speaking, there are multiple factors that contribute to first-generation Chinese immigrants' negative attitudes toward African Americans: language barrier, individual experiences of interracial conflicts, exposure to mainstream media's racist portrayal of African Americans, structural discriminations faced by both groups in American society, and mediating influence from ethnic organizations and informal personal networks.

As has been noted by many scholars in American studies, racial formation in the United States is oftentimes a class formation as well.[18] Because of the deeply entrenched stereotype of "the Model Minority,"[19] there are relatively few studies on the heterogeneity among Asian Americans.[20] Nevertheless, some scholars in Asian American studies have noted that class mobility and new immigration among Asian Americans have eroded the cross-racial coalitions of the civil rights era and created strategic new alliances between whites and a segment of Asian Americans—some middle-class immigrants may distance themselves from whiteness as culture and simultaneously identify with whiteness as power through their class aspirations.[21] I would argue that middle-class Chinese Americans like Mr. Moy are practicing a strategic colorblindness, which is manifested by a strategic manipulation of "color lines" in order to seek economic and political advancement of one group of Asian Americans at the expense of another. For middle-class Chinese Americans like Mr. Moy, social mobility is both a class and racial project: it works in tandem with the colorblind racial ideology of multiculturalism to distance them from poor African Americans and Latinos and to ally themselves strategically with whites.[22]

An important collusion between whites and middle-class Chinese Americans is the shift of interracial oppression toward intraracial exploitation within the historical context of globalization and postindustrial urbanization.[23] Drawing from the experience of early Chinese immigrants in the United States, Lisa Lowe notes a contradiction between the expansion of U.S. capitalist economy, which allows the exploitation of cheap immigrant labors, and the political integrity of the nation-state, which seeks to put these alien populations under control.[24] The solution is the racialization of Asian immigrants by a series of restrictive immigration and naturalization laws, which construct a collective identity for Asian Americans as "nonwhite." Today this intersection of race and class takes on a new meaning when American businesses are shifting to Third World countries and poor immigrant communities for cheap and un-unionized labor. Because of the existence of a group of middle-class ethnic business brokers, the direct exploitative relation between American capital and immigrant labor is shielded by an apparent intra-ethnic conflict. This flexible accumulation of U.S. capital not only further downcasts working-class immigrants to the isolation of ethnic enclaves, but also fosters class differentiations within minority immigrant communities. Due to their knowledge of the English language and American culture, middle-class Chinese Americans like Mr. Moy monopolize the ethnic market and cater almost exclusively to new Chinese immigrants. On the one hand, this makes it easier for the daily life of new immigrants: they can function without learning English. On the other hand, it increases their dependence on life in the ethnic enclave and ties them further to restaurant work or other manual labor that provides little prospect for upward mobility. I was once at a citizenship rally where several social service agencies provided free service for immigrants who wanted to apply for U.S. citizenship. One Chinese man who works in a suburban restaurant told me, "I went to a Chinese lawyer and asked him to fill out the application form for me. He charged me $800 for that. If my wife and I apply together, we had to pay $1600." In the Chinese American case, the model minority is not only an artificial community created by the U.S. immigration policy,[25] but also the result of intra-ethnic exploitations.

In his analysis of ethnicity and opportunity in urban American, Ulf Hannerz notes the strategic use of ethnicity to cover up intra-ethnic exploitations:

[E]thnicity may be employed strategically by members of groups distributed in a variety of ways over the urban opportunity structure....since the relationship is not systematically governed by reciprocity, it can be used as a gloss to cover a more or less exploitative relationship, where one party makes real gains in exchange for the other party's sense of conducting himself in line with a moral duty.[26]

There are at least three explanations within the middle classes' strategic use of Chinese ethnicity. First, it offers a nonconfrontational venue for middle-class Chinese Americans to express their ethnic solidarity under the auspice of current U.S. racial ideology of multiculturalism and color-blindness. Second, by appealing to new Chinese immigrants' feelings of obligation or loyalty to an essentialized notion of Chinese culture, ethnic solidarity can be commercialized by middle-class Chinese Americans and used as a safeguard for intra-ethnic exploitation. Third, ethnicity may become a handy tool for middle-class Chinese Americans to function as gate keepers and mediators in managing the racial learning of working-class immigrants. This monitored racial learning is often couched in cultural terms with an emphasis on family structure, hardworking ethics, and education of the young.[27]

Among the working-class youth I interviewed, there is evidence of both accommodation and resistance toward this middle-class colorblind teaching. Emphasizing the difference between the city and the suburbs, David, another Chinese American youth, takes pride in the diverse environment in the city:

Suburban people are more likely to prejudice against Blacks, because there are almost no Blacks in their places. But I grow up in the city and I have Blacks as classmates and I know them. City people are more independent and one can do whatever one wants. My suburban friends are very family oriented. They have curfew time, and they are not allowed to go out alone.

Countering the popular conception that Chinatown is the quintessential embodiment of Chinese identity, David said,

All my suburban friends go to Chinese school to learn how to write Chinese. Their parents make them go. Because in the suburb, there is so few Chinese thing and their parents want them to learn more about Chinese culture. Here in Chinatown and I'm surrounded by Chinese so nobody bothers with us learning the language. So it is the suburban kids who know more about Chinese culture.

David's differentiation between the city and the suburbs is really a class differentiation. It serves to deconstruct the family-orientated model-minority kid as a middle-class image fostered in the segregated environment of the suburbs. By distancing himself from the suburban way of life, David is also distancing himself from a middle-class racial ideology dressed up in essentialist cultural terms.

When asked why he didn't fight back in time of harassment, Steve said, "I don't know. It's like the thought of being a Chinese kid, bearing responsibilities for your parents, staying away from trouble. My parents always tell me not to do any thing to damage my grade report. I always dreamed of getting rich and moving out of the place." In *Landscape for a Good Woman*, Steedman argues that her mother's desire for a New Look coat should be legitimized as female working-class consciousness.[28] I want to point out that Steve's longing to get rich and move out of Bridgeport is not so much an internalization of the model-minority myth, as an overt expression of his consciousness of being both a working-class youth and a racialized minority youth. This imagined social mobility not only provides a much-needed consolation for working-class youth's traumatic experiences of racism, it also illustrates how race and class work together in structuring the daily life of working-class Chinese immigrants. Although the two variables in this article, race and class, are not fixed entities and are constantly changing, the experiences of emotional injuries in the life of working-class immigrants of color are powerful social realities that draw attention to interrelated levels of structural inequalities in a rapidly changing U.S. society.

So far this paper has demonstrated that there are variegated racial fault lines, as opposed to clear-cut racial boundaries, between Chinese Americans and African Americans, which speak of the multiple layers of complexity in interminority relations, of which class difference is just one example.[29] It also aims to go beyond the Asian-shopkeeper and African American–customer model in theorizing Asian-Black relations and examines how interethnic relations are mediated by intra-ethnic differences.[30] Because of their crucial position in navigating the color line between Black and white, Asian Americans cannot be viewed simply as another racial minority added to the multiracial U.S. landscape.[31] In this context, understanding class differentiation among Asian Americans offers a productive window on the rearticulation of whiteness and the contemporary transformation of U.S. multicultural politics.[32]

ACKNOWLEDGMENTS

This research was supported by a fellowship from the Center on Democracy in a Multiracial Society at the University of Illinois at Urbana-Champaign, and a Dissertation Travel Fellowship from the Graduate College of the University of Illinois at Urbana-Champaign. Special thanks go to Professor Nancy Abelmann, who read through the article and provided helpful comments. My other dissertation committee members, Professors Martin Manalansan, David Roediger, and Arlene Torres, are also sources of valuable insights in the formulation of this research project.

NOTES

1. Frank Guridy, "Racial Knowledge in Cuba: The Production of a Social Fact" (PhD diss., Michigan: University of Michigan, 2002).

2. Chicago Commission on Race Relations, *The Negro in Chicago* (Chicago: University of Chicago Press, 1922); Chicago Commission on Human Relations, *Report on 3309 South Lowe Avenue* (Chicago: Chicago Historical Society, 1964).

3. *Chicago Tribune*, March 25, 1997 and November 10, 1997.

4. *Census 2000* (Washington, DC: U.S. Census Bureau).

5. Otto Santa Ana, *Brown Tide Rising: Metaphors of Latinos in Contemporary American Public Discourse* (Austin: University of Texas Press, 2002).

6. I get inspiration from Omi and Winant's idea of "racialization" and Lewis' idea of "overlapping diasporas" in my formulation of the concept of "overlapping racializations." See Michael Omi and Howard Winant, *Racial Formation in the United States from the 1960s to the 1990s* (New York: Routledge, 1986); Earl

Lewis, "To Turn as on a Pivot: Writing African Americans into a History of Overlapping Diasporas," *American Historical Review* 100, no. 3 (1995): 765–787. For a more detailed analysis, please see my article "Chinese Americans in Multiracial Chicago: A Story of Overlapping Racializations," *Asian American Law Journal* 13 (Spring 2006).

7. Richard Alba and Nancy Denton, "Old and New Landscapes of Diversity: The Residential Patterns of Immigrant Minorities," in *Not Just Black and White: Historical and Contemporary Perspectives on Immigration, Race, and Ethnicity in the United States*, ed. Nancy Foner and George M. Fredrickson (New York: Russell Sage Foundation, 2004), 237.

8. Peter Kwong, *The New Chinatown* (New York: Hill and Wang, 1987).

9. George Lipsitz, *The Possessive Investment in Whiteness* (Philadelphia: Temple University Press, 1998); Douglas Massey and Nancy Denton, *American Apartheid: Segregation and the Making of the Underclass* (Cambridge: Harvard University Press, 1993).

10. For a strong criticism of the model minority and the urban underclass dichotomy, see Nancy Abelmann and John Lie, *Blue Dreams: Korean Americans and the Los Angeles Riots* (Cambridge: Harvard University Press, 1995).

11. For comparison, see Charlotte Brooks, "In the Twilight Zone between Black and White: Japanese American Resettlement and Community in Chicago, 1942-1945," *The Journal of American History* (March 2000), http://www.historycooperative. org/journals/jah/86.4/brooks.html (accessed November 5, 2005); James Loewen, *The Mississippi Chinese: Between Black and White* (Cambridge, MA: Harvard University Press, 1971).

12. Susan Koshy, "Morphing Race into Ethnicity: Asian Americans and Critical Transformations of Whiteness," *Boundary* 2, no. 28:1 (2001): 153–194.

13. I choose not to explore the fine distinction between accommodation and internalization in order to leave room for specific social actors to negotiate their multipositionality in situated contexts. See Lewis, "To Turn as on a Pivot."

14. Aihwa Ong, *Flexible Citizenship: The Cultural Logics of Transnationality* (Durham: Duke University Press, 1999).

15. Mary Waters, *Black Identities: West Indian Immigrant Dreams and American Realities* (New York: Russell Sage Foundation; Cambridge, MA: Harvard University Press, 1999), 324.

16. Bonnie Urciuoli thus makes the distinction between racializing and ethnicizing: "Racializing is defined by a polarity between dominant and subordinate groups, the latter having minimal control over their position in the nation-state....In ethnic discourses, cultural difference is safe, ordered, a contribution to the nation-state offered by striving immigrants making their way up the ladder of class mobility." See Bonne Urciuoli, *Exposing Prejudice: Puerto Rican Experiences of Language, Race and Class* (Boulder, CO: Westview Press, 1996), 15–16.

17. David Roediger and James Barrett, "Making New Immigrants 'Inbetween': Irish Hosts and White Panethnicity, 1890 to 1930," in *Not Just Black and White: Historical and Contemporary Perspectives on Immigration, Race, and Ethnicity in the United States*, ed. Nancy Foner and George M. Fredrickson (New York: Russell Sage Foundation, 2004), 187.

18. See David Roediger, *The Wages of Whiteness: Race and the Making of the American Working Class* (New York: Verso, 1991); Earl Lewis, *In Their own Interests: Race, Class, and Power in Twentieth-Century Norfolk, Virginia* (Berkeley: University of California Press, 1991); John Jr. Hartigan, *Racial Situations: Class predicaments of Whiteness in Detroit* (Princeton, NJ: Princeton University Press, 1999); John L Jackson Jr., *Harlemworld: Doing Race and Class in Contemporary Black America* (Chicago: University of Chicago Press, 2001); Sherry Ortner, *New Jersey Dreaming:*

Capital, Culture, and the Class of '58 (Durham: Duke University Press, 2003).

19. The term was first used by William Petersen in 1966. In the *New York Times Magazine*, January 6, an article entitled "Success Story, Japanese-American Style," Petersen praised Japanese Americans as the model minority in opposition to Blacks because of their hardworking cultural values. For a critique of the model minority myth, see Stacey Lee, *Unraveling the "Model Minority" Stereotype: Listening to Asian American Youth* (New York: Columbia University, 1996).

20. A few exceptions are Aihwa Ong, "Cultural Citizenship as Subject Making: Immigrants Negotiate Racial and Cultural Boundaries in the United States," *Current Anthropology* 37, no. 1 (1996): 737–762; *Flexible Citizenship: the Cultural Logics of Transnationality* (Durham: Duke University Press, 1999); *Buddha is Hiding: Refugees, Citizenship, the New America* (Berkeley: University of California Press, 2003). Lisa Lowe, *Immigrant Acts* (Durham: Duke University Press, 1996).

21. See Yen Espiritu and Paul Ong, "Class Constraints on Racial Solidarity among Asian Americans" in *The New Asian Immigration in Los Angeles and Global Restructuring*, Paul Ong, Edna Bonacich, and Lucie Cheng, eds. (Philadelphia: Temple University Press, 1994): 295–321; Koshy, "Morphing Race into Ethnicity," 153–194.

22. Omi and Winant, *Racial Formation*, 2nd ed. (1994); Sherry Ortner, *New Jersey Dreaming: Capital, Culture, and the Class of '58* (Durham: Duke University Press, 2003).

23. Edna Bonacich et al., *Behind the Label: Inequality in the Los Angeles Apparel Industry* (Berkeley: University of California Press, 2000); Saskia Sassen, "Whose City Is It: Globalization and the Formation of New Claims," in *Cities and Citizenship*, ed. James Holston (Durham: Duke University Press, 1999), 177–194.

24. Lisa Lowe, *Immigrant Acts: On Asian American Cultural Politics* (Durham: Duke University Press, 1996).

25. Vijay Prashad, *The Karma of Brown Folk* (Minneapolis: University of Minnesota Press, 2000).

26. Ulf Hannerz, "Ethnicity and Opportunity in Urban America," in *Urban Ethnicity*, ed. Abner Cohen (London: Tavistock Publications, 1974), 42.

27. It must be noted that not all middle-class Chinese Americans are fully aware of the negative structural consequences in the choice of ethnicity over race. In fact, people like Mr. Moy firmly believe that they are contributing to the wellbeing of the Chinese community. At the time of our meeting, Mr. Moy had just donated a large amount of money to a Chinese American social service agency whose major clients are new immigrants. By listing some of the possible consequences of a middle class strategic colorblind racial learning, I hope this paper may prompt Asian American scholars and social activists to explore alternative ways of doing Asian American politics, for example, coalition building with African Americans and Latinos.

28. Carolyn Kay Steedman, *Landscape for a Good Woman* (New Brunswick, NJ: Rutgers University Press, 1986).

29. Tomas Almaguer, *Racial Fault Lines: The Historical Origin of White Supremacy in California* (Berkeley: University of California Press, 1994); Fredrik Barth, introduction to *Ethnic Groups and Boundaries: The Social Organization of Cultural Difference*, ed. Fredrik Barth (Boston: Little, Brown and Company, 1969), 9–38.

30. John Lie, "The Black-Asian Conflict?" in *Not just Black and White: Historical and Contemporary Perspectives on Immigration, Race, and Ethnicity in the United States*, ed. Nancy Foner and George M. Fredrickson (New York: Russell Sage Foundation, 2004), 301–313.

31. Frank Wu, *Yellow: Race in America beyond Black and White* (New York: Basic Books, 2002).

32. Vijay Prashad, *Everybody Was Kung Fu Fighting: Afro-Asian Connections and the Myth of Cultural Purity* (Boston: Beacon Press, 2001).

Old Rituals in New Lands

(Original Title: A Change in Direction: Bringing the Ancestors Home)

Roberta S. Greenwood, PhD

For the Chinese, the exchanges between the living and the dead represent a reciprocal relationship. Through the presentation of food and other observances, the descendants hope to insure a good life for themselves in the form of wealth, health, good harvest, and offspring.

Historically, it was the wish of most Chinese who came to this country for work in the gold fields, railroad construction, farms, or other jobs, to be buried in the homeland. As far back as the Gold Rush and well into the 1930s and even later, literally tens of thousands of individuals who were buried in temporary graves throughout the west were regularly disinterred and the remains shipped back to the native villages. The total will never be known. From Sacramento alone, the bones of 1,200 Chinese railroad workers were sent home in 1870, and it is estimated that the bones of 10,000 individuals left the United States in 1913. As late as 1937, the remains of 850 Chinese were disinterred from a single cemetery in Los Angeles. Women, infants, and victims of violence were less apt to be removed.

In years past, part of the yearning for return to the ancestral land resulted from the prejudice, isolation, and hostility experienced in America. In recent years, the trend is being reversed. As recent generations have established permanent residence and roots in this country, ties to the homeland have loosened and the obligations of the traditional spring and fall observances have become burdensome. Yet, the continuing association between the living and the dead is of paramount importance, and maintaining the original place of burial has been secondary throughout history. It is the safety of the remains and access to them that is important. So that proper respects can be paid, some families are choosing to disinter ancestors buried in China and bring them to America for local reburial. In this way, they can maintain the traditional spring and fall customs of paying respect without incurring the long and costly trips to China.

Details of the historical background and customs, and the personal experience of one family in accomplishing such a relocation, are available in the new book, *Chinese American Death Rituals: Respecting the Ancestors,* published by Alta Mira Press (2005).

The Alien Files or A Files

The Missing Link

Jennie F. Lew, Jeanie W. Chooey, and Daniel Nealand

FLORENCE TU, MODERATOR

This presentation will showcase a new, as yet barely explored "source frontier" in American immigration and ethnic and family historical research: the huge U.S. government investigative case file group known as *Alien Registration Files* or *A Files*, which encompass the fabric of America with immigrants entering from every country worldwide. In Chinese American Studies, these files contain informational and evidentiary documents that are vital for family historians and essential for understanding such subjects as American immigration policy/practices and the Chinese diaspora, as well as many other social science areas.

A BRIEF HISTORY OF THE A FILES AND THEIR RECORDS APPRAISAL STATUS

Daniel Nealand

The National Archives and Records Administration conducts "appraisals" of "current use" and longer-lasting historical values for U.S. government records. Enduring public historical research possibilities play a major role in determining which federal records will be kept forever and become part of the National Archives. Approximately 2 percent of federal government records are appraised as having permanent historical value. Traditionally, twenty to thirty years after creation, these are supposed to—and often do—go into the custody of the National Archives for preservation and public research.

Under the Alien Registration Act of 1940, all aliens in the United States were required to register with the Immigration and Naturalization Service (today the U.S. Citizenship and Immigration Service). Investigative files created for every alien registered were called *Alien Registration* or A Files. In the 1950s, INS headquarters decentralized and consolidated A Files with many older files at its field offices. Beginning in 1956, records of any active INS investigation were "uploaded" into A Files.

In following decades, the value and volume of A Files—the main file system for all INS activities regarding immigrants—increased dramatically. In 1998, A Files at most NARA Federal Records Centers, except for those still stored at FRC San Bruno, were relocated to a central FRC in Missouri. All A Files remain covered by an older appraisal calling for destruction seventy-five years after closing.

Regional research communities know that NARA-USCIS now favors permanent retention for the A Files. However, they differ with NARA-USCIS's proposal to transfer to the National Archives only A Files covering persons born 105 or more years prior to transfer. They propose instead that the first transfers to National Archives include A Files for immigrants born in 1925 and before. Not confronted yet is where A Files brought into the National Archives would be housed. Researchers hope the San Bruno FRC files will go to the San Francisco regional archives in accordance with demonstrated public-historical interests there.

THE ULTIMATE A-FILE OF "NATIVE HAWAIIAN BORN" SUN YAT SEN!

Jennie F. Lew

The intent of this panel presentation is to reveal how an examination of certain Alien Files holds more than an exploration into personal histories. They can be a huge asset and invaluable resource in important research related to issues of public policy as well as the dynamics that affect both national and world history.

For example, one of the most famous Alien Files discovered at the National Archives and Records Administration is that of Sun Yat Sen, the "founding father" of the Republic of China. Though generally acknowledged as a giant in leading China to end thousands of years of dynastic rule, a handwritten note in Sun Yat Sen's Alien File reads—"Weller says that he gave the passport back to the Chinaman."

Early in Sun Yat Sen's A File are records that he attempted to enter the United States in June of 1896 with official documents from the Consulate General of Shanghai, China, claiming to be a "native born Hawaiian." Two farmers living in Oahu even submitted written testimony of growing up with Sun Yat Sen in the Hawaiian Islands and knowing his parents there.

However, as U.S. immigration officials began to discover the true identity of Sun Yat Sen, both Chinese and U.S.

government officials began to debate the pros and cons of providing refuge to a leading world revolutionary. Hence, what began as a simple and even very common story of a Chinese immigrant attempting to circumvent the severe restrictions imposed by the Chinese Exclusion Act, evolved into a documentation of the twists and turns of American immigration policy, the ebb and flow of foreign relations between two great nations, and the nuances of both political protocol and precedence.

ACCESS TECHNIQUES FOR A FILES

Jeanie W. C. Low

Each Alien File or A File represents an individual's twentieth-century American immigration and naturalization history. In some instances, the case file may span thirty or more years. An A File contains from 2 to over 150 pages. They include personal photographs, family history details, immigration interviews, subsequent investigations, and naturalization documents.

Of particular interest is a sample Chinese American "confession and amnesty" files. There are approximately 130 pages: 70 pages of entry immigration with an additional 60 pages of subsequent "confession and amnesty" proceed-ings dated thirty years later. That particular A File includes the following government forms: Record of Illegal Alien Apprehended or Located, Request for Record Check (criminal—police, sheriff, and welfare departments), Agency Name Check, Report of Investigation, Record of Sworn Confession Statement with true family history, witness statements, permanent resident and naturalization applications, and a copy of the Certificate of Naturalization.

At present, access to the restricted A Files requires a letter or a Freedom of Information/Privacy (FOIA) request through the U.S. Citizenship and Immigration Service. Information needed and the FOIA form is outlined at the USCIS website: *http://uscis.gov/graphics/aboutus/foia*. Individuals and/or their families may request the files with the first 100 electrostatic copies and two hours of search time free of charge. Researchers need written authorization or proof of death to request those files, and are responsible for research and electrostatic copy fees.

Through analysis of oral interviews and A File documents, the following questions may be addressed: (1) Was the testimony consistent with family units? (2) Do global events affect the treatment of focus immigrants? (3) Is the immigration experience easier with overseas contacts? (4) How did the immigration experience and subsequent investigations affect the individuals, their families, and the community?

Rooted in the Americanization Zeal

The San Francisco International Institute, Race, and Settlement Work, 1918–1939

Andrew Urban

The Chinese and Japanese come from the Asiatic zone ineligible to citizenship. This means that the impulse to serve them has never been rooted in the Americanization zeal which has played so large a part, spoken or unspoken, in the attitude of Americans toward other transplanted folk.

—Letter from Ethel Bird of the National Services Division of the YWCA to Mrs. Emily Price, Member of the Executive Board of the San Francisco International Institute, March 9, 1934

INTRODUCTION

This essay will explore how the work and philosophy of the International Institute, a settlement house located in downtown Sa n Francisco, relates to the larger historiography that has attempted to understand the role of settlement houses and social work in regard to race and cultural pluralism. As a settlement house that directed its resources toward San Francisco's Asian immigrants as well as the city's American-born Asian population, the International Institute offers a unique look into how race informed "Americanization" work and imbued it with unavoidable contradictions.

The settlement house movement that emerged in the first part of the twentieth century defined among its primary goals the making of good American citizens who would contribute to the nation and become part of its social fabric. As the San Francisco International Institute noted in its 1934 Annual Report, "The International Institute thinks of itself as society's agent in trying to help the foreign-born and their children become so adjusted in and identified with American life that they will cordially cooperate as responsible citizens."[1] In another document articulating why it was worthy of receiving funding from San Francisco's municipal philanthropic organization, the Community Chest, the Institute would state as its purpose, simply, "the protection and integration of foreign born and racial groups into our civilization."[2]

The International Institute's self-described goals of making "responsible citizens" and facilitating "integration" were not applied universally to all of the nationality groups that the organization worked with in San Francisco. As the quote at the beginning of this essay illustrates, Asian immigrants living in the United States were "ineligible" for naturalization. In seeking to help assimilate immigrants into the nation, the International Institute was nonetheless limited to the prevailing legal definition of which groups were racially eligible for incorporation into the nation. As Annie Clo Watson, Executive Secretary of the San Francisco International Institute, would note in speaking before the National Conference of Social Work, no amount of Americanization work could change the fact that Asians were "a permanent body of non-citizens, who cannot hold property and establish homes for their families, who are cut off from the institutions of government, who are socially, culturally, and legally isolated."[3] In extending its services to the American-born Chinese population in San Francisco—citizens by birth—the International Institute performed a different type of Americanization work that framed citizenship as being contingent on cultural qualities. In this manner as well, the International Institute grappled with how race informed fitness for national inclusion.

BACKGROUND OF THE INTERNATIONAL INSTITUTES

In 1918, the International Institute in San Francisco opened its doors, joining nineteen other Institutes already in operation across the United States. Conceived of as a department of the Young Women's Christian Association (YWCA), individual Institutes were affiliated with both the national organization of the YWCA, to which they reported and on which they relied on for funding, as well as local branches of the YWCA in the cities where they operated. In San Francisco this meant that the International Institute worked closely with both the Chinese YWCA and Japanese YWCA (often referred to as the Chinese and Japanese Centers), despite maintaining its own offices and a separate staff.

The San Francisco International Institute was modeled as a settlement house; although its employees did not reside in its main building, the Institute was located in downtown San Francisco at 1860 Washington Street and maintained an open-door policy to the communities it served. The International Institutes oriented their work around the idea that the different nationality communities possessed specific needs, and as a result, assigned programs and staff by nationality. In 1923, for example, the Institute employed on its staff a Greek visitor, a Spanish-speaking visitor (working primarily with the city's Mexican population), a Russian visitor, in addition to a Japanese visitor and three Chinese visitors, one of whom worked as a full-time liaison at the Chinese Center.[4] Visitors had the job of cultivating contacts among individuals representing the different nationality communities of the city, promoting the Institute's groups and clubs, as well as responding to needs in the areas of employment, medical care, and interpretation and translation.

The Institute's headquarters at 1860 Washington Street provided a common venue for the different nationality groups that the organization worked with in San Francisco. The Institute believed that events held in the main building fostered a cosmopolitan appreciation between nationality groups, as well as among native-born Americans who could attend and learn "to understand the foreigner" and avoid being "guilty of American arrogance." In accordance with the philosophy of many prominent individuals within the settlement house movement, the Institute in San Francisco theorized that Americanization could occur ostensibly without erasing the cultural traits immigrants brought with them to the United States. Rather, the Institute sought to foster a type of cultural pluralism and served as "sympathetic interpreters of those traditions, social laws, beliefs, and customs valid in the homeland, and also fundamentally valid here," while also facilitating the "slow wearing away of those customs and habits which are of the surface, and are the badge of ignorance; and which can bring only grief and failure in America."[5]

THE SETTLEMENT MOVEMENT AND THE RACIAL IDEOLOGIES OF SOCIAL WORK

In looking broadly at settlement house work and issues of race, most scholars have focused on how mainly Protestant settlement workers interacted with predominantly Catholic and Jewish European immigrants. In addition, scholars have explored how settlement houses responded to the "Great Migration" of African Americans into Midwestern and Eastern cities. Settlement workers understood the differences of Italians and Russian Jews, for example, to be racial.[6] Nonetheless, despite examples of biological racism—the belief that race was an innate genetic quality—most settlement houses advocated a definition of "race" that, in line with the liberal sociologists of the era, considered it to be a cultural and contingent category of identity that would yield to and eventually allow for assimilation into a pluralistically American culture. Edith Terry Bremer, the founder of the national federation of International Institutes and a friend and associ-

ate of Jane Addams, articulated this belief: "We are committed to the philosophy that all races of men are intrinsically of equal worth and that the economic and social arrangements should be such as to permit each to work out its own unique life and contribution to mankind."[7]

Settlement houses were often located in white immigrant neighborhoods that, while segregated, bordered on areas inhabited by African Americans. Like the European immigrants that settlement houses were initially created to serve, African Americans coming north in the early part of the twentieth century also faced difficulties in finding housing, jobs, and acceptance from already established and often hostile communities. With these factors in mind, it would seem that the settlement houses would extend an invitation to African American migrants to participate in programs and services, alongside their original mission to assist European immigrants.

This was markedly not the case in the majority of instances. Most settlement houses accepted the commonly held perception that there should be a natural social space between African Americans and whites. Although there were some exceptions, most settlement houses banned African Americans from their programs, often in the process spinning off segregated and autonomous branches to deal with African Americans who sought inclusion. In extreme cases, settlement houses closed down rather than integrate. As Thomas Philpott comments cynically of the settlement houses, "their specialty as social workers was to appreciate neighborhood realities."[8] As institutions with budgets, reliance on outside funding, and a need to attract as many participants as possible, settlement houses believed it was a risky prospect if not outright organizational suicide to try to serve both constituencies. As Robert Woods and Albert Kennedy noted in their influential book, *The Settlement Horizon*, "Large groups of colored people in a neighborhood predominantly white may force a settlement, against its inclination, to choose between the two. In this case the soundest practice is to establish a separate branch."[9] This mentality led to the creation of African American settlement houses with limited access to resources and for the majority, short life spans as "separate and unequal" institutions.[10]

Although settlement houses geared toward white immigrant populations took into account what they believed to be the practical outcomes of racial integration, they also justified their refusal to work with African American through a racialized understanding of what they considered to be African Americans' cultural limitations. Even though social workers were relatively progressive in eschewing popular theories of the time that presented race as being biologically determined, they understood race, as a cultural manifestation, to be deep-rooted and inherited. Jane Addams herself, the most famous of settlement workers, felt, as Elisabeth Lasch-Quinn argues, that slavery had "obliterated morality, family integrity, social organization, and even culture and civilization itself." Due to the traumas and lasting effects of slavery, in Addams' estimation, African Americans ranked significantly lower than European immigrants in terms of their potential to assimilate. Whereas Addams felt that Greek and Italian immigrants had illustrious cultural pasts to draw upon and utilize in their adaptation to American society, she felt that African Americans were hopelessly disadvantaged in this regard.[11]

In San Francisco, while the International Institute did not establish separate houses to maintain segregation between whites and Asians, race played a constant factor in its day-to-day operation. Comparable to the manner in which settlement houses downplayed the racial difference of African Americans yet nonetheless isolated their needs as belonging to a race apart, Asians in San Francisco were never simply just another nationality group. How white, native-born Americans compared the capacity of Asians to assimilate to that of Europeans cannot be analyzed without understanding how different races have been socially constructed in the United States. As Henry Yu points out in his discussion of the Survey of Race Relations that was conducted by the University of Chicago Sociologist Robert Ezra Park in the 1920s, "Park was not coming all the way out to the West Coast just to argue that anti-Asian prejudice was the same as other forms of prejudice."[12]

Kay Anderson has theorized that the long history of white fascination with Vancouver's Chinatown does not mean that the neighborhood possessed an inherent "Chineseness" prompting such intense attention. Rather, "in an important and neglected sense, 'Chinatown' belongs as much to the society with the power to define and shape it as it does to its residents."[13] Representations of Chinatown as an exotic, foreign location in the heart of San Francisco with roots in the "Orient," coexisted with the neighborhood's real isolation. Prevented from living in ethnically mixed neighborhoods like members of the various white European nationality groups, the physical barriers of Chinatown reinforced and gave salience to the barriers associated with a racial identity. The Institute highlighted the role white intermediation could play in making Chinatown safe and accessible to the city's white population. As the minutes of a 1924 meeting at the International Institute note, the YWCA's presence at the Chinese Center reassured the "very many tourists who call at Chinese headquarters; sometimes they have a sort of hazy idea that something uncanny is lurking in the background but when they see the triangle over the door, their fears are dispelled."[14]

FROM GROUP WORK TO CASEWORK

From its beginning, the International Institute divided its work with San Francisco's various nationality groups into two main categories: group work and casework. Group work took the form of organizing activities such as promoting the Father-Daughter banquet (a competition hosted by the Institute that brought together different nationality groups), offering English language courses to foreign-born women, and providing classes that centered on domestic skills considered essential to the "respectable" American woman, such as cooking, sewing, and lessons in personal hygiene. Group work of this nature had been the traditional domain of the YWCA for many years, although through the International Institutes it was directed exclusively at foreign-born women and their daughters. Casework comprised providing assistance in settling domestic disputes, attempting to mediate intergenerational conflicts between native-born children and their foreign-born parents, and offering legal advice on questions regarding citizenship, deportation, and immigration.[15]

Although both group work and casework had the putative goal of helping to make "good" Americans, the varied methods involved in each type of social work ultimately fomented irreconcilable tensions between the San Francisco Institute and the YWCA, which would result in the Institute declaring its independence from the national organization in 1934. With the break, the San Francisco International Institute joined a number of other Institutes nationwide that had already established autonomy. In a 1930 speech, the Institutes' National Director, Edith Bremer, foreshadowed separation by voicing some of the concerns that would emerge explicitly in years to come:

> Personally, it always seemed to me that central to the question of the future of International Institutes lay this other question—what is the greatest need among the foreign peoples today?—is it for an agency championing their interests in a more general way? or is it for one working especially for women? with particular attention to the transition taking place in the homes? Do women represent the most handicapped group, socially speaking, within the immigrant nationalities?

For Bremer, at least at the time, the answer was "yes." Whereas members of the International Institutes' staff sought to become increasingly involved in the politics and legalities of immigration, by refocusing their attention to incorporate in their work the needs of immigrant men and families through casework, Bremer articulated a continuation of group work. As Bremer exclaimed, "Many a woman owes her first personal release to a church bazaar! Why shouldn't these oncoming 'newer Americans' have the soul luxury of participating in some sort of genuine 'social' service?" Bremer believed that wresting immigrant women from their restrictive cultures and engaging them in "American" activities was the most important service that white, native-born women could perform.[16]

Eventually, the desire of Institutes located in cities with large Catholic, immigrant populations, alongside the goal to serve men and families, provided the main reasons for leaving the YWCA.[17] When it became apparent that the San Francisco International Institute would split from the national YWCA, members of the Institute's executive board sought to maintain its direct link with the local Chinese and Japanese YWCAs so as to preserve access to their largest constituencies. This initiative would ultimately meet in failure, as both the Chinese and the Japanese Centers voted to remain branches of the YWCA. As Ethel Bird of the National Services Division of the YWCA explained to the Institute's Board, in part this reflected the Protestant orientation of the San Francisco YWCA branches, which dictated that the majority of Asians and Asian Americans in contact with the Institute through the YWCA were those who had converted to Protestantism. In addition, Bird pointed out that, "In San Francisco the erection by the Y.W.C.A. of the two lovely buildings tends to emphasize the Chinese and Japanese as racial groups. The lack of buildings, as for example in Oakland, has meant that Chinese and Japanese were drawn in as nationalities into an international grouping with Portuguese, Mexican, and Italian."[18]

The Chinese Exclusion Act, passed in 1882, ensured that the Chinese community in the United States would experience a steady decline among not only new immigrants, but also as a result of the departure of those who chose to resettle in China.[19] This decline, coupled with the persistence of Chinatown as a well-demarcated physical community, informed not only the decision of the Chinese Center to stay part of the YWCA, but, to a larger context, the manner by which the needs of the Chinese were defined. The Chinese in San Francisco were treated as a community with boundaries, resources, and customs that could not necessarily be worked upon to fit a larger conceptualization of the social order, but one that remained essentially outside the (white) social order altogether. The tensions that defined the Chinese community in which the International Institute had contacts and worked with—Protestant, yet ineligible for citizenship, a national community yet permanently racial in that its members could not realize what were considered to be the tangible benefits of Americanization—dictated the limits of the goals the International Institute wished to affect.

Ethel Bird of the national YWCA would remind the San Francisco International Institute that its efforts toward the Chinese could not be "rooted in the Americanization zeal" but were better served by the "missionary zeal."[20] The Chinese could be converted but not made Americans. Group work, which focused on the "betterment" of individual women, coincided with the missionary effort to inculcate Christian mores. Casework toward the Chinese and Japanese communities inevitably confronted legal barriers that race posed. Although the International Institute would maintain associations with the Chinese and Japanese Centers, the decline in the number of Chinese and Japanese individuals it worked with in years subsequent to the separation and its shift toward casework is revealing. While in 1923 the Institute recorded 456 contacts through group work or household visits with Chinese individuals, and 382 with Japanese, by 1934, those numbers were 85 and 17 respectively.[21]

THE "SECOND GENERATION"—SOCIAL WORK AND AMERICAN-BORN CHINESE

Despite defining its mission as being geared toward members of nationality groups whose foreignness required assistance in adaptation to American life, the San Francisco International Institute focused a great deal of attention on the plight of American-born children of Chinese immigrants. The so-called "second-generation Chinese" warranted great scrutiny in the minds of the staff workers who believed that members of this cohort required special needs in order to be made American. In determining whether the second-generation Chinese would be recognized culturally as citizens, white Americans scrutinized their families, religious beliefs, and other practices to make sure they were free of "Oriental" influences.

As Mae Ngai has argued in presenting the concept of "alien citizenship," the racial ideas encoded in immigration laws and restricted naturalization bestowed upon American-born Asians a type of "alien" citizenship that "cast them as permanently foreign and unassimilable to the nation."[22] The very language used in discussions of Chinese Americans reveal the ingrained, racial assumptions underlying what it meant to be American. Although "American" in citizenship, the second-generation Chinese in the United States remained "Chinese." As an (aptly titled) mission worker with the YWCA observing second-generation Chinese "social relations with Americans" noted, "so much of the intercourse between Chinese and Americans is on an artificial basis, i.e. participants of the two groups not being on the same social and educational levels. So often, too, contacts are on the basis of adding atmosphere or color to situation not real nor genuine basis of approach."[23]

In her 1930 "Survey of Chinatown," Rose Chew would note that among the difficulties perceived by young Chinese Americans, respondents to her questionnaires ranked employment as perhaps the greatest hurdle that barred them from integration into the larger social life of San Francisco. As Chew would observe, "the problem is not so acute with the first generation, as the majority of them are absorbed in the various businesses in the community itself," yet their children, fluent in English and recipients of high school and college degrees, felt continually reproached in their attempt to acquire jobs outside of Chinatown. Those among the second generation, especially women, felt that their only options for work were jobs in which they performed the stereotypical role of the "Oriental." As Chew put it:

> For the second generation girls, her employment frequently takes her outside the community in work where her costume is a requirement, such as waitresses in tea-rooms and restaurants, stock girls, elevator operators, etc. Herein is also a problem which must be met—the effect of such employment on character—employment dependent primarily upon attractive costumes rather than upon qualifications and ability to do the work.

These racialized expectations were grounded in white representations of how a Chinese woman should act; the second generation, as Chew commented, listened to American music, watched American films, and tended not to join the familial and benevolent associations their parents belonged to. As Chew explained, "A large number of the second generation would find it difficult to give a talk in Chinese."[24]

In 1930, these observations for Chew must have had particular resonance, as a member of the second generation who had successfully gained employment outside the traditional career path of Chinese women. Straddling the divide between Chinatown and the settlement house, where white, middle- and upper-class Protestant women sought to produce knowledge and explain the increasingly "foreign" city around them, Chew occupied the role of translator. Chew came from a very prominent Chinese family in San Francisco, and her father Ng Poon Chew was the editor of a number of local papers. One author in the 1930s would go as far as to state that the Chew family's success "attest[s] to the value of the work which was begun by missionary enthusiasts of the seventies and eighties."[25] Chew's role as an interpreter was not only a means to show-off a "successful" example of assimilation, but also was necessitated by the International Institute's belief that Chinatown remained an impenetrable space hindering Americanization even among the American-born. While the International Institute attributed many of the problems of the second-generation Chinese to discrimination, alternatively, staff members did not feel one could be American in Chinatown. It was a "Ghetto" with "bad housing" and "petty strife," a "dragon devouring itself."[26] Only those who were able to make contact with the surrounding world outside Chinatown were "greatly affected by modern influences, that is, influences other than Chinese."[27]

The Institute's "Chinese Survey of Chinatown" bears a good deal of resemblance to the publications authored by white sociologists and missionaries during the same time period. Revealing the cultural dimensions of citizenship, Albert Palmer attempted to convince his readers through the voice of the Chinese American graduate student he interviewed, that "'the Chinese young people are psychologically American,'" while Allan Hunter wrote of discrimination that, "They go from one disillusioning experience to another. Small wonder that many of those educated American-born Orientals cry out: 'Only in name have we all the citizen's rights; but in fact we are men without a country.'"[28] William Carlson Smith, a close colleague of Park's who also worked on the Survey of Race Relations, subtitled one of the chapters in his *The Second Generation Oriental in America*, "Oriental in Appearance But Not in Reality." Throughout *The Second Generation Oriental in America*, Smith appears to be attempting to compensate for the fact that their race precluded American-born Asians from being recognized as equals, to the point where he emphasizes over and over again their strong work ethic, the lack of crime in Chinatowns and Japantowns, and the ingrained deference Asians have for the authority of elders.[29]

Like the International Institute, however, these commentators on the Chinese second-generation could not escape race even when dismissing its significance. As Henry Yu notes, "Culture, rather than being a mere description of the mores or folkways of a certain group of people, assumed causal force in the sociologists' narratives." For example, Hunter heralded the role Christian social workers could play in guiding American-born Asians through rituals such as marriage, so as to circumvent the prearranged marriages that could not be reconciled with American individuality.[30] For the children of Asian immigrants to become Americans, they had to distance themselves from the customs of their race, which stood as barriers to inclusion.

In the immediate aftermath of the separation between the San Francisco International Institute and the YWCA, much of the work directed toward the Chinese nationality community was cut off altogether. The Institute, beginning in 1935 when Rose Chew was rehired as a temporary caseworker, eventually returned to the issues of the second generation. Yet if the speech Frank Harris, vice president of the Institute's board, gave to the California Personnel Managers' Association Meeting is indicative, the scientific needs and strict empirical logic of casework shifted focus from discrimination to racial explanations of why second-generation members of San Francisco's nationality communities were not finding work. Although Harris acknowledged that prejudice existed among the city's white workers, he commented that:

> The personality impression made by some, is not favorable, particularly when they are competing with old-stock Americans, for a job. Their dress may be a bit peculiar. Their personal grooming and personal hygiene may not be up to the American standard. The odor of cooking in the clothing, or of garlicky food in the diet are fatal to office or mercantile employment—particularly when the public is to be met. Then too, there is frequently a faulty personality adjustment to American groups. The person of immigrant background, due to consciousness of language difficulty or other evidence of "foreignness," holds himself aloof, resists friendly advances, and otherwise introverts himself. The reverse of this is found in the person who adjusts to American groups, laughs off ridicule of his foreign characteristics and his name which is hard to pronounce, and makes his way successfully toward integration.

He added,

> We need give little thought to the second-generation of English-speaking, Scandinavian, and German nationalities. These, in the second-generation have no language difficulty; they have lost all trace of "foreignness" in appearance and manner; and in general are as fully integrated as they ever can be, limited only by their personalities, as are old-stock Americans. The problem is quite different for the racial groups who do not thus lose their nationality characteristics,—the Orientals, the Mexicans, and of course the Negroes.[31]

Harris was intent to convince the managers he met with that "Orientals," and other racial groups could be transformed into white workers, but only after they had been stripped of their inhibiting cultural qualities.

CONCLUSION

It is important to note that the International Institute, in a period often marked by virulent, biological racism, stood out as a consistent advocate for amending legislation that barred Asians from naturalization. Before the National Conference on Social Work, Annie Clo Watson urged settlement workers across the country to petition for the revision of exclusion laws to allow for citizenship.[32] During the height of the Great Depression, when both state and federal governments contemplated enacting legislation that would tie relief to legal citizenship, the International Institute attempted to dissuade such policies. In a letter to Dewey Anderson of the California State Relief Administration, the president of the Institute's board of directors pointed out that such laws were "discriminating doubly" against the Chinese and Japanese who had no means of legally acquiring citizenship.[33] In an internal report, the International Institute astutely observed of the relief issue and the fate of all noncitizens during the crisis times of the Great Depression, that "it [is] difficult to see how the interests of the alien can be nicely and neatly separated from those of the citizen."[34]

Still, such positive contributions do not mask that in spite of its rhetoric, the International Institute consciously and inadvertently played a role in the racialization of Asians in San Francisco. In the case of San Francisco's Filipino population, the Institute's role in reinforcing the racial prerogatives of federal immigration laws is even clearer. In 1934, as part of the Tydings-McDuffie Act, which granted the Philippines' autonomy and eventual independence from the United States, Filipinos ceased to be colonial subjects and were allowed free movement between the insular possessions and the mainland, becoming instead barred immigrants from the Asiatic Zone of Exclusion.[35] Despite maintaining a mission that ostensibly sought to help with integration, the San Francisco International Institute, in accordance with immigration officers at Angel Island and the Department of Labor, took responsibility for facilitating the forced repatriation of Filipinos in the Bay Area, a task considered the "high spot of the year."[36] In a confidential supplement to the 1936 Annual Report, an anonymous worker at the Institute described the situation of Mrs. Garay, a Filipino widow living in San Francisco with ten children, nine who were born in the city. According to the report, Mrs. Garay and her late husband were "natives of one of the remote islands of the Philippines where life is backward and living conditions primitive." Insinuating that Mrs. Garay was both promiscuous and indolent, the worker assigned to the case described how she "had at first expressed a desire to [repatriate], but had begun to vacillate when she considered the attractions of a city where there is one Filipino woman to more than 100 men and where half-orphans are provided for rather generously by the State."[37] Although members of the Institute rarely expressed such explicit and cruel racial comments, it nonetheless captures the extreme divide between the rhetoric surrounding integration and the rhetoric invoking the need for repatriation.

Although the members of the San Francisco International Institute might have truly believed they were fostering a pluralistic model of assimilation for the United States, the pluralistic society they desired had built-in racial boundaries determining who could be legally and culturally included. Social policies toward Asians in San Francisco, such as the ones enacted by the International Institute, could not function in a vacuum, free of the legal codes that defined race. The San Francisco International Institute's "Americanization zeal" had to be recast and even dropped when confronted by Chinese immigrants whose race had left it predetermined as to their ability to be legally or, in the case of the Chinese American-born, socially American.

Author's Note: I would like to thank the participants in "Branching Out the Banyan Tree" for their comments and feedback. In addition, at the University of Minnesota, I would like to thank Anna Clark, Doug Hartmann, and especially Erika Lee for their thoughtful suggestions on how to transform this essay from a seminar paper into an article.

NOTES

1. The papers of the International Institute of San Francisco (SFII Papers) are housed in the Immigration History Research Center (IHRC) at the University of Minnesota, as part of its General/Multiethnic Collection. The IHRC is also in possession of the personal papers of Annie Clo Watson, who served as the San Francisco International Institute's Executive Secretary in the 1930s. Citations in this paper will denote the record group of the collection being cited, box number, file folder, and the page number within the document when given. Annual Report, 1934, IHRC, SFII Papers, 168:1:13, 2.
2. "Discussion of the International Institute as a Private Agency in San Francisco, Presented to the Section on Family Welfare of the Relief Council of the Community Chest," May 10, 1934, IHRC, SFII Papers, 168:34:9.
3. "Special Nationality Problems of the Pacific Coast—Presented at National Conference of Social Work, Kansas City, Missouri, May 22, 1934," IHRC, Papers of Annie Clo Watson, 54:1:3.
4. Annual Report, 1923, IHRC, SFII Papers, 168:1:2.
5. Annual Reports, 1924, 1925, IHRC, SFII Papers, 168:1:3, 4. The creation of an international setting was an undertaking the International Institutes took on quite consciously. In the 1925 Annual Report, for example, one of the questions the individual Institutes had to address and report back on to the national organization was how their various programs contributed to "the 'atmosphere' of an 'international' interest." "The International Institutes Founded by the YWCA: Purpose, Program, Organizations and Achievements," 1933, IHRC, SFII Papers, 168:14:1.
6. For an example of a work that looks at the racialized response of Jane Addams and Hull House to eastern and southern European immigrants, see Rivka Shpak Lissak, *Pluralism and Progressivism: Hull House and the New Immigrants, 1890-1919* (Chicago: University of Chicago Press, 1989). On settlement houses and African American communities, see Elisabeth

Lasch-Quinn, *Black Neighbors: Race and the Limits of Reform in the American Settlement House Movement, 1890-1945* (Chapel Hill: University of North Carolina Press, 1993), and Thomas Philpott, *The Slum and the Ghetto: Neighborhood Deterioration and Middle-Class Reform, Chicago, 1880-1930* (New York: Oxford University Press, 1978), both of which focus mainly on the midwest.

7. Edith Terry Bremer, "A Forward Look for International Institutes," 1930, typescript of speech given to the national conference of International Institutes, IHRC, SFII Papers, 168:14:2.

8. Lasch-Quinn, *Black Neighbors*, 22–24; Philpott, *The Slum and the Ghetto*, 301.

9. Robert A. Woods and Albert J. Kennedy, *The Settlement Horizon* (New Brunswick, NJ; London: Transaction Publishers, 1990 [1922]), 337. Interestingly, *The Settlement Horizon* omits any discussion of the "racial" difficulties that might arise when a settlement house was located in a neighborhood consisting of both white and Asian populations. In Eliot Mears's 1928 study, he does note that in San Francisco, the YMCA, which also maintained a separate Chinese branch, had had little luck at integrating its swimming facilities. As a letter from the General Secretary of the YMCA in San Francisco to Mears noted, "Even one [Asian] in the swimming-pool brings resignations from American members." Eliot Grinnell Mears, *Resident Orientals on the American Pacific Coast: Their Legal and Economic Status* (Chicago: The University of Chicago Press, 1928), 378.

10. Philpott, *The Slum and the Ghetto*, 315.

11. Lasch-Quinn, *Black Neighbors*, 10.

12. Henry Yu, *Thinking Orientals: Migration, Contact, and Exoticism in Modern America* (New York: Oxford University Press, 2001), 42, 47.

13. Kay Anderson, *Vancouver's Chinatowns: Racial Discourse in Canada, 1875-1980* (Montreal, Canada and Buffalo, NY: McGill-Queen's University Press, 1991), 10.

14. "Report of Minutes," January 1924, IHRC, SFII Papers, 168:1:3.

15. Annual Reports, 1924, 1925, 1926, 1927, 1928, 1929, and 1930, IHRC, SFII Papers, 168:1:3–9. The annual reports provide numerical compilations of the amount of group work and casework staff members were doing respectively.

16. Edith Terry Bremer, "A Forward Look for International Institutes," 1930, IHRC, SFII Papers, 168:14:2. Bremer eventually left the YWCA as well, joining the National Institute for Immigrant Welfare, which became the umbrella organization for International Institutes that had opted out of their affiliation with the YWCA.

17. "The Place and Future of International Institutes," report made from the committees that met at the national conferences in 1926 and 1927, completed in 1929, IHRC, SFII Papers, 168:14:2. In a letter to Elsie Newton, Executive Secretary of the Los Angeles International Institute, explaining why the San Francisco Institute had chosen to become independent of the YWCA, Annie Clo Watson would reiterate the same themes. Annie Clo Watson to Elsie Newton, September 17, 1934, IHRC, SFII Papers, 168:10:16.

18. Ethel Bird to Emily Price, March 9, 1934, IHRC, SFII Papers, 168:14:2.

19. Erika Lee, *At America's Gates: Chinese Immigration During the Exclusion Era, 1882-1943* (Chapel Hill: University of North Carolina Press, 2003), 238. Although the San Francisco International Institute also lost its affiliation with the Japanese YWCA, most of its records and files are devoted to its relationship to the Chinese YWCA and what it considered to be the needs of San Francisco's Chinese community.

20. Ethel Bird to Mrs. Price, March 9, 1934, IHRC, SFII Papers, 168:14:2.

21. Annual Reports, 1923, 1934, IHRC, SFII Papers, 168:1:2, 13.

22. Mae Ngai, *Impossible Subjects: Illegal Aliens and the Making of Modern America* (Princeton, NJ: Princeton University Press, 2004), 7–9.

23. Rose Chew, "Chinese Survey of Chinatown," March 19, 1930, 19, IHRC, SFII Papers, 168:14:3.

24. Chew, "Chinese Survey," 21–23.

25. Albert Palmer, *Orientals in American Life* (New York: Friendship Press, 1934), 34.

26. "Special Nationality Problems of the Pacific Coast."

27. Chew, "Chinese Survey," 21.

28. Palmer, *Orientals in American Life*, 139; Allan Hunter, *Out of the Far East* (New York: Friendship Press, 1934), 43.

29. William Carlson Smith, "The Second Generation Oriental in America," Preliminary paper prepared for the second general session, Institute of Pacific Relations, Honolulu, Hawaii, July 15–29, 1927, 5, 12–13.

30. Yu, *Thinking Orientals*, 103; Hunter, *Out of the Far East*, 100–103.

31. "Personnel Managers' Association Meeting," May 26, 1937, speech delivered by Frank Harris, IHRC, SFII Papers, 168:1:15.

32. "Special Nationality Problems of the Pacific Coast."

33. Mrs. James Reed to Dewey Anderson, January 19, 1939, IHRC, SFII Papers, 168:34:13.

34. "October 1938, Report," 4, IHRC, SFII Papers, 168:34:12.

35. For a detailed history of this chapter on the relationship of the United States and the Philippines, see Ngai, *Impossible Subjects*, 96–126.

36. "President's Report, February 19, 1935," 2, IHRC, SFII Papers, 168:1:14.

37. "Confidential Supplement to Annual Report of 1936," IHRC, SFII Papers, 168:1:15.

Detention at Angel Island
First Empirical Evidence
Robert Barde and Gustavo Bobonis

This paper draws on new data found in ledgers of the Pacific Mail Steamship Company for the period from 1913 to 1919, representing over 29,000 of its "alien passengers" (including native-born American Chinese) coming from Asia and from Central America. The Federal government charged the PMSS for upkeep of its passengers at the Angel Island Immigration Station from which we can determine which passengers were detained, how long they were detained, and under which "exempt" status Chinese passengers were allowed to enter the United States.

The data, representing fewer than 10 percent of those who were detained at the Angel Island Immigration Station during its thirty years as a functioning immigration service facility, confirm our basic impression of Angel Island: that Chinese made up most of the detainees and were detained longer than other groups. But the data also add interesting and important new findings.

We now know for certain that many Chinese were not detained at all. Most Chinese were detained for relatively short periods, the median period of detention for Chinese being six days, with a relatively small number held for rather long periods. There was great variation in the length of time that Chinese were detained, significantly correlated to, but not entirely explained by, the type of "exempt" status under which they claimed eligibility for admission. Many of the people detained were not even trying to enter the United States but were in transit to a third country. Traveling in cabin class, for Chinese, as opposed to steerage, was associated with a slightly shorter time in detention for those in first class but with a longer time for those in second class. Chinese women were much more likely to be detained than Chinese men but were not detained appreciably longer. Japanese were significantly more likely than Chinese to be detained but for substantially shorter periods. Substantial numbers of non-Asians, including many coming from Latin America and Russia, were detained.

This paper, jointly authored by Robert Barde and Gustavo Bobonis, and presented by Barde at the conference, has appeared in the Spring 2006 issue of *Social Science History*. It is available at *http://ssh.dukejournals.org/cgi/content/refs/30/1/103*.

On Chinese American Political Participation Since the Post-war Period

Critical Studies from Mainland China

(Original English title: On Chinese American Post-war Political Activities)

戰後美國華人參政研究的若干問題

Zhang Yinglong, PhD

張應龍

中國大陸研究美國華人問題主要集中在五個方面：(1) 美國華人移民史研究；(2) 美國排華研究；(3) 美國華人對中國的貢獻；(4) 美國華人人才研究；(5) 美國華人參政研究。在這五個方面的研究當中，移民史研究、排華問題研究和美國華人對中國的貢獻的研究起步較早，成果也多。至於美國華人人才與美國華人參政研究主要是在90年代左右才逐步興起。美國華人參政活動是作為研究戰後美國華人社會變遷的一個重要方面得到關注，因為研究美國華人社會融入當地主流社會的過程，華人參政活動是一個重要的指標。同時，在海外華人參政活動中，美國華人的參政活動佔有重要的地位，是研究海外華人參政活動的主要對象。作為發達國家華人參政活動的主要代表，研究美國華人參政活動，對研究海外華人參政活動，顯然具有重要的意義。

本文主要是對中國大陸有關美國華人參政活動的研究概況作一般性的述評，同時也就美國華人參政活動與馬來西亞華人參政活動作一個簡單的比較，以便對美國華人參政問題進行一些討論。

隔洋觀察：中國大陸美國華人參政研究述評

有關美國華人參政問題的研究，在中國大陸還不是熱門。

根據中國期刊全文資料庫和暨南大學圖書館華僑華人文獻信息中心專題資料庫的記錄，自1980年以來中國大陸發表的美國華人參政活動的論文大約28篇。這些成果以90年代以後發表的居多，尤其是90年代後期以後佔了18篇。隨著美國華人參政活動的發展，中國大陸對於美國華人參政問題的研究也將越來越多。

表1, 1978－2005年中國大陸美國華人參政問題研究成果統計

年份	1980－85年	1986－90年	1991－95年	1996－2000年	2001－05年
數量	1	6	3	6	12
比例	3.1%	21.4%	10.7%	21.4%	42.9%

此表是作者根據中國期刊全文資料庫 (1994－2005年) 和暨南大學圖書館華僑華人文獻信息中心專題資料庫的記錄編制而成。

表2, 中國大陸美國華人參政問題研究內容分類

內容	華人參政史	華人與美國大選	華人政治團體	社會政治環境
數量	18	2	4	4
比例	64.3%	7.1%	14.3%	14.3%

資料來源：同上表。

中國大陸對美國華人參政的研究主要集中在下列幾個問題：

(1) 華人參政歷史研究。主要有梅偉強《美國華人參政史探》,《世紀之交的美國華人：從漠視政治到積極參政》,陸宇生《美國華人參政的回顧與前瞻》,沈立新《美國華人參政的歷史與現狀》,李其榮《向主流社會邁進—近三十年美國華人參政分析》,莊國土《從移民到選民：1965年以來美國華人社會的發展變化》,郭玉聰《美國華人的參政熱潮及存在的問題》等。

梅偉強 將美國華人參政的歷史分為三個時期：(1) 萌芽期 (1943年以前)。以1895年陳德等土生華人發起組織的同源總局為開端,以夏威夷華人參政活動為萌芽階段,其表現是有好幾個華人當選為夏威夷准州參議員、眾議員、市議員等職。(2) 迅速成長期 (1943年—70年代)。1882年排華法案的廢除,60年代美國民權運動的興起,為華人參政創造了新的社會環境。華人參政意識興趣增強,在各級權力機構中任職的華人人數增多,在華人人數較少的邊遠州,華人參政活動有了起色,華裔婦女精英嶄露頭角。(3) 開花結果期 (80年代以後)。特點是參政人數多,任職範圍更廣,官階高,群體意識增強,婦女政績突出,知識階層起到領導作用。梅偉強認為,早期美國華人參政之所以夏威夷最為突出,原因是夏威夷華人人數較多,經濟實力較強,文化程度較高,受孫中山民主革命思想的薰陶,夏威夷排華活動和種族歧視比美國大陸輕。而當代美國華人參政熱潮的出現,原因主要是：(1) 美國政府對華人移民政策的轉變,為華人參政創造了前提條件。(2) 華人經濟實力大大增強,為華人參政創造了物質條件。(3) 華人文化程度提高,知識階層形成,為華人參政創造了領導條件。(4) 從落葉歸根到落地生根意識的轉變,是華人參政的思想基礎。(5) 土生華裔的增長,是華人參政的催化條件。(6) 中美建交,中國國際地位的提高,為華人參政開闢廣闊的前景。

李其榮 將美國華人參政分為兩個時期：(1) 20世紀40–70年代初期,特點是個別華人單槍匹馬進入政壇。(2) 70年代以後,特點是華裔精英分子群起參與美國政治；華人參政意識增強；大選中華人投票熱情高漲；華人參政人數多,層面廣,官階高；一批華裔政治女強人脫穎而出；反對種族歧視,維護華裔合法權益。沈立新 的分期與此相同。

莊國土 則以80年代中期為界,認為80年代中期以前華人的參政主要是通過個人的努力和選區的支持,80年代中期以後華人政治家的成功在相當大的程度上是依賴華人選民的支持。

關於美國華人政治參與度不高的原因。大多數學者認為,影響美國華人參政活動的擴大和參政水準的提高的原因是：(1) 華人社會幫派林立,缺乏團結協助的精神。(2) 不關心政治,政治參與熱情不高。(3) 美國主流社會的歧視。認為如果能夠走出派別、區域、黨派等的差別,以一個統一的聲音,為一個共同的目標—爭取華裔權益而奮鬥,就能迎來華人參政的新氣象。以上這些描述是對的,但只是表面的描述。事實上,社會是多元的,政治更是多元的,我們看不到那個國家那個族群有一個統一、一致的政治訴求。

(2) 美國華人與美國大選。主要有彭湛東《美國華人社會對美國大選的反應》,萬曉宏《從2002年美國中期選舉看華人參政》等。萬曉宏從2002年美國中期選舉中華人的表現,分析華人參政取得的進展和存在的問題,如較多華裔參選人分散了華人選票的作用,有些華人選民不瞭解候選人的綱領,只認定誰獲勝率高就投給誰,具有盲目性。該文也提出未來華人參政途徑的看法,如候選人的參政理念、競選政綱和做法需要更新,以便與選民形成良性的互動等。

(3) 華人政治團體研究。主要有沈燕清：《百人會與美國華人社會》,莊禮偉：《百人會在美中關係及華裔權益問題上所起的作用》,萬曉宏：《"80/20促進會"與美國華人參政新策略》等。

沈燕清與莊禮偉的論文對百人會 (Committee of 100) 的成立經過、宗旨和作用都做介紹。認為百人會的成立是美國華人參政達到一個新階段的標誌。百人會對促進華人的參政活動,提升華人的參政意識,維護華人的政治利益,促進中美關係的良性發展均發揮重要的作用。至於80/20促進會 (80/20 Initiative),萬曉宏的論文重點探討80/20促進會成立的原因、目標和宗旨,美國華人對80/20促進會競選策略的爭議,80/20促進會在大選中的影響力評估。最後,著重分析80/20促進會對美國華人參政新策略的影響和意義,認為80/20促進會的出現是美國華人參政意識趨於成熟和理性的表現,是美國華人參政方式的重大突破，提高了亞裔整體參政意識，是亞裔參政邁出的歷史性一步。

(4) 社會環境與華人參政的關係。主要有陳文鑫：《中美關係視野中的美國華人》，陳奕平《當代美國亞裔參政問題分析》，莊禮偉《美國政治環境與美國華裔：衝擊與反應》等。

莊禮偉認為美國華人參政受到文明衝突論、中美關係的波動，美國政治週期的變化的影響。陳文鑫認為美國華人作為一個相對邊緣的群體，其參政活動必須要與美國主流社會的政治傾向保持一致，其作用受到美國主流社會政治議程的影響。陳奕平認為美國亞裔（包括華人）參政水準較低的原因有政治經濟、社會環境、社會心理、社會文化、制度與歧視等因素的影響，所以，亞裔的參政水準不如黑人和西裔。

在中國大陸有關美國華人參政的研究當中，王少如對第一次世界大戰到第二次世界大戰期間三藩市和紐約唐人街政治風潮的研究是為數極少、較為具體的美國參政史研究。他以三藩市的美洲工藝同盟總會、革命工餘俱樂部和紐約華僑衣館聯合會為重點，分析了兩次世界大戰期間唐人街的政治活動。可惜，這種具體的研究個案在以後的研究中沒有得到延續。

回顧中國大陸海外華人研究的變化過程，中國大陸的海外華人研究也是經歷了從"落葉歸根"到"落地生根"的變化。即：過去從中國的立場出發，注重研究海外華人與中國的關係、海外華人對中國的貢獻等問題；現在從海外華社的立場出發，注重研究海外華人社會在當地的生存與發展問題。這種研究立足點的變化，對正確認識海外華人社會的變遷，提升中國大陸海外華人研究水準是很有幫助的。

總的來說，中國大陸研究者對美國華人參政問題的焦點聚集在華人參政史和中美關係變動對華人參政的影響這兩大方面，在展望美國華人參政前景時絕大多數人喜歡將中美關係與華人參政的前途結合起來討論。顯然，研究參政史是必要的，分析參政背景、原因也是必要的，但要推進研究的深入，僅僅是宏觀的敍述是不夠的。雖然中美關係的變化對華人參政產生一些影響，但不是很大，過多強調中美關係變化與美國華人參政的關係，容易造成忽視華人參政主流發展的傾向。

從中國大陸有關美國華人參政研究的狀況來看，主要存在以下幾個問題：

(1) 沒有形成一個穩定的隊伍。研究者基本是個人行為，沒有形成一個研究團隊，資料不能共用，研究者本人缺乏長期的跟蹤研究，從而影響到研究的深度和廣度。從事海外華人研究，毫無疑問需要在研究對象國進行實地調查，獲得感性認識，以便在解讀資料時能夠抓住問題的本質。實地調查還可以獲得更多的第一手資料，這對開展研究都是十分重要的。可是，中國大陸研究美國華人參政問題的學者大多數沒有這樣的經歷，因此，其研究成果的品質、水準存在不少問題。

(2) 缺乏專業的背景。作為美國華人研究的學者，應該具有美國史專業出身的背景，應該以美國歷史與現狀為研究對象。研究美國華人參政問題，不能離開美國具體的社會環境，只有將華人參政問題放到美國社會政治的大背景下才能得到符合實際的解釋。可是，中國大陸研究美國華人參政問題的學者只有少數是以研究美國問題為主攻方向的。因而，研究成果有時難免有與實際不符的感覺。從事參政問題研究需要有政治學的專業訓練，掌握相關研究技能，但中國大陸研究美國華人參政問題的學者差不多都是歷史學專業出身，雖然在實際研究中試圖使用政治學的研究方法，但實際上所擁有的專業素養相當有限，這對他們進行華人參政問題的研究工作產生很大的影響。

(3) 研究以宏觀敍述為主。顯而易見，中國大陸對美國華人參政問題的研究以宏觀研究為主，微觀研究、個案研究極少，在資料的利用上也是大同小異，所分析的原因和結論也相差不遠，總之，給人的印象有雷同的感覺。

(4) 研究資料來源單一。從中國大陸有關美國華人參政的研究論文中可以看出，其資料的收集和利用基本上局限於華文報刊資料，對許多外國學者的用英文寫成的研究成果極少利用，這在很大程度上限制了中國大陸學者利用外國研究成果來提高自身研究水準的可能性。

比較視野：馬來西亞與美國的華人參政活動

馬來西亞華人參政活動是海外華人參政活動一個重要的範例。從比較的視野將美國華人參政問題與馬來西亞華人參政問題作一個比較，也許有助於我們更加深刻、全面的認識海外華人參政問題。

馬來西亞華人參政活動至少可以追溯到19世紀。回眸馬來西亞華人政治史，百餘年來的華人政治經歷了四大高潮：辛亥革命，抗日救國運動高潮，社會主義運動高潮，民主政治高潮。這四大政治高潮構成馬來西亞華人政治史的基本框架。伴隨四大政治高潮的政治思潮是愛國主義和民族主義，社會主義，民主自由思潮。其領導力量在第一和第二次高潮時是華團領袖，在第二次高潮是政黨，在第三次高潮是政治精英（"三結合"、"華團宣言"、"兩線制"是由依託華團的精英人士大力提倡，然後由政黨承接進行）。四大政治高潮的不同之處是政治目標不同，共同之處是實現了社會政治大動員。

回顧馬來西亞華人政治史，華人政治參與的取向首先決定於政治認同的異同。在20世紀上半期，華人的政治認同對象以中國為主，並含有對馬來西亞的政治認同。二戰結束後，對中國的政治認同迅速減低，對馬來西亞政治認同佔了上風，雙重認同逐步匯合成對馬來西亞的單一認同。受政治認同的影響，在二戰以前，華人社會除了一部分人（如華人社會領導層、土生華人、部分文化人，等等）比較積極參與當地的事務之外，大部分華人比較關心中國的現實問題，而對當地的政治不甚感興趣。當日本不斷擴大對中國的侵略活動時，在愛國主義、民族主義的激勵下，華人社會掀起面向中國的大規模政治活動。儘管華人以中國為對象的大規模政治活動似乎與馬來西亞無關，但它為華人日後進行其他對象的政治活動奠下基礎。當認同對象變化時，華人就能用比較成熟的方式開展政治活動。由於有了前期的"實習"，華人社會很快就適應獨立後馬來西亞議會民主的制度安排，能夠很快從僑民心態轉變過來，以國家主人翁的姿態組織本土色彩的政黨，提出黨綱，發動民眾，通過選舉等途徑，直接參與馬來西亞的國家政治建設，展開自己政治鬥爭和政治追求。

獨立以來馬來西亞華人參政熱情先是高漲，後趨於平緩。在90年代以前，面對民族利益的整體危機，馬來西亞華人表現出非常昂揚的政治熱情，即使為此身陷牢獄也無畏無懼，前仆後繼。90年代以後，在政治局勢日趨緩和的背景下，華人的熱情逐步減少，重要華人社團出現解去政治化的傾向，對反對黨的支持力度也大不如以前，華人政治思潮更加多元化，而不是以前的兩元化對立。

馬來西亞華人參政活動的特點主要有：

(1) 以華人社會為基礎。馬來西亞的政治特點就是以族群為基礎進行政治活動，馬來西亞三大民族的執政黨都只限于本族人民的參加，華人執政黨馬華公會 (Malaysian Chinese Association) 明文規定只有華人才能加入。雖然也有一些政黨以跨族群的名義出現，但在實際上是以某個族群為主導的運作模式，例如民政黨 (The Gerakan Raayat Malaysia)、民主行動黨 (Democratic Action Party) 等。馬來西亞歷史上曾經出現一些跨族群的政黨，最後都以失敗告終。曾經幾次組建過多元族群政治聯盟，也是很快就解體。馬來西亞華人政黨以及政治組織的政治綱領是以華人利益為依歸，不論那個華人政黨或者政治派別，在從事政治活動和大選中，都標榜自己是華人社會的政治代表，自己是捍衛華人社會利益的鬥士。一些華人政黨，由於政治夥伴的約束，有時在關係華人社會利益上表現含糊，便遭到華人社會的大力抨擊，結果在大選時被華人選民所拋棄。

(2) 擁有雄厚的群眾參政基礎。從辛亥革命以來，馬來西亞華人在各種政治運動的薰陶下，歷經歷練，參政意識相當高。不但在歷次大選中華人群眾踴躍投票，而且在遇到關係華人社會根本利益時群起相應。獨立以後，馬來西亞華人掀起的一次次政治運動就是例子。

(3) 同時擁有華人執政黨和反對黨。華人執政黨有馬華公會、民政黨和沙撈越人民聯合黨 (The Sarawak United People's Party) 等，反對黨有民主行動黨。無論是執政黨還是反對黨都擁有一批忠貞分子，相對而言，城市華人多支持反對黨，鄉村華人多支持執政黨。

(4) 華人在全國人口總數中所佔的比例較高。在新加坡未脫離馬來西亞之前，華人是第一大族群，如果不算新加坡，華人人口在1957年馬來亞獨立時佔有35.6%，即使到現在，華人所佔比例仍佔有24.5%。因此，華人族群很難被邊緣化，而華人社會參與國家政治的主動性很強。

(5) 擁有傑出的政治領袖。馬華公會創始人陳禎祿、華文教育領袖林連玉、反對黨領袖林吉祥等在不同歷史時期扮演華人社會政治領袖的角色，這些魅力型的政治領袖對推動華人社會的參政活動起到很大的作用。

不過, 馬來西亞華人與美國華人面臨著同樣的問題:

(1) 種族歧視問題。馬來西亞在法律上明文規定馬來人優先的基本原則, 馬來人在政治上、經濟上、文化上、教育上均擁有不可爭辯的優勢。同時, 馬來人優先的原則是不可置疑和挑戰的, 否則就是"違法", 是"種族主義"。總之, 在受歧視方面, 馬來西亞華人面臨的困難不比美國華人小。

(2) 內部不團結問題。華人社會不但存在不同的政治派別, 而且還存在支持執政黨和反對黨的分歧。在大選時, 馬來西亞不同政治派別的華人集中在華人社會內展開爭奪戰, 情況激烈, 每次都產生嚴重後遺症。馬來西亞華人社會認識分裂影響華人政治力量的表現, 曾經發動過幾次團結運動, 最後卻以分裂告終。

(3) 在民主制度下受到非民主的排斥。在馬來西亞, 執政者喜歡標榜馬來西亞擁有民主制度, 即使在種族關係緊張以及政治局勢處於動盪的情況下, 馬來西亞的大選從來沒有因此延期或者取消, 以此宣揚民主制度真實性。可是, 馬來西亞執政者常常運用制度與法律的手段壓制華人社會, 限制華人社會的合法權益。在美國這個號稱民主的國度裏, 以民主制度的名義對少數族裔的排斥也是司空見慣。

美國華人社會與馬來西亞華人社會不同的是:

(1) 華人人口在美國全國人口中占的比例較小。華人只占美國總人口的1%左右, 分佈在廣袤的國土上, 華人參政活動難以出現馬來西亞那樣的洶湧澎湃的場面。不但如此, "靠強調少數民族問題和華人投票而希望當選的任何華人, 不會有多大收穫"。因此, 目前人們熱衷討論的觀點就是華人可以成為"關鍵的少數", 以此激勵華人積極參政, 踴躍投票, 以間接方式施加政治影響力。

(2) 沒有建立全國性的華人政黨。在美國現行的政治制度下, 美國華人很難自己組織政黨作為華人社會的政治代表, 負起政治動員和政治領導的責任。華人參政活動基本上被納入美國的兩黨政治體系, 美國華人主要是通過組織各種政治組織來進行各種政治活動。

(3) 華人政治代表面向的是選區的全體選民。例如, 駱家輝所在的華盛頓州, 居民89%是白人。駱家輝當選華盛頓州長是因為他的政治主張和價值觀得到大多數選民的認同和支援, 並不是華人社會支持的結果。出任各級官員的華人, 情況也與此相差不遠, 他們所依託的政治基礎不是以華人社會為主。華人政治人物之所以能夠在華人人數很少的地方勝出, 可能與美國文化有關。有一種觀點認為, 在美國, 個人意識和種族群體之間的互動和演變相當普遍, 像黑人歌星黑人球星喜歡自認是美國歌星和美國球星。白人選民支持駱家輝大概是認為他是美國人而不是華人。

(4) 與此相聯繫的是, 華人政治人物與華人社會基層普羅大眾的關係不是十分密切, 互動關係比較薄弱。對於華人社會來說, 政治人物的象徵意義大於實際意義。政治精英們一般是追求本階級的利益, 往往攀附主流社會的一些勢力集團, 以此培植本身集團的利益。而在馬來西亞, 許多華人議員服務的選區居民基本是華人居民為主體, 雙方的互動很密切。

(5) 美國華人社會的構成遠比馬來西亞複雜。馬來西亞自獨立以來, 限制外來的華人移民, 馬來西亞華人人口的增長基本是本土出生人數的增長。美國作為移民國家, 華人社會的來源包括本土出生的土生華人、臺灣移民、港澳及其他國家的移民、中國大陸移民, 這些移民到達美國的時間也不一致, 教育背景、思想意識、行為習慣、政治立場、經濟地位等相差甚遠, 因此美國華人社會呈現多元化的鮮明特徵。就對中國的政治立場來說, 美國華人社會存在親大陸與親臺灣的政治分歧, 而在馬來西亞, 這種政治分歧只是發生在獨立時期。美國華人社會的複雜性還在於她的變動性, 即不斷有新移民的移入。

從馬來西亞和美國華人參政歷史來看, 土生華人在參與當地政治方面比"新客"(華僑)要積極的多, 最初華人參政除了華人社團領袖被當地政府委任為某種官職之外, 自己主動參與當地政治的是土生華人或者當地化程度較深的華人。同時, 政治思潮對激發華人參政高潮起到非常重要的作用。例如, 60年代馬來西亞的社會主義運動與美國的民權運動等。

戰後美國華人參政的代表是走出唐人街的社會精英, 是融入當地社會的社會精英。從當選各級政治代表的華人的個人經歷來看，基本屬於這種模式。戰後美國華人參政所取得的成就，主要是參政者對美國政治文化的認同和社會責任感的認同，他們的思想意識、行為習慣、價值觀符合主流社會的口味。通過選舉或者通過委任出任各種公職的政治精英，大多數不是來自華人社會的推動，不是來自華人社會的支持。不像在馬來西亞，通過選舉，華人執政黨可以根據大選的成績分配相應的政府官職。由於美國華人沒有自己族群的政黨，華人參政主要依託的政黨是美國共和民主兩黨，所以，即使在華人人數很少的地方或者華人選民根本不起作用的地方也能通過選舉成為議員，這在馬來西亞是難以想像的。

美國華人參政活動，常常面臨種族認同與社會認同的困擾，並造成華人民眾參與政治活動時的不同取向：到底是積極融入主流社會，爭取華人平等權益的保障，改善生存環境，還是以族群為界線，只選擇涉及華人利益議程的政治活動？採取種族認同的華人，只關心看到涉及華人利益議程，對融入主流社會，通過社會參與來維護華人的權益的途徑有些淡漠，因此，對參加選舉投票不是那麼熱心，認為結果都一樣。當然，影響華人投票熱情還有其他的原因。對於那些被當作華人驕傲的政治代表，不少華人認為他們不是代表華人的利益。客觀事實表明，不積極融入主流社會，積極參與社會活動，只限于華人社會的小圈子，華人參政活動難以取得成效。客觀事實也表明，華人政治精英如果不積極加強與華人社會的聯繫和互動，便可能陷於"解去華人化"，難以成為真正的華人社會政治代表。種族認同與社會認同的衝突，應該是影響美國華人參政廣度與深度的主要因素。

毫無疑問，這些年來美國華人參政活動空前活躍，出任國會議員、州議員、市議員以及各級政府官員的華人可以列出長長的名單。據介紹，目前在美國31個州之中，有2000多名亞裔通過選舉或者委任擔任各種公職。布什總統在第二任開始6個多月裏，就任命了289位亞裔出任聯邦公職，其中大部分是華人。今年9月中旬，紐約州長和紐約市長雙雙造訪紐約中華公所，決定將3200萬美元撥給華埠，作為發展建設之用。由此可見，華人參政活動取得重要的進展，在社會上發揮了越來越大的作用，而華人的政治力量也受到美國政府的重視，這些都是華人積極參政的結果。

結　語

不同國家的華人社會由於所處具體環境以及歷史背景，社會文化的不同，其參政的經驗也有很大的不同。

美國華人與馬來西亞華人分別代表兩種類型的華人參政模式。在美國，走出唐人街的華人參政熱情較高，成就也顯著，但他們主要不是依靠的華人社會的政治支持，因此，其政治特徵具有跨族群性。儘管有眾多的華人進入政治領域，但一般華人的政治參與度依然不高，換句話說，兩者的互動關係不強，結果，華人政治人物的數量與華人社會的政治參與度難以成正比。在馬來西亞，華人政治人物的命運常常決定于所在選區華人的政治參與態度，兩者之間存在密切的互動關係。馬來西亞華人政黨和政治人物的生存決定于華人社會的政治熱情與支持。在馬來西亞，華文教育議題是整個華人社會最關切的議題，為了維護華文教育的權利，馬來西亞華人掀起一次次政治運動，並形成華教運動，這種運動得到不同黨派不同政治立場的華人的共同支持，從而推動了馬來西亞華人參政活動的發展。雖然，有關華人合法權益、平等權益等議題也備受關注，但它無法像華文教育議題一樣激起整個華人社會的熱情。在美國華人參政活動中，顯然缺乏一個能夠激起全體華人社會政治熱情的議題，這大概也是美國華人參政的一個重大瓶頸。

比較不同國家華人的參政經驗，其意義不在於獲得一種標準來作為實踐的指導，而在於可以使我們獲得一種新的感受，可以引起我們更多的思考，從而加深我們對所研究問題的認識。

Reclaimed Stories
Chinatown, Oakland, California
(Original Title: Oakland's Chinese Pioneers: A Forgotten Generation)
William Wong

The story of Chinese America is complex and multifaceted. One significant segment is the adaptability and survival of the immigrants and descendants of the so-called Pearl River Delta Chinese, those who founded many Chinatowns in the United States in the mid-1800s. First-person accounts of the earliest immigrants are practically nonexistent. It is now impossible to capture their stories. But capturing the stories of their descendants is possible, especially descendants of first-generation U.S.-born children who grew up in or near a Chinatown in the 1910s and 1920s.

My oral history project, "Reclaimed Stories: Chinatown, Oakland, California," attempts to capture a piece of the first-generation's story. That generation represents an important link between the Exclusion Era and the post-World War II generations, some of whom grew up at a time when legal segregation against ethnic Chinese in the United States had ended.

Art Tom's mother, Emma Hoo Tom, was a pioneer. She and Clara Lee were the first two Chinese American women to register to vote in the United States. Both women were from Oakland's Chinatown. They made history in 1911, when California women were given the right to vote by the California Legislature. That was nine years before other American women were given the right to vote. Emma Hoo Tom's son, Art, opened the first Chinese-owned gasoline station in Oakland's Chinatown. In 1935, he became the first Chinese American employee of the California Department of Motor Vehicles. Art Tom passed away in March 2006 at the age of 93.

Jean Moon Liu is one of the surviving granddaughters of Lew Hing, a rarity in his day as a Chinese American industrialist who founded the Pacific Coast Canning Company in 1904 in West Oakland. Jean Moon Liu was a rarity herself, having graduated from the University of California at Berkeley in 1939, when relatively few Chinese American women got a higher education. Her daughter, Carol Liu, is a member of the California State Assembly, representing Pasadena.

Dr. Richard Fong was the first son of the legendary Fong Wan, an Oakland herbalist who gained fame nationally through his aggressive marketing in mainstream English-language newspapers. Dr. Fong was one of the first Chinese American medical students in St. Louis, Missouri. He was one of the earliest Chinese American interns at Highland Hospital, in the early 1940s. He had a successful Western medical practice in Oakland until his death early in 2005.

These are but three of the stories this oral history project hopes to document, in authentic, first-person voices. Visit *http://www.oaklandchinatownhistory.org* for a work-in-progress website housing their stories.

Driven Out
Roundups and Resistance of the Chinese in Rural California
Jean Pfaelzer, PhD

Early Friday evening, February 2, 1885, David Kendall, a city councilman, was caught in the cross fire as two Chinese men shot at each other in Eureka, California, a small fishing and lumber town on the foggy north coast. Kendall died instantly, and a crowd quickly gathered, chanting "Burn Chinatown." In less than twenty minutes, some six hundred white men met in Centennial Hall, a few blocks from Chinatown, and determined that all Chinese had to leave Eureka. A committee of six men was chosen to go to Chinatown and tell the Chinese they had twenty-four hours to leave. That night an effigy of a Chinese man hung from a gallows on the edge of Chinatown. Pinned to the gallows was a sign announcing "Any Chinese seen on the street after three o'clock today will be hung." Two Chinese men fled into the redwoods and were caught; the rest complied. By Saturday morning, twenty-three loads of Chinese people and their clothing and household goods were gathered on the docks. Small skiffs carried the Chinese to two steam ships that happened to be in Humboldt Bay; 135 people were loaded onto the *Humboldt*, 175 were loaded onto the *City of Chester*. By nightfall, the tide was out, and the laden ships could not set sail until early Sunday morning. With a strong wind from the north, the ships reached San Francisco early Monday. The Customs House was still closed from the weekend, and the Chinese people disembarked quickly and disappeared into the safety of Chinatown. Meanwhile, in Eureka, the citizens immediately regathered and announced that all remaining Chinese people in Humboldt County would be expelled, that no Chinese could ever again settle in Eureka, and that no one in the county could ever again rent to or hire a Chinese person. In two days the Chinese community in Eureka was erased. But on Monday afternoon, the Chinese who had been expelled from Eureka regathered in San Francisco and announced that they were going to sue Eureka for being the objects of mob violence, for the loss of their property, and for being driven out.

"Driven Out: Roundups and Resistance of the Chinese in Rural California," stems from my forthcoming book *Driven Out: Roundups and Resistance of Chinese People in the Pacific North West, 1850-1906* (Random House 2006) and describes the expulsions of Chinese people from over one hundred rural towns, from Southern California to including Washington Territory—in Eureka, Truckee, Red Bluff, Crescent City, and Fresno. Opening with the story of the Eureka's "roundup," "Driven Out" exposes and analyzes the purges and the failed purges, and describes the many successful efforts of Chinese resistance—legal, militant, legislative, and passive—as well as what I believe to be the first lawsuit for reparations in the United States, *Wing Hing v. the City of Eureka, 1886*. It considers the mass actions of passive resistance by 110,000 Chinese people in 1892–1893 who risked deportation by collectively refusing to carry photo-identity cards under the Geary Act. The talk includes slides of the various roundups, from the 1871 lynching in Los Angeles to the burning of Chinatown, San Jose. "Driven Out" ends with photographs of the 1906 "final" roundup of Chinese cannery workers along the Eel River near Ferndale, California (who were held in railroad boxcars on "Indian Island" or Gunther Island in Humboldt Bay—the site of the 1862 massacre of the Wyott tribe), successfully refusing deportation until they were paid for their full season's contract.

The relationship between China and the overseas Chinese and the relationship between China and the United States put these expulsions in a global context of migration, trade, and expansion. In many ways the expulsions of Chinese people were connected to movements against indigenous peoples and to lynchings and land deprivation of African Americans during Reconstruction. The model for these expulsions came first from the Black Codes of the Southern Democrats who, by the 1880s, had taken over California's governor mansion, state legislature, and many local county boards, mayors, and so on, and second, by the mass removal of native people onto reservations, which was happening close by. The roundups of Chinese immigrants foretell the ideology and methods of later expulsions against Mexican immigrants and Japanese Americans.

In order to resist the purges and assure legal remedies for being driven out, early Chinese Americans redefined the concept of "belonging" by attaching legal status to a diasporic community. Not only did they create original legal definitions of the duty of cities to protect all of their residents, but they also redefined the Fourteenth Amendment, appropriating its language of the right of "persons"—not just citizens—to due process of law. They filed early lawsuits for police harassment in San Jose. The appropriation of the law helped to forge and sustain early Chinese communities during the era of the roundups, claim restitution, and assert "belonging" to the country that was redefining its own geographical and ethnic identity. In particular, in the first lawsuit for reparations in 1886, fifty-five Chinese people sued Eureka in the U.S. Circuit Court to recover $132,000 in damages ($75,000 for injuries to property and $58,000 for the loss of business, for the loss of opportunity to collect debts owed by their white customers, and for being driven out of the city by a mob). Ultimately, the Chinese lost the suit because they did not and could not own land in Eureka, could not testify against whites, and were prevented by vigilante activities from returning to the area. But in the act of bringing *Wing Hing*, the expelled community quickly regrouped, and the lawsuit itself became an effective warning and sounded across the state against similar treatment of the Chinese. It put other cities on guard.

Other actions did prevail: China and the overseas Chinese forced the U.S. government to provide $140,000 in indemnity for the violence against the Chinese in the infamous Rock Springs riot; $8,000 for the Tacoma, Washington, riots; and financial compensation for the purge in Redding, California. The Chinese consuls forced legal actions against vigilantes in Wheatland and Sacramento. These cases undercut the view that China left its immigrants stranded, that their homeland denied their very presence abroad. These lawsuits by Chinese immigrants anticipated legal actions pursued by Japanese Americans for reparation and restitution of property following their removal to camps during World War II.

In the process of testifying on their own behalf, the nineteenth-century Chinese left a hitherto unread set of writings about their own lives. These testimonials against the roundups are the most expansive voices of nineteenth-century Chinese Americans, and speak to their transnational self-definition. These testimonials become a place where the silenced voices of nineteenth-century Chinese immigrants from rural towns can be heard.

Aggressive resistance to the purges supports the view that Chinese immigrants were profoundly engaged with the institutions and possibilities of life in the United States, and hence did not view themselves as "sojourners." These responses—legal cases, Chinese labor strikes, purchasing arms from China, flatly refusing to leave towns, and ultimately the refusal to wear identity cards—also dispute a set of cultural stereotypes of the Chinese. The roundups, purges, expulsions, and pogroms of Chinese people in the nineteenth century reveal both similarities and differences in anti-Chinese and anti-black discrimination; they reveal how the particularities of difference—immigration and enslavement, geography and demography, familiarity with dominant cultural practices based on the duration of residence in the United States—become critical to our understanding of Chinese American history. The Chinese acts of resistance to purges is built on the assumption within critical race theory that focuses on a desire not merely to understand the vexed bond between law and racial power but to change it.

Return of the "Heathen Chinee"
Stereotypes in Chinese American Archaeology
Kelly Fong

The following paper is an excerpt from my University of California, Berkeley, Anthropology senior honors thesis on Chinese American historical archaeology and stereotype, that is, pervasive, preconceived, and usually racialized notions regarding a particular group of people. While the full paper goes into more detail regarding stereotype's influential role in archaeology and its alarming consequences, this segment examines and evaluates the field in light of powerful, hegemonic, nineteenth-century stereotypes.

In 1850, a New York public school surveyed its upper-grade students on their knowledge of China. The results proved to be mixed, contradictory, and conflicted; in addition to a girl's statement that "China is known for tea and also for the peculiar caracter [sic] of its inhabitants," numerous responses commented on "the Chinese taste for puppy dogs, cats, rats, or other vermin."[1] Culturally immersed in this line of thought from childhood, anti-Asian sentiment in the realm of children echoed the cries of the adult world. According to Presbyterian missionary Reverend Ira B. Condit:

> As an illustration of the feeling toward the Chinaman, the children in one of the primary schools in San Francisco had brought an American flag for their use. When the teacher asked them for some sentiment to inscribe upon it, one little fellow said, "The Chinese must go."[2]

With generations raised to believe that this phenomenon was irrefutable truth, the prowess of the "heathen Chinee" stereotype grew stronger, and the image became more vividly defined and pervasive. The representation effectively functioned like folklore—that is, it was passed from generation to generation like a prized family heirloom, something everyone knew and impossible to entirely smother.

Since mainstream American society accepted and, to a certain degree, continues to accept this "heathen Chinee" as factual common sense, this image became *the* representation of Chinese Americans. This history therefore falls victim to the fate of marginalized (and, in the eyes of hegemonic society, "lesser") populations. Deemed as unimportant compared to the largely white male elite, the documentary record has tended to overlook these people, providing only minimal evidence of their existence in dry governmental documents. Mainstream popular ideas and representations fill the gaps, yielding an overpowering, stereotype-driven fable in history's master narrative. Consequently, history rendered these groups voiceless by a lack of self-representation.

"As one of the few objective sources of data available for reconstructing" the past, archaeologists Marley R. Brown, III and Kathleen Bragdon write, "archaeological remains become very significant."[3] By drawing upon multiple lines of evidence to interpret the past, historical archaeology possesses great potential to overcome historical biases, omissions, and errors. Because all individuals, regardless of ethnicity or socioeconomic status, impact the archaeological record, archaeology ideally equalizes people in the past. It can become "the unearthing, literally and figuratively, of a history once silent—of individuals, of families, and of businesses that were rarely acknowledged" by written history.[4]

Consequently, archaeology can be, as Asian Americanists Yuko Matsukawa and Josephine Lee, and Asian Americanist/archaeologist Imogene L. Lim call for, "a revisionist project."[5] Focusing specifically on researching Asian American communities, Matsukawa, Lee, and Lim advocate this kind of project to confront "the conspicuous absence of Asian Americans in 'official' histories and correcting stereotypes, myths, and false assumptions."[6] Archaeology can be used to "supplement and corroborate the documentary record" with material culture, which is "superior to the historian's documents for studying changes in ethnic boundaries."[7]

Archaeology in reality, however, deviates from the field's potential to provide more proportionate representations of history than written history. Not only do archaeologists covet particular sites, but material culture is also subject to researchers' conscious and unconscious interpretive biases, similar to those reflected in the documentary record—the very biases they attempt to evade. This is precisely what Asian American archaeology suffers from under the influence of stereotype. Since the mid-nineteenth century when Chinese immigrants began arriving in the Americas, they have been constant victims of Western obsession, awe, amazement, and Orientalism. Western society clearly expressed these sentiments in derogatory, racist representations—that is, the opium-addicted, rat/cat/dog-eating, abnormal, foreign, exotic, alien, and therefore nonassimilable "heathen Chinee."

This image, while over one hundred years old, has not disappeared over the course of the twentieth century. Deeply embedded in the psyche of mainstream American society as a "fundamental assumption of American culture," essentializing stereotypes of the Chinese continue to persist through time.[8] They manifest themselves in a variety of media from the mass media to literature and, most importantly to this paper, archaeological analyses. While adopting these manufactured racial assumptions is likely to be unconscious and entirely unintentional, the outcome is the same as if it were intentional; stereotype-infused analyses contribute to stereotype perpetuation.

William Wu wisely observes that "[s]uch an assumption [as stereotype] is especially dangerous, when it is unrecognized, and can cause Americans to evaluate current events, for instance, in a particular way without a sound rationale."[9] I extend Wu's argument to include the peril of not recognizing the effect of stereotype in contemporary interpretations of all media of history. Acknowledging its powerful role in Chinese American archaeology is therefore crucial to the field's future development. How does archaeology, remaining under the sway of antiquated preconceptions, effect and further perpetuate warped history? How can Chinese American archaeology avoid stagnation in this nineteenth-century perspective and move away from the dangers of racialized biases?

By criticizing stereotype's influential role in past analyses, my intent is to condemn neither historical archaeology nor its undeniably significant contributions, and to these questions, I offer no one answer. Instead, I seek to raise archaeology's level of awareness by examining the field's history and acknowledging its shortcomings. I seek to augment an existing body of work by encouraging new methods of self-reflexivity, potentially via interdisciplinary work that integrates Asian American Studies into archaeological analyses.

As a discipline, historical archaeology has only recently begun moving beyond Euro-Americans, in terms of both who prominent historical archaeologists are and their subjects of study. Chinese American archaeology emerged in the late 1960s, but existing projects have been overwhelmingly limited to the realm of the Cultural Resources Management (CRM)—that is, archaeology in a salvage archaeology context. Legal requirements such as the 1966 National Historic Preservation Act forced developers to hire archaeologists, who realized these sites had been occupied by historic Chinese Americans.

In sites excavated out of law-induced necessity and allotted a short time frame, unfortunately, analyses involve less specialized archaeologists trained to interpret a variety of sites from prehistoric to historic, Chinese to Anglo to Native American. Roberta Greenwood, an archaeologist noted for her Chinese American CRM work, notices these researchers usually lack sufficient knowledge required for accurate and comprehensive analyses.[10] This may result in incorrect identification and cataloging of artifacts as well as the inability to read necessary non-English languages. Greenwood consequently deems these researchers unqualified for adequate work on non-English American sites. Despite her 1993 criticism, Asian American archaeology remains without the specialized knowledge she believes is essential for more accurate analyses. Instead, the field perpetuates the pattern of the Euro-American studying the "Other" from a Euro-American perspective—that is, an "etic" (outsider/descriptive) perspective instead of an "emic" (insider/understanding) analytical framework.[11]

Stereotype and the "etic," sadly, have traditionally dominated Chinese American historical archaeology. Stereotype most notably appears in archaeologists' overwhelming research interest in opium habits, foodways, and the question of assimilation/acculturation (or lack thereof) into mainstream Euro-American society. Regarding opium, for example, many archaeological reports spend a great deal of time discussing this sensationalized topic, from detailing Chinese opium habits and the proper way to prepare and smoke opium, to attempting to analyze and classify pipe fragments and other related materials. An example of this is in Priscilla Wegars' 1993 edited volume *Hidden Heritage: Historical Archaeology of the Overseas Chinese*, where approximately 75 pages, or nearly 20 percent of the text, discuss opium habits. Likewise, Riverside Chinatown's 1987 report contains a large volume of text devoted to opium. Studies on the drug and its paraphernalia make up nearly 60 percent of the 120-page section devoted to "The Pleasures" and almost 14 percent of the report's massive, 500-page second volume as a whole. Assuming these works proportionally discuss Chinese American lifestyles, it is difficult to believe opium consumed 14–20 percent of the average Chinese American's time. They draw, however, from the overly simplified reduction of opium smoking as inherent to Chinese culture, yielding the racialized image that Chinese men are incorrigible opium-addicts who wasted their free time in a smoke-induced stupor.

Studying foodways is similarly problematic, where stereotypes surrounding Chinese cuisine run rampant. Stereotype dictates that the Chinese consumed rats, cats, and dogs—species Western standards deemed inedible and repulsive. Shades of this rhetoric appear in Chinese American archaeological analyses, which describe Chinese cuisine as "highly distinctive" and "eclectic."[12] The influence of food preconceptions permeates further into analyses when archaeologists study faunal remains, calculating species ratios, and specifically noting the presence or absence of cat, rat, and dog bones as well as duck and pig feet.

Most notably and most pervasive (verging to the point of obsession) is the use of archaeological remains to answer the notorious assimilation/acculturation question—that is, whether the Chinese joined the Great American "melting pot" or if they retained their "distinct," "foreign," and "exotic" ways. This quest for an archaeologically-derived answer frames research questions and dictates how archaeologists execute their analyses. The research inquiry for a cannery site, for example, was to determine "how they [the Chinese] adopted [sic] to the dominant American culture" because "[t]he variety and types of artifacts of non-Chinese origin associated with artifacts of Chinese origin were expected to provide information about Chinese self-sufficiency and degree of acculturation."[13] To answer this question, analyses guided by these agendas commonly adopt what I describe as the "theory of replacement." The "theory of replacement" is the methodology in which archaeologists categorize artifacts by their supposed ethnicity and then calculate ratios to "scientifically" reach conclusions via statistics. Under this methodology, statistics yielding higher proportions of "American" artifacts to "ethnic" artifacts indicate an assimilated population and the inverse indicates nonassimilation. Overly simplified, not only does this explanation reduce Chinese American life to a black and white binary of assimilation or nonassimilation, but it also overlooks a wide range of external factors affecting individual choice and contributing to this archaeological pattern, such as access to particular goods. This methodology, then, effectively ignores historical context in favor of answering the ever-popular, unanswered assimilation question.

With these problematic practices, Chinese American historical archaeology clearly has much work to do. While the field must also increase its supply of cultural relativism and historical context in analyses, it is absolutely essential that Chinese American archaeology shifts from a Euro-American "etic" epistemology to an "emic" analytical perspective that centers the voice of the studied population. While this initially requires self-reflexivity to identify stereotypes, the process of divorcing its influence may be as simple as changing ceramic taxonomy from the descriptive Euro-American names based on perceived function or design to the names that the archaeological population utilized. Furthermore, following African American historical archaeology's example, as with the work of Teresa Singleton (1985, 1999) and Maria Franklin (2000), Chinese American archaeology would benefit from incorporating Asian American Studies and Asian American historical archaeologists into the discipline.

As a "decentering model," Asian American Studies would incorporate the descendant voice into archaeology, yielding a more "emic" perspective.[14] This new direction will permit archaeologists to interpret the archaeological record from the eyes of the community and consequently reduce the influence of stereotype. It would redirect the field from the historically-rooted Occident-Orient paradigm to one that ideally centralizes the voice of the studied population. This, in turn, will refocus archaeological research agendas from answering the assimilation/acculturation question to simply investigating the everyday life of these populations. Most importantly, this shift will encourage historical archaeology to become increasingly responsible for accurately representing the voices and histories of documentary-marginalized communities through what they leave behind—that is, the archaeological record. Thus, while my evaluation of Asian American archaeology makes the history of the field look grim, it is possible for archaeology to free itself from the powerful hold of pervasive (and invasive) hegemonic stereotypes through self-reflexivity. And once it is free from the influence of these powerful preconceptions, Asian American historical archaeology can continue striving to meet its potential to shed light on marginalized but undoubtedly important Asian American pioneer communities.

NOTES

1. John Kuo Wei Tchen, *New York before Chinatown: Orientalism and the Shaping of American Culture* (Baltimore, MD: Johns Hopkins University Press, 1999), 155, 156.
2. Ira M. Condit, *The Chinaman as We See Him* (Chicago, New York, and Toronto: Fleming H. Revell Company, 1900), 87–88.
3. Marley R. Brown, III, and Kathleen Bragdon, "Research Design," in *Archaeological and Historical Studies of the IJ56 Block, Sacramento, California: An Early Chinese Community,* ed. Mary Praetzellis and Adrian Praetzellis (Rohnert Park, CA: Cultural Resources Facility, Anthropological Studies Center, Sonoma State University, 1982), 39.
4. Imogene L. Lim, "Pacific Entry, Pacific Century: Chinatowns and Chinese Canadian History," in *Re/collecting Early Asian America: Essays in Cultural History,* ed. Josephine Lee, Imogene L. Lim, and Yuko Matsukawa (Philadelphia: Temple University Press, 2002), 28.
5. uko Matsukawa, Josephine Lee, and Imogene Lim, introduction to *Re/collecting Early Asian America: Essays in Cultural History,* ed. Josephine Lee, Imogene L. Lim, and Yuko Matsukawa (Philadelphia: Temple University Press, 2002), 2.
6. Matsukawa, Lee, and Lim, *Re/collecting,* 2.
7. Randall Rohe, "Chinese Camps and Chinatowns: Chinese Mining Settlements in the North American West," in *Re/collecting Early Asian America: Essays in Cultural History,* ed. Josephine Lee, Imogene L. Lim, and Yuko Matsukawa (Philadelphia: Temple University Press, 2002), 33; Randall H. McGuire, "The Study of Ethnicity in Historical Archaeology," *Journal of Anthropological Archaeology* 1 (1982): 161.
8. William F. Wu, *The Yellow Peril: Chinese Americans in American Fiction, 1850-1940* (Hamden, CT: Archon Book, 1982), 208.
9. Wu, *Yellow Peril,* 208.
10. Roberta Greenwood, "Old Approaches and New Decisions: Implications for Future Research," in *Hidden Heritage: Historical Archaeology of the Overseas Chinese,* ed. Priscilla Wegars (Amityville, NY: Baywood Publishing Company, Inc., 1993).
11. Alan Dundes in "From Etic to Emic Units in the Structural Study of Folktales" (1962) discusses Kenneth Pike's distinction between the "etic" and the "emic" within the context of folklore. According to Dundes, "[t]he etic approach is nonstructural but classificatory in that the analyst devises logical categories of systems, classes, and units without attempting to make them reflect actual structure in particular data" whereas "the emic approach is a mono-contextual, structural one" that must be studied relative to a particular context (101). See Alan Dundes, "From Etic to Emic Units in the Structural Study of Folktales," *The Journal of American Folklore* 75 (1962): 95–105.
12. Edward Staski, "The Overseas Chinese in El Paso: Changing Goals, Changing Realities," in *Images of the Recent Past,* ed. Charles E. Orser, Jr. (Walnut Creek, CA: AltaMira Press, 1996), 181; Roxann Prazniak, "The Chinese in Woodland California:

A Social History of the Canton Delta Region, 1850-1880, in Connection with Archaeological Findings at the Woodland Opera House Site," in *The Chinese Laundry on Second Street: Papers on Archaeology at the Woodland Opera House Site,* ed. David L. Felton, Frank Lortie, and Peter D. Schultz (Sacramento: State of California, Resources Agency, Department of Parks and Recreation, Resource Protection Division, Cultural Resource Management Unit, 1984), 131; Vincent Moses and Kate Whitmore, "Table of the Dragon: Foodways of the Overseas Chinese of Riverside, 1885-1920," in *Wong Ho Leun: An American Chinatown* (San Diego, CA: The Great Basin Foundation, 1987), 2:257.

13. John L. Fagan, "The Chinese Cannery Workers of Warrendale, Oregon, 1876-1930," in *Hidden Heritage: Historical Archaeology of the Overseas Chinese,* ed. Priscilla Wegars (Amityville, NY: Baywood Publishing Company, Inc., 1993), 222.

14. Matsukawa, Lee, and Lim, *Re/collecting,* 2; Chris Friday, "Asian American Labor History: 'What *Do* You Do?'" *Amerasia Journal* 26, no. 1 (2000): 183.

Activating Legal Protections for Archaeological Remains of Historic Chinatown Sites

Lessons Learned from Oakland, California

(Original Title: Rediscovering Oakland's San Pablo Avenue Chinatown)

Anna Naruta

While state law protects archaeological resources, a major redevelopment project planned for the site of one of Oakland's earliest Chinatowns showed community members they had to struggle to get the developer to meet their legal obligations. This paper discusses a few of the lessons learned in activating legal protections for unique and significant archaeological sites.

ACTIVATING LEGAL PROTECTIONS

The California Environmental Quality Act (CEQA) not only protects historic buildings and landscapes, it protects unique and significant archaeological remains.[1] City Planning departmental reviews of whether a development project will adversely impact the environment are therefore legally required to assess potential "impacts" to historic buildings and potential archaeological remains. If the project will impact a resource, and the impact cannot be avoided, the project is required to "mitigate" the impact in a manner that compensates for the damage to or loss of an irreplaceable cultural resource. In designing mitigations, the guiding principal is that after the project is complete, the mitigated resource should be at least equal to the resource that was destroyed. For a potentially unique and significant archaeological site, if a project cannot be designed to avoid impacting the site, the site must be studied and excavated by a qualified archaeological team, an extensive report published, and the archaeological documents and artifacts curated in a permanent repository accessible to researchers.

That's the theory, anyway. But when a national development corporation started the Environmental Impact Review process for a project that would redevelop the site of one of Oakland's earliest Chinatowns, we found there's nothing automatic about the process of assessing and mitigating a project's impacts. It's up to community members to activate the legal protections for significant cultural resources.

In our case, the site was what long-time Oaklander Edward Chew records as the site of the "'official' Chinatown" of the late 1860s and 1870s, created along San Pablo Avenue near today's 20th Street. Chew writes that this Chinatown was established after city authorities refused to allow the rebuild-

ing of the first "'official' Chinatown" on Telegraph near today's 17th Street, after it was destroyed in a fire. The next year, the City extended its main street, Broadway, northward through the former Chinatown site. The dislocations continued; residents of the San Pablo Avenue Chinatown were "consigned" to live at the City's industrial south shore, and the Charter Avenue Chinatown site (today's Grand Avenue) resulted from an 1880s redevelopment of the San Pablo Avenue Chinatown site. Very little is known of these historic Chinatown sites, although their existence is well established through a few mentions in historic newspapers and the federal census. The paucity of information about the Chinatowns underscores the legal significance of any potential archaeological remains.[2]

While the draft Environmental Impact Report for the project acknowledged that the project area had a high likelihood of containing archaeological remains of the historic Chinatown, it initially made no provision for archaeological study. Instead, the only "mitigation" was to have archaeological monitoring during construction. This procedure usually fails either in adequately mitigating the archaeological resource or in keeping the project on schedule, or—most frequently—both.[3] A pre-construction archaeological study was essential for the developer to be able to meet the legal protections for potentially unique and significant archaeological remains.

To activate the legal protections, community members spent countless hours spreading the word about the archaeological issue, calling and writing City Council members, and speaking at public meetings. Recognizing the importance of the potential archaeological site, the City Council adopted a requirement for a full pre-construction archaeological study into their agreement with the developer. The mitigation measures that the City Council adopted incorporated a public review process for the archaeological testing and treatment plan, specifying that the City would seek comments on the draft archaeological treatment plan from "established local Chinese-American organizations, including the Chinese Historical Society of America and the Oakland Asian Cultural Center."[4]

While it was hard won, the public review procedure was not an extraordinary measure. In terms of how local governments conduct Environmental Impact Reviews, seeking public comment on the archaeological testing and treatment plan merely brought the proposed archaeological mitigation plan into the same sort of public review process routinely undertaken for proposed mitigations to impacts on historic buildings, traffic patterns, or air or water quality.

The remainder of this paper shares lessons we learned in this process.

METHODS MATTER

In the world of cultural resource management, doing a "pre-construction archaeological study" can mean virtually anything. Some methods to discover existing intact historical archaeological remains are proven to fail but are still commonly used in legally mandated studies. One example of an investigation method proven to fail is geotechnical soil bores or auger testing. This method may be appropriate for discovering sites such as Native Californian shellmounds, sites that are meters deep and wide. But these soil bores are likely to miss remains of sites such as early U.S.-period California towns. Another method, backhoe trenching, tends to discover archaeological remains simultaneous with destroying them, or, at best, while removing significant contextual data that is required for archaeological interpretation.[5]

Mechanical methods can be employed to good effect, however. A backhoe with a flat-edged bucket can be an effective tool that allows archaeologists to rapidly expose a wide area of historic soil at one time and excavate by hand when potential archaeological remains are encountered. Such "areal" or "horizontal" excavations provide the archaeologist with a better chance to observe the relationships between archaeological deposits and to form a discovery method that is efficient, cost effective, and appropriate to historical archaeological remains. An additional factor that can determine whether effective archaeological interpretations of the site will be possible is whether there is adequate observation and recording of geomorphological data. This is the data that speaks to when and how the archaeological deposits were created and lets those of us who were not on-site for the excavations "see" what the site looked like.[6]

Whether the archaeological study would conduct the historical research necessary to perform an adequate assessment proved to be another issue. We found that contracting archaeologists did not necessarily utilize the basic set of historic documents that could reveal early land uses. Instead of conducting basic land-use research using documents such as property records, chains of title, and the federal census, contractors frequently relied on historical accounts found in secondary and tertiary sources as well as maps that post-dated the time period for which legally-significant archaeological remains may exist.[7] In the future, mitigations may need to specify either the general scope of landuse research required or specifically name documents and records that must be studied.

SELECTING A "QUALIFIED ARCHAEOLOGIST"

The Secretary of the Interior provides standards for who can be considered a "qualified archaeologist." The standards require that the archaeologist have a proven track record of bringing archaeological work from excavation and analysis through completing the final stage, public reporting. These are minimum standards. It's also relevant to ask how a particular contractor meets the Secretary of the Interior's standards with regards to archaeology of a site associated with historic Chinese Americans. Relevant questions include: (1) what experience the archaeological contractor has in the archaeology of that region; (2) whether the contractor has demonstrated full completion of projects on historic sites associated with Chinese Americans; (3) whether the contractor has qualified Chinese Americanists on staff or will consult with qualified Chinese Americanists during all phases of the study, and not merely at the end of the project; and (4) whether the contractor has a proven track record of completing and fully reporting basic analysis and cataloging of materials.[8]

OVERSIGHT

Review of an archaeological treatment plan is analogous to the established city planning procedures of design review for new construction projects, or a Landmarks Board review of proposed alterations to a historic site. Despite this established precedent, City oversight of the archaeological process does not seem to be as firmly established. We found an important question to be whether the City's reviewing agency, such as planning staff or a Landmarks Board, has archaeological expertise available, or whether the State Historic Preservation Officer may need to be called on to review the mitigation plan for adequacy. As our City government does not have a staff archaeologist or archaeological expertise represented on the Landmarks Board, public participation in review of the plan formed an essential step in helping the project meet CEQA guidelines for adequate treatment of potential archaeological resources.[9]

Oversight of the final archaeological plan and in-progress archaeological project is an area where the mitigation measure language failed. In this language, the oversight role is assigned to an entire City agency, the Community and Economic Development Agency. A particular overseeing staff member should have been named. The consequences are not trivial—to date we are still awaiting response regarding who at the City is overseeing the project to ensure compliance with CEQA and the adopted mitigation measures.

A concurrent redevelopment project made clear that the mitigation measure language should be altered to ensure both accountable oversight and a better procedure for community participation. This redevelopment project impacted an area that was the site of either the immediate neighbors of the Chinatown or the historic Charter Avenue Chinatown itself. Community research demonstrated the existence of the Chinatown, and the contracting archaeologist concurred the site was likely to contain historical archaeological remains. With community members advocating for the potential archaeological remains, the developer at the last minute voluntarily adopted mitigation measures that seemed to be identical to those adopted for the San Pablo Avenue Chinatown site. The developer agreed to a focused community review of the archaeological study "prior to construction" and additionally called for stopping all work and allowing archaeological evaluation if a single archaeological artifact was discovered during construction.[10]

In this case, that the community review of the archaeological plan was slated to happen "prior to construction" instead of "prior to any removal of foundations or other ground-disturbing activities" meant that it never happened. Instead, the work demolishing the existing historic structures flowed into removing soil in preparation for the new construction. After the buildings were demolished, earthmoving equipment was brought in to stir up and then compact what was euphemistically called the project area's "unconsolidated historic fill"—that is, the potential archaeological site. By the time the project hit the mitigation measure's trigger, the commencement of construction, there was likely no intact site left. The archaeological monitoring plan, which required construction workers to call a halt to the project if an historic artifact was found, also failed. Although casual observation of the project area showed the demolition and other ground-disturbing work exposed buried historic items, and therefore would have triggered an archaeological assessment within twenty-four hours, an archaeologist was never summoned. It may never be known if unique and significant archaeological resources were destroyed.[11]

CURATION

Since the intended goal of mitigations is that the cultural resource remaining at the end of the project is at least equal to the cultural resource that existed before the project, CEQA guidelines have been amended to specifically state that if the impact cannot be avoided, mitigation measures can include curation of the resultant archaeological collection. The mitigation measures adopted for the San Pablo Avenue Chinatown unfortunately have left the curation stage of the archaeological collection as something yet to be negotiated. Adequate curation poses a challenge. Facilities that curate archaeological collections in accordance with the State of California's "Guidelines for the Curation of Archeological Collections" routinely charge $1,000 per each cubic foot (a bankers' box worth) of materials. Even so, most such facilities are no longer accepting new collections due to lack of space. The

solution for the final curation plan should be specified in the mitigation measures.[12]

PROACTIVE STUDY

Activating legal protections for the rediscovered San Pablo Avenue Chinatown highlighted the need for further work that could identify existing cultural resources relating to California's Chinese heritage before they might be threatened by redevelopment. Hometown Oaklander Kelly Fong, then a senior in archaeology at the University of California, Berkeley, conducted a volunteer research project to identify further historic sites associated with nineteenth- and early twentieth-century Chinese Oaklanders. Fong compiled the lists of Oakland Chinese businesses from three sources: the *1882 Wells Fargo Directory of Chinese Business Houses*; the first one hundred Oakland Chinese Merchant Partnership case files generated as part of the enforcement of the Chinese Exclusion Act and now preserved at the National Archives, San Bruno; and the businesses, residences, and other establishments labeled as "Chinese" on the surviving volume of the 1889 Sanborn Fire Insurance Company map of Oakland. She produced a database of early Chinese businesses by street address, and plotted the locations on a map. The results not only expand ideas about early Chinese Oaklanders, demonstrating that many early Chinese Californians lived and worked outside of established Chinatowns, but also provide a first step in proactively protecting historic buildings or potential archaeological remains associated with these sites. The results of Fong's study are on file with the City of Oakland's Cultural Heritage Resource Survey, where the information will be included in future city planning assessments.[13] Placing such studies in the regional governmental repository for archaeological records (such as the California Archaeological Site Survey Northwest Information Center) can increase the likelihood the data will be incorporated in Environmental Impact Reviews.

CONCLUSION

Our experience with activating legal protections for significant potential archaeological resources taught us a number of lessons. Mitigation measures should spell out the who, what, where, when, and how of all steps in explicit detail. Long-term curation procedures, if applicable, need to be addressed as part of the project's initial Environmental Impact Review. We demonstrated that public review by community members and other archaeological practitioners provides a better opportunity for planned mitigations to meet legal obligations for protecting significant cultural resources. Our experience also highlights the current gap in standards for and oversight of archaeological projects, at both the local and state level. Perhaps most of all, our experience highlights the need for active community involvement in researching and preserving historical and archaeological resources. With redevelopment projects continuing to impact significant sites of our Chinese heritage, it will be communities who ultimately decide the fate of these cultural resources.

NOTES

1. The complete CEQA guidelines can be found on the state's website, *http://ceres.ca.gov/ceqa*. (Any project that draws on federal funds is subject to more stringent review, under Section 106 of the National Historic Preservation Act.)

2. Edward W. Chew was the son of Ng Poon Chew (1866–1931), a civil rights crusader who edited and published San Francisco's major turn-of-the-century Chinese-language newspaper, *Chung Sai Yat Bo*. A resident of Oakland since the 1906 San Francisco earthquake, Edward Chew's father—if not Edward Chew himself—was likely to have been in direct communication with the people who had lived in the San Pablo Avenue Chinatown. In 1952, on the occasion of Oakland's 100-year anniversary, Edward Chew published a special article in the *Oakland Tribune* relaying the history of Oakland's early Chinatowns and preserving important community oral history. Chew's article provided clues that allowed discovery of further information about the San Pablo Avenue Chinatown. See Willard T. Chow, "The Reemergence of an Inner City: The Pivot of Chinese Settlement in the East Bay Region of the San Francisco Bay Area" (Ph.D. diss., University of California, Berkeley, 1974); Anna Naruta, *Oakland's San Pablo Avenue Chinatown: A Compilation of Research to Aid the Upcoming Archaeological Sensitivity Study and Treatment Plan to Be Drafted by the Archaeological Contractor for Forest City's Uptown Redevelopment Project, UptownChinatown. org*, January 2005 (on file at the Oakland Cultural Heritage Survey, Oakland Public Library, and the Oakland Asian Cultural Center); Anna Naruta, "Creating Whiteness in California: Racialization Processes, Land, and Policy in the Context of California's Chinese Exclusion Movements, 1850 to 1910" (Ph.D. diss., University of California, Berkeley, 2006), 139–177.

    Archaeological remains that can provide information unavailable from other sources meet CEQA criteria for a legally significant archaeological resource. (See the CEQA code for other significance criteria.) A review of archaeological investigations of California Chinatown sites demonstrates that while archaeological research has substantial accomplishments, the current archaeological sample is so small that any potential archaeological site associated with Chinese Americans meets the CEQA criteria for a unique and significant (and therefore legally protected) cultural resource. See Naruta, "Creating Whiteness," 71–77, 136–138, 229–233.

3. One of the problems of archaeological monitoring is that it frequently produces out-of-context materials, a situation that renders archaeological interpretation impossible. For a discussion of the failure of archaeological monitoring at a site identified as the location of Oakland's first Chinatown, see Naruta, "Creating Whiteness," 145–148. The identification of Oakland's current City Hall location as the site of the earliest Chinatown is given in L. Eve Armentrout Ma and Jeong Huei Ma, *The Chinese of Oakland: Unsung Builders*, ed. Forrest Gok and the Oakland Chinese History Research Committee (Oakland: Oakland Chinese History Research Committee, 1982), 32; and L. Eve Armentrout Ma, *Hometown Chinatown: The History of Oakland's*

Chinese Community (New York and London: Garland Publishing, Inc., 2000), 29.

4. As an aid to other communities facing threats to potential archaeological resources, the full text of the cultural resource mitigations and public review process that Oakland City Council adopted for Forest City's Uptown Mixed Used Redevelopment Project is provided below and at *http://UptownChinatown.org*. This paper discusses some of the areas where the adopted language falls short, such as in specifying curation of archaeological materials, and naming specific staff charged with overseeing the archaeological mitigations measures. We will likely discover additional shortcomings as the mitigation process proceeds.

The following language was adopted by Oakland City Council on July 30, 2004 for inclusion in the Mitigation Monitoring and Rep orting Plan (MMRP):

New HIST-2a and HIST-2b REFLECTING CITY REVISIONS AND RECOMMENDATIONS TO COUNCIL 6-30-04

Mitigation Measure

HIST-2a: A pre-construction archaeological testing program shall be implemented to help identify whether historic or unique archaeological resources exist within the Project site. Examples of potential historic or unique archaeological resources that could be identified within the Project site include: back-filled wells; basements of buildings that pre-date Euro-American buildings that were constructed on the Project site; and back-filled privies. For these resources to be considered significant pursuant to CEQA, they would have to have physical integrity *and* meet at least one of the criteria listed in *CEQA Guidelines* section 15064.5(a)(3) (for historic resources) and/or CEQA section 21083.2(g) (for unique archaeological resources). These criteria include: association with events that have made a significant contribution to the broad patterns of California history and cultural heritage; association with the lives or persons important in our past; embodiment of the distinctive characteristics of a type, period, region, or method of construction, or represents the work of an important creative individual, or possesses high artistic values; yield, or may likely yield, information important in prehistory or history; contains information needed to answer important scientific research questions and be subject to a demonstrable public interest in that information; have a special and particular quality such as being the oldest of its type or the best available example of its type; or be directly associated with a scientifically recognized important prehistoric or historic event or person.

The testing program shall be guided by a sensitivity study (including a history of previous land uses) and shall use a combination of subsurface investigation methods (including backhoe trenching, augering, and archaeological excavation units, as appropriate). The purpose of the sensitivity study and testing program is to: (1) identify the presence and location of potentially-significant archaeological deposits; (2) determine if such deposits meet the definition of a historical resource or unique archaeological resource under section 21083.2(g) of the CEQA statutes; (3) guide additional archaeological work, if warranted, to recover the information potential of such deposits; and (4) refine the archaeological monitoring plan.

Representatives of established local Chinese American organizations (including the Chinese Historical Society of America and the Oakland Asian Cultural Center) shall be invited to participate in a focused community review of the sensitivity study and plan for the subsequent testing program prior to initiation of subsurface investigation. The City shall consider the community comments in finalizing the sensitivity study and testing program.

If historic or unique archaeological resources associated with the Chinese community·are identified within the project site and are further determined to be unique, the City shall consult with representatives of an established local Chinese American organization(s) regarding the potential use of the archaeological findings for interpretive purposes.

Implementation Procedure

(1) Project Sponsor shall retain an archaeologist to implement a pre-construction archaeological testing program, as described in the mitigation measure.

(2) Archaeologist shall provide the sensitivity study and plan for the archaeological testing program for focused community review by representatives of established local Chinese American organizations (including the Chinese Historical Society of America and the Oakland Asian Cultural Center). Community reviewers shall be provided 14 days to review sensitivity study and archaeological testing program and provide written comments. The City shall consider the community comments in finalizing the sensitivity study and archaeological testing program.

(3) Archaeologist shall prepare a plan for additional data recovery of archaeological material, if deemed necessary.

(4) If additional data recovery of archaeological material is deemed necessary, Archaeologist shall submit the plan to focused community review by representatives of established local Chinese American organizations (including the Chinese Historical Society of America and the Oakland Asian Cultural Center). Such community reviewers shall be provided 14 days to review the plan and provide written comments.

(5) Project Sponsor shall consult with representatives of the Chinese American community regarding the potential use of archaeological findings.

Monitoring Responsibility

(1) through (5): City of Oakland Community and Economic Development Agency, Planning Division.

Monitoring and Reporting Action

(1) Receive notice that an archaeologist has been retained.

(2) Verify that appropriate groups have been contacted to review sensitivity study and archaeological testing program. Verify community comments have been collected and reviewed and considered.

(3) Verify that a research design is prepared.

(4) Verify that appropriate groups have been contacted to review research design and plan for additional data recovery. Verify community comments have been collected and reviewed and considered.

(5) Verify that the appropriate groups have been contacted regarding archaeological findings within the Project site.

Monitoring Schedule

(1) through (4): Prior to approval of any permit that authorizes removal of foundations or work below finished grade.

(5) During Project construction.

Non-Compliance Sanction

(1) through (4): No approval of any permit that authorizes removal of foundations or work below finished grade.

(5) City issues corrective action or stop work order.

Mitigation Measure

HIST-2b: Archaeological monitoring of ground-disturbing construction in the Project area shall be conducted, as appropriate and if necessary, based on the results of the pre-construction testing program and the potential for encountering unidentified archaeological deposits. Upon completion of the pre-construction testing program specified in Mitigation Measure HIST-2a, the extent of archaeological monitoring during Project construction will be assessed, and the scope and frequency of the monitoring required by this mitigation measure shall be based on the findings of this assessment. Monitoring shall be conducted by a cultural resource professional approved by the City who meets the Secretary of the Interior's Professional Qualifications Standards for Prehistoric and Historical Archaeology.

Upon completion of such archaeological monitoring, evaluation, or data recovery mitigation, the archaeologist shall prepare a report documenting the methods, results, and recommendations of the investigation, and submit this report to the NWIC (Northwest Information Center). Public displays of the findings of archaeological recovery excavation(s) of historical or unique resources shall be prepared. As appropriate, brochures, pamphlets, or other media, shall be prepared for distribution to schools, museums, libraries, and—in the case of Chinese or Chinese American archaeological deposits—Chinese American organizations.

Implementation Procedure

(1) Project Sponsor shall retain an archaeologist to monitor ground-disturbing activity within the Project site, as described in the mitigation measure.

(2) Archaeologist shall halt work in the vicinity of the archaeological resource until findings can be made regarding whether the resource meets the CEQA definition of an archaeological or historic resource.

(3) If identified archaeological resources meet CEQA criteria for archaeological or historic resources, they shall be avoided by demolition or construction activities. If avoidance is not feasible, then effects to the deposit shall be mitigated through a data recovery strategy developed by the evaluating archaeologist, as described in the mitigation measure. This report shall be submitted to the NWIC.

Monitoring Responsibility

(1) through (3): City of Oakland Community and Economic Development Agency, Planning Division.

Monitoring and Reporting Action

(1) Receive notice that an archaeologist has been retained.

(2) Verify that work is suspended if archaeological resources are found.

(3) Review and approve the archaeological resources mitigation plan, if one is prepared.

Monitoring Schedule

(1) Prior to approval of any permit that authorizes removal of foundations or work below finished grade.

(2) During demolition or Project construction.

(3) During Project construction.

Non-Compliance Sanction

(1) No approval of any permit that authorizes removal of foundations or work below finished grade.

(2) City issues corrective action or stop work order.

(3) City issues corrective action.

5. An Oakland mitigation project obtained a false negative when using soil bores to assess whether significant historical archaeological remains might be present. The estimation that nineteenth-century historical archaeological remains would have been eliminated through the mid-twentieth-century construction of buildings with "extensive basements" also proved to be incorrect. For the preconstruction assessment, see Jan M. Hupman and David Chavez, *Archaeological Resources Investigation for the Oakland Administration Building Project, Oakland, California* (David Chavez & Associates, P.O. Box 52, Mill Valley, CA 94941), submitted to Environmental Science Associates, Inc. (301 Brannan Street, San Francisco, CA); California Archaeological Site Survey Northwest Information Center file #S-16863 (June 1994), 22–23, 34–35, 61. During construction, the archaeological monitor found intact historical archaeological deposits and recovered objects dating to as early as 1840, as reported in Colin Busby, *Archaeology Services, City Administration Building—Project L74021: Final Monitoring Report*, letter to City of Oakland Project Manager Jack Young, April 22, 1996 (Basin Research Associates, 1933 Davis Street, Suite 210, San Leandro, CA); California Archaeological Site Survey Northwest Information Center file #S-18536 (1996). For a discussion of how these mitigations failed to meet adequate treatment for archaeological remains under the legal protections of CEQA, see Naruta, "Creating Whiteness," 146–148.

6 For a discussion of how geomorphological data plays an essential role in archaeological interpretation of Chinatown sites, see Naruta, "Creating Whiteness," 71–138, 214–216. One resource for archaeologists is Stewart Reed, Nathan Bailey, and

Oghenekome Onokpise, *Soil Science for Archeologists*, vol. 1, ed. Michael Russo and Virginia Horak, Florida Agricultural and Mechanical University and Southeast Archeological Center, National Park Service, June 2000, *http://www.cr.nps.gov/seac/soils-index.htm.*

7. This was the case for the above-mentioned archaeological mitigations reported in Hupman and Chavez, *Oakland Administration Building Project,* and Busby, *Final Monitoring Report*, and also an archaeological mitigation for Upper Chinatown that formed after the dislocation of the San Pablo Avenue Chinatown, Archeo-Tec, *Cultural Resources Evaluation for the Broadway–West Grand Project*, submitted by Allen Pastron, Archeo-Tec, to Patrick Van Ness, Signature Properties, for City of Oakland, Case File Numbers ER03-0022, PUD03552, PUDF03553, September 15, 2004. For the San Pablo Avenue Chinatown, a compilation of basic research was prepared and donated to the project to give the archaeological contractors a better starting point for their research. See Naruta, *Oakland's San Pablo Avenue Chinatown.*

8. While we prepared a list of Bay Area historical archaeologists who met the Secretary of the Interior's Standards with regards to previous work on Chinatown sites (see *http://UptownChinatown.org*), the developer apparently did not seek bids from any of them.

    It's worth stipulating that the archaeological contractor must complete the full preliminary analysis and cataloguing of artifacts, including determining minimum number of specimens represented by the fragmented artifacts and checking ceramic fragments for "crossmends" with fragments from other deposits from the same site. If fragments from different deposits show themselves to have been part of the same item, this provides data about the relationship between the different deposits. Analyzing ceramics through determining crossmends is therefore part of the basic reporting of a site. See Naruta, "Creating Whiteness," 208–217.

9. Community review helped redirect the archaeological contractor to areas that primary source documents indicated were likely to contain archaeological remains of the San Pablo Avenue Chinatown. See Allen G. Pastron and Allison Vanderslice, *DRAFT Archaeological Sensitivity Study and Testing Program for the Uptown Mixed-Use Project, City Of Oakland, Alameda County, California*, submitted to Forest City Residential West Inc. (785 Market Street, 14th Floor, San Francisco, CA 94103), by Archeo-Tec (5283 Broadway, Oakland, CA 94618), *http://www.oaklandnet.com/government/ceda/revised/planningzoning/MajorProjectsSection/environmentaldocuments.html, 2005);* Anna Naruta to Claudia Cappio, Development Director, City of Oakland, letter on behalf of the Chinese Historical Society of America Re: Uptown Redevelopment Project MMRP Hist 2a and 2b, Initial Review of Draft Archaeological Plan Dated January 2005, prepared by Archeo-Tec (available at the City of Oakland, Community and Economic Development Agency and *http://UptownChinatown.org*, May 19, 2005).

10. Naruta, "Creating Whiteness," 150.

11. City of Oakland, Planning Commission, Staff Report, Broadway–West Grand Project, City of Oakland Case File Numbers ER03-0022, PUD03552, PUDF03553, December 1, 2004, 28–31; Naruta, *Oakland's San Pablo Avenue Chinatown*; Naruta, "Creating Whiteness," 148–151; Doug Park, Project Manager, Signature Properties, Signature Properties community meeting to discuss the Broadway–West Grand Project, May 25, 2005; Naruta, letter to Claudia Cappio, Development Director, City of Oakland Community and Economic Development Agency, on behalf of the Chinese Historical Society of America, Re: Broadway–West Grand Mixed-Use Project, Case File Numbers PUD03552, PUDF03553, ER030022, April 20, 2005.

12. State Historical Resources Commission, Department of Parks and Recreation, "State of California Resources Agency Guidelines for the Curation of Archeological Collections," (Sacramento, Office of Historic Preservation, 1993). For a typical cost of archaeological curation, see Museum of Anthropology and Repository for Archaeological Collections, California State University, Bakersfield, "Storage Guidelines," *http://www.csub.edu/musanth/GdlnsRep.htm* (9001 Stockdale Highway, Bakersfield, CA 93311). Part of the expense associated with archaeological curation is that in order for such facilities to meet their long-term curation goals, they must use only the interest on the curation fee to cover operating costs. "The San Francisco Bay Area currently suffers from a shortage of acceptable curation facilities," note Allen G. Pastron and Allison Vanderslice, *Archaeological Sensitivity Study and Testing Program for the Uptown Chinatown Project, City of Oakland, Alameda County, California*, submitted to Forest City Residential West Inc. (785 Market Street, 14th Floor, San Francisco, CA 94103), by Archeo-Tec (5283 Broadway, Oakland, CA 94618), November 2005, 133 (see also 132–134).

13. Kelly Fong, "Nineteenth-Century Oakland Chinese Businesses," report with maps prepared for Anthropology 197 (Independent Research in Oakland Cultural Resources and Cultural Heritage), instructor Anna Naruta, supervisory professor Kent Lightfoot, University of California, Berkeley, Spring 2005 (Oakland, CA: *UptownChinatown.org*, June 2005); on file at the Oakland Cultural Heritage Survey, Oakland Public Library, Oakland Asian Cultural Center, and the Chinese Historical Society of America. For more on the Chinese merchant partnership files, see Bill Greene, Bob Glass, and Daniel Nealand, *A Guide to Records of Asian Americans and Pacific Islanders at the National Archives and Records Administration Pacific Region–San Bruno*, National Archives and Records Administration, Reference Information Paper 111, January 2004.

    Fong's research also discovered the additional significance of the 1880s Victorian Italianate false-front stores, part of the nineteenth-century redevelopment of the San Pablo Avenue Chinatown, that still stood on the site of Chinatown. Following the 1906 San Francisco earthquake, they became home to merchant tailoring firm Hing Chong & Company and part of a thriving early twentieth-century Chinese garment district. The story of the rediscovered additional historic significance of buildings and resilience of community presence in that area is recounted in Rick DelVecchio, "Oakland: New Twist in Roots of Chinatown/Effort Under Way to Save Historical Buildings," *San Francisco Chronicle*, East Bay ed., August 5, 2005; Momo Chang, "Digging Up Old Chinatown's Roots—Downtown Oakland Buildings Marked for Demolition May Hold Key to Hidden Past," *Oakland Tribune*, November 6, 2005; and Momo Chang, "History Amid Old Chinatown Demolition—Storefronts Slated for Uptown Wrecking Ball Reveal Past Culture," *Oakland Tribune*, December 6, 2005. Articles are archived at *http://UptownChinatown.org.*

Finding Home Again

The Story of the Chinese Historical and Cultural Project (CHCP) and Its Efforts to Reclaim the Forgotten Historic Chinatowns of San Jose, California

(Original Title: The Chinese Historical and Cultural Project)

Rodney M. Lum, OD
President, Chinese Historical and Cultural Project

San Jose, California, had a key role in the anti-Chinese movement of the 1880s as the Chinese fought valiantly to remain in a valley that repeatedly tried to oust them—by arson, police harassment, local legislation, and unconstitutional ordinances. While the Chinese endured, all of their historic communities have been lost.

The most significant findings on the Chinese American community within the past two decades have emerged from archeological digs within the metropolis of San Jose, the heart of Silicon Valley. It was progress and development that uncovered the detritus of two historic Chinatowns. Another planned redevelopment in the coming few years will uncover the site of yet another Chinatown.

San Jose's Chinese communities of the nineteenth century, long neglected in history, have been brought to light by the work of the Chinese Historical and Cultural Project. The Ng Shing Gung Museum, the book publication of *Chinatown, San Jose, USA*, the film *Homebase: A Chinatown Called Heinlenville*, and the ongoing educational and cultural activities of CHCP showcase the magnitude of the struggles of the Chinese pioneers as they survived, flourished, and in the end triumphed over adversities.[1]

INTRODUCTION

San Jose, Calif ornia, once counted as many as six settlements considered Chinatowns. As there have not been any Chinatowns locally for approximately seventy-five years and since many of these sites have been overlaid with modern development, even longtime residents of our area are often unaware they ever existed and ignorant of their locations. Few remaining inhabitants of these settlements survive, and, therefore, as time passes these sites have faded not only out of existence but out of memory too.

The past two decades have brought great redevelopment to the metropolitan San Jose area, once a primarily agrarian region known as "The Valley of Heart's Delight" but today known better for its high technology industries. The sites of two Chinatowns have been rediscovered, and in the next few years a third will be added to the list. The inevitable wave of progress benefits us in that whenever there is development, regulations dictate that before work can proceed, archaeological studies must be done. Archaeologists working these locations, in conjunction with historians and cultural experts, turn their findings into stories that can provide a coherent view of the historical, social, and cultural life of a lost community.

MARKET STREET CHINATOWN

In 1985, development began in downtown San Jose to build a grand new hotel to be known as the San Jose Fairmont. Excavation for the garage revealed the site of the historic Market Street Chinatown of 1866. Only established for a few years, a fire in 1870 had gutted the town, but the determined citizens soon rebuilt in the same location. At one time the home to 2,000–3,000 inhabitants, this Chinatown was in the heart of downtown near the business district and across from the new City Hall. Unfortunately, its prominent location targeted it to be cited as a blight on the community, and another fire, likely arson, burned it down once again in 1887. The *San Jose Daily Herald* duly reported, "Chinatown is dead. It is dead forever."[2]

WOOLEN MILLS

After the Chinese were burnt out of the Market Street Chinatown, some resettled in an area called the Woolen Mills Chinatown, named for the local factory that provided employment to many of these Chinese. A fire in 1902 later destroyed this settlement also. Nearly a century later, construction on State Route 87 led to archaeological studies being performed by Past Forward, Inc. Their findings revealed that "the Woolen Mills Chinatown was a well-organized and planned community" with an "elaborate sewer and hydrant system."[3] The San Jose Chinatowns were shown to be well-constructed communities despite the fact that they were forced by outside agencies to relocate themselves frequently.

HEINLENVILLE

The most recent Chinatown in San Jose's past was called Heinlenville. As with the Woolen Mills Chinatown, its inhabitants had also been displaced by the 1887 Market Street fire. Rather than allow themselves to be driven from San Jose, their representatives quickly located a sympathizer in a German American named John Heinlen. Despite great public opposition in the press and at rallies, and official injunctions against it, a new Chinatown rose. Dubbed by some as "Heinlen's Hell-hole," the community was well built of fireproof brick with an eight-foot high wall topped with barbwire against intruders. Ironically, the same architect, Theodore Lenzen, built both Heinlenville and San Jose's City Hall. A key building in this Chinatown was the Joss House called Ng Shing Gung, which functioned not only as a house of worship, but also as a meeting space, Chinese school, storehouse, and temporary lodging. Heinlenville became a more permanent location for the Chinese, existing from 1887 until the 1930s. By that time the Chinese and their American-born children were able to move more freely out into mainstream society, and the Great Depression led to the Heinlen family's bankruptcy. These factors caused the demise of the last Chinatown in San Jose. Creditors received the property, the buildings were razed, and the city took over the area to be used as a storage yard. Only one building, the Ng Shing Gung temple, survived until 1949 when it was also demolished. Fortunately, some far-thinking community leaders made the effort to store away the altar and some of the furnishings of the temple.

THE CHINESE HISTORICAL AND CULTURAL PROJECT

CHCP was organized for a purpose: to replicate Heinlenville's temple and restore its altar, thus creating a museum to document the history of the Chinese in Santa Clara Valley and a monument to the legacy of the pioneering Chinese immigrants to the area. CHCP arose from a broad community effort that involved people from various walks of life, different ethnicities, and different political parties. Despite being a "grassroots" effort originated by community activists, including members of the Chinese American Women's Club of Santa Clara, the effort to recreate the temple gained widespread public support. This support expanded to include people from all levels of society, government, education, and business. But only coordination and cooperation among these organizations, professionals, and government agencies enabled the project to succeed. This assemblage of concerned and motivated citizens banded together to create CHCP in 1987, significantly one hundred years after the Market Street Chinatown fire.

The "project" was to have lasted only a few years, and once the building was dedicated and deeded over to the city of San Jose, the job could be considered completed. However,

the great momentum that was generated led CHCP to continue with further endeavors. Soon a "Chinese Summer Festival" of various entertainment and cultural displays became a regularly scheduled event at the site. The extensive research involved in the project also led to a curriculum on Chinese American history and culture that was created and distributed widely in the local school districts. A grant program was added to help educators and students interested in studying about or creating their own programs on multiculturalism. CHCP also provides scholarships for students and support for writers, artists, performers, film festivals, and other cultural groups, and participates in community activities and events.

CHCP has formed deep ties with individuals of varied professions. From the archaeologists to the anthropologists and historians who provided the studies, to the community activists and politicians who pushed the project forward, and to the architects and designers who created the space for the exhibits—all have played vital roles. Then there are the directors and staff of History San Jose who do the fine work in their role as managers of the museum. There is also another group that keeps everything going. These are people who volunteer their time, their labor, their financial support, and their spirit to CHCP. From our dedicated museum docents and volunteers at our festivals and events to our volunteer webmasters, they all provide essential manpower. And lastly there is the volunteer governing structure of CHCP: A board of directors and a board of trustees charged with oversight for the museum. These are dedicated individuals, many of whom have been there even before CHCP was formed.

CHCP has been the recipient of several awards from various distinguished institutions. Most recently the Society of Historical Archaeologists has given their Award of Merit to CHCP for their contributions in the Woolen Mills Chinatown studies. Previously a Caltrans Award was given as well as an Albert B. Corey Award, also from the American Historical Society. These awards from professional groups reflect the extent to which CHCP honors the archaeological history of the site in recreating for the public the many stories of the Chinatowns. These awards also display the professional respect and cooperation that CHCP and their partners share. From the original Market Street findings by Archaeological Resource Service, Inc. twenty years ago, to more recent collaborations at the Woolen Mills with Past Forward Inc. and with the Market Street Archaeological Project at Stanford University, these have been fruitful relationships. The end results are brought to the public's attention through different avenues, most notably the museum with its exhibition design by prominent designer Daniel Quan Associates, and also in the curriculum guide *Golden Legacy*, the books *Chinatown, San Jose, USA* by CHCP Board Member Connie Young Yu and *Life Along the Guadalupe River* by archaeologists Rebecca Allen and Mark Hylkema, and the film *Homebase: A Chinatown called Heinlenville* by Connie's daughter Jessica Yu. Lastly, a website (chcp.org) supplies a wealth of data on local Chinese American history and culture, plus a link into the workings of CHCP.

Led by cofounders Lillian Gong-Guy and Gerrye Wong, CHCP continues its mission into the twenty-first century. CHCP has expanded beyond its original "project" but stays true to its ideals to "preserve, educate, and promote the history and culture of the Chinese and Chinese Americans in America, particularly in Santa Clara Valley, California."

PRESENT-DAY ACTIVITIES

CHCP continues to help operate its museum and is involved in the extended care of the site through a forward-thinking Long-Term Maintenance Agreement with the city of San Jose and with History San Jose, the managing organization. All three parties in this agreement work closely with the goal of maintaining the museum and ensuring its availability to the viewing public.

CHCP is currently in the final stages of enhancing our museum to showcase Cantonese Opera as a popular entertainment, and we are installing new exhibits on the recent findings from the Woolen Mills Chinatown. CHCP has been blessed to work with excellent professionals from the staff of History San Jose to the knowledgeable experts in the community and the many archaeologists who provide the data that is the basis for our exhibits. A shard of pottery, a pork bone, or a woman's comb can tell us a lot about the intricacies of the social fabric or the commerce of the community.

Other ways CHCP maintains relevance is to participate in today's events, not only with festivals, sponsorships, and outreach activities, but also by means of active involvement with various organizations and groups in our community. CHCP is not an advocacy group and has no political agenda, as dictated in the bylaws of our organization. However, these restrictions do not mean that CHCP should not have an influence on what is happening. On the contrary, we take an active role in our community. First, we are in the business of education; what we present to the youth of today will help them understand society better and their roles within it. As our future, the youth need to know about the injustices and prejudices encountered by the immigrants, and the youth need to be shown examples of how others have found the determination and the means to overcome them. CHCP supports organizations such as Vision New America or the Asian Pacific American Leadership Institute at DeAnza College, both training young people to be politically and socially involved. We also encourage groups such as Asian Americans for Community Involvement as they provide new immigrants with legal, medical, and social assistance.

CHCP'S FUTURE ACTIVITIES

Heinlenville has sat buried for over fifty years in the midst of Japantown, underneath what the city calls the Corporation Yard. Restricted access to the public meant that citizens could not even walk the site of historic Heinlenville. But soon San Jose will relocate the Yard and open the site to redevelopment for housing and commercial use. Next year when the earthmovers come, we intend to have archaeologists to monitor what they unearth. This will provide a wealth of fresh data and new stories to interpret and present to the public.

But just as important, CHCP is actively involved in the redevelopment process with the City. We are representing the Chinese American community, with full intention to inform all involved parties about our history on this parcel of land. Of course, no one expects a "New" Chinatown to rise. There no longer exists the social or commercial need that originally created these enclaves. But we expect any development to respect our past while also reflecting our future. The formal documents guiding developers interested in this property contain wording carefully constructed from public input, including that of CHCP representatives:

> Given the long and powerful history of the site as the last Chinatown in San Jose, the history and culture of the site needs to be clearly and meaningfully integrated into the redevelopment."[4]

The Chinese were long ago removed from Heinlenville and had little say in the matter. This time we expect our voices to be heard and not neglected when this piece of our history is reclaimed. Only through proactive participation in community processes can we succeed. The pioneering Chinese were denied many of the rights and resources now available to all Americans and suffered as a result. CHCP promotes respect and understanding of other cultures to avoid the injustices of the past. It also encourages and supports active participation in our community, whether through political, social, or educational means.

CONCLUSION

All immigrants seek some place to find security and safety in a difficult, sometimes threatening new environment. And it was the same for the pioneer Chinese. To quote Connie Young Yu, "Chinatowns were sanctuaries, offering physical and emotional protection…a cultural homebase."[5] San Jose's Chinese pioneer immigrants faced great hardships to remain in the area yet displayed grit and resilience in the face of adversity. Their chances to succeed were greatly enhanced by these Chinatowns, created by the two factors of a common sociocultural environment and the need for protection from a hostile environment. Along with family and, for some, religion, there is no concept so vital as that of a "home."

The basis of America is in its immigrants, and the triumph of this nation has been the integration of all these people of different backgrounds. However, the past shows that it has not been an easy process, and the present shows that there are still conflicts to be resolved. Although the immigration stations of Ellis Island and Angel Island are now historic sites, immigration to the United States is still happening and this continues to change the "face" of this nation.

This year's Chinese American Studies conference is subtitled "A Changing Chinese America" to stimulate discussion on the changing Chinese American population. This idea of a changing demographic is also applicable to Asian America on the whole. Whether it's due to the influence of mixed marriage or to suburban flight leading to an influx of new residents, Chinatowns and Japantowns are becoming more multiethnic. For example, in San Jose's Japantown you now find Hawaiian stores and restaurants representing the most diverse Asian American state in the United States and a neighboring population largely of Latinos. Fortunately, strong local activism and leadership appear to ensure that this Japantown, one of the last three in America, will not vanish like the six Chinatowns of San Jose. When redevelopment commences in San Jose Japantown and the long-buried Heinlenville is unearthed there, we expect to find artifacts of that old Chinatown to further enrich our understanding of the Chinese in San Jose. Furthermore, we are excited for the day when once more the public will be able to walk these grounds freely and see monuments and tributes to what was once San Jose's last Chinatown.

An organization like CHCP needs to be aware that we may be losing our natural audience. We tell the story of the Cantonese from Toishan and Zhongshan, rather clannish people who were among the first Chinese to immigrate to our area. But these early inhabitants and their descendants have largely assimilated into the general population. It is the recent immigrants from various other provinces of China and especially Taiwan who are bringing their new influence to the area. This is "the face of a changing Chinese America" in the Silicon Valley. For these newcomers, the stories in our museum are not specifically theirs. Yet there is a commonality to the immigrant experience that should resonate within them and all Americans. To quote CHCP Trustee Dr. Jeffery Lee, "Remarkably, the community sensed a special kinship to the old town of Heinlenville, although few had childhood experiences in San Jose."[6] And even more so, there is nobility in the great stories of struggle, survival, and triumph that should touch every person regardless of his or her own particular origins. It is our responsibility to inform people of all colors about our stories, because they truly are universal tales for every American to know. With further exploration of new archaeological sites, we will continue to bring the story of our Chinese past to life, even as we promote our future by participating to our fullest extent as Americans.

NOTES .

1. As cited in the preface, Connie Young Yu, *Chinatown, San Jose, USA* (San Jose, CA: San Jose Historical Museum Association, 1993).
2. Yu, *Chinatown*, 30.
3. Rebecca Allen and Mark Hylkema, *Life along the Guadalupe River—An Archaeological and Historical Journey* (San Jose, CA: Friends of the Guadalupe River Parks and Gardens), 51.
4. San Jose Redevelopment Agency, "Goals, Objectives and Developer Responsibilities (Attachment)," June 27, 2005, 3.
5. Yu, *Chinatown*, 21.
6. Yu, *Chinatown*, (afterword), 112.

Forming a Chinese Identity When Everyone Else Is Either Black or White

John Jung, PhD

Ethnic identity[1] involves the cultural aspect of an individual's sense of self. These beliefs, attitudes, and values are acquired to a large extent from experiences of interacting with others from one's own ethnic background, especially during the early formative years. For example, American-born Chinese growing up in a place like San Francisco with a large Chinese community, form a Chinese identity because they live, play, and attend school and church with mostly Chinese friends and family in Chinatown and nearby areas. But is the process of forming ethnic identity different in its characteristics when the only available contact with people of one's ethnicity is limited to one's parents and siblings, as was the case for me growing up in the Deep South as a member of the only Chinese family in town?

The Chinese in the South were severely isolated as there were only 190 Chinese men and 55 women living in the entire state of Georgia in 1930. My parents came to America in the late 1920s and ran a laundry in Macon, near the geographical center of Georgia. It had a population of about 55,000 when I grew up during the 1940s. We were the *only* Chinese in Macon at that time although there had been three Chinese laundrymen and as many as eleven Chinese in 1908, but they had all left by the time my parents arrived. When we eventually left Macon by the mid-1950s, there was not a single Chinese left in town.

Growing up, I learned from my parents that there were a few other Chinese in the South, more or less as isolated as we were. These Chinese laundrymen had come from the same Taishan villages of Guangdong province. As a child, I thought it curious that Chinese immigrants in the South, many of them relatives of my father, were also in the laundry business. Thus, nineteen or twenty of the male descendants of my great-great-grandfather came to own or operate Chinese laundries in Georgia, Alabama, and Tennessee, starting from about 1915 until the 1960s, with one still operating. Five of his grandsons, and eleven of his great-grandsons left China to escape economic hardship in the early part of the last century and ended in the Deep South running laundries. This could hardly have happened by chance. Most likely, the first of his descendants to leave China headed for the South because he had either a relative or a friend from his village there who helped him get settled, and, in turn, he assisted other relatives to come to the South.

CHINESE AND RACE RELATIONS IN THE SOUTH

The Deep South is infamous for its long history of racial segregation and violence against blacks. Fortunately, as a child I was not exposed to or aware of the extremely violent forms of racism toward blacks, and in a few instances toward Chinese, that occurred in the South. However, I was well aware of racial segregation and Jim Crow traditions because it was so apparent in all forms of daily interactions that favored whites over blacks. Drinking fountains, public toilets, schools, movie theatres, and bus seating sections were strictly segregated.

But Chinese are neither black nor white, so how did our family fit in in Macon? The townspeople, black and white alike, often treated us as foreigners, approaching us with some mixture of curiosity, hostility, superiority, and ridicule. Since there were only six members of our family, most Maconites were unlikely to have acquired their knowledge and attitudes about Chinese from direct interactions with them.

Media played a larger role in shaping their images and attitudes toward Chinese. For example, in 1908 the local newspaper[2] announced the New Year's celebration by Macon's "celestials," as Chinese were called then, focusing on foods from China such as "dried fish with staring eyes," bird's nests, and other delicacies (see Figure 1). This mocking tone toward Chinese customs encouraged racial intolerance. Newspaper accounts mocking our food and fluency in English could only serve to foster and reinforce attitudes of American superiority over Chinese ways not just in Macon, but throughout the South.

In addition, images of Chinese, mostly negative, in motion pictures also fueled derogatory attitudes toward the Chinese. I was spared knowledge of evil Chinese villains like Fu Manchu as I somehow never saw these films when I was growing up. But in one of my favorite action comic books, *Blackhawk*, I had to suffer the indignity of how the Chinese sidekick was depicted. This squadron of action heroes featured Blackhawk,

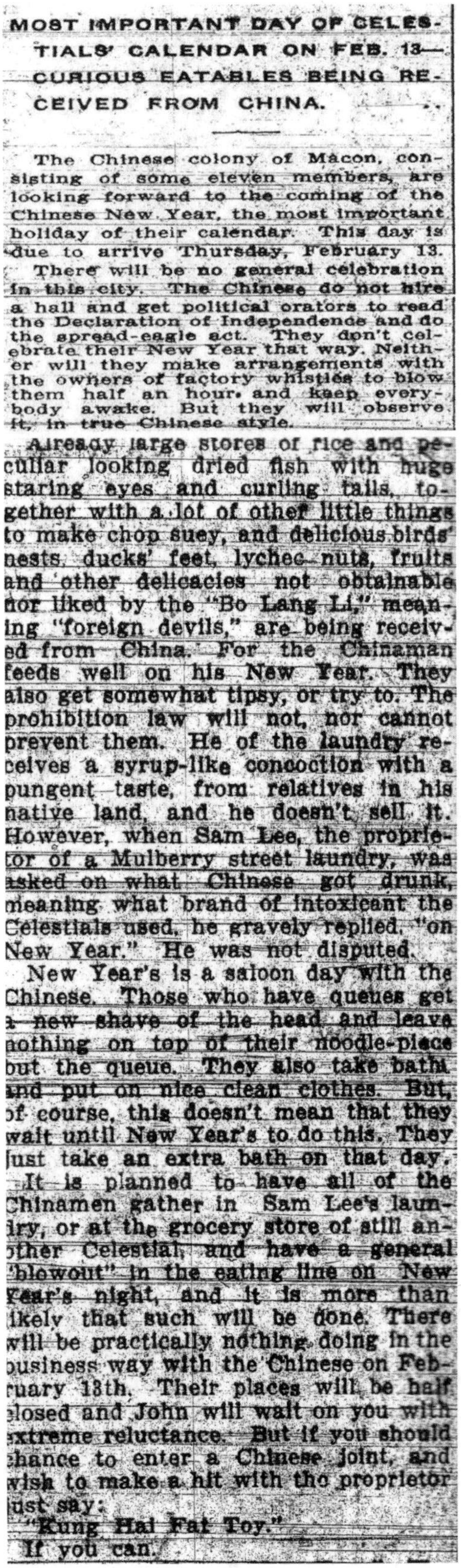

**MOST IMPORTANT DAY OF CELES-
TIALS' CALENDAR ON FEB. 13—
CURIOUS EATABLES BEING RE-
CEIVED FROM CHINA.**

The Chinese colony of Macon, consisting of some eleven members, are looking forward to the coming of the Chinese New Year, the most important holiday of their calendar. This day is due to arrive Thursday, February 13.

There will be no general celebration in this city. The Chinese do not hire a hall and get political orators to read the Declaration of Independence and do the spread-eagle act. They don't celebrate their New Year that way. Neither will they make arrangements with the owners of factory whistles to blow them half an hour and keep everybody awake. But they will observe it, in true Chinese style.

Already large stores of rice and peculiar looking dried fish with huge staring eyes and curling tails, together with a lot of other little things to make chop suey, and delicious birds' nests, ducks' feet, lychee nuts, fruits and other delicacies not obtainable nor liked by the "Bo Lang Li" meaning "foreign devils," are being received from China. For the Chinaman feeds well on his New Year. They also get somewhat tipsy, or try to. The prohibition law will not, nor cannot prevent them. He of the laundry receives a syrup-like concoction with a pungent taste, from relatives in his native land, and he doesn't sell it. However, when Sam Lee, the proprietor of a Mulberry street laundry, was asked on what Chinese got drunk, meaning what brand of intoxicant the Celestials used, he gravely replied, "on New Year." He was not disputed.

New Year's is a saloon day with the Chinese. Those who have queues get a new shave of the head and leave nothing on top of their noodle-piece but the queue. They also take bath and put on nice clean clothes. But, of course, this doesn't mean that they wait until New Year's to do this. They just take an extra bath on that day.

It is planned to have all of the Chinamen gather in Sam Lee's laundry, or at the grocery store of still another Celestial, and have a general "blowout" in the eating line on New Year's night, and it is more than likely that such will be done. There will be practically nothing doing in the business way with the Chinese on February 13th. Their places will be half closed and John will wait on you with extreme reluctance. But if you should chance to enter a Chinese joint, and wish to make a hit with the proprietor just say:

"Kung Hai Fat Toy."

If you can.

Figure 1. Macon newspaper (1908) belittled Chinese New Year customs.

a white American leading a group that included a Frenchman, Dutchman, Norwegian, and Chinese with the condescending name Chop Chop. Whereas all of Blackhawk's white crew members wore dark blue military uniforms, had revolvers, and piloted their own fighter planes, Chop Chop wore Chinese-style garb, had a pigtail, buck teeth, and rode in the back seat of Blackhawk's plane. The other members used their firearms to fight the villains while Chop Chop ran around using only a meat cleaver as his weapon. He was about as good as it got in those days for any positive Chinese male role model. Chinese female characters were even less frequently portrayed and never in a positive way. Thus, the only Chinese woman in a comic strip I saw was the sinister and slinky "dragon lady" from *Terry and the Pirates*.

With these demeaning and condescending stereotypes, it is not surprising that both whites and blacks would sometimes query me about exotic customs and practices in China, make fun about our customs and language, or speak mock Chinese, often while stretching their eyelids to mimic slanted eyes. Much of the racial prejudice that we experienced was more in the form of a banal curiosity from ignorant hicks, albeit often in an insensitive manner rather than from malevolent intent. For the most part, whites interacted with us in a superficial and sometimes patronizing way. Still, that was preferable to the ridicule, hostility, or, on occasion, threats, we faced from a handful of townspeople. We were allowed to attend white schools, and because we were good students as well as well behaved, we faced no problems at all. In other ways, we were accepted as "white" inasmuch as we could attend movie theaters and use white-only public toilet and drinking facilities.

Most of our laundry customers, black and white, were friendly or civil, but a few were demanding or even rude to us. Some of these rude customers may have been drinking, but others may have been angry about something else and took it out on us. This abusive behavior toward my parents in the laundry, I felt was racist, because I never witnessed such rudeness from either white or black customers in stores run by whites.

HOW RACISM AFFECTED ME

Growing up, there was no escaping the fact that I was Chinese. My parents spoke to me in Chinese, so it was my first language, and Mother cooked meals with Chinese ingredients or prepared American foods in the Chinese style of stir frying. More significantly, Mother periodically cautioned us about how whites discriminated against Chinese to prepare us for our inevitable encounters with racism. She warned us to avoid confrontations and to ignore racial insults because she felt we had no power to deal with hostile people.

She told us about times when white children would come by the laundry and taunt her and my father, with chants of "Chinese eat rats!" During the war years, they would follow her on the street, making nonsensical sounds, pretending they were speaking Chinese, or they would make derogatory comments such as "Chinese eat dogs." She recited many instances of violence against Chinese, including homicide, in cities all over the United States that she had learned about in the Chinese newspaper. She would tell us how China suffered when England forced opium into China in the middle of the nineteenth century to destroy the will and resistance of the people to British domination.

Mother also told us, on numerous occasions, how Father, like other Chinese immigrants, had to resort to buying false documents to enter the United States as a paper son. I was upset, angry, and surprised that the United States treated Chinese so unjustly by excluding them, and no other group, from the opportunity to enter the country legally. I was torn between feelings of shame for being "illegal" and fear that someday my parents would be apprehended and deported. It also bothered me because I felt that if my parents lied to enter the United States, they were doing something wrong.

I hate to admit it, but there were times when I was growing up that I truly wished that I were *not* the child of Chinese immigrants because that meant that you were a target of ridicule and racism. You were painfully different from everyone else. Many times I secretly wished that there were at least a few Chinese Americans who were famous, such as star athletes, movie stars, or public leaders. However we soon came to realize that no matter how "American" we children may have felt or wanted to be, in the eyes of others, we would always be seen as "Chinese," even if we hardly knew the culture of China or its language.

One striking personal example to illustrate this point was the visit of Madame Chiang Kai-Shek, the first lady of China, to Macon in 1943 during her historic visit in the United States to rally support for U.S. aid for the war effort against the Japanese. When she was an adolescent, she had lived in Macon because her two older sisters attended Wesleyan College in the early 1900s. In recognition of her prominence, Wesleyan decided to bestow an honorary doctorate upon her. It was decided that we Jung children, being the only children in town of Chinese descent, should be invited to attend the festivities. We were paraded out for public display simply because we were Chinese. I was only six, and none of the proceedings meant much to me, although the press release gushingly described our encounter of a few seconds with Madame Chiang as a thrill that we "tiny Jungs" had eagerly awaited.

PRIDE IN BEING CHINESE

Our parents often reminded us of the positive aspects of our Chinese heritage. They told us the history of China and how it had been a great and successful civilization over thousands of years, but that it had suffered from some inept emperors who were responsible for the country's downfall in modern times. We also learned in school about the great achievements of Chinese civilization, which made us proud to be Chinese.

A major factor in my understanding of what was involved in being Chinese was our Uncle Joe who had a laundry in Atlanta, about 100 miles north of Macon. Uncle was separated from his wife and three sons who were still in China and unable to come to America until around 1950. Not having his own family with him in Atlanta, Uncle would come by train to visit us every few months on a Sunday, his only work-free day. This was very exciting for us, not only to see an uncle who was very indulgent and eager to see his nieces and nephews, but because he was the only Chinese person we knew outside our own family. In turn, Father would take me, and sometimes my sisters, on an occasional Sunday trip by train to visit Uncle in his laundry.

During the typical visit, the two brothers spent a lot of time gossiping about relatives or discussing worldly matters that I was too young to comprehend. When we visited Uncle in Atlanta, we sometimes met a few other Chinese laundrymen. Listening to their conversations about other Chinese men from their home villages who also had laundries in other southern towns, I formed the erroneous impression that all Chinese in America ran laundries. Father sometimes squeezed in a short visit to a distant cousin who also had a laundry in Atlanta. He had five children, and although we scarcely got to know them because our contact was only for an hour or two each time, these rare visits were special because they were the only Chinese children we ever met in Georgia.

On a few Atlanta visits, father took me to the Chinese association hall on the second floor of a downtown building not far from the train terminal. It served as a place where the old and not-so-old Chinese men would congregate from Atlanta and nearby small towns to socialize on Sundays, their day off. They would gamble, gossip, share useful information, and reminiscence about the old country. These contacts greatly enriched my knowledge and understanding of the lives of these Chinese laundrymen and provided me with a stronger realization of my Chinese identity than I could have ever formed in Macon where we were the only Chinese.

MOVING TO A CHINESE COMMUNITY

As we children grew up, we increasingly questioned our parents' plans and expectations for our future because our experiences were so different from theirs. We had white schoolmates and playmates, and of course, no Chinese friends or age mates. My parents realized that there was an urgent need to move the family to California when my sisters reached adolescence. In San Francisco, because of its large Chinese population, our parents hoped we could meet, and hopefully marry, Chinese. If we remained in Macon, they feared that we might enter mixed-race marriages, which my parents did not consider desirable, especially in the South.

When we moved to San Francisco, I thought (at age 15) that I had a good idea of what it meant to be Chinese. I had a rude awakening because I discovered I was quite different from my American-born Chinese peers in San Francisco. They had grown up immersed in Chinese ways and had lived in close proximity to many other Chinese for all of their lives. I now discovered that I did not really know how to be "Chinese."

In San Francisco, I had ample opportunity to develop new friendships through social contact with Chinese Americans. Most of the Chinese of my age whom I met were second generation. I had some difficulty identifying with the Chinese American students at school, because the Chinese Americans in San Francisco seemed so different from me in many ways. Most of them had grown up in Chinatown, and had attended *de facto* segregated schools that were predominantly Chinese. They were influenced by Chinese customs and culture all of their lives and were thoroughly self-identified by their Chinese heritage. They not only could speak Chinese much better than I could, but some could read and write Chinese because from an early age their parents had sent them to Chinese language school after their American school hours.

No sooner had I become "Chinese," living in the San Francisco area during my high school and college years, then I lost awareness of much of my Chinese identity because I would be living over the next decade in regions with relatively few Chinese. First, I spent three years working on my PhD at Northwestern University, located in a predominantly upper-middle-class white community just north of Chicago. Then, in 1962, I assumed a teaching appointment in Long Beach, California, where there were few Chinese at that time. Three years later, I taught at York University in Toronto, where the population was primarily white. During this decade I found myself again isolated from contact with other Chinese. I came to resign myself to the fact that I lived and worked in a primarily white-dominated and non-Chinese world. I resolved to make the best of things and tried to focus on the best qualities of both the Chinese and white aspects of my experiences.

It was not that I thought of myself as "white" as much as I found it futile to obsess about being "Chinese." Once in a while I might catch a glimpse of myself in a reflection and suddenly remember, "Oh, I'm Chinese," but most of the time I ignored or suppressed awareness of my ethnicity. My solution was flawed because one's ethnicity does not vanish even though one ignores it because many others still focus on it. This can be positive; for example, while I did not think of myself as a "Chinese" psychology professor, many of my students, mostly non-Chinese, did. By noticing my ethnicity at a time when there were very few Chinese psychology professors, they saw that a Chinese person could successfully teach psychology.

IDENTITY CONFUSION AND CONFLICTS

Among whites, I often wanted to assimilate or pass as one of them to avoid the stigma of being Chinese. The racist stereotypical images of Chinese that emphasized slanted eyes, straight hair, queues, sing-song Chinese music and spoken language, idiographic Chinese written characters, and exotic clothing items like coolie hats had subtly poisoned my desire to identify as Chinese.

Yet among whites, I was regarded as an authority on matters related to the Chinese. As Chan[3] similarly observed, "My sense of ethnic identity changed when I am in a non Chinese community, where I am perceived as an expert about Chinese culture by virtue of my ethnicity and teased when I talk about Chinese events or customs with anything but certainly." Among Chinese, I wanted to be accepted as one of them but I often felt that they did not think I was Chinese enough. As Chan noted, "It changes again when I am in Chinatown where the majority of the residents are recent immigrants from areas of China…about which I know very little. I do not assume that I understand their experiences." These predicaments exist to some degree for all ethnic minorities. But they may be greater for ethnic minorities who, like the Chinese, are few in numbers in a society where race issues have up to now been seen only in terms of black or white.

Finally, as noted in research by psychologists,[4] there is considerable variation in the form and content of ethnic identity even within a specific ethnic group. Initially formed in Georgia under minimal contact with Chinese, and later altered by an overnight move to San Francisco where I was almost totally immersed in contact with Chinese people and lifestyle, the shaping of my Chinese identity involved a different process and outcome than for Chinese who lived under different social conditions than I did.

NOTES

1. Jean Phinney, "Ethnic Identity in Adolescents and Adults: A Review of Research," *Psychological Bulletin* 108 (1990): 499–514.
2. "Macon Chinese Colony to Observe New Year," *Macon Daily Telegraph* (1908): 4A.
3. Elaine Chan, "Ethnic identity in Transition: Chinese New Year through the Years," *Journal of Curriculum Studies* 35, no. 4 (2003): 409–423.
4. Phinney, "Ethnic Identity." 510.

A Snapshot of the Asian Community in 1930s San Diego

Murray K. Lee

In 1930 the Asian community remained in eight blocks of the downtown area of San Diego. While some of the Chinese (240) and Japanese (119) in the district were raising families, Filipinos (10), who were the most recent arrivals, were all bachelors. Data from the U.S. Census of 1930 was used to look at all 568 people living in these eight blocks. Because of housing restrictions, almost all of the Asians living in the city were in this district. The census allows one to virtually enter the homes of all the people in the area and identify the families and the occupants. It listed by name the head of each household, the wife, the children, and other family members or lodgers. Included were age, sex, marital status, birthplace of residents and parents, language spoken, date of entry, and citizenship status. Other important data included were education, occupation, employment, and veteran status.

A map of each block in the district was created to show the residences, businesses, and organizations. Almost all the children in the area were from Chinese and Japanese families. Non-Asians living in the area were lodgers in hotels and boarding houses. Some remnants of the former red-light district were also present. Housing in the area was deficient in amenities and in short supply. The Asian families lived in cramped quarters, some above or behind their businesses, with many children, relatives, and lodgers. The most ethnically diverse block was located here. It included Chinese, Japanese, Filipinos, Whites, Blacks, Mexicans, Hawaiians, and a Native American. With the census, city business directories, oral histories, and historic photos, a snapshot of a unique period in the life of San Diego's Asian community is provided. (See map.)

Market Street

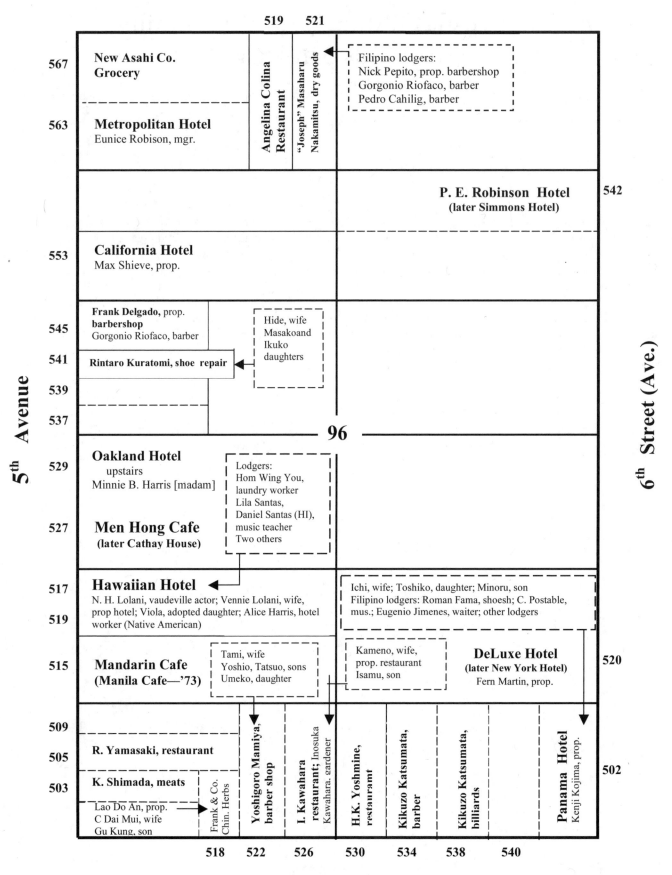

519   521

New Asahi Co. Grocery		Filipino lodgers:
567		Nick Pepito, prop. barbershop
		Gorgonio Riofaco, barber
563 **Metropolitan Hotel**		Pedro Cahilig, barber

567   New Asahi Co. Grocery

563   Metropolitan Hotel
Eunice Robison, mgr.

Angelina Colina Restaurant

"Joseph" Masaharu Nakamitsu, dry goods

Filipino lodgers:
Nick Pepito, prop. barbershop
Gorgonio Riofaco, barber
Pedro Cahilig, barber

P. E. Robinson Hotel
(later Simmons Hotel)

542

553   **California Hotel**
Max Shieve, prop.

545   **Frank Delgado,** prop. **barbershop**
Gorgonio Riofaco, barber

Hide, wife
Masakoand
Ikuko
daughters

541   **Rintaro Kuratomi, shoe repair**

539

537

96

529   **Oakland Hotel**
upstairs
Minnie B. Harris [madam]

Lodgers:
Hom Wing You,
laundry worker
Lila Santas,
Daniel Santas (HI),
music teacher
Two others

527   **Men Hong Cafe**
(later Cathay House)

517   **Hawaiian Hotel**
N. H. Lolani, vaudeville actor; Vennie Lolani, wife,
prop hotel; Viola, adopted daughter; Alice Harris, hotel
519   worker (Native American)

Ichi, wife; Toshiko, daughter; Minoru, son
Filipino lodgers: Roman Fama, shoesh; C. Postable,
mus.; Eugenio Jimenes, waiter; other lodgers

515   **Mandarin Cafe**
(Manila Cafe—'73)

Tami, wife
Yoshio, Tatsuo, sons
Umeko, daughter

Kameno, wife,
prop. restaurant
Isamu, son

DeLuxe Hotel
(later New York Hotel)
Fern Martin, prop.

520

509

505   **R. Yamasaki, restaurant**

503   **K. Shimada, meats**

Lao Do An, prop.
C Dai Mui, wife
Gu Kung, son

Frank & Co. Chin. Herbs

Yoshigoro Mamiya, barber shop

I. Kawahara restaurant; Inosuka Kawahara. gardener

H.K. Yoshmine, restaurant

Kikuzo Katsumata, barber

Kikuzo Katsumata, billiards

Panama Hotel
Kenji Kojima, prop.

502

518   522   526   530   534   538   540

MKL 9-04

Island Avenue

5th Avenue

6th Street (Ave.)

The Development of Chinese Ethnic Communities in Greater Boston

(Original Title: Change and Continuity: Boston's Chinese American
Community at the Turn of the 21st Century)

Shauna Lo

Since the 1870s, Chinatown has been the center of the Chinese community in Greater Boston and the only neighborhood with a significant concentration of Chinese Americans. However, Boston's Chinatown has faced numerous threats. Since the 1950s, its land area has been reduced by one-third due to urban renewal projects and institutional development. More recently, Chinatown has been undergoing a process of rapid gentrification as real-estate developers rush to build high-rise office buildings and market-rate or luxury housing.

As Chinese looked elsewhere to settle, two new Chinese communities began to form in Quincy and Malden in the 1980s. These two cities are within ten miles of Chinatown, are accessible by subway, and offer affordable housing, and while the Chinese population has increased dramatically over two decades in Quincy and Malden, it has remained more or less constant in Chinatown. Indeed, the Chinese population in Quincy prior to 1980 was only a few hundred; it is now estimated at 16,000 to 20,000, many times larger than Chinatown's population.

Although the Chinese populations in Quincy and Malden both have a high proportion of immigrants and a large number of limited-English speakers, they are at a somewhat better socioeconomic level than their counterparts in Chinatown. Their household income is higher, poverty level is lower, and rate of homeownership much higher.

Chinese in Quincy and Malden still have strong ties to Chinatown but have less need to rely on Chinatown since the amount of social services, cultural offerings, restaurants, and other businesses in both cities is increasing. However, the Chinese communities in Quincy and Malden still need more culturally and linguistically appropriate services, stronger community organizations, and greater influence in city affairs.

The History of Two Taoist Temples

The Baiyunguan in Shanghai, China, and the Bok Kai in Marysville, California

(Original Title: Two Daoist Temples: The Baiyunguan (White Cloud Temple) in Shanghai and the Bok Kai Temple in Marysville, 1880s until Present)

Joan Mann

There is an old Chinese proverb, loosely quoted, that says: "Seeing for oneself is better than hearing it from others."

While spending a year teaching in China, I visit a Taoist temple and witness a traditional Taoist ceremony where ten priests, dressed in traditional blue gowns and black flat hats take turns reading long prayers. As they finish, each one bows toward the altar as incense burns and the smoke curls up from each of the deities chosen to dispense blessings. Seven other priests play the fundamental Taoist music with their traditional musical instruments and together these sights, sounds, and smells of the temple begin to envelop my senses. I notice there are candles being lit throughout the temple as an ancient ceremony is being performed to honor the hundredth birthday of a deceased relative. I am told that this ritual is the commission for the continuation of lengthy afterlife rites and the descendants have paid for this service to ensure that the wishes for the happiness and wealth of their ancestor in the afterlife are still being carried out.

Attending rituals like this at the Baiyunguan (White Cloud) temple in Shanghai, China, was once reserved for members of the temple, or for those who lived in the surrounding neighborhood, to allow the people in the community to come face to face with their ancient rites of Taoism. However, now intruding tourists and visitors like myself are invited to visit and view these temple rites and celebrations in an effort to sustain the temple both culturally and economically.

Across the Pacific Ocean in California, in a town named Marysville, another Taoist temple is holding a celebration that will bring back to the community not only its slowly vanishing members but also many visitors from the large cities in the area, such as Sacramento and San Francisco, to a Chinese community that has grown smaller and smaller throughout the years. This is the only temple in the United States that still celebrates Yee Yeut Yee, or "Bomb Day,"[1] a holiday honoring the deity known as Bok Kai, the God of the North and Protector of the Floods.[2] This holiday, usually held on the second day of the second month of the Chinese lunar calendar, derives its name from the shooting off of "bombs," which contain good-fortune rings, and has been an ongoing holiday in the Marysville area for over a century. The two-day holiday begins quietly with religious observances on the first day and ends with the bombs and a parade featuring the Golden Dragon. This Golden Dragon is said to have been brought to America sometime before the turn of the century. It was exhibited at the World's Fair in New York and was last used in the 1937 parade in Marysville.[3] Now, in later years, a newer, shorter dragon is used in the parade.

Marysville, at the junction of the Feather and Yuba rivers, was once an entrance to the goldfields of the Sierras and served as a jumping-off point for both prospective miners and their goods during the days of the gold rush. The temple, located next to a levee, was prone to flooding, and Bok Kai, the principal deity of this temple, was believed to offer protection from the often occurring floods.

During the Bok Kai celebration, this local temple is filled with community members, visitors, and tourists alike who come to light incense sticks to a particular deity to express gratitude for the blessings they have been granted or the good fortune they hope to receive. There are no longer any Taoist priests at this temple to perform prayers or rituals, so usually an individual is left to worship on his or her own. If, during your visit, you ask an attendee how he or she knows which rites are being performed, you are told that any explanation of the rituals of this Bok Kai temple are only ones that have been passed down in families for many generations through oral translation and tradition.

Since my research is in the field of the religion/philosophy of Taoism and its temples, when walking in a Chinese mainland city such as Shanghai, Beijing, or Xian and looking for Taoist temple structures, I am always genuinely surprised when I see the "construction" of a Taoist temple. It would be the same when I visit the California cities of Marysville, Oroville, Weaverville, and Mendocino, several locations of the remaining semi-active Taoist temples in the United States. Here again, as in China, I would be surprised that the buildings I viewed were actually "temples." In the West, we tend to think of temples as large, ornate structures and as such, it was always unexpected, when I found a temple structure, to see that it was usually a small, nondescript building looking on the outside very much like an ordinary, small wooden house. Both the "old" Baiyunguan temple in Shanghai and the Bok Kai temple in Marysville are of this type, where one can hardly discern anything of a religious nature other than some ornate carvings around a doorway or a roof with curling eaves. I would find my most recognizable feature of both of these temples especially during temple holiday celebrations, and it would not be the physical construction but rather how each temple had reconstructed itself to be, for those few special days not only a place of worship, but also a local and visitor tourist attraction.

So we must begin to ask ourselves why Taoism, and more importantly its representative temples, are becoming important to the occasional visitor or tourist, both Chinese and Chinese American. Is it because today's visitor is beginning to recognize that the Taoist temple of yesterday could well be the symbolic reflection of a changing society in both China and the United States? I believe we must look at the example of these two Taoist temples, their past, their present, and hopefully their future, as a blueprint to the changing Chinese and Chinese American communities that are reflected in a changing Chinese culture. The term I use here, "Chinese American," will be used in its broadest sense and is meant to include all Chinese, both citizens and noncitizens. Before 1943, Chinese immigrants were prevented by law from becoming naturalized citizens; because this law was discriminatory, my definition of Chinese Americans will include all of those permanent residents who have spent most of their lives in America. On the other hand, my definition of "Chinese" is meant to refer to those who live in mainland China.

The Taoism of Chinese culture found its way to America in the nineteenth century during the time of the California gold rush. Many Chinese had immigrated to California from the southern provinces of China where poverty, famine, and war had become the norm. Enticed by dreams of a better life, their mass immigration created the development of communities that would predominately follow the lifestyles of their hometown in China, where Chinese customs and culture were an important part of everyday life. When the Chinese who worked the mines came to America and found instead of wealth and security, mostly discrimination and oppression, the Taoist temple would be built as a place where they could once again practice harmony, balance, and a sense of order in their lives. The temple was in many ways their fortress against all that was unpleasant in the new country. It was a continuing part of their culture that gave wholeness and meaning to their existence, and it was able to generate within the heart of the worshipper the courage to return to the harsh realities of the outside world and to work patiently toward the future by following the "Tao," the path of long suffering but of eventual victory.[4]

Taoism would also remain an important staple of Chinese religion/philosophy for those who remained in mainland China. Today one still finds not only Taoism but four other active major philosophies/religions practiced in China:

Buddhism, Islam, Catholicism, and Protestantism. There are also a variety of folk beliefs/religions practiced in areas that are inhabited by ethnic minority groups. All of these groups still maintain their houses of worship whether they be temples or yurts, churches or cathedrals, or once again just the small altar in their homes. Taoism, however, is the only one of these religions/philosophies that is indigenous to China as each of the other four were brought into China and had their origination in a foreign country.[5] Taoism would become the major religion/philosophy of the Chinese people during the second century AD and it is Taoism, along with Buddhism and Confucianism, that has endured in the Chinese community into this new millennium.

It is difficult to give an exact number of believers of Taoism in this twenty-first century because there are no recorded rituals for conversion to become a Taoist practitioner and thus there are no records or statistics available to give the exact number of believers. However, the Taoist Associations of both Beijing and Shanghai have reported their number of members in China to be over 100 million, and the International Taoist Association numbers its followers in the hundreds of millions.[6]

Informal interviews with members of today's mainland Chinese population about any organized religion/philosophy such as Taoism have raised some interesting points: first and foremost is that any and all Taoist beliefs stem from China's oldest historical and cultural tradition of Confucianism. It was Confucianism that would become China's official ideology far back in the second century BC, and it is Confucianism that remained the major philosophy in China for over two thousand years until the end of the Qing Dynasty in 1911. Confucianism calls for a set approach toward society known as *filial piety*, or honoring one's leaders and elders, with attention focused on the practical problems of morality and ethics. Because of Confucianism, ancient China was regarded as a "State of Ceremonies,"[7] and its traditional culture would develop to include not only Confucianism, but also Taoism, which historians now recognize as having complemented each other for long periods of time in Chinese history. These two schools of thought are understood by the West to be similar and yet different in their common belief that by using a "natural hierarchy," harmony will come to all. It is my opinion that this is the basic tenet of the China of the past, but also an apt description of the China I visited and lived in this present year.

What is most interesting in the study of Taoism and its temples is that the differences in the teachings of Confucianism, Taoism, or Buddhism are not an important component of any religion/philosophy practiced in China today. A person may be a believer of Buddhism while frequently going to the Taoist temple for worship. Yet this same person will most likely also honor the moral and ethical teaching of Confucianism. Interestingly, conflicts of a religious nature have seldom occurred in China, unlike in Europe where religious wars were constantly being fought during the Middle Ages. Thus it is sometimes difficult for those of us in the West to understand the practices of a Chinese religion/philosophy, as we who do choose to worship must choose only one religion/philosophy to believe in and one sect of that religion to follow.

Taoism is the only pure Chinese religion/philosophy among the major five in China and it has a history of over 1,800 years. Most historians agree that Taoism came into being in the second century AD and followed a unique process of development. During the Han Dynasty, from 206 BC to AD 220, it would be known as the study of Huang and Laozi. Huang is believed to have been the mythical ancestor of the Chinese Nation, and Laozi was a historiographer of the Zhou Dynasty, 1100–221 BC. Taoism was developed on the basis of two indigenous beliefs or sects, the Five Dou (measure of grain) Sect and the Taiping (peace) Sect, as the way to self-cultivation, helping one not only to concentrate the mind and act unobtrusively, but also to care for all things on earth by following the natural order of things. The former sect required only that to be a member one must donate five dou of rice for payment as admission to the sect. This sect regarded Laozi (the philosopher of the Spring and Autumn period dating back 2,500 years ago who wrote the *Tao Te Ching*, as its leader) and the *Tao Te Ching* and the Great Way as the central text of its philosophy. It taught people to purify their souls through confession, and its priests used incantations to treat diseases and ills. It is believed that the Five Dou Sect was Taoism in its embryonic form, and Taoism as it was practiced by this sect would continue to develop into the Taoist religion/philosophy that would be practiced in the following centuries. By the third century AD, this sect had changed its name to Heavenly Teacher's Sect, and during the Tang (618–907) and following dynasties, this Heavenly Teacher's Sect was to receive many honored titles and rewards from their emperors.

As Taoism gradually developed into a full-fledged religion/philosophy, its main claim would be to help mortals become immortal. Thus, with the support of the ruling class to whom immortality was a major goal, Taoism became attached to the imperial courts. However, Taoism also became a "popular" religion/philosophy because in many ways it was associated with sorcery and incantations that supposedly were able to ward off evil spirits, treat diseases, and usher in good luck. As such, "official" Taoism and "popular" Taoism did not compete against one another as all Chinese of both the upper class and the peasant class were interested in becoming "immortal."

What merits special attention to Taoism is that during its long, time-honored history of development, it has exerted far-reaching influences on literature, the arts, chemistry, medicine, and science. Joseph Needham, noted historian of science, wrote in his 1956 *Science and Civilization of China,* that many of the most attractive elements of the Chinese characters derive from Taoism. China without Taoism, Needham says, would be a tree of which some of its deepest roots have perished.[8]

Taoism in early turbulent Shanghai was still a somewhat secret Chinese religion/philosophy that was very different from the simple Taoism practiced at the time by the the Chinese mining community in Marysville. Shanghai, then known as the "Whore of the Orient" or the "Paris of the East," had an open-door policy that had attracted a conglomerate of British, Russian, German, Japanese, Italian, and American people in the early part of the twentieth century. During its period of infamy, Shanghai was made up of many of these expatriate "societies," but often forgotten—yet more important—was the Chinese "secret society" with its recondite culture and customs that in reality was the exotic face of China. Hidden in the "secret societies" of the Shanghai Chinese community was the ancient religion/philosophy, with its secret elixirs and spells, known as Taoism, with its temples that served those in the faith. It was Taoism that captured the imagination of the underworld of Shanghai during that time, but it would be Taoism and its many deities that would ultimately sustain the Chinese people during the long years of both Nationalist and Communist rule when many of the temples were desecrated and destroyed. In my many interviews I was told that in place of the temples, their members would place small hidden altars in their homes during these years, where prayers could still be offered to the deities and incense was still burned to ask for protection and the promise of life after death.[9]

The Baiyunguan temple in Shanghai was rebuilt after being destroyed by both the invading Japanese army and the warring Nationalist and Communist armies. The Bok Kai temple in Marysville was rebuilt after numerous floods. Both temples date their beginnings to the 1800s, and both temples are still semi-active today. It is evident that the religious life of the people in both places is tightly woven into the history, economics, language, and cultural fabric of their neighborhoods, yet both temples are experiencing major problems as the communities, societies, and culture around them continue to change. The Baiyunguan was recently moved from the Xilain Back Road Alley outside Laoximen, back to its original site that is located at the North Gate of what is left of the original Old Shanghai Wall. This famous temple was, and still is, the headquarters of the Complete Perfection Sect.[10] The temple, as it stands now, was rebuilt in 1882 during the eighth year of the reign of Emperor Guangzu of the Qing Dynasty. It was originally founded by Complete Perfection priest Xu Zhicheng, and the temple originally worshipped the Thunder God, Lei Shen, during that period. Today the Baiyunguan has become the Temple of the Orthodox Oneness Tradition, where eight gilded bronze statues built during the Ming dynasty are enshrined.[11] The most important statues from this period that hold places of honor in the temple are the five standing statues of the Heavenly Generals (Tian Jiang), which are each approximately eight feet tall. There are also the statues of two of the Celestial Masters (Tian Shi), and these are about six feet tall. There are several lesser statues placed in alcoves throughout the temple, but unfortunately, none of these statues are original.[12] Today those who come to the Baiyunguan mainly worship the Great Jade Emperor, Yu Huang.

The Baiyuunguan slumped into a gradual decline in the early twentieth century, and during the Cultural Revolution from 1966 to 1976, nearly all of its precious paintings and books were destroyed. After 1978, both the State and local government placed greater emphasis on rebuilding and revitalizing Taoism. By 1984, the Baiyunguan was finally allowed to resume its Taoist activities.[13] Since that time, the temple has become the seat of the Shanghai Taoist Academy, where it also maintains the Institute of Shanghai Taoist Culture in Shanghai.

In comparison, Taoism found its way to Marysville in the nineteenth century during the time of the 1849 California gold rush with the many Chinese who emigrated from the southern provinces of China. Those Chinese who settled in Marysville built their first temple there in 1865, and it was located about a half mile from the site of today's temple site in the vicinity of First and B Streets. In 1866, a great flood is said to have destroyed the temple, and local legend says that one of the temple tablets was found in the mud and silt following the flood. That spot, which was a bathhouse at the time, was chosen as the site for the present-day Bok Kai temple. Although this temple is known as the Bok Kai (Water God) temple, there are several other deities that hold places of honor. Historically these gods of Taoism were once human beings who lived in a specific time and place, and who displayed exemplary qualities while living. Upon their death they have been deified as legends and the myths of their skills have been related to generation after generation. Rituals during Bomb Day and other ceremonies in the Bok Kai temple remain unchanged from times past, and the Chinese Americans who celebrate at this temple still see the deities as benevolent beings or high officials who can help mortals in exchange for food, drink, and money.[14]

Examples of this kind of testimony can be found in reading the local Marysville newspaper, the *Appeal-Democrat*, when reporters conducted interviews with visitors during the Bok Kai Bomb Day festivities. Below are several excerpts from a recent Bomb Day celebration:

> [O]ur family has gotten continuous good luck over the years, said Eric Young of San Francisco, who counted among the recent blessings, graduations, promotions, job offers, and his two-year-old daughter....[A] lot of people get their wishes and they come back to thank the gods" said Kathy Ng from Oakland....[Y]ou don't ask for anything unreasonable....I asked that everybody be safe and healthy...if someone in the family is sick, you can ask that they be healed....[15]

The Bok Kai temple still works in the old style of "caretaker," says Daniel Barth, current president of the Marysville Historical Society. "A visitor decides they have a request for Bok Kai because they have heard that the Bok Kai temple has a very good track-record for granting requests. However,

once they arrive at the temple they find it closed. They see a phone number posted on the side wall of the temple and they make a call. If good fortune is on their side, a caretaker will answer, and after a wait the caretaker arrives to open up the temple. He lights the incense, and the lucky visitors make their prayers and requests. They may also ask to toss the divinations blocks if they are looking for answers to a specific question, or they can use oracle sticks to consult for answers from the Oracle Book."[16] Visitors are usually cautioned not to take photographs, and after the visit to the temple is over, the caretaker expects to be paid. The author notes here that I did as was expected of me, as this is the Taoist "Way."

Does this intrusion by visitors, tourists, and even historians such as myself represent for many Chinese Americans a way back to the temple for the generations who have grown away from their religious/philosophical roots? Or has time changed not only the Taoist "temple," but more importantly how both today's Chinese and Chinese Americans view themselves, the temples, and their heritage? These are some of the questions that must be addressed before we can arrive at a viable definition of what it means to be Chinese or a Chinese American living in the twenty-first century.

Those Chinese Americans living on the West Coast of the United States who, over the years, have adapted to the values and cultures of American life with very little knowledge of the religious philosophy of Taoism are the ones who will one day be heir to any Taoist temple legacy such as that found at the Bok Kai in Marysville. Will any proposed restoration of the temple also restore some Chinese religion/philosophy and its basic teachings to any of the people? Or even more importantly, is it important for Chinese Americans as a way to retain or regain their "Chineseness"?

For the Chinese who live in mainland China and have been subjected to the fluctuations of acceptance of their religion/philosophy by government changes, there have also been dramatic differences in their experiences both within and without their Taoist temple and its culture. The Shanghai city government's moving of the "old" Baiyunguan temple to make way for roads and buildings to accommodate the World Exposition in Shanghai in 2010 meant that the "old" temple structure would be moved from a Chinese neighborhood to a tourist neighborhood. It would be located closer to well-known venues visited by tourists, like Nanjing Road and Yu Yuan Market, both on the Shanghai visitor circuit. This also meant that the "old" Baiyunguan would receive some much needed repairs that in reality would ultimately lead to a virtually "new" temple.

The "old" Baiyunguan temple was located down an alley from a small side street in the Huangpu District of Shanghai called "Nanshi" or Old Town, and was far away from any tourist venue or activity. As one of the oldest temples in Shanghai it was smaller in size than either the Confucian temple or the Buddhist temples located in the same general area of Old Town, and it sat for over one hundred years under the protection of the branches of a huge old tree. This same "old" Baiyunguan temple, also known at one time in the nineteenth century as the "Temple of the White Clouds," owes its name to the 8,000 scrolls it received from the temple of the same name in Beijing.[17] The "old" Baiyunguan still had its terracotta soldiers on the roof to keep watch, I was told by temple members, to ensure that nothing disrupted the serene atmosphere that surrounded the temple. This "old" temple, which I was privileged to visit in the Fall of 2004, was still an active and busy temple at the time, with many of its local congregation also still active and busy in attendance at all hours of the day, either folding the small yellow triangles used to hold the ashes from the incense burner (and considered to have special powers) or preparing the vegetables that had been brought to the temple for the meals cooked for the priests. However, just as I had started my exploration of every nook and cranny of the "old" Baiyunguan's proud history, I saw this very special Taoist temple suffer the indignities of relocation and separation from its community at the end of 2004, and its new congregation and new neighborhood take on modern and more Western characteristics, very much like the Chinese American population in the United States.

Chinese and Chinese American history is a living, continuous history that has weathered many changes in its long and unique past. Chinese Americans in particular have taken a number of paths to identify their ethnicity. According to historian Barbara Fields,[18] race is either an illusion that does ideological work or an objective biological fact. In the case of Chinese or Chinese Americans, race is a biological fact, but any "Chineseness" seems to have become an illusion seen only by non-Chinese. Has the exotic face of the "Orientalism" that Edward Said[19] wrote about some years ago been systematically deconstructed by those effected? I would hope not. That luminaries of Chinese American society, such as Him Mark Lai and Albert Cheng have chosen to develop the "In Search of Roots" Program for constructing identity through family history research tells me that through organizations like the Chinese Culture Foundation of San Francisco, "Chineseness" will remain an important part of the discovery of Chinese American identity. In China, where the government is now openly supportive of restoring historic buildings, although not necessarily their functions, I hope that the recognition of all Taoist temples will be included as the component complementary to the reidentification of one's cultural history.

ENDNOTE

This document uses a mixture of pinyin, romanization, and commonly accepted transliterations. Interviews cited in this paper were conducted by the author in Shanghai, China. Specific names have not been used so as to protect the privacy of both the priests and the members of the Baiyunguan temple.

NOTES

1. National Register of Historic Places, *A History of Chinese Americans in California* (2002), *www.nr.nps.gov/RedBooks/75000498. red.pdf.*
2. Paul G. Chace, *Returning Thanks: Chinese Rites in an American Community* (PhD diss., University of California, Riverside; Berkeley: University of California Press, 1999), 75.
3. Chace, *Returning Thanks,* 416.
4. Daniel Wong, Doris Wong, and George Williams, "Chinese Temples of Northern California," in *The Life, Influence, and the Role of the Chinese in the United States, 1776-1960: Proceedings, Papers of the National Conference held at the University of San Francisco, July 10–12, 1975* (San Francisco: Chinese Historical Society of America, 1976).
5. Cheng Manchao, *The Origin of Chinese Deities* (Beijing: Foreign Language Press of Beijing, 1995).
6. Ibid.
7. James Legge, *Confucian Analects, The Great Learning and the Doctrine of the Mean,* vol. 1 (London: Dover Publications, 1971).
8. Joseph Needham, *History of Scientific Thought,* vol. 2, *Science and Civilisation in China* (London: Cambridge University Press, 1956), 164.
9. Hong Yi Huang, interview by author, Shanghai, China, November 8, 2004.
10. Yie Wang, *Daoism in China* (Beijing: China Intercontinental Press, 2001).
11. Wang Lixian, Chair Master, Baiyungun Temple, Shanghai, China, interview by author, Shanghai, China, December 2, 2004.
12. Ibid.
13. "Temple Is Witness to Taoism's Ups and Downs," *China Daily/ Shanghai Star,* September 26, 2002.
14. Guang Yun and Yi Cheng, (Bejing: Foreign Language Press, 1999).
15. "Annual Bomb Day Celebration at Bok Kai Chinese Temple," *Marysville Appeal-Democrat,* February 2004.
16. Barth,Daniel, "Notes on the Bok Kai," e-mail to author, January 6, 2003.
17. Guang Yun and Yi Cheng, *A Taoist Miscellany.*
18. Barbara Fields, "Slavery, Race and Ideology in the United States of America," *New Left Review* 181 (May/June 1990): 95–118.
19. Edward W. Said, *Orientalism* (New York: Random House, 1979).

Two Critical Points on
Chinese Language Literature Overseas
海外華文文學的兩點困惑

Frank Cheng
程寶林

我不是職業的評論家, 因此, 並沒有對海外華文文學的發展源流與現狀, 進行系統的、高屋建瓴式的研究。但是, 作為一名寫作者, 對於美國海外華文文學的現狀, 或多或少有一點直觀的感受。讓我感到困惑的, 當代海外華文文學, 至少在兩個重大層面上存在著缺失或者缺位:

其一: 海外華文作品中, 缺乏對於海外華人既不能回歸祖國, 又不能真正扎根美國的那種文化上的 "孤懸感" 進行深達靈魂的展示和解剖, 由此產生的許多華人心理深處暗藏的精神創傷, 本來可以成為極具開拓價值的文學礦藏。這種缺失或缺位, 部分原因在於海外華文文學創作隊伍中, 從事長篇小說寫作的成熟作家並不多見, 而篇幅短小、主要抒寫個人經歷與感受的散文, 無法承擔海外華人心靈史這樣重大的使命。

其二: 由於語言、文化等的障礙, 大多數美國華文作家, 與美國主流文學無法產生互動。他們對於美國當代的文學發展和現狀既缺乏了解, 對於祖國的文化和文學, 也產生了難以逾越的隔絕和疏離。更重要的是, 身處海外, 生活在範圍很小的華人圈子裏, 無論對於美國社會, 還是中國社會, 都缺乏聲氣相通、血肉相聯的認同感。這就必然使得他們的寫作, 喪失了作品應有的 "氣場"。與之相一致的, 是美國華文文壇的評論家嚴重缺乏。沒有學術機構的資料與資源作為後盾, 也缺乏對美國當代主流文學的對比參照, 美國華文文學的評論, 還停留在圈子內無謂拔高的狀態, 沒有進行整體性把握的能力。在我看來, 某些評論家, 對於美國華文作家的成就所進行的不負責任的拔苗助長, 更主要的, 恐怕是借以確立自己的評論家地位, 因為 "皮之不存, 毛將焉附" 的古理, 對於作家與評論家的依存關係, 是同樣適用的。

那麼, 如何解決這樣兩個問題呢? 首先, 我們應該拓寬海外華文文學的涵蓋面, 而不應該在題材上, 對海外華文文學進行作繭自縛的限定。我們絕不可以將海外華文文學, 局限在 "海外華人, 寫海外生活" 這樣的層面上。由于前面已經說過的海外華文作家的天生不足一我們只有圈子生活, 至多社團生活, 而無社會生活, 許多作家的筆觸, 都自覺不自覺地伸向、探向祖國的社會與生活。這對於海外華文文學的發展, 不是損失, 而是收獲, 因為, 這些作家, 利用了身處美國, 對中國歷史、社會現實的審視角度有所不同的優勢。比如, 最近旅居灣區的著名作家嚴歌苓, 完成了寫中國土改運動的長篇小說《第九個寡婦》。如此重大的題材, 很可能具有開拓性的意義。對於主要從事散文寫作的作家來說, 我們不應該將自己的寫作, 局限在海外生活的細微和瑣屑中。我一向認為, 缺乏悲劇感的文學, 一定是膚淺的文字。而美國華文文學, 尤其要呼喚具有悲劇美感、悲劇思想力度的作品。

其次, 我們應該同時涉及、介入中國與美國的現、當代文學, 既從中國的文化、文學中吸取營養, 也從美國的文化、文學中得到養份。有部分作家不具有英語能力, 這並不構成真正的障礙, 因為中國大陸對於美國當代文學是極其關注的, 美國文壇出現的重大作品, 很快都會有中譯本出現。只有與中國、美國的當代文學同步發展, 吸取其有利於海外華文文學的營養, 美國華文作家才能利用自己足踏兩塊大陸、身處兩種文化的優勢, 寫出具有獨特藝術價值和思想深度的作品。

就我個人而言, 寫作也走過了兩個階段。第一個階段, 是痴迷於詩歌的年代, 從1982年7月, 在吉林省的《長春》月刊(現為《作家》)發表第一首詩開始, 到1991年12月,由四川大學出版社出版《程寶林抒情詩拔萃》, 並獲得第三屆 "成都市金芙蓉文學獎" 為止。這一段時間, 將近10年, 基本上確立了我作為詩人的地位和影響力, 寫出了《雨季來臨》等代表性詩歌作品。可惜的是, 在這一段時間內, 我完全忽視, 甚至蔑視散文寫作, 對散文作家不屑一顧, 荒誕地認為, 寫不出詩, 也寫不出小說的人, 才寫散文。慶幸的是, 這一期間我閱讀了大量的西方長篇小說, 培養起了對於長篇小說的閱讀興趣和整體閱讀把握能力, 為我今後的寫作轉向奠定了基礎。

第二個階段, 是從1991年到2005年, 時間跨度超過10年。這是我的散文寫作期, 詩歌祇是偶爾為之, 作品雖然數量不多, 但質量尚可, 基本維持住了我作為詩人的身份。我的散文, 歸納起來有三種類別, 其一是以白描手法, 抒寫中國社會底層人物的悲歡離合, 特別是農民, 代表作有萬字散文《歸葬》等。其一是以性靈文字為主要特色, 具有美文特徵的散文, 代表作有《廢園紀穎》等。

其三是具有雜文特色、以社會批判、文化抨擊為特色、語言犀利、思想深刻的作品, 代表作有《英語雜談》系列散文等。就散文寫作而言, 我目前面臨的困境是, 如何增加自己散文作品中的文化、哲學內涵, 使它能將上述三種特色融為一爐, 自成一家。這一個階段, 使得我完成了由純粹詩人, 到全方位文人的轉變。我的寫作領域旁涉到評論、翻譯, 即使我在創作上江郎才盡, 在這個兩個領域, 也還可以有所建樹。

第三個階段, 可以從2005年5月, 我獲得舊金山州立大學創作系藝術碩士學位算起。經過多年的語言準備, 和寫作練習, 我感覺到, 自己作為一個未來的小說家的人生閱歷已經充足, 思想和文化的準備也基本具備, 在英語和漢語的層次上, 已經具有從事雙語寫作的基本條件。在今後的三年內, 我的寫作計劃, 包括兩本長篇小說、一本寫實文學, 初步規劃用英文寫出, 以美國主流社會讀者為閱讀對象。目前我已將閱讀範圍, 主要限定在美國當代小說名著方面。如果在不放棄中文詩歌、散文寫作的前提下, 堅持10年的英文創作, 很難說最終一無所獲。對于自己語言感悟能力和思想敏銳度的自信, 將激勵我鼓勇前行。

Chinese Language Literature in America
A Historical Development
美華文學的歷史發展

Maurice Chuck
黃運基

文學是人學。而人是歷史的創造者，所以，文學是離不開歷史的。美華文學已經有很長的歷史。以我不成熟的看法，美華文學大致可劃分為四個歷史階段：從1785年-1888年描述早期被"賣豬仔"到美國的華工的文學作品為第一階段；第二階段則從1888年至1943年間，美國煽起了殘暴的排華風潮，迫使華人由鄉野遷居城鎮，導致美國各城市唐人街的形成，孕育了華人社會的雛型。直至第二次世界大戰後，由於華人的不斷抗爭，美國政府撤銷了排華法案，引起了華人社會的變化。然後，第三階段從1943年到1979年的36年期間，隨著美國少數族裔民權運動風起雲湧，華人也捲進了這個與他們息息相關的運動中去，為爭取自身應享的權益而進行了各種形式的鬥爭，使華人較前有更多的機會進入美國各個行業中去。第四階段是從1979年到現在，由於美中兩國關係正常化導致華人社區發生了巨大變化。可以這麼說，在這漫長的歷史長河中，華人先驅，創業維艱，對美經濟，貢獻鉅大；華人地位，稍有提高，面臨問題，仍然不少；美國社會，決非熔爐，而是一盤"沙拉"或"八寶飯"，彩色繽紛，代表移民美國的各個不同族裔。華僑歷史、文化習俗，已成為美國歷史、文化的重要組成部分；美華文學也成為反映美國華僑、華人特定的生命形態和特定的文化思維的文學。

1. 早期與抗日時期的美華文學

什麼是美華文學？目前還沒有一致的定義。各種說法都有：美國華文文學，美國華人文學，美國華僑文學，美國華族文學，等等等等。我們在1995年創辦的刊物《美華文學》(前身為《美華文化人報》) 在創刊詞中就標明了宗旨："除了以文會友外，更要通過多樣化的文藝形式—小說、詩歌、散文、雜文、戲劇、評論、報告文學等，從廣度和深度上反映華僑文化，反映華僑、華人今昔創業的軌跡。"十年來，《美華文學》一直努力循著這個宗旨發表大量具有濃郁"僑味"的多形式的作品，反映美國華僑、華人的生命形態與特定的文化思維。而這種"生命形態與特定的文化思維"就是美國華僑、華人從初始移民美國時的"落葉歸根"思維改而紮根美國本土的"落地生根"思維的轉化過程。

早期的美華文學，比較集中反映的有阿英編的《反美華工禁約文學集》(1960年代初由北京中華書局出版)，內容分五卷，第一卷詩歌；第二卷小說；第三卷戲曲；第四卷事略；第五卷散文。1882年美國國會通過法案禁止華工入境，1884年國會又修訂了該法案，進一步擴大限制華工來美。復於1888年通過法令，禁止暫離美國回中國探親的華人重返美國。這一連串的排華法案，激起了華人的抗爭，《反美華工禁約文學集》的整體內容，就是反映這個時期，中國工人被美國資本家誘騙到美國西部海岸等地，從事開礦、築鐵路等勞動，長期遭受侮辱、剝削和迫害的悲慘命運。這部文學集真正是"華工血淚史"，華人被白種人虐待的慘況，令人髮指，感人至深。

舊金山有個小島叫天使島。名字很動聽，但它絕對是沒有"天使"的孤島，它其實是一個移民拘留所。從1910年到1940年，有20多萬華僑被拘禁在天使島，等候移民局的審查，他們過著非人的屈辱生活。他們在拘禁的木屋牆上刻寫詩詞，以發泄他們心中的苦惱、憤怒、沮喪、彷徨、絕望、自憐、念鄉、思親和希望，人類最複雜的情感都在我們這些被拘禁的祖輩們的心靈深處流露無遺了。這些刻在木牆上的詩是在1970年才偶然被人發現的。後來由華僑歷史學家麥禮謙和林小琴、楊碧芳等人編譯成《埃崙詩集》，於1980年出版。可以說，這也是反映早期華僑來美遭受歧視、拘禁歷史的美華文學。1979年4月28日，天使島博物館開幕那天，數以千計的華人，其中有幸存的老華僑們，帶領兒孫來到天使島，默默地凝視著大理石刻書的對聯："別井離鄉飄流羈木屋，開天闢地創業在金門"，追思他們那段辛酸的歷史。

在 30 年代和 40 年代期間，居美華僑、華人，在風起雲湧的抗日救亡運動中，也推動了華僑文學的茁壯成長。《華僑文陣》、《輕騎》、《新苗》、《戰鬥》等華僑文學刊物相繼出現。這個時期，美華文學另一重要部分是戲劇的蓬勃發展。這也是抗日救亡運動所推動起來的。當年舊金山較有影響的青年組織，一是新文字會，一是盧烽劇社，還有屋崙的野火社。他們演出過許多抗日話劇。戰後，於 1946 年由加州青年救國團改組成立的加州華僑民主青年團（簡稱"民青"），文化活動也非常活躍，演出過多部話劇及演唱過《黃河大合唱》，也表演中國民族舞，并出版期刊。

2. 草根文群的形成

從 60 年代至 90 年代期間，美華文學有了喜人的發展，可謂大豐收的年代。來自大陸、台灣、香港的作家群，壯大了美華文學的創作隊伍。在這 40 年間，白先勇、陳若曦、聶華苓、於梨華、紀弦、謝冰瑩、喻麗清、李黎、木令耆、非馬、許達然、嚴歌苓、吳瑞卿、曹又方等，創作了一大批優秀的作品，其中有小說、詩歌和散文，尤以小說的影響最大。

在 80 年代出現一批新銳作家、被國內文學評論家稱作"草根文群"的有黃運基、劉荒田、老南、宗鷹、程寶林、劉子毅、關維杭、鄭其賢、梁應麟、穗青、陳中美、覺虹、陳雪丹、王性初、黃文湘、呂紅、曾寧、招思虹、伍可娉等。他們的作品，無論是小說、散文或詩歌，均以美國華僑、華人在東西文化的碰撞中的生命形態為其主題，表現特定的文化思維。從內容到形式，都與早期的美華文學和留學生文學截然不同。一方面，他們既傳承了中華民族、民俗文化的"根"，又汲取了西方以個體為中心的文化養料，這使他們創作出一批"僑味"無窮、"洋味"十足、獨具藝術風格的"美華文學"。中國山東大學文學院曾與美國華文文藝界協會合作，由黃萬華教授主編了一本《美國華文文學論》(2000 年 5月山東文藝出版社出版)，是論述"美華文學"最詳盡的一本書。書內對"草根文群"以及"新移民作家群"的研究，均有詳細論述，大家可找來參考，我就不在這裡贅述了。

3. 邊緣與主流

海外華僑、華人或華文文學，既不被認定屬於中國文學的一部分，亦不被認定屬於華僑華人在居住國文學的一部分；哪麼，它究竟應如何定位呢？到目前為止，文學界還沒有一致的認知。然而，這種現象並不防止學者們對海外華文文學這一新興的文學領域的整體研究。於是，在海外的華人作家群中，長期存在著"邊緣"與"主流"文學的議論。

然而，任何一個作家的文學創作，都是心裡有話要說，有感而發的；他在動筆(電腦)之前絕不會想到自己寫(打)出來的作品是屬於什麼文學。他也不會感覺到自己是"邊緣人"，他的作品被"邊緣化"。至於這些作品能否進入文學的"主流"，則應視乎作品本身的主題張力和它的藝術感染力。文學作品很難有確定的、一致的標準，連獲諾貝爾文學獎的《靈山》亦如是，有評論家認為它是一部"偉大的、輝煌的"作品，也有評論家認為它是"一座文化垃圾山"。

文學，就其本質而言，是人學。作家要表達的是人對精神與物質狀況的反應，是人對周圍環境引起的心靈感受。著名作家葉君健說，"文學是一種靈魂的活動"。對美國的華人作家來說，他們都不是專業作家，他們必須有固定的、足以維生的職業。他們在工作之餘，僅靠有限的精力和時間從事創作。他們長期遠離故國家園，在一個陌生的異域謀生，時刻體驗到東西文化的碰撞，他們的"靈魂的活動"的複雜性可想而知。一方面，在他們的身上既傳承了中華民族民俗文化的"根"，又汲取了西方以個體為中心的文化養料，這使他們創作出一批"僑味"無窮、"洋味"十足、獨具藝術風格、彩色斑斕的"美華文學"。

當然，文學很難亦不適宜歸類。但就作品的主題而言，我們習慣於把描寫留學生的校園生活，以及他們在美國這片"新土"體驗到的東西方文化衝突所引起的異域感、流放感和放逐感，從而激發他們一種無形的衝動，他們要透過文學作品來發洩他們內心"懷念故土"、尋找"文化回歸"的夢，故稱之為"留學生文學"。反之，在歷史上，移民來美國的華僑，儘管他們世世代代飽受白種人的歧視，深感"海外孤兒"之苦，他們亦日夕盼望有朝一日"衣錦還鄉"。不幸的是，一百多年來，祖國總是處於兵荒馬亂的劣境，使他們有家歸不得。這樣，代代相傳，他們選擇了"歸化"為美國公民。因此，不同於"留學生文學"，老一代華僑在美國的生活經歷，即從"華僑"到"華人"這一歷史性轉變，反映到文學上，便從"落葉歸根"選擇了"落地生根"。

4. 歸根與生根

從"華僑"到"華人"，需要一個過程；從"落葉歸根"到"落地生根"也需要一個過程。而在漫長的歷史進程中，華僑選擇"歸化"為美國公民，受到多個客觀因素的推動：一是美國在1943年取消了"排華法"；二是二次世界大戰時中美兩國是盟邦，居美華人效忠美國政府，與美軍並肩作戰，在歐洲戰場打擊德國納粹侵略，在亞洲戰場對抗日本倭寇。戰後，美籍華人在中國的妻兒子女和父母都可以合法移民來美，他們這些親人並最終成為美國公民；三是中國變天後，千千萬萬的海外華僑、華人曾歡欣了一陣子。然而，曾幾何時，由於人所共知的原因，中美兩國隨即變"友"為"敵"。緊接著的是中國政治運動不斷，天災加人禍，國家弄得支離破碎，傷透了華僑的心。在這種情況下，既然他們"落葉歸根"的心願難圓，只好面對現實，腳踏實地，紛作"落地生根"的打算。

這種時空的變異，中美關係風雨陰晴的反復，反映到美華文學方面，自然也發生了劇變。即便如此，美華文學離不開中華本源文化和美國本土文化的影響。因此，不管作者是來自母國或是在美國土生土長，他們用華文創作或用英文創作，與白人作家不同的是，他們主要還是寫華人或亞裔的故事。而華人"落地生根"的結果，從文學的層面而言，作家們將可能更著重於以中華本源文化思維進行創作美國本土華人帶有西方文化情感載體的作品來，"魂繫中華、心連祖國的情結"的"海外孤兒"心態將會隨著時空的變異而顯得"相對淡薄"。

在這次研討會上介紹的幾位作家，與會者將從他們的發言中，透過他們的作品，讓大家深切體會到作者"從華僑到華人"，從"落葉歸根"到"落地生根"過程中的思想、心靈變化。

像近年極受關注的華文作家劉荒田的作品，如果我們用心細嚼，就不難體會到他在九十年代出版的《北美洲的天空》、《舊金山抒情詩》、《異國的粽子》和《唐人街的地理》等幾本詩集中所流露的"厚厚的一迭鄉愁"(著名詩人邵燕祥評語)。但劉荒田在新世紀出版的多部散文集中，我們現在看到的是他的《假洋鬼子》系列、《仿真洋鬼子的胡思亂想》、《美國世故》、《星條旗下的日常生活》等等；又如程寶林的《美國戲台》、《國際煩惱》、《心靈時差》；劉子毅的《八年一覺美國夢》、《愛的莊園》；宗鷹的《異國他鄉月明時》、《月曲情濤》、《宗鷹文集—中短小說卷》、《宗鷹文集—散文小品卷》；呂紅的《女人的白宮》；展我的《展我散文集》；招思虹的《金山之路》系列等等，均已明顯紮根於美國本土、又努力把東西文化融為一體的"特定的文化思維"。

筆者強烈感覺到，這種"特定的文化思維"很可能就是今後海外華人作家努力的方向，至少對我個人來說是這樣。拙作長篇小說《異鄉三部曲》—《奔流》、《狂潮》、《巨浪》，正是透過小說裡幾代的眾多人物在美國動蕩的不同年代的悲歡離合的命運，反映這種"特定的文化思維"。

不庸諱言，每年有大批華人新移民來到美國新大陸，即使他們之中不少都是專業人士，但由於他們絕大多數都有語言障礙，很可能在一段很長的時間內，是難以繼續任職本行的，如醫生、護士、工程師、會計師、教師等等專業。因此，這些新移民在適應美國新生活之前，便難免因東西文化的碰撞、生活習慣和美中兩國關係的變化而滋生"鄉愁"的情緒來，這是每一個新移民都經歷過的一個階段。美華文學亦然。這就是從"華僑"到"華人"，從"落葉歸根"到"落地生根"的涵義。

Dear Mother,
I Am Trying My Best to Come to You
母親啊, 我正努力向您走來

Ray Lau

劉荒田

舊金山 "美華文協" 出版的《美華文學》雜誌, 已經走過了10年的路程。看著書架上厚厚的一疊, 從開始到現在, 已經出版了60期。由此想起非馬先生的名詩《醉漢》: "把短短的直巷/走成一條/曲折/回蕩的/萬里愁腸//左一腳/十年/右一腳/十年/母親啊/我正努力/向您/走/來"。

我所以有這樣近似荒誕的聯想, 也許是因為二者都有 "十年" 吧?想下去, 咦, 美華文學的同仁, 不都是這樣的 "醉漢" 嗎?醉於中華文化, 醉于以方塊字排列的文學, 醉于凌駕生存壓力和文化衝突的精神漫游, 所以, 在這裏集結。"醉枕美人膝, 醒掌天下權", 据說是政治家如當今日本首相小泉純一郎的抱負。我們這群血液裏含著濃度不等的文學 "酒精" 的小人物呢, 醒時為衣食奔波, 醉時在以英語為主景觀的百花園裏, 也謙卑也驕傲地栽上姚黃魏紫牡丹和觀音竹, 這些從東方古國移植的芳菲。

回顧十年, 《美華文學》雜誌出了60期, 加上它的前身《美華文化人報》, 這份無論從年資上看還是從質量上看, 無論影響力還是覆蓋度, 在美國華文文壇, 如果不宜僭稱 "獨一無二", 至少 "獨當一面" 的純文學刊物, 讓我們想到太多太多。

不能忘記社長黃運基先生, 和他的夫人與女兒。這位遠遠不算 "大富" 的著名報人和作家, 紐約散文大家撰文尊為 "文壇孟嘗君" 的舊金山文壇領袖, 從雜誌開辦伊始, 都由他擔任董事長的時代公司獨力支撐, 印刷費、郵費加上其他開銷, 至今早已突破10万美元。這麼多期的稿件, 手寫稿件都由黃運基夫人打字, 直到眼睛出了毛病, 才停下來。黃社長從公司退休後, 由女兒小堅接任, 她在公司營運遭遇困難的一年, 果斷決定, 寧可將雜誌從雙月刊改為季刊, 也要辦下去。

不能忘記主編劉子毅, 副主編老南、王性初、鄭其賢、穗青、李碩儒, 曾擔任常務編輯的程寶林, 把《美華文學》推上網絡的詩人王明玉。他們都是義工。在草創階段, 每期《美華文化人報》, 是幾位正副主編在紙版上貼成的。雜誌出版後, 老南和穗青開車到處跑, 送到分銷點去, 送了許多年, 風雨不改。如今老南已成古人, 他的勞績與詩文仍舊由許多期雜誌記載著。

不能忘記畫家李曉軍, 《美華文化人報》自1998年6月改為《美華文學》迄今, 每期封面的美術都是由他義務精心設計的。不能忘記書法家趙鋒強先生, 《美華文學》的刊名題字出自他的手筆。而黃健威則負責每期的電腦排版工作。

不能忘記眾多的作者, 10年間所凝聚的投稿群體, 主要是美國的打工族, 還有留學生和退休者。此外, 稿件來自全球各洲。至於以海外華文作家為對象的評論和推介, 則要歸功于國內的評論家們。所有投稿者, 都沒有領過稿費, 純然的奉獻。

不能忘記眾多的讀者, 沒有他們的愛護和支持, 雜誌辦不下去。其中一位叫黃漢中, 是屋崙唐人街中餐館貧寒的侍應生, 差不多每次他和我見面, 都掏出一百元來, 托我轉給《美華文學》, 作為贊助。

"醉漢" 的 "左一腳" 是 "十年", 路在前面, 漫長, 且愈來愈寬廣。"母親啊, 我正努力向您走來", 中華文化, 就是我們共同的母親。《美華文學》雜誌同仁, 是母親派遣到西方文化腹地來的別動隊。我們在這個和母體隔離的新大陸, 並非作血腥廝殺, 而是在和主流文化的融合中, 自我發展, 自我完成, 從而構建全新的屬於中華文化的文學品種。

The Association of
Overseas Chinese Language Literature
A Brief Introduction
美國華文文藝界協會簡介

Ziyi Liu

劉子毅

美國華文文藝界協會是一個非牟利的民間組織, 其成員包括來自中國大陸、台灣、香港、東南亞等地的華文作家、畫家、攝影家、歌唱家、書法家, 以及文藝愛好者。其宗旨在團結美華文藝界的創作者和愛好者, 弘揚中華文化, 開展各項文藝創作與文化交流活動; 它具有最廣泛的包容性, 即不分成員來自地區, 不問成員之間的意識形態、政治理念、宗教信仰和學術流派的差異, 我們堅持純文藝和高品質的健康方向。

美華文協主辦了一份《美華文學》雙月刊 (現為季刊, 前身為《美華文化人報》), 已進入第十個年頭。美華文協還出版了一套《美國華僑文藝叢書》, 作者有黃運基、劉荒田、老南及宗鷹。美華文協還與山東大學文學院合作出版了一本專著《美國華文文學論》, 全面介紹美國華人作家和他們的文學作品。

過去八年, 美華文協邀請及接待了眾多的中國作家、藝術家來美國訪問, 進行富有意義的文化交流活動。最新一批應邀訪美及接待過的是佛山作家代表團。應邀訪美及接待過的中國作家還包括: 張炯、董乃斌、徐乃翔、張抗抗、顧艷、鄭心伶、施建偉、洪三泰、譚元亨、黃偉宗、黃海歌; 畫家李徵、燕陵; 北京電影製片廠、中央電視台代表團: 製片人李曉婉、導演李小紅、編劇鄭重、王要、主任編輯于振鐸, 等等。

Perspectives on Cultural Attributes
and Identities in Overseas Chinese Literature
海外移民文學視點：文化屬性與文化身份

Lu Hong
呂紅

摘要：海外華文作家獨具風格的寫作，將個體、民族特質融合在文化屬性和文化身份的尋找中。這種新的人文特質、新的書寫困惑，糾纏徘徊在故鄉他鄉、原鄉異鄉之間，在身份認同、國籍認同、語言認同之間。經過陌生的異域文化衝擊之後，正逐漸摸索著建立一種超越地域身份超越有形無形之藩籬的精神歸屬。

關鍵詞：身份焦慮，文化身份，
多元文化，文化融合

一、 身份的一般意義

所謂身份，一般指的是在某個社會結構中人所具有的合法居留標識，及其所處的位置。

作為從心理學引入文化研究的重要概念，身份認同其原意是 "一個個體所有的關於他這種人是其所是的意識"。作為文化研究的一個分析工具，身份是 "人們對世界的主體性經驗與構成這種主體性的文化歷史設定之間的聯繫"，換言之，身份是一個族群或個體界定自身文化特性的標誌。而所謂 "身份焦慮" 就是指身份的矛盾和不確定，即主體與他所歸屬的社會文化傳統失去了聯繫，失去了社會文化的方向定位，從而產生觀念、心理和行為的衝突及焦慮體驗。

任何一個尋夢者，不管你來自哪個國家，在美國想要待下來首先都會面臨著 "status" 或 "identity" —身份轉換或身份認同問題。

在黃運基的長篇小說 "異鄉三部曲" 中，以主人公余念祖的經歷深刻觸及了長期存在卻被忽略的現實：正常的移民史是第一代移民到這個國家後，第二代與第三代都是移民國出生，並且在語言文化上完全融入移民國。然而，美國歷史上的排華政策造成一個奇特的歷史現象：早期移民的三代華裔都是先後在祖籍國出生成長，每一代移民都從頭經歷第一代移民特有的掙扎與成長過程。

當小小的余念祖冒名來美，從踏上海船的那一刻起就面臨了身份的困惑，他被大人反復叮囑必須記住有關自己身份查詢的細枝末節；緊接著被囚禁在移民拘留所裏等候身份辨別；成年之後，又因 "非美言論" 和父親的身份坦白而再度陷入身份困境。被剝奪國籍、不名譽退伍、沒有工作和生存權利等種種艱難陡然壓下來。但主人公沒有屈服命運，在郊外務農種菊花的同時進行艱難的訴訟，與美國政府打了長達10年的官司，終於贏得一個 free man 自由人的身份和權利。

在過去海外華人文學作品中，"身份" 的焦慮並沒有凸顯出來。因早期華人移民數量畢竟不比現在，文化層次也不比現在。隨著地球村意識出現，人們對外部世界了解增多，移民潮暗濤洶湧。各種國際因素變化使美國這個最大的移民國家移民法趨嚴，條件愈來愈苛刻。(無論你去租房、求學、打工、去 DMV 考駕照、去醫院看病、去銀行申請信用卡或貸款等，方方面面，幾乎任何地方都會被問到 "什麼身份？" 不同的身份有不同的待遇。有無 "身份" 便左右了其生存意識和生存狀況。) 在這一漫長過程中，以敏感反映移民社會生活和移民情緒的海外華人文學，身份焦慮亦愈來愈多成為描述和深層開掘的主題。新移民文學在身份書寫中又有了更細膩感性的刻劃。

譬如，嚴歌苓旅美最初的創作體驗："人在寄人籬下時是最富感知的。" 撞車了有沒有人問傷？跌倒了有沒有人問疼？沒有。更多的時候，生存的迫急，使生活的目的變得堅硬而直接—"擺脫貧困，就是勝利"。"拿到綠卡，就是解放"。這是每一代移民都曾有過的狀態。當信念成為事實，剩下的，便是生命的虛空。小漁磕磕絆絆，一路小心，終於熬到了領取綠卡的那天，她猶豫了，她問，我為什麼呆在這兒？我在這兒幹什麼？似乎任何一條理由都不充分，任何一條理由一旦成立，就立即顯出了荒誕。《少女小漁》以巧妙的構思在人們司空見慣的現象裏發掘出人生的荒誕意味。

加拿大華人女作家張翎的長篇小說《郵購新娘》、灣區女作家嘯塵的中篇小說《覆水》等也都以不同的視角及筆調透出了移民身份未定的隱忍和焦慮。在《郵購新娘》中，被男人相中的女人以未婚妻身份進入了陌生的異國他鄉，不料，婚姻在即將成為現實的關口化為泡影。女人面臨要麼回國要麼留下來的抉擇。類似的例子應該說在美國加拿大都不乏其人，難得的是女作家在表現此類題材時，不以故事取勝，而是關注故事背後蘊含的生命本體，關注在社會背景變異中的人的命運。如小說《戀曲三重奏》，一開頭便通過女主人之口，點出了"身份"問題。透過王曉楠、章亞龍的情感糾葛，表現一雖有身份卻內心彷徨的女人和一身份不明卻內心強大的男人的命運反差對比。

在小說《覆水》中，女主角依群25歲來到硅谷，用了20年的光陰，從一個弱不禁風(心臟病)，目不識丁(英文盲)的中國南疆小城裏街道鐵器廠的繪圖員，成為美國頂級學府柏克萊加大的EE(電子工程)碩士、硅谷一家中型半導體設計公司裏的中層主管。如此鮮明的反差是她驕傲的依據，也是她憂傷和苦澀的理由。因為這樣的"神話"並不是她一個人創造的，還有一個決定性的合作者，她的丈夫、美國人老德，共同努力的結果。那是上帝預先的設定，也是內心傷痛的根源。女人的人生正精彩，男人的人生卻要落幕了。命運既相互影響著，也彼此獨立著；每個人只能承受自己的命運，每個人必須為自己的選擇負責。作品梳理了移民複雜網絡中的豐富經驗，從男女跨國、跨齡、跨文化背景的婚姻中，去檢索文化、身份、身體、利益、價值等諸多問題。讓人物始終在情感和理智、得與失之間經受著考驗。

虹影的自傳體小說《飢餓的女兒》對身份的追尋貫穿始終，對過去貧瘠荒蕪年代的回顧、命運的錯綜糾葛、肉體與精神的雙重痛苦以及人性的深刻挖掘，給讀者帶來強烈的震撼。荷蘭的華文女作家林湄在飽經飄泊人生之後，以10年功夫磨出一部《天望》。在自序中她如此感嘆，"現實改變了我的生活境遇、文化背景和審美意識，也改變了我的身份和命運。我是誰？像一棵樹嗎？移植在天涯海角的另一片土壤裏"。

在我的小說《海岸的冷月》、《英姐》等作品所彌漫的飄泊情緒，以及中西文化碰撞、生存現狀所帶來的精神落差，無不觸及了這一移民文學焦點：身份困擾。對所有移民而言，異國經歷是一個顛覆心智的過程，是探險與心碎的混合：它打開了一切事物的可能性，同時也侵蝕了傳統信仰與習慣。華人在新舊拉扯間左右為難、痛苦掙扎的困境，不正體現了生活之紛繁複雜、人性之紛繁複雜嗎？作為自尊自強的女性典型，她們的精神追求和人生命運具有某種代表性。在夢想追尋的過程中，身份的不自由；殘酷的生存壓力生存環境；情感的壓抑和犧牲；坐"移民監"的痛苦鬱悶；都通過一柄"精神懸劍"淋漓盡致的表現出來。

諸多困惑同時也反映在同胞遭受不公平待遇等問題上。譬如李文和案，這時"身份"已經不是外在形式上的，而是膚色標識。令人感到，所謂排外意識、種族歧視往往是潛隱在諸多理由和借口之下的，並錯綜複雜地滲透到骨髓裏。那麼即便你是入了籍，是有身份地位的美籍華人，但在保守者眼中，從骨子裏你還是異類。這，當然又是另一話題甚至是文學創作進一步挖掘的主題。可以預料，將會有愈來愈多的海外作家對這一透著文化身份及屬性的題材作深入透徹的刻劃和描述。

大凡新移民，如果不是由祖輩或者父母傳下的親屬移民、婚姻移民或是拿"6.4"綠卡者，一般從求學到尋找工作、尋覓情感歸宿，皆有一番心酸或一番苦鬥，甚至包括不堪回首的經歷。在華文媒體上，我們也不時看到有關對移民身份問題關注，提到"新移民入境安身難如意"，更點出"追求綠卡，甚於追月"。一部移民史就是一部為爭取身份自由平等的血淚史。身份焦慮應如影隨形伴隨著華人移民生涯中。因此，當人們歷經艱辛走出黑暗的隧道口時，竟有長吐一口氣和苦盡甘來的欣慰感：終於可以做個自由人了！

二、從身份狀態調整到深層精神尋覓

美國著名的精神分析學家埃里克在其論著中將"identity"表述為"同一性"，即所謂的認同也就是人們對於自我身份的確認。(注1)身份認同帶有歷史和社會的影響及烙印。移民文學與其說表現了一種認同感的匱乏與需求，不如說是深刻的現實焦慮的呈現；與其說是對自我身份的建構，不如說是對自我身份的解構和由此產生的焦慮。人們所關心的已不是如何通過自己的力量去實現自我，而是如何在身份中獲得認同。人成了一個非中心化的主體，無法感知自己與過去、現實、未來的切實聯繫。個體生存因此失去了內在根基，沉入孤獨漂泊的困境，最終陷入深深的焦慮之中。

其實，從文化層面來說，現代社會人們無論身處何方，對定義自己身份都有無法解說的惶惑。換句話說，每個身份都形成一個集合，而這無數多個集合交匯的那一點，恰是自身所在的坐標。在社會急速流動的今天，這些集合在不住的變化，人的矛盾身份也在不斷地游移，沒有一個固定的所在。由此而構成了身份焦慮。透過身份焦慮可以折射出社會背景轉換以及人類遷徙的漫長歷程。

"新生代、新移民創作的異同讓人感覺到了一個民族內部跨文化因素的出現，也顯示出身份、傳統、邊緣這些課題將越來越影響一個民族的文學。"(注2)這種體驗有時是共通的。從諸多新移民永不停息的奔波尋找中，從窮學生、打工者到擁有綠卡身份、洋車豪宅和安穩的生活之後所面臨的精神困惑；既充實同時又很空虛，既擁有一切又似乎一無所有的心理狀態，從而揭示出更深刻的哲學命題。譬如，當身份轉換後，尋常人也許就滿足了異國他鄉過安寧平淡的日子，但依舊有人惶惑：這是我夢寐以求的歸宿麼？魯鳴發出"海外華人共同的痛"之慨嘆；劉荒田在散文書寫中坦露心跡，對"英文橫行"的異域的疏離及對母語的熱愛，最終仍要回到自己心靈安身立命之處、華文為根基的故園。

詩人王性初以感性的詩句表現漂泊者"根"與"家"分離無奈的同時，"孤獨已從相對外在的懷鄉，發展成為對生命的一種更普遍也更深刻的內視"。"孤獨不再是對往昔的牽掛，喧喧大千，孤獨是對世界既排拒又滲入的一種認知和態度。……這是哲學問題，要去詢問金字塔前的斯蒂克若。"(注3)從兒時的故居到異國的豪宅；從詩仙李白"何處是歸程？"到哲聖尼采對人的精神家園的拷問，李碩儒無語問蒼天：家歸何處？迷失在洪荒大野，再難找回自己的家。

何處是歸？何時歸？我從何處來？到何處去？從文學描述的"身份焦慮"上升到哲學意義的思考。而表現這種精神迷失和追尋的，在大陸留學生文學的代表作《叢林下的冰河》最為典型。當小說主人公回答教授說，她到美國來，是為了看看、找找，其印度裔教授的話語則顯得意味深長：看看是可以的，找什麼 就很難說了，等你找到，也許就不是你所要找的了。(這里順便提一句，以往說

到"海歸派"多半是側重他們回國創業什麼的，其實從某種意義來講，又何嘗不是華人走過萬里長路之後更高層面的精神回歸呢？)

這也就是說，華人移民在下一代學業完成或成家立業之後，亦有再度尋求精神寄托的彷徨。譬如你有了美國公民或者綠卡身份，你有了在這個國家生存的基本條件，但是你究竟是主流還是邊緣化的？是受重視還是被歧視？都是決定你的精神生活是否充實的重要因素。東方文化背景顯然成為不了西方國家的主流。西方讀者往往更傾向華人作品對過去時代的反思和尋索，而並非關注移民困境或表現移民生態的文學。

"文化身份"也是海外華人在創作中關心的主題。涉及諸如關於父母子女之間的關係、孤獨、如何融入主流等問題。多元文化中的"文化身份認同"是一個重要母題。它包涵在生活經驗、工作、教育、階層、語言等具有文化象徵意義的因素中，也包涵在一些命題中。不少敘述者對自己童年和青年時期的反思，以及對自己上輩生活故事的講述，反映了種族混合的社會狀態。同時亦表現他們無效地為融入主流社會所作的努力，並在很大程度上因為這種努力的無效而痛苦。

華人的文化屬性和文化身份，到第二三代移民身上就基本上模糊了。從出生到成長都是在種族熔爐裏的土生華人，既沒有華夏民族數千年文化精髓和傳統包袱，也就不存在什麼文化碰撞的尷尬。但文化影響仍或多或少的存在於他們的作品中。一些土生作家，漸漸以英文或其他語言創作，表達他們尋找祖宗根文化或者文化認同的困惑。"對于逐步失去中國人特徵、已經失去使用漢語能力的土生華人而言，這種疏離和曲解也是通過努力才獲得的。它既是一條彎路，也是一條漫長的曲線的開始"。(注4)文化之間的震蕩，以及同種文化內部理想價值與現實價值的衝突都體現在文本中，將故事鑲嵌在移民的歷史和文化背景之上。新一代移民對於文化身份的認同已經與老一代人顯示出差異。相對於上一輩人來說，傳統意識淡化—其身份情結是離散的、更加有一種無根感。

從女作家於梨華的《又見棕櫚，又見棕櫚》中"無根的一代"，湯亭亭的《女勇士》，到譚恩美的《喜福會》等都表現類似的主題。《喜福會》通過描繪四對華人母女關係，表現了在"中國移民母親"和"美國出生的女兒"之間，交織著由語言差異及文化衝突所展現的代溝問題。母親無法跟女兒溝通，正是語言作為生存本身而包含的文化

衝突。語言轉換"意味著一個人身份的根本性變更"。母女都相對處於失語的境地。該作品成為新移民語言命運的一種寓言和象徵。

失語失聲之所以首先成為新移民筆下反復渲染的情境，是因為新移民對自己失卻"存在之源"的傷痛有著深刻的體驗，身份的建構存在于語言屬性中，失語往往意味著身份的遮蔽乃至失落。與第一代移民出國主要是謀求物質生活改變不同，當新移民有著強烈的跨文化精神交流的願望時，他們在語言(包括母語的繼續使用和居住國語言的學習)上的多向努力就顯得更加自覺、強烈。(注5)

一種潛在而深刻的認同危機在不同層面、不同程度上侵擾著新移民：生存或欲望、個人或民族、社群或地域。由於獨特的社群結構和移民文化，使得異域生活的每個個體都無法迴避這種多元化的鏡像，因此，對文化身份的追問與認同，成了海外華人社會的文化母題。在這裏，身份不是通過其他諸如一種國籍或一種經濟上的實力體現，而是通過代代相傳的故事、歷史，來獲得自己在文化上的根基。亦為此間建立了身份表述，成為獲取文化認同的諸多路徑之一。

三、文化身份認同與文化融合

一個人必要首先確立自己的文化身份，才能在人文舞台上發出獨立的聲音。知識分子都具有相似的離散經驗。自我放逐者則不再於現有的身份體係之中努力，轉而試圖進入另外一個身份體係之中尋求。毋庸置疑，人之身份不能脫離既有坐標體係而被定義。對身份的追求從某種意義上來說體現價值觀念和文化認同，在這個過程中人們常常忽略甚或無視邏輯和秩序中根深蒂固的利益、種族、文化歧視與偏見，以及貫穿始終的經濟、政治和話語上的不平等。

身份，這種不斷試圖向另外一個點移動的努力，便可以稱之為奮鬥。通過一個個坐標點來定位生活，找到自己在這個世界裏所處的位置。同時，不斷地對自己現有的身份懷著焦慮，指向未來坐標體係，而這種潛藏的焦慮，則是動力。正是文化的無所不在，改變了人類數千年來對精神、物質以及自身生存意義的固有認識和界定，也創造著、生成著新的身份觀。

其實，在社會群體中獲得承認或身份的嘗試幾乎從人類文明誕生的那一天起就存在。而這些力圖做到標新立異別具一格的人，則希望在這個複制生產的年代尋找到自己特殊的身份與 歸屬感。"不僅如此，一如安迪.沃霍爾在其著作《從A到B与其重複:安迪.沃霍爾的哲學》中宣稱的那樣，當下創作與時常行為之間界限的模糊，可以使那些最沒有天賦的人有機會輕鬆地實現自我"。(注6)

"身份並非是一種界定或者歸宿，而是對自身擁有的文化資源的不斷開掘。如果我們能更關注這一過程包含的悖論、矛盾，更關注文化情感、生存策略對身份書寫的影響，華文文學中的身份認同會呈現出更豐富的意義"。(注7)

過去國內對海外移民文學有邊緣化的漠視或遲鈍，資訊欠缺亦導致對海外移民作家創作主題的隔膜與疏離。尤其是評論界缺乏具體生存體驗孕育的"現場感"。這種"不在場"的位置使其對移民文學的文化生存狀態缺乏真切的體認，因此難以從複雜的社會背景來全面考量海外華文文學的歷史與現實際遇。這，大概也是文學批評終竟滯後或僅停留在表象或抽象術語層面的深層次原因吧。

文學的邊緣位置和文化身份建構的困境，觸及了"失語"與邊陲文學的語言表徵之困境，經典缺席，文學史敘事的結構與文化政治的懸浮狀態，而"身份焦慮"更凸顯出來。作為一種文化需求，它試圖提供的不僅是在酷烈的現實面前對自身身份的幻象，而且更重要的是通過自我建構，可以超越固定身份的刻板局限。"其實，對于海外華文文學而言，全面地吸取其它族裔文化、中華文化以及西方文化的精華，把它們視為自己的文化資源并且轉化為文化資本，可能是發展的更為積極的一種策略"。(注8)

作為一種離散族裔文化表徵的海外移民文學置身於各種思潮的旋渦中，藝術取向的差異也造成了文本表述的巨大分野。紀實性風格更多地體現在顯性的題材、主題層面；而現代主義傾向的文本則滲透在語言的肌理血脈中，變形誇張、扭曲或佯裝復古等處心積慮的語言策略，其深處，同樣訴說著文化身份的焦慮。而焦慮中的困惑、飄泊里的無奈、壓抑中的奮起，在北美出版的《一代飛鴻》所聚集的40多位新移民作家作品的字裏行間，在全球華人各類文學社團的風起雲湧中不難尋覓。"這真是外面的世界好精彩，海闊天空，天外有天，而且，中西文化在這裏交匯、撞擊、融合，生成了一種新質的文學品種:有忠實的寫主義傳統，也有前衛的現代派手法;有嚴肅的社會批

判精神, 也有全新的文學理念；有精美典雅的華文篇章, 也有探秘索隱的西方心理分析". (注9)

這種新的人文特質、新的書寫困惑, 糾纏徘徊在故鄉他鄉、原鄉異鄉之間；在身份認同、國籍認同、語言認同之間, 經過西方文化衝擊之後, 正逐漸摸索著建立一種超越地域身份、超越有形無形之藩籬的精神歸宿。因此, 有些海外華裔作家就選擇了跨越兩邊的文化及生活方式, 在東西方之間自由穿梭和來回游走, 借以擴展文化交流融合的空間。

應該說, 文化是一個共同體的社會遺產和話語編碼, 不僅有民族創造和傳遞的物質產品, 還有包括各種象征、思想、信念、審美觀念、價值標準體系的精神產品與行為方式。這意味著文化無優劣, 而只有差異；尊重文化的差異, 是世界之潮流。美學大師宗白華曾經提出功利-倫理-政治-學術-藝術-宗教這個縱軸, 這是橫亘于古今中西的境界之軸, 是個不斷超越的過程。在經由了藝術境界的洗練之後, 最後領悟到天地人神四重根的渾然一體。學者認為, 當今語境中全球化不是西化, 也不等于本土化, 而是包含了多層面的選擇。

當代德國哲學家雅斯貝爾斯提出 "軸心時代" 觀點, 認為第一個軸心時代正是在西方產生柏拉圖、亞里斯多德等思想大師, 而東方產生了孔子、孟子和老子等思想文化大師的先秦時代；經過歷史的流變而產生不同的文明和文化藝術流派。當今世界正進入第二軸心時代, 文化的衝突碰撞必然要產生文化的交匯融合。西方文化, 相對于東方文化是人類整體文化的一極, 亦不可能成為中心。人類文化就像太極圖般地呈現出互補結構。西方的陽剛與東方的陰柔互補, 才能達至陰陽平衡。

另外, 以文化融合為宗旨的 "新時代運動" (New Age Movement), 從美國加州起始逐漸影響至全球。預示著 "人類由追求社會的、物質的、科技層面的進步, 將演進到注重 '心靈' '精神' 層面的探索, 找到超越人種、膚色、民族、國籍以及宗教派別的人類心靈的共通點, 認知人類的 '同源性' 和 '平等性', 從而達成 '四海一家' 與 '和平' 的遠景"。(注10)

而方興未艾的海外華人文學將在此一歷史過程中, 以視野廣闊和無羈的精神活力, 擔當承前啟後的重任及多元文化融合的獨特角色。

參考文獻：

1. 《同一性：青少年與危機》, 埃里克.H. 埃里克森著。
2. 《在旅行中 "拒絕旅行"》, 黃万華, 參見《美華文學》2003年秋季號。
3. 《一個孤獨旅人的繁富世界》, 劉登翰, 序《孤之旅》。
4. 《印尼土生華人文學曾經的 "尋根" 之旅》, 王列耀, 13屆世界華文文學研討會論文集。
5. 《語言還鄉：海外創作心靈栖息地的尋找》, 史進, 13屆世界華文文學研討會論文集。
6. 《尼斯主義:黑啤酒和身份焦慮》, 朱步沖著。
7. 《多元文化語境中的華文文學》序言, 黃万華主編。
8. 《華文文學後殖民批評的可能性及限度》朱立立, 《福建論壇.人文社會科學版》2004年第11期。
9. 《一代飛鴻》前言, 陳公仲, 僑報副刊2005年10月27日。

On Literary Vitality
文學的命力

Zhao Sihong
招思虹

把文學融入生活、融入社區，更能顯示出文學的生命力。

　　本人創辦由陳香梅和黃運基擔任正副團長的"金山之路讀者慈善團隊"為社區驅寒送暖的一波又一波行動，就力證了這一點。

　　不少人認為，要報效祖國或幫助弱勢人群，為社區驅寒送暖，要等到成為百萬富翁才能行動。其實非也。只要你有一顆助人之心，哪怕你是一個只領取有限的退休金之退休工人，也可以微薄之力去幫助社會上的弱勢人群。

　　"金山之路讀者慈善團隊"凝聚的一個龐大讀者群，就以實際行動向社會釋放出一個訊息——有一分力，發一分光。

　　本人是《金山之路》一書的作者，同時也是《星島日報》和《金山時報》的專欄作者。以文會友。多年來，我就凝聚了那些願意盡一分心力去為社會驅寒送暖的讀者，他們捐出十元、二十元不等去為大陸水災災民、地震災民、華人非牟利機構、九一一事件遇難者家屬、中國大西北貧困學童、南亞海嘯遇難者、為孤兒捐贈玩具、為弱能兒童捐助。我們這支北美洲天空下獨一無二的讀者慈善團隊，集腋成裘，到目前為止，籌募到的善款已超過七萬美元。七萬美元對於那些捐款大戶來說，這是一個微不足道的數字。然而，這裡卻凝聚著讀者們的一顆顆愛心。

　　假如，我們把身邊的"晨運友"、"麻雀友"、"卡拉OK友"一齊去有一分力，發一分光，這對於促進社會良性的互動，將會是一股不可估量的力量。

　　"金山之路讀者慈善團隊"有一分力，發一分光的精神，曾得到中央電視台、中國國際廣播電台、三藩市市長、市參議會和中國領事館的嘉許和褒揚。

Chinese Language Literature and the Chinese in America
A Shared Historical Destiny
美華文學與美國華人的共同歷史命運

Zong Ying
宗鷹

在美國華人歷史學會的學術討論中談及美華文學，首先想到的議題就是：美華文學的歷史命運與美國華人的歷史命運有何關聯？依我的淺見，兩者儘管不能劃個完全等號，但又密切攸關。美國華文文學的萌發、興起以至旺盛，大體上與美國華人的社會歷史、社會地位同步。沒有華人在美國的社會地位的歷史性變化發展，就沒有華人文學尤其是華文文學的興旺發達。

華文文學的發展，有其必然的社會因素和堅實的社會基礎。華文文學研究，務必注重這社會因素和社會基礎，也務必避免兩個極端的偏頗。忽視社會因素和社會基礎，為文學而文學，就文學研究文學，這種孤立研討的偏頗，實在無法作出恰當的評析。等同甚至混同文學與社會，機械地、生硬地尋找社會因素和社會基礎，也有百害而無一益。

首先，讓我們試來把美國華僑華人的歷史命運做個粗淺的勾勒。1987年，我在論文《崛起在多元美國華文文壇的"草根文群"》中試作探討：美國華人既有一部待於挖掘、整理的"消逝"的歷史、"塵封"的歷史，也有一部急需記錄、留真的"活著"的歷史，"行進"的歷史。大體而言，美國華僑華人的歷史命運可以分為三個階段：被動被為－自動自為－奮為奮進。

過去式、過去完成式的美國華僑華人史，尤其是早期，主要是被動被為而受辱受役史。在這個標榜人道、人權的文明之邦，留下無數對華人無人道、無人權的不文明記錄。黃運基的《殺戮者》等，儘管反映的是這個階段時較晚時期的社會生活，但是以烈火和熱血，展示了美國社會的種族歧視和奴役，給人們留下深刻的印象。

經歷了漫漫長期的掙扎、抗爭，華人逐漸奮起，進入一個較為自動自為的過渡時期。但是受侮辱、受歧視依然深重而不斷。天使島的歷史文物就是很好的見證。在那時期，華僑華人不同層次有不同境遇，但是不管層次多高，"黃皮膚就是黃皮膚"，終究都受到不平等對待，甚至遇到相似相同的侮辱歧視。工作的歧視，生活的歧視，處處可見。這種歧視侮辱，最明顯的體現在工作、居住的不平等待遇。那時代，美國相當歧視東方人，把東方人和黑人一樣看待，黃種人和黑人不許露面，只能在地下室幹活。華人大學生連每小時七角五分美元待遇的售貨員工作都不能做。一些住宅區，華僑華人即使有錢也不能住，更不能買。因為那些社區一旦有黃皮膚的人"闖進"，白人住戶就要遷走，房產也要大跌。我曾經訪問過芝加哥大學東亞圖書館前館長、現任榮譽館長錢存訓教授和夫人。四十年代後期，錢教授奉中國北平圖書館之派來美，後來應聘在東亞圖書館任職。在芝加哥無法租房。經大學負責人多方幫助，才找到住房。我也曾經電話訪問紐約吳阿姨服務中心創辦人吳世珊女士。四十年代，她在上海結識了美國白人軍官，結婚後隨丈夫來美。她先生原來在大學任教，只因為娶了"黃臉"太太，原校不接納他回去任教。他們夫婦甚至連房子也租不到。這從側面反映了華僑華人的處境和命運。

現在完成式、現在式和現在進行式的華僑華人史，釀於四五十年代，始於六七十年代，盛於八九十年代，進入一個奮為、奮進，成功而耀目時期。華人的奮為奮進主要集中在科技方面。既有如同錢學森等已回國的傑出科學家，也有吳健雄、袁家騮等傑出科學家，楊振寧、李政道、丁肇中、李遠哲、朱棣文等諾貝爾獎獲得者，丘成桐這樣的菲爾茲數學獎獲得者，貝聿明、鄧文中等建築大師，名牌大學第一位華裔校長田長霖等相繼出現，使美人、世人對華人的觀感發生突變，好比石破天驚。這個潮流繼續湧動，並擴及文化、教育、藝術、商務、工程、法律各個方面。近年來，華裔從政也取得相當成就，陸續出現許多華裔市長、議員。第一位華裔州長駱家輝是傑出從政的範例。許多普通華人的努力也匯進這洪流。近十年來, 中國大陸的學生、學者和移民也接連取得可喜成就, 嶄露頭角。

美國華人自身的奮為、奮進時期, 華人社會形成和趨向大變動的時期, 又恰逢中國國力空前增強、國際威望空前提高, 中美關係儘管曲折起伏但總體上向前發展。前者為美國華人地位的提高提供了具體的環境, 後者為美國華人地位的提高提供了大的環境、大的氣候。

華人的社會地位的歷史性變化, 大的環境變化和具體環境變化兩者的結合, 既使華人社會迅速壯大, 日顯活力, 也使華文文學根基更豐厚而日見旺盛。這是美國華文文學興旺的社會因素、社會基礎。

美國華文文學, 與美國華僑華人同命運共呼吸。無論逆境還是順境, 無論悲遇還是幸遇, 都在美華文學中有所呼應和反映。進入奮為奮進時期的華人社會, 也激發和催動了美國華文作家的奮為奮進。在全美各地湧現了大批華人華文作家和作品。如同哈金這樣以英文寫作為主的華人作家, 直接進入美國主流社會。而許多堅持華文寫作的華人作家, 不但面向美國華人讀者, 也面向祖國和世界華人讀者。金山灣區擁有大量高質的作者, 包括來自港臺、大陸和東南亞的新移民作者、留學生作者。其中包括集結在《美華文學》的草根文群。難能可貴地堅持了十一年的純文學園地《美華文學》, 既團聚了又孕育了許多華文作家。往程艱辛, 前途跋涉。但我深信, 只要華人奮為奮進之勢繼往開來, 華文作家奮為奮進之志日益彌堅, 我們依然可以在創作上大有作為。我們有理由相信: 美華文學迎來新的春天。

（2005年10月7日臨時發言, 11, 25日整理。）

What Is Chinese American Art?

Mark Johnson, Ch'ingche Lo, and Jade Snow Wong

IRENE POON ANDERSEN, MODERATOR

Our current exhibition "Remembering C. C. Wang" sparked the question for the panel—"What Is Chinese American Art?" Is C. C. Wang, who was a naturalized U.S. citizen living and working in New York for many decades, a Chinese American artist, or is he a Chinese artist living in America? This was the question posed to the three panelists, Mark Johnson, Jade Snow Wong, and Lo Ch'ingche.

MARK JOHNSON, MFA

Professor and University Art Gallery Director, San Francisco State University

The question for today's panel, "What is Chinese American art," was raised by Lorraine Dong during a conversation with Irene Poon. It was posed in relation to the exhibition of C. C. Wang, being planned for the Frank H. Yick Gallery at the Chinese Historical Society of America Museum and Learning Center. Although C. C. Wang spent virtually his entire professional artistic career in New York and studied at the Art Students' League there, his work is often discussed and appreciated within the context of "Chinese literati painting" or "Chinese Diasporic art"—and not Chinese American art. At the opening of the exhibition of his work, Wang's friend and student Arnold Chang wondered if anyone had ever asked Wang if he perhaps considered himself a "Chinese American."

Rather than comment on possible subtleties that these definitions imply, I would like to comment more generally about the long history of art produced by persons of Chinese ancestry in the United States. For the past fifteen years, I have been part of a community of scholars that have researched Asian American art in California from the Gold Rush until 1965. That community has included faculty, staff, and students from diverse institutions including San Francisco State University, the University of California in Los Angeles, Stanford University, and the Smithsonian Institution Archives of American Art. In California alone, we have identified more than one thousand artists active during this time period, and a significant number were of Chinese ancestry. However, as citizenship was not available to these immigrant artists in early periods, the words "Chinese American" must be qualified. They are here meant to imply simply that artists of Chinese ancestry were working in the United States even in the mid-nineteenth century.

Two important figures from that period were Lai Yong and Mary Tape. Yong was a successful portrait painter and photographer who was active in the 1860s and 1870s. Today, his works appear as very skilled, displaying photographic verisimilitude and fine glazing techniques. His portraits of Caucasian subjects do not hint that the artist was Chinese. Yet, we know from historical documents that Yong was a coauthor of an important 1873 statement that was read before the San Francisco Board of Supervisors that protested U.S. policies toward China and the treatment of the Chinese in America. This points to Yong's community engagement at the same time he was working as an artist. Similarly, Mary Tape was an "amateur" artist in the 1880s and 1890s, working in media including oil painting, china painting, and photography. Her paintings sometimes integrate Chinese decorative motifs with oil paint on wood or canvas. Yet Tape is best remembered for her 1884 appeal to allow her children to attend public school in San Francisco that was allowed by courts in San Francisco but overturned the following year by California's superior court. Again, for these artists, art and community engagement goes hand in hand.

The decades of the 1920s and 1930s were a rich time for Chinese American artists. Several art clubs and associations were founded in California, including the Chinese Revolutionary Artists' Club in San Francisco and the Chinese Art Associations that appeared in cities including New York, Seattle, and San Francisco. In addition, several groups were multiethnic in membership, such as the East West Art Society in San Francisco and the Oriental Artists Group in Los Angeles. Artists associated with these clubs often developed a more self-consciously "transnational" expression. Examples include Chee Chin S. Cheung Lee's "Mountain Fantasy," where a nude woman at the base of a tall waterfall confronts a cliff face below a California landscape. The cliff face writhes with figures and embodies the living "qi" of the landscape in an anthropomorphic way. Lee participated in exhibitions organized by both the East West Art Society and the San Francisco Chinese Art Association. Yun Gee's "Where is My Mother" is an image in a cubist-related style that shows the weeping artist in a beret in front of a Chinese landscape, where the artist's mother looks out over the sea where a ship departs. Gee was the founder of the Chinese Revolutionary Artist Club and founded a modern art gallery on the edges of Chinatown with his teacher Otis Oldfield. Images like this are both personal and political, referencing Gee's own status as a "paper son" who was able to immigrate to the United States because of the loss of his father's birth records during the 1906 earthquake while his mother was never able to join her family. The photograph of Eva Fong Chan and Stella Wong from the 1935 Artist Parilla Ball provides powerful visual evidence of the role of women artists during this period. Both Chan and Wong were involved with the Chinese Art Association during this time. Dong Kingman is perhaps the best known artist to have exhibited with the Chinese Art Association, although it was only after the artist had moved to New York after the Second World War that he became so renowned—perhaps the most famous American of Chinese ancestry during his lifetime.

Several other generations of artists appeared in ensuing decades, and many were born in the United States. A new generation of artists immigrated after the 1949 Communist Revolution in China. These include C. C. Wang, Tseng Yuho, Chen Chi-kwan, and even the renowned Chang Dai-chien. All of these artists were trained in classical traditions of Chinese painting, yet all of them developed innovative approaches to ink painting while living and working in the west. In fact, their contributions have great relevance to both the lineage of "Chinese" painting, and the internationalization of American art in the Twentieth Century. Perhaps for now, it is best not to worry about the limits of the definition of Chinese American art, but instead to celebrate the incredible richness and diversity of art produced in America by individuals of Chinese ancestry.

JADE SNOW WONG

Ceramic Artist, Writer

This is such a vast topic that it's best to try to define the parameters of this category. Once I took a semantics course from S. I. Hayakawa in which he emphasized how ambiguous words can be. "The Map is not the territory," he told us over and over again, so if you mention the words, "Chinese American art" to a hundred people, the hundred people would have a hundred different impressions.

The words "literature" and "art" defy exact definition. Literature can be fiction, nonfiction, poetry, short stories, many forms. Art can be in many media or mixed media. Some considered the recent Burning Man project in the Nevada desert "art."

When I began making pottery in a Chinatown window sixty years ago, the local residents laughed at me. To them I was a female college graduate in the days when none of my high school classmates went to college, and I was trying to make a living getting my hands covered with mud in public. Mainstream art critics said ceramics was a "craft" and craft cannot be in the category of art. Now I am considered a

member of the Post World War II California Arts and Crafts Movement.

So the definition of art changes with the passage of time. A couple hundred years ago, what is being featured in today's museums might not have been considered art.

As a writer and ceramic artist in two media—pottery and enameled metal, I would define literature and art as the creator's mental concepts, transformed into the reality of words or into objects a viewer can appreciate. He has labored to transmit his ideas to the world. The words or objects may not be well received, but the artist has completed his creativity. He considers himself a writer or an artist. If what he produces sells, he can be called a published writer or professional artist. If he can't sell his work, he can still consider himself a writer or an artist.

Regarding the words, "Chinese American," I assume the word "Chinese" is used as an adjective while "American" is the noun it modifies. So a person of Chinese descent who is born in America and writes or creates art would earn the label "Chinese American artist."

But you can make another assumption—to use both words as adjectives—Chinese and American influences on personal creative endeavors. Does it really matter? A creator can claim the work is both. I don't think the reader or viewer really cares. He just reacts to the written or visual work with whatever has created his taste and judgment. He completes the communication process. In fact, I started both my writing and art careers within five years of each other, during a time when my Chinese race was a liability in the American business world. In the art and writing world, my Chinese identity was intriguing. I encountered no prejudice. I transformed my inspiration and thoughts into a book that I typed out on a manual typewriter, and my clay into beautifully glazed objects. I utilized my time and my hands in media that would inform the American public's opinion about my Chinese cultural heritage, and I interpret art in my style as works of Chinese influence with American technology.

Can you say that an American of the white race who has studied the technique of Chinese art in China and paints in the Chinese style is creating American Chinese art? Is not her name a distinctive personal identity? I am thinking of the late Alison Stillwell who had a loyal following of collectors. I do not think they regard her so much as an American Chinese as the late General Stillwell's daughter, who was presenting her idea of beauty to the world.

The important consideration in the topic "What is Chinese American art" is the noun, "art." Once, a doctor told me, "When the ordinary person sees blue, you will see it bluer." It's the sensitivity of the artist together with how he executes his creation that's important. How good is the art?

Do we have to say the "Spanish-French painter, Pablo Picasso" or the "French-Polynesian painter, Gauguin"? It isn't the label that's important; it's the quality of the art.

[Editor's Note: Jade Snow Wong passed away on March 16, 2006. This was one of her last public appearances.]

LO CH'INGCHE

Artist, Poet

Professor, Department of Chinese,
Fu Jen University, Taiwan

The central purport of Western aesthetics is *mimeses*, and its aftermath, such as artistic representation, scientific reproduction, and image simulation, has become the core of Western cultural development. The ultimate concern of Chinese aesthetics is *hsing* [*xing*], the aesthetic of contingency that operates through Confucianism, Daoism, and Chan Buddhism with literary and artistic lyricism and individual linear expressionism. These two major worldly trends of ideas and their graphic signifier practices are both deeply rooted and nourished in the modes of thought derived from their verbal and written signifier systems respectively.

An artist can only work comfortably and innovatively in the graphic language that springs from and corresponds to the verbal and written language in which he thinks, meditates, and reflects primarily and freely. An examination of the art of C. C. Wang (1907–2004), an artist-collector born and educated in China, who migrated to New York for over fifty-five years, will prove that it is only with the artist's brooding artistic concerns in the verbal and written language in which he is most familiar, that the results of his graphic performances mirror those concerns accordingly and faithfully, profoundly, and creatively.

Wang's early work showed that he was caught between East and West traditions and was constantly entangled in a dilemma of aesthetic confusion. However, in his more mature artistic performance, he demonstrated that only when he was working with his indigenous calligraphic linear movement lyrically was he able to express his artistic power in the most energetic and creative way possible, in spite of whatever graphic techniques he visually inherited/borrowed or utilized either from his own or from other traditions.

The Visual Dialectics of Golf, Leisure, and Beauty in Eva Fong Chan's Paintings

(Original Title: Racialized Images in 1920s and 1930s San Francisco: The Paintings of Eva Fong Chan)

Di Yin Lu

Eva Fong Chan (1897–1991), a Chinese-American artist who actively painted and exhibited her work between 1925 and 1940, painted *Bo Kay Chan Golfing, Thomas Kwan Watching* (1931) and *Portrait of Tom Yuk Lan* (1930). Born in Sacramento, this California native studied art in San Francisco and exhibited in local institutions such as the San Francisco Art Association at the Palace of Fine Arts.[1] Though briefly affiliated with the Chinese Revolutionary Artists' Club, an avant-garde Chinatown-based painter's coalition that studied abstract painting, Chan's own work stuck closely to realistic landscapes, portraits, and flower paintings that betray the influence of American oil masters such as Winslow Homer.

The uniqueness of Chan's paintings lie in the strange everydayness of her style and subject matter and the way in which that everydayness engages visual constructions of race and class in California's 1930s Chinese American community. *Bo Kay Chan Golfing, Thomas Kwan Watching* resembles images of golf outings that frequently appeared in period American newspapers and magazines such as *McLure's* and *Frank Leslie's Popular Monthly*. Chinese Americans, however, hardly populated California golf courses, much less golf courses in the larger United States. Portraits of beautiful Chinese women, like Chan's *Portrait of Tom Yuk Lan*, certainly flooded the Chinese and American retail market. The great majority of these images, however, were calendar posters: glossy lithographic advertisements for consumer products such as cigarettes, beauty products, and medication. Courtesans and actresses often modeled for these advertisements. This was hardly the demographic with whom Chan, a piano teacher, an organist and Sunday school teacher at the San Francisco Chinese Congregational Church, and the wife of a prominent Canton businessman, associated.

The contradictory choices and experiences that Chan's paintings record eloquently project the privileges and constraints of a female, Chinese American, upwardly mobile, and *fashionable* individual. Chan's paintings carry on a nervous flirtation with contemporary images of privileged leisure and metropolitan life. They confront their audience with images that link Chinese Americans with that double-edged sword, sobriquet, "model minority."

The lived reality of Chinese Americans, like those Chinatown denizens of the Chinese Revolutionary Artist's Club, did not encompass the social mobility that Chan's paintings implied. Of all the members of the painting club, Chan was likely the only one who could afford to buy her own set of paints, canvases, and art classes—the rest were largely Chinatown laborers. The members' professional lives overlapped with the rowdy 1920s and 1930s employment disputes surrounding Asian laborers in California. Asian women in 1920s and 1930s California did not fare much better than Asian laborers. The 1924 Immigration Act kept Chinese women from entering the United States for permanent residence. By the 1930s, new marriage laws stripped citizenship from female citizens who married those without citizenship.[2] According to these laws, Asian American females, whose families may have resided in the States since the 1880s, could not retain their citizenship if they chose to marry an illegal immigrant or choose a mate from China. Asian females also received a particular sexualization in United States media, especially through films that highlighted prostitution. Despite social reformers' reports that, with the exception of San Francisco, the overwhelming number of prostitutes in American cities were white, "Chinese prostitutes" retained a larger-than-life notoriety in the United States.[3]

Compared to the vast majority of Asian Americans living in San Francisco's Chinatown during the early twentieth century, or even under today's standards, Chan belonged to a privileged class. Her family could afford her taking music lessons, going to art school, and attending a music college. Noted for her beauty, Chan won the 1915 Chinatown Queen contest.[4] Before her 1919 marriage to Bo Kay Chan, Eva spent a few years vacationing in Canton and Shanghai, two cities that were the hub of metropolitan life during the Early Republican Era. Her husband hailed from a prominent Canton family with nationalist affiliations. Together the Chans owned a restaurant and an export-import company with branches in San Francisco and China. In 1949, within a few years of their first daughter's birth, the family moved out of Chinatown and into a townhouse near San Francisco's affluent Russian Hill. In 1986, former mayor Willie Brown presented Chan with a California State Assembly resolution that commended Chan for her life achievements.

Indeed, the very subject and style of Chan's paintings betray the wide socioeconomic gap between her and her

Chinese-American painting fellows. Members of the Chinese Revolutionary Artist's Club, including the well-known artist Yun Gee, painted Chinatown cityscapes, street musicians, and other subjects within close range of Chinatown's observable environment.[5] Chan's 1931 landscape, *Bo Kay Chan Golfing, Thomas Kwan Watching*, portrays her husband, Bo Kay Chan, playing golf with his friend on a beautiful green complete with mountains rolling in the background and lush pine trees framing the foreground (see Figure 1).[6] The specific dating of the painting (October 30, 1931) and Chan's own writing on the back of the canvas, "Bo Kay Chan Golfing, Thomas Kwan Watching," indicates that this painting portrays an actual event, not an imaginary outing. On October 30, 1931, accompanied by Chan, who recorded the event, and Kwan, a golfing buddy, Bo Kay Chan traveled to one of the many well-pruned golfing greens in California and played rounds of golf while his wife sketched on her canvas. In comparison, Chan's fellow painters rarely left Chinatown, and given their stretched economy, did not consider golf a viable option on their rare days off.

During the turn of the twentieth century, golf was one of the dominant forces behind the creation of new country clubs in America.[7] The Scottish import began attracting members of the affluent American middle class by the 1920s.[8] By the 1930s, golf became an important part of privileged, white, middle-class, American culture; newspapers touted its contributions to physical health and published photographs of lithe, clean-cut young men enjoying a round of golf on a picturesque green. Country clubs around the country opened up membership quotas in order to draw more members and golf players onto their well-maintained grounds.[9] By recording this golf outing, Chan associated herself, her husband, and Thomas Kwan with this affluent, American cultural phenomenon and displayed that association to whoever examined her painting.

Figure 1. Eva Fong Chan (1897-1991), Bo Kay Chan Golfing, Thomas Kwan Watching, *October 30, 1930, oil on canvas. Private collection of Rosalind Chan Wong, San Francisco, CA.*

Chan's very recording of this outing betrays the values of an upwardly mobile, middle-class, Chinese American family of the 1930s. Of Chan's ten or so extant works, this painting alone records an event—this event is not a birthday party, a wedding, or any other gathering that might mark significant events in modern family life; it is a leisurely afternoon of golf with friends. Something about this outing made it more worth recording than the myriad of other equally important vicissitudes in Chan's life in 1931. I believe that "something" was the privilege and middle-class stability that golf outings represent. Chan tells us, through this painting, that not only did the Chan family have the time and money to indulge in lengthy, leisurely activities, they indulged in affluent, white, middle-class American activities such as golf.

Positioning herself as an unseen observer who watches from behind the golf players, Chan offers the viewer two perspectives—that of her husband, the expert golf player, and that of herself, an accomplished woman, able to produce paintings comparable to those in classical American genre painting. Caught in the moment after he completed his swing, Bo Kay Chan expertly wields his club above his shoulder while he surveys the trajectory of his golf ball. He wears golf shoes, socks, and pants, as well as a hat, as does his partner Thomas Kwan. These accoutrements imply that Chan's husband regularly plays the game, enough to own the appropriate clothing and a set of golf clubs, which rest alongside him.

In fact, the composition of figures and scenery in Chan's painting matches that of golf advertisements in contemporary newspapers and country club brochures (see Figures 2 and 3).[10] Chan's own painterly perspective directs the viewer's eye toward the painting's setting—a beautiful expanse of rolling California hills. Tall pine trees that frame the edges of the painting direct the viewer's eye to a small clubhouse nestled in a grove of trees in the middle ground of the painting. The viewer looks past the well-pruned, grassy green to uniformly aligned shrubs that dot gentle mountain ridges. Regardless of which California golfing green this painting represents, the historic Lincoln Park golf course by the Legion of Honor or the exclusive Lake at Olympic Club golf course, the difference between this idyllic escape and those congested urban streetscapes that other Chinese Revolutionary Art Club members painted and lived in is vast. Chan's depiction of her family's very access to these lush surroundings, as well as this opportunity to enjoy leisure, indicates an economic standing that sets her apart from other members of her art club.

Artists in the Chinese Revolutionary Artist's Club focused their studies on abstract painting (see Figure 4).[11] They painted avant-garde works of art that veered away from realistic depiction, played with the use of color, and distorted three-dimensional form. The club members saw avant-garde painting as representative of new and modern forms of expression.[12] Learning to paint in this method signified a turning away from established artistic genres, be that method Chinese literati painting, which some of the club members

Figure 2. Picture taken from Andrew Lang, "Pleasures and Pains of Golf," Frank Leslie's Popular Monthly 32, no. 1 (July 1891): 108.

Figure 3. Artist unknown, print advertisement in McClure's Magazine 52, no. 1 (January 1920): 65.

Figure 4. Yun Gee (1906-1963), A Minimal Vision—Furniture with Painting, 1915, oil on canvas. Private collection.

studied and then relinquished, or perspectival painting as taught in traditional painting studios.[13]

Chan's paintings, on the other hand, retained the realistic representation taught by older masters in California art schools. The difference in visual representation here hints at Chan's position in regard to the Western painterly tradition. She associated with, but ultimately abandoned, the in-vogue, avant-garde painterly path that absorbed the edgier students in California art schools. As a Christian wife and stay-at-home mother, she, the occasional painter, studied the traditional American genre painting style of Winslow Homer and not the avant-garde painting style of Otis Oldfield.

Chan's life choices paralleled the more traditional leanings that her paintings already imply. Although she and Bo Kay purchased a home near the more polished, Russian Hill district, she stayed close to her Chinatown community, taught Sunday school, and continued teaching those piano classes that earned her respect and prestige in the Chinese Congregational Church of San Francisco. While Chan painted with professional ease and exhibited her paintings regularly, she did not claim painting as a career. In fact, she gave up painting a few years after giving birth to Rosalind, her daughter. While she carried on her profession as a piano teacher, she did not leave home—Chan's students came to lessons in her living room. Indeed, if avant-garde painting represented the new, the modern, and the relinquishing of traditions for other members of the Chinese Revolutionary Artist's Club, Chan's rejec-

tion of avant-garde painting represented her self-alignment with more traditional, white, American middle-class values as they percolated through Chinatown's rising merchant families.

The socioeconomic aspirations in Chan's 1930s paintings bring a unique historical perspective to the 1960s media designation of Asians as model minorities. During the 1960s, American media cited Asian Americans' higher academic and financial attainments, as well as their expertise at math and technology, despite the long history of anti-Asian immigration laws and hostility toward Asian Americans in the States. These reports designated Asian Americans as *model minorities*—the minority race that achieved, through hard work, a privileged status.[14] Facing the threat of the 1960s Black Civil Rights movement, American media chose to draw upon Asian Americans' historical groping toward white, middle-class privileges in order to create model-minority Asians, as opposed to sly, ruthless, untrustworthy Asians, who simultaneously existed in the racial vocabulary of the time.[15]

The visual allusions to white American upper class, country clubs, and privilege are crucial to the historical importance of Chan's work. The 1931 landscape's racialized investment in golf's socioeconomic footprint negotiates Chan's lived reality, namely her association with Chinatown laborer/artists and other members of the Chinatown working class, with the display of her own middle-class stability. The painting represents what she achieved—a systematic investment in American identity and privilege, and what she relinquished in return for those achievements—the possibilities of which are too numerous to list.

Chan's willing alignment of herself and her painting style with American genre painting is precisely what makes her 1930 painting, *Portrait of Tom Yuk Lan*, so strange (see Figure 5).[16] The portrait draws stylistic elements from advertisement calendar posters: large, consumer-oriented lithographs of beautiful Chinese women. Having lived in Chinatown and Shanghai, Chan was steeped in the advertisement calendar posters that circulated in Shanghai and overseas during the 1920s and 1930s. Although Chan designed the portrait so that Tom Yuk Lan resembles a dignified, composed lady, the visual allusions to beautiful women in calendar posters give the portrait an edgy, sexual undertone that contemporary viewers would have immediately recognized. Why would Chan, a member of Chinatown's privileged, older establishment, choose to create this sexually charged portrait of a woman who might presumably have been a member of her social circle?

Figure 5. Eva Fong Chan (1897–1991), Portrait of Tom Yuk Lan, 1931, oil on canvas. Private collection of Rosalind Chan Wong, San Francisco, CA.

At the turn of the twentieth century, Shanghai commercial advertisers used lithography, a Western import, to design highly popular and successful posters that circulated throughout China and the overseas Chinese community.[17] By the 1920s, these posters by and large depicted urban beauties—beautiful women in modern, westernized Shanghai.[18] Merchants from professions as different as butchers, grocers, booksellers, and magazine publishers commissioned these posters and gave them to customers. They also sold the posters to buyers willing to pay the cost of producing the posters.[19] Bazaar stalls sold calendar posters on street corners.[20] Overseas Chinese merchants likewise sold and gave away these posters to their customers in San Francisco and New York's Chinatowns. Calendar posters propagated through Shanghainese popular culture and became part of the visual culture of the 1920s and 1930s for Chinese and overseas Chinese communities. Some of these posters even became prized collector's items for art connoisseurs.

The models that posed for calendar poster artists included known courtesans, prostitutes, and, in later years, movie stars.[21] Although these pictures borrow from traditional visual references to beautiful women in Chinese popular media, such as prints in the *Illustrated Biographies of Worthy Women* and the *Illustrated One Hundred Beauties*, the overwhelming visual reference for women in the calendar posters come from images of Qing dynasty courtesans and Early Republican Period prostitutes.[22] Urban guides to Shanghai featured illustrated biographies of famous courtesans and prostitutes,[23] newspapers such as the *Dianshizhai Buabao* fea-

tured titillatingly illustrated stories about public courtesan behavior,[24] and popular romantic fiction, such as Mandarin Duck and Butterfly literature, featured prints of courtesans on their publication covers.[25] Indeed, as early as the 1880s and certainly in the 1920s and 1930s, images of urban beauties were an inescapablepart of modern life.

The ubiquitous flood of early twentieth-century calendar posters transformed courtesans into urban beauties who actively participated in fashionable metropolitan life.[26] Images of the urban beauty symbolized Shanghai's glamour, commercial might, and urban follies, while the urban beauty herself was admired for her looks, clothes, and accessories. These women wore the latest hairstyles, dressed in fashionable Western and Eastern-style clothes, lived in lush, modern interiors, and entertained themselves by going to popular Shanghai dancehalls.[27]

Overseas Chinese communities displayed advertisement calendar posters in much the same way as their counterparts did in China. In addition to using the posters as calendars, people separated the images from the calendar and used them for decoration.[28] As the 1925 *Chinatown Studio Photo* from the Bancroft library demonstrates, images of urban beauties stood alongside framed copies of calligraphy, photographs of family relatives and a myriad of other knick-knacks that Chinese Americans hung on their walls during the early twentieth century (see Figure 6).[29]

A comparison between *Portrait of Tom Yuk Lan* and contemporary calendar posters will show the many similarities between the women's hairstyle, makeup, and choice of clothing. Despite the Western pedigree in Chan's use of oil paint and a frontal, three-quarter pose, the painting draws visual references from calendar posters to depict Tom Yuk Lan as a well-dressed, well-manicured, and well-groomed lady—an urban beauty who stands at the height of Chinese metropolitan fashion. Chan's painting, however, reveals an important difference from its Shanghainese source—and perhaps this is the answer to why Chan would use the risqué calendar poster girl as a reference. Although in her portrait, Tom Luk Yan looks every bit the urban beauty, her lack of jewelry, her air of reserve, and her choice of clothes filter out the posters' allusions to courtesans and everyday Shanghainese consumer culture. Chan's painting gentrifies the urban beauty image into that of a privileged, middle-class woman.

Some of the most popular and widely circulated urban beauty images of the 1920s and 1930s came from the hand of Xie Zhiguang (1900–1976), a commercial artist who created innumerable illustrations for newspapers and magazines, as well as hundreds of advertisement calendar posters and

Figure 6. Unknown photographer, Untitled (Chinatown Studio Portrait), ca. 1925. Bancroft Library, University of California, Berkeley.

Figure 7. Xie Zhiguang (1900-1976), Girl Holding Ken-i-kocho-jo Box, advertisement calendar poster for Ken-i-kocho-jo Tablets, 1931.

Figure 8. Xie Zhiguang (1900-1976), Girl Holding a Lily, advertisement poster for Russia-China Tobacco Manufacturing Company, 1930s. Collection of Agnes Tabah, Washington, DC.

hangers. Not only were Xie's work popular in China and overseas, they were representative of other urban beauty images circulating in advertisement calendar posters in the 1920s and 1930s. Two examples of Xie's work from the 1930s include *Girl Holding Ken-i-kocho-jo Box* and *Girl Holding a Lily* (see Figures 7 and 8).[30] *Girl Holding Ken-i-kocho-jo Box* advertises medicinal tablets made for the Japanese Ken-i-kocho-jo Company, whose products are featured prominently in the lower right-hand corner of the poster. Like many cigarette advertisements of the 1930s, *Girl Holding a Lily* features no products, though the name "Russia-China Tobacco Manufacturing Company," boldly printed in Chinese and English, makes clear the poster's intent.

The urban beauty in *Girl Holding Ken-i-kocho-jo Box* represents a more outgoing, modern beauty: she sports a carefully maintained, short, curly bob, and lives in a spacious, modern home that only wealthy Shanghainese could afford in the congested 1930s urban housing market. The mix of Eastern and Western accoutrements in the room indicates her access to the wealth of foreign and domestic imports in Shanghai—the chandelier, fireplace, and couches reflect European tastes, while the Chinese prescription for Japanese medication on her marble-top table remind the viewer of Shanghai's importance to international and interregional trade. The urban beauty drips with jewelry, as if further underlining her metropolitan affluence. She wears two long pearl earrings, while two jewel-encrusted rings adorn her left hand. In fact, Xie turns the woman's hand

unnaturally forward so that the center of this image focuses on the medicinal pills and the large stones on her rings.

The calendar poster entitled *Girl Holding a Lily* represents a more demure, traditional variety of urban beauty. Portraits of beautiful women holding flowers appear so often in Ming, Qing, and Early Republican Chinese art that the pose became a cliché.[31] This urban beauty also sports a fashionably short bob but covers her ears with her hair and shyly conceals her body from the viewer by sitting sideways. She wears a traditional one-piece mandarin dress that has fashionably widened sleeves and a shorter hemline. Here, Xie again employs his stylistic display of the urban beauty's jewelry, in this case her ring and bracelets. This urban beauty's accessories, however, are much less elaborate and gaudy in comparison to that in the medicinal advertisement. Furthermore, while the urban beauty in *Girl Holding Ken-i-kocho-jo Box* wears translucent fabric that tempts the viewer to peep through the clothing at her underlying skin, the school-girlish urban beauty in *Girl Holding a Lily* sits primly in an opaque, one-piece dress, contemplating her sprig of lilies.

Tom Yuk Lan's slick, short, curly hairstyle resembles that of the two urban beauties in Xie's advertisement calendar posters. Like the westernized urban beauty in *Girl Holding Ken-i-kocho-jo Box*, she brushes her hair away from her face to reveal her forehead and ears. The frontal perspective of the painting and the close-up focus on her face, however, gives her hairstyle the smooth, traditional respectability of the urban beauty in *Girl Holding a Lily*. Tom's finely drawn eyebrows have the same pencil-shaped quality as the neatly plucked and shaped eyebrows in Xie's posters. The three women have identically applied eye makeup and similar nose and lips, as if Chan used the ideals of beauty pictured in advertising calendar posters as a model for her own portrait of a San Francisco urban beauty. Even the application of oil paint in Chan's portrait gives Tom Yuk Lan's features a graphic, flat quality that highlights the similarities between this oil painting and its lithographic cousins.

Despite the similarity in hair, makeup, and dress, Chan's San Francisco urban beauty has a seriousness that the alluring, calendar poster women do not. Tom Yuk Lan has a solemn face and an observing gaze that make the viewer aware that she looks back as much as the viewer looks at her. In contrast, the urban beauty in *Girl Holding Ken-i-kocho-jo Box* looks askance and smiles at someone beyond the viewer's immediate surroundings, simulating a friendly, almost flirty conversation wherein she recommends the health tablets to one of her friends or admirers. Compared to this smiling gamine with an inviting smile, Tom Yuk Lan's firmly pressed lips remind the viewer that she is a lady of quality, one who does not laugh and smile for any consumer's entertainment.

Even the urban beauty in *Girl Holding a Lily*, whose downward gaze and shy smile more closely resembles Tom Yuk Lan's contemplative quality, exudes a flirty invitation that Chan paints out of her portrait. While Tom Yuk Lan gives the viewer no indication of whether she wants the viewer to step further into her space or otherwise, *Girl Holding a Lily* turns toward the viewer and rests her arm on an imaginary ledge behind her, opening up the space around her body to the approaching individual. The urban beauty in *Girl Holding a Lily* even begins to smile, assuring the viewer that, yes, the space next to her has room for two. Tom Yuk Lan, on the other hand, cocks her head to the side with the seriousness and propriety of a woman whose sense of status and social etiquette makes her approachable only under more formal social circumstances.

The composition of Chan's portrait also imposes a rigid formality on Tom Yuk Lan that filters out the more blatant sexual messages in Xie's calendar posters. Tom's bust-length portrait cuts off her arms and torso, rendering only the most concealing parts of her *qipao* accessible to the viewer. Unlike the urban beauty in *Girl Holding Ken-i-kocho-jo Box*, whose translucent sleeves fall teasingly away from her arms and whose billowing clothes cling to her body, Tom wears a thick silk fabric that reveals none of her underlying skin; in fact, the mandarin dress creases around her shoulders, implying that the clothing falls relatively loosely on her body. Both women have the accoutrements of wealth—the San Francisco urban beauty as indicated by her elaborate heavy-silk qipao and the Shanghainese urban beauty as indicated by her jewelry and luxurious surroundings. Chan's composition, however, erases the urban beauty's accessibility by turning the woman's body away from the viewer and shielding the woman's body with the accoutrements of her wealth.

Even Chan's composition indicates that her visual intensions for Tom Yuk Lan's dress are different than Xie's for his urban beauty. In *Portrait of Tom Yuk Lan*, the qipao's elaborate design, its pearlescent, silky sheen, and the color resonance between the fabric and the woman's makeup opened up the painting's dark background. The bright colors flatten the perspective and keep the viewer's eyes on the painting's surface. The urban beauty in *Girl Holding a Lily* wears a loose fitting qipao, similar in design to Tom Yuk Lan. Xie's composition of *Girl Holding a Lily*, on the other hand, pulls away from the Shanghainese urban beauty in order to reveal the soft drape of a dress of undeterminable material, which enhances the urban beauty's fashionably slim body underneath the dress.

Looking at the three urban beauties, one immediately notices that in Chan's portrait, Tom Yuk Lan wears no jewelry, whereas Xie's two urban beauties twist and turn their bodies in such a way that their jewelry appears as much on display as the women themselves. In *Girl Holding Ken-i-kocho-jo Box*, the rubies, diamonds, and pearls take as central a space in the poster's composition as the urban beauty herself. Even the more reserved gamine in *Girl Holding a Lily* positions her arms and her lily so that her ruby ring and cloisonné bracelet appear in plain view. Tom Yuk Lan, on the other hand, does not even have pierced ears.

In the visual culture of calendar posters, Tom Yuk Lan's lack of jewelry may indicate Chan's unwillingness to associate this portrait with visual indicators of prostitution and courtesan life. Newspaper reports on Shanghai courtesan life often describe the women's wealth of jewelry and their catty fights over each other's jewelry; the newspapers' accompanying illustrations likewise highlight the urban beauties' jewelry-encrusted attire. In fact, admirers and customers often used jewelry as a way of introducing themselves to courtesans and prostitutes. One famous story about a particularly lavish dancehall customer documents him as giving bejeweled hairpieces to each of those courtesans and prostitutes who entertained him. When one greedy courtesan took two, the customer bid the servant holding the jewelry box not to scold the courtesan, but to allow her to take as much as she liked. A 1923 short story, written for the Zi Lan Hua Pian by Zhou Shou Juan, a student who traveled to Shanghai to make his living as a writer, describes his astonishment that a prostitute who could not afford jewelry wore electric bulbs to attract customers' attention.[32] In the narrative, Zhou's friend confirms that many lower-level prostitutes in city brothels wear electric bulbs as jewelry.[33]

In contrast to those courtesans and prostitutes, whose jewelry delineate their commodified status in Shanghai's consumer culture, Tom Yuk Lan's bare ears and her lack of a necklace gentrifies her. Her lack of jewelry reminds the viewer that this woman cannot be purchased by jewelry, nor does she reveal her gaudiness by displaying her jewelry to all and sundry. By filtering out rings, necklaces, and bracelets, Chan filters out a significant element of her urban beauty's association with the courtesans and prostitutes who model for calendar posters, making Tom Yuk Lan at least a woman of quality, if not a woman of the upper class.

Some might argue that Chan's San Francisco urban beauty takes after those more gentrified versions of advertisement calendar posters that portrayed women as mothers and housewives. Certainly such posters existed and circulated with equal ubiquity in China and overseas in the early twentieth century. Xie Zhiguang himself depicted a well-to-do, gentrified mother figure in his 1930s advertisement for the Haofen Cigarettes Company entitled *A Mother and Her Children* (see Figure 9).[34] What underscores the role of the woman in Xie's poster as a mother, however, are the telltale markers of motherhood and marriage, not her physical appearance.

The urban mother in *A Mother and Her Children* is also covered in jewelry. Xie turns her body toward the viewer to reveal her large jade ring, the matching, long jade earrings, and her elaborately decorated qipao. Much like the other urban beauties in Xie's and other calendar posters, her carefully drawn face, well-groomed attire, and luxurious accessories keep her in the visual formula of an inviting, alluring urban beauty. It is her three children, one of whom she holds in her arms and the other two of whom cling and clamor for her attention, that conceal her body and designate her as a mother. The idyllic country house in the background further underlines her comfortable, suburban lifestyle. Without the context of her house, her children, and the placement of the ring on her ring finger, the urban mother in *A Mother and Her Children* does not differ greatly from the urban beauties in *Girl Holding Ken-i-kocho-jo Box* or *Girl Holding a Lily*. The urban mother's smile, glittery wardrobe, and her very appearance on a cigarette poster designate her as a beauty to be admired by consumers.

What is extraordinary about Chan's paintings are their careful selection of visual elements from select sources in early 1930s visual culture and Chan's own volition to do so in her upper-middle-class, San Francisco social circle. As previously mentioned, San Francisco's rhetoric on prostitution in Chinatown cast a particularly sexualized light on Chinese American women living in early twentieth-century San Francisco—with so many purported prostitutes, madams, and pleasure houses in San Francisco's Chinatown, how can a casual visitor distinguish a well-dressed woman from a well-dressed prostitute? The proliferation of calendar posters featuring titillating illustrations of Chinese urban beauties, as well as foreign companies' steady investment in the production of these posters in China and overseas, did not help the situation.[35]

Figure 9. Xie Zhiguang (1900-1976), *A Mother and Her Children*, advertisement poster for the China Haofeng Tobacco Company, 1930s. Collection of Ellen Johnston Laing.

American film media likewise marked Asian women with a particularly sexual image. Films such as Sternberg's *Shanghai Express* titillated audiences with Marlene Dietrich, the sexually promiscuous "Shanghai Lily," who associated with Chinese prostitutes. Alan Crosland's 1927 film, *Old San Francisco*, features Asian American film star Anna May Wong as a "Flower of the Orient," a prostitute with connections to San Francisco's opium ring and white slave trade.[36] The tensions between privileged, middle-class consumers, Chinatown laborers, and these sexualized urban beauties in American as well as Chinese popular culture come to a head in Chan's paintings. Tom Yuk Lan's concealed body, her solemn expression, and the formal three-quarter pose structure of her portrait filter out the sexual markers prevalent in calendar posters because this San Francisco urban beauty wants no association with those prostitutes in American media nor those courtesans and prostitutes in Shanghainese popular culture. Instead, Chan's portrait gives Tom Yuk Lan markers of Asian American, middle-class privilege and propriety—the costly, dazzling yet conservative heavy silk mandarin dress makes clear Tom's comfortable economic status, the formal composition gives the painting the propriety of a formal portrait, and the lack of jewelry makes Tom a modest, chaste member of Chinatown's privileged class.

The markers of privilege and class in Tom Yuk Lan's portrait indicate an investment in upper-middle-class, white American culture that underlies immigrant upward mobility in the early twentieth century. Like the 1931 landscape, whose leisurely golf outing represents social and economic privileges that the working-class members of the Chinese Revolutionary Artists Club had little access to, the urban beauty's luxurious accoutrements in advertisement calendar posters represent social and economic privileges that everyday Shanghainese people and overseas Chinese American laborers had little access to.[37]

Despite Chan's careful filtering of visual markers in her paintings, however, contemporary audiences would have considered her work edgy, even somewhat racy. Chan's Christian Chinatown community, with which her family socialized for four generations and in which her husband conducted his entrepreneurial ventures, were steeped in calendar posters. Similarly, the older Chinatown residents were directly involved in the economic tensions between newer and older immigrants.

Since I first visited Rosalind Chan, Eva Fong Chan's daughter, and saw Chan's work, her paintings have both puzzled and fascinated me. They illustrate, in an artistically polished, visually satisfying, yet contentious way, the complicated dynamics of Chinese Americans who tasted, and continued to strive for, middle-class status in early twentieth-century San Francisco. The painter's willful choosing and relinquishing of specific visual markers brings up the question—how many of her choices were dictated by her aspirations to middle-class American life, and how many are dictated by middle-class American life itself? The rigor of raising a family in San Francisco, her responsibilities as a prominent member of the Chinese American community, and her social aspirations marked her paintings as well as her artistic legacy.

Chan stopped painting shortly after her daughter Rosalind Chan's birth in 1940, although she continued to display her painting in her home as well as the homes of relatives across America.

NOTES

1. This exhibition record was gathered from an exhibition label on Chan's 1932 painting, *Seascape*. The painting resides in the private collection of Rosalind Chan, Eva Fong Chan's daughter.
2. Laura Hyun Yi Kang, *Compositional Subjects Enfiguring Asian/American Women* (Durham and London: Duke University Press, 2002), 139.
3. Robert G. Lee, *Orientals: Asian Americans in Popular Culture* (Philadelphia: Temple University Press, 1999), 90.
4. All personal information on Eva Fong Chan's life come from interviews conducted with her surviving relatives, such as Mei Ping Wang, who lived with the artist until her death, and Rosalind Chan, the artist's daughter.
5. Lee, *Popular Culture,* 201.
6. See Figure 1. Eva Fong Chan, *Bo Kay Chan Golfing, Thomas Kwan Watching*, October 30, 1930, oil on canvas, private collection of Rosalind Chan Wong, San Francisco, CA.
7. Richard J. Moss, *Golf and the American Country Club* (Urbana and Chicago: University of Illinois Press, 2001), 21.
8. Ibid., 83.
9. Ibid., 102.
10. See Figures 2 and 3. Figure 2, picture taken from Andrew Lang, "Pleasures and Pains of Golf," *Frank Leslie's Popular Monthly* 32, no. 1 (July 1891): 108. Figure 3, artist unknown, print advertisement in *McClure's Magazine* 52, no. 1 (January 1920): 65.
11. See Figure 4. Yun Gee, *A Minimal Vision—Furniture with Painting*, 1915, oil on canvas, private collection.
12. Judith Tannenbaum, "Yun Gee: A Rediscovery," *Arts Magazine* 54 (May 1980): 165.
13. Ibid., 165.
14. Jean Kim, "Asian American Identity Development Theory," in *New Perspectives on Racial Identity Development: A Theoretical and Practical Anthology*, ed. Charmaine L. Wijeyesinghe and Bailey W. Jackson, III (New York and London: New York University Press, 2001) 69.
15. Kim, "Asian American Identity," 69.
16. See Figure 5. Eva Fong Chan, *Portrait of Tom Yuk Lan*, 1931, oil on canvas, private collection of Rosalind Chan Wong, San Francisco, CA.
17. Ellen Johnston Laing, *Selling Happiness Calendar Posters and Visual Culture in Early Twentieth Century Shanghai* (Honolulu: University of Hawaii Press, 2004) 3.
18. Ibid., 93.
19. Ibid., 29.
20. Ibid., 3.
21. Ibid., 103.
22. Catherine Vance Yeh, "Creating the Urban Beauty: The Shanghai Courtesan in Late Qing Illustrations," in *Writing and Materiality in China: Essays in Honor of Patrick Hanan*, ed. Judith T. Zeitlin and Lydia H. Liu (Cambridge and London: Harvard University Press, 2003), 397–98.
23. Ibid., 400.
24. Ibid., 413.
25. Lu Hanchao, *Beyond the Neon Lights Everyday Shanghai in the Early Twentieth Century* (Berkeley, Los Angeles, and London: University of California Press, 1999), 59–60.
26. Yeh, "Creating the Urban Beauty," 432.
27. Laing, *Selling Happiness Calendar Posters,* 132–35.
28. Ibid, 3.
29. See Figure 6. Unknown photographer, Untitled (Chinatown Studio Portrait), ca. 1925, Bancroft Library, University of California, Berkeley.
30. See Figures 7 and 8. Figure 7, Xie Zhiguang (1900-1976), *Girl Holding Ken-i-kocho-jo Box*, advertisement calendar poster for Ken-i-kocho-jo Tablets, 1931. Figure 8, Xie Zhiguang (1900-1976), *Girl Holding a Lily*, advertisement poster for Russia-China Tobacco Manufacturing Company, 1930s, collection of Agnes Tabah, Washington, DC.
31. Laing, *Selling Happiness Calendar Posters,* 101.
32. Zhou Shou Juan, "Small Electric Bulbs on Prostitutes [researcher translation]," in *Jiu Shanghai Feng Qing Lu*, ed. Yu Zhi and Cheng Xin Guo (Shanghai: Wen Hui chubanshe, 1998) 149.
33. Ibid., 150.
34. See Figure 9. Xie Zhiguang, *A Mother and Her Children*, advertisement poster for the China Haofeng Tobacco Company, 1930s, collection of Ellen Johnston Laing.
35. Many of the companies using advertisement calendar posters were Western, such as the British American Tobacco Company, the aforementioned Russia China Tobacco Company, My Dear Cigarettes, and so on. Though the calendars primarily targeted Chinese audiences, many calendars featured bilingual printing, implying that the advertisements targeted foreign as well as Chinese readers. Considering the number of foreigners traveling for pleasure in Shanghai during the early twentieth century, Western audiences certainly saw these posters; Western collectors amassed several large advertisement calendar poster collections, such as that of Agnes Tabah of Washington, DC. Laing, *Selling Happiness Calendar Posters,* 3.
36. In Chinese media, the term "flower" is synonymous with prostitute. Popular Chinese fictional magazines featured successive covers that depicted "famous flowers (prostitutes) of society," early twentieth-century newspapers famously published "huabong," or flower lists, which refer to a list of famous prostitutes in any given city.
37. As social historian Lu Hanchao eloquently points out, "While Shanghai has the reputation of having a diverse and rich cuisine, the standard breakfast for the people of Shanghai was, and remains, tasteless *paofan* and pickles. In high fashion, the city led the nation (the Paris of the east), but ordinary people seldom purchased clothes off the rack at a fashionable shop. What most Shanghainese wore was made either by the handy housewife (as most of them were) or a Ningbo or Suzhou tailor, whose shop most likely sat right on the corner of the alley.... While automobiles were found in abundance on the streets of Shanghai, most people had never taken a taxi; for the majority, to ride in a sedan would have been considered a once in a lifetime experience" (Lu, *Beyond the Neon Lights,* 14).

On the Term "Chinese Language"

(A Preliminary Manuscript)

(Original English title: Teaching Huayu Chinese versus Teaching Guoyu, Putonghua, or Hanyu)

華 語 正 名 說 (初 稿)

Leung Puichee

梁 培 熾

日常有不少朋友或學生家長問我，在我們華文學校裏教的究竟是臺灣的中文，還是中國大陸的中文，或是香港的中文呢？

這的的確確是我們華文教育上常常遇到困擾的問題。事實上也是一個要我們大家必須明白的課題。由於兩岸三地歷史發展的成因，這一問題，常常把我們弄得也無可奈何。臺灣用的是繁體字，講的是"國語"；香港用的也是繁體字，講的卻是廣州話；而中國大陸用的是簡體字，講的是"普通話"。這樣，自然是不少人以為是三種不同的語言了。怎麼樣學呢？究竟學那一地那一種的呢？

還有，在我們日常生活、工作和學習的各方接觸中，華語又叫普通話、國語、漢語、中國話和唐話等。華文則叫中文、漢字，或叫漢文、唐字。眾說紛紜，不知究竟，無所適從，怎不教華童滿頭霧水泥？

要解決這個問題，首先要明確我們華文教育的對象是什麼人，確定我們華文教育的屬性，作出適當的定位，弄清我們華文教育的路向，然後再瞭解各個概念的內涵及其演變，才能給我們弄清楚它的究竟。

一、

那麼，什麼是我們華文教育的對象呢？我們華文教育的屬性又是什麼？

我們華文教育的對象，毫無疑問，當然是"華人"，是先後來自中國大陸，來自臺灣，來自香港，來自澳門，來自世界五湖四海的炎黃民族子孫及其後裔。我們的教育對象是華裔的美國人，而不是"中國人"，也不是傳統的"華僑"。今天在美國的華文教育，是我們華人的族裔語言和文化的教育。（詳見拙文《美國華文教育發展的新理念》、《美國華文教育發展的深層思考》。）

什麼是華僑，什麼是華人和華裔？它們間又有什麼樣的關係？

華僑、華人與華裔，看來這似乎是三個不同名稱的叫法，但其實，它們的具體含義卻是不同的。這種不同，就會直接地關係到我們華文教育的定位不同。不同的屬性，有不同的定位。我們的華文教育，是面向華人或華裔而不是華僑，這是我們進行華文教育時必須要弄清楚的首要前提。

這是因為，華僑是保留了中國國籍而又工作或生活在中國國境之外的中國人。華僑既受到中國法律的保護，也要盡中國公民的義務；他們既不受其生活所在國的保護，也不需要向生活所在國承擔任何的國民義務。當然，他們一定需要遵守生活所在國和當地的法律和法規。簡單地說，華僑就是生活在中國以外的中國人，但不是居住國的公民。

那麼，華人又是什麼？？

華人者，凡是生活在中國以外的，他們既持有中國護照，又還沒有所在國的國籍，但又具有所在國永久居留權的中國公民，這類人或遲早都會向所在國歸化而放棄中國籍的，或是已歸化了所在國的第一代移民，我們都把他們稱呼為華人。

至於華裔，那是出生在中國以外的華僑和華人的後代及其子子孫孫。

由於當代國際形勢的變化發展，尤自第二次大戰之後，中國境外的華僑，都先後向華人轉變。美國在其憲法第十四款中有明確的規定："凡在美國境內出生或歸化，而且屬其法權管轄之一切個人，均屬美國國民"。又據1980年9月10日第五屆全國人民代表大會第三次會議通過《中華人民共和國國籍法》第九條也明確地規定："定居外國的中國公民，自願加入或取得外國籍的，即自動喪

失中國國籍"。不論美國, 還是中國, 其立法都是不採取
雙重國籍的。所以, 不論華人也好, 華裔也好, 他們都變成
了所在國的公民, 成為美國多元民族中的一元。從國籍法
的角度看, 他們已經不是 "中國人", 而是 "美國人" 了。那
麼, 美國的華文教育, 其對象已不是 "中國人" 而是 "美國
人"。更具體地說, 是華裔的美國人。這麼說, 並不是要我
們數典忘祖, 事實上我們淵源自中華民族, 但我們是美國
的公民, 是美國多元民族大家庭中的一元。所以, 今天美
國的華文教育, 已不是傳統的僑民教育, 而是真真正正的
華文教育。

為什麼呢?

這是因為僑民教育, 它是對謀生和居住在國外而又
保留自己原有國籍的僑民及其子女, 施行與本國政府教育
制度基本相一致的教育, 它是本國政府對自己國民的教育
在國外的延伸。今天美國的華文教育, 則是在美國的華人
群體, 或作為一個少數民族, 對自己的族裔進行本民族的
語言和傳統文化的教育。它與傳統的僑民教育在本質屬性
上是不同的。這是我們必須要弄清楚的。這都是關係著我
們華文教育的定位和華文教育的任務。

當然, 傳統的僑民教育, 孕育了今天我們的華文教
育。華文教育是脫胎自僑民教育的, 而且, 它們今生今世,
母子相隨, 很難分離。但我們也必須要分清楚僑民教育與
華文教育在本質上的不同。只有這樣, 我們才能找到華文
教育的路向, 明確我們的目的, 才能使我們有所為和有所
不為, 才能推動我們華文教育的不斷發展, 才能完成我們
族裔所託付的神聖使命!

當今我們的華文教育, 所面向和立足的是華人, 在
法理上不是 "中國人"。美國的華文教育, 無疑是要服務
於美國的廣大的華族, (這裡只是借用華族這一概念, 以
方便論述華文教育等有關問題, 至於是否已構成為美國
的華族, 或是否已具備了構成華族的民族遷移的標準等
問題, 這有待社會學家、人類學家、民族學家、和歷史學
家去論斷。這已不是本文所要討論的, 下同。) 是在美國
的華人族群對其後代進行祖語和傳統文化的教育。既然
我們是華人, 那麼我們所說的當然是 "華語", 這是 "名
正言順" 的。這樣的正名, 對我們族裔的成長, 對我們華
人族群迅速地融入美國主流社會, 與其他族裔一起, 攜
手邁進, 是很有幫助的。當然, 我們的 "根" 在中國, 我
們的祖語是 "中國話", 但不是美國的 "國語"。因為 "國
語" 者, 一個國家之共同語言也。中國的 "國語" 不是美
國華人的 "國語"。我們身為 "美國人", 美國的 "國語" 是

英語, 而不是中國話的 "國語"; 如果 "美國人" 以 "中國
話" 為 "國語", 不論從哪一個方面來看, 都是說不過去
的。若我們整天叫中國的 "漢語" 或 "普通話" 或 "國
語" 為我們美國華人的 "國語", 試問又怎樣去向美國人和
美國的社會交代呢? 這對我們華裔的成長是沒有好處的。
我們不要只看成僅僅是一個名稱的改變, 但它反映出我們
身份的變化, 社會地位與處境的根本不同。

所以, 我們在華文教育中教的是華語。如果我們仍
然把它稱之為 "國語" 或 "普通話", 這是很不合時宜的。

二、

那麼, 我們的華語究竟是以哪一種華人方言為普遍使用
的共同語言? 是廣州話還是四邑話? 是 "國語" 還是 "普通
話"? 等等。這又是我們要解決的課題。

要知道, 從 "國語" 到 "普通話", 在廣義的層面來
說, 兩者的意義基本上是相同的, 在一定的歷史時期內發
揮著它們的功能。

"國語" 或 "普通話" 名稱, 雖是近代才出現, 但
其含義, 在中國傳統文化中, 卻是古來有之, 它是有一個
悠長的發展過程的。我們只有瞭解了它的發展過程中的
演變, 才能找到我們 "華語" 的標準, 才能確立我們 "華
語" 的規範。

要知道, 中國自古以來就是一個幅員廣大、方言複
雜的大國, 各地方言的分歧也就相當的明顯。春秋戰國的
時候, 各地諸侯國間的頻密往來, 自然不能各自都說自己
的方言土語, 而是說一種共同明白的語言, 當時叫做 "雅
言"。所謂 "雅" 者, 就是 "正" 的意思, 就是大家互相明白
的、共同遵守的、共同使用的語言。孔子對這種語言, 是非
常重視和提倡的。他說 : "子所雅言, 詩、書、執禮, 皆雅言
也"。可見孔子在他誦讀詩書和執行典禮的時候, 不是用他
魯國的家鄉方言, 而是使用各地都通行的雅言。這種 "雅
言", 就是當時周王朝中央政府所在地的豐鎬 (今陝西省
西安市西南灃水東岸地區) 話, 它被認為是當時最純正、
最典雅、最規範的語言, 周王朝也藉著京城豐鎬 "雅言",
進行有效的交際與溝通, 從而有效地控制著全國各地的
諸侯國。由秦而漢, 不叫雅言, 而稱 "通語"。漢朝楊雄《
方言》就曾多次使用 "通語"、"凡語"、"通名" 等稱謂。
可見它們所指的就是當時流行的共同語。從商、周、而至
北宋, 都有交際場合中的共同語, 雖然它沒有明確的語音
標準, 但很顯然的人們在日常交際中的說話和寫的文章,

都必然會以某一種方言為其基礎的。這種方言流行的地方,就是當時的政治和經濟的中心,也就是當時的京城。在歷史發展的長河中,周、秦以後,由於改朝換代和京城的遷移改變,"雅言"的基礎方言也隨之重新被"雅正"。長安、洛陽、開封,自古以來,都是中國的帝都京城。也即是說,全國通用的共同語,它的基礎方言就是以長安和洛陽為中心的中原地區方言。更具體地說,秦、漢時的關中話,唐代的長安話,宋代的汴梁話(今河南開封地區),分別成為各自朝代的標準"雅言"。從元、而明、而清,以至現代,由於歷史發展的結果,北京代替了中原。那麼,人們日常的共同語,則以北京話為標準基礎方言的"雅言"。

明代把這種共同語稱作"官話"。所謂"官話"者,就是指官場上通行的話,就是官吏們所說的話。因為當時無論在京城還是到外省去做事,都不可能講京城人和外省人都聽不懂的家鄉話,這在客觀上就逼著官吏們就必須要學會說"官話"。這種"官話"就是我們今天別稱為"國語"。"國語"在英語裏叫做"Mandarin",它就是"滿大人"的音譯,過去在西方人的眼中,滿大人所說的話,不就是"官話"嗎?這不就是中國的"國語"嗎?官話這一稱謂,就是到今天,我們有時仍還在沿用。不過,它的內涵已經有些變動了。今天的"官話"只是漢語北方話的統稱而已,而不是指今天以北京話為語音標準的漢民族共同語而言的"普通話"。今在英語裏仍稱之為 Mandarin,這也已經是時過境遷,在英語裏我們現代應該叫它 Standard Chinese 才是適當的。

到了清末,特別是中、日甲午戰爭之後,民族與社會的危機,空前的深重,

一些有識人士便紛紛提出向西方國家學習,尤其是向明治維新之後強盛起來的日本尋求富國之道。1902年,京師大學堂第一任總教習吳汝倫便赴日本考察學政,他深受以東京話為標準音的日本"國語"的統一和教育普及的影響,回來後即給管理大學堂事務的大臣張百熙寫信建議,要學日本的經驗,推行以北京話為標準音的中國"國語"。他認為"此音儘是京城口音,又可使天下語言一律"。張氏採納了此意,便於翌年聯同張之洞和榮慶在奏定學部章程時,就明確地提出了"予以官音統一天下之語言,故自師範以及高等小學堂均於國文一科內附入'官話'一門"。到了1909年的宣統元年,清政府的資政院開會,江永議員就正式提出要把"官話"正名為"國語"。從此,"國語"一名,便正式在官方和民間開始採用了。1910年,學部召開中央教育會議,隨即通過了"統一國語辦法法案",準備

審定"國音"標準,編輯國語課本和國語詞典等。1912年民國成立,同年7月在北京召開的"臨時教育會議"上便即肯定了"國語"這一名稱,並決定在全國推行國語。第二年2月又在各省都有代表參加的"讀音統一會"上,議定每個漢字的國音讀音和拼寫國音的符號"注音字母"。"五四"新文化運動的前夕,即1918年,胡適先生發表了他著名的《建設的文學革命論》,更明確地指出:"我們所提倡的文學革命,只是要替中國創造一種國語的文學。有了國語的文學,方才可以有文學的國語。"於是,他提出"國語的文學,文學的國語"的口號,隨著"五四"新文化思想的深入發展,國語的推行和提倡白話文運動,便緊密地結合在一起,形成了聲勢浩大的全國性的提倡國語運動。1919年北洋政府的教育部正式成立了"國語統一籌備會",主張"語"與"文"合一,並把全國學校的"國文"科改名為"國語"科。國語運動從此也變成了一項持久推動的工作,"國語"一名,自此也深入全國,普遍流行,80多年來,它也陪伴著我們這一代和上一代人的成長。

迄後,歷北伐、抗日戰爭和國共內戰,於1949年下半年,中國國內形勢發生了變化,以國民黨所領導的國民政府,退居到了臺灣。由於當時臺灣客觀社會發展形勢的急切需要,推行國語運動,雷厲風行,僅僅在10年時間裏面,就在臺灣全省普及了國語。"國語"一名,便從島內到島外,隨著海外僑教的推廣,數十年來,在海外廣為流行,一直到現在,無遠弗屆了。

惟在中國大陸,1949年10月中華人民共和國成立,對國語的推行也不遺餘力,1955年便召開"全國文字改革會議"和"現代漢語學術會議",會議決定,以"普通話"作為漢民族的民族共同語正式名稱,已不再沿用原來的"國語"。1956年2月國務院頒佈了《關於推廣普通話的指示》,正式規定了普通話的內容,要"以北京語音為標準音,以北方方言為基礎方言,以典範的現代白話文著作為語法的規範"。這就使得從"國語"到"普通話",其內容作了一個具體的飛躍,也對普通話作出了全面的、具體的明確的解釋。

其實,北京話也好,北方方言也好,都是屬於漢藏語系的漢語方言。漢語乃是漢民族共同使用的語言。但是,為什麼不稱"漢語",不叫"國語"而正名為"普通話"?

這是因為中國是一個多民族的國家,除了漢民族之外,還有五十多個其他的少數民族,如果把北京話稱為"國語",這就抹煞了中國是一個多民族國家的事實。況且漢語的方言有很多,大概的劃分就有北方方言、粵方

言、閩方言、湘方言、吳方言、贛方言、客家方言等, 它們間的方音分歧也是很大的。因為方言是民族共同語的地區分體或地方變體, 漢語的本身也需要統一。因為北京話本身也是漢語方言, 所以, 北京話並不是中國的 "標準語", 也不是漢民族的民族共通語, 更不是中國的 "國語"。中國的標準話是 "普通話", 它是以中國北方話方言為基礎, 以北京話的語音為標準音, 以典範的現代白話文學著作為語法的規範的。它是全國各地各族人民普遍使用的共通的語言。所以現在中國的 "國語" 是 "普通話" 而不是 "國語"。

　　一個國家的共同語言就是這個國家的國語。每一個國家都有自己的共同語言, 也就是它的 "國語"。中國 "國語" 一名, 自1909年從 "官話" 正名為 "國語" 於今, 已經有九十多年了。臺灣和海外於今一般來說仍是此稱。惟自1955年起, 中國大陸已不再沿用此稱而改為 "普通話"。香港和澳門, 原也叫 "國語", 但自上世紀80年代開始, 隨著兩地社會情勢的變化, 已慢慢地改稱 "普通話" 了。然新加坡不叫 "國語", 也不叫 "普通話", 而命名為 "華語", 因為新加坡的 "國語" 是馬來語。日本卻常常把它稱作 "中國語", 其他地方是不作這樣叫的。至於 "漢語" 一名, 主要在中國國內流行, 惟其一般都是用在學術著作中, 有時是指漢民族的共同語而言, 有時是指方言而稱。"華語" 一名, 最早是由新加坡用開的, 隨後在臺灣和中國大陸, 也時有所用。現在, "華語" 一名, 在世界各地, 包括中國大陸和臺灣, 都已相當普遍地使用了。

　　當今普天之下, 我們海外的華人, 都是同種同文, 同為炎黃民族的子孫, 但是在很多時候, 對同一種事物的表達或稱呼, 卻有多種不同的用詞, 為了我們共同的事業, 為了發展我們華人文化, 為了我們民族的凝聚, 我們華人共同語名稱上的協調規範, 是十分重要的。那末, "華語" 究竟仍以 "國語" 或 "普通話" 稱呼? 又或者稱它為漢語? 這都是需要我們弄清楚的。

　　按普通話和國語, 已如前述。它們有明顯的相對性, 只有在一定的國度裏面才能展示出了它的內涵, 表現了它的功能。因它們只有明顯的共性, 而無明顯的個性, 隨意性也很大。它們都沒有具體地說明那個國家的官方語言和它的民族共同語是什麼, 它們只是一個泛指詞, 缺乏了明確的 "內容" 和明顯的 "個性"。因為每一個國家都有該國的 "國語", 這種國家的共同語, 也可以說是該國的 "普通話"。法語是法國的 "國語", 也是法國的 "普通話"; 日語是日本的 "國語", 也是日本的 "普通話"; 葡語是葡萄牙

的 "國語", 也是它的 "普通話"; 德語是德國的 "國語", 又是它的 "普通話", 等等。當然, 中國話就是中國的 "國語", 這 "國語" 就是中國的普通話。可見, 在我們美國華文教育的領域裏, 教學華語, 仍稱 "國語" 或叫做 "普通話", 顯然是很不恰當的。

　　在過去一個多世紀以來, 由於美國華僑社會的特殊性, 四邑話 (或臺山話) 成了美國華僑及華裔的 "雅言"。但現在的社會情勢變了, "國語" 和 "普通話" 將會漸漸成了美國華人的共同語, 這是美國華人社會發展的必然; 華語的標準音將以 "普通話" 為其標準和規範, 這也是華語歷史發展的必然。

三、結語

基於我們今天的華文教育對像是美國華人的子女, 或者說是美國華人。今天美國的華文教育, 不是往日的僑民教育。因為美國華人是作為美國多元民族中的一元, 當今的華文教育也不僅僅是華人華裔對其 "祖語" 語言的學習或其言語的習得。今天我們的華文教育乃是美國華人的族裔文化教育。所以, 應該把它的語言定位為 "華語", 也叫它做 "華語", 甚至全世界的海外華人都應作如是觀。"華語" 不是中國的 "國語", 也不是中國的 "普通話"。雖然漢語是華語的 "祖語", 是華語的生身阿母, 但仍稱之為 "漢語" 也是不恰當的。所以 "華語" 就是 "華語", 就是我們華人所使用的語言。"華語" 的標準音, 不是廣州話、客家話、上海話、潮州話或其他中國的方言。基於我們華人族群中內部方言的複雜性和多樣性, 為了促進華人族群的團結, 增強族裔的凝聚, 為了傳承和發展華人文化, 就需要我們華人的共同語, 這樣華人的語言也就需要統一, 要統一就必須要有一個標準。我們 "華語" 的標準, 基於其歷史發展背景及其遞變, 毫無疑義應該是以中國的 "普通話" 為其標準, 以 "普通話" 為我們華人共同遵守的統一的規範。這樣, "華語" 與英語、法語、德語、葡語、日語、西班牙語等是並立的。同時, 它還可以和 "華文" 相配。"華文" 與 "華語", 正像 "英語" 和 "英文", "德語" 和 "德文", "日語" 和 "日文", "西班牙語" 和 "西班牙文" 的相配一樣。諸賢大家, 以為然否? 尚祈博雅君子, 不吝教正, 不勝感幸。(匆匆成文, 未及列出注解和主要參考文獻。)

(2005年10月5日 三藩市 金門橋畔 寓所)

Mirrors and Windows
Chinese American Filmmakers
Felicia Lowe, Simon Mah, and Valerie Soe
VALERIE SOE, MODERATOR

The filmmakers in this roundtable discussed the ways in which their work reflects and interprets the concerns of the changing Chinese American community, including constantly shifting definitions of culture and identity, the Chinese diaspora, representations of Asian Americans in popular culture, and the ways in which film can be used as a means of social change. Panelists reflected several different aspects of the Chinese American media arts community—new immigrants, American-born Chinese, established filmmakers and emerging artists, and working in a variety of genres and techniques. Each filmmaker screened a brief sample of their current work and discussed its relationship to themes and issues in the Chinese American community at large.

Felicia Lowe screened excerpts from *China: Land of My Father* and *El Barrio Chino*, describing them as bookends twenty-five years apart that examine similar stories of family, culture, and identity. Simon Mah excerpted *Kung Fu Mon Amour* and discussed issues of Asian masculinity, representation, and pop culture. Valerie Soe screened *Mao Redux* and showed excerpts from *Mixed Blood*, mentioning her interest in art and activism. Other topics discussed included educational distribution of Asian American films, reaching mainstream audiences without diluting the impact of the work, funding for Asian American filmmakers, and venues for Asian American films. Audience members queried whether Asian American films had any impact in society and how beginners could get started in making their own work. They were also interested in representations of Asian Americans in children's television and how Asian Americans can become more influential as viewers trying to impact television programming.

Sing Tao Daily's Overseas Edition and the Globalization of Chinese Language Newspapers
星島日報海外版與華文報章全球化

Joseph Leung
梁建鋒

星島日報歷史簡介

星島日報於1937年八月一日在香港創刊。星島日報創辦人胡文虎先生原意是命其子胡好先生於當年在廣州籌創星粵日報，但適逢發生七七事變，胡文虎便將辦報計劃轉移到香港。1949年，星島日報創辦了英文的香港虎報。

除了不斷壯大發展香港的星系報章外，星島日報亦致力發展海外業務。早於1961年，星島日報便年開始每日透過空運至三藩市發售，代理商是昌記棧。這可以說是星島日報創建全球報業團的第一步，也是華文報業中全新的全球經營理念。

接著在1963年，星島日報首次在三藩市發行航空版。1965年，星島日報在紐約開設辦事處，並開始發行美東版星島日報。1975年，三藩市辦事處創辦星島日報美西版，同年星島日報歐洲版創刊。1978年，洛杉磯版及多倫多版星島日報創刊。1982年，澳洲版星島日報創刊，翌年，增設加拿大溫哥華版。至1988年，再增加拿大卡加利辦事處。

至今，星島日報已經是一份每日在全球四大洲發行的中文報紙，亦都是首份全球性發行的華文報章。

星島日報由一份香港報紙，發展成為一份球性報章，並不是單純出自個別創業家的私人夢想，而是與過去六十多年的全球華人歷史的發展密不可分的。報章，本身就是一種以人為本，以讀者為本的事業，它的發展必須緊貼讀者群，否則便會被淘汰。星島從創刊起，由廣州遷到香港，便是受到歷史環境因素所影響。星島發展海外版，也是與華人移民歷史緊扣在一起的。

對海外華文報業的衝擊

中國知識分子喜歡辦報，所以，在稍為華人集中的海外城市，都會有華文刊物出現。星島日報選擇三藩市作為走出海外的首個據點，但其時三藩市本來就已經有多份中文報章，不乏歷史悠久的地方大報，如少年中國晨報及金山時報。為什麼一份從老遠香港而來的報章能夠打入當地市場呢？從星島在三藩市首創海外版起至今，海外華文報業經歷了三個不同時期。

鄉愁時期

六十年代末至七十年代初，美國移民社區結構發生變化，因為取締排華法案而導致移民法的變更，中港新移民潮出現。對比過去一段較長時間，新移民數目增長緩慢，各地僑社類近密封式，當地報章是純為本地服務，除了中港台新聞外，本地僑社各類活動成為新聞為主流。

而星島日報海外版最大特式是中港台新聞量多並且新鮮。除了迎合傳統僑社對家鄉新聞外，最重要是成為新移民保持與家鄉的一份連繫。於是有其他香港報紙加入，紛紛發行海外版，如明成新、電視日報及信報等。主要是滿足新移民的一份家鄉情。一些爭著到海外發行衛星版的香港報紙，更加在香港重點向準移民招手，提供優惠讓他們預訂衛星版，甫到埗便能即時看到家鄉報紙。這與當時餐館不論是否正宗，也流行以港式招徠是同一道理。果真是：物離鄉貴。

隨著移民人口的增加，華人經濟逐漸發展，華文報章也受惠，不論在銷量和廣告兩方面都同步增長。與傳統僑社報相比，這些香港報章雖然歷史不及他們長，但在經營模式、資本和版面內容方面，都是故有華文社區報章所不能相比的，於此消彼長之勢形成。舊有社區報銷路與收入都不斷走下坡，而紛紛結業。

扎根代時期

正如美國華人歷史學家麥禮謙先生的觀察，華人歷史的發展階段是由落葉歸根慢慢發展到落地生根。最初帶著鄉愁而來的新移民, 逐漸以本地為家, 也明白到下一代亦將以美國為家。他們關心的層面也從故鄉, 慢慢轉移增加對美國以及本地生活的興趣。

星島日報在1982成立本地新聞編採部, 採訪本地新聞。逐漸將星島美西版, 從一份外來報章, 成功轉化為一份本地華人報章。而原先從香港來的幾份中文報, 雖然在香港都是頗知名的大報, 但由於沒有發展本地新聞, 也逐漸失去市場, 最終全部撤回香港。這顯示海外華人對新聞資訊的需求的另一轉變, 先前有親切感的家鄉味, 現在反而顯得遙遠及不夠切身。

步入九十年代, 星島美西版繼續深入本地社群, 加強對與華人生活息息相關的社會政治新聞的報道, 擔負溝通主流社會與華人社區的橋樑作用。與此同時, 星島美西版也堅持為民喉舌的社會責任, 美西社評以中英雙語刊出, 將華人社區聲音向主流社會直接反映。在首篇評論三藩市市長施政的社評刊出後, 市長辦公室即時有反應, 市長佐敦本人更親自到訪星島編輯部, 就社評內容與編輯交換意見。

除此之外, 星島日報更積極鼓勵本地華人參與政治, 以保障和爭取華裔社區利益。星島一方面詳盡報告選舉相關新聞, 另一方面也深入報道華裔候選人動向, 並且作出選舉推薦, 帶動華裔社區關心政事, 參與選舉。經過十餘年的耕耘, 灣區華裔選民力量日漸成熟, 華裔參選公職也蔚然成風。

至今, 三藩市星島日報已成為本地政客溝通華裔選民的主要工具, 候選人不分族裔都爭取星島支持, 這不是星島的成功, 而是同步反映華人社區力量和政治影響力的增強。據一位州參議員候選人在今年所做的民意調查, 灣區華裔選民中, 超過四成會認同星島對選舉的推薦, 而排在第二位的中文報, 只得到一成多為選民的認同。這是客觀反映了星島努力推動華人參政的成績。也說明星島美西版已經成為一份百分百的本地華人報章。

華人地球村時期

踏入廿一世紀, 星島日報的發展踏也入一個新里程。這主要是受到中國改革開放成功, 促使經濟起飛的影響。加上互聯網的快速發展, 各地新聞資訊可作即時交流, 令到海外華文報業有了本質的改變。

自從中國實施改革開放政策以來, 前來西岸經商及留學的中國人士大幅增加, 三藩市華埠也由過去的流行台山話, 八十年代轉而流行廣州話, 到廿一世紀, 普通話已經在華埠以至整個灣區普遍使用。而中國經濟逐步發達, 海外華人與中港台的互動頻繁, 特別是商貿的來往, 不純是家庭或是個人的往來。在灣區的華裔移民, 以來自中國大陸的佔多數。他們對資訊的需求, 直接影響了本地華文報章的內容取向。中國大陸移民讀者, 已經成為目前灣區各華文報章的共同爭取對象。因而在報章內容方面, 不但相應加強了中國新聞, 並且已經成為各報競爭的熱點所在。二零零二年, 星島日報在深圳設立製作中心外, 增強吸納中國大陸資訊速度和力度。

過去的華人社區是寄人籬下, 忍辱偷生, 海外華人只是零散的獨立社群。而與社區緊扣在一起的星島日報, 也是服務當地的華人社群為主。各地星島分社, 可說是各自為政的。但踏入廿一世紀, 華人地球村已經成型。當中國國際地位不斷提升, 對兩岸三地, 以至世界各地華人新聞的興趣也普遍提升。海外華人不再是一個活在有限空間的孤立社群, 生活在不同國家地區的華人, 他們不一定都認同單一的政治理念, 但那種血濃於水的精神連繫日益增強。中國的正面發展, 凝聚了對海外僑社的一股向心力。

從2000年起, 在香港星島日報在全新管理層的領導下, 也掌握了新形勢, 全面強化全球作業模式, 將過去各分社獨立運作的情況, 改為全球一體化。並加強各地華人社區的新聞資訊交流, 並集中力量提供各地華人所共同關心的新聞資訊, 每天推出環球直擊版。在美加的華人想知道更詳盡的中港台新聞, 在歐洲或澳洲的華人可能希望知道美國的政情, 星島日報擔當了融滙全球華人資訊的角色, 成為建立華人地球村的工具。最新例子是在今年九月, 開通了星島環球網, 目標是要成為最完備的全球華人資訊平台。

美西星島日報則是扎根本地, 面向華人地球村, 既是一份本地華人報紙, 也是全球華人資訊網的一分子。美西星島所走過的路, 每一步都反映了社區的發展階段, 既是配合社區的發展, 而在某程度上也有著推動和帶領的作用。

The Development of Chinese Language Television in Northern California
北加州華語電視發展史

Franklin Wu
吳育庭

電視媒體, 已經是人類文明, 汲取新知識的來源和休閒生活不可或缺的工具。其所發揮的功能和影響是相當深遠的。本人從事" 華語媒體" 相關事業, 已經有三十年之久。經歷過華語電視媒體的興衰起落, 前仆後繼的全部歷程, 足以見證北加州華語電視媒體的一部發展史。

目前北加州播出華語電視節目的管道有下述三種系統: (1)兩個地區性的無線電視 (KTSF-TV26 和 KMPT-TV32)。(2)有線電視系統, 除 KTSF-26 (華語節目) 和 KMPT-32 (世界電視, 新唐人衛視) 之外, 另有翡翠台 (Jade Channel), 東森美洲衛視 (ETTV), 中天衛視 (CTI-TV), 中國中央衛視 (CCTV-4)。(3)經由衛星傳送的華語衛星節目有三十四個頻道, 其中來自台灣的衛星節目(13家), 中國的衛星節目(12家), 香港的衛星節目(3家), 美洲綜合衛星節目(6家)。在美國的華人電視節目, 除少數是自製本地的新聞和訪談節目外, 絕大部分都是轉播外來的連續劇, 新聞和綜藝節目。從表面來看, 目前的華語電視節目好像非常的多, 但不是每個人都能過隨時收看任何的節目; 而收視的方法可用最簡單也是最原始的方法, 是架設一般的屋頂天線, 免費收看當地的無線電視台節目, 或安裝有附加華語節目的有線電視和解碼器, 也可選擇性的裝設小耳朵, 收看自己喜歡的特定衛星頻道節目。

約在150年前, 先後約有一萬七千多名來自中國大陸東南沿岸的華人投入加州淘金熱和美國跨西岸鐵路段工作, 也從此走入不歸路。在三十年前, 即1975年的整個大灣區, 總共約有14萬華人, 講粵語的約佔85%, 講國語的佔極少數。自從1977年以後, 中南半島船民, 1982年後的中國大陸開放和1997年香港的回歸等等因素, 因而有大量華人湧入美國。直到2000年人口普查, 在灣區九個縣703萬人口中, 華裔有515,451人; 華裔人口的增長, 造就了多元的社區和繁榮的市場也改變了整個原來較保守封閉的華人社區型態; 也由於移民的辛勤耕耘,促進工商百業發達, 創造科技重鎮奇蹟; 而華語電視事業亦相對突顯其重要性。

本人是在1973年移民來美國, 當時能閱覽到的報紙有十家。在三藩市的中國城有一家廣播電台另外有四家戲院, 在華埠小巷裡到處可聽到麻將洗牌聲音, 獨獨缺乏華語電視節目。1975年創辦海華電視公司, 開始每晚有了華語電視節目和新聞, 引起了廣大的迴響。從此華人的生活作息和休閒習慣也起了相當大的變化。在那個時候, 欣賞華語電視的確是華人和社區的一大盛事, 也是茶餘飯後的主要話題。

三十年前的大環境, 全都是講英語的電視台, 而灣區各城市都有獨立的有線電視系統(共約有五十多家), 互不相通, 也無法聯播。其中三凡市有線電視公司 (Viacom Cablevision) 地下管線尚未普及華人住宅區(包括大埠, Richmond 和 Sunset District)。自從海華電視在1975年開播後特別要求逐步沿路安裝管路, 才有今日在建築物牆腳處處看到電視管線的景象。有線電視 (cable television) 是在1950 年代開發的,其最早的設計是代替室外天線; 有的用來播放節目和社區動態或作電視教學。在1976年間中華電視, 天祥電視, 華語廣播電視相繼出爐。1991年香港的TVB(USA) 翡翠台, 也播出香港無線電視節目。從此也開始了電視媒體的白熱化競爭。在當時可以用 "爭先恐後, 當仁不讓" 來形容。到現在, 整整三十年間, 華語電視的起起落落,只有身歷其境的經營者, 才能真正體會和感受其艱辛的過程。

FCC 修訂章則促使在灣區原有的50幾家 cable companies 整合成為 TCI 和 Viacom 大集團。後再被 AT&T Broadband 併購。在2003年初再轉讓給今日獨家壟斷的 Comcast 有線電視系統。

1976年灣區無線電視 KTSF-TV26 正式開播, 海華電視也是在該台首先播出的華語電視。四年後(1980年) KTSF-TV26 將晚間時段全部租給 Star TV 供播放 Showtime 付費電視。海華電視節目被迫移到 KEMO-TV20 播出,半年後 KEMO-20 出售, 因而在1982年海華電視改在

San Jose KSTS-TV48 試辦付費電視。直至1984年 Star TV 公司破產, KTSF-TV26 再度恢復商業電視後, 海華電視和中華電視分別在黃金檔時間播出, 另外的時段和週末則有聯合華語, 世華, 華聲電視播出。

1985年由華人組成的太平洋無線電視公司獲得 KPST-66 經營執照。1986年包括華人的少數族裔集團 West Coast United Broadcasting Inc. 也購得 KWBB-TV38 執照。然而1985-1996十年期間, 此兩家華人擁有的無線電視台執照 KPST-66 (1985-1996) 和 KCNS-38 號台 (1986-1994) 被高價收購拱手讓出執照。

1989年 KTSF-TV26 收回了海華電視時段自己經營記續播出華語新聞和連續劇, 而海華電視又轉到 KCNS-TV38。KMTP-TV32 (公共電視台) 在1991年曾轉播由台灣傳送的半小時衛星新聞。1994年 KPST-66 出售給 Silver King Broadcasting Co. 其承諾繼續華語電視節目五年。1996年KCNS-TV38 讓售給 Ramcast Broadcasting Co. 之後, 再轉售給購物頻道。2002年初 KPST-66 由西班牙語系電視集團 Telefutura (Univision) 收購,同時終止華語節目。在這三十年間, 以承租電視台時段的八家電視公司, 有者因財務不繼, 或因轉換經營方式或因電視台轉讓執照而先後停播。目前只有 KTSF-26 台自營華語節目, 獨領風騷, 但洋人老闆是否願意永續經營仍是一個變數。

而 KMPT-TV32 每晚也有兩小時的華語節目, 因是公共電視台, 其能發展的空間也有限。

至於衛星電視是利用衛星發射電視訊號, 經由碟形天線(俗稱小耳朵)接收, 才能收看電視的一種新趨勢。1986年以後才開始有華語衛星電視, 直到現在已有三十四家衛星電視頻道, 大部分是二十四小時播出。可以用 "群雄並起" 來形容當前的現況。目前有四顆衛星提共轉播華語電視; 而北美兩大衛星電視系統 Direct TV 和 Dish Network。也轉播付費華語電視節目。由於各家都是自立門戶, 更因各有特定收視群, 觀眾市場分散, 雖然付出的成本代價極高, 但卻未得到相對的收視和酬報率的預期效果。

網際網路電視將會是媒體未來的寵兒; 一些華語地區的電視台紛紛利用網站播送。目前最新的趨勢是, 結合電腦寬頻網路, 電話和電視 (IPTV/Internet ProtocolTV), 網羅各國電視電影節目在線上播放。

華語電視新聞的發展歷程相當坎坷。當時受限於新聞資訊取得不易和電視台播送與製作設備簡陋; 初創階段困難重重。惟在30年前,1975年四月十五日開播的海華電視新聞以後,堅持原則努力排除萬難, 能為華人廣開視野和提供新資訊,深得讚賞和肯定的結果以引為傲。

有關新聞素材除有本地採訪和取得 KRON-TV4 和 CNN 同意插播相關新聞外, 另有香港電視提供香港新聞和台灣中國電視(中視)提供一週新聞錄影帶, 惟仍受到中國大陸和台灣的中華民國政府均屬行新聞管制,須先送請新聞當局審核後才能放行的限制。1976年海華電視在 KTSF-26 台首次播出台灣電視新聞, 擴大新聞資訊。1989年5月20日台灣的國民政府解除禁令後, 台視堤供每天即時新聞由中華航空直飛空運, 提升新聞時效。1991年9月16日利用衛星傳送台灣新聞, 更是大放異彩。

華人媒體能否生存或發展, 廣告的營收, 是主要的因素。在此呼籲在創業或營運中的工商企業, 無論是刊登廣告, 還是專案贊助, 或多或少, 都能幫助媒體的生存; 各界人士, 除熱心捐輸公益外更有義務帶動華人媒體的發展, 如同有心回饋社會的德意和認同華語媒體存在的實質意義。衷心建議成立 "在美華人電視基金會", 用以設立智庫, 和廣籌財源累積基金, 短程可隨時透過本地電視台或衛星頻道為華人出聲爭取權益。長程為儲備和培訓相關專業人才, 並爭取自營電視頻道的目標邁進; 藉此發揮華語電視的主導作用和加強整合現行眾多的華語衛星集團, 創造電視業者和觀眾雙贏的機會。

目前電視媒體的多元發展, 競爭極烈。雖然各擁有一片天, 然收視率卻互有消長, 廣大觀眾仍都有顧此失彼之遺憾, 傳統的電視節目, 特別是 "電視新聞報導" 的方式, 也會隨著時代潮流, 面臨改革的命運。而現今我華人的電視媒體, 仍處於二三十年前的型態, 未見有開創性和可取的優點, 毫無向上提升的作為, 實有待努力。我華人移民來自海峽兩岸各地, 有不同的國家認同和民族意識, 各有強烈家鄉觀念和眾多地域方言等等錯綜複雜的存在因素, 實在看不到有團結和統合的契機。切望有識之士, 能為我華人電視媒體的發展和前途多費一點心機。

無論是開路先鋒的先進, 或是後來居上者,都曾經奉獻過心力。走過的一步一腳印, 都已成為歷史痕跡, 也曾累積不可磨滅的貢獻。其留下我華人媒體的斑斑史頁, 是值得懷思並加以珍惜的。美國華人歷史學會自創立以來, 對華人在美國的歷史和社會的研究與探討, 扮演了承先啟後, 繼往開來的實際標竿作用, 實難能可貴。尤其最重要的是, 讓後人能瞭解到前人艱辛創業的精神和歷程, 必能激發起勇于開創自己一片美麗燦爛的天空, 努力向上, 奮鬥不懈。

More to the Chinese Side
The Ruminations of a Fifth-generation Chinese American Filmmaker
William Gow

My Chinese American experience is probably different from yours. We, fourth- and fifth-generation Chinese Americans, represent only about 10 percent of the entire Chinese American population. Many of us, like myself, don't look typically Chinese, our mixed-race blood often masking our Chinese heritage. Because our great-grandmothers and great-grandfathers were part of the original wave of Chinese immigration in the 1860s, 1870s, and 1880s, ours seems the experience most often relegated to the history books. The railroad worker, the cook or laundryman, the prostitute: our families' stories have become caricatures forever trapped in the past.

Like so many Asian American artists, I became a filmmaker to see myself represented. I was tired of watching the same film about the tribulations of the white middle class that I had seen the week before. I was equally frustrated with the state of Chinese American cinema, where the majority of films seemed to be about the struggles between present-day ABCs (i.e., American-born Chinese) and their Chinese-born parents. As a fifth-generation Chinese American of mixed descent, I knew that the diversity of stories in our community was much greater than what was being represented in either community or mainstream media. Fueled by a desire to see my Chinese American experience represented, I became a filmmaker.

Although I never connected my passion for movies with my racial identity while I was growing up, my experiences as a college student at New York University showed me how strong the link actually was. NYU attracted me because I knew that it was the school that Spike Lee attended, and I related to the political bent of many of Lee's films. I arrived at the Tisch School of the Arts at NYU thinking, or at least naively hoping, that I would be taking classes with scores of people of color who shared my political passions and moral sensibilities. The reality of my experiences could not have been farther from the truth. Despite its placement in one of the most diverse cities in the world, NYU's Tisch School of the Arts remains a bastion of whiteness. A few high-profile alumni and professors, like Ang Lee, Christine Choy, and Spike Lee, serve to mask a student body that is overwhelmingly white, suburban, and upper middle class. I realized soon after arriving that I was chosen, in spite of my less than stellar high school grades, because I added a speck of color to NYU's sea of lily white. I was accepted to NYU in part because I am Chinese American.

At NYU, I put a human face to the type of people who create the images that the vast majority of Americans watch in movie theaters every weekend. NYU is one of a triumvirate of schools—along with USC and UCLA—that provides the bulk of Hollywood "talent," and I could see even from my classmates' student films that they would follow in the footsteps of the classes that had come before them. The content of the work that my classmates at Tisch created, while technically adroit, reflected the lack of diversity at the school. I saw amusing student films about bowling in the woods and about giant killer mice but few films featured any actors of color, and I never saw a film that seemed to be driven by a developed political or moral argument.

Surrounded by suburban whites, I felt strangely out of place at NYU. My interest in classic Japanese cinema, modern Hong Kong films, and movies by Asian Americans made me somewhat of an anomaly at a school where my classmates' favorite directors were David Lynch, Woody Allen, or even Steven Spielberg. When my department offered an upper-division class on Chinese cinema before the fifth generation, I was one of three students who enrolled, a reflection no doubt on the interest—or lack thereof—of my classmates.

As I got to know my classmates, I realized that these future Hollywood moguls and producers didn't make films about the suburban white middle class because they wanted to exclude other voices. They made movies about the white middle class because these stories reflected their own life experiences. If their films were vapid—albeit sometimes engaging—uncontroversial fluff, this was in part a reflection of the suburban strip-mall culture that had bred them. With few classmates of color to speak of, I became patently aware that the next generation of mainstream Hollywood films would be no more diverse than the last. While I didn't see it at the time, later in life this realization would further my commitment to grassroots community media.

I left NYU with a good grounding in film history, theory, and criticism and waded head first into a sea of personal debt. I had yet to take a filmmaking class. My two attempts to enroll in film production classes had been rebuffed by the long waiting list imposed on anyone from outside the film production department. As I stood among a crowd of purple that graduation afternoon in late May of 1999, I looked forward to putting my prestigious $100,000 film degree to use in discussions back home with friends about the movies we had rented from the local mom-and-pop video store. My first film would have to wait another two years until I was a graduate student in Asian American Studies at University of California, Los Angeles, and enrolled in Bob Nakamura's EthnoCommunications course.

I arrived at UCLA's Asian American Studies program not knowing quite what to expect. I knew of the grassroots history of the field of Asian American Studies, and I arrived hoping to find a department still deeply rooted in the community. Sadly, I found a department, and indeed an entire field, grappling with its proper place in academia. In many ways UCLA's Asian American Studies Department had reached an apex: on the one hand, the program was on the verge of becoming the first Ethnic Studies Program at the university to be given full departmental status, and yet on the other hand, this new academic standing had brought to the forefront internal conflicts on the direction the program should be taking. A vocal minority of professors felt that the program should remain rooted in the community while many others felt that the program should focus on producing future academics to lead the field. The department did a good job of teaching a few large introductory lecture courses to hundreds of interested UCLA Asian American students, and it also turned out a half dozen MA candidates each year, but its presence in the various Asian American communities around Los Angeles was almost nonexistent.

In many ways, Asian American Studies has become a victim of its own success. Back in 1969, in San Francisco, Asian American Studies started out as a way to bridge the community-academy divide. Thousands of Asian American activists waged a prolonged student strike to establish a department that not only taught about the experiences of Asian Americans but also acted outside the academy to better the life experiences of the entire community. Bringing then underrepresented Asian American students into the university to work on projects that would be helpful to the Asian American community was the original purpose of Ethnic Studies. But as the years wore on, much of this original mission became lost in the mélange of unintelligible, post-structuralist psychobabble that is, even now, slowly consuming our discipline.

Professor Nakamura, a tenured professor of Film and Asian American Studies and long-time social activist and artist, realized the need for a course that would give Asian American students specific skills that could be used in the betterment of their various communities. EthnoCommunications teaches Asian American Studies students with no filmmaking experience how to make video documentaries in the hopes of training a legion of Asian American community filmmakers. In this age when one is more likely to hear "Foucauldian Biopower" in a graduate level Asian American course than be required to go out into the community, EthnoCommunications is a throwback to another era.

The EthnoCommunications program provides a refreshing alternative to the established film schools around the country that fail to seek out students of color to admit, and then fail to educate the students of color they do admit, about anything other than how to light a shot or which lens to use at which distance. The need for our communities to have people to represent our stories properly and realistically in visual media such as film and video is paramount. Ethnocommunications fills a needed void by teaching Asian American Studies students who already have an understanding of the issues facing our communities about how to make documentaries.

Over the course of three quarters, students in EthnoCommunications learn how to bring a documentary from proposal to screening. In the first quarter, students learn how to write a treatment of their ideas and how to turn that treatment into a viable grant application. Bob Nakamura and Vivian Wong, the program's assistant director, teach students the basics of camera work and editing, thereby giving the students the requisite skills to turn their treatments into short ten-minute video documentaries. In the second quarter, students perfect their editing skills, while workshopping their short documentaries as a class. In the third quarter, the students fine-tune their videos, sometimes lengthening them to fifteen to twenty minutes. Guest professional filmmakers visit the class, giving the emerging student filmmakers criticism and encouragement.

Thus after four years of attending one of the most prestigious film schools in the country, I finally took my first film class as a grad student at UCLA. My first film, *More to the Chinese Side,* was written, directed, and edited with my good friend Sharon Lee. The treatment we had written called for us to explore the life of my grandfather, Edward W. Gow, and his life growing up in the Southern California farming town of Oxnard. Logging hundreds of miles in Sharon's car, we made the drive from Los Angeles to San Francisco no less than five times in order to interview members of my family about their remembrances of my grandfather. We hoped to juxtapose these stories of my grandfather that the various members told to us with a discussion of their views on their own identity, thus showing a bridge between my grandfather, his children, and his grandchildren. It wasn't until we started editing that we realized we had conceptualized a film a little bit more complex than could fit in our allotted ten minutes. So we focused the theme of the video solely on identity, specifically the ways in which Edward Gow's grandchildren negotiate their identities as biracial Chinese Americans.

Although originally we began with a documentary much broader in scope than the one we ended up with, in editing *More to the Chinese Side,* we were quite conscious of the ways that Chinese Americans and mixed-race people had been represented in popular culture. Although the film does not overtly reference other texts, we saw *More to the Chinese Side* very much in dialogue with both dominant mainstream and community representations of Chinese Americans. On this critical level, we had two specific goals with *More to the Chinese Side*: first, we tried to represent the life of a fifth-generation Chinese American family, thus challenging the largely held conception that Chinese Americans are all recent immigrants; and secondly, we hoped to present an image of a multiracial family that was wholesome and well adjusted, thereby showing that not all mixed race families or mixed race people were mentally disturbed or psychologically maladjusted.

As has been documented elsewhere, one of the most common Chinese American representations in mainstream cinema is that of the perpetual foreigner. From Fu Manchu to Jackie Chan, Chinese in America have been represented as the Yellow Peril, the unassimilable other against which white society defines itself. We are the domestic Orient to the American Occident. The body of literature on this subject is massive and need not be repeated here. But it was this understanding of Chinese Americans being seen as perpetual foreigners that influenced our work on the documentary.

Likewise we were conscious of the extent to which Asian American films were often built around the conflict between second generation Chinese Americans and their American-born parents. From *Chan Is Missing* to *Joy Luck Club* and *Wedding Banquet*, this conflict, which is both generational and cultural, drives so many of the films made by Asian American filmmakers. While this is no doubt a reflection of the high number of first- and second-generation filmmakers in the Chinese American community, this image silences the voices of those of us who have been here longer.

These films often hinge on the idea that Chinese from China are more Chinese than Chinese born in America because of their proximity to the culture and fluency in the language. Likewise, ABCs in these films are often portrayed as less Chinese because of their birth in the United States and their less-than-perfect Chinese language ability. In this type of construct, language ability and birth are privileged over action and personal choice. This type of cultural reading of Chinese American identity is problematic on a number of fronts. First of all, by privileging culture over action, these filmmakers make Chinese American identity into something that is bestowed on individuals based on their place of birth rather than being something that is grappled with, performed, and negotiated. In reality, of course, the extent to which people embrace their ethnic identity and see themselves as members of ethnic communities is determined not by the place of one's birth or the fluency of ones language skills but by the extent to which a person participates in a community.

More to the Chinese Side is constantly in dialogue with this cultural concept of identity. The documentary argues that even though my fifth-generation family doesn't speak Chinese or stay in contact with relatives in Asia, we are still Chinese American. While the issues of who and how people are included in our community may seem irrelevant to some, in fact these issues lay at the heart of who we are as a community. As a fifth-generation Chinese American who looks white, I find more resistance within the community to my identifying as a Chinese American than I do in the broader white society. On a number of occasions after showing the film, I have been challenged by members of the "progressive" Asian American community on the way I choose to identify myself. Offended by the idea that someone who is half white and doesn't speak Chinese would claim to be an Asian American, these progressive Asian Americans have been vehement in their demands that I acknowledge that I am half white, as if this in some way invalidates my Chinese heritage. While I never deny that I am part white, neither will I let that stop me from identifying myself as a Chinese American.

Phenotype aside, people have a hard time accepting me and other fifth-generation Chinese Americans like me because, discursively, my generation does not exist. In mainstream and community media alike, the image of the Chinese American is too often that of the recent immigrant. Our great-grandfathers are allowed into the history books because at the time they still had queues and wore straw conical hats and thus fit nicely with the stereotype of Asians as perpetual foreigners. But our great-grandparents are then frozen in time, bachelors without families that never bore children. The very existence of us, their great-grandkids, causes confusion in the representational universe because we are so far from this image of the inassimilable Other. One of our goals with *More to the Chinese Side* was to put the story of my generation on the small screen, thus combating this representational absence.

The second common mainstream representation that we actively engage in in *More to the Chinese Side* is less well documented but no less apparent, and that is the constant conception that mixed race people are at best socially maladjusted and at worst psychologically deranged. Historically, this conception has been perpetuated in two ways, first by the presence of mixed race characters in film who are deranged—think Warner Oland in yellow face as the villain in *Shanghai Express*—and second, by having mixed race actors play roles as monoracial characters, thus denying the audience the opportunity of seeing mixed race characters on screen as "normal" individuals.

In *More to the Chinese Side* we were very conscious to show a multiracial family made up of well-adjusted individuals. We didn't portray my mother as a crazy sinophile, nor did we portray my father as a whitewashed yappie. Rather we showed them for who they are, two people whose paths crossed and who fell in love with each other. Indeed the scene in the film that seems to elicit the most audience reaction is when my mother pretends not to be a vegetarian so that she can go and buy a hotdog from my father's hotdog stand in order to have a chance to talk to him. While it is common in film to see white men desiring Asian women as objects, instances of white women courting Asian American men are close to nonexistent.

In the same way, the video sets out to show my brothers and cousins as individuals who each have chosen to negotiate their Chinese identity in their own ways. For my cousin Jonathan this has meant being an Asian American Studies major. For my brother Eddie this has meant believing in Chinese superstitions, while for my brother Max this has meant having an "Asian" car. While their Asian American identities are much more complex than this, the parts of their identity that they choose to highlight in the interviews are telling. While in many ways all people perform their identities, for many multiracial people, like myself, the ways in which we choose to perform our identities often determines the degree to which we are accepted by our peers. For many of us, the performance of our identities is a constant negotiation between our phenotype and the expectation and assumptions placed on us by other members of our community. Multiethnic Asian Americans must often "prove" their identities in ways that others in the community do not have to do.

Despite the occasional challenges at screenings over the way I choose to identify myself, the documentary in general is nearly always well received. Often audiences marvel at how loving my family appears to be. Both Sharon Lee and I have always taken this as a compliment as this was one of the goals we set out to achieve in making the film. While our film is not overt in its political content, it does in many ways try to raise complex social issues while highlighting for other Asian Americans a voice that is often unheard.

My second film was quite a different venture. *Revisiting East Adams* was a project that my friend Jenny Cho and I did together for the Chinese Historical Society of Southern California. I wrote, edited, and produced the documentary while Jenny served in all these capacities as well as being the film's director. *Revisiting East Adams* is a film that captures the history of one of Los Angeles' oldest and now nearly forgotten Chinese American neighborhoods. In the early 1930s when Los Angeles's Old Chinatown was demolished to make way for Union Station, most Chinese residents fled to one of three other communities: New Chinatown, the smaller City Market Chinatown, or the adjacent East Adams neighborhood, which had ample cheap housing and no restrictive covenants. East Adams then came to serve as a bedroom community for many of the Chinese working in and around the City Market Chinatown. Our documentary covers the history of the East Adams neighborhood from its inception in the1930s through its disintegration in the 1950s. Through interviews with former residents we paint a picture of what it was like to grow up in this diverse Chinese American community.

Few films have been made of this first group of second-generation Chinese Americans who came of age in the 1930s and 1940s. This was the generation that lived through the Depression, that witnessed the internment of their Japanese American neighbors, and that fought in World War II. These experiences and others have made this group as a whole see themselves not as Chinese living in America, as most previous generation had, but rather as Chinese Americans. Most of the men who fought in World War II are proud of their service to the United States. These veterans present a side of the Chinese American experience rarely seen in mainstream society.

Making this film we saw many similarities between this original group of ABCs and the current group of second-generation Chinese American youth. These second-generation Chinese Americans who came of age in the 1930s and 1940s played in their own sports leagues and founded their own clubs. Like many Asian American youth today, they were interested in cars and racing. They attended Chinese school and helped in their parents' grocery stores. They negotiated the largely integrated public schools of Los Angeles and had friends from other ethnic groups. Yet when it came time to serve in World War II, many of these young men saw themselves as completely American. Unlike their Japanese and African American neighbors, most Chinese Americans were placed in all white units and most returned proud to have fought in a war they saw as just.

Their story challenges the representational norm for Chinese Americans in film in so many ways that it is difficult to know where to start. Simply representing older Chinese Americans speaking English without an accent is a challenge to representations of Chinese Americans as perpetual foreigners. Indeed, the complexity of the individuals who appear in *Revisiting East Adams* is a challenge to the one-dimensional caricature of Chinese Americans seen in most mainstream media. And while their story does draw parallels to the Chinese American films that deal with the experiences of second-generation youth today, the details of their story put an unconventional twist on the prevailing genre.

I feel blessed and humbled that both the documentaries I have worked on have been as well received as they have. *More to the Chinese Side* played at a number of film festivals and was nominated for the Golden Reel Award at the Visual Communications Film Festival before being picked up for distribution by NAATA. Likewise, the response to *Revisiting East Adams* by former residents of the neighborhood was nothing short of astounding. We distributed hundreds of DVDs to former community members and sold out our first public screening at the David Henry Hwang Theater in Los Angeles' Little Tokyo.

Despite their success, both documentaries were made with inexpensive consumer cameras and little equipment other than a tripod and a lav mike. They were both edited on Mac PowerBooks and shot completely on DV tape. *More to the Chinese Side* was made for about $500 and *Revisiting East Adams* for about $5,000—miniscule budgets when compared to even the cheapest of independent films. The speed of advancing technology has given our community the power to tell the stories of our experiences in a relatively presentable way for little money. Indeed, distribution remains the biggest obstacle for determined new filmmakers, and even this obstacle, with the proliferation of websites showing videos online, is slowly crumbling.

As the technology improves, it is imperative that we invest in programs like EthnoCommunications that teach young people how to document their own lives. These programs must not be limited to elite universities like UCLA but must be brought into our public high schools, middle schools, and community centers. With the power to make our own media and capture the real experiences of our community in all its complexities, we no longer have to waste our money to see the mindless commercial drivel Hollywood turns out. The right type of investment in the right type of organizations can insure that even Chinese Americans living in the poorest neighborhoods in our community can represent and speak for themselves, thus ensuring that the stories of our community are preserved in all their diversity and complexity for generations to come.

The 1905 Anti-American Boycott as a Transnational Chinese Movement

Jane Leung Larson

That Chinese living overseas have had a crucial impact on China's political development is only slowly being acknowledged by scholars. More than a decade ago, Harvard historian Tu Wei-ming's provocatively termed "transformative potential of the periphery" referred to the influence of overseas Chinese dissidents (the "periphery") on Chinese politics (the "center"). Tu speculated that when China's central government is weak and ineffectual, Chinese activists overseas can take the initiative to set the political and intellectual agenda for their homeland.[1]

The history of China has generally been studied in isolation from the history of overseas Chinese, both by historians of China and historians of overseas Chinese. The two fields of study usually are subsumed under different broad disciplines (history versus ethnic studies), with research disseminated through separate professional associations and journals. Multidisciplinary thinkers who go beyond these boundaries have been rare. Among them are philosopher/historian Tu, whose book *The Living Tree* explored the concept of "Cultural China," and anthropologist/historian Arif Dirlik, who, in writing about Chinese transnationalism, noted that "with a few notable exceptions, Chinese overseas have long been kept out of the study of 'China.'…Chinese overseas have played a significant role in the unfolding of mainland history since the nineteenth century."[2]

Dirlik goes on to cite the 1905 anti-American boycott as one of those politically transforming events that originated outside of China. This paper aims to contribute to a transnational Chinese history by exploring in detail one facet of the 1905 boycott—its connection to the overseas Chinese reform organization, the Baohuang Hui.

The significance of the 1905 boycott stems not from its impact on the U.S. policy of Chinese exclusion, which was minimal, but from its transformation of China's political landscape and of the political consciousness of the Chinese people. The anti-American boycott of 1905–1906 marked the beginning of mass politics and modern nationalism in China.[3] Never before had shared nationalistic aspirations mobilized Chinese across the world in political action, joining the cause of Chinese migrants with the fate of the Chinese nation. All Chinese could sympathize with Chinese immigrants detained for months in wooden sheds, stripped and examined for diseases, questioned harshly, and often deported, their chances for a decent livelihood lost. That image personalized the impact of foreign powers over Chinese people, and, by extension, over China.

Millions of Chinese in China and abroad were moved by the boycott action, which they learned about in newspapers or novels if they could read or in speeches, plays, and songs if they could not. Boycott rallies attracted thousands. Merchants stopped buying and selling American products, or if they refused, boycott committees put on the pressure. A number of local and imperial officials sympathized with the movement, but they did not lead it in any way.

The boycott's power is revealed by the apprehension provoked in both the American and Chinese governments about the growing weight of Chinese public opinion, with its potential to resist foreign abuses on the one hand and to turn against the Qing court on the other. From the very beginning of the movement, the boycott ideology linked China's weakness with American imperialism. A strong China would have been able to protect its people overseas, the argument went. Furthermore, during negotiations in 1905 over the renewal of an Exclusion treaty between the United States and China, Chinese Americans feared that their government would be too weak to stand up to the American government, even though the Qing court had stated it did not want to sign the treaty. Baohuang Hui Vice President Liang Qichao argued for a boycott of American goods because "if the power of the citizens does not provide a back-up force, the government still might timidly bungle matters."[4]

In fact, both reformers and revolutionaries found the boycott fertile ground to pitch their broader political messages, and boycott leaders became players in the constitutional and revolutionary movements that would follow. For example, ideas of popular sovereignty that had been introduced by the Baohuang Hui in the years before the boycott, became common currency during the boycott movement as a result of Baohuang Hui publicity and remained at the core of the constitutionalist movement that continued the political transformation begun by the boycott. The 1905 boycott was followed by a 1908 boycott against Japanese goods (see below), in which the Baohuang Hui became increasingly assertive in advocating political reform and connecting it to the boycott message. With its widely accepted nationalistic ideology that gave precedence to people over governments, the 1905 boycott heralded a change in consciousness that would ultimately lead to overthrowing the Qing.

Was the 1905 boycott a Chinese American protest? Or a Chinese protest? I argue that analysis of the boycott that disregards its international context is misleading and that the 1905 boycott must be seen as a transnational Chinese protest. Indeed, Ling-chi Wang pointed out that those Chinese in America who thought of themselves as American, such as the Native Sons of the Golden State (which became the Chinese American Citizens Alliance), participated little in the boycott because they saw no reason to ask the Chinese government to intervene on their behalf.[5] For most Chinese in America in 1905, however, opportunities in the American political structure (and legal system) were diminishing with the continued tightening of the Exclusion policy, and a mass protest would have been impossible. On the other hand, they had the freedom to organize political associations such as the Chinese Empire Reform Association—which could not openly operate in Qing China—making possible the growth of powerful organizations that could aid and abet movements inside China. It was only through transnational means that Chinese could effectively promote their cause.

In a paper given in 1999 at the Sixth Chinese American Studies Conference in San Diego and published in 2002,[6] I presented a detailed case for the pivotal role of the Baohuang Hui in shaping the boycott movement. This paper used the Tom Leung (Tan Zhangxiao 譚張孝) collection of documents at UCLA[7] to show how the Baohuang Hui's highly organized, transnational network of perhaps 70,000 members, was key to the boycott's initiation and strength. The Baohuang Hui widely publicized the idea of a boycott beginning in 1903, mobilized Shanghai merchants and pressured Qing officials to support the boycott, articulated the meaning of the boycott for the Chinese nation and people, and sustained the movement through continual financial support from its members and the dissemination of key ideology and information through its newspapers. The present paper takes a broader approach to the boycott by seeking to explore its transnational characteristics and again relies on the Tom Leung papers and focuses on the Baohuang Hui's boycott activities.

The Tom Leung papers are significant in revealing new information about the Baohuang Hui's role in initiating and sustaining the boycott. The organization's president, the exiled reformer Kang Youwei, spent much of 1905 with Los Angeles Baohuang Hui leader Tom Leung, having arrived in the United States in February, after years of being thwarted by the Exclusion policy. The Tom Leung collection includes several important letters written to Kang about the boycott as well as group letters sent to Baohuang Hui leaders worldwide.

Briefly, the direct links of the Baohuang Hui to the call for a boycott are as follows: In late April or early May, Kang sent a telegram from Los Angeles to Baohuang Hui leaders in Shanghai, Hong Kong, and Yokohama telling them of the imminent negotiations over the Exclusion treaty in Beijing. "This is a matter of life and death," he wrote, and he called for the leaders to "organize a rally and urge everyone to send telegrams to our government and to provincial governors appealing for help." [8] Coordinating the response was Baohuang Hui Vice President Liang Qichao in Yokohama, who reported that "I have had constant and urgent communications with Shanghai and Hong Kong by letter and telegram to discuss how to handle this problem." Recalling the 1903 proposal by Baohuang Hui newspaper editor Chen Yikan for a boycott to protest the Exclusion policy, Liang deemed this "the best foreign affairs strategy," and Shanghai, "the number one commercial city in China," was chosen to initiate the boycott. The Baohuang Hui was represented in Shanghai by the small but influential newspaper, *Shi Bao* 時報, which had been founded by Liang in 1904. "I had the paper publish the telegram from President Kang and every day write articles to explain and criticize, as well as describe in detail the importance of this matter." Furthermore, hitherto undocumented contacts took place between *Shi Bao* staff members and the Shanghai Chamber of Commerce, setting off the boycott. These contacts are described by Liang and in two letters from *Shi Bao* staff. The editor, Luo Xiaogao, writes that after receiving Kang's telegram, "first, we talked secretly with two of the most respected and influential people in Shanghai [he later identifies them as Metropolitan Minister Yang Shiqi 杨士琦 and Shanghai Chamber of Commerce leader Zeng Shaoqing 曾少卿] and decided to boycott American products."[9] This letter goes on to describe contacts with official sympathizers, all the way up to a Qing prince, and lays out *Shi Bao's* plans for a national campaign with fliers, a survey of American goods, and activists to travel into the interior to lobby for the boycott "so that the whole country will react and act." Three other documents in the Tom Leung collection, written during the summer of 1905 by Baohuang Hui activists in Hong Kong, Rangoon, and Shanghai, verify the seminal role of Kang's telegram and recount how *Shi Bao* staff members spurred Shanghai businessmen into action.

Why did the cause of a hundred thousand Chinese in America inspire millions of Chinese to join the protest, when, for most of them, it had no connection to their lives, and, for some, it meant an economic loss? Self-interest is surely part of the reason for the involvement of the Chinese in America as well as Chinese living in other countries who either feared that American exclusion practices would be applied to them, or, as in Canada, were already victims of a similar policy. But self-interest alone—especially for Chinese in China—cannot account for the mass movement that resulted.

Instead, one must credit the formation of a shared Chinese nationalism across boundaries that linked Chinese in China with their compatriots abroad. The boycott embraced what would become a common theme of Chinese protests—China and Chinese as victims of foreign oppressors—a theme as alive today as it was one hundred years ago, though with far less unifying resonance for Chinese living outside of China.

A boycott handbill from early June 1905, published by a Baohuang Hui chapter in Rangoon, Burma, and sent to chapters throughout the world, expresses the power of this shared nationalism:

> The United States has extended the exclusion treaty in order to put an end to Chinese people's livelihood there. This is a national disgrace second to none. Everyone is furious and aggrieved…. Now, all the Chinese people in the United States are making every effort to achieve the goal of taking back the national rights [of the Chinese people] and saving Chinese people's livelihood. Noble-minded people in Shanghai and Hong Kong and the charitable organizations in Guangdong province have all responded enthusiastically. They have worked together in full cooperation. They held meetings to discuss protest and defense measures. They communicated with each other through letters and telegrams to encourage one another to do a citizen's duty.[10]

Along with the sense of shame and humiliation from being victimized by foreign powers, there was an even stronger feeling of exhilaration from the act of collective protest. Liang Qichao describes the atmosphere in Shanghai, where the boycott was declared in May 1905:

> In the last month, everyone in Shanghai has been thinking about and talking about the Exclusion Treaty. From millionaires to poor workers, millions of people are of one mind, and we must not stop until we win back our rights. Oh! We [disciples of Kang Youwei] have been working on these matters for many years, but have never seen more success than this time.
>
> …[A]ll the foreigners in Shanghai have become worried, saying that China, the sleeping lion, has awakened . Since the Treaty ports were established [1842], there has never been any activity like this. It shows that we Chinese are not easily bullied.[11]

As participants in this transnational protest, Chinese Americans could not boycott American goods themselves, as did overseas Chinese in places like Singapore where the American consul reported that "every firm here handling American goods reports trade at a standstill with the Chinese."[12] However, Chinese Americans could support the boycott in China with their donations. Shanghai boycott organizers sent a telegram to Kang in America saying, "we are not able to raise funds in Shanghai. We expect support from the United States. Without financial support, we cannot mobilize the public. This is a good cause. We hope you can raise funds in America."[13]

Chinese Americans were the most generous financial donors to the boycott cause, with funds flowing through many channels to recipient organizations in Shanghai, Guangdong, and Hong Kong. They also sent home vivid descriptions of life under Exclusion and provided accurate information about the current status of the Exclusion treaty negotiations and legislation in Congress, which were printed in Chinese newspapers or read aloud at boycott rallies, and a few even returned to China to speak about their experiences. But for most Chinese in America, the boycott was a movement allowing only their indirect participation.

Who was the boycott directed to? The array of targets in itself was transnational. Certainly, the boycott was explicitly aimed at the American government by putting pressure on its business interests in China. American public opinion was also seen to play a role in the shaping of American policy, and Chinese boycott propagandists in the United States occasionally sought to influence it, through speeches by Kang Youwei[14] and others to American church and business groups as well as interviews and articles in the American press. A secondary target was the Chinese government, which was seen as requiring a strong showing of popular support to reinforce China's side in the bilateral negotiations. Finally, and perhaps most important, many of the boycott leaders had grander goals—inspiring in boycott followers new experiences of nationalism, confidence, and political participation so that after the boycott they could be recruited to the mission of reform or revolution.

Given the diverse interests of the boycott participants, which themes resonated across the United States, China, and among overseas Chinese? How was boycott ideology disseminated across the world?

Guanhua Wang devotes a chapter of his book on the 1905 boycott to the movement's ideology, and, after analysis of the copious boycott literature (including novels, newspaper articles, songs, speeches, and essays), delineates a broad spectrum of justifications for the boycott.[15] What is most surprising is how eclectic and wide-ranging were these justifications and how they would appear again and again in subsequent political movements. Briefly recounted, here are the predominant themes in boycott literature that Wang found:

- the injustice of the Exclusion policy and its harsh implementation
- America's ingratitude toward the Chinese laborers who had been so essential to building the new nation
- the boycott as an effective strategy in the evolutionary life-and-death struggle between the American and Chinese peoples (as perceived in the Social Darwinist ideas of the time), presented as the only possible way a weak China could overcome the powerful United States
- a pervading sense of deep national crisis and a perception that China's survival was at great risk, which a successful boycott could help overcome
- the racial self-awareness that resulted from the perception that "all Chinese, and only Chinese, were discriminated against in U.S. immigration law"
- Chinese should be treated as equals with other nationalities, as envisioned in the traditional Chinese moral concept of universal humanity
- a development of the concept of "nation," which was described as an extended family, whose future was as vital to

oneself as the future of one's children, and which belonged to the Chinese people rather than the Qing government

- the boycott as a populist vehicle, allowing people to use their power as citizens to join together for a common cause apart from their government

"Boycott nationalism," in Wang's view, transformed the boycott into something much larger than a protest against the Chinese Exclusion Act: "Beginning as a campaign for specific immigrant rights, it had become a broader social movement dedicated to social justice and profound change.... Boycott nationalism included a sense of racial awareness, of group solidarity, and of the rights and responsibilities of the people."[16] From this list of motifs, one can see that the Exclusion policy itself was but one note in a complex tune.

The Tom Leung papers give us a more focused but widely disseminated perspective on boycott ideology, since the Baohuang Hui's propaganda on the boycott was developed by Kang, Liang, and others who had direct experience of the Exclusion policy and who had spent years thinking about the broader issues of Chinese nationalism and civic participation.

A far more practical argument for fighting Exclusion policy than the themes Wang outlined above was Kang Youwei's initial justification for taking action. In Kang's urgent telegram from Los Angeles to his leading activists in Asia, which set off the cascade of Baohuang Hui contacts with Qing officials and Shanghai merchants that ended in the boycott announcement on May 10, he described the fate of Chinese immigration to the United States (and the Exclusion treaty) as bound to the economic and social future of the Chinese people:

> This concerns the livelihood of the Chinese people, especially the Cantonese, because they earn tens of millions of dollars here every year. If we are able to get rid of the treaty, it could greatly increase our annual income. Chinese people's lives are impoverished. If the laborers are completely cut off from working in the United States, then the situation inside China will certainly turn into great disorder.[17]

In a later communication to his followers, Kang expanded the economic argument and claimed that if Exclusion were ended, "in ten years, we will have one million people here. In that case, we cannot estimate the income of the Guangdong people....This money will return to Guangdong and in turn will benefit the whole nation to support industry, business, schools, weapons, etc. In addition we can set up our own navy. As a result, we can wipe out the humiliations we suffer."[18]

Just as Kang segued from the economic argument to the building of the Chinese nation, so did the Baohuang Hui fill in the dots connecting the humiliating experiences of Chinese immigrants with populist nationalism, linked by the themes of anti-Americanism and a more general "anti-foreignism." Here, Liang Qichao passionately calls for united resistance:

> Due to the abuses resulting from the exclusion of Chinese laborers, our Chinese have suffered inhuman treatment, establishing many harsh precedents. Among the 400 million Chinese, there may be at least 100,000 who have suffered in person. In Shanghai alone, many can describe the events that they endured or witnessed in the past. Even more have been told repeatedly by their relatives or friends to let the people of China, whether rich or poor, know about all the bitterness that Chinese laborers have endured.

> For these reasons, Chinese people's hatred and anger due to the bitterness caused by the Exclusion Treaty did not just begin today, nor is it limited to only a portion of our people. Since this act brings disgrace to our country and hurts business, it does only damage and brings no benefit. This really has filled the whole country with bitter hatred and [caused us to] plot a way to resist. This has been in the minds of the people for a long time. Now, taking advantage of the opportunity to change the treaty, the Chinese are compelled by their shared hatred of this act to plan a way to deal with it. This is a patriotic development of the Chinese people.[19]

The emotional transformation from disgrace to resistance is eloquently achieved in a song that may have been written by Kang and was included in a handbill from the Baohuang Hui chapter in Rangoon, Burma, in early June 1905. The excerpts below illustrate perhaps better than any other document in the Tom Leung collection how the plight of Chinese immigrants to America symbolized China's predicament:

> Watch a European with a dog wagging its tail, both landed, walking away slowly.

> Chinese should be grieving, lower than a dog.
> Why so despicable, so disgraceful?
> Our own country is too weak, no good,
> Tears come down like rain
> when looking at the general situation and our fatherland.

> Even one as honorable as a royal prince was hit by a flying stone; and a Minister can be demanded to show his passport.
> See the embassy guard trampled to death,
> how much more do we workers and merchants [suffer]?
> Alas, we have no country
> and can only blame our empress dowager for her lack of virtue.

> We lament that with such difficult lives and so poverty-stricken,
> we cross the ocean.
> How distressed we are! Looking at the vast land, we hesitate.
> There are restrictions on the other four continents, and it's also hard to go back home.
> We are so sorrowful that our navy was destroyed and cannot be rebuilt;
> Our military strength is weak and no one comes to protect us.
> We just wait for the boat to sail.

> There are 100,000 Chinese in this country [United States].
> We can pool together as much as 100,000,000 dollars.
> Since we have such rich resources and powerful strength, why are we afraid of the small nation?

> We vow to resist the great oppression.
> We vow to work together and cooperate with one another.
> We vow to wipe out our shame and disgrace.
> We would risk our lives to fight against exclusion and to accomplish our goal.
> My fellow 100,000 compatriots, do you hear me?[20]

The connection between China's weakness and discrimination against Chinese in North America was the dominant theme that first emerged in Baohuang Hui propaganda as early as 1903 when Chen Yikan, the editor of the Association's Hawaii newspaper, *New China Daily* 新中國日報 proposed a boycott of American goods to protest Chinese exclusion.[21] Chen argued that a strong country protects its people overseas and that if Chinese didn't protest their treatment in America, other countries would also exclude them. A boycott would not involve the government and would work because the Americans would not want to lose its China trade.

On May 4, 1905, perhaps after receiving Kang's telegram, Liang Qichao's newspaper *Xinmin Congbao* 新民叢報 contrasted the weakness of the government with the "magical power" 魔力 of the people. The article also predicted that within one or two months the power of the Chinese people would send a shock wave to the world, thrusting Chinese public opinion into the U.S.-China relationship with the message that "China can not be bullied." But, the writer warned, if the actions of the Chinese people failed, China's international status would be weakened even more.[22]

Kang and Liang recognized the potential of the anti-American boycott as a powerful, populist cause in which Chinese could participate as citizens, and it is clear that they saw it as a test of the strength of voluntary associations, the agility of Baohuang Hui's transnational network of followers, and the influence of its newspapers and journals.

Indeed, near the end of the boycott, late March 1906, U.S. Consul Samuel L. Gracey reported from south China that he and other foreign observers agreed that the boycott would live on in something "more virulent that will last and spread"—"the spirit of antagonism to foreigners and especially just now to American foreigners. This is being encouraged by many Chinese officials, the gentry-literati and the native merchant, in order that 'China for the Chinese' may become a national and popular sentiment."[23]

The transnational diffusion of "boycott nationalism" as well as news and strategies of the movement was surprisingly swift, using the well-established telegraph system (including trans-Pacific lines) for communications among activists and on-the-scene reports from correspondents to their newspapers. Particularly effective in dispersing its version of the boycott message was the Baohuang Hui's worldwide network of 160 chapters and at least one dozen newspapers.

Linking the Baohuang Hui chapters was a constant flow of correspondence, including printed "public letters" sent to other chapters, many of which were headed by local Chinese leaders of considerable prominence, such as Tom Leung, a prosperous herb doctor. Thus, the informal networks of the Baohuang Hui activists extended widely within their communities. Inside China, most notably in Shanghai, the Baohuang Hui activists such as the *Shi Bao* publicists were part of a growing circle of literati, officials, and businessmen interested in reform. Outside of China, Baohuang Hui membership was much more diverse and in some cases included a majority of the Chinese community in a city.

Newspapers had the greatest value in spreading boycott ideology, and in 1905, the Baohuang Hui media network reached much of China and the major overseas Chinese communities, both through local newspapers and the widely disseminated *Xinmin Congbao* and *Shi Bao*.[24]

Shi Bao was the preeminent source for boycott information and served as "a hub linking participants in the movement," according to Guanhua Wang.[25] It published daily news of the boycott for months on end, including lists of those who had pledged not to buy American goods as well as announcements and resolutions by the boycotting organizations, and distributed news stories and commentary to other papers in China.[26] Above all, the newspaper mobilized public opinion. Liang Qichao said of *Shi Bao* that "every opinion it publishes is admired and followed by the whole country." He pointed to its earlier primacy in informing the public of "debates over the case of the Canton-Hankou railroad and the case of the murder by a Russian sailor [of Zhou Shengyou in 1904] which aroused the whole country. This time, *Shi Bao* yielded even greater results. Looking at these [results], we can see more clearly that the power of a newspaper can withstand four thousand Mausers."[27] Though Liang may be exaggerating,[28] *Shi Bao*'s powerful influence on public opinion, in these two cases, and on the 1905 boycott continues to be affirmed by historians.[29]

Finally, *Shi Bao* played both overt and covert activist roles in the boycott. Covertly, *Shi Bao* staff made secret contacts with Shanghai businessmen and Qing officials and princes associated with the Foreign Ministry to promote the boycott cause. Overtly, they were the conduit for fundraising—Tom Leung, among others, sent funds he collected to *Shi Bao* to be used for the boycott.[30]

While the anti-American boycott eventually died out in 1906 soon after the San Francisco earthquake in April, the transnational Chinese boycott as a popular mode of "civilized protest" had been born. Furthermore, many of the same strategies and themes reemerged in the large mass demonstrations that erupted throughout the following decades, such as the May 4, 1919 movement. Likewise, the anti-foreign targets of these demonstrations inspired nationalistic feelings in movement participants, and these feelings were exploited by political groups like the Baohuang Hui to carry a broader political message quite unrelated to the original target.

The next major anti-foreign boycott occurred in 1908—the first Chinese boycott against Japan, again supported heavily by the Baohuang Hui. This followed another painful humiliation by a foreign government—the Qing government's apology and payment of an indemnity to the Japanese government after Chinese officials (tipped off by reformers) detained the *Tatsu Maru* in Macao and seized its cargo of smuggled weapons intended for Sun Yatsen's revolutionaries in China. Once again, Baohuang Hui chapters throughout the world helped mobilize a transnational movement, with the San Francisco chapter leading the American response.[31] In China, Liang Qichao's Political Information Club (Zhengwen She 政聞社) had been recently established in Shanghai and immediately became involved in the protests.[32] Zhengwen She's secretary general was the respected Shanghai educator and public orator Ma Xiangbo 馬相伯, a 1905 boycott leader with long ties to Liang Qichao.[33] More so than in 1905, the protestors turned much of their wrath on the Qing government for its weakness, even holding a number of "National Humiliation" meetings in Guangdong and accusing the Foreign Ministry of disloyalty for agreeing to Japan's terms.[34]

Hand in hand with promoting the 1908 boycott for the Baohuang Hui were increasingly assertive moves advocating political reform, taking advantage of the Qing government's reluctant commitment to the goal of constitutional monarchy. For example, in connection with the 1908 boycott, the Baohuang Hui newspaper in Australia, *Dong Hua Bao* 東華報 and local Association leaders solicited donations for a Naval Fund to build a Chinese navy to prevent future aggression by countries like Japan. However, the Australian Chinese added the stipulation that the Naval Fund, which apparently had been started by Chinese in the United States, would be turned over to the Chinese government only if a parliament were formed.[35]

Most challenging to the Qing were several Baohuang Hui petitions submitted to the court by Zhengwen She in 1908 during the boycott movement. These derided the Qing's procrastination in implementing a constitutional government and called for a parliament to be convened soon. No petition was considered more inflammatory by the Qing than one written by Kang Youwei and signed by members of two hundred overseas Baohuang Hui chapters [now called Xianzheng Hui]. It asked the government to immediately convene a national assembly, adopt a constitution, build a navy, restore the emperor, and abandon the distinction between Manchus and Han, among other demands.[36] Perhaps most enraging to the Qing was the suggestion that China's name be changed to Zhonghua Guo (or China) from Da Qingguo (the Great Qing Empire), symbolizing the transformation of dynasty to nation-state. In closing, Kang wrote: "This petition is written for merchants and other people. They say that there need to be very basic measures taken to save the country. Millions of people share this idea. They represent the vast majority of the Chinese people. They hope that reform will be implemented."[37] The Qing court met to discuss the petition and took action by disbanding Zhengwen She in August 1908, being unable to reach across the ocean to quash the Xianzheng Hui. The latter managed to continue activities in China by sending representatives to China to join the constitutional movement and presenting further petitions in Beijing.

The first decade of the twentieth century not only marked the first Chinese mass protests directed toward foreign targets but a concomitant flowering of Chinese nationalism as individual Chinese began to identify with the emergent nation. This sense of being Chinese, not simply a subject of the Qing, seemed to be as potent for Chinese living outside of China as those within its borders. Indeed, it was the overseas Chinese, led by reformist and revolutionary political parties active abroad, who saw more clearly than their compatriots back home that the national humiliation that led to the anti-foreign boycotts was largely due to the failings of their own government. Many of the ideas first widely discussed during the 1905 and 1908 boycotts, from the meaning of citizenship to the need for an effective navy, served to undermine confidence in the Qing.

Transnational Chinese protests continue today, mostly directed against Japan and the United States. Peter Gries in *China's New Nationalism* asserts that young Chinese nationalists have revived a pre-1949 view of themselves as victims of foreign aggression, recalling again and again in their polemics China's "Century of Humiliation."[38]

Note the resilience of the anti-Japanese movement among first-generation Chinese Americans, as expressed in such organizations as the Truth Council for World War II in Asia and the Global Alliance for Preserving the History of World War II in Asia. These organizations are part of the transnational Japanese war crimes redress movement, which seeks an apology from the Japanese government for the Nanjing massacre and other atrocities and is protesting the bid by Japan to join the United Nations Security Council, among other activities. The Truth Council visited a large World War II Japanese prisoner of war camp in Shenyang, China, and persuaded the local Cultural Bureau to make the campsite a memorial museum, which was dedicated this year. In 2005, Chinese cities have been rocked with sometimes violent demonstrations against Japan, with huge crowds of young people expressing outrage about Japan's treatment of Chinese during World War II, a war that ended sixty years ago.

Anti-American sentiment likewise continues to well up, an especially striking instance being the spontaneous transnational protests in 1999 against the accidental American bombing of the Chinese embassy in Belgrade, broadly believed by native Chinese in both China and in the United States to be a deliberate strike.

The Chinese government has tried to shape (or, some would say, provoke) and co-opt anti-Japanese and anti-American incidents, but frequently has had to clamp down on them when foreign relations with Japan and the United States as well as internal stability have been threatened. Perhaps because of the relative strength of the Chinese government compared to the weakness of the Qing court, popular Chinese nationalism today largely lacks the China-directed reform critique that grew out of late Qing anti-foreign movements and undermined the Chinese empire.

NOTES

1. Tu Wei-ming, "Cultural China: The Periphery as the Center," in *The Living Tree: The Changing Meaning of Being Chinese Today*, ed. Tu Wei-ming (Stanford: Stanford University Press, 1994), 34.

2 Arif Dirlik, "Transnationalism, the Press, and the National Imaginary," *The China Review* 4, no.1 (Spring 2004): 11–25.

3. Recent publications expressing this view are Sin Kiong Wong, *China's Anti-American Boycott Movement in 1905: A Study in Urban Protest* (New York: Peter Lang, 2002); Guanhua Wang, *In Search of Justice: The 1905-1906 Chinese Anti-American Boycott* (Cambridge: Harvard University Asia Center, 2001); Yong Chen, *Chinese San Francisco; 1850-1943: A Trans-Pacific Community* (Stanford: Stanford University Press, 2000); Wang Lixin, "Zhongguo jindai minzuzhuyide xingqi yu dizhi Meihuo yundong" 中國近代民族主義的興起與抵制美貨運動 [The rise of modern Chinese nationalism and the anti-American boycott movement], *Lishi Yanjiu* 1 (2000): 21–33; Jin Xijiao "Dizhi Meihuo yundong shiqi Zhongguo minzhongde 'jindaixing'" 抵制美貨運動時期中國民眾的"近代性" [The modernity of the Chinese masses during the time of the anti-American boycott movement], *Lishi Yanjiu* 4 (1997): 92–107.

4 Liang Qichao, "Liang Qichao zhi gebu liewei tongzhi yixiong shu" 梁啟超致各埠列位同義兄書 [Printed letter from Liang Qichao to all comrades in all cities] in *Kang Youwei yu Baohuang Hui—Tan Liang zai Meiguo suocang ziliao huibian* 康有為與保皇會一譚良在美國所藏資料匯編 [Kang Youwei and the Baohuang Hui: A compilation of materials collected by Tom Leung in America], ed. Fang Zhiqin (Tianjin: Tianjin guji chubanshe, 1997), 113 (#578, June 7, 1905).

5 Talk on Chinese Americans and the 1905 boycott given at the Third International Convention of Asia Scholars, Singapore, August 2003.

6 Jane Leung Larson, "The Chinese Empire Reform Association (Baohuanghui) and the 1905 Anti-American Boycott: The Power of a Voluntary Association" in *The Chinese in America: A History from Gold Mountain to the New Millennium*, ed. Susie Lan Cassel (Walnut Creek, CA: AltaMira Press, 2002), 195–216. A subsequent development of this paper was published as "The Chinese Empire Reform Association (Baohuang Hui) and the 1905 Anti-American Boycott: The Transnational Connection in China's First Nationwide Movement," in *Wenming kangzheng—jindai Zhongguo yu haiwai Huaren lunji* 文明抗爭—近代中國與海外華人論集 [Civilized protest—assembled papers on modern China and overseas Chinese], ed. Wong Sin Kiong (Hong Kong: Hong Kong Educational Publishing Company, 2005), 244–301.

7 The original documents collected by Los Angeles Baohuang Hui leader Tom Leung are in the UCLA East Asian Library. Documents cited in this paper are numbered as they are on the originals by an earlier researcher; all dates are in the Western calendar. Most of the documents concerning the Baohuang Hui are available in Fang, *Kang Youwei and the Baohuang Hui*.

8 Liang Qichao, "Printed letter from Liang Qichao to all comrades in all cities," in Fang, *Kang Youwei and the Baohuang Hui*, 113–28. All subsequent quotes in this paragraph come from this letter.

9 Gao De and Gao Shan to Kang Youwei, "Gao De Gao Shan zhi Kang Youwei shu" 高德高山致康有為書 [Letter from Gao De and Gao Shan to Kang Youwei], in Fang, *Kang Youwei and the Baohuang Hui*, 321–22 (#183, June 22, 1905). According to a personal communication from Pei-yi Wu, Columbia University, this letter and two others from Luo Xiaogao, who wrote Tom Leung in 1901 and 1906, are in the same hand.

10 "Ju Jinyue chuandan—lü Mei Huaren lai gao" 拒禁約傳單—旅美華人來稿 [Leaflet opposing the Exclusion Treaty—manuscript from Chinese living in America] in Fang, *Kang Youwei and the Baohuang Hui*, 379–83 (#577, June 1905).

11 Liang Qichao, "Printed letter from Liang Qichao to all comrades in all cities," in Fang, *Kang Youwei and the Baohuang Hui*, 127.

12 Wong, *China's Anti-American Boycott Movement*, 102.

13 "Leaflet Opposing the Exclusion Treaty," in Fang, *Kang Youwei and the Baohuang Hui*, 383.

14 Kang was frequently interviewed by the American press during his ten-month stay in the United States in 1905, much of which was on the road. He met with a variety of American politicians, from mayors and governors to President Theodore Roosevelt (twice), and spoke before such groups as the American Baptist Missionary Union Convention in St. Louis, which passed a resolution calling on Congress to modify the Chinese Exclusion Act. [Robert Leo Worden, "Chinese Reformer in Exile: The North American Phase of the Travels of K'ang Yu-wei, 1899-1909" (PhD diss., Georgetown University, Washington, DC, 1972).]

15 Wang, *In Search of Justice*, 134–59.

16 Wang, *In Search of Justice*, 158–59.

17 Liang Qichao, "Printed letter from Liang Qichao to all comrades in all cities," in Fang, *Kang Youwei and the Baohuang Hui*, 113.

18 "Leaflet Opposing the Exclusion Treaty," in Fang, *Kang Youwei and the Baohuang Hui*, 379–80.

19 Liang Qichao, "Printed letter from Liang Qichao to all comrades in all cities," in Fang, *Kang Youwei and the Baohuang Hui*, 122.

20 "Leaflet Opposing the Exclusion Treaty," in Fang, *Kang Youwei and the Baohuang Hui*, 379–80.

21 Zhang Cunwu, *Guangxu sayinian Zhongmei Gongyue fengchao* 光緒卅一年中美工約風潮 [Agitation against the Sino-American Exclusion treaty] (Taipei: Zhongyang yanjiu yuan jindaishi yanjiusuo, 1965), 27–28.

22 Zhang, *Guangxu sayinian*, 78–79.

23 Samuel L. Gracey to Assistant Secretary of State Robert Bacon, letter, March 28, 1906, *Dispatches from U.S. Consuls in Foochow, China, 1849-1906*, Record Group 59, roll 1007, National Archives.

24 Local Baohuang Hui–run newspapers in China in 1905 included *Yangcheng Ribao* and *Lingnan Bao* in Guangzhou and *Lianhe Bao* and *Shang Bao* in Hong Kong. Other overseas Baohuang Hui papers extant in 1905 were: *Donghua Bao* [Sydney, Australia]; *Minyi Bao* [Manila]; *Bincheng Xin Bao* [Penang]; *Rixin Bao* (China Reform Gazette) [Vancouver, Canada]; *Wenxing Bao* [San Francisco]; *Xin Zhongguo Ribao* [Honolulu]; *Yang Jiangxin Bao* [Rangoon]; *Zhongguo Weixin Bao* and *Niuyue Ribao* [New York City].

25 Wang Guanhua, *1905-1906 nian Huaren dizhi Meihuo yundong—shehui yundong shijiaode zai tantao* 1905-1906 年華人抵制美貨運動—社會運動視角的再探討 [The 1905-1906 Chinese boycott against American goods—a reexamination from the perspective of social movements], in *Civilized Protest*, 96, ed. Wong Sin Kiong.

26 Wang, *In Search of Justice*, 2, 114–15, 182.

27 Liang Qichao, "Printed letter from Liang Qichao to all comrades in all cities," in Fang, *Kang Youwei and the Baohuang Hui*, 120.

28 Barbara Mittler, in her book on the commercial newspaper *Shen Bao*, contends that his statements about the power of the press were "part of Liang Qichao's self-constructed myth" and that Chinese newspapers contributed less to fomenting the

1905 boycott than Liang Qichao suggests, simply reporting on it, often in a neutral tone. See *A Newspaper for China? Power, Identity, and Change in Shanghai's News Media, 1872-1912,* (Cambridge and London: Harvard University Asia Center, 2004), 23, 371–77.

29 Joan Judge, *Print and Politics: 'Shibao' and the Culture of Reform in Late Qing China* (Stanford: Stanford University Press, 1996), 50 (Guangzhou-Hankou Railway), 113 (Hu Shi on Zhou Shengyou case).

30 He Qingyi to Tan Zhangxiao, "He Qingyi zhi Tan Zhangxiao shu" 何擎一致譚張孝書 [Letter from He Qingyi to Tan Zhangxiao] in Fang, *Kang Youwei and the Baohuang Hui,* 327 (#196, December 14, 1905).

31 L. Eve Armentrout Ma, *Revolutionaries, Monarchists, and Chinatowns: Chinese Politics in the Americas and the 1911 Revolution* (Honolulu: University of Hawaii Press, 1990), 126–27.

32 Wu Xianzi, *Zhongguo Minzhu Xianzhengdang dang shi* 中國民主憲政党党史 [Party history of China's Democratic Constitutional Party] (San Francisco: Chinese Constitutionalist/Reform Party, 1952), 53–56; Ding Wenjiang, ed., *Liang Rengong Xiansheng nianpu changpian chugao, shangce* 梁任公先生年譜長編初稿, 上冊 [First draft of Mr. Liang Rengong's chronological life, long version, volume 1], (Taibei: Shijie shuju, 1962), 265–66.

33 Judge, *Print and Politics,* 210; Wang, *In Search of Justice,* 97, 131, 133.

34 Edward J. M. Rhoads, *China's Republican Revolution: The Case of Kwangtung, 1895-1913* (Cambridge: Harvard University Press, 1975), 137.

35 Wu Longyun, "Aozhou Huaren yu 1908 nian dizhi Rihuo yundong" 澳洲華人與 1908 年抵制日貨運動 [Overseas Chinese in Australia and the anti-Japanese boycott of 1908], in Wong, *China's Anti-American Boycott Movement,* 222–43.

36 Ma, *Revolutionaries, Monarchists, and Chinatowns,* 126–27; Jungpang Lo, *K'ang Yu-wei: A Biography and a Symposium* (Tucson: University of Arizona Press, 1967), 212–13, 274; Akira Iriye, "Public Opinion and Foreign Policy: The Case of Late Ch'ing China," in *Approaches to Modern Chinese History,* ed. Albert Feuerwerker, Rhoads Murphey, and Mary C. Wright (Berkeley: University of California Press, 1967), 226–28; Prasenjit Duara, "Nationalists among Transnationals: Overseas Chinese and the Idea of China, 1900-1911," in *Ungrounded Empires: The Cultural Politics of Modern Chinese Transnationalism,* ed. Donald M. Nonini and Aihwa Ong (New York: Routledge, 1997), 49; Wu, *Party history of China's Democratic Constitutional Party,* 54.

37 Kang Youwei, "Haiwai Ya Mei Ou Fei Ao wuzhou erbaibu Zhonghua Xianzheng Hui qiaomin gongshang qingyuanshu" 海外亞美區非澳五洲二百埠中華憲政會僑民公上請願書 [Petition from overseas Chinese in the Constitutional Society from two hundred cities in the five continents, Asia, America, Europe, Africa, and Australia], in *Buren Zazhi Huibian, Chu Ji* (Taibei: Zhongguo tushu chubanshe, 1968), 2:986.

38 Peter Hays Gries, *China's New Nationalism: Pride, Politics, and Diplomacy* (Berkeley: University of California Press, 2004), 43–53.

Branching Out
Chinese American Literary Studies in Taiwan
Te-hsing Shan, PhD

Some of the writings are also, or rather, especially, autobiographical or autocritical, in the sense that I speak of my own identity not as a theorist but as a practicing writer. As a general rule, I do not like to confuse the two roles, but sometimes it is necessary... to turn to one's own experience....

—Umberto Eco, Introduction to *On Literature*

While the "Branching Out the Banyan Tree" conference focuses primarily on the branching out of the Chinese people and their culture in America, this paper tries to address another direction of "branching out," namely, the spread of Chinese American literary studies from the United States to Taiwan. As a deeply involved observer-participant in the institutionalization of minority literary studies in Taiwan, I am here to offer a "witness report" on the development of this branch of American literature on the other side of the Pacific Ocean, hopefully, without too much self-indulgence.

Like everywhere else, English and American literary studies in Taiwan used to focus on mainstream literature at the expense of works by minority writers. As an MA student at National Taiwan University in the late 1970s, the only minority text I read was *Invisible Man* by the African American novelist Ralph Ellison, and it was in a seminar on modern American fiction. No trace of any Asian American writer was to be found. In other words, English students of my generation were totally ignorant of Asian American literature.

The early 1980s witnessed the beginning of the publication of Chinese American literature in Taiwan. "The Albatross Exorcised: The Rime of Frank Chin" by Joseph S. M. Lau 劉紹銘, then a professor at the University of Wisconsin at Madison, was published in *Tamkang Review* in Fall 1981.[1] Appearing in an English journal devoted to Chinese-foreign comparative literature, this paper marked the beginning of scholarly publications on Chinese American literature in Taiwan. The first Chinese paper, "Understanding and Misunderstanding: The Mutual Description of Immigrant Writers and the Writers of the Chinese Descent" 了解與誤解：移民與華裔在創作文學中的互描, by Marlon K. Hom 譚雅倫, was collected in the Festschrift in honor of the eighty-second birthday of Vincent Yu-chung Shih 施友忠 in 1982. Although some papers did appear afterward, Taiwan's academic climate was not yet ready for this emergent literature. Moreover, most of the publishing scholars were neither based in Taiwan nor trained in Asian American literature.

It was not until 1987, when Lin Mao-chu 林茂竹, the first PhD specializing in Chinese American literature, returned to Taiwan that Taiwan could claim to have a scholar trained in Chinese American literature. From the title of the doctoral dissertation Lin submitted to the University of Minnesota—"Identity and Chinese-American Experience: Study of Chinatown American Literature since World War II"—it can be clearly seen that the author focused on the identity issue and literary expressions of post-war Chinatown.[2] A comparison of this dissertation with the first book published in the field, *Asian American Literature: An Introduction to the Writings and Their Social Context* (1982), by Korean American scholar Elaine H. Kim,[3] showed that Lin's methodology was similar to Kim's, though he focused more specifically on the experiences and literary productions of the ethnic minority with which he was more familiar.

Five years later, the second PhD on Chinese American literature, Hsu Li-tsui 許儷粹, also graduated from the University of Minnesota, with her dissertation on "Images and Identity: Chinese Americans in Euro-American and Chinese American Fiction, 1970-1989."[4] The title showed that "identity" was still one of her foci, the other being "images." The scope of her research expanded from Chinese American literature to Euro-American. In addition, three characteristics could be discerned: genre-wise, this study focused on fiction; time-wise, it concentrated on a more recent period, namely, 1970–1989; and theme-wise, it dealt with one of the long-time concerns of comparative literature, namely, the study of images and/or mirages. Both Lin and Hsu taught at universities in Taiwan and went on to write academic papers on Chinese American literature.

The 1990s witnessed the rapid growth of Chinese American literature both in the United States and in Taiwan. At that time, the study of Chinese American literature was often included in minority discourse or postcolonial discourse. A lot of dissertations focused on the issue of ethnicity and gender. Young scholars who graduated from U.S. universities in the first half of the 1990s, such as Kate Chiwen Liu 劉紀雯, Pin-Chia Feng 馮品佳, Chiung-Huei Joan Chang 張瓊惠, and Iping Joy Liang (梁一萍), are all female and have become the new blood in this emergent field.[5] These U.S.-trained scholars were one of the two main forces devoted to Chinese American literary studies in Taiwan in the late 1980s and 1990s.

The other force came from academic institutions in Taiwan itself, especially from the Institute of European and American Studies, Academia Sinica (hereafter abbreviated as IEAS), which is the only area studies institute in Academia Sinica, the highest research institution in Taiwan, Republic of China. IEAS covers a wide variety of disciplines, including literature, history, philosophy, legal studies, political science, sociology, and education. With sufficient budget and complete academic autonomy, Academia Sinica encourages team efforts to pursue intellectual excellence and unique contributions to the academic discourse. In order to capitalize on the particular speaking position of English and American literary researchers in Taiwan, one of the major projects was targeted at Chinese American literature, with Lee Yu-cheng 李有成, Ho Wen-ching 何文敬, and me as members.

Choosing to undertake this research project was by no means accidental, as it closely related not only to our bicultural or transcultural backgrounds, but also to our previous research. As a student of English and comparative literature, Lee has been a pioneering scholar in Jewish and African American literature, and has applied his expertise in ethnic American literature and comparative literature to the study of Chinese American literature. Trained as an Americanist, Ho's study of William Faulkner had already touched upon race issues. He has also published comparative studies on African American writer Toni Morrison and Chinese American writer Maxine Hong Kingston. Also trained in comparative literature and American literature, I have been working on American literary historiography since the late 1980s by investigating the shifts and trends in American literary canons, literary histories, and literary anthologies. The Reconstructing American Literature Project of the 1980s, which took on literary study from the perspective of race and gender, left an indelible impression on my mind. Moreover, as a Fulbright postdoctoral research fellow at University of California, Irvine, from 1989 to 1990, I offered a course on the comparative studies of Chinese and American narratives in the spring quarter of 1990. One of the textbooks I used was Maxine Hong Kingston's *The Woman Warrior: Memoirs of a Girlhood among Ghosts* (1976). Among the thirty-odd students I taught, about half of them were of Asian descent, and they were especially interested in the Chinese intertexts appropriated by the author in her work. Historically, it is also interesting to note that I attended Amy Tan's 譚恩美 book tour for her first book, *The Joy Luck Club*, and the title of her lecture was, significantly, "Finding a Voice in American Literature." Based on the above

background, the three of us decided to embark on this new exploration by making use of our "intersectional as well as transgressional speaking position"[6] in the hopes that we might carve out a niche of our own and generate significant dialogues with scholars at home and abroad.

In order to lay a firm foundation for the newly emergent field and to attract the attention of scholars and students in Taiwan, we decided to hold conferences. Altogether, three national and two international conferences took place in ten years. In the history of IEAS, this series of conferences was one of the most consistently focused conferences on a chosen topic in a specific area. Moreover, in order to facilitate exchanges with scholars abroad, each of the national conferences also invited a representative Asian American scholar from the United States to present a paper.[7]

The choice of the conference themes was based mainly on the following considerations: to highlight the characteristics of Chinese American literature, to make connections with current scholarly trends and social concerns, and to provide an open forum and discursive space for interested scholars and students at home and abroad. In order to achieve the above-stated goals, the theme of the first national conference, held in February 1993, was "Cultural Identity" 文化屬性, because this was a significant issue not only in the context of Chinese/Asian American literature,[8] but also as regards the concerns of Chinese/Asian Americans and the research orientations of Taiwan scholars. It was also hoped that with this theme, the conference would be able to help orient future directions. In addition to inviting a limited number of scholars in Taiwan to present papers, scholars and graduate students in English departments were also notified of this conference wholly devoted to the study of Chinese American literature, the first of its kind in the world. In addition, I also invited King-Kok Cheung to participate, and published an interview with her in *Chung-Wai Literary Monthly* before her first visit to Taiwan so as to facilitate exchanges between her and local scholars. A symposium was organized to allow panelists and audience to exchange views on this new research area. The huge turnout and warm dialogue in the conference testified to the success of this conference.

In order to share the research results, each paper was revised by the author and reviewed by two anonymous reviewers before it was formally accepted for publication. The transcript of the symposium was also sent to the panelists for revision. Moreover, my interview with Cheung was included to mark the first scholarly exchanges between scholars at home and abroad at the initial stage of Chinese American literary studies in Taiwan. With the help of my research assistant, I also compiled an annotated bibliography of Chinese and English papers and degree theses on Chinese American literature in Taiwan to provide a map for interested students of literature.

In short, this conference and its subsequent publication followed the standard operational procedure of IEAS: allocating the budget, choosing the theme, inviting paper presenters, convening the conference, revising the papers (including translating Cheung's paper into Chinese), reviewing, editing, and publishing. In addition to conference papers, the resultant *Cultural Identity and Chinese American Literature* 文化屬性與華裔美國文學 (1994), coedited by Ho Wen-ching and myself, also contained my introduction to the volume, the record of the symposium, my interview with Cheung, and an annotated bibliography.[9] As the first collection of critical essays and assessment on Chinese American literature in the Chinese-speaking world, this book was a landmark and cleared a new discursive ground for scholars and graduate students alike. Therefore, this volume carries both historical and scholarly weight.

In fact, while we expected to create a certain academic climate by organizing a conference, we were not quite sure about the result. However, the warm responses from the participants as well as the effects of this conference were somewhat beyond our expectations. With encouragement from local scholars and our American participant, we began to devote ourselves to preparing for the second conference, with its theme "Politics of Representation."

As the first conference set up an efficient model, "Politics of Representation: The Second Conference on Chinese American Literature" was held in April 1995. As a Harvard-Yenching visiting scholar that year, I was unable to attend the conference in person and could only have my paper read by a colleague back in Taiwan. However, I was able to contact Kingston and Ling in the United States. So, in addition to paper presentations and discussions, Kingston appeared as a special guest and read passages from her manuscript of *The Fifth Book of Peace*.[10] Moreover, the volume from the previous conference, which took two years to prepare, was published just in time to be on display at the conference venue, a witness to the first concrete achievement of the study of Chinese American literature in Taiwan.

As expected, the second conference was also well received, and all the papers were reviewed and edited before formally being included in the conference volume. This book also included my interview with Kingston and the enlarged, updated, and annotated bibliography. The new volume, entitled *Politics of Representation and Chinese American Literature* 再現政治與華裔美國文學 (1996) was once again coedited by Ho Wen-ching and myself. In comparison with the previous volume, the second no longer focused so much on a single author and proved to be more diversified and multifaceted.[11]

With the firm foundation laid by the first two conferences, it became a matter of course to hold a third. "Invention of Tradition: The Third Conference on Chinese American Literature" was held in April 1997, with Sau-ling Cynthia Wong from UC, Berkeley. The major difference this time was that in order to meet the increasing demand for journal publications, the conference papers, after the standard reviewing process, were published in the December 2002 issue of *EurAmerica*,

the official quarterly of IEAS for over thirty years as well as *the* leading European and American Studies journal in Taiwan.[12]

After several years of effort and three national conferences, Chinese American literary studies not only gained a secure footing, but also became one of the most eye-catching areas of study in Taiwan. The appearance of many conference and journal papers as well as dozens of degree theses testified to the enthusiastic acceptance it found outside of the United States as well as how quickly it took root in Taiwan. When we first conceived of the conference, we purposefully chose Chinese as the working language with a view toward cultivating people's interest in Chinese American literature and spreading it out in the Chinese-speaking world. However, we fully realized that to promote international exchanges and to gain international visibility, we had to resort to English. After years of preparation, we judged that the time was ripe for an international conference and as a result, "Remapping Chinese America: An International Conference on Chinese American Literature" 重繪華美圖誌：華裔美國文學國際研討會, the first international conference wholly devoted to Chinese American literature, was held in June 1999.[13] In his call for papers, Ho Wen-ching stressed that it was high time that we remapped Chinese American literary and cultural terrains at the turn of the millennium by focusing on the problematics of race, class, gender, and sexuality and by re-viewing the relationship between Chinese American and mainstream American as well as other ethnic American literatures. In addition to re-viewing the past, this conference also hoped to map out some directions for the future.

Therefore, the first international conference aimed at providing a platform for scholars at home and abroad to renavigate Chinese America from their respective positions. The enthusiastic participation and discussion demonstrated that internationalization was indeed urgently needed, for it would certainly serve to promote the exchange of ideas across national and cultural borders and would also reflect various ideas regarding the field at the end of the last millennium.

Witnessing the fast growth of ethnic literature in the English-speaking world and attempting to explore a broader territory, IEAS later convened "Negotiating the Past: An International Conference on Asian American and Asian British Literatures" 與過去協商：亞裔英美文學國際研討會 in November 2003. By that time it was already ten years after our first national conference. The theme of this international conference clearly indicated the effort to re-visit and re-view the past with an attempt to face the present and to plan for the future. What was most significant was the expansion of the investigation from "Chinese" to "Asian" and from "American" to "both American and British." In addition, the word "Literatures" in the plural form further indicated the endeavor to acknowledge and facilitate complexity, diversity, and multiplicity.

The call for papers written by Lee Yu-cheng extended Stuart Hall's discourse on the past and pointed out that people continuously make use of memory, re-memory, post-memory, and so on in order to confront and understand the present. In addition, many Asian American and Asian British writers delve into the hidden past in order to draw inspiration for their literary creations. The efforts in this new direction indicated that scholars in Taiwan were trying to expand their vision by making use of the foundation they had laid in Chinese American literature. In so doing, new issues were being discussed, new territories explored, and new challenges met. Moreover, the expansion of the conference theme further provided interested scholars at home and abroad an opportunity to exchange views from various perspectives, and the result was more than satisfactory.

To sum up, the three national conferences on Chinese American literature in 1993, 1995, and 1997 used Chinese as their working language so that this new research area could take root in foreign soil. As the intellectual climate became more and more mature after years of concerted effort, the two international conferences in 1999 and 2003 used English as their working language, with an attempt to go global and to provide a public forum for international scholars. The targets and themes of these conferences were clearly defined, and with their unique speaking positions, scholars in Taiwan tried to carve out a niche of their own, so to speak, from which they could begin dialogues with colleagues from different parts of the world. All this has proven that with a vivid vision, workable procedures, sustained efforts, sufficient resources, and the determination to reach out, much can be accomplished. As I pointed out in my introduction to the special issue:

> Before the 1990s, there was a wholesale acceptance of the English and American mainstream values in the English and American literary studies in Taiwan. Consequently, the main focus had been placed upon English and American literary classics at the expense of ethnic literary studies. However, after the 1990s, with the devotion of the scholars in Taiwan and the necessary institutional support, the number of academic papers and degree theses in Chinese American literature has grown rapidly and has made this emergent research area one of the most eye-catching and fruitful ones. Pin-chia Feng's studies bear this out with clear statistics and annotated bibliography.[14]

As mentioned earlier, IEAS, with its institutional status, had devoted numerous resources to cultivate this new field. Therefore, in his foreword to the special issue of Asian American literature coedited with Chang, Tee remarked at the outset that, "The efforts of the research fellows at IEAS in promoting Chinese American literature in the 1990s were witnessed by the academic circle in Taiwan. And the number of young students of literature devoted to Chinese American literary studies has been steadily on the rise. Within ten years, a certain amount of academic energy and scholarly results have been accumulated."[16] This special issue also included Tee's "Examining" essay in which he further specified:

> With its combined human resources, its holding of national and international conferences on Chinese American literature, its publication of collections of essays as well as journal articles

in *EurAmerica*, its research fellows' offering Chinese American literature courses in the graduate programs in several universities, IEAS has become *the* driving force of the institutionalization of Chinese American literature in Taiwan. As a consequence, Chinese American literature has rapidly become the emergent phenomenon in the English and American literary studies in our country and IEAS itself has become the bastion of Chinese American literary studies in Asian-Pacific area.[18]

Coincidentally, Feng has the following observation to make:

> [T]he fact that Chinese American literature has gained such a rapid growth is because several research fellows at IEAS have spared no efforts to promote Chinese American literature in Taiwan—from the holding of national and international conferences to the publication of books. Consequently, they have laid a firm foundation for Chinese American literary studies in Taiwan, far surpassing the research results produced by the scholars of similar linguistic and cultural background on the other side of the [Taiwan] Strait.[19]

However, two things must be pointed out here. First, although IEAS as a research institution has had some achievements in this newly emergent field over the past twelve years, it is by no means complacent. Multicultural studies of literature have always been one of the major goals of IEAS, and we have been fortunate to be able to do the right thing, at the right time, and in the right way. The quick blossoming of Chinese American literature in Taiwan as one of the dominant literary discourses, if not *the* dominant discourse, can be attributed to the institutional support which were targeted to the needs of English and American literature scholars in Taiwan. This is indeed a rare case in the international scene and shows another kind of continuity and discontinuity, inheritance and deviation, in relation to the scholarship done in the United States. Second, it should also be pointed out that scholars in mainland China have expressed strong interest in Chinese American literature, world literature written in Chinese 世界華文文學, and Overseas Chinese Studies 海外華人研究. With more and more scholars and institutions devoted to these fields, they are also rapidly producing academic papers and Chinese translations.

As for myself, I have been privileged to have joined the research team at IEAS at the start and have had the opportunity to present papers at related national and international conferences at home and abroad. A collection of my Chinese papers written in the 1990s, entitled *Inscriptions and Representations: Essays on Chinese American Literature and Culture* 銘刻與再現：華裔美國文學與文化論集 was published in 2000. From the particular bilingual and bicultural perspective of a Taiwan scholar, I have striven to approach Chinese American literature from an angle different from those of my American counterparts and to produce some unique contribution in this transcultural discursive space. I have conducted research on some representative Chinese American writers as well as literary and cultural texts. Moreover, I have also conducted field studies by visiting some historical sites and interviewing some representative Chinese American writers, critics, and historians. This book addresses subjects such as literary and historical representations, literary historiography, cultural identity and imaginaries, politics of representation, the invention of tradition, multilingualism, biculturalism, visual texts, and cultural studies. A closer look at the book reveals that historically it deals with subjects ranging from the poems carved on the wooden walls of the Angel Island detention camp as early as 1910 to literary works of the late 1990s. Linguistically, in this book I try to go beyond English to redefine Chinese American literature from a translingual and transcultural perspective. In addition to dealing with representative writers of both genders, this book discusses a variety of subjects, such as literary texts, literary criticism, literary historiography, and photographic and visual texts. As a result, it became a combination of literary *and* cultural studies. As the first book of this kind by an individual author in the Chinese-speaking world, it not only conducts in-depth analyses of the emergence and significance of Chinese American literature and culture in American society, but also embodies the critical intervention of a Taiwan scholar into American literary and cultural studies from a non-mainstream speaking position. The cultural politics that lie therein are more than obvious.

The observations made so far are meant to serve as an observer-participant's eyewitness report concerning the speedy institutionalization or "branching out" of Chinese American literary studies in Taiwan. However, looking back on its development over the past one-and-a-half decades, we also discern some characteristics or even "drawbacks" which need to be addressed with more critical awareness if this field wants to maintain its vitality, flexibility, and multiplicity. Six critical reflections are in order.

1. *The broadening of visions and themes.* First, so far as Asian American literature is concerned, Taiwan scholars have focused too much on Chinese American literature. Some linguistic, literary, cultural, and historical factors have been involved, of course. And there is no denying the unique position occupied by Chinese American literature in Asian American literature. Still, if we look at the scholarly output on Chinese American literature and other branches of Asian American literature in Taiwan, we will find that up to now there are less than ten papers dealing with Japanese American literature, fewer papers on Korean American literature, let alone other branches of Asian American literature (as for literature of Indian descent, it has been more commonly included in new English literature or postcolonial literature due to India's relationship to its former colonizer). Not only is this self-imposed limit unnecessary, but it prevents studying Chinese American literature and culture from a broader Asian American context, which is a loss to both sides. Second, the research up to now has been so over-focused on a handful of authors that some less-famous writers have been neglected.

Third, genre-wise, fiction has attracted much, probably too much, attention. After fiction comes drama, but overall, very little research has been devoted to poetry. Although more and more attention has been paid to cinema due to the blooming of Cultural Studies, a lot of it has focused on the Chinese American director Ang Lee 李安 and fails to provide more comprehensive investigation of Chinese American visual culture in general. Fourth, little research has been devoted to the relationship between Chinese American literature and other ethnic American literature, especially African American literature. Lastly, a comprehensive Chinese American literary history remains to be written.

2. *The deepening of history and the contextualization of research.* Literature never comes out of a vacuum but instead is produced from a specific social and historical context. This is especially true for ethnic literature. As a result, ethnic literary studies pay more attention to historical background and cultural-political implications. Sensitively reflecting the outer environment, literature always plays a unique role in expressing ethnicity-related issues. On the other hand, literature must not be regarded as an instrument only; otherwise, its value will only be debased. In fact, literary and cultural studies have long transcended theories that regard literature as merely a mechanical reflection of its outer environment. More efforts should be made to delve into the complexity and multiplicity of its contexts and to explore its historical and cultural specificities so as to construct a more inclusive and multicultural picture. This is even more imperative for ethnic literature and culture.

3. *The case for more refined and oppositional theorization.* Theory posits an abstract and universal nature, appeal, and function. However, theory also comes from "somewhere" and has its specific intellectual context. Therefore, in applying a certain theory, more critical attention should be paid to the applicability and adaptability of the particular theory at hand. For instance, many researches on ethnic female writers have made use of postcolonial discourse, minority discourse, and (mainstream) feminist discourse to discuss female writers operating under the dual pressure of race and gender. Sometimes there are comparative studies of female writers of Chinese descent and other ethnic American female writers or Third-World female writers. This is a prevalent and powerful approach in its own right and serves to situate Chinese American female writers in a larger context. However, when many scholars apply similar theories to the study of similar authors and works with a similar reasoning process, and reach similar conclusions; what is produced is often a universal impression devoid of ethnic and cultural specificities and a lack of the unique power of literature. In short,

theory (etymologically meaning "clear seeing") does highlight some characteristics. However, those who appropriate theories for their studies need to recognize the costs and avoid using theory in a repetitive, uncritical, and mechanical way. The relationship between theory and text should not be unidirectional, but reciprocal. Rich and multifaceted literary texts can also highlight the characteristics and supplement the inadequacies of theory. In the study of ethnic literature, more attention should be paid to the relationship of minority literature and dominant theory so that ethnic literature is not once again subjugated to dominant theory. Whenever possible, efforts should be made to emphasize the counter-memory and counter-history that are unique to ethnic literature, to propose an alternative narrative and discourse, to conduct some kind of meta-criticism, and even to develop theories of ethnic literature to contest mainstream theories. Otherwise, the prevalence and repetitive use of theories might result in the lack of imagination and multiplicity, to the detriment of both prevailing theory and minority literature.

4. *The adoption of a multiple and transdisciplinary approach.* With its focus on literary texts, the study of minority literature is by no means limited to literary texts or certain literary and cultural theories. Approaches from other disciplines, such as history, sociology, and anthropology, to name just a few, also provide useful theoretical frameworks and concrete instances that shed light on hitherto neglected texts and contexts and help save important writers from oblivion. In this respect, the active intervention and multiple approaches advocated by Cultural Studies offers an important impetus.

5. *The imperative of going international and global.* Studying English and American literature in Asia is already an international act—the internationalization of English and American literary studies. When it comes to Asian American literary studies, scholars in Asia have more confidence and competence to engage in dialogues with scholars in the United States and to produce another version of the interaction between globalization and localization. Moreover, American literature scholars in Asia have been looking toward the United States and, as a result, they are much more familiar with what is happening in the United States than in their neighboring countries. Therefore, internationalization here means having more dialogues with scholars of other Asian countries as well as with their American colleagues. For instance, while attending an international conference on American Studies in Korea in 2003, I personally witnessed Korean scholars' strong interest in Korean American female writer Theresa Hak Kyung Cha's *Dictee.* As that book contains many allusions and references to Korean language, literature, history, and politics, Korean scholars are in a privileged position to provide

information, explanations, and annotations that will be of tremendous help to scholars and general readers alike. Similarly, each Asian country may adopt measures suitable for its environment. So, regional cooperation between Asian countries will help provide a more comprehensive picture from an international perspective.

6. *The cultivation of multilingual and multicultural perspectives.* The American Constitution has never designated an official American language. Therefore, multilingual and multicultural perspectives will indeed do more justice to this country of immigrants. For instance, instead of "English only," Werner Sollors and Marc Shell have been advocating "English plus" in their LOWINUS Project (the Project of Languages of What Is Now the United States). In terms of Chinese American literature, it means that Chinese-language writings published in the United States can legitimately claim their position in American literary and cultural history. This re-cognition expands the scope and landscape of American literature and culture to an amazing degree. Moreover, according to Itamar Even-Zohar's translation theory, when Chinese American literary texts in English are translated into Chinese, they become part of the "literary polysystem" of Chinese literature.[20] However, I want to point out that these translated texts can be contextualized in a number of different ways and gain different meanings in what I coin as a "literary multisystem." Namely, in this literary multisystem, the translated Chinese American literary texts can be situated in four different literary contexts, at least, and produce different meanings, respectively. These contexts are *Zhongguo wenxue* (中國文學, Chinese literature proper, which fits in Even-Zohar's conceptualization), *Huawen wenxue* (華文文學, literature written in Chinese, including that produced in the United States), *Meihua wenxue* (美華文學, Chinese American literature, or literature written in English by the Americans of Chinese descent), and *Huaren wenxue* (華人文學, literature written by people of Chinese descent).[21]

There are bound to be some overlaps and intersections among these critical observations and reflections. Moreover, they are made on the basis of Chinese American literary studies in Taiwan. In comparison with the American academic community, English and American literary studies in Taiwan are already marginalized, and doing ethnic literary studies is even more so. Paradoxically, due to the characteristics of Chinese American literature and the cultural and academic conditions, the originally marginal and marginalized Chinese American literary studies has rapidly been institutionalized in Taiwan and has even become one of the most dominant discourses. The main reason behind this peculiar phenomenon is the specific position and perspective of those engaged in the study of minority literature on this side of the Pacific Rim.

This also serves as an example of how originally marginal and marginalized scholars, by making use of their marginality, are able to create a niche of their own. What is more impressive is that as organic intellectuals, scholars obtain their agency with their scholarly intervention and interventionist scholarship. Equally important is the constant self-awareness and self-critique that allows them to reflect honestly upon the past, together with its merits and defects, gains and losses, to have a critical understanding of where they stand now, and to plan for a more inclusive, open-minded, and, hopefully, just future.

ACKNOWLEDGMENTS

Special thanks go to Lee Yu cheng, Ho Wen-ching, and the "Branching Out" conference participants for their comments and to Judd Kinzley for his editorial assistance. An earlier Chinese version of this paper was read at "Querying the Genealogy: An International Forum on Chinese American Literature and Chinese Language Literature in the United States," sponsored by the Center for the Study of Chinese World Literature, Fudan University, Shanghai, June 1—3, 2005. I want to express my gratitude to Jennie Wang for giving me the opportunity to address a Chinese-speaking audience, and to Lorraine Dong and Ling-chi Wang for the English-speaking one.

NOTES

1. Joseph S. M. Lau 劉紹銘, "The Albatross Exorcised: The Rime of Frank Chin," *Tamkang Review* 12, no. 1 (Fall 1981): 93–105.

2. Marlon K. Hom 譚雅倫, "Liaojie yu wujie: yimin yu Huayi zai chuangzuo wenxue zhong de humiao" [Understanding and misunderstanding: a mutual description of immigrant writers and writers of Chinese descent], in *Wenxue, shixue, zexue: Shi Youzhong xiansheng bashi shouchen jinian wenji* [Literature, history, philoso phy: Festschrift in honor of the 82nd birthday of Professor Vincent Yu-chung Shih], ed. Chang Chen-ao 張振翱 and Cheng Peng-hsiang 陳鵬翔 (Taipei: Shihpao, 1982), 201–30. For a survey and critical evaluation of the institutionalization of Chinese American literature in Taiwan, see Tee Kim Tong 張錦忠, "Jianshi Huayi Meiguo wenxue zai Taiwan de jianzhihua (1981-2001)" [Examining the institutionalization of Chinese American literature in Taiwan], *Chung-Wai Literary Monthly* 29, no. 11 (April 2001): 29–43. For an understanding of Chinese American literary studies in Taiwan, see my annotated bibliography in Shan Te-hsing 單德興, *Minke yu zaixian: Huayi Meiguo wenxue yu wenhua lunji* [Inscriptions and representations: Chinese American literary and cultural studies], (Taipei: Rye Field, 2000), 365–87, hereafter cited as *Inscriptions*.

3. Lin Mao-chu 林茂竹, "Identity and Chinese-American Experience: Study of Chinatown American Literature since World War II" (PhD diss., University of Minnesota, 1987).

4. Elaine H. Kim 金惠經, *Asian American Literature: An Introduction to the Writings and Their Social Context* (Philadelphia: Temple University Press, 1982).

5. Hsu Li-tsui 許儷粹, "Images and Identity: Chinese Americans in Euro-American and Chinese American Fiction, 1970-1989" (PhD diss., University of Minnesota, 1992).

6. The topics of their dissertations are as follows: Kate Chiwen Liu, "De/constructing National Identity: The Historiographical Metafictions of John Barth, Joan Didion, and Maxine Hong Kingston" (PhD diss., State University of New York at Stony Brook, 1993); Pin-Chia Feng, "Rethinking the Bildungsroman: Return of the Repressed in *The Bluest Eye*, *Sula*, *The Woman Warrior*, and *China Men*" (PhD diss., University of Wisconsin–Madison, 1994); Chiung-Huei Joan Chang, "Neither-Nor or Both-And: A Study of Chinese American Writers" (PhD diss., University of Oregon, 1994); and Iping Joy Liang, "The Lure of the Land: Ethnicity and Gender in Imagining America" (PhD diss., University of Massachusetts–Amherst, 1995).

7. Shan, *Inscription*, 26.

8. King-Kok Cheung 張敬珏 of UCLA, Amy Ling 林英敏 of University of Wisconsin–Madison, and Sau-ling Cynthia Wong 黃秀玲 of University of California at Berkeley attended these conferences, respectively. It is worth mentioning that Kingston and Ling were visiting Taiwan in the same group. As a result, Kingston also attended the conference. What is also interesting to note is that all these pioneers of Asian American literature were trained in other areas. Their active participation and solid contribution helped pave the way for this new field.

9. For instance, a lot of Chinese/Asian American literary works and studies have focused on cultural identity. Even though Frank Chin 趙健秀 and a number of people were quite critical about this topic, their strong objection to this theme indicated that this was indeed a focus of concern and even controversy. In fact, if we look at Chin and his comrades, we would find that either the so-called Asian American sensibility which is neither Asian nor American emphasized by them in *Aiiieeeee!* in the early 1970s, or the heroic tradition of Asian American literature they tried to establish in *Big Aiiieeeee!* two decades later, expressed their strong motivation and strategy to fight mainstream American society in different historical contexts. And it is not too far from the fact to say that these "manifestos" carry a strong sense of essentialized identity.

10 It could be clearly seen from the table of contents of this volume that more than half of the papers focused on Kingston, reflecting the beginning stage of the institutionalization of Chinese American literature in Taiwan.

11. I met Kingston on October 2, 1994, in Boston during the stage performance of *The Woman Warrior*. Later on, I conducted an interview with her through correspondence to prepare for her first visit to Taiwan and the upcoming conference. An excerpt of the interview was published in the literary supplement of *United Daily News* on April 7 and 8, and that of *World Journal*, the leading Chinese-language newspaper in North America.

12. Since I translated Cheung's paper for the first book, I translated Ling's for the second book. It is sad to remark that though Ling and I had been working closely to bring her work into publication in a Chinese volume, we never met each other.

13. Shan Te-hsing 單德興, "Chuangzhao chuantong yu Huayi Meiguo wenxue zhuanti xulun" [An introduction to the symposium on the invention of tradition and Chinese American literature], *EurAmerica* 32, no. 4 (December 2002): 621–39. See the special issue and the long introduction I wrote. A comparison shows that while about two-thirds of the first volume focused on Kingston, the second and the third volumes proved to be more diversified, indicating the gradual coming of age of this discipline in Taiwan.

14. According to the Call for Papers, this was going to be "The 'First' International Conference on Chinese American Literature."

However, later on the word "First" was dropped in order to maintain more flexibility.

15. For instance, over the years, courses related to Chinese American literature have been offered in different universities around the island. As far as I am concerned, I have offered seminars on Asian American literary and cultural studies in the graduate programs of National Taiwan University and National Chiao Tung University. In addition, Wong and I coedited a translation series of Chinese American literature with the support of the National Bureau of Compilation and Translation and the Rye Field Publishing Company and, subsequently, published Ho's translation of *Homebase* by Shawn Wong and Chang's translation of *Among the White Moon Faces* by Shirley Lim. This translation project served to combine translation with scholarship and to introduce Chinese American literature to a much wider reading public beyond the academy.

16. Shan, "Introduction" 632. According to Feng's research, there were only eight entries on Asian American literature in the 1980s. However, eighty-odd entries appeared in the 1990s, more than ten times that of the previous decade. And the year 2000 alone witnessed the publication of thirteen papers. Almost all of them dealt with Chinese American literature. As a result, it became the most popular ethnic American literature in Taiwan. And two of the most popular ethnic American writers were none other than Morrison and Kingston. See Feng Pin-chia 馮品佳, "Taiwan diqu de xin Yingwen wenxue ji Meiguo ruoshi zuyi wenxue yanjiu: xulun" [Studies of new English literature and American minority literature in Taiwan: an introduction], research project sponsored by the Humanities Research Center, National Science Council, Taiwan, ROC, p. 14.

17. Tee, Jianshi Huayi Meiguo wenxue, 10.

18. Tee, Jianshi Huayi Meiguo wenxue, 35.

19. Feng, Taiwan diqu, 10.

20. Shan Te-hsing 單德興, *Duihua yu jiaoliu: dangdai zhongwai zuojia pipingjia fangtan lu* [Dialogues and interchanges: Interviews with contemporary writers and critics], (Taipei: Rye Field, 2001). This is a collection of my interviews with Chinese American writers Jade Snow Wong 黃玉雪, Maxine Hong Kingston, Gish Jen 任璧蓮, Wing Tek Lum 林永得, Chinese American historian Him Mark Lai 麥禮謙, and Chinese American literary critic Cheung. After its publication, I also interviewed the Chinese American writer and editor Russell Leong 梁志英 when he visited Taiwan.

21. Itamar Even-Zohar, "Polysystem Theory," rev. version, 1997, *http://www.tau.ac.il/~itamarez/papers/ps-th-r.htm* (accessed October 30, 2005).

22. If it is situated in the context of the Chinese diaspora, more complexity is bound to occur. I will not discuss it here since this is not the focus of this paper.

Motherland and Chinese Diaspora

Da Zheng, PhD

In 1975, Chiang Yee took a trip to China from April 15 to June 15. It had been forty-two years since he left China in 1933. Upon his return to New York, Chiang gave public speeches, showed slides at gatherings, and discussed the unprecedented changes he had witnessed in China. Simultaneously, he quickly recorded his thoughts and experiences, which came out in a book entitled *China Revisited*, posthumously published in 1977. On the dust jacket is his Chinese painting of Mao Zedong, sitting on top of the mountains and appreciating the surrounding beautiful landscape of the country. This China visit seemed to have been a transforming experience; Chiang appeared like an entirely different person after the trip. His close friend and colleague at Columbia exclaimed: "Chiang Yee has become a revolutionary."

Indeed, Chiang Yee's viewpoints and his description of the experience in China in the book *China Revisited* are unusually candid and emotional compared to his earlier works. Now that thirty years have passed since the publication of the book, it is apparent that some of his views and understanding of China were not accurate for epistemological and historical reasons. Still those drastic changes after his visit prompt us to ask these questions: Had he really been converted to communism after the trip? How should we explain those sudden changes in him? What had been the cause of those changes, and what are the conclusions we may draw from that? All these questions are important because the answers may help us understand not merely the changes in Chiang himself only, but also some fundamental issues related to Chinese diasporas in general concerning their indissoluble bond to the motherland.

Chiang Yee was born in 1903 in Jiujiang, Jiangxi Province. In 1911, the Manchuria emperor was dethroned, and the feudal system was replaced with a new republic. Chiang went to college in Nanjing and graduated in 1926 with a bachelor of science degree in chemistry. He aspired to help bring prosperity to China with an extensive training in science. Unfortunately, the country, under the Nationalist government, was plagued with civil wars, famines, corruption, crimes, and poverty. Influenced by his older brother, who served in the Nationalist government, Chiang joined the Northern Expedition, hoping to defeat warlords and unite the country. Later, he served as county magistrate for three years in three different counties, including his hometown, Jiujiang.

He attempted to bring about reforms and improve the lives of the people. He promoted education, effected tax reform, and curbed bribery and other crimes. His lofty ideals, however, collided with the interests of some local officials. He opted to resign from office after the new provincial governor took the office. Chiang went to England to study foreign government at the University of London for a year, intending to bring about social reforms in China in the future. Unexpectedly, for various reasons, including the subsequent Japanese invasion of China, the Second World War, and the political situation in China, he stayed abroad, first in England and then in America as faculty at Columbia University.

During his sojourn overseas, Chiang became known for his *Silent Traveller* series, which consisted of a dozen volumes that cover various cities and countries in Europe and Asia. These volumes, decorated with illustrations, Chinese calligraphy, and poems, appeal to readers of all ages and backgrounds as original, refreshing, and entertaining. On various occasions, Chiang has explained that he wrote these volumes in order to underline the commonalities among people between the East and West. He writes about natural landscape and sociocultural practices in the West, and he loves to "defamiliarise the world" around him and transform a common scene—such as a waterfall or snow scene in the West into an unfamiliar sight in the East or an ancient Chinese painting.[1] For members of diaspora like Chiang, writing is more than a mere inscribing practice: it is a medium with which the writer searches for home and constructs an imaginary home. The act of defamiliarization here is an important part of the home-construction efforts, allowing the diaspora to come to terms with displacement and homelessness.[2]

Chiang's return to his original homeland in 1975 disrupted and complicated the home-construction process by introducing these two new elements: disorientation and re-orientation. When Chiang returned to China, he was confronted with a motherland entirely different—yet with some degree of strange familiarity—from what had been registered in his memory. He describes his bewilderment at the site of his childhood home in Jiujiang near the end of *China Revisited*.

> Every inch reminded me of something, yet everything looked so different from what I had known before. I insisted on being taken to where my old home had been, but there was no trace of

it, or of my old official residence, for both had been destroyed by the Japanese invaders in 1938. I gazed at the stones on the road and the walls of the new houses, and that my past had gone forever. "How could this be?" I asked myself, but no answer came.[3]

Like Rip Van Winkle in Washington Irving's story, Chiang is totally disoriented. Such an incredible transformation that has taken place in his hometown within such a short time period is too baffling: a formerly small town where a small textile mill was the only industry in the early 1930s has now metamorphosed into "a sort of cosmopolitan place" with "eighteen good-sized factories producing tools, engineering tools, machine parts, as well as other light industries making products like fertilizers, matches, and toothpaste."[4] The memory of the old China which he has tenderly preserved and harbored as the guiding map and lens for this search fails to match and measure the reality.

The stage of re-orientation began subsequently in the United States when he started to re-evaluate the home-returning experience and the meaning of home. The two layers—a present China versus the old one—collided and collaborated in his presentations and writing of the book *China Revisited*. It was re-orientation that corrected the vertigo of the disorientation and enabled Chiang to reassess the facts he had just witnessed during the trip, adjust the lens of the present and the past, and set his mind to "face the present and future."[5] Needless to say, the socio-political situation played a critical role here. The improved Sino-U.S. diplomatic relationship and less restrained political atmosphere in the post-McCarthy era allowed Chiang to voice his opinions more openly and freely.

China Revisited, the last travel book he published, appears somewhat like just another volume in his Silent Traveller series. However, there are some fundamental differences. First of all, this book does not have Chiang's signature phrase, "The Silent Traveller," in the title, such as *The Silent Traveller in Boston* or *The Silent Traveller in San Francisco*. Second, this is a book about his home country while all other *Silent Traveller* books deal with cities and countries overseas. Third, when writing *Silent Traveller* books, he always attempts to underline the commonalities among all cultures, especially between the East and the West. Nevertheless, this China book tries to bring out the sharp differences between the two Chinas: the post-1949 China versus the China of the past. He wants to display and highlight the stark contrasts through detailed comparisons. Finally, the China book is the most candid and outspoken among all his travel writings. Chiang seems to have cast off all precautions and tells the world, for the first time in his career since 1933, about his true feelings in regard to politics, personal life, and motherland.

Chiang manifests at the beginning of *China Revisited* that the book is an account of his "personal experiences in China before 1933 and forty-two years later."[6] Indeed, it begins with a chapter, entitled "Why I Left China for England," that gives an introduction to his experience in China before 1933.

Chiang writes about his aspiration for making contributions to bring about a strong China and his political experiences as county magistrate in three different counties, an experience that eventually only led to his disillusionment and displacement. It is followed by two chapters that narrate his experience overseas: "In England" and "In America." Chiang tells about his difficult path toward literary and artistic successes in the West. Displacement from home is unquestionably the source of irreparable loss and pain to the diaspora. The poignant and emotional tone is filled with longing and memory in those chapters.

Starting from the fourth chapter, the book switches to an exuberant and buoyant tone, presenting Chiang's recent trip to China. He acknowledges that, though he had been reading about China and had followed the latest development there as closely as he could during all those forty-two years abroad, he could not help being impressed with the changes he has witnessed, particularly socioeconomic, cultural, and political changes.

China has become an entirely different country socioeconomically. "[T]he feeling of peace and prosperity in the air everywhere was the most striking change from the past," Chiang states.[7] People in China appear cheerful, healthy, and content, and there is no trace of beggars, hunger, or crime. On a street in Beijing, Chiang stops to chat with a farmer, who is busy selling vegetables from a heavily loaded pushcart. Chiang wants to find out what would happen to the vegetables left unsold at the end of the day. The farmer tells Chiang that he goes home in the evening and leaves all the items where they are. It is perfectly safe to leave them there even though no one will stay nearby guarding the pushcart at night.[8] In Shanghai, there used to be a district where prostitution was rampant in the first half of the century. Half-naked girls could be seen loitering on the street, and foreign sailors would go there to seek prostitutes. Poverty and venereal diseases were widespread. When Chiang revisits the area, vestiges of prostitution were nowhere to be seen any more. Some of those former prostitutes and beggars have been married and working in the factories. It is a "remarkable achievement" that the government has succeeded in eradicating this social evil within such a short time [9]

The most impressive of all is the fact that China has grown independent and self-reliant. Shanghai, a world-renowned industrial city, for example, used to be controlled not by Chinese but by the Westerners. Cotton mills were mostly owned by English and Japanese entrepreneurs, and many foreign products could be found in the markets. Nevertheless, such a phenomenon has become a remnant of the past. China is now capable of producing cars, tractors, cameras, bicycles, and many other goods for both domestic consumption and export. Aside from its development in light and heavy industries, China has improved its agricultural products as well. Dazai Commune in Shanxi Province exemplifies this aspect. Originally a large piece of barren land at the base of a rugged mountain area, it has been turned into fertile terraced fields where wheat and corn grow. There is no famine any more. The commune has become a national model for its revolutionary spirit, determination, and collective efforts.[10] Impressed with such a good organization of the new government and the power of collective efforts, Chiang writes the following poem on the evening of the visit:

> Like a long stem where hang many bitter melons,
> With one heart and combined effort, they plough and
>   harrow together!
> The treacherous hills and wicked water are all trans-
>   formed,
> In the yellow soil of Dazai, blossoms everywhere.[11]

As a poet and artist, Chiang is sensitive to the important changes in cultural aspects. He observes that all big stores in Beijing—not just department stores but also bookstores—are crowded with customers in the afternoon. "This told me that the people now had money to spare for some extra food or clothing. They were also interested in reading. What a different attitude and situation now from what I knew of the masses before 1933." Again, Chiang is impressed with the changes in contrast to the past he is familiar with. When he was a county magistrate in the early 1930s, hardly any peasants could read and write. Most of them could not afford to send their children to school for elementary education. At the time, only 20 percent of the 400 million Chinese were literate. But now elementary and often middle school education has become mandatory and popular. Approximately 90 or even 95 percent of the 800 million have had some education.[12] Chiang praises the government policy of sending the educated youths to work in the countryside or factories to broaden and raise the level of knowledge and science.[13] Besides, universities are no longer ivory towers. They run a factory on campus and often send students to work in the countryside; in the meantime, factories and farms also run schools that teach practical subjects to the selected workers and peasants. Higher education has thus "become a useful social and economic means to combine study and production."[14]

At various points in the book, Chiang enthusiastically commends the achievements China has made in regard to cultural development and refutes the accusations some foreign reports have made as inaccurate or distorting. While in Beijing, he visits the Temple of Heaven, which consists of the Hall of Prayer for Good Harvest, the imperial Vault of Heaven, and the Altar of Heaven. After rendering an introduction to its history and description of the architecture, Chiang writes:

> For myself, I think these three structures as a whole form the most beautiful construction I have ever seen in the whole world. I have traveled as widely as I could during the past forty-two years, but have found nothing like the Temple of Heaven anywhere. I admire the present government in Peking for having repaired and restored it to its original grandeur as one of the most strange but beautiful pieces of architecture that was ever designed by man.

> Before I returned to China, rumors that most of the ancient buildings had been destroyed or torn down were widespread in Europe and America. The Temple of Heaven with its ancient beauty should give the lie to all these baseless rumors.[15]

Chiang manifests his pride in China's cultural heritage. He has visited several handicraft factories and art stores in China, where veteran and young craftsmen—both male and female—are working on jade carving, ivory sculpture, pottery, painting reproduction, and embroidery. He points out that, because of the renovation in techniques and design, these traditional crafts have not only been preserved but also have kept pace with the modern age.[16] But most important of all, he has noted that art, which used to be considered mysterious and yond the reach of the ordinary, working-class people, has been mastered by and appreciated by the masses. He cannot conceal his joyful astonishment at the visit to Hu County in Shanxi. Some of the art products by the talented peasant-artists there, he claims, "could be compared with *Women in the Field Working* by the French artist Jean Francois Millet or Vincent van Gogh's *Potato Eaters*."[17]

Changes in political system receive much emphasis in the book, as Chiang emphasizes that social order and peace are prevalent across the nation. On May 1, Chiang is invited to visit Summer Palace, a famous park in Beijing, for the festive Labor Day celebration. Colorful hangings on the trees and platforms can be seen everywhere. There are a variety of activities, such as dancing, orchestras, singing, acrobats, and martial arts, and around forty thousand people participate in the celebration there that day. "Gaiety and merrymaking filled every corner," Chiang writes. "In the past fifty years or so I have never seen so many people assembled and mingling together in such an orderly way without the slightest disturbance anywhere." The lantern festival had been his favorite in childhood, yet the fond memories are inevitably mixed with unpleasant incidents that occurred such as pickpocketing. In comparison, Labor Day celebration at the Summer Palace is an immaculate success. He expresses "his greatest admiration" for those organizers, and he stresses that the social order and peace are indicative of a government that serves its people and takes their interest as its priority.

Chiang's admiration of the new government under the leadership of Mao is evident. His visit to Jinggang Mountain in Jiangxi where Mao established the first revolutionary base in 1927, offers Chiang a key to an understanding of the success of communist government. He perceives that the Mao revolutionaries' solid determination to do good for the people "enables it to eventually overcome every obstacle."[18] Contrary to that, the Chiang Kai-shek government had been negligent of people's welfare, and the officials were only interested in how to "squeeze money from the people for themselves."[19] In 1938, the Nationalist government had ordered bombing of the Yellow River, leaving sixty to seventy thousand civilians consequently drowned and many thousands more homeless. The Nationalist army leaders "showed no remorse for their evil action."[20]

Chiang's return to China seems to have brought some fundamental changes in his long-time apolitical stance. In the late 1920s and early 1930s, he had served under the government before leaving for England. In addition, his elder brother Ta-chuan had been a high government official. Nevertheless, Chiang was never a politician by nature. He did not like to flatter, bribe, or please higher officials in exchange for promotion or personal favor. His experience as county magistrate only led to his disillusionment and disdain toward politics. Having witnessed corruption, bribery, treachery, and power struggle among Nationalist bureaucrats, he had become thoroughly disgusted with politics. He had coined a pen name for himself soon after he left for England: Silent Traveller. The word "traveller" suggests his exile status, and "silent" indicates the pains and suffering he endures in his heart. As he explains, *yaba chi huanglian, youku shuo buchu* (A dumb person tastes the bitter herb—suffering its bitterness in silence). Silence becomes the most powerful nonverbal expression of emotional distress and political disillusionment. Indeed, "only experienced political exiles can understand what I went through," he proclaims in *China Revisited*.[21]

In all his previous books, Chiang has consistently circumvented politics. He would comment on art, calligraphy, literature, legends, social customs, or historical anecdotes, but the subject of politics was always like a minefield carefully avoided. He distanced himself from the Nationalist government and turned down the invitation to serve at the United Nations on behalf of the Chiang Kai-shek government after 1949. Much later, for the same reason, he refused to accept an honorary degree that a Taiwan university planned to grant him. But Chiang had never become a revolutionary communist and never supported the Communist government. In fact, owing to his historical ties to the Nationalist government, he was hesitant and fearful when exploring the possibility of a China visit after 1972. He suspected that he might be executed by the government upon his return to China, and he expressed to a friend his apprehension. The misgiving itself reflects both his fear and a lack of knowledge about the new government in China.

In *The Politics of Home*, Rosemary M. George gives the following definition of home:

> One distinguishing feature of place called home is that they are built on select inclusions. The inclusions are grounded in a learned (or taught) sense of a kinship that is extended to those who are perceived as sharing the same blood, race, class, gender, or religion. Membership is maintained by bond of love, fear, power, desire and control....Home is a place to escape to and a place to escape from. Its importance lies in the fact that it is not equally available to all. Home is the desired place that is fought for and established as the exclusive domain of a few. It is not a neutral place. It is community. Communities are...only extensions of home, providing the same comforts and terrors on a larger scale."[22]

During all the years Chiang sojourned overseas, the motherland occupied a sacred place in his heart. His family, his friends, and his hometown were constantly in the back of his mind. Writing and painting served as a unique way for him to express his emotional longings toward the faraway motherland.[23] In many of his poems and writings, Lu Mountain, a famous mountain located right next to Kiu-kiang (Jiujiang), is often mentioned.

> After my departure, I have revisited Lu Mountain in my dreams,
> As we used to gather in the south of the city.
> There is one thing worthy of boasting in the year that has passed:
> Admiring mountains overseas can never be overindulging.[24]

To the poet, mountains overseas become a surrogate for the Lu Mountain in the homeland. And the act of "admiring mountains overseas" may help lessen his intense nostalgia for artistic activities and friendship in Jiujiang by allowing him to enjoy an imaginary homecoming. His appreciation of the natural scenery overseas thus becomes an indirect way to lessen homesickness. Yet, such imaginary homecoming can offer only tentative promises and is never thoroughly gratifying. In another poem that is included in *The Silent Traveller in Paris* (1956), for example, he writes about a crag in a park in Paris:

> The crag is like another in Eastern lands;
> Its reflection in the water is more beautiful still.
> If another scene is just as lovely,
> Why should I think of Kiu-kiang [Jiujiang]?[25]

The poet seems to have reached a reasonable and satisfying understanding that the scene overseas is at least equally beautiful, a fact that makes homesickness unnecessary; but the last line of the poem, if read closely, actually poses self-questioning, which reflects the equilibrium just established and becomes a perpetual call for reconciliation. In other words, the diasporic poet can never truly feel at home overseas.[26] That is why he was so proud of this line from his 1934 poem: "When spring comes, every dream takes me back to the south of the River [Yangtze]."[27] He had recited this line over and over again during the stay overseas, and he had it carved into a seal, which he frequently applied to his calligraphy and artwork.

Though unable to return to the motherland, Chiang cared about everything that happened there: the Japanese invasion in 1937; China's alliance with the United States and Britain in 1943; the surrender of Japan in 1945; a communist government founded in 1949; the Korean War in 1950; the three-year natural disaster in the early 1960s; the successful test of the nuclear bomb in China in 1964; the beginning of the Cultural Revolution in 1966; and Nixon's visit to China in 1971. Truly, China underwent significant political and economic changes during the four decades, which Chiang monitored and followed closely. During the Second World War, he attended many fundraising activities in England, giving lectures or donating his artwork to support Aid to China efforts and to fight for the sovereignty of his motherland. One of the most exciting events was on January 11, 1943, when the

United States and Britain signed bilateral treaties with the Chinese government for the relinquishment of extraterritorial rights in China. After the news was announced on that day, the Chinese Nationalist flag was raised together with the English, French, Russian, and American flags in London's Piccadilly Circus. Chiang was in Oxford at the time, but he "especially went down to London to walk about near the Chinese flag all morning and afternoon like a young child."[28] To a diasporic Chinese, nothing could be more exhilarating than a strong independent motherland. For a century, China had been invaded and dissected by the foreign powers, and the memory was painfully fresh in Chiang's mind. In the summer of 1914, he accompanied his elderly grandfather for his daily walk. As they strolled to the British and Japanese concession on the bank of the Yangtze River, Grandfather, exhausted, seated himself on a public bench. But a foreign police officer, brandishing a baton, ordered him to get up from his seat immediately. They noticed an elderly foreign lady with a huge dog sitting on an adjacent seat but not being bothered at all. Chiang had been indignant, and the incident left a permanent scar in his memory.[29] Later as county magistrate, he refused to permit American Texaco Oil Company to illegally purchase a piece of land for construction of an oil refinery in the area. He got himself into conflict with the national government and lost his job afterward. It was a steep price he paid for his own moral integrity and national pride.[30]

The diaspora's love toward the motherland often transcends politics, geography, and language barrier. In the early 1970s, with the improvement in the U.S.-China relationship, some renowned Chinese American scientists, engineers, medical doctors, and economists as well as tourists had the opportunity to visit China. *Chinese American Scholars on Their Visits to China* (1974) is a collection of speeches and writings by thirty eminent Chinese American scholars, such as Chen-Ning Yang, Yuen-Ren Chao, Chien-Shiung Wu, Chih-Kung Jen, and so on.[31] Most of them had left China before 1949 when the country was still under the Nationalist government. Even though they held different political affiliations and their political opinions were even opposed to each other, they unanimously expressed their admiration for the unprecedented progress and improvements they had witnessed in China, and they felt unusually proud of all those nationwide accomplishments. Just as in *China Revisited*, exhilaration, amazement, and excitement were the prevailing motifs in their speeches and writings. China, formerly known as the "Sick Man in East Asia," had become a prosperous, independent, and respectable nation in the world arena. "In the motherland there is bright sunlight everywhere. Scenes everywhere were exciting and so memorable," wrote one of them.[32]

Chiang believed that he was best qualified to make an accurate and objective judgment about China. Before he made up his mind to apply for a visa to China in 1975, he read about the reactions of those who had just visited the country. In his collection was a copy of *Chinese American Scholars on Their Visits to China*, and he personally knew many of the contributors to that volume. In late 1974, when Sir Rutherford N. Robertson, a biology professor of the Australian National University, was traveling with his wife in the United States, Chiang arranged a dinner party for them in a New York Chinese restaurant. Robertson had just been back from a "most interesting and very successful" trip to China. While in China, he tried to get in touch with two of Chiang's old friends but failed. Among other guests at their New York dinner were Professor Tsung-Dao Lee (a Nobel Laureate in physics) and his wife, Professor and Mrs. T. C. Yu, Professor Chien-Shiung Wu and her husband, as well as Professor Hans Bielenstein. All the guests had visited China recently, and the conversation, as Robertson recalls, was "largely on our impressions of what had happened there, with favourable comments on the effects of liberation except for the Cultural Revolution and its impeding effects."[33] After his careful observations, Chiang concluded that he was in a better position than anyone else to make a reliable judgment since he was familiar with China, both old and new. According to him, those who had visited China could be divided into three groups: (1) Chinese American intellectuals who were born in China and came to the United States when they were young, (2) American-born Chinese, and (3) European and American intellectuals. He believed that none of these groups had a solid understanding about what China had experienced in the past to merit a good comparison and contrast. Even those in the first group had scarce knowledge in that regard since they left China at a young age and, their being mostly city-dwellers, had little contact with the peasants in China before 1949.[34]

It needs to be emphasized that the socio-political situation in the early 1970s favorably facilitated Chinese Americans' search for a return to China. With the Civil Rights Movement in the 1960s, the change in the immigration law in 1965, President Nixon's historic visit to China in 1972, and reformation of the U.S.-Sino diplomatic relationship, Chiang and other Chinese Americans could speak of their China connection more openly and freely. During the McCarthy Era, when Chiang had just moved to the United States, he had to be very discreet in his talk about China. Even mentioning that he had a family and relatives in China could incur undesirable suspicion and investigation.[35] It was impossible for him to visit China because of the political shift in the Chinese government; nor was he allowed to visit Taiwan after he became a U.S. citizen for his visa application was denied by the Nationalist government. The only place where he could enjoy the "home" atmosphere was his New York apartment. Along the walls were bookcases filled with thread-bound volumes of Chinese classics. On the walls and tables were Chinese painting and calligraphy scrolls. Whenever he came back from teaching at Columbia, he would change into a Chinese robe and enjoy the surrounding Chinese cultural and traditional artifacts. His apartment was like "an enclosed private oasis," providing him with "replenishing sources of cultural nourishment."[36] However, Chiang grew more outspoken in the 1970s. In *Hong Kong Zhuzhi Poems*, published in 1972, for example, he begins with these two poems, which speak of his deep yearning with such heartbreaking poignancy and honesty.

> I have been talking about home returning overseas year after
>   year,
> And the fragrance of the harbor greets me before I reach my
>   home.
> In the distance I can see white clouds, unchanged as before,
> And there underneath those white clouds stands the Chiang
>   Village.
>
> Mr. Jia drove me to Lo Wu,
> At the Wen Jin Dock I cried out loud:
> Having missed China for forty years,
> I wonder if China still remembers the Silent Traveller.[37]

Chiang declares in the book *China Revisited*, "I am neither a propagandist, nor an ideologist."[38] Having confronted all those unprecedented changes in the "strange" motherland, he feels perplexed, excited, and exhilarated. He has witnessed a government that is genuinely dedicated to its people and is capable of organizing the whole society to work for the interest of everyone, regardless of gender, age, and social class. In those changes, he has seen "a sure sign not only that she is revitalizing herself, but also that she will infuse new life into the other nations of the world." His response to those unprecedented changes in China is emotional, sincere, and unguarded.

> Forty-two years ago, most of the Chinese I saw were the most miserable and the most impoverished in the world. After forty-two years have passed, I returned to the motherland to see that everyone had food to eat, had clothes to dress, had a job and medical care, a world entirely different from the old China. How could I not feel touched and emotional?[39]

Nevertheless, there is somewhat a degree of reservation in his joy and pride: "I need to see more of China and to give more proof of these hopeful thoughts and predictions as long as I have life and strength."[40] Clearly, he was not a revolutionary; however, changes in China surely brought revolutionary changes in him.

NOTES

1. Chiang Yee, *The Silent Traveller in Edinburgh* (1948; Edinburgh: Mercat, 2003), xi. Citations are to the Mercat edition.
2. Da Zheng, "*Zhongguo wenhua de guoji shizhe*" [The international diplomat of Chinese culture], in *Meiguo yanjiu* [American Studies] 17, no. 1 (2003): 108–21.
3. Chiang Yee, *China Revisited* (New York: Norton, 1977), 130.
4. Ibid., 131.
5. Ibid., 130.
6. Ibid., 14.
7. Ibid., 162.
8. Ibid., 86.
9. Ibid., 115.
10. Ibid., 95–98.
11. Ibid., 99.
12. Ibid., 165.
13. Ibid.
14. Ibid., 116.
15. Ibid., 85–86.
16. Ibid. 89.
17. Ibid., 77.
18. Ibid., 145.
19. Ibid., 32.
20. Ibid., 101–2.
21. Ibid., 34.
22. Rosemary M. George, *The Politics of Home* (New York: Cambridge University Press, 1996), 9.
23. Several critics have noted this feature. For example, Theodor Adorno states, "For a man who no longer has a homeland, writing becomes a place to live." Rosemary George argues that "the search for the location in which the self is 'at home' is one of the primary projects of the twentieth-century fiction in English." For that reason, she reads "all the fiction in terms of homesickness." See Adorno, *Minima Moralia*, trans. E. F. N. Jephcott (London: NLB, 1974), 87; George, *Politics*, 3.
24. Chiang Yee, *Chiang chungya shi* [Poems by Chiang Yee], (n.p., n.d.), 21.
25. Chiang Yee, *The Silent Traveller in Paris* (New York: Norton, 1956), 80.
26. See Da Zheng, "The Traveling of Art and the Art of Traveling: Chiang Yee's Painting and Chinese Cultural Tradition," *Studies in the Literary Imagination* 37, no. 1 (Spring 2004): 169–90.
27. Chiang, *China Revisited*, 105.
28. Ibid., 43.
29. Chiang Yee, "*Yangren yu gou*" [Foreigners and dogs], in *Haiwai chizi Chiang Yi* [Overseas Chinese Chiang Yee], ed. Jiang Jianlan and Liu Naicong (Jiujiang: n.p., 1992), 9–10. Hereafter cited as *Overseas Chinese*.
30. Chiang, *China Revisited*, 31–32.
31. *Liumei Huayi xuezhe chongfang Zhongguo guangan ji* [Chinese American scholars on their visits to China], 2nd ed. (Hong Kong: The Seventies Journal, 1974). Hereafter cited as *Chinese American Scholars*. Chiang Yee had a copy of the book in his collection.
32. Wang Shengguang, "Harvard Medical Doctor Wang Shengguang," in *Chinese American Scholars*, 316.
33. Rutherford N. Robertson to Chiang Yee, May 1, 1974, in Paul Andrew, "The Silent Traveller: A Study of the Life and Works of Chiang Yee."
34. Chiang, *China Revisited*, 53–54.
35. Ibid., 48–49.
36. Zheng, "The Traveling of Art," 187–88.
37. Chiang Yee, *Yaxingzhe Xianggang zhuzhici* [The Silent Traveler's Hong Kong Zhuzhi Poems], preface by Lo Kang-lit (Hong Kong: privately printed, 1972). There is no pagination in the book, and the two poems are the first two poems. The book is in Chinese and the translation is mine.
38. Chiang, *China Revisited*, 179.
39. Chiang Yee, "*Yaxingzhe fanghua guilai hua jinxi*" [The Silent Traveller on the present and past after visiting China], in *Overseas Chinese* 30.
40. Chiang, *China Revisited*, 180.

Chinese Crossing Borders
A Roundtable Comparing Chinese in Canada and the United States

Imogene Lim, Edgar Wickberg, PhD, and Larry Wong

HENRY YU, PhD, MODERATOR

The panel on Chinese Canadian history focused on differences between Chinese Canadian and Chinese American history. Edgar Wickberg explained the goals of the new (2004) Chinese Canadian Historical Society of British Columbia. CHSA has been a partial model for CCHSBC, but CCHSBC, of necessity, will be different because of its later formation and because Chinese Canadians and Chinese Americans have different trajectories. Larry Wong pointed out that the Canadian government between the 1880s and 1940s limited Chinese immigration by use of both a head tax, paid only by Chinese, and a severe exclusion law. Those policies were finally terminated largely due to the efforts of 600 Chinese Canadians who fought for Canada in World War II. Their numbers, when compared to those of Chinese American veterans of that war, were small; but their achievement was great. Imogene Lim noted the historic cross-border connections of Chinatowns. She also urged a continuing awareness that Chinese Canadian history is not merely a story about Chinatowns in cities. Chinatowns in small towns in British Columbia have a history and sets of experiences that are often very different from those in places like Vancouver. Research on such places is often less about archives and more about archaeology, oral histories, and family genealogies. Henry Yu, as facilitator of the panel, expanded on these observations by drawing on his experiences of teaching Asian American and Asian Canadian history at University of California, Los Angeles, and University of British Columbia. He particularly noted the differing reactions of UBC students when confronted with Los Angeles Chinatown and UCLA students when confronted with Vancouver Chinatown.

The New Chinese Canadian Historical Society of British Columbia

(Original Title: Founding a Chinese Historical Society in Canada:
Challenges and Lessons from the United States)

Edgar Wickberg, PhD

In May 2004, a dozen of us formally established the Chinese Canadian Historical Society of British Columbia. We began accepting members in October and held our founding event in November. That was a two-day workshop on doing Chinese Canadian genealogy and local history. We invited three CHSA members, Him Mark Lai, Marji Lee, and Russell Leong, to come and act as an informal panel discussing how similar organizations have been established in the United States and some related issues. One hundred fifty people attended, and most of them signed on as members of CCHS. Within the space of two months we went from twelve members to two hundred members. Part of that surge was due to the attractiveness of the program—the panel referred to and the genealogical discussions. It was also related to the bargain price of membership, $20, that we had set. But part of it was clearly a definite interest in the subject and the goals we were setting ourselves. In January 2005, we held a Research Fair in which twenty of our members who were doing independent research on aspects of Chinese Canadian history in British Columbia displayed their work. This event was held in a museum on a rainy Saturday. Normally, that museum draws about seventy-five visitors on such days. But on that day about three hundred people went through our fair. The publicity around the fair also drew considerable response, especially callers, to a phone-in radio show. Since then we've sponsored or cosponsored a variety of events, all of them well attended. At our next Annual General Meeting in January 2006, we will find out how well we maintain that initial surge of membership and interest.

A major thrust of our work right now is preparing an application to the government for charitable status, which, once achieved, will allow us to issue tax receipts to donors. We hope to have that in hand by some time in 2006. We are presenting ourselves as essentially a nonprofit public education organization. Our mandate is broad. Fundamentally, it is to bring out the unknown roles of the Chinese in the history of our province. To do this we will work to preserve research materials on Chinese Canadian history and facilitate their availability to researchers and the public, promote research, encourage the teaching of the subject in the schools, and promote public awareness. We hope that we may thereby take a step toward rewriting the history of British Columbia in multicultural terms. Multiculturalism is the official national policy in Canada. But that fact has not resulted, so far, in any multicultural histories of the country or of individual provinces.

As can readily be seen by the references to our province, we are not aiming to be a national organization. We are not the Chinese Canadian Historical Society of Canada; we are the Chinese Canadian Historical Society of British Columbia only. The reason is simple. In Canada organizations of this kind that try to go national immediately almost always fail. In our case the two major centers of Chinese population in Canada are Vancouver and Toronto. The two cities (and their provinces) do not communicate well with each other. We are better off starting small. There is plenty to do in British Columbia. Toronto is free to start its own historical society focused on the Province of Ontario. Some day we and they may bring together these two poles and everything between in Canada, but not now.

I've often been asked questions about CCHS, at international meetings, especially. Why hasn't Canada established something like this before, especially given the American example of thirty or forty years ago? Why are we establishing such an organization now? Is it like the Chinese Historical Society of America? The CHSA has had considerable influence on the thinking of some of us. I have been a member since the 1970s. Others have been aware of CHSA as a possible example for Canada, and today, in some ways, it has become just that. But in the 1970s and 1980s we were not ready to go down that path. There was plenty of history-related activity going on in Canada's Chinatowns but seemingly not in that direction.

To understand this we can try looking at the differing histories of the United States and Canada where ethnic Chinese are concerned. The seemingly similar trajectories of American and Canadian Chinese histories conceal important differences. Granted, both had exclusion laws from the 1880s onward and those Chinese who did get in suffered discrimination. Both revised their Chinese-related policies in the 1940s, and both liberalized immigration rules in the 1960s.

But there the similarities seem to end. First, there were different political environments. This becomes apparent in the 1960s and 1970s. In the United States, the 1960s were a time of demands for radical changes. Ethnic-related movements, based in communities and the universities, were prominent. These included demands for historical rectification. In Canada, radicalism, milder than that in the United States, took other forms. Canada was just emerging to full independence during the 1950s and looking for a new identity. In the early 1970s, the Canadian government preempted any possible demands for radical social change by declaring Canada a multicultural country. It was now government policy that our population of diverse cultural origins should be proud of its various heritages and preserve them. There was to be no assimilation, or even, any longer, the "Anglo Conformity" of the past (the Canadian equivalent of the "melting pot" idea). This initiative seemed to pose the question for everyone: how to make multiculturalism work?

Second, professionals and students who formed the spearhead for CHSA and Asian American Studies were not present in sufficient quantities in Canada to make their voices heard or even to create and sustain the kinds of organizations that appeared in the United States. To understand this we need to look again at the exclusion laws and related legislation and policies. Canada's ways of limiting or excluding Chinese were more complex than those of the United States. Canada had a head tax of $500 from 1903 to 1923, followed by a very strict exclusion law from 1923 to 1947. The result of both of these by the 1960s was that there were fewer Chinese families in Canada and hence smaller cohorts of local-born Chinese in proportion to the population than was the case in the United States, hence, also, a smaller number of professionals in the population and a smaller number of Chinese students in the universities. The broad subject of demographic differences between the Chinese populations of the two countries will need more study. But what I know of it now convinces me that the emergence of significant numbers of second and third generation Chinese was much delayed in Canada compared to what was happening in the United States.

The United States and Canada both liberalized their immigration laws in the 1960s, and a large number of Chinese then began to come in. The result of that now (2005) in Canada is that a quarter of the population of Vancouver is of Chinese background and one-third or more of the students at the University of British Columbia are likewise. But my argument here is that back in the 1960s when CHSA and Asian American Studies appeared in the United States, there was not a critical mass of locally born generations in Canada that would be ready for and could effectively demand such a thing. In Vancouver, the Chinese population was just beginning to expand in the 1960s and really boomed only in the 1980s. In Toronto, the other major center of Chinese settlement today, the Chinese population had been small. A population surge occurred in the 1970s, but these were newcomers with no interest in the history of the Chinese who were already there.

Third, unlike the United States, where Chinese demanding change were part of many parallel groups of like mind,

such as African Americans, Mexican Americans, and others, there were no such groups in Canada. The Chinese were the largest of the so-called "visible minorities." They had no large allied groups.

Fourth, there were the distractions of specific problems with government and within Chinatowns, especially in Vancouver, that occupied the attention and energies of Chinese Canadian activists. In Vancouver Chinatown, people stopped the City's plan for a freeway through the community and altered its urban renewal schemes to become self-help programs. There were other city planning issues that mobilized Chinatown for resistance. There were also broad national issues with local repercussions. Canada recognized the People's Republic of China in the early 1970s, and the Vancouver Chinatown "Left" and moderates took over direction of the Chinese Benevolent Association from its Taiwan-affiliated leadership. Media discrimination was a frequent issue that had to be addressed. And, from the early 1980s, when the Canadian Charter of Rights was instituted and Japanese Canadians began to fight for redress of their relocation outrage, Chinese Canadians took up a similar task, one that is still ongoing.

There were cultural and social activities in both Vancouver and Toronto, ones with historical implications. In Toronto, Tony Chan taught night-school courses on Asian Canadian history and published a book on the Chinese in North America. He also led the way in publishing the *Asianadian* magazine, which lasted for several years in the 1970s and early 1980s.[1] Individual research projects also went on, some of them historical in nature. In Vancouver, the Chinese Cultural Centre was established and for a time involved itself in Chinese Canadian history. The "Pender Guy" group, named after Chinatown's main street, did oral histories of elders, several months of radio programs, and the like. The Asian Canadian Writers Workshop, led by Jim Wong-chu, encouraged a sense of British Columbia Chinese community history and kept the faith for decades before it became a widely admired success at the end of the century. Toronto, by the late 1970s, had the larger Chinese population; but Vancouver had the history behind it and, as it turned out, the environment in which a historical society would emerge.

It is not that there was an absence of historical writing before the 1990s. Besides Tony Chan, the Chinese school principal David T. H. Lee published a very informative history of the Chinese in Canada in Chinese.[2] Peter S. Li produced a sociological study emphasizing systemic anti-Chinese racism in Chinese Canadian history.[3] But it is significant that the only detailed history of the Chinese in Canada in English was published by a mixed group of Chinese community members and non-Chinese academics, under contract to the Canadian government.[4] Many Chinese Canadians had private collections of materials suitable for research, and some informally shared their materials. But there was no systematic assembling and depositing of these in public venues.

In the late 1980s, Chinese Canadian literature began to receive popular attention in British Columbia and especially in Vancouver, where writings by Wayson Choy, S. K. Y. Lee, Denise Chong,[5] and others were widely recognized. So were newly produced histories. Paul Yee published his outstanding history of Vancouver Chinatown, *Saltwater City*,[6] by far the best thing on the subject. Geographer David Chuenyan Lai published *Chinatowns: Towns within Cities in Canada*,[7] and historian Wing Chung Ng's book, *The Chinese of Canada* focused on the period 1945–1980.[8] At the provincial level, the growing public sense of the importance of the now sizeable and often influential Chinese population resulted in the appointment of David Lam as lieutenant governor of the province. He and others moved toward broader, more inclusive social measures and attitudes. In Vancouver in particular, the city was feeling a growing sense of itself as multicultural and of the importance of the Chinese part of its population and their history. Civic institutions "discovered" the Chinese as they became too numerous and visible to be ignored. Chinese Canadians began to appear on the governing boards of universities. It then became possible to consider course work in this area and to formalize some of the relationships between campuses and the now various "Chinese communities." In 2003, Henry Yu began teaching courses on Asian Canadian history in the UBC History Department under a sharing agreement between UBC and UCLA.

In this new environment several people both inside and outside of local Chinese society began to talk about the possibility of a Chinese Canadian historical society. It is not that the subject had never been broached before. It had been, probably as far back as the 1960s and 1970s. But for reasons mentioned above, no such specifically historical society ever reached viability. The Writers Workshop was the nearest thing. But now the time seemed ripe for a historical organization. The group that formed the CCHS organized itself before anyone else did and had specific goals and plans. Reflecting upon the differences between the 1960s and the 2000s, our organizers and board members from the start were both Chinese and non-Chinese individuals.

We thus could build on both the new cultural and institutional environment and also the years of work of dedicated activists in local Chinese society. Building on that we could launch sustained efforts to promote preservation of research materials and public education efforts, and study, teach, and more. We could also, from the perspective of the 2000s, reflect on the experience of CHSA and learn from it.

In the United States, Chinese American Studies in universities is part of Asian American Studies. Is that likely to happen in Canada? As a kind of answer I will pose some questions. Do we intend to follow the American examples on this? There is great strategic value to putting all Asian American issues and studies together, as is well recognized. But in British Columbia, at least, that may be difficult to achieve. Clearly the groups most interested in academic work, and

other projects, are the local ethnic Chinese. That is one of our problems. Will we have an Asian Canadian Studies program in name that is de facto a Chinese Canadian Studies program? That might happen. Can we get support from all the relevant groups (at this point, it's hard to call any of them "communities"): Japanese, Koreans, Filipinos, Indians, and Pakistanis?

Is the term "Asian" viable here? In Vancouver we have the Asian Canadian Writers Workshop and Asian Heritage Month. But otherwise, our thinking tends to be national. That is at least partly a result of our acceptance of official multiculturalism, which encourages us to think in terms of national identity units. These may prove to be artificial and unhelpful. Alejandro Portes, writing about immigration policy in the United States, has commented on the problems of using invented identities such as "Hispanic" or "Asian."[9] In Canada, such terms are used. But when the Institute of Asian Research was developed at UBC it was found that donations of support were usually available only on a nation basis: Korean business, for instance, would donate only for Korean Studies under an Asian Institute umbrella. Even the Japanese, who had provided much of the funding for the Asian Centre Building years before, were reluctant to finance anything other than Japanese Studies. It is no surprise that the Chinese, the largest population group, are interested in a Chinese Canadian Historical Society. But it is unclear how far they would support an institutional umbrella of which Chinese Studies was only one subordinate unit. We also are aware that in Asian American Studies programs in the United States, it often happens that one such group becomes dominant, and the others lag behind. We will face such problems.

But, in another way, our lateness gives us a different kind of advantage. In the United States, Asian American or Chinese American history programs were started in the atmosphere of the 1960s—one in which arguments were about "claiming America" and claiming one's own history. Starting now as we are, we are not claiming Chinese Canadian history as belonging only to Chinese Canadians and a proof of their being here and deserving to be. We can skip that stage. Forty years and a multiculturalism policy later, we can and do appeal not just to local-born Chinese, but to newcomer Chinese and to non-Chinese as well. We actively seek as broadly-based an organization as we can manage. And though we are about the past, the past now includes not only the stories of the local-borns of the pre-1980s but also the pasts of the newer arrivals from everywhere, whose own history in Canada dates only from the 1980s. We may turn out to be, like CHSA, pretty much an organization of people who are locally born. Necessarily the history of the *lo wah kiu* (pre-1980 self-designated local-born Chinese) is what we have to preserve and develop first because the oldest members of this group are slipping away as time passes. But we are not ignoring all the other groups and have begun to reach out to some of them. Our history, as we propose to write it, is not a history of Chinese Canadians in and for itself. It is a history of the Chinese Canadians as part of the histories of the many groups that have made up and make up today the population of British Columbia. We see ourselves as part of the mainstream of history study in this province, contributing to better histories of what has happened here.

We plan, and are trying to maintain, a very active website, one where student research papers and the writings of CCHS members, whether academic or otherwise, can be posted. We do as much as we can electronically. Most news and announcements are done that way. But we do have an in-print occasional newsletter to hand or mail out. We partner with the major local universities (UBC and Simon Fraser), the Vancouver Historical Society, Vancouver Museum, Centre A (an organization that promotes current Asian art in Vancouver), the Vancouver Public Library (VPL), and Historica, which works in the schools. Our members are involved in the VPL's creation of a website devoted to Chinese Canadian genealogy and in a database project of Chinese language historical materials in British Columbia designed by the UBC Asian Library. We are associated with a project to digitize the *Chinese Times (Da Han Gong Bao)* daily newspaper, published in Vancouver from 1914 to 1992.[10] We have recently completed a study of five traditional Chinese associations in Chinatown and their heritage buildings as part of the City of Vancouver's "Chinatown revitalization" program.

Some of our problems are these: We have a large agenda and we want to do everything right away, but we obviously have to work out priorities and sequences of development. We are devoted to both popular history and academic history writing. How are we to balance these? What are the best methods for developing the various areas of interest and commitment that we have? Clearly the experience of CHSA and other American programs will help us deal with these and other issues.

These are some of our current issues and dilemmas and some of our anxieties about them. The feelings of excitement but frustration that we now have must once have been part of CHSA somewhere in its earlier days. I would welcome any comments from long-time CHSA members or others.

NOTES

1. Anthony Chan, *Gold Mountain: The Chinese in the New World* (Vancouver: New Star Books, 1983). A complete set of the *Asianadian* (1978–1985) is available at the UBC Library.
2. Li Donghai [David T. H. Lee], *Jianada Huaqiao shi, A History of Chinese in Canada* (Vancouver: Jianada ziyou chubanshe, 1967).
3. Peter S. Li, *Chinese in Canada*, 1988, 2 ed. (Toronto: Oxford University Press, 1998).
4. Edgar Wickberg, ed., *From China to Canada: A History of the Chinese Communities in Canada*, by Harry Con, Ronald J. Con, Graham Johnson, Edgar Wickberg, and William Willmott (Toronto: McClelland & Stewart Ltd., 1982).
5. Wayson Choy, *The Jade Peony: A Novel* (Vancouver: Douglas & McIntyre, 1995); Sky Lee, *The Disappearing Moon Café* (Vancouver: Douglas & McIntyre, 1990); Denise Chong, *The Concubine's Children: Portrait of a Family Divided* (Toronto: Viking, 1994).
6. *Saltwater City. An Illustrated History of the Chinese in Vancouver* (Vancouver: Douglas & McIntyre, 1988). An updated version is expected to appear in May 2006. Yee's many children's books—some of them prize winners—are now used in Canadian schools.
7. David Chuenyan Lai, *Chinatowns: Towns within Cities in Canada* (Vancouver: UBC Press, 1988).
8. Wing Chung Ng, *The Chinese in Vancouver, 1945-80: The Pursuit of Identity and Power* (Vancouver: UBC Press, 1999). Ng has also contributed the essay on Canada in Lynn Pan, ed., *Encyclopedia of the Chinese Overseas* (Singapore: Chinese Heritage Centre, 1998), 234–237.
9. Alejandro Portes and Ruben Rumbaut, *Immigrant America: A Portrait*, 2 ed. (Berkeley: University of California Press, 1996).
10. *Da Han Gong Bao* (Chinese Times) (Vancouver: Chinese Freemasons, 1907–1992). An almost complete set of extant issues, covering 1914–1970 and 1985–1992, may be found in the UBC Library.

The Canadian Chinese Exclusion Act and the Veterans Who Overcame It

(Original Title: Comparing Chinese Exclusion and the Veterans Who Overcame It)

Larry Wong

The 1923 Immigration Act, often referred to as the Chinese Exclusion Act, was an accumulation of the Canadian government's attempt to frustrate the migration of the Chinese to Canada. Unlike the United States, which imposed the Exclusion Act in 1882, the Canadian government in the year 1885 levied a head tax of $50 for each Chinese entering the country. This policy was initiated by the province of British Columbia where many of the Chinese arrived from China and the United States.

The provincial government of the day was dismayed by the number of Chinese who came for the Fraser River gold rush in 1858 and the Cariboo Gold Rush in 1861 and again during the building of the transcontinental railroad from 1881 to 1885. When the railroad was completed, some 14,000 Chinese found themselves unemployed, much to the consternation of the white population. Most of the Chinese turned to low-paying jobs, for example, working as houseboys, laundrymen, and general laborers, but nonetheless they were perceived as a threat to the general economy, and the provincial government forced Ottawa to take action.

The solution was simple. The federal government was persuaded by the British Columbian government to impose a $50 head tax on each Chinese entering Canada as a means to discourage further migration from China. The Chinese however, much to the chagrin of everyone, kept coming, and in 1901, the tax was increased to $100. Again, the Chinese were able to finance the head tax. In response, the government increased the tax to a whopping $500 in 1903.

The Chinese Exclusion Act came into effect on the first of July, 1923. The Act was the only act in Canadian Parliament aimed specifically at a particular race. In the Chinese communities across Canada, no Chinese joined in the festivities of Dominion Day, no business was open, no Canadian flags were flown. The Chinese called it the Day of Humiliation.

There were exceptions to the Exclusion Act. Chinese students and ministers of the cloth were allowed and, of course, diplomatic staff and Chinese born in Canada. However, the Chinese born in Canada were never considered citizens; they were classified as aliens. The Chinese had been listed on electoral lists as far back as 1867 but lost the right to vote in 1874.

The Chinese communities across Canada were mainly a bachelor society and more so after 1923, being cut off from friends and families in China. The Chinese reacted by a letter-writing campaign to protest the racist act. The protest was ignored.

Chinatowns across Canada became stagnant, and in the 1930s, some Chinese returned to China, including sixty-five mental patients whom the provincial government of British Columbia did not care to look after. In the depression years, unemployment rose; some Chinese lost their homes, and some ultimately, in a despondent state, committed suicide. There were however, some means of getting around the Act, such as the buying and selling of genuine Canadian birth certificates to persons wanting to assume such identity to come to Canada.

By the 1930s, the Sino-Japanese War was uppermost in the minds of the Chinese. Fundraising efforts to help China fight the Japanese came in the form of special performances of local Chinese opera companies, banquets, bazaars, tag days, and campaigns to sell Chinese war bonds.

When the Second World War was declared by Canada in 1939, loyalty to Canada was fiercely debated in Chinatown. One side of the community wanted to fight the war for Canada while others questioned the need to fight for a country that did not want them. They argued that the Chinese were not welcomed in Canada, so why should they fight for a country that discriminated against them, first with the head tax and now the Exclusion Act, to say nothing of the blatant discrimination in everyday life. Even the job opportunities were closed to them; a university-trained person was denied professional memberships, for example, to accounting, law, and pharmacy groups, on the grounds they were not Canadian citizens. But the young men and women wanted to fight for Canada to prove that they were as worthy as anyone else and by doing so, earn the right to citizenship. They were tired of being treated as second-class citizens.

In the early years of the war, the Chinese volunteered their services. Those who wanted to enlist with the navy and air force were in for a shock. Both the navy and the air force's regulations specified that a recruit must be a British subject and of the white race. In British Columbia, racism was acute, and the Chinese were rarely accepted by the recruiting offices. There were exceptions of course. Victor Louie from Vancouver, for example, on his own, went to China to fight the Japanese in the 1930s. He returned to Canada to join the Canadian Army after 1939 and fought again in Japanese-occupied territories.

Besides the soldiers, there were civilians such as nurses, doctors, and pilots who went to China. I can think of two pilots, who were brothers, who were refused by the Royal Canadian Air Force. They went on to become instructors for the British Commonwealth Air Training Plan but were offered jobs with the China National Air Corporation (CNAC), which was half-owned by the Chinese government and Pan American Airways. The two Canadian pilots flew from their base in northern India, over the "hump" of the Himalayas to destinations in China delivering fuel, supplies, weapons, and food.

In contrast, the Chinese in the United States were readily accepted into the armed forces. They were American-born of Chinese immigrants with full rights as compared to their Canadian counterparts. In Canada, some 600 Chinese Canadians served their country while 13,000 Chinese Americans served in the American armed forces. There were enough Chinese American men and women to form full divisions while in the Canadian forces, a single Chinese face was common in a group of Caucasian soldiers.

When the war shifted to Asia, it was recognized that Asians were needed, particularly for undercover work. There was a specially trained unit called Operation Oblivion. A select group of Chinese was chosen for their abilities and skills. The thirteen candidates were recruited by military intelligence from across Canada and met together at a secret base in the Okanogan Valley in British Columbia. The base was remote, at a lake called Goose Bay, far from prying eyes and the nearest town. This was where the Chinese recruits were trained in the art of sabotage using, for example, weapons, unarmed combat, demolition, guerrilla tactics, survival, and wireless communications. They were given Chinese language lessons as most of the Canadian-born spoke little or no Chinese. The group was transported to Australia where they learned parachute jumping before shipping off to India for their final training. They were being trained for a particular operation called Operation Oblivion. It was a dangerous assignment to frustrate the Japanese in Hong Kong, and they were told not to expect to return from their mission. If captured, they would use a cyanide pill. They were to operate in cells of no more than four men. Each cell worked independently, not knowing what the others were doing. This was so that, in the event that they were captured by the enemy, they would not give away valuable information. The mission however, was cancelled at the last minute.

Operation Oblivion was disbanded, but Force 136 was born. It was also known as Special Operations Executive. Like Operation Oblivion, the men worked in cells of four. Four men of the original group found themselves in the head-hunting country of Borneo. The mission of the four Chinese was to seek out the anti-Japanese forces and train them in the art of sabotage. In return, they were shown how to use blow pipes and survive in the jungle. The war ended in August of 1945, but in the jungle, many of the Japanese refused to surrender, let alone admit the defeat of their empire. For the remainder of the calendar year, the four Chinese sought out the Japanese soldiers and eventually persuaded them to repatriate. For their efforts and duty, the four were awarded the highest military medal in the field.

There are other war stories. Frank Wong from Vancouver enlisted in 1942 and took part in the Normandy Invasion at Juno Beach. His unit later moved through Europe and liberated the Netherlands. Richard Mar from Victoria was the only Chinese Canadian to serve in the First Canadian Parachute Battalion and took part in the drop for the Rhine crossing in 1945. Quan Louie enlisted in the RCAF in 1942 and received his bomber aimer's wings. On a mission just short of his thirtieth, his bomber was shot down over Germany. He was twenty-three years old. In 1996, the province of British Columbia proudly named a lake after him. Roy Mah, Harry Con, and Bill Chow were three Chinese sergeants who led the first all-Chinese contingent overseas from England to India, ready to spring into action. After the war, both Roy and Harry were active community leaders in Vancouver's Chinatown. Douglas Sam was rejected by the RCAF but tried again when the new regulations were issued in 1942. He flew in bombers that took part in the raids against Germany. On his final run over France, his bomber was shot down, but he managed to parachute to safety where he was picked up by the French Resistance. He worked with the Resistance and took part in the liberation of Paris. For his services to France, he was awarded the Silver Cross.

Bill Chong was in a unique position. Born in Vancouver, he became a secret agent in China for the intelligence unit of the British Army. He was visiting Hong Kong when he was caught in the Japanese take-over of that city. He volunteered to serve the British Army by gathering intelligence on the Japanese and escorting downed airmen and families from Japanese-occupied China to the relative safety of Macau. One family he helped was the Kwan family who had a five-year-old girl. Bill adopted the girl who eventually moved to Los Angeles with her parents. In 1960, she appeared in a movie called *The World of Suzie Wong*. The girl's name was Nancy Kwan.

In all, some 600 Chinese Canadians fought. Those who did join found something interesting—once in the King's uniform, they were treated as equals outside of Chinatown. The uniform gave them the respect and recognition not possible in Chinatown. In fact, they were allowed to vote because of the uniform. The military regulations were that everyone who wore the uniform had all rights, regardless of their status. During the war, because China was fighting the Japanese, it brought the white Canadians closer to the Chinese communities because of the patriotism being shown.

At war's end, the Chinese veterans and the community leaders continued to press for the rights to vote and citizenship. Finally in 1947, the infamous Exclusion Act was repealed and the franchise restored. The right to vote changed forever the social landscape of Chinatown. Not only were they now Canadian citizens, but professional societies welcomed them, allowing opportunities far beyond their dreams. For example, a young war vet named Douglas Jung, who was one of the original thirteen I spoke of earlier, attended law school and became one of the first Chinese Canadian lawyers. By 1957, he joined a political party and ran for a seat representing Vancouver Centre, which included Chinatown. He was successful in his bid and became the first Chinese Canadian elected to Parliament. Jung was appointed by the government to represent Canada at the United Nations Headquarters. Of his experience there, he was fond of telling the story of sitting at his appointed desk only to have an usher tell him, "I'm sorry, Sir, but this is for the Canadian delegate."

"I *am* the Canadian delegate," he told the embarrassed usher.

That moment in history saw Canada come of age and the Chinese become proud citizens.

Homeland Origins and Political Identities among Chinese Americans

Pei-te Lien, PhD

The Chinese population in the United States consists of persons with multiple origins and diverse histories. In what ways do Chinese Americans of various ancestral homeland origins identify themselves politically in the United States? How does homeland origin explain the ethnic group identity and other political preferences for immigrants and their descendants in the adopted homeland? Through analyses of individual political behavior, this paper seeks to understand the scope and sources of political identities among U.S. residents of Chinese descent whose families originated from the Chinese mainland, Taiwan, Hong Kong, and elsewhere in Asia. After profiling the contemporary Chinese American population with U.S. census and immigration data and brief accounts of its recent trans-Pacific community formation, we discuss the nature and types of identity formation for a heterogeneous, transnational, and nonwhite minority population in the United States. Then, we use a large-scale opinion survey of Chinese Americans in Southern California to examine the direction and sources of ethnic, national, and political ideological identities and their relationship to homeland origins, transnational ties, and adaptation experiences in the United States.

FROM DIFFERENT SHORES: A SOCIODEMOGRAPHIC PROFILE OF CHINESE AMERICANS

According to the U.S. Census Bureau, there were close to 2.9 million Chinese persons in the United States in 2000. Individuals of full Chinese descent accounted for 23.7 percent of the national Asian population. Including the 447,000 Chinese of mixed-race descent, about one in four Asians in the United States could claim to be Chinese. A full seven in ten Chinese were foreign-born in 2000. Among them, only 24 percent arrived before 1980; about a third arrived between 1980 and 1990; and 43 percent arrived after 1990. Between 1971 and 1980, close to 238,000 immigrants arrived from China, Taiwan, and Hong Kong; another 445,000 and 529,000 arrived in the 1980s and 1990s, respectively.[1] The recentness of their immigration directly affected their rates of language use and citizenship acquisition. In 2000, about 85 percent of all U.S. Chinese reported speaking at least some Chinese at home; exactly a third of the U.S. Chinese reported not having acquired U.S. citizenship yet.

The sudden and persistent rise of the Chinese immigrant population after the mid-1960s can be attributed to factors found on both sides of the Pacific. Key actions include the liberalization of the U.S. immigrant policy in 1965, the restructuring and transformation of the Pacific Rim economies after World War II, the fall of Saigon and the exodus of ethnic Chinese from Vietnam, the anxiety over the future of Taiwan after the normalization of U.S.-China relations in 1979, the anxiety over the future of Hong Kong after the Chinese takeover in 1997, and the deterioration of Taiwan's international status and internal social order.[2] Different from the nineteenth-century labor migration, which was dominated by uneducated males from Guangdong, China, many in the post-1965 wave of Chinese migration originally arrived as college-educated students pursuing advanced graduate studies in U.S. institutions. Others arrived as skilled workers or professionals who were able to either bring their own families along or sponsor the entry of their direct and extended family members under the family reunification provision of the 1965 Immigration Act. These immigrants brought with them not only their labor skills and capital but social networks, cultural practices, and lingering political tensions. The close transnational ties of these immigrant parents inevitably affected the ethnic identity and political behavior of the U.S.-born generations.[3]

Because of the divided status of the homeland in Asia for Chinese Americans, three sets of immigration statistics are reported by the U.S. Citizenship and Immigration Service. In fiscal years 1989 to 2003, immigrants born in China represented 70 percent of the nearly one million legally admitted Chinese immigrants to the United States; those born in Taiwan represented 18 percent, and those born in Hong Kong represented 12 percent. Among persons who became legal permanent residents during fiscal year 2003, California was the top state of permanent residence for 28 percent of the China-born, 43 percent of the Hong Kong-born, and 51 percent of the Taiwan-born. New York was the second most popular state of residence for 21 percent of the China-born, 18 percent of the Hong Kong-born, but only 7 percent of the Taiwan-born. Among the China-born, 54 percent were admitted as immediate relatives of U.S. citizens, 25 percent were admitted under family-sponsored preferences, and 18 percent were admitted under employment-based preferences. In contrast, only 15 percent among the Hong Kong-born and 29 percent among the Taiwan-born were admitted as immediate relatives of U.S. citizens. Moreover, about seven in ten of the Hong Kong-born and just over one in three of the Taiwan-born were admitted under family-sponsored preferences. Another indicator of differences among immigrants from the "three Chinas" is their occupation. Whereas about one in four among the Taiwan-born and one in five among the Hong Kong-born held managerial or professional jobs, only one in eight among the China-born was in a similar occupation.

The sharp differences in immigration history, population share, place of settlement, admission classification, and occupation status among the three groups of Chinese immigrants who became permanent residents in 2003 give a snapshot of the current sociodemographic divide within Chinese America. It raises the question of whether it makes sense to lump together these persons of diverse origins and disparate social standings under a single umbrella—a (pan-) ethnic label. A major purpose of this study is to empirically assess the meanings of the term "Chinese Americans" as compared to other self-identities in the contemporary U.S. Chinese population.

STUDYING IDENTITY FORMATION AMONG CHINESE AMERICANS

Although the issue of identity formation is of prime importance to the study of any ethnic group, studies on overseas Chinese identity, including Chinese American identity, have largely remained qualitative and discursive in nature and seldom engage rigorous social science research methods.[4] When social investigations are involved, most focus on the experiences of the U.S.-born generation.[5] Adopting the theory of and research on transnationalism in Asian American studies, we posit that the process of ethnic identity formation for individuals in an immigrant majority community of color may be influenced by forces on both sides of the Pacific, such as U.S. domestic racial and social conditions; U.S. immigration, citizenship, and racial categorization policies; and transnational, homeland-related cultural identities, practices, and politics. Thus, ethnic self-identity labels preferred by individuals of Chinese and other Asian descents may be varied and the negotiated outcome of several competing forces, such as between assimilation and ethnic attachment, or between ethnic specific and panethnic, racialized identification.

That the nature of ethnic identity is fluid and multilayered is observed by anthropologist Franklin Ng (1998) who comments that, like Chinese from elsewhere, migrants and their descents from Taiwan can consider themselves either as Taiwanese American, Chinese American, Asian American,

and American, and the identity choices depend on the situation, the community, and the individuals involved.[6] Another anthropologist Melissa Brown (2004) emphasizes that identity is really a matter of politics, and its formation is based on common social, cultural, economic, and political experiences, which can be "passed down from one generation to the next as oral history, with events that have been especially important or galvanizing handed down in more detail and for more generations."[7] One galvanizing event for many Taiwanese people was the brutal crackdown of the 2/28 Incident in 1947 by the Chinese Nationalists who took control of Taiwan after the retreat of the Japanese colonial power at the end of World War II.[8] Although the Nationalists were able to effectively suppress this political uprising and halt any immediate challenge to its rule, the 2/28 Incident symbolized the mistreatment of the Taiwanese by the Chinese mainlanders.[9]

Despite the fact that nearly all residents in Taiwan can trace their ancestral origin to the Chinese mainland, memories of these Taiwanese grievances proved to be a powerful tool used by supporters of Taiwanese independence—especially those U.S.-based organizations—to forge a separate Taiwanese ethnic identity. The pro-independent sentiment has loomed larger since the early 1990s with the oppositional Democratic Progressive Party's (DPP) successes in eroding and eventually overturning the Nationalist political order in 2000.[10] Similarly, for people from the Chinese mainland, one galvanizing event was the crackdown of the student protesters in Tiananmen Square on June 4, 1989. The 6/4 Incident came after a long series of political suppression used by the Chinese Communists against the ordinary people. It symbolizes the length the Chinese Communist government would go to crack down on any aspiration for freedom and democracy. Understandably, the idea of the Chinese takeover of Hong Kong in 1997 triggered widespread, trans-Pacific concern over the democratic future of Hong Kong and the century-old British territory's continued ability to practice capitalism and freedom of speech.

Focusing on identity formation in the Chinese diaspora, Laurence Ma (2003)[11] echoes the opinion of Aihwa Ong (1999)[12] and confirms the existence of the flexible and strategic, but also the hybrid and transnational nature of cultural and political identity and citizenship among the Chinese overseas, who differ in their relationships with the host populations. Although the Chinese in Hawai'i may be found to get along well with other local ethnic populations,[13] numerous accounts of the historical and contemporary experiences of the Chinese in the U.S. mainland point to a mixed success of integration and the continuing significance of race and ethnicity in identification and treatment.[14] The concept that people of diverse ethnic origins can come together and consider each other as belonging to a common community is called *panethnicity*. Despite their profound interethnic differences in history, identity, culture, and class, Yen Espiritu (1992) argues that peoples of Asian descent in the United

States are capable of showing situational solidarity because of the common experiences of racial lumping and mistreatment and the political needs to fight group-based discrimination and for political representation and empowerment.[15] In her later writings, Espiritu (2003, 2004) notes that panethnic consciousness can be forged not only out of U.S. domestic experiences but of transnational concerns over the impacts of (post-) colonialism, neocolonialism, and imperialism in the Asian homelands.[16]

Although, in the context of Asian American studies, the term "Chinese American" is an ethnic-specific rather than a panethnic expression, it may be considered a panethnic label when compared to other more parochial, place-based labels such as "Taiwanese American" and "Hong Kong American." Here, a similar process that explains the development of pan-Asianness may characterize the formation of pan-Chineseness. Namely, regardless of a person's homeland origin, the "one China" policy officially supported by the United States (and by both the People's Republic of China and—until the late 1990s—the Republic of China) may impose a pan-Chinese identity on all persons of Chinese descent in the United States. This process of panethnicization or racial formation[17] is reinforced by the tendencies of the mainstream media and politicians to treat all U.S. Chinese as one and the same by conflating Chinese government's and Chinese Americans' interests as illegitimate foreign aggression.[18] It may also be forged by a common concern over the welfare of the homeland people and the need for liberalization and democratization in homeland governance.[19] As a result, we hypothesize that the panethnic "Chinese American" label may be adopted by more individuals than the place-specific ones. However, the rate of the adoption may not be evenly distributed across persons of various homeland origins. It may be highest among those migrated directly from China and lowest among those migrated from Taiwan because of the active mobilization by pro-independence Taiwanese American groups for a separate ethnic identity from being Chinese.[20] Support for Taiwanese independence, nevertheless, may be highest among the U.S.-born generations because of the passing on of memories of the 2/28 Incident and the pro-independence groups' broad-based appeals for democracy, human rights, and self-determination—values that are consistent with the American creed.

Thus far, the literature shows that both memories of and transnational ties to the ethnic homeland as well as the adaptation experiences of nonwhite immigrant minorities in the United States can shape the political identities of Chinese Americans. Much of the longstanding debate between assimilation and ethnicity, nevertheless, is currently not a debate over whether immigrants can and want to adapt to the American system and culture but one over whether immigrants get to keep their cultural practices and "old" political loyalties without being suspected as "un-American" in the process.[21] Paul Watanabe (1999) warns that Asian Americans are in a vulnerable position, for their interest in shaping foreign policy toward Asia or lobbying on behalf of the ethnic homeland may backfire because ethnicity is often mistaken for loyalty and their activism may be misunderstood as disloyalty and thus "a conflict of interest."[22] The Chinese American situation is being complicated by the fact that the Chinese mainland is ruled by communism, both Hong Kong and Taiwan are former colonies, and the democratic Taiwan is anxious to establish its own independent state, a stance against the U.S. "one-China" policy.

How does the nationalist orientation expressed as support for an independent Taiwan affect the political identity preferences of Chinese Americans? And how does it compare to the role of the democratic orientation expressed as a concern over the future of Hong Kong under the Communist rule? We hypothesize that an individual's political identity choices may depend on his or her own homeland origin and the associated forms of political transnationalism practiced. Not all transnational ties are equal, however. Motivation behind the concern over the democratic future of Hong Kong may be related to but is not the same as that over the sovereignty status of Taiwan. Moreover, political transnationalism that promotes a parochial and adversarial stance to the prevailing U.S. foreign policy interests, such as support for Taiwanese independence, may facilitate homeland-specific identification but impair the development of and identification with U.S. national identity.

DATA AND METHODS

To answer the research questions and empirically assess the relationship between homeland origins and political identities, we analyze a unique public opinion survey of Chinese in Southern California conducted by the *Los Angeles Times* that took place on the eve of the returning of Hong Kong to Chinese rule and just weeks before the Senate hearings on illegal Chinese campaign contributions. In addition to the survey's fortuitous timing, the research site of Southern California is particularly valuable for the study's purpose because of its large community of immigrants of Chinese descent from diverse homeland origins.

Voting-age Chinese residing in six Southern California counties were interviewed by telephone between May 9 and 27, 1997. A list of Chinese surnames was used to draw the sample from phone directories in the counties of Los Angeles, Orange, San Diego, San Bernardino, Riverside, and Ventura. Of the 773 interviews completed, 45 percent were conducted in English, 29 percent in Mandarin, and 26 percent in Cantonese. The margin of sampling error is plus or minus four percentage points. Only weighted results adjusted to conform to census figures on demographic characteristics such as gender, age, and region are reported. About half of the respondents were female (52 percent) and have college or advanced degree (46 percent). The average age is forty-five and about four in ten are forty-five years in age or older. Two-thirds were married. Sixty percent were employed full-time or part-time or self-employed. Citizenship rate is 72 percent; naturalization rate among the foreign-born is 68 percent. Eighty-six percent were immigrants. The average length of permanent U.S. stay for immigrants is fourteen years.

Among the foreign-born, 204, or 26 percent of the respondents were born in China; 187, or 24 percent, were born in Taiwan; 174, or 23 percent, were born in Hong Kong; and 106, or 14 percent, were born elsewhere (mainly Vietnam). Among the 100 respondents who were U.S.-born, 80 percent belong to the second generation. Because about 14 percent of those born in any of the "three Chinas" did not grow up in their place of birth, an indicator of socialization context is created where respondents born in China and raised in Taiwan have their place of socialization coded as "Taiwan." Likewise, those born in China and raised in Hong Kong have their place of socialization coded as "Hong Kong;" those born in China or Hong Kong or Taiwan but raised in the United States have their place of socialization coded as the "United States." This practice finds 25 percent of the respondents socialized in China, 23 percent in Taiwan, 21 percent in Hong Kong, 20 percent in the United States, and 12 percent in other Asian places. By using place of socialization rather than place of birth as the social marker, this study is able to compare the attitudes and opinion of the U.S.-born or U.S.-raised Chinese to those of their foreign-born and -raised counterparts—a beneficial feature not typically found in most studies on Chinese Americans.

Our basic argument is that homeland origins, as measured by socialization context, matter in political identity preferences. Additionally, the process in making these choices may be influenced by the individual respondent's level and type of transnational political and cultural ties; U.S. social, political, and economic adaptation experiences; and basic sociodemographic background, such as education, age, gender, and extent of exposure to the U.S. society and system. The dependent variables of political identity choices are measured in terms of one's preferences in ethnic self-identity and the adoption of U.S. national identity or citizenship. The key independent variables are transnational ties, which involve political and cultural types. In this study, transnational political ties are the awareness, interest, and concern over ethnic homeland development that may occur among both immigrant and nonimmigrant sectors of the ethnic population and over a sustained period of time. This conceptualization is to tap into the broad concept of political transnationalism that is practiced by the masses, without their actually crossing the national borders, and without governmental or organized group intervention.[23] Two distinct homeland political issues regarding Chinese Americans are investigated: the transition from British to Chinese rule of Hong Kong and the pursuit of Taiwan independence. We gauge respondents' concern over the democratic future of Hong Kong following its transition to the Chinese rule with a five-question index assessing respondents' levels of satisfaction with the Chinese government and its handling of Hong Kong as well as the expected impact on Hong Kong's politics, economy, and press freedom under the Chinese rule.[24] Their opinion on the status of Taiwan is gauged by a single question.[25]

In addition, we assess respondents' extent of transnational cultural ties by their level of contact with the ethnic culture.[26] For measuring the significance of U.S. experiences, we test the effect of three types of indicators: the personal experience of discrimination,[27] the level of political integration as indicated by the respondents' citizenship status and adoption of mainstream political ideology, and the level of economic integration as indicated by the respondents' financial investments in the United States.[28] For measuring the significance of the respondents' socioeconomic background, we examine the role of six items: educational achievement, martial status, age (in raw year), employment status, gender, and the percentage of U.S political life (calculated as "one" if U.S.-born, but as a fraction of one's length of U.S. stay over age, if foreign-born).[29]

In the following pages, we first report the percentage distribution of political identities and transnational concerns over the status of Taiwan by place of socialization (Tables 1a to 1e). Then, we report multivariate results assessing the independent impact of socialization context and other factors on political identities dealing with ethnic identity and U.S. citizenship. Logistic regression results based on maximum likelihood-based estimations (MLE) of the incidence of each of the four types of ethnic identity are reported in Table 2. Foreign-born respondents' likelihood of acquiring U.S. nationality is reported in Table 3.

THE CONTOURS OF CHINESE AMERICAN POLITICAL IDENTITY AND PREFERENCE BY PLACE OF SOCIALIZATION

To what extent do Chinese in Southern California identify themselves as "Chinese Americans"?[30] Table 1a shows that although the term "Chinese American" was mentioned by less than half of all the respondents, it is—as hypothesized—the most popular identity label for respondents of all socialization contexts. The second most common ethnic label among the respondents is "American Chinese" (17 percent), followed by "Taiwanese American" (9 percent) and by "Hong Kong American" (7 percent) and "Chinese" (7 percent). Only 5 percent of the respondents chose the label "American" over the other labels. Persons who are most likely to self-identify as "Chinese American" are those socialized in China (52 percent), the United States (53 percent), and "other" places in Asia (54 percent). Even among those respondents socialized in Taiwan or Hong Kong, the label "Chinese American" is preferred over the homeland-origin labels of "Taiwanese American" and

TABLE 1A. ETHNIC IDENTITY CHOICES AMONG CHINESE IN SOUTHERN CALIFORNIA (PERCENT)

Socialization Place	China	Taiwan	Hong Kong	Other	United States	All
Chinese American	52%	38%	40%	54%	53%	47%
American Chinese	28	9	11	10	24	17
Taiwanese American	-	33	-	1	5	9
Hong Kong American	1	-	29	2	1	7
American	2	2	5	3	7	4
Chinese	11	7	5	12	1	7
Other	-	8	5	12	5	5
Not Sure	6	3	6	6	3	5

Source: Los Angeles Times Poll Study #396: A Survey of Chinese Residents of Southern California.

TABLE 1B. POLITICAL IDEOLOGY AMONG CHINESE IN SOUTHERN CALIFORNIA (PERCENT)

Socialization Place	China	Taiwan	Hong Kong	Other	United States	All
No Attention	3	2	-	1	-	1
Very Liberal	8	5	12	5	8	8
Liberal	19	17	14	22	23	19
Middle	32	28	38	41	30	33
Conservative	14	26	21	13	32	22
Very Conservative	3	5	1	5	5	4
Not Sure	21	16	14	12	2	14

TABLE 1C. U.S. CITIZENSHIP ACQUISITION AMONG CHINESE IN SOUTHERN CALIFORNIA (PERCENT)

Socialization Place	China	Taiwan	Hong Kong	Other	United States	All
Citizen	61	65	74	69	96	72
Expect Citizenship	90	74	84	85	100	83

"Hong Kong American." The label "Taiwanese American" is favored by only one-third of those raised in Taiwan, and the label "Hong Kong American" is favored by less than one-third of those raised in Hong Kong.

Among the Chinese in Southern California, as with average Americans, the most common category of political ideology is "middle-of-the-road," which is favored by one-third of the respondents (Table 1b). A slightly higher percentage of the respondents prefer to identify themselves as politically conservative rather than as liberal, but the percentage of the very liberal is twice as large as that of the very conservative. About one in seven respondents are uncertain of their ideological orientation; the percentage is highest among those born and raised in China (21 percent). Compared to the Chinese socialized elsewhere, those socialized in Taiwan or in the United States are more likely to identify themselves as politically conservative.

Table 1c shows that about seven in ten of all foreign-born respondents are naturalized citizens. Those socialized in the United States have the highest citizenship and expected citizenship rate. Those from Hong Kong have the second highest, and those from China have the lowest citizenship rate. This seems to contradict some past research on the effect of repressive regime over naturalization.[31] However, those socialized in China have a higher expected citizenship rate than any group socialized outside of the United States. This suggests that their lack of citizenship is less about their lack of identity than the ability to satisfy the time-dependent qualification for naturalization.

Respondents generally express very high levels of transnational concerns over the political transition of Hong Kong to Chinese rule through their attention to homeland news (tables not shown). Two-thirds of those who grew up in the United States followed either very closely or somewhat closely the events leading up to the Hong Kong handover. However, this amount of news attention pales compared to the levels exerted by those socialized in Asia, especially those

TABLE 1D. PERCEIVED PERFORMANCE OF THE CHINESE GOVERNMENT IN DEALING WITH HONG KONG AFFAIRS (PERCENT)

Socialization Place	China	Taiwan	Hong Kong	Other	United States	All
Very Satisfied	13	5	8	9	3	7
Satisfied	41	24	28	29	34	32
Unsure	33	27	28	46	30	31
SW/Dissatisfied	11	33	25	12	25	22
Very Dissatisfied	2	12	11	4	8	8

TABLE 1E. PERCEIVED CURRENT AND PROSPECTIVE STATUS OF TAIWAN (PERCENT)

Socialization Place	China	Taiwan	Hong Kong	Other	United States	All
Is part of China today	79	37	62	52	27	52
Should become part of China	2	2	6	1	3	3
Should become independent	1	22	10	8	32	15
Should remain as it is	4	26	16	16	24	17
Not sure	14	13	6	23	15	13

from Hong Kong (92 percent). In terms of the perceived performance of the Chinese government in its ruling over China and its dealing with Hong Kong affairs, those born and raised in China are significantly less likely to express dissatisfaction than those socialized elsewhere (Table 1d). By contrast, those socialized in Taiwan show the highest level of dissatisfaction with the Chinese government. Those socialized in China also express the least amount of pessimism about the impact of the political change on Hong Kong local politics, economy, and press freedom (tables not shown). Importantly, it is those who are socialized in the U.S. context that show a higher or as high a concern over the negative impact of the transition over the politics, economy, and press freedom of Hong Kong than those socialized in Taiwan or Hong Kong.

When asked if Taiwan is currently part of China, Table 1e shows that about half of all the respondents answer positively; the percentage is much larger among respondents socialized in China (79 percent) or Hong Kong (62 percent) than those socialized in Taiwan (37 percent) or the United States (27 percent). Just over one in five of those raised in Taiwan would support the push toward the creation of an independent Taiwan state, ten percentage points lower than the opinion of those Chinese raised in the United States. Overall, 15 percent of all respondents support Taiwanese independence. About one in four of those socialized either in Taiwan or the United States believe that Taiwan should remain the way it is—neither part of nor separate from China. Fewer than one in seven persons in each of the socialization places are uncertain of how the relationship should be. In the multivariate analysis, we measure the degree of support for Taiwan independence by assigning a score of one to those who believe that Taiwan is part of China today, two to those who believe that Taiwan should become part of

China, three to those who are uncertain, four to those who prefer the status quo of de facto independence, and a score of five to those who support the push for political independence.

SOURCES OF POLITICAL IDENTITIES BY HOMELAND SOCIALIZATION CONTEXT AND OTHER FACTORS

To assess the empirical relationship between homeland socialization context and political identity among Chinese Americans, we hypothesize that this relationship may be influenced by the respondents' transnational homeland ties, U.S. adaptation experiences, and sociodemographic background. We measure the effect of homeland socialization by comparing the significance of one's being socialized in China, Taiwan, Hong Kong, or other places in Asia, as opposed to socialization in the U.S. context. Entries in the first two major columns of Table 2 show that, compared to the U.S.-born or raised, those respondents socialized in China or "other" places are more likely to self-identify as "Chinese American." Support for Taiwan independence is negatively associated with the label; so are being ideologically conservative and young in age; on the other hand, possessing U.S. citizenship and spending a greater share of political life in the U.S. context are both positively associated with the label. Among those who self-identify as being "American Chinese," they are more likely to be U.S-born or raised, marginally less supportive of Taiwanese independence, having greater contact with the Chinese language and culture, possessing U.S. citizenship, being ideologically conservative, older in age, and employed. From these results, we learn that identifiers of "Chinese American"

TABLE 2. PREDICTING ETHNIC IDENTITY PREFERENCE AMONG CHINESE AMERICANS

	Chinese American		American Chinese		Taiwanese American		Hong Kong American	
	b.	s.e.	b.	s.e.	b.	s.e.	b.	s.e.
(Intercept)	–1.517	.809	–3.125	1.147	–6.559	1.914	–2.366	1.898
Place of Socialization (ref. = U.S. A.)								
China	1.226**	.433	–.735	.593	–2.458#	1.304	–1.749	1.319
Taiwan	.541	.430	–1.893**	.636	.869	.926	–18.16	3015.7
Hong Kong	.527	.413	–1.581*	.600	–19.63	3059.1	2.324*	1.060
Other	1.194**	.441	–1.703*	.653	–2.273#	1.237	–1.291	1.266
Transnational Ties								
Concern over Hong Kong Transition	–.014	.108	–.120	.145	.239	.237	.006	.258
Support Taiwan Independence	–.172*	.061	–.161#	.087	.587**	.128	.035	.151
Cultural Contact	–.301	.306	.948*	.432	.970	.739	1.873*	.873
U.S. Adaptation Experiences								
Experienced Discrimination	.020	.121	–.055	.166	.469*	.241	–.029	.256
Citizenship	.507*	.227	.731*	.331	.730	.501	–.362	.538
Political Ideology (Conservative)	–.425*	.197	.658*	.255	.343	.394	–.211	.489
Financial Investment	.325#	.191	–.387	.257	–.363	.403	–.400	.437
Sociodemographic Background								
Education	.015	.044	.077	.059	.166	.108	–.018	.103
Married	.003	.198	.201	.273	–.346	.439	–.773#	.422
Age	–.009*	.004	.015**	.005	–.011	.011	–.033*	.013
Employed	–.347#	.184	.553*	.256	–.175	.395	1.070*	.488
Female	.006	.166	–.068	.222	.845*	.358	.543	.391
% U.S. Political Life	1.497*	.586	–.215	.826	–3.075*	1.339	–1.658	1.356
N = 690								
–2 Log Likelihood	902.9		563.6		235.6		204.8	
Model Chi-square	57.9		74.7		198.4		146.7	
% Predi. Correct	62.4		82.2		93.0		93.3	

Source: see Table 1a. Note: The parameters are estimated using logistic regression procedures. Each of the dependent variables is a binary variable. The reference category is R's self-identity as being "Chinese." b = unstandardized logit coefficient; s.e. = standard error. **$p \le .005$ *$p \le .05$, #$p \le .10$.

are very different from those who self-identify as "American Chinese" in terms of place of socialization, attitude toward Taiwanese independence, cultural contact, ideological orientation, age, employment status, and exposure to U.S. life. They do share the attribute of possessing U.S. citizenship.

Entries in the right half of Table 2 show that, whereas being socialized in Taiwan does not make a respondent more likely to self-identify as "Taiwanese American" than those socialized in the U.S. context, the reverse is true among identifiers of "Hong Kong American," where being born or raised in Hong Kong is the strongest predictor of identification. Being supportive of Taiwanese independence is a significant predictor of identification as "Taiwanese American," but this

identification is also positively related to experience of ethnic discrimination, being female, and having a shorter amount of exposure to U.S. politics. Having greater concern over the Hong Kong transition is not significantly associated with the "Hong Kong American" identification. It is the cultural, not the political, ties that may increase a respondent's chance of identification with this particular place-based label. Being young in age and employed are also positively associated with being "Hong Kong American." Neither U.S. citizenship nor political ideology is significantly related to either of the two place-based ethnic labels.

Table 3 shows that, among Chinese immigrants, those originating from Hong Kong may be more likely to adopt the

U.S. nationality than those originating from elsewhere. It also shows that, whereas neither having greater concern over the Hong Kong transition nor having closer contacts with the ethnic culture is significantly associated with the acquisition of U.S. citizenship, those immigrants who are more supportive of Taiwanese independence are uniquely less likely to adopt U.S. nationality. Moreover, while none of the indicators of the adaptation experiences is found to have any significant relationship to the incidence of U.S. nationality among the Chinese, it can be greatly enhanced by one's exposure to U.S. political life, followed by marital status, age, and employment status.

In sum, the multivariate results show that the ethnic identity preference of Chinese in California may be influenced by one's homeland socialization, transnational ties, and U.S. adaptation experiences. Nevertheless, the extent and the direction of the relationship may be conditioned by the specific type of ethnic identity, the specific nature of the transnational ties, and the specific type of the transnational political tie. Everything else being equal, homeland socialization context is significant in predicting ethnic identity

TABLE 3. PREDICTING THE ACQUISITION OF U.S. NATIONALITY AMONG CHINESE IMMIGRANTS

	b.	s.e.
(Constant)	−6.421	1.073
Place of Socialization		
(ref. = Other)		
China	.068	.353
Taiwan	.628	.394
Hong Kong	1.224*	.403
Transnational Ties		
Concern over Hong Kong Transition	.088	.163
Support Taiwan Independence	−.234*	.095
Cultural Contact	.281	.484
U.S. Adaptation Experiences		
Experienced Discrimination	.230	.180
Political Ideology (Conservative)	.499	.308
Financial Investment	.428	.280
Sociodemographic Background		
Education	.001	.060
Married	1.490**	.294
Age	.037**	.007
Employed	.930**	.265
Female	.096	.246
% U.S. Political Life	8.693**	.875

N = 584, −2 Log Likelihood at intercept = 477.0, Model Chi-square = 277.0, Percent predicted correct = 82.6, Pseudo-R-square (Negelkerke) = .517
**p≤.005 *p≤.05, #p≤.10.

choice except for "Taiwanese American" identifiers. None of the ethnic identity preferences is affected by the respondents' transnational concern over the democratic prospect of Hong Kong, but support for Taiwanese independence can be negatively associated with the "Chinese American" identity while positively associated with the "Taiwanese American" identity. Having greater transnational cultural ties are found to increase a respondent's chance of identification as "American Chinese" and "Hong Kong American." Having personally experienced discrimination may impact identification, but only for Taiwanese American identifiers. Possessing U.S. citizenship helps increase identification either as "Chinese American" or "American Chinese," but being a political conservative has the opposite effect. Neither U.S. citizenship nor political ideology has a significant relationship to the two place-based labels. And none of the ethnic identity preferences is affected by personal financial stakes in the United States, educational achievement, or marital status. Among the immigrants, factors that predict ethnic identity preference, with the important exception of sociodemographic variables, appear to be useful in explaining the acquisition of U.S. nationality as well. Thus, socialization context matters, and findings of the differential impact of the two measures of transnational political ties as well as the negative association of the pro-independence sentiment with the acquisition of U.S. nationality are consistent with the hypothesized direction. However, Chinese immigrants' identification with the U.S. national identity is related much more strongly to time-dependent, sociostructural factors than to attitudinal and contextual, socialization factors.

CONCLUSION AND IMPLICATIONS

This study is a preliminary attempt to understand the complicated relationships between homeland origins and political identities among Chinese Americans. Using the experiences of Chinese in Southern California prior to the Chinese takeover of Hong Kong in 1997 as an example, this study finds that homeland origins as measured by socialization contexts and the associated transnational political and cultural ties may be significantly related to ethnic identity and other political preferences at both aggregated and individual levels. As hypothesized, the panethnic "Chinese American" label was adopted by more individuals than the place-specific ones. We also find that respondents who migrated directly from China were the most likely, and those migrated from Taiwan were the least likely, to identify themselves as "Chinese American." In addition, we find that support for Taiwanese independence was highest among the U.S.-born generations. The multivariate results confirm the differential impacts of homeland origins and transnational political concerns. For example, we find that homeland origin has a significant relationship to various ethnic self-identity choices except "Taiwanese American," which can be predicted by attitudes toward Taiwanese independence but also by experience of ethnic discrimination in the United States, being female, and having a shorter proportion of political life in the United States. Transnational concern over the democratic future of Hong Kong, on the other hand, does not have an independent impact on the ethnic self-identity choices or the adoption of U.S. national identity. Moreover, we find that political transnationalism that promotes a parochial and adversarial stance to prevailing U.S. foreign policy interests, such as support for Taiwan independence, may facilitate homeland specific identification but impair the development of and identification with the U.S. national identity.

These empirical findings provide important modification to the theoretical debates over the relationship between immigrant assimilation and transnationalism. Whereas recent analyses of the political participation of Latino and Asian American immigrants seem to support a null or even a complementary relationship,[32] this research finding that being supportive of a transnational nationalistic political cause such as Taiwanese independence may boost the chance of identification as Taiwanese American but eclipse the chance of acquiring U.S. nationality points to a zero-sum relationship for a certain type of transnational political practice. The findings reported here support the admonition issued by scholars of long-distance nationalism[33] that it may be a double-edged sword that may both invigorate political participation and hurt the political incorporation prospects of immigrant communities in the United States. However, the general null findings regarding the more universalistic form of transnationalism concerning the Hong Kong transition suggests the need to unpack the term and avoid over generalization. Much more research is needed to test the observed relationships on other transnational issue areas, immigrant groups, and beyond the Southern Californian region.

Adaptation and Organization

The History and Heritage of the Chinese in the Riverina and Western New South Wales, Australia

(Original Title: Adaptation and Organization: The History and Heritage
of the Chinese in Western New South Wales, Australia)

Barry McGowan, PhD

The most significant study of the rural Chinese in Australia is Cathie May's *Topsawyers: The Chinese in Cairns, 1870 to 1920*, published in 1986. Likewise, the most important American study is Sucheng Chan's *This Bitter Sweet Soil. The Chinese in California Agriculture, 1860-1910*, also published in 1986.[1] In Australia, later studies have included work by Rod Lancashire, Maxine Darnell, and Warwick Frost. Lancashire has written on the Chinese in the vineyards of northeast Victoria, Darnell has discussed the use of indentured Chinese laborers in New South Wales prior to and immediately following the gold rushes, and Frost has provided a critique of past and present studies of Chinese farming in Australia. Frost remarked that the broadest agricultural histories made no mention of any Chinese contribution at all. Australian historian Ian Jack has also commented upon a similar neglect in the area of historical archaeology.[2]

More recently in 2004, Janis Wilton wrote a very well-illustrated and well-researched account of the material culture and archival evidence for the Chinese in regional rural New South Wales, and two compendiums of Chinese-Australian studies were published.[3] The focus of the latter two publications was strongly oriented toward urban and goldfield studies, but some contributions included accounts of Chinese market gardening activities in Australia. A feature of all three publications was the departure by most authors from the now well-trodden paths of victimization, discrimination, and violence on the goldfields toward a more nuanced view of the Chinese in Australia, with an emphasis on agency and participation.[4] A heritage study of the Chinese in central-west New South Wales has a publication date of 2006.

My objective is to discuss the significance of Chinese migration and settlement in the Riverina and western New South Wales (Figures 1 and 2) and to draw comparisons with California and some other regions in Australia. There is an important caveat to the Californian comparison. Chan's work focuses almost exclusively on agricultural workers. The main farming industries in the Riverina and western New South Wales (NSW) at the turn of the nineteenth century were pastoralism (sheep farming) and wheat farming. My discussion focuses on the Chinese involvement in land clearing and in ancillary activities such as market gardening and the heritage and technological significance of the gardens. Large-scale irrigation industries were to become increasingly important in the Riverina in the early twentieth century and beyond, but by then the Chinese population had fallen significantly. The role of the Chinese in these industries is still under review, but it was clearly nowhere as significant as in California. There are now very few descendants of the Chinese left in the region. Many of the towns in which they lived have succumbed to the passage of time and today are not even names on a map. It is in this context that the physical evidence is significant.

STATISTICS

First, the statistical evidence for the Chinese in rural and regional Australia must be reviewed. By the time of Australian Federation in 1901, the Chinese experience in the two most populous colonies/states, Victoria and NSW, was still predominantly rural and regional. In the third largest colony/state, Queensland, it was emphatically so. Statistics on occupations are equally illustrative and emphasize strongly the shift over time from gold mining to rural, pastoral, and other activities. By 1901, the percentage of Chinese in Victoria and NSW who were working in market gardening was far higher than in gold and tin mining.[5] The numbers involved in pastoral work were much smaller by comparison, but this under-enumeration can be attributed partly to the dual occupation status of many Chinese and deficiencies in the Census recordings.

In the Riverina and western NSW, several thousand Chinese men were employed in land clearing (scrub cutting and ringbarking), market gardening, and ancillary activities. The land was used for wheat growing and pastoral activities, in particular, sheep grazing. Some guidance to the number of Chinese people in the Riverina and Western NSW is provided by an 1883 report (subsequently referred to as the Brennan report) on Chinese camps prepared by Martin Brennan, the NSW sub-inspector of police, and Quong Tart, who was at that time NSW's leading Chinese entrepreneur and one of the colony's most respected citizens. Also important is

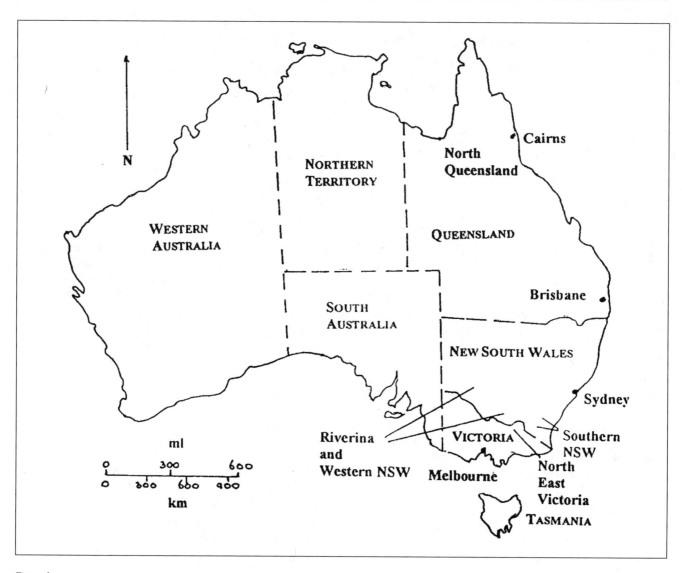

Figure 1

an 1878 NSW Parliamentary paper on Chinese residents in country towns.[6]

In the Brennan report, the Chinese population in the five largest towns (Narrandera, Wagga Wagga, Deniliquin, Hay, and Albury) in the Riverina district was 869, which suggests that the total Chinese population in the Riverina and adjacent districts was well over 1,000. In the 1878 paper, there were a total of 1,100 residents in the Riverina and adjacent districts, of whom 571 were living in the five above-mentioned Riverina towns.[7] If it were assumed that the overall Chinese population increased at about the same rate as that for the five largest Riverina towns, there would have been a Chinese population in the Riverina and adjacent districts of about 1,600 in 1883.

But this is an understatement for the region as a whole, for by the mid to late 1880s, the scrub cutting and ringbarking frontier and the Chinese population moved sharply northwards. The catalyst was a boom in copper mining commencing in the early 1880s, followed by gold mining in the 1890s. Most of these new towns either did not exist at the time of the 1878 report or were excluded from the report. A comparison with the better-known Cairns District in North Queensland is useful. It had a peak population of about 2,550 at the time of Federation in 1901.[8] If the Chinese residents in the Riverina and western NSW towns excluded in the 1878 report were included, the total Chinese population would be comparable. These numbers may appear small by Californian measures, but in Australia they are significant and representative of an important and prolonged pattern of internal migration. In the early 1880s, in some towns, every second man was Chinese. Chan has made a similar point concerning the representation of the Chinese in the Californian town and country labor force.[9]

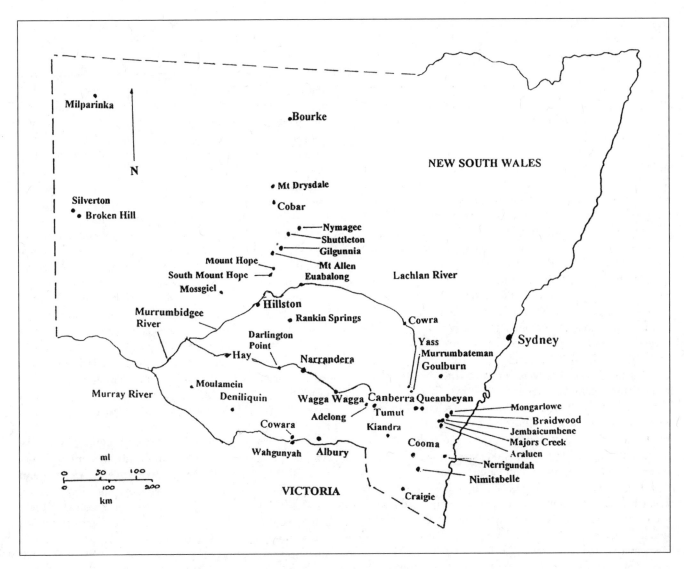

Figure 2

RACE RELATIONS

I turn now to the question of race relations. The most serious incident identified to date is a riot between the Chinese and Europeans in Hillston in 1895, on Chinese New Year's Day. On that day, a number of Europeans visited Chong Lee's market garden. They were well treated at Chong Lee's, but some of the more inebriated went into the garden and began pulling fruit from the trees. No notice was taken of the protestations of the Chinese, and a fight ensued. The Europeans were driven from the gardens, and both parties were joined by more of their compatriots and clashed on the bridge. About thirty Chinese and twenty Europeans were involved in the brawl. One Chinese man was killed and three severely wounded. Ten Europeans were brought to trial, but they were all acquitted of manslaughter. At a subsequent trial, one

European was sentenced to two years imprisonment for starting the brawl, but one other culprit, possibly a "phantom" made up by the other defendants, was never found.[10]

How bad were race relations in Australia, and how do they compare with California?[11] A comparative study by Andrew Markus in 1979 shows that there were important qualitative differences. According to Markus, the Chinese in California were "outside the pale of the law," exploited by the government and mistreated by officials. Discrimination and violence existed in both countries, but in Australia the Chinese had the full protection of the law and could seek redress through the courts, a process facilitated by the British obsession with law and order, and the rapid establishment of goldfield administrations. Where these forces were absent or inadequately provided, serious, but usually not fatal, violence occurred, the two most infamous examples of which were at Lambing Flat in NSW in 1861 and at the Buckland in Victoria in 1857.[12] Another factor working for "better" race relationships in Australia was the absence of the widespread unemployment that afflicted America in the 1870s.[13]

In Australia, there is an absence of the type of organized violence that beset the Chinese agricultural community in California from 1876 to 1879, in 1886, and from 1893 to 1894.[14] The Hillston incident could be seen, therefore, more as a one-off occurrence, unusual for a rural town, and probably one over which the police had little immediate control. The Chinese were also subject to acts of preclusion, particularly where they were seen to be competing directly with European workers, for instance as sheep shearers. Otherwise, most racial incidents identified to date within the region constitute the usual array of taunts, cowardly assaults, and bullying, some of which had serious consequences. For instance, at Wahgunyah (a border town in northeast Victoria) a Chinese man was killed as a result of stone throwing. Two boys were arrested and arraigned on a charge of manslaughter.[15] Most racial incidents were often dealt with in the courts, the magistrates and the press often reminding the townspeople that regardless of what they may think of the Chinese as a race, as individuals they were entitled to the same legal protection and penalties as everyone else.[16]

The topic of Chinese Australian race relations in rural Australia is still in need of much research, but the general picture emerging is one predominantly of tolerance. An important ingredient to that attitude was the favorable view of the Chinese as workers compared to many Europeans, and their economic importance. Observations made by May and Lancashire support this view. May commented that in the Cairns District in North Queensland, the Chinese were noted for their lawfulness and generosity in local causes and were an accepted part of everyday life and individually tolerated. They were not in threatening occupations and served important economic functions in opening up the land and as suppliers of goods, services, and cash flow.[17] Lancashire made similar comments in his study of the Chinese in northeast Victoria, many of whom worked extensively in the local vineyards and in pastoral work in NSW. He attributed this empathy to the close interaction between the Chinese and Europeans, and the value placed upon Chinese participation in the local economy.[18]

LABOR ORGANIZATION

In the Riverina and western NSW, the economic value of the Chinese people is undisputed. A pastoralist in the Nymagee district well north of Hillston commented in 1888 that Europeans were no good at scrubbing and ringbarking:

> They can't do it at the price, and if they take a contract they only do so to get a draw of rations and then clear out and take the tools with them. It's quite different with the Chinese; we only

deal with the head man, and whatever price he accepts the work is always done, even when they can't earn tucker at it, and then they don't get drunk, and kick up rows.[19]

A *Sydney Morning Herald* correspondent stated in 1890 that nearly all the pastoralists to whom he had spoken had the same opinion of the Chinese. It was not so much that they were cheaper, for in many cases the Chinese received the same wages or even more than the Europeans; it was because they were steadier and more reliable. He stated that as cooks and gardeners they were invaluable and produced nearly all the vegetables grown in the bush. They also turned their hand to rabbiting in some cases, and were found ready to do nearly all the rough work on the stations.[20]

Similar observations were made by Lancashire in northeast Victoria. He argued that it was not so much the cheapness of the Chinese labor that was attractive to employers, but their greater reliability. According to one correspondent, the Chinese were regarded as "sober, persevering, industrious and trustworthy," whereas the European was "very apt to go upon a spree or to strike for higher wages at the very moment it is most essential that the operations of the vineyards should be pursued without an hour's intermission." The wages paid to the Chinese were generally lower than those paid to Europeans but not significantly so and could be more a result of expectations by the Chinese laborers rather than oppressive bargaining by the wine producers.[21]

A comparison can be made between California and NSW on the questions of organization and payment of labor. In NSW, the Chinese men were very well organized and equipped for ringbarking. George Gow, a station manager and later a stock agent, wrote a detailed account of these activities. One of the men who helped organize the gangs was Wong Gooey. He would inspect the proposed contract and property and then bargain for terms. Gow stated that the "contracts were sublet to a body of Chinese, who gave Gooey five per cent for organi[z]ing the job. Sometimes he had several jobs going at once, extending into thousands and thousands of acres, and he would move to and fro inspecting them." After making his inspection he would return to Narrandera and discuss the contract with Sam Yett, a Chinese storekeeper and financier, who supplied the rations and took the men to the job. Gow commented that the Chinese were very well provided for and lived "exceedingly well."[22]

The organization and payment of Chinese rural labor in California was very similar to the system applied in NSW. Chan refers to the existence of pseudo labor organizations as a type of employment agency for the recruiting and hiring of Chinese labor for seasonal jobs. The extent to which formal organizations were used is less clear in NSW, although Gammage has stated that the Narrandera Chinese were members of the See Yap Society, which operated as a cooperative and was particularly strong in Victoria. In NSW, as in California, much of the recruitment took place in the local Chinatowns or Chinese camps, although laborers were also recruited from the cities.[23] The similarities in labor organization for Chinese workers in the Australian pastoral industry and the Californian agricultural industry are striking.

Lancashire has commented that there was evidence of "widespread organi[z]ed networking of Chinese into the Riverina from Victoria." Recent evidence supports this conjecture emphatically. Chinese market gardens were established at Deniliquin in the Riverina in 1864. Of note were the comments on gardening techniques including the use of liquid manure. The garden was referred to as "a perfect oasis in the surrounding desert."[24] But the market for this produce was not only local. In April of the following year, a cart loaded with cabbages was sent to the Victorian goldfields, for instance at Bendigo. The local press stated that "the profits on their persevering toil will not be inconsiderable and whatever these may be they are well deserved."[25] There were frequent reports in the Bendigo press of other incidents involving the Chinese at Deniliquin in matters such as court appearances, and there was considerable liaison between the two communities in social matters.[26]

ENVIRONMENT

From both a demographic and an environmental aspect it is important to have some concept of the extent of land clearing. By any measure, the size of the contracts and the environmental impact were enormous. In 1881, a correspondent in the *Sydney Morning Herald* reported that ringbarking of trees upon pastoral leases had increased "to an alarming extent" as there were "perfect armies of Chinamen [sic] going about ringbarking every tree at the rate of 9d per acre." He had a particular aversion to pastoralists who used Chinese labor to ringbark all trees, including the more valuable ones. Throughout the 1880s, newspapers advertised thousands of acres of "ringing and suckering." Almost all of this work was conducted by Chinese labor.[27] In 1888, there were about 200 Chinese cutting and burning scrub on Coan Downs, a property of 240,000 acres (97,100 hectares) north of Hillston, while 60,000 (24,280 hectares) were to be cleared at Yathong, and large contracts had been let on various other runs. Two years later, the manager of Coan Downs remarked that if it had not been for the Chinese laborers the station would never have been cleared. As a consequence, he had ringbarked more land than any other station in the neighborhood, increasing the stock-carrying capacity enormously.[28]

The effect of these activities was to remove an enormous number of trees. On one station the landowner employed Chinese laborers to such good effect that he nearly bankrupted himself with payment of their contracts. However, in the process he increased the carrying capacity of his property by the 1890s from 90,000 to 300,000 sheep.[29] Some observers have attributed the rapid spread of pine scrub to this activity, but more critically, the removal of trees also hastened the loss of topsoil in the dry years.[30] In the drought-stricken years of the mid-1890s and early 1900s, the consequences would have been very severe. This adverse impact differs enormously from the environmental benefits associated with Chinese market gardening, land reclamation, and flood mitigation in California, and can be regarded as a strong negative.

THE MATERIAL EVIDENCE

In some towns, remnants of Chinese camps can be found. More common, however, are the remains of the market gardens. Many of these sites are located in the arid or semi-arid environs of the far west, and illustrate the innovative harnessing by the Chinese gardeners of scarce water resources, their inventiveness in the use of technology, and the adaptation and modification of farm machinery. Of particular note is the integrity of many of these sites. Chan has implied that such evidence is largely absent in California.[31] I question this, but in fairness her remarks were made two decades ago, and possibly in Australia a similar conclusion would have been reached. It is only now that a concerted effort is in progress to ensure that such sites are recorded and where possible, placed on a heritage register. It should be noted that nowhere in Australia is there an example of a Chinese town as remarkable as that of Locke in the Sacramento Delta region.[32]

On Conapaira station near Rankin Springs southwest of Hillston, there is a strong local memory of a large Chinese camp where the Chinese were reputed to have had a fine vegetable garden, the remains of which can be seen today.[33] On the Lachlan River at Euabalong north of Rankin Springs, there were allegedly Chinese market gardens and at least one joss house, which suggests that there must have been a large camp in that area. There was also a Chinese garden at Darlington Point, farther west. It was described as "fearfully and wonderfully irrigated," and a "spectacular success...washed by the Murrumbidgee River, watered by two wells, and traversed throughout by canals."[34]

I now turn to the dry, bordering on arid, landscape, north and west of Hillston. Court records indicate that there was a Chinese camp at Mossgiel, an abandoned town west of Hillston. Between Hillston and Cobar, but not including those two towns, there was a peak population between 1890 and 1910 of at least ten thousand, courtesy of the mining industry. There are today barely two hundred residents. The copper- and gold-mining booms gave rise to new towns such as South Mount Hope, Mount Hope, Nymagee, Mount Allen, Shuttleton, Gilgunnia, Mount Drysdale, and the largest of them all, Cobar. A correspondent for the *Town and Country Journal* in 1888 stated that the population of Nymagee included about 1,200 Europeans and a large number of Chinese, of whom there were between 800 and 1,000 in the district. They had about a dozen bark houses and huts in the eastern part of the town and were engaged primarily in scrub cutting and ringbarking, although they also had several market gardens around the town.[35]

At the former gold-mining town of Gilgunnia, a market garden was established by Charley Chin, who conveyed water to the garden by a water race from the gold battery dam.[36] Remains of his garden can still be seen today and include the water race, an internal dam, parts of a wooden, iron, and wire fence mounted on an embankment, which surrounded the garden, and two live quince trees. A market garden was also located on Bedooba station north of Gilgunnia. Remains include a dam, a fruit tree, household items such as cast iron stoves, and an array of improvised agricultural items one of which is a single blade plough and seeder.

Gardens also existed at Nymagee and at Nimagee station. The former is now the site of a new town dam, but part of the Chinese camp and a few mulberry and quince trees remain. More remarkable still are the gardens on Nimagee station. Water was diverted to the garden from a soakage and overflow area by a wing dam and small race. The remains of the garden are still in existence today and include the embankments, beds, parts of the fences, internal channels, reservoirs or pits, countless mulberry, fig, quince and other fruit trees, and a slab hut.[37]

Further north is the much larger and more resilient mining town of Cobar. Here there were several large Chinese gardens. My information on the Chinese people at Cobar has been gleaned from the reminiscences of several local residents.[38] The main garden was owned by Mah Mong and existed into the 1940, until a fire leveled his large two-story building, which was located in the garden. It is today the site of a housing development and motel. There were upwards of five hundred Chinese in the town (some accounts suggest up to three hundred, which is still significant), almost all of whom worked for Mah Mong, either on the gardens or as contract laborers on pastoral stations.

The siting of the Cobar gardens shows an innovative attention to the harnessing of scarce water resources, for although the fall of land is not large, the storm-water flows were captured from several directions via railway culverts and large eroded gullies on the edge of the roads. During storms, the water and silt were channeled into stone and wooden sluice gates, and then conveyed into two large dams in the gardens. From the dams the water was pumped into a tall water tower, and from there, reticulated into 440-gallon (2,000-liter) ship tanks placed at strategic points around the garden. They were partly sunk in the ground and their tops cut out so that cans could be filled. There was an additional unauthorized water source, for water piped from the town dam conveniently bypassed the council's meter box.

A second garden in Cobar also utilized storm-water flows from the railway culverts. The water was channeled into two large dams and from thence pumped to the gardens and a large tank. Remarkably, part of the gardens, including the two dams, the tank, pipes, and remains of the petrol-powered pump can still be seen today. The use of storm-water flows and accompanying silt depositions is similar to the methods utilized in the more fertile and heavily populated areas of China, as recounted by Franklin King in 1911.[39] A similar practice must have been used in the more arid areas of China as well, though King did not visit them.

Another market garden is located on Mount Drysdale station, about 34 kilometers north of Cobar. The station was the site of important gold-mining activity in the 1890s and 1930s, which gave rise to two towns, Mount Drysdale and West Drysdale. These gardens are largely intact and include wooden, iron, and wire-netting fences, a gateway, a pipe that took water from the base of a large mine dam to a small holding tank sunk in the middle of the garden, irrigation channels, and stockyards. According to the owners of Mount Drysdale, Michael and Shirley Mitchell, several hundred Chinese men were engaged in ringbarking on an adjoining property.[40]

There was a large Chinese camp and several Chinese market gardens at Bourke further north toward the Queensland border. A large garden was located near the weir on the Darling River, and there are indications that water would rise in a similar manner to that described by Franklin King, although in later years a petrol-powered pump was used. Water was channeled into open 200-gallon (900-liter) tanks and taken from the tanks by watering cans on shoulder yokes. The garden was abandoned in the 1920s. There were three other gardens in town, the largest of which covered 6 acres (2.4 hectares) and employed eleven men. Water was obtained by wells and distributed originally by hand; pumps were introduced later. Bourke was one of the few towns in western NSW where there were also European gardeners. There were Chinese employment agencies and contractors in Bourke for gardeners, cooks, and ringbarkers, one local recalling his invitation to a feast by sixteen such workers in about 1910. The ringbarking frontier had obviously spread well north of Cobar by the 1890s and by the turn of the century possibly into Queensland as well.[41]

Market gardens were also located at the mining towns of Broken Hill, Silverton, and Milparinka near the South Australian border. At the former locale, a garden is located on Clevedale station, about 5 kilometers east of the town. The embankments for the garden and some internal galvanized fencing similar to that at Mount Drysdale still remain together with two ship tanks for storing water, a large boiler, and the remains of an elderly motor vehicle. Water was obtained from a nearby well, now the site of a windmill. Gardens were also established in the town, though their location has not yet been established. At Silverton, the precursor to Broken Hill, the Chinese gardeners were among the first business people to arrive in the town and, by May 1884, had commenced work on the establishment of a garden.[42]

Chinese market gardeners also played a very important part in the sustenance of the then typhoid-stricken gold-mining town of Milparinka, located in the arid and remote northwest of NSW. The gardens were situated on the floodplain of Evelyn Creek, which is more often dry than running, and were watered from a well.[43] In 1881, the Warden commented that the improvement in the general health of the inhabitants was "in some degree…attributable to the good supply of vegetables raised by the Chinese gardeners," of whom there were eight employed on two gardens. In the following year, he commented that the gardeners had been very successful in supplying vegetables at reasonable prices. They had grown potatoes and in the following year, they expected to have peaches, pears, and grapes in bearing.[44]

CONCLUSION

The Chinese presence in southern and western NSW was significant, both demographically and economically, and evidence of an important pattern of migration from the goldfields and gold mining to other rural areas and rural occupations. This shift can be seen in terms of a large and sustained migratory movement across the landscape, spanning a period of well over fifty years. Outside the more familiar gold rushes, it constitutes one of the most significant examples of intranational ethnic migration in Australia. Their degree of technological adaptation and innovation in the use of scarce water resources is also significant and is attested to by the large number of market garden sites that remain. In a similar vein, Chan has commented upon the substantial physical presence of the Chinese people in California, and more important, their legacy in the development of Californian agriculture.[45]

Can the Chinese people be regarded as pioneers? In my view the answer is a resounding yes, particularly as the migration extended across colonial and state boundaries. Without this labor force and initiative, the spread of pastoralism would have been much impeded and the health and vitality of many mining and rural towns adversely affected to a serious extent. The Chinese adaptation to and impact on the landscape may be a key issue in arguing for a reinterpretation of the relationship between their experiences and mainstream Australian stories about land and nationality and the place of the Chinese people in the pioneer iconography. At the very least there is a need to reconsider the importance of the Chinese in Australian rural society. Possibly the same is the case in America. The points of comparison and contrast with the American experience are strong in many other respects, such as race relations and material culture, and point the way to an exciting field of research in both countries.

NOTES

1. Sucheng Chan, *This Bitter Sweet Soil: The Chinese in California Agriculture, 1860-1910* (Berkeley and Los Angeles: University of California Press, 1986); Andrew Markus, *Fear and Hatred* (Sydney: Hale & Iremonger, 1979); Cathie May, *Topsawyers: The Chinese in Cairns, 1870 to 1920*, Studies in North Queensland History 6 (Townsville: History Department, James Cook University, 1984).

2. Rod Lancashire, "European-Chinese Economic Interaction: A Pre-Federation Rural Australian Setting," *Rural Society* 10, no. 2 (2000): 229–241; Warwick Frost, "Migrants and Technological Transfer: Chinese Farming in Australia, 1850-1920," *Australian Economic History Review* 42, no. 2, (2002): 113–131; Maxine Darnell, "Master and Servant, Squatter and Shepherd: The Regulation of Indentured Chinese Labourers, New South Wales, 1847-1853," in Henry Chan, Ann Curthoys, and Nora Chiang, *The Overseas Chinese in Australasia: History, Settlement and Interactions* (Canberra and Taipei: Australian National University and National Taiwan University, 2001), 54–68; Ian Jack, "Some Less Familiar Aspects of the Chinese in 19th-century Australia," in *The Overseas Chinese in Australasia*, 44–53.

3. Janis Wilton, *The Chinese in Regional New South Wales, 1850-1950* (Haymarket; New England Regional Art Museum in association with Powerhouse Publishing, 2004); Heather Nicholls, Barbara Hickson, and Barry McGowan, *Tracking the Dragon though the Central West*, Progress Report to New South Wales Heritage Office (Mudgee, NSW, Australia: Barbara Hickson, 2005).

4. *Active Voices: Hidden Histories: The Chinese in Colonial Australia*, special issue, *Journal of Colonial History* 6 (2004); Sophie Couchman, John Fitzgerald, and Paul Macgregor, eds., *After the Rush: Regulation, Participation, and Chinese Communities in Australia, 1860-1940* (Melbourne: Otherland, 2004).

5. C.Y. Choi, *Chinese Migration and Settlement* (Sydney: Sydney University Press, 1975), 30–31.

6. Martin Brennan, "Chinese Camps," New South Wales Legislative Assembly, vol. 2 (Sydney: *Votes and Proceedings*, 1883–1884). The total population of the camps was 942, of whom 800 were Chinese men, 68 were children, and 36 were European women married to Chinese. There was one Chinese woman and 37 European prostitutes. "Chinese (Information Respecting, Resident in the Colony)," New South Wales Legislative Assembly 7 (Sydney: *Votes and Proceedings*, 1878–1879).

7. "Chinese (Information Respecting, Resident in the Colony)," 2–3; Brennan, "Chinese Camps," 6.

8. May, *Topsawyers*, 13–14.

9. G. L. Buxton, *The Riverina 1861-1891* (Melbourne: Melbourne University Press, 1967), 224; Chan, *This Bitter Sweet Soil*, 305, 351–355.

10. *Hillston Spectator*, February 2, 1895; *The Riverine Grazier*, February 5, 8, 19, and April 5, 1895.

11. The topic of European Aboriginal relations in Australia has been discussed and debated intensely for many years and is ongoing. It is the most contested area of history in Australia. For a good account of the current debate, see Stuart Macintyre and Anna Clark, *The History Wars* (Melbourne: Melbourne University Press, 2003). Other large ethnic groups included the Japanese and Malays, most of whom worked in the pearling industry, and Pacific Islanders who worked on sugar plantations in North Queensland. For further insights into late nineteenth-century European-Asian race relations, see Henry Reynolds, *North of Capricorn* (Sydney: Allen and Unwin, 2003).

12. Andrew Markus, *Fear and Hatred* (Sydney: Hale & Iremonger, 1979). Also see David Goodman, *Gold Seeking: Victoria and California in the 1850s* (St. Leonards: Allen and Unwin, 1994).

13. Iris Chang, *The Chinese in America* (New York: Penguin, 2003), 116–129.

14. Chan, *This Bitter Sweet Soil*, 370–396; Markus, *Fear and Hatred*, 50–52.

15. *Argus*, August 18, 1876.

16. *The Riverine Grazier*, June 1, August 13, 1881 and January 18, June 14, 1882; John Merritt, *The Making of the AWU* (Melbourne: Oxford University Press, 1986), 144–149, 176, 186–187, 199–205.

17. May, *Topsawyers*, 143–168.

18. Lancashire, "European-Chinese Economic Interaction," 238.

19. *Town and Country Journal*, May 19, 1888.

20. *Sydney Morning Herald*, December 30, 1890.

21. Lancashire, "European-Chinese Economic Interaction," 232–235.

22. Barellan Progress Association and Improvement Society, *Early Days in Barellan and District* (Barellan: n.p., 1975), 35–40.

23. Lancashire, "European-Chinese Economic Interaction," 237–240; Bill Gammage, *Narrandera Shire* (Narrandera: Australian National University, 1996), 141–145; Chan, *This Bitter Sweet Soil*, 292–350.

24. *Bendigo Advertiser*, November 14, December 20, 1864.

25. *Ibid.*, April 15, 1865.

26. *Ibid.*, February 25, 1891; *Ovens and Murray Advertiser*, June 19, 1897.

27. Buxton, *The Riverina*, 247–248; *The Sydney Morning Herald* in *The Riverine Grazier*, June 11, 1881.

28. *Town and Country Journal*, May 19, 1888; *Sydney Morning Herald*, December 30 1890.

29. Peter Freeman, *The Homestead: A Riverina Anthology* (Melbourne: Oxford University Press, 1982), 150.

30. Buxton, *The Riverina*, 248.

31. Chan, *This Bitter Sweet Soil*, 402.

32. Jeff Gillenkirk and James Motlow, *Bitter Melon: Inside America's Last Rural Chinese Town* (Berkeley: Heyday Books, 1997).

33. No Chinese artifacts have yet been found, although this could be explained by subsequent European occupation and the deposition of topsoil drift.

34. *The Riverine Grazier*, May 4 and June 8, 1881; *The Dusts of Time: Lake Cargelligo and District, 1873-1973*, (n.p., 1973), 54.

35. *Town and Country Journal*, May 19, 1888.

36. Leila Alderdyce, *Gilgunnia: A Special Place* (Young: Leila Alderdyce, 1994), 22, 24–25, 28–29.

37. Dolly Betts, *Our Outback Home: Memories of Nymagee* (Dubbo: Nymagee CWA, 2003), 30.

38. Discussions with Alan Delaney, 2003, and information provided by local residents to Barbara Hickson, 2004 and 2005.

39. Franklin Hiram King, *Farmers of Forty Centuries: Organic Farming in China, Korea and Japan* (New York: Dover Publications, 2004), 173–175.

40. Information provided by Michael and Shirley Mitchell.

41. Information provided by Barbara Hickson; *Western Herald*, April 13, 1973; *Bourke Banner*, March 1, 1899; *History of Bourke*, no. 10, 24.

42. *Adelaide Observer*, May 17, 1884.

43. G. Svenson, "Marginal People: The Archaeology and History of the Chinese at Milparinka," (MA thesis, University of Sydney, 1994), 131.

44. NSW Department of Mines, *Annual Report* (Sydney: NSW Department of Mines, 1882), 98–99; NSW Department of Mines, *Annual Report* (Sydney: NSW Department of Mines, 1883), 115–116.

45. Chan, *This Bitter Sweet Soil*, 403.

Exile between Two Continents

Ettie Chin's War Experience in China (1937–1944)

Jin Feng, PhD

Those who study Chinese American experiences in the early twentieth century often face the challenge of the paucity of written materials produced by ordinary Chinese Americans themselves. Ettie Len-Toy Chin [Hong] (1913–2005) is such a case in point. Having worked as an instructor of physical education in an American-founded missionary college in wartime China from 1937 to 1944, her experience as a second-generation Chinese American living in the old country would have shed light on the construction of Chinese American identity from a unique perspective. However, she left behind very little writing representing either her wartime experience in China or her continued efforts to develop exchange relationships between Chinese and American institutions of higher education after she returned to the United States in 1944. Therefore, the goal of my project is not just to retrieve some lost pieces of an individual life, but also to explore effective ways to examine Chinese American experiences where "authentic" written materials of their own creation are scarce or even nonexistent due to various historical circumstances. By situating the most extensive of the few available written accounts of Chin's experience in wartime China—a letter written by her, dated July 1938—in its particular historical and textual context, I hope to explore the means by which Chin negotiated her way through complex cultural forces and systems of knowledge at a critical moment in both Chinese and Chinese American histories.

Sau-ling Wong has argued that second-generation ethnics have to contend with three cultural systems: "the 'ideal' Old World Values" as presented by their parents, "'real' Old World values" as actually mediated by these same parents, and "'real' New World values as seen from the vantage point of Americans by birth."[1] Chin's experience would add yet another layer to this already complex story. To paraphrase Wong's terminology, she also had to contend with the "real" Old World values as she wrestled with the challenge of living in her parents' native country during the war. Caught in the crossfire of Chinese and American cultural values, such as individualism versus collectivism, or filial obligations versus institutional allegiance, while carrying with her the burden of racial stereotypes, Chin encountered plenty of thorny situations in wartime China. In order to investigate how Chin interacted with the different cultural forces from her particu-

lar locale of wartime China, I will first provide a biographical sketch of Chin, then offer an institutional snapshot of Ginling College, the missionary college where Chin taught during the war years, and last examine her letter in light of both its historical and textual context.

FORMATIVE YEARS IN THE UNITED STATES DURING THE EXCLUSION ERA

From records at the Smith College Archives, we know that Ettie Chin was born in Worcester, Massachusetts, in 1913, and received her bachelor's degree in history from Smith College in 1936 and her master's degree from the University of Michigan in 1937. After her graduation from Michigan, Chin set out to join the Physical Education Department at Ginling College, an all-women's college that had been established by female American missionaries of multiple denominations in Nanjing, China, in 1913, and which later became a sister college to Chin's alma mater, Smith College. By the time she reached China, however, the Japanese occupation had forced Ginling College to leave Nanjing. Chin joined a unit of Ginling students in Shanghai, and in 1938 she accompanied them to Chengdu, Sichuan in West China, which became the site of Ginling-in-exile from 1938 to 1946. Chin worked in the Physical Education Department at Ginling's Chengdu campus until 1944, when she returned to the United States and joined the faculty at Smith. She served as an assistant professor in Smith's Physical Education Department until 1953. Chin was an active member of the Smith Alumnae Committee for Ginling for a number of years after her return to the United States, not the least because her first-hand experience at Smith's sister college made her a valuable and popular spokesperson. In 1953, she married Edward Lim Hong, a restaurateur, and the couple settled in Freeport, Long Island, New York.[2] She passed away in August of 2005.

Furthermore, my oral interviews with Chin's family members also reveal that Chin's parents were first-generation Chinese Americans from Toisaan (Taishan) County, Guangdong Province. They were the first Chinese family to settle in Worcester, though the town had seen single Chinese men whose presence predated their arrival. Her father ran a dry goods store in town and later operated a family laundry and restaurant. We may find it surprising that Chin was able to hold degrees from prestigious institutions of higher education as the daughter of Chinese nationals, especially since at that time Chinese Americans were subjected to discrimination under the Chinese Exclusion Act while her family was eking out a living in a mostly "white" town. But Chin excelled in Worcester's public schools and earned a scholarship to Smith.[3] As the youngest of five children, with four older brothers before her, one suspects that she may have also enjoyed some degree of parental indulgence and sibling doting and was thus able to pursue her dreams of higher education. Although all of Chin's brothers, except for the oldest, received a college education, it is known in her family that it was her youngest older brother, Rockwood Chin, then a Yale student, who encouraged her to attend college by declaring: "No sister of mine is not going to college!"[4] This incident gives us a rare glimpse into the intriguing shift of expectations of Chinese American women's education and career in an immigrant family, when the second-generation ethnic's experience outside of home ushered in fresh ideas and more daring ventures. However, in order to focus more on Chin's experience in wartime China, I will refrain from delving too deep into its significance at this point.

Chin's trip to China was actually a collective family project, since it had originally been instigated by her parents, who had often encouraged their children to visit China, and it was joined in by her two older brothers, Luther and Rockwood Chin. In August 1937, after the recent deaths of their parents, Chin and her two older brothers started out for a country that was up to that point known to them only through their parents' stories. This journey, both filial and patriotic in the historical context of the Sino-Japanese War, heralded the beginning of her complex, though often understated and truncated, self-representation as a Chinese American P.E. instructor at Ginling College in China during the war.

THE GINLING FAMILY

In addition to Chin's experience of having spent her formative years during the time of the Chinese Exclusion Act, Ginling's particular institutional temperament also played an important role in the way that Chin represented herself. Ginling College boasted an institutional history strongly influenced by the vicissitudes of twentieth-century Chinese history. It was founded in 1913 through the united efforts of eight American women's missionary boards—Baptists, North and South; Disciples; Episcopalians; Methodists, North and South; and Presbyterians, North and South—and officially opened its door in Nanjing, China, in 1915, with six faculty and eight students. Ginling's birth can be attributed to a fortuitous combination of various national and international factors, particularly the Student Volunteer Movement and the

Social Gospel Movement in the United States that recruited many female college graduates for the mission field in China, and the Chinese government's more receptive attitude toward "new learning" as a result of its repeated defeat and humiliation suffered at foreign hands. While Ginling's origin already implies that both its Chinese and American constituencies must carry more than their share of cultural and emotional baggage, Ginling also witnessed the many cultural and political convulsions of early twentieth-century China during its lifetime. Before Chin arrived on the scene, Ginling had already experienced two large-scale collective traumas. In 1927, American faculty members had to evacuate Nanjing when the Nationalist Northern Expedition Army recaptured it and engaged in anti-foreign activities such as arson, looting, and shooting, causing considerable chaos and distress within the college community. In 1937, the whole college was yet again dispersed, as they were forced to scatter to different parts of China by the invading Japanese army.

Added to this mixture of tumultuous historical events was also Ginling's dominant ethos. Attempting to maintain Ginling amidst increasing political turmoil and nationalist fervor, the missionary faculty created and propagated the discourse of "the Ginling Family" in order to establish a unified collective identity and group cohesion. That is to say, in order to ward off charges of cultural imperialism from radical Chinese intellectuals, they not only institutionalized a family spirit at Ginling, but also expanded the trope of the family from the institutional to the national level. Through daily interactions with students in and out of classroom and the establishment of institutional rituals such as the Founders' Day celebration, the missionary faculty helped their students to build a collective self-image as both the Christian savior of their people and the pioneer in China's nation-building project and thereby cultivated among their students a unifying sense of *noblesse oblige* toward their nation and people.

What would happen, then, when somebody like Ettie Chin joined Ginling? As a Chinese American born to Chinese parents yet with an American education and perhaps even a completely American mindset, her group affiliation could not be so clearly defined as belonging to either the group of Caucasian missionaries or that of the native Chinese faculty and students, as either the benevolent benefactor and transmitter of Western civilization or its Chinese beneficiary. This in-between position often proved more a liability than an advantage for Chin at Ginling despite, or, precisely because of its family rhetoric. This we can see most clearly by juxtaposing Chin's letter with the materials generated by her colleagues at Ginling.

THE LEGENDARY LONG TREK

As I have mentioned, one of the few available written accounts of Chin's war experience in China is a letter written by her. It records part of the legendary long trek from Shanghai to Ginling's home in exile in Chengdu, Sichuan, undertaken by a group of fifteen women: five Ginling faculty (two of them foreign missionaries), eight Ginling students, and two students from other institutions. The group left Shanghai on July 14, arrived in Hankou, Hubei Province, on July 30, and stayed there until August 8 or so, when they took a riverboat to sail for Chongqing, Sichuan Province, and, finally, a bus from Chongqing to Chengdu, to the campus of Ginling-in-exile in mid-August. Their long trek covered between 2,500 and 2,600 miles, utilized every means of transportation, and took more than two months to complete. It later became a permanent part of the institutional lore at Ginling both because of its unprecedented length and because of the grave war situation that added a heady mixture of danger, excitement, and heroism to this legend.

Florence Kirk, a Canadian missionary who was a member of Ginling's English Department, took up the role of the official recorder of this journey by keeping fairly detailed diary entries between July 12 and August 1, 1938. In comparison, Chin's letter, the only other surviving account of the long trek, spans only three days, from July 27 to August 2, 1938. She wrote this letter to Ginling's Board of Control in New York on the train from Jiulong to Hankou, and described the activities of the group as they trekked across war-torn China from the coast of Hong Kong to unoccupied interior China. Although the letter itself sheds some light on Chin's wartime experience in China, it nevertheless only provides a slice of a rich and complex period of her life. In what follows I will first analyze Chin's own letter in some detail and then examine it in conjunction with letters, diary entries, and reports produced by Chin's Chinese and American colleagues at wartime Ginling College.

Chin's letter started on July 27, 1938, typed by her own hand while the train her group rode on was stranded by a Japanese air raid. They were then only a day from Changsha, Hunan Province. The letter first backtracked the group's activities, mentioning the starting point of the long trek, when they left Shanghai on the *Empress of Japan* on July 13, and arrived in Hong Kong on July 15. They stayed in Hong Kong from July 15 to 25, until they were finally able to board a train from Jiulong to Hankou after quite a few false starts and a last-minute scramble. When Chin started this letter, the group had been riding on the train for two days, and had suffered unrelenting heat, soot, air raids, and general uncertainty. Interestingly enough, however, in Chin's letter we can scarcely notice any signs of her own apprehension about physical hardship and danger or other psychological strains brought on by the war.

Chin told her reader first about their delightful trip from Shanghai to Hong Kong. Although Kirk worried that the bright moon under which they set sail would invite Japanese bombing,[5] Chin only enthused over such facts as

> The steward was very good to us and the girls had special privileges and a special morning breakfast. The Captain was perfectly

grand to us and we visited the navigation bridge and had a bit of education on navigation. The trip from Shanghai was short and comfortable. Some of the Ginling alumnae were at the boat to greet us.[6]

This tone of optimism is also typical of her account of their uncomfortable and dangerous trip on the train from Jiulong to Hankou. They had to cook their own food, constantly cover their mouths and noses with pieces of wet cloth to keep out the soot, sleep in the hallway of the train when temperature in their compartments rose to over 100° F, and take refuge in rice paddies and rustic houses when air raids were on. Chin's former students who also undertook the journey recalled sleeping next to a pigsty in the farmhouse and some cases of lice infestation among them.[7] Nevertheless, Chin chose to focus on the positive aspects of the trip only. She stated: "the train was most comfortable, I think, and we all slept fairly well with the exception of the one night when we stopped in Yuchow [Yuezhou], because of Japanese air-raid," and "Our trip up on the whole was a safe one without much alarm along the way with the exception of one time when there was an air raid warning." She was light-hearted enough to note that the food situation was satisfactory:

> We spent fifteen dollars and we got some grand noodles which tasted exceptionally good especially when we cooked them ourselves on the train. I had brought a pot pan with me and we had the ingredients to make it delicious. Then there was a continuous fire on the platform where our water for drinking was boiled for us and we could use the fire for cooking.

Chin also found the company of her colleagues and students congenial: "One of the most wonderful things about this whole group was the way they accepted what had happened and kept a cheerful face and optimistic outlook upon everything even in the face of disaster and suffering." At the end of the trek, she even claimed to have found the key psychological element that would sustain the Chinese people through the war: "I think this [optimism and forbearance] must be the attitude of nearly all the people in China during the present."

In praising China's beautiful scenery and Chinese people's heroic forbearance during the war, Chin's observations very much resembled those uttered by her more experienced missionary colleagues who had worked at Ginling much longer than she had. For instance, her British colleague Eva Spicer, who also went on the trek, mentioned "heat and beauty" when asked about her impression of the trip. Florence Kirk voiced similar enthusiasm about the "greatness" of China: "What a wonderful piece of luck that I am here to see these lovely provinces of China! They strengthened my consciousness of the greatness of China's resources, both human and material."[8] Those foreign faculty members at Ginling who did not take the long trek also echoed each other in their admiration of Chinese people's capacity for suffering during the war. As Catherine Sutherland, a member of the Music Department, remarked, "The tolerance of the crowd under such circumstances always amazes me, and is just another sample of the quiet submissiveness wrought out of long experience that has helped this wonderful race to persist thru all these long years."[9]

However, although Chin resembled her missionary colleagues in providing a fairly superficial and romanticized commentary on the China situation from the perspective of an alien observer, she differed from them in her insistence on finding common grounds between her American and Chinese heritages:

> Many times I thought that the trip along the embankments with mountains towering high above and a large stream of water flowing just below were like the trips I have taken in America. One time especially I was reminded of my trip to Yellowstone. China is indeed beautiful and there is more beauty than we can imagine.

Undoubtedly Chin was genuinely inspired by what she saw on this trip and sought to assimilate her new experience by comparing it to what had been more familiar to her up to that point in her life: her experience in the United States. Yet considering the constant signs of war-induced ravages and life-threatening danger, how should we interpret her overly bright narrative tone?

Of course, we must consider Chin's age and experience in 1938. Not yet twenty-five and never out of school before she went to China, she may have found her war experience a source of stimulation and excitement as well as that of danger. Moreover, she was a P.E. instructor accustomed to an active lifestyle. Her youth and health must have made it easier for her to endure physical discomfort than it was for her more sedentary and older colleagues. Indeed, Kirk noted in her report that Chin even insisted on taking photos when they were taking shelter from a Japanese air raid in the rice fields. One of her former students also recalled that Chin taught them how to sing "Old Father Time" while the group was sailing by the treacherous terrain of the Three Gorges of the Yangzi River.[10] But, other than these factors, the audience of her letter played a more important role in determining her narrative tone.

Chin was by no means insensitive to the dangers and hardships caused by the war despite her age, experience, and personality. In fact, she described them to her friends back in the United States in far franker terms than what she had adopted in the letter around the same time. For instance, she found Wuchang, the destination of their train ride, "desolate," and noted the fact that although it was midnight when they arrived, they "made haste to cross over to Hankow [Hankou] by the last ferry, for in the morning there was no telling but that the station might be bombed. Already many attempts had been made on it."[11] In contrast, since she was writing a letter to the U.S. sponsors of Ginling College, she assumed an optimistic tone in order to impress upon her American correspondent the indomitable will of the group in general and her own strength of character in particular. In fact, at the beginning of the war it was common practice among the Ginling faculty and students, whether they were Chinese or foreign, to write to their U.S. correspondents across the ocean in just such a heroic and optimistic tone.

For example, in the critical year of 1937 when Ginling College was first dispersed, Ginling's Chinese president, Wu Yifang, sent a telegraph on October 29 to the groups in Changsha and Wuchang in anticipation of the annual Founders' Day celebration: "Our national struggle challenges Ginling family to actively seek and sacrificially share the Abundant Life. Romans 8:35, 37." On October 30, obviously considering the first telegram insufficient to express her vision, she sent another telegraph to the Shanghai and Hong Kong groups: "May the Ginling family be worthy of the Founders' and College ideals by humbly strengthening ourselves and sacrificially sharing in the national crisis. Romans 8:35, 37—Alma Mater." The Wuchang group sent back to her a telegraph on October 31—"Dispersed but not dispirited. Through one faith, one hope, still one. Long life to Alma Mater"—while students and faculty from everywhere wrote letters and reports to talk about the various Founders' Day celebrations they had carried out in various locations. In response, Ginling's U.S. sponsors took due notice of the optimism and heroism typical of the written materials sent to them from China. As an article published by the Ginling office in New York declared, "The sense of unity in work and ideals which the war has brought has become very important to Ginling morale....Founders' Day has become one of the symbols of unity of spirit, and each year is celebrated by Ginling women wherever they are."[12]

For a physically disembodied Ginling, the sense of solidarity must be maintained in its members not only through the reenactment of rituals and ceremonies that they had once shared in more peaceful times, but, more importantly, through the construction of narratives that could signify to distant correspondents their shared memberships in both the Ginling family and their national family. Fortunately for the Chinese students and faculty, in the early years of the war their identities as "daughters of Ginling" and citizens of China meshed well with each other, for the dangers and hardships they had endured as Chinese citizens also heightened their hope for a reunited Ginling family, a haunting dream that they thought only a peaceful and unified China could turn into reality. As such, the abundant descriptions of hardships proclaiming the narrators' unremitting loyalty to Ginling in the years 1937 to 1940 also facilitated their efforts to swear their allegiance to their native or adopted country.

However, while the Chinese and American constituencies at Ginling sought to both demonstrate their morale and group cohesion to the U.S. side and to contain the hardships and dangers they had to endure everyday through the very act of narrating and sharing such experiences, Chin's letter differed from their accounts in that she completely erased any unpleasant and life-threatening situations, though she was not averse to sharing those with her friends in the United

States. Seen in this light, Chin's bright narrative tone and her strategy to focus on the little delightful details of the trip while overlooking the general grave picture functioned as a way for her to claim membership in a group of people to whom she was a relative newcomer and a junior member. On the other hand, it also pointed out the significant differences between her colleagues and herself in the way they perceived of and coped with the war, thus foreshadowing her experience among them as a second-generation Chinese American who would always be subjected to implicit stereotypes.

LIFE AT GINLING-IN-EXILE: THE UNTOLD STORY AND UNSUNG HEROINE

Similar to Chin's letter discussed above, her intentionally rosy representation of her experience as a P.E. instructor on Ginling's Chengdu campus during the war also reveals her wish to be included in the charmed circle of the Ginling family that was, nevertheless, not always as welcoming as she had hoped for or described to her American audiences later. This can be seen most clearly in the business correspondence between Wu Yifang, the Chinese president of Ginling College, and Ginling's New York office.

Wu belonged to the first class of five students who graduated from Ginling in 1919 and were the first Chinese women to have received a fully accredited bachelor's degree in China. She later went to the University of Michigan for graduate study and received her doctorate degree in entomology in 1928. In the same year, Wu was invited to return to Ginling as its first Chinese president. Although an American-educated Chinese woman, Wu seemed to harbor some suspicions about the work ethic of Chinese Americans. In her letter to the Ginling New York office dated February 7, 1945, she stated: "From our experience with American-born Chinese on the faculty, we have found that if the woman has a Christian background or affiliation, we can at least be sure of certain fundamental conceptions toward life. Otherwise there is the chance that the American-born Chinese may have lost the Chinese culture and, at the same time, may not yet have gotten enough from the West to have a worthwhile working principle of living."[13] Although Wu did not specifically cite Chin as a negative example in her letter, she had not been very satisfied with her work either, for in the same letter she asked for a Chinese candidate for the P.E. Department, explaining: "I should tell you, very confidentially, that Ettie will do better as a teaching member of the faculty than carrying the administrative duties of running a department. Furthermore, there is bound to be contact with the outside, such as the education authorities and physical education schools in the country, and that work Ettie is not able to take up at all." Wu considered Chin a less effective faculty member than her Chinese colleagues at Ginling ostensibly because of Chin's insufficient administrative and publicity skills.

Chin's alleged lack of PR skills was probably inevitable since she spoke little Mandarin and her working experience was limited to her short stint at Ginling, at a time of war emergency and in a remote locale in China as different from her East Coast educational and family background as it could be. But justly or not, Wu also found Chin's sense of family obligation an anathema to the kind of whole-hearted devotion to Ginling that she had expected of all faculty members. In 1944, Chin's continued employment at Ginling arose as an issue because: "[She] has family debt to help pay off, so has to know the salary offered by Smith. If not accepting, she may remain or try to find work with the American army" (April 29, 1944). We do not know the details of this alleged family debt that had caused Chin to rethink her appointment at Ginling. Yet, rather than acknowledging the historically lower salary scale of faculty members at Ginling as compared to faculty members of other missionary colleges in China, though she had done so on another occasion (April 23, 1945, 5), Wu expressed more irritation than understanding in this letter. To be sure, Wu refrained from making harsh judgments on such "self-centered" behavior, prevaricating with remarks such as: "[Chin] is a fine person and as she sees the need for her [at Ginling], she has changed somewhat her former definite decision....Personal problems are always difficult, and when there were recent frictions it becomes more so...." Nevertheless, Wu looked on Chin's defection as another nuisance added to Ginling administration's already chaotic scramble for qualified faculty members in wartime Sichuan, if not as an utter betrayal to Ginling's family spirit. In another letter discussing personnel issues with Ginling's New York office, Wu forthrightly admitted: "I have been greatly disturbed by the condition of self-seeking cliques among the faculties of the big universities and I am very thankful that my college is small and I am not troubled by such delicate questions. Then all the more I have to be very careful in the qualifications of new people we are seeking to invite" (April 29, 1944, 3). Seen in hindsight, it was unreasonable of Wu to demand exclusive loyalty of Ginling's faculty members at a time when they had to wrestle with more challenges than ever in order to support their own families because of the raging war and rocketing inflation.[14] Nor should she have passed judgment on the ethical and cultural makeup of Chinese Americans as a group or on Chin as an individual. However, we can see that Chin occupied a rather precarious position at Ginling as far as her relationship with the college administration was concerned.

While the Chinese president of Ginling questioned Chin's "Chineseness," Chin was meanwhile seen as "Chinese" and treated as a junior faculty member who should defer to her seniors by her Western missionary colleagues. Although neither Kirk's nor Chin's account of the long trek to Sichuan highlighted the fact, Chin was assigned, together with three Chinese faculty members of Ginling, to take care of the Chinese students, eating and sleeping at first in third-class passage on the ship and then in a second-class compartment on the train, while her more senior Western colleagues, Florence Kirk and Eva Spicer, partook of better accommodations on both occasions. Moreover, although a bona fide instructor and paid according to the salary scale of that rank,[15] at Ginling, Chin was expected to pick up all the practice sessions that her Chinese colleagues were not able to teach. As Wu explained to the New York office in a letter dated April 29, 1944: "With P.E., we would also like to have some young person to give the practical courses, because our own graduates get married and are able to give only the theory courses when babies come along to interfere." Chin's teaching duties resembled those of several recent Ginling graduates who stayed on to teach phyiscal education at a reduced salary as "Teaching Assistant" (zhujiao), to the extent that even those students close to her sometimes misunderstood her rank.[16] Chin not only gave students P.E. classes, she also taught foreign faculty members how to play badminton.[17] This sport later caught on in Chengdu since the primitive conditions for P.E. instruction in inland China and the increasing difficulty in securing import supplies caused the replacement of tennis by badminton as the college-sanctioned sport. Moreover, Chin refereed volleyball games, organized indoor and outdoor sports meets and field days, initiated a cheer-leading group,[18] as well as taught Physical Education, though she was not able to do what was dearest to her heart: to teach fencing. She had been on the Smith fencing team as an undergraduate and even received a Smith blazer as recognition of her achievements in that sport.[19] However, Ginling's refugee years in Sichuan did not allow luxuries such as fencing. Unfortunately, Chin could not augment Ginling's traditional strength in dance instruction, considered by the college administration both as an acceptable genteel exercise for their female students and a good showpiece for publicity materials because every performance always drew large crowds of Chinese audience. It can be seen that while she worked hard at Ginling, Chin was unable to make full use of her own talent and passion in P.E. instruction.

Instead, in Chengdu, Chin taught a much simplified version of Physical Education together with her colleagues, which included track and field, volleyball, basketball, gymnastics, softball, Chinese boxing, rhythm, group games, archery, tap dance, recreational sports, and advanced dance. Rather than possessing the kind of facilities available at Ginling's Nanjing campus, which had aroused the envy of all and sundry, now they had to make do with a one-floor small gym of simple design: one 40' x 25' room, with rooms at the side for an office, reading room, storeroom, and two dressing rooms, one for faculty and one for students. For equipment, they tried to train local workmen to supply their needs. For example, in archery they modified the Chinese bows and arrows according to their teaching needs. As imported articles became more and more difficult to secure, they had all their basketballs, volleyballs, baseballs, and other equipment locally made.[20] These kinds of conditions must have been a far cry from what Chin had been used to at Smith or Michigan. It was a tribute to Chin's commitment to both Ginling and China that she stayed on and worked with the students for more than six years, almost to the end of Ginling's exile in Sichuan. Chin contributed to the overall achievements of the P.E. Department at Ginling-in-exile, including their impressive achievements at joint sports meets where they claimed the majority of championships from their peer competitors at other missionary or state colleges. As a young instructor with an outgoing personality, she was also well liked by her Chinese students, who were drawn by her youth, energy, and less formal way of interaction, and some even found in her a unique combination of Chinese courtesies and American openness.[21] However, she did not receive her fair share of accolades. As I have mentioned earlier, she was dismissed as a junior faculty member with a questionable racial background by the administration and only caught their attention when her departure could give rise to staffing problems, while among her colleagues she was more the work horse than their peer or leader.

While Chin was surreptitiously belittled by her colleagues at Ginling College in China, despite its pervasive family rhetoric and the overall happy and harmonious surface, her identity in the United States was equally suspect during that period. The Chinese Exclusion Act of 1882 disqualified foreign-born Chinese immigrants in the United States for naturalization and forbade Chinese laborers to enter the United States. With the eruption of World War II, especially the incident of Pearl Harbor on December 7, 1941, Chinese Americans suddenly became the "good Orientals" while Japanese Americans were rounded up for internment camps. Chinese Americans were allowed to participate in the U.S. war effort as they joined the army and the navy, and worked side by side with American workers to build ships, planes, and other weapons. In 1943, the Exclusion Act was finally repealed when it became an embarrassment to the U.S. government, who declared to its ally, the Nationalist Chinese government, that the discriminatory bill that had lasted more than eighty years was a "historic mistake." We do not know what Chin thought of the Repeal. But she was able to return to Smith as a faculty member in 1944, when previously Chinese Americans were subjected to racial discrimination in employment, as few of them had been able to find employment in their specific fields of training.

But more importantly, Chin made other attempts at self-signification in addition to the letter that I have discussed, despite the adverse circumstances facing her both in China and in the United States. For her Smith audiences, she transformed her experience of marginalization at Ginling into a positive self-portrait both as a valued P.E. instructor and an intimate friend to the missionary faculty at wartime Ginling. To be sure, Chin established congenial social relationships with her colleagues, for she recalled being consulted by her

American colleagues on issues of fashion while in Chengdu, since all of them had been cut off from the United States and women's fashions for quite a few years by the war. But she was more likely far lower on the social hierarchy rather than the "Acting Head" of the department that she had represented herself to be to her audiences at Smith.[22] Such efforts of self-signification were not necessarily motivated by desires of self-aggrandizement, either, for she took upon herself the responsibility of speaking for China and the Chinese people during the war.

Not only did Chin woo her Smith audiences with her speeches about her war experience in China, but she also virtually became the spokesperson of Chinese patriotism and China's ultimate victory in the war in the local Worcester newspaper, *Worcester Telegram and the Evening Gazette*. In an article dated September 23, 1939, which cited her letters extensively, she predicted China's "great resources" and "the ability of the people to adjust and adapt themselves to new environment" to be the definitive elements that would lead to a Chinese victory against Japanese invasion. She shared with her readers her impressions of Chinese patriotism: "Everywhere little children of all classes up to the older folks sing with fervor their patriotic songs which are beautiful to hear." She particularly rhapsodized about the young people of China while urging her American audience to pay attention:

> The youth of China today is worthy of notice. They are strong and sturdy and plying themselves to study and at the same time, giving service. These years have burned into them a greater sense of responsibility, of new and practical ideals—of building themselves up for the growth of a new China and resistance to Japanese aggression.

Most significantly, Chin assumed the role of the bridge between Chinese and American cultures and people when she claimed: "The Chinese people are very much like Americans. We have a good sense of humor, are hard working people, and get along well with others. We try to make the American soldiers feel at home [in Sichuan, China]."[23] As we can see, in one brilliant discursive move, Chin simultaneously conjured up the image of the overseas U.S. soldiers fighting side by side with the Chinese people, an emotionally charged picture that must have resonated strongly with American readers; spoke for the "hardworking" Chinese people who had "a good sense of humor"; and, most importantly albeit subtly, claimed her membership among both the Chinese and American people, now that she had established meeting grounds between the two groups by invoking both their shared war effort and the cultural values allegedly dear to both.

Chin's attempts at integrating her Chinese and American heritages, thus forming a coherent and meaningful identity for herself in the particular milieu of post-World War II United States, cast a poignant light on her experience both in China and in the United States. Ironically, it was precisely because many of her values and ways of dealing with situations seemed more American than Chinese to her colleagues at Ginling that created problems, since her colleagues, fairly or not, held certain expectations of her way of thinking and behaving because of her Chinese racial heritage. Meanwhile, although her appearance in the local media may have made her a celebrity in Worcester, Chin could not, and should not, be expected to surmount the deeply ingrained and widespread racism in the United States at the time.

From the discussion above, we can see that Ettie Chin's experience in China and the United States between 1938 and 1944 reveals her awkward position of being caught between two cultures and two nations, neither of which she could lay full claim to and neither of which would accept her as its full-fledged member. Chin's war experience shows that for American-born Chinese Americans, their parents' moral instruction based on their fond memories of the Old World could not forestall the second-generation's marginalization in China, while in their adopted new country, the avowed values of freedom and equality did not always ring true for them, either. Seen in this light, Chin's attempts at self-representation, whether through words or deeds, illustrate her attempts at self-signification despite the overwhelming odds against them.

Chin's experience also illustrates that in order to engage more effectively with the few written records produced by Chinese Americans themselves, we as researchers should not only bring in varied types of data including written and oral records produced by both Chinese Americans and others, but also "read against the grain" by examining their mutual interactions in their particular historical and cultural context. As Lisa Lowe has argued, writings by Chinese Americans prove to be "an aesthetic product that cannot repress the material inequalities of its conditions of production; its aesthetic is defined not by sublimation but rather by contradiction."[24] My case study of Ettie Chin reveals that historicization and contextualization can expose the irreconcilable contradictions both within her self-representation and between the accounts produced by herself and by the others, thus dismantling the image of a homogenized nationalist subject as required by the discourse of cultural assimilation circulated in both the old and the new country. Ultimately, in challenging the master narratives of nationalist subject formation in China and the United States, Chin's wartime experience also highlights for Chinese Americans the space of self-empowerment at the margins of two cultures.

NOTES

1. Sau-ling Wong, "Immigrant Autobiography: Some Questions of Definition and Approach," in *Women, Autobiography, Theory: A Reader*, ed. Sidonie Smith and Julia Watson (Madison: University of Wisconsin Press, 1998), 302.
2. *http://www.library.yale.edu/div/colleges/Smith/bios/Chin_Ettie. html*.

3. Rockwell Chin, "Biographical Notes for Ettie Chin Hong's Funeral," August 2005.

4. Rockwell Chin, oral interview with author.

5. All quotations of Florence Kirk can be found in her report of the long trek, Smith College Archives, Box 1338.

6. All following quotations from Chin's letter can be found at *http://www.library.yale.edu/div/colleges/Smith/bios/EC_3.html.*

7. Loretta Pan, oral interview with author.

8. Kirk, "Report of the Long Trek," 14.

9. Typed letters, December 26, 1937, Smith Archives, Box 1338.

10. Loretta Pan, "A Tribute to Ettie Chin on Her 85th Birthday," May 3, 1998, 2.

11. *Worcester Telegram and the Evening Gazette,* September 23, 1939.

12. "Ginling College in China," *Newsletter 1938-1939,* Yale Divinity Library Archives, Group 11, Box 158.

13. All letters by Yifang Wu cited in this paper can be found at the Yale Divinity School Library Archives, Group 11, Box 149.

14. For example, Chin's description of buying a pair of shoes for $10, 000, in *Worcester Telegram and the Evening Gazette,* April 8, 1945.

15. Salary report for 1937–1938, Yale Divinity School Library Archives, Group 11, Box 148.

16. Yizhen Chen Wang, oral interview with author.

17. Florence Kirk, typed report of Shanghai Unit, March 27, 1938, Smith College Archives, Box 1338.

18. Yizhen Chen Wang, oral interview with author.

19. Newspaper clippings, Smith Archives, Box 697.1.

20. Chen En-tsi, "A Report of the Physical Education Department Since 1937 and the Outbreak of the Sino-Japanese War," typed excerpts, Yale Divinity School Library Archives, Group 11, Box 159.

21. Loretta Pan, Mingzhang Lu Liao, and Yizhen Chen Wang, oral interviews with author.

22. *http://www.library.yale.edu/div/colleges/Smith/bios/Chin_Ettie.html.*

23. "Former City Girl Writes of Experiences in China: Miss Ettie Chin, Smith Graduate, Relates Adventures as Teacher," *Worcester Telegram and the Evening Gazette,* September 23, 1939.

24. Lisa Lowe, "Canon, Institutionalization, Identity: Contradictions for Asian American Studies," in *The Ethic Canon: Histories, Institutions, and Interventions,* ed. David Palumbo-Liu (Minneapolis: University of Minnesota Press, 1995), 54.

Youth Empowerment:
Employing Opportunities

Polly Kam Yan Fung, David Lin, Anna Liu, and Jeffrey Ng

MICHELLE C WU, MODERATOR

INTRODUCTION

CYC (formerly Chinatown Youth Center): MYEEP (Mayor's Youth Employment and Education Program) presented a panel of Youth Peer Leaders for "Branching Out the Banyan Tree," the 2005 Chinese American Studies Conference cohosted by the Chinese Historical Society of America and San Francisco State University's Asian American Studies Department. These youth discussed the history and impact of San Francisco's largest after-school employment program through the MYEEP Collaborative. CYC, serving the Chinese community since 1970, is one of twelve agencies in the collaborative. The youth reviewed the history of the program as well as the structure of positive youth development. While sharing the personal story of one of their own, the Peer Leaders examine growth and community building of youth in search of skills, and belonging in immigrant America. This paper will look at the impact and structure of MYEEP as well as reviewing one youth's journey through CYC's youth development practice.

CYC was incorporated in 1970 as a private, nonprofit agency. Its founders were concerned about the manner in which problems associated with Chinatown were affecting the area's Asian youth. Since its inception, the agency rapidly gained a reputation for working with Chinatown's at-risk youth and their families. CYC has expanded from its San Francisco Chinatown roots and has extended our services to include an employment office in the Richmond district and an outreach office in Visitacion Valley. Our culturally appropriate programs target youth ages ten to twenty-five in areas of education, delinquency prevention and intervention, employment, and leadership development. Today, CYC continues to respond to the complex challenges faced by its clients on issues such as family conflict over acculturation, difficulties in school, economic hardships, and gang membership through its many programs. CYC envisions empowering youth to reach their highest potential as individuals and to develop a positive self/cultural identity. Our mission is to strengthen and empower high-need Asian youth and their families by providing comprehensive youth development through education, employment training, advocacy, and other supportive services. Today, CYC serves over two thousand youth yearly; MYEEP is one of CYC's fifteen programs.

HISTORY AND BACKGROUND
(JEFFREY NG)

MYEEP provides job opportunities to high school youth. It envisions a society of confident, self-directed, responsible, and independent youth who engage in productive activities, play an important role, make positive contributions to the larger community, and achieve personal happiness. MYEEP has a long history of evolution since 1970. Before understanding the impact of the program, one must look at its humble and laborious journey to appreciate this program as it stands today.

In 1970, federal funding was available for youth employment services through the Comprehensive Employment and Training Act (CETA). Federal funding was originally provided for the after-school youth employment program and later extended to include a summer youth employment program. Community organizations that work with youth competed for this funding. The competition occurred twice a year; agencies could either work for the after-school employment or the summer employment program. Many agencies from MYEEP today were the ones that competed for and provided the youth employment services back then.

In 1983, federal funding was cut drastically; CETA was replaced by the Federal Job Training Partnership (JTPA). The after-school youth employment program was cut; funding was only available to cover the summer employment program. This led to the intense lobbying of the city by advocates who supported youth employment services. In response, Mayor Diane Feinstein funded the program temporarily with local revenues. As a result, the after-school employment program was back in gear. Unfortunately, in 1985, Proposition 13[1] made it difficult for California to raise revenues. Once again, the after-school employment program was cut.

During his 1988 campaign, Mayor Art Agnos rallied for the support of youth employment services. With the help of youth services in the city, he fulfilled his promise by establishing the

Mayor's Office of Children, Youth, and Families (MOCYF). In 1989, MOCYF established and managed the Mayor's In School Youth Program (MISYP) that reinstated school youth employment services. At this time, city commissioners and youth advocates agreed that two million dollars should be made available to MISYP programming to be used to fund the community organizations that had previously worked with the after-school youth employment. One of their ideas was to divide the money equally among various agencies, so that they could serve the same number of youth throughout the city. There were eleven agencies that worked with the after-school youth employment program; one of the agencies worked with disabled youth.

The eleven agencies that provided for programming as part of MISYP included Bernal Heights Neighborhood Center, Community Educational Services, CYC, Horizons Unlimited, I.T. Bookman Community Center, Jewish Vocational Services, Morrisania-West Inc., Potrero Hill Neighborhood House, Vietnamese Youth Development Center, Visitacion Valley Community Center, and Young Community Developers. MOCYF decided that it was not their role to directly manage the service; therefore, they awarded the contract to be administered by Japanese Community Youth Council (JCYC). Under JCYC, the program was renamed MYEEP. The MYEEP Collaborative was designed so that each area of the city had one agency that could work with the program. The collaborative expanded from eleven to twelve agencies.

In 1991, Proposition J became effective.[2] The Children's Fund was created, and the Department of Children, Youth, and Families (DCYF) was established. It increased funding to MYEEP, so each neighborhood agency also expanded employment slots.

MYEEP continued to grow over the years. Back then, MYEEP had no formal ties to youth education and/or development; it only focused on job training and providing income to youth. As the MYEEP Collaborative developed through the years, it included two main goals. The first one is to develop job skills, provide work experience, and increase career awareness and future employability. The second is to increase knowledge of educational opportunities and community issues.

MYEEP also received state funding to operate the School-to-Center Program that partnered with four public schools and added work-readiness components to the academic curriculum. College tours to college campuses, later known as University Day, were added to the program in 1994. As a result, youth were introduced to the college campus and preparation before they graduated from high school. That same year, San Francisco Day was added to the program. Youth tour and participate in work activities at businesses throughout the city. They get to pick which career they want to learn more about, and then they go observe what the career is like.

In 1995, federal funding was cut again. MYEEP worked with the Board of Supervisors, the Chamber of Commerce, and Mayor Willie Brown to raise funding for the summer employment program. The Coordinator in Training (CIT) youth leadership program was established in 1995 and was later renamed Counselor in Training.

MYEEP was honored as an exemplary program by the Promising and Effective Practices Network (PEPNet) of the National Youth Employment Council. PEPNet uses nationally accepted criteria to identify effective programs and to expand the knowledge base of what works for youth. MYEEP continued to be honored by PEPNet with the award in 2003.

In 2000, Proposition J was reaffirmed, and the Children's Fund continued to give funding to MYEEP. In 2002, the Leadership in Training (LIT) program was created; it helped youth to develop their leadership skills. The Menagerie of Reflection, Growth and kNowledge (MORGAN) workbook was also added to the program. This workbook lets the youth and worksite supervisors express their thoughts and experience by writing; it eases communication efforts and provides a bridge for both the youth and the workers.

Between 1970 and 1990, federal funding was available for the Summer Youth Employment and Training Program. This meant that in some districts in the city, different organizations provided summer youth employment services, rather than MYEEP. Federal funding for the summer youth employment program started to diminish, causing hundreds of youth to picket City Hall to make the government aware of the need for a summer youth employment program.

In 2001, the summer youth employment program was transferred to MYEEP, which gave MYEEP a year-round youth employment program in each area of the city. The agencies that work for MYEEP continue to be stable over the years. MYEEP currently provides jobs for over one thousand youth every year.

STRUCTURE OF MYEEP (ANNA LIU)

MYEEP is structured to provide youth with experience and training to develop their employment skills and career awareness. It fosters the building of self-esteem and facilitates the reduction of delinquency. Youth participate in job-seeking workshops, which focus on interviewing skills, resume writing, job search techniques, job application procedures, and computer skills training. Job development, readiness, training, and placement are the primary objectives of CYC's employment programs. The goal of the program is to support the development of youth in San Francisco by engaging them in employment, career, leadership, and community involvement opportunities.

MYEEP serves low-income youth aged in every geographic neighborhood in San Francisco. Program recruitment and selection target youth whose ability to access employment opportunities may be limited as a result of disability, limited English proficiency, juvenile probation, teen parenthood, or other factors. Most program participants have no previous work experience. In order to qualify, youth must be a resident of San Francisco County, fourteen to nineteen years old, up to twenty-one if enrolled in and attending a high school or GED program. In addition, participants must be attending middle school, high school, or a GED program, and legally eligible to work in California.

Every MYEEP participant is placed in a subsidized after-school job at a nonprofit or public agency under the supervision of a volunteer worksite supervisor. This work experience provides participants with the opportunity to develop work skills in a real work environment. Each participant also attends mandatory training, which includes a pre-employment period and ongoing workshops. These program elements are supplemented by other program activities, including community service, career portfolio development, career and educational exposure events, nonsubsidized job placement services, and youth leadership development. Community service is a program-wide effort and is an integral part of the MYEEP experience. Each youth participates in at least one community service event during their participation in the program.

After completing a year of the program, youth have the opportunity to be a CIT, which stands for "counselor-in-training." Participants of this program assist the MYEEP program coordinators at their agency by facilitating workshops and organizing activities.

Work placements are based on each youth's interest assessment, education, and career goals. Second-year participants will not be placed in the same worksite unless the coordinator can demonstrate learning opportunity exists there. Participants work ten hours per week during the school year and twenty hours per week during the summer. Participants spend approximately 80 percent of their time at the worksite.

Supervisors are more than just supervisors. Worksite supervisors become one of the primary adults with whom the young people form a relationship during the program. They provide participants with training, career exposure, and adult role modeling. To help build this adult-youth relationship, MYEEP ensures that the adult-to-youth ratio at the worksite is no more than one to three and that supervisors work with the young people one on one.

Believing that education is an important piece of the process that leads to adult success, many of the MYEEP program services focus on the development of educational awareness and success. The academic progress of each participant is monitored twice yearly by the agency coordinator. Youth who are identified as being academically at-risk attend MYEEP tutorial sessions. MYEEP field trips and workshops expose youth to their training and college options after high school and guide them in setting short- and long-term educational goals. For example, University Day allows youth to visit local colleges and universities; this provides youth with an opportunity to explore a college campus, visit college classes, and make plans for college admission and financial aid. MYEEP partners with academic counseling programs to help youth review their current graduation status and make plans for college admission.

As mentioned earlier, MYEEP has a youth development program known as the Counselor-in-Training Program. CITs work with each other and the MYEEP Coordinator at each individual agency, such as CYC, with the administration of the program. They create and facilitate learning experiences that matter and are a fun part of in a teenager's life. They also manage participant files and monitor partnerships between youth participants and their worksites. The CITs at CYC for this year are Polly Fung, David Lin, Anna Liu, and Jeffrey Ng. We help our coordinators run MYEEP at CYC.

As CITs, we work with fellow CITs from around the city to maintain relationships with community agencies throughout San Francisco. During the summer all the CITs in the MYEEP program go to a retreat at the U.C. Santa Cruz campus. There we meet all the other CITs from the entire city. Over forty CITs help run a program serving over 1,200 youth a year. We learn how to work as a team through the games we play and activities we have. For example, we play human knot where about ten of us hold each other's hands and made a huge knot. Our task is to untangle ourselves. It may sound simple, but it really isn't. We have to go under and over each other, trying to unknot ourselves without letting go of each other's hands. This activity helps facilitate the teamwork and communication skills needed to untangle ourselves. We receive training in workshop facilitation, conflict mediation, group management, and teambuilding activities.

As CITs, we also facilitate workshops, plan various activities, and provide input and perspective as MYEEP makes program changes. Participants are required to attend mandatory workshops. Youth will attend pre-employment workshops, run by their CITs, before being placed at a worksite. In the pre-employment workshop, participants will learn what is expected of them, the worksite rules and responsibilities, what to do if they get sexually harassed, how the payroll and timesheet system works, and the history of MYEEP and CYC. During the school year, participants will attend workshops once a week—no youth is paid for work during scheduled workshops. Workshops include topics like planning for college, developing teamwork, preparing for future careers, and developing better communication skills.

We receive training from our project coordinator (PC). In other words, they are like our CITs. They conduct workshops like we conduct workshops for our participants. When we are in Santa Cruz for five days, we have workshops every day covering topics like facilitation skills and feedback, communication skills, workshop planning, and conflict resolution. Like our participants, we also have weekly workshops at JCYC, which is the main MYEEP agency from which we receive training. For example, when we have a communication workshop, we learn that there are different styles of communicating and learning. It's helpful to know that there are different learning styles because some people learn visually, physically, or by hearing. When we run a workshop for our participants, we include all these styles to make sure everyone will understand and absorb the information.

We also attend and support city-wide and agency-specific MYEEP events. When we went to Santa Cruz, we didn't pay a single penny. All expenses were covered by MYEEP. We helped fundraise for this trip. For example, in August we sold lumpias at the Nihomachi Street Fair at Japantown.

I was a participant prior to becoming a CIT. It was a big transition because CITs have a lot of responsibilities. We are in charge of over a hundred participants. We are responsible for correcting all their timesheets and distributing their paychecks. Moreover, it's essential that we train them well. We want to have great youth workers, so we can keep the worksite. It's important to know the welfare of our participants. We have worksite visits, where we can talk to the youth one on one. If there are any problems, they can feel comfortable talking to us.

While participants only attend workshops, CITs attend and facilitate workshops. Before I facilitate a workshop, I must have everything planned and written out in an agenda format. This increases my communication skills and helps me learn to plan things ahead of time. Additionally, we are able to build relationships with our participants, as well as give them a sense of belonging. When they are scared to talk to the coordinator or any adult, they talk to us. A lot of CYC: MYEEP's participants are immigrants from China. By giving them a sense of belonging, they will not feel isolated from the rest of America. Immigrants such as David, who will share his own personal experience with CYC: MYEEP, feels comforted and welcomed at CYC.

CASE STUDY
(DAVID LIN)

I would like to share my own experiences of how being part of CYC has changed my entire life. CYC helped to change my life by showing me awareness in the community. This organization showed me a sense of belonging and provided opportunities to improve myself. When I first started, I never thought I could have done this without the help and support of CYC.

During my freshman year at George Washington High School, I met some new friends and we started hanging out together during school and after school. When we hung out together, we always broke school rules, vandalized school property, and messed around with other students in school.

Most of the time, we didn't get caught or anything. But one time when my friends and I were hanging out in the hallways, we saw this one kid who owed my friend money. We went up to him and started asking for money. We started to pocket check him[3] and didn't find anything but trouble. A teacher saw us pocket checking the student and reported it to the dean. I didn't think that asking someone for money who owed money to my friend was a violation.[4] I considered myself lucky that I only got suspended for four days and didn't get kicked out of school. As a result of missing work, my best GPA was 2.33 that year.

During sophomore year, I did the same thing for another year. Going to school but not progressing, I still hung out with a big group of people during school and after school. We had nothing to do and nowhere go; most of the time we would just hang out at the esplanade. It was so immature, but we did that day after day until an incident occurred. We got into a fight with another guy; later, he filed a police report. Deans and security started pulling people out from their classes and took them to the office to talk. Unfortunately, I was one of them. By telling us that this fight was gang-related, they took us "downtown" to a place known as YGC. They did not explain anything to us. We were confused, and after all the security systems and different checkpoints, we realized what YGC was: Youth Guidance Center, a jail or prison for minors. We did everything we could, thinking that we were helping the school. But instead, we were locked up.

It was like my worst nightmare. Imagine a fifteen-year-old student going through something very shameful but all alone. In prison, we were handcuffed day and night; security watched us every second. Any freedom you had was gone. We spent a week in a tiny room with a bed for us to sleep in and a window that we couldn't even see through. How about going to the bathroom? Knock on the door just like how a dog would bark to their owner saying they need to use the bathroom. Finally, I received a phone call from my probation officer saying I could leave. I was so happy that I couldn't wait until my grandma came and picked me up. I was so happy that I could go back out and enjoy my freedom. The first thing my grandma told me when I got out was, "You've just ruined your whole future all by yourself." Now, try to imagine for one minute how you are so happy, thinking you are free, but the next minute, you are so upset and sad because someone whom you love so dearly told you that your future was just ruined. I felt really bad for what I had done.

I was on suspension for a full month. Everyday, I needed to go to court and do all the extra stuff before I could get back on track. Luckily they let me go back to George Washington High School, but they warned me that it was going to be my last chance to stay in that school. By the time everything was over and I got back to school; sophomore year passed just like that.

My family was extremely disappointed with me. They always tell me that I should take advantage of what I have right now; and that our lives are a lot better than the people in China. So I decided to go back to China and try to experience how life really is in China compared to the United States. It was very different in China. You need money, knowledge, and everything in order to survive in the community, even as a youth. It is even more competitive than the United States.

During junior year, I learned a lot over the past summer vacation in China. I realized that knowledge is the key for you to be successful in society. With that in mind, I started everything new and pushed myself to the limit in order to be successful. I decided to apply to CYC to find myself a job. But when I first applied to CYC, I didn't think having a job could make me change so much. After being accepted to CYC: MYEEP as a participant, I worked at the Richmond District Library. There, I met Doriene, my supervisor. She was very supportive of me and treated me as a friend, not as a supervisor to a subordinate. She started advising me on school AND life. I remember she once told me that "a split second of decision making can make a real difference in life," encouraging me to think twice about all I do.

When the program ended, I reapplied for the summer. When I turned in the application, I saw that CYC: MYEEP was recruiting for counselors-in-training. I gave a shot at the open recruitment and attended an orientation. At the interview, I facilitated a workshop as well as answered questions for a REAL job interview. There were many reasons why I wanted to be a CIT. The most important one was because I didn't want any more teenagers to be involved in street life. CITs are positive role models for the participants and are like representatives for youth. They give the youth a sense of belonging. CIT also increased my learning environment and sharpened a lot of my skills, including communication skills, leadership, conflict resolution, facilitation, and so on.

When I received the phone call that I was offered the job as a CIT, I was extremely happy. But I was also nervous because I knew that the program accepted over a hundred students every year at CYC. I had a lot to learn and was very excited about training. Within a short period of time, I started facilitating workshops, doing worksite visits, and learning to speak for myself instead of having an adult speak for me.

CYC really made an impact on my life. It helps youth a lot, like getting job opportunities and exposing youth to new things while sharpening their skills. They believe that every single person has a lot of potential. They give us a sense of belonging with opportunities to challenge ourselves.

I remember thinking that getting a part-time job at CYC wouldn't change me much, but I was wrong. After joining CYC: MYEEP, I realized that they helped us more than we know. We didn't even realize all the things they do for us. Imagine what I would be doing if I didn't join CYC: MYEEP. I bet I would be getting into lots of trouble. CYC made me feel there is a sense of belonging, something I can depend on when I need help, and somewhere I can go when I have no place to go. It made me feel I really belong to something other than the street life. Once, my coordinator told me that when you make the choice to do something, you choose to not do something else at the same time. As I choose to join CYC: MYEEP, I choose not to hang out on the streets. I have no idea of what I would be doing right now if I hadn't join CYC: MYEEP. Maybe I wouldn't be here sharing my story with you. Joining CYC: MYEEP changed my life from a no-life student to a helpful person in the community.

YOUTH DEVELOPMENT
(POLLY KAM YAN FUNG)

CYC provides many positive youth development experiences through the programs they serve. In order to ensure positive youth development through programs, CYC needs to provide five key experiences. These five key experiences are safety, relationship building, youth development, community involvement, and skills building.

The first key experience, safety, includes both emotional and physical safety. By providing physical and emotional safety, young people will feel secure and can take risks that will help them grow. For example, at CYC, emotional safety means no put downs, no biases, and no cruelty to everyone. The second element of safety, physical safety, means no violence and fights. No one wants to work in a dangerous environment; that is the same for us. We don't want them to be at risk at their worksites or at the agency. CYC finds worksites that are safe for youth to grow and learn. Also, we provide workshops to participants where they can learn about worksite safety, and issues such as sexual harassment in the workplace and in the community. We provide them with such workshops because we want them to learn how to prevent it and understand what to do if they ever become a victim.

The second key experience is relationship building. By providing multiple supportive relationships, young people are able to receive guidance from adults as well as emotional and practical support from both adults and peers. Elements of relationship building include guidance, emotional support, and practical support. It is easy for teenagers to be influenced by bad people, follow the wrong path, or go astray. They might start to smoke, do drugs, and drink alcohol under age. To prevent this, youth needs to be surrounded by positive role models and appropriate guidance. CYC staff, as their tagline states, is there to motivate youth to succeed. Sometimes, students would feel angry, upset, crazy, or high, and need someone to support them when they are going through an emotional rollercoaster. CYC staff cares for them, as do CITs, and we want them to feel a sense of belonging. For a teenager, the road to maturity is really important. We ensure that they stay on the positive road. In ensuring that they stay on the right path, we also provide practical support to help youth move on, such as college preparation workshops, job opportunities, and health education.

The third key experience, meaningful participation, includes providing a role in decision-making for youth, a sense of belonging, and community involvement. We have workshops where they have opportunities to practice their decision-making skills regarding their group projects and team efforts. This will help them learn how to make important decisions in the future and take ownership in the group projects as well. Additionally, by speaking the same language as our clients, who are mostly immigrants from Asia, we ensure that they feel welcomed and comforted in our agency and our programs. Using language as a bridge, we provide a sense of belonging to the many immigrant youth who are new to America, providing a community for them in a new society. Community involvement, the last element of meaningful participation, provides an opportunity for young people to gain an understanding of community so that they feel they are able to make an impact and be a productive part of their community. Additionally, this allows them to access different resources for issues such as teenage pregnancy, health education, and job placement.

The last key experience to ensure positive youth development is skills building. Youth need tasks where they are challenged. By providing different projects and group work, CYC: MYEEP ensures team effort as well as provides new experiences. As a result, there is a sense of growth and progress in youth knowledge.

In past years, CYC: MYEEP received many applications resulting in an extensive waiting list. We have waiting lists that have 75 people one year, 150 the next, and over 200 the year after. These are all new lists, with new applications year after year. CYC is just like a big family, we would never give up on any participant, no matter how long the waiting list becomes! People might think that because we have so many people in our waiting list, our goals are reached. But in my opinion, I think our goals are neverending. It goes on forever; we help the community every day. And the community grows every day. So if the community never stops growing, our goals will never end since we have reached only part of our goals!

CONCLUSION

The youth development approach mentioned was adapted from Community Network for Youth Development (CNYD). It has been developed in response to about twenty years of youth policy and programming in the United States that have focused on young people's deficits. This approach focuses on the positive youth development of adolescents. Through the five key experiences (physical and emotional safety, relationship building, meaningful participation, community involvement, and challenging and engaging youth experiences), CYC: MYEEP is able to provide youth, such as David and the other CITs, a positive and healthy alternative to street life. Hence the goal of youth empowerment programs, like all youth services at CYC, is to improve the quality of life for the young people on whose behalf we labor. We believe in youth empowerment; we believe in a higher potential to be filled. We are in the business of employing youth; we are in the business of employing opportunities.

NOTES

1. Proposition 13 establishes an acquisition-value assessment system for tax collection in California. As a result of tax limitations, the city was unable to leverage necessary funding for the program. Proposition 13, Section 2 of Article XIIIA of the California Constitution was enacted. For detailed information see *http://www.leginfo.ca.gov/cgi-bin/waisgate?waisdocid=0927553 902+9+0+0&waisaction=retrieve*.
2. Proposition J, also known as the Children's Amendment, created the Children's Fund, whereby it guaranteed funds for children in its city charter. Under the initiative, mandated set-asides will be applied to property taxes in future years. The set-asides are designed to expand children's services beyond past levels of support and to establish a base of support for children, which the city must maintain.
3. "Pocket check" is a slang term used to refer to the checking of pockets for valuables or items (in the way that a cop pats down a robber), usually in the form of all pockets being patted down and checked.
4. According to school policy, violating someone's property and safety will result in up to five days of suspension and possibly expulsion from school.

Youth Empowerment:
Language, Barriers, and Opportunities

(Original Title: Asian Pacific Islander Youth Leadership Development Program)

Lucinda Huang, Jiyang Liu, Calvin Jia Xing Ruan, and Wai Kit Tam

HUBERT V. YEE, MODERATOR

On October 7, 2005, at the Seventh Chinese American Studies conference in San Francisco, CYC (formerly known as Chinatown Youth Center) presented a panel. As the first-ever high school group from a community organization to present at a Chinese American Studies conference, the Youth[1] from the Asian Pacific Islander Youth Leadership Development Program (APIYLDP) chose to present on the issue of language. Language has been viewed as a barrier but seldom seen as a tool that can lead to opportunities for social change.

"Too often Asian American Students are left on their own to manage and mediate their experiences in school and society. Community interventions then become critical to support [Y]outh development," stated Peter Nien-chu Kiang.[2] CYC assists over two thousand Youth a year in school and social settings. The agency, incorporated in 1970 as a nonprofit, seeks to address the needs of high-risk and at-risk Youth in Chinatown. Over time the agency has grown and expanded into providing services in the multiple and diverse districts and neighborhoods of San Francisco. The services have expanded from jobs to other services such as parent groups, after-school educational programs, and Youth development. CYC "envisions empowering [Y]outh to reach their highest potential as individuals and to develop a positive self/cultural identity." Through the program APIYLDP, CYC helps Youth develop skills to become not just navigators of systems[3] in society such as government and institutions, but to become leaders who will reform and build new systems to address the needs and concerns of all Youth. APIYLDP provides opportunities for young people to learn about needs assessment, community development, advocacy, and organizing, and to develop leadership skills to address issues of racial and social justice.

The issue of language has serious implications in our lives. One only needs to sample the events in literature from Leland Saito, John Horton, and Timothy Fong, who covers the English-Only Movement in Monterey Park.[4] Another incident is the fight over bilingual education in 1998 over Proposition 227 titled *English Language in Public Schools*.[5] Both incidents show that language is an important issue in the lives of the Chinese in America.

Many studies have been done on social movements and electoral politics as a form of empowerment. Youth movements have been excluded. Youth voices and concerns are unheard and not studied.[6] As recipients of the systems, Youth are important stakeholders. The following stories by Youth exemplify the challenges faced by Chinese Youth. This paper is by no means a comprehensive analysis on the intersection of Youth, language, and systems. The essay is only a guide to the exploration and analysis of the intersection.

Through the four panelists, this paper provides a glimpse of the positive and negative challenges Youth face with languages. This paper by Lucinda Huang, Jiyang Liu, Calvin Jia Xing Ruan, and Wai Kit Tam, with moderator Hubert V. Yee, shares their experiences and thoughts on the barriers and opportunities that language offers. The students attend Phillip and Sala Burton High School in the southeast sector of San Francisco. They are Chinese American Youth, ages fourteen to eighteen. In the conclusion, the Youth will offer their ideas and insights on how to manage the use of language in their lives.

Following the stories will be a list of recommendations by the Youth to address issues of language in their life and a statement. The moderator concludes the paper by pointing out certain aspects of the Youth's lives that needs to be noticed because of their relations with systems. Chinese American Youth fight two fronts of subjugation, the systems that restrict them from growth and the society that confines them through stereotypes.

LANGUAGE AND FAMILY
(LUCINDA HUANG)

Since the time my mom and dad came to the United States, there was a huge language barrier that always prevented them from getting where they wanted. They came here thinking and hoping that life would be easy and that they might even become rich once a few years passed by. To them, it was impossible for things to go wrong in such a wealthy country. They thought everything that was real in their minds could be within their grasp in real life. Unfortunately, that didn't happen. Although it was better here than it was back in China, they still had to suffer. My parents had to work extremely hard to find decent paying jobs. My mom knew that nobody would want to hire her if she had no work experience whatsoever, so my mom even told lies about it. At that time, my parents didn't know how to drive and they didn't know how to take the public transportation, so they rarely got the chance to go anywhere to get what they needed. She didn't know anyone here except for her sisters. She even contemplated going back to China when she lost one of her jobs. My mom had to take English classes, work a part-time job, and take care of my sister and me.

My mom tells me how I should never grow up to have the kinds of jobs that she had because it's not worth the time. She tells me how she never gets the respect that she wants and how they never treat people like her fairly. When she was newly arrived in America, she worked in restaurants. One of her bosses took advantage of her and made her do more work than she was supposed to by forcing her to do chores at her boss' house. But my mom was desperate for money and it showed, so she couldn't do anything about it. That's why she wants me to excel in everything that I do. She wants me to have a completely different life. Her inability to speak English wasn't something she could naturally change, but I do speak it, and she said that if I worked hard enough, I wouldn't have to endure so many hardships.

It has also been hard for me because, as their daughter, I wasn't always able to provide all the help that they needed, especially when I was younger. I didn't understand that much about the business world, and yet they expected me (and still do) to read and translate their letters, help them communicate with non-Chinese speakers on the phone and outside of home, and basically be their stepping stone. For example, when we went out to shop for new furniture, they wanted me to talk to the salespeople and I was really uncomfortable and reluctant about that, especially when I was nine or ten years old, because I had no idea what to say to them. In a way, it helped me be more of the independent person that I am now because I knew I couldn't always expect my parents to help me when they couldn't even speak fluent English. For example, right now, they don't have any idea what kind of classes I should be taking in order to have a better chance of getting into a "good" university. They have no idea what I'm learning in school, so I always have to depend on myself to take the full responsibility of getting myself on the right track and making sure that I understand what I'm learning in my classes.

Then again, my ability to speak Cantonese started to diminish during my years in middle school since I focused so much on getting good grades and trying to improve my own English-speaking skills. All of a sudden, everything that came out of my mouth was in English—even when I spoke to my parents, so of course they disapproved of it. At that time, my Cantonese still wasn't fully developed, so the more

English I learned, the less I cared about Cantonese, and eventually, it became harder and harder for me to take that one big mistake back. This is the one thing that is really frustrating for my parents and me because it lessens our ability to communicate and understand each other fully like a family should. They look down on me for being another Chinese American who bears the shame of not knowing her own native language. There are times when my relatives call to have conversations with my mom, and they would ask about my sister and me. My mom would say the usual things about us doing well in school, but, she would add, we can't speak Chinese. Then after that, I already know that they will immediately assume that I'm some sort of rebellious child who has lost touch with the Chinese traditions. And it does offend me to a certain degree because I know that there's a lot more to me than that. Since I'm not as comfortable with the language as I am with English, I rarely speak it outside of home, but I still understand a reasonable amount of it.

My parents themselves have their negative opinions about me not being able to speak Cantonese like they do. For the most part, my dad can never get over the fact that we live in America. I always get into fights with him because he always tells my mom that I'll never grow up to be a proper Chinese American. What he means is that he thinks I'll be partying too much, doing drugs, have no objective in life, and just get involved in nonsense that he wouldn't allow when I become an adult. He lives in an illusion where he believes that no child who is born in America will survive without falling into those kinds of traps. That's the reason why he doesn't like the fact that I speak so much English. He emphasizes more the fact that he doesn't want his daughters to be Americanized because being Americanized means that we'll forget about all of the struggles he and my mom had to overcome before having a financially stable family. I remember that he and my mom joked a couple of times about how I wouldn't come visit their graves when they die. And it really hurt me when they said that because I just really can't believe that they think I will grow up to be so heartless.

But realizing where I went wrong also made me want to try harder to communicate and build a better relationship with my mom. I knew that if I continued at this rate, I wouldn't know a single word in Chinese by the time I am an adult, and, of course, I didn't want that to happen. Unlike my dad, my mom was more patient with me, and she and I could actually have a conversation where I could talk to her about almost anything. Since my parents don't speak English, I was helping myself improve my Chinese by speaking it as much as I could around my parents. It was never easy to begin with because I could never find the right words to express myself, but I knew I had to push myself beyond my limits in order to get back to where I wanted to be. It motivated me to spend more time with my mom during meals and just whenever she was home. I would watch Chinese shows or listen to the

Chinese radio station with her, and whenever I didn't understand what someone was saying, I would ask her about it. My mom encouraged me to listen to as much Chinese as I possibly could because it was a way of training my ears to understand more of it.

LANGUAGE AND VIOLENCE
(WAI KIT TAM)

When I first came to San Francisco, I had difficulties communicating with other people. On the first time I went out to buy stuff in Safeway by myself, I didn't really understand what they were talking about when I was about to pay my money. Their English accent is a bit different than the English accent I learned in Hong Kong. Maybe it is because I learned the British accent in Hong Kong. The Safeway workers spoke too fast for me to understand, so I asked them to slow down a little bit in my limited English. I used to have trouble understanding the lectures that the teachers gave in class. Now I have been in the United States for about four years. I'm starting to get used to the way people speak. My listening skills are better than when I first came to the United States. Reading is not one of the biggest problems I have now; although I think I still need to work more on writing. Also I'm getting used to the American lifestyle.

For many people who don't understand much English when they face problems like violence, they get beaten up in school or after school, or violence happens among family members. They won't be able go up to the teacher or police and tell them what happened because of some language barrier. They don't know how to express their feelings. I faced the same thing before. I didn't know what I should do.

This happened when I was in seventh grade. On the first day I went to Visitation Valley Middle School, I got beaten up near school by three Mexicans after school when I was heading to the nearby bus stop. The next day when I went back to school, I tried to tell the principal what happened, but my English was pretty bad. I wasn't able to express my feelings. He really didn't get what I said. I think it was because of the British accent I had back then. Also I was using Chinese grammar to speak English. I had no idea what the principal was telling me. I guess the principal wanted me to go with him to class and point out the students who had hurt me.

Three months after I came to San Francisco, my parents started fighting because of some money problem. My mother's arm was injured, so I decided to call 911 for help. When I reached 911, I had a very hard time telling them what happened. I don't remember the details of the conversation I had with 911. I remember I had to ask them to send someone to help my mother. I just said my mother injured her arm accidentally. After a while, an ambulance came to our house and took my mother to the hospital.

There are a lot of organizations that provide services free of charge to assist with issues of violence. For example, CYC is part of the Asian Pacific Islander (API) Youth Violence Prevention Network. There they provide services to API Youth with the aim of reducing violence. Besides CYC, there are a lot of different organizations that help Youth with issues of violence in their first language, the language that they know the best. My first language has helped me a lot to avoid violence. It is easier for me to express my feelings in my first language than in English.

LANGUAGE AND EDUCATION
(JIYANG LIU)

I believe that education is one of the most important things for Asians. It is the same for me. I found some challenges in high school, and most of those are related to language.

First, when I study science classes such as biology, chemistry, and physics, I don't understand the academic words even though the books give their definitions. It is not because my English is poor but because we do not know scientific terminologies. We get the words' meanings, but not their scientific context. I am studying for Advanced Placement (AP) Chemistry by myself. When I study, I feel that I have to spend a lot of time with the words in my dictionary. Most of the time I can't find the meaning for the technical words. Even though I ask my chemistry teacher to explain it to me, I still don't get it. If I don't solve the problem, I can't assimilate the knowledge. You might say, "You don't get the meaning in English; how can you be sure that you can get the meaning in your mother tongue?" Whether this applies to other language speakers, I don't know. But based on my Chinese background, I can say this is useful.

My reasons are the following: Chinese words make more sense to me. I don't need to worry about forming sentences, arranging words, and so on. I only need to read the words, and then the meaning will appear in my mind. Many scientific words do not appear in a regular dictionary. They always appear in the larger dictionary that is impossible to take to school everyday. The Chinese have a saying, "You have to spend ten minutes to study again, if you don't pay attention one minute in class." Therefore, it is impossible to spend my time checking the dictionary in class, especially a large one. In the AP Free Response Test, we have to finish some labs. Sometimes the objects use their real name, not the scientific name. For example, $CaCO_3$ is called "lime." I wish the Education Department could create a Chinese glossary for science books, just like the Spanish translation glossary at the end of history textbooks.

Second, I don't know what kinds of books or, say, what level of books I need when I'm in the library. If we had a reading list for English as a Second Language (ESL) students,

I think this would be easier. Reading the correct books is important for immigrants. It helps me understand at what reading level I should be. For example, it is impossible for me to read the *Da Vinci Code* well. Although I have learned English for about six years, the novel is still too hard for me. It is a waste of my time to check for definitions in a dictionary. Even though I can find all the words in the dictionary, I don't think that I can understand the metaphor implied by these words.

My friends said that my English sounds a little bit different from the Chinese born in the United States. I really want to practice with a good English speaker and have them correct my speaking mistakes.

Lastly, other people can benefit from my improved English. When I do community service I can help the Chinese-only speakers. I can help them to fill out forms, and I can also translate them. I recently volunteered at the Autumn Moon Festival, which was on September 10 and 11. On those days, I translated many things for people who do not understand English. I helped sellers build booths and used Chinese to introduce people. I helped the Pepsi Company booth. I will be working with the Department of Elections to help people translate English for the Chinese-only speakers. In school, I can introduce more things about the traditions of China and the lifestyle of the Chinese. For teachers, most of the time their favorite thing is Chinese food. Talking with my teachers not only helps me to practice my English, but also lets us know more about each other, including lifestyles, experiences, and knowledge. I talk with my teachers many times, and they help me correct my English, decrease my mistakes, and make me a better speaker.

LANGUAGE AND FRIENDS (CALVIN JIA XING RUAN)

People are always moving from place to place to find a suitable environment to settle down, but once they settle down, they inevitably need to adjust themselves to adapt to their new environment. As Charles Darwin stated, "when species change their habitat, they will also change themselves in order to be 'successful.'" Language barriers between different language-speaking people cannot be avoided. Not being able to communicate with others is a very big obstacle. This language barrier secluded me from other people who spoke a language different from mine.

When I first came to America, I found it extremely difficult to communicate in school using English, a completely different language. It was very hard to talk to my classmates or to make friends with them. Sometimes my classmate would make fun of me by saying something that I did not understand. Because of this language barrier, I was limited in my ability to interact with these people. For this reason, all of my friends are either Chinese or speak the same language as

me. The disadvantage of this was that I was prevented from having a chance to learn about and blend into the "American" mainstream culture. Using a different language to communicate is very difficult and challenging for me.

Sometimes when my friends talked to me in English, I would often misunderstand the meaning of their words, and this would cause a gap between my friends and me. Because of this, I am inclined to make Chinese friends. All the elders are always saying that it is very easy for a child my age to learn English and adapt to this new environment, but they are wrong. I have been through many obstacles and difficulties. It was and still is very hard to assimilate into this strange society and speak their language. There is and will be always laughter, embarrassment, and mis-enunciation that often surround me because of my Chinese accent, that classmates and friends think is funny. Thus, people always make fun of my pronunciation.

It took me a while to learn how to pronounce the word "discrimination." Discrimination means a treatment based on characteristics. Often in school, my non-Chinese friends would look down on me. They often put me down like I do not belong to them just because we do not share the "same" language. It is immoral and unfair to laugh at someone who is not familiar with their language. If they were in my shoes, they would also feel remorseful and shameful, being laughed at. Because of this, I usually never make an attempt to communicate with other non-Chinese-speaking people. It was this period of time that I went through that taught me a lot about moral principles that I would never have contemplated about in my daily life. If we could stand in other people's positions and think about their concerns, then we would be able to be more considerate and thoughtful of other people, and also be great listeners.

A language barrier is a very big problem for immigrants who are unfamiliar with the new language. They would encounter a lot of problems, just like me. There have been a lot of obstacles that I have been through that no one knows. English is the dominant language, so it was set to be the default language for every American and in other parts of the world. Because of this, I can use it to learn about other cultures and pick up new languages from my non-Chinese friends. I would always ask my Spanish-speaking friends about any problems that I encounter when I do my Spanish homework. This helps me a lot in my academics. Besides this, I can also learn about the cultures of other countries, such as Korea, Japan, Philippines, Mexico, and a lot of others. Learning English can enable me to go almost anywhere I want since English is the primary language of the world, and it will allow me to get to know more friends and travel in the world.

Although English is a very powerful language, it is difficult for an immigrant to learn. There are positive and negative things that I have gotten from this language. Meeting new friends and being able to travel through many countries would be considered a good thing, while humiliation and embarrassment are negative, which we as a whole should work together to eliminate.

CONCLUSION

Though their experiences, the panelists drew up a list of recommendations to ease the adaptation or negotiation of the English language in their lives.

- Youth and Support Networks
  - Promote students to join more outside activities like CYC so they can meet new friends and improve their language skills.
  - Create a support network and forum for immigrant Youth to share their experience.
- Language and Study Groups
  - Form language conversational study groups for the ESL speakers.
  - Provide translations for those who don't understand English, especially on important letters and store products.
  - Create more after-school programs that can tutor the students with their English and homework.
- Safety and Government Systems
  - Designate a specific extension for 911 callers who are Chinese immigrants.
  - Assign 911 staff members to immigrant callers to reduce lag time.
  - Allocate police officers to patrol school sites and create better rotation times to reduce gaps in coverage.
- Educational Institutions and Assistance
  - Produce a glossary for meanings of scientific words in Chinese at the end of the textbooks.
  - Create a book reading-level list for new immigrants to improve their English.
- Family and Communication
  - Encourage parents to be more patient with their children when they're trying to improve their Chinese.

Through the essays provided by the panelists, a few points emerge from their lives that we must examine closely. Lucinda's parents associate being Americanized with being less Chinese. America's prejudices have defined Chinese as being not Americans but foreigners. Chinese in China believe that overseas Chinese are in fact not ethnically Chinese because of the lack of Chinese culture. From this perspective, it is important that Chinese American Youth receive a safe space to define themselves as they grow rather than having society impose stereotypical constraints on them. Such constraints may lead to self-hate and limited growth because of stereotypes.

Wai Kit cites CYC as a tool for creating and deconstructing confusing paths of systems for Chinese American Youth in society. As Peter Kiang states, institutions play an important part in the lives of Asian Youth. They represent Youth in many aspects of their lives, such as case managers at detention centers, lobbyists at the government level, and teachers at after-school educational programs. What is important to note is that institutions must become culturally competent. They must be aware of cultural differences and not follow the white model of services. Imposing a white model of services only result in ambiguous consequences, and broken family and Youth relations.

In school Jiyang faces many educational challenges because of his limited English ability. He recommends a terminology list in Chinese be added to scientific texts because they have it in Spanish. Currently 31.6 percent of the San Francisco Unified School District is comprised of Chinese American Youth. From 1996 to 2005, the population of Chinese American Youth has jumped 4 percent, which amounts to an increase of approximately 1,400 Youth.[7] As the population of Chinese American Youth increases and Chinese American Youth identifying that their home language is Chinese, systems of government need to accommodate them by assisting them in their educational transitions through translations embedded in school texts.[8]

Language defines friends for Youth. Because of Calvin's language limitations, his friends are predominately Chinese or Asian. He faced discriminatory actions by other Youth because of his limited language capacity. The forming of cliques on school grounds should not be seen as a segregation effort by Youth. We must recognize that language can be a barrier to interaction with other Youth. To bring about an inclusive setting where Youth interact in a healthy manner, school teachers, administrators, and principals must make a concerted effort to encourage interaction regardless of language.

Social movements have not been inclusive of Youth. Youth voices and concerns must be included and studied. Adults must make an effort to eliminate ageist attitudes toward Youth. Chinese American Youth in San Francisco face distinct challenges. These concerns and needs must be heard and met by people who work within the systems with which Youth interact such as government, institutions, and families, which can be divided into two fronts, system and society. Yet these concerns must be tied with the Youth of Color movement because of similar concerns that overlap. The strength in numbers will change these systems and models of services that are inadequate and constrain the growth of Youth. Language offers opportunities and barriers for Youth. Lucinda finds that Chinese can be an opportunity for her to communicate and develop a stronger relationship with her mother. Jiyang uses Chinese and English to assist people at the Autumn Moon Festival in Chinatown. Yet there are shortfalls such as Wai Kit trying to navigate the 911 emergency system and Calvin facing discriminatory actions by others. While there is a balance of positive and negative, Youth voices and community institutions play an important role in creating a healthier and stronger community through taking advantage of the opportunities language offers and breaking the barriers that exist with languages. Power to the Youth and the organizations that challenge systems that exclude Chinese American Youth and Youth of Color.

NOTES

1. "Youth" is defined as between the ages of 5 and 18 years. The word is capitalized to show its importance in society. It also signifies an aspect of empowerment.
2. Peter Nien-chu Kiang, "K-12 Education and Asian American Youth Development," *Asian American Policy Review* 10 (2001): 40.
3. "System" is defined as a maze of nodes that control access to resources. Government, school districts, or community organizations fall under this term.
4. Timothy P. Fong, *The First Suburban Chinatown* (Philadelphia: Temple University Press, 1994); John Horton, *The Politics of Diversity* (Philadelphia: Temple University Press, 1995); Leland T. Saito, *Race and Politics: Asian Americans, Latinos, and Whites in a Los Angeles Suburb* (Chicago: University of Illinois, 1998).
5. Paul M. Ong and David E. Lee, "Changing of the Guard? The Emerging Immigrant Majority in Asian American Politics," in *Asian Americans and Politics: Perspectives, Experiences, Prospects,* ed. Gordon H. Chang (Stanford: Stanford University Press, 2000), 153–172.
6. Peter Nien-chu Kiang, "Asian Pacific American Youth: Pathways for Political Participation," in *Asian Americans and Politics: Perspectives, Experiences, Prospects,* ed. Gordon H. Chang (Stanford: Stanford University Press, 2000), 232.
7. San Francisco Unified School District, "San Francisco Unified School District Historical School Data," *San Francisco Unified School District,* August 5, 2005, *http://orb.sfusd.edu/schdata/hist/hist-100.htm* (accessed November 13, 2005).
8. San Francisco Unified School District, "SFUSD School Profiles 2004-2005 (Fall 2004)," *San Francisco Unified School District,* May 16, 2005, *http://orb.sfusd.edu/schdata/hist/hist-100.htm* (accessed November 13, 2005).

Mainstreaming and Professionalizing Chinese-Language Education

A New Mission for a New Century

Stella Kwoh, EdD

[Author's note: For a discussion of the historical development of the Chinese-language education in the Chinese heritage schools, please refer to "Retention of the Chinese Heritage, Part I and Part II" by Him Mark Lai in Chinese America: History and Perspectives, 2000 and 2001.]

Since 1990, Chinese (Mandarin and Cantonese) has satisfied the California foreign-language requirement and has been a part of the curriculum of many public schools and universities throughout the state of California. Many students from Chinese heritage schools take Chinese classes in mainstream schools. The number has increased partly because of the beginning of SATII-Chinese in 1993. Due to a diverse student population, the growing number of second- and third-generation Chinese American students learning Chinese, and the AP Chinese courses and tests to be started by the College Board in the high schools in 2006 and 2007, Chinese programs at the K–16 (kindergarten to college senior) levels are on the increase. In addition, worldwide cultural and economic exchanges between China and the rest of the world make schools and parents more enthusiastic about starting a Chinese program for their students. We can indeed say that this new century is the century for moving Chinese language education from heritage schools to mainstream schools and the society.

CURRENT CONDITION AND DEVELOPMENT OF CHINESE-LANGUAGE EDUCATION IN THE UNITED STATES

The Start of AP Chinese: Before and After

Before the College Board announced the start of AP Chinese in 2003, there were more than 200 elementary, middle, and high schools that offered Chinese-language education. Many teachers did not have a valid state teaching license to teach Chinese. After the College Board announced its plan to start AP Chinese courses in 2006 and AP Chinese tests in 2007, more than 2,400 K–12 (kindergarten to high school) mainstream schools planned on starting Chinese programs.

Teachers in Chinese Heritage Schools

With a severe shortage of qualified and experienced Chinese-language teachers, the teachers in Chinese heritage schools became possible candidates to teach mainstream K–12 schools. Based on a survey conducted by the National Council of Associations of Chinese Language Schools (NCACLS) in 1995, there were 5,540 language teachers teaching in its member schools. The Chinese School Association in the United States (CSAUS) conducted a similar survey in 1996 and reported 1,300 language teachers teaching in its member schools. Unfortunately, there has not been a systematic teacher-training program among Chinese schools and neither Chinese school associations have come up with a plan to encourage their teachers to receive training and to get certified. Fortunately, the author has been able to observe some efforts made by both NCACLS and CSAUS to find ways to work with teacher-training institutions to certify teachers in their member schools.

Challenges Faced By Mainstream Schools

Teacher Shortage. With the prediction of a severe teacher shortage and the lack of a certification program for Chinese-language teachers in teacher-training institutions, the teacher shortage will inevitably last for a long time. School administrators will need to be very creative and resourceful to recruit their teachers for the Chinese programs.

Curriculum, Pedagogy, and Instructional Model Selection. This will inevitably bring up the debate of traditional and simplified characters, the different phonetic systems (mainly Zhuyin and Pinyin), and teaching Chinese as a foreign language or in a dual-language immersion program. Fortunately, we have started to see some agreeable approaches that best serve Chinese-language learners.

With regards to the debate between traditional or simplified characters, more scholars and teachers agreed that it is necessary for students to learn both types of characters. In today's shrinking world, the students should be able to surf websites using both traditional and simplified characters.

Furthermore, they should be able to use both forms of the Chinese characters for their travel and work. Some people choose to teach traditional characters first and then simplified characters. Some teach simplified before traditional. The author prefers teaching simultaneously: reading traditional and writing simplified.

As for the phonetic systems, the majority of teachers and students prefer Hanyu Pinyin. Even Chinese heritage schools that traditionally teach Zhuyin have started to teach Hanyu Pinyin in the higher grades. The College Board has announced that the AP Chinese test will be a computer test. This will make more students learn Pinyin simply because the input or typing is easier.

CURRENT DIFFICULTIES FACING CHINESE-LANGUAGE TEACHERS

Insufficient State Regulations and Standards

Each state has its own regulations and standards for foreign-language teachers. Every teacher in California must take and pass all sections of the California Basic Educational Skills Test (CBEST). Additionally, he/she must prove his/her subject-matter competency by completing a subject-matter program or by taking the California Subject Examinations for Teachers (CSET). For a Mandarin teacher, he/she must take and pass all sections of the CSET Mandarin. Finally, verification of knowledge of the Constitution of the United States of America is a state requirement for teachers.

In California, the current regulations and requirements for foreign-language teachers cannot ensure teaching competency in the foreign-language classroom. All the requirements mentioned above plus the courses offered in a credential program do not really enhance the necessary knowledge or teaching methodology in the target subject. For example, a person pursuing a Mandarin teaching *credential* (term used for a teaching license in California) will take all courses required by the State. All candidates take the same courses including teaching methods courses (California State University, East Bay, is the only university that offers one Mandarin teaching methods course). A person with a valid California teaching credential in any subject can get an additional credential to teach Mandarin after passing a subject matter competency test entitled California Subject Examinations for Teachers in Mandarin (CSET Mandarin). (Please note that the credential teacher must have already satisfied the CBEST and U.S. Constitution requirements.) This person, although holding a valid credential in Chinese, might not know how to teach Chinese if the language pedagogy course does not include Chinese pedagogy. Some Chinese-language teachers do not even have the additional credential in Chinese and are just assigned by the school to teach Chinese because they are native speakers.

Furthermore, anyone holding a teaching license in any subject issued by a foreign country, or completing a teacher-training program in a foreign country in the past, would most likely be able to get the California teaching credential after taking a language pedagogy course (not necessarily Chinese pedagogy) and satisfying the three requirements previously discussed, namely, CBEST, CSET, and U.S. Constitution. (For a person holding a bachelor of arts degree in Chinese literature, CSET Mandarin could most likely be waived because the bachelor of arts degree in Chinese is considered a subject-matter program.) Again, earning a valid credential in Chinese without training on the teaching of Chinese would no doubt jeopardize teaching and learning in the classroom. A Chinese-language teacher without proper training will usually create learners with low motivation and will even make the classroom chaotic. In addition to Chinese pedagogy courses, Chinese-language teachers need training in cross-cultural communication in order to appreciate cultural diversities and to perform properly in U.S. classrooms.

Lack of Teacher Education Program in Higher Education

In California, all universities approved by the California Commission of Teacher Credentialing to offer a foreign-language teaching credential, can offer a Chinese teaching credential. With the arrival of AP Chinese, several state universities have started to promote a Chinese credential program. However, with insufficient state requirements, most Chinese credential programs do not even offer a Chinese pedagogy course. Generally speaking, Chinese credential candidates will take pedagogy courses with candidates who will teach other subjects. Although some pedagogy courses are designed for foreign-language teachers, the Chinese candidates will usually find themselves learning Spanish pedagogy. At the time of this writing, only the two teacher education programs offered by the California State University, East Bay, offer Chinese pedagogy courses. The author believes this phenomenon is mainly due to the lack of sufficient State regulations and the lack of faculty members in the field of professional development for Chinese-language teachers.

Professional Background of Chinese-Language Teachers

A majority of today's Chinese-language teachers, including those who are teaching in mainstream schools, are not properly trained in teaching Chinese. Some Chinese-language teachers holding a valid California teaching credential are trained in teaching English, and some are trained in teaching other subjects such as math and science. There are also teachers who are holding a bachelor of arts or master's degree in Chinese and using an emergency credential to teach Chinese in the public schools. In other words, some of them are teachers trained in another subject who have gotten a job to teach Chinese for a variety of reasons. Again, Chinese-language teachers with no proper training will usually create learners with low motivation and will even make the classroom chaotic.

Living in our ever-shrinking global village, Chinese-language students need to learn the different forms of Chinese language as much as possible. Putting political issues aside, today's Chinese-language learners will have opportunities to go to many different cities where Chinese is used daily. Mandarin learners working for businesses like Intel and IBM may visit a branch office in Beijing in the morning and then visit a branch office in Taipei in the afternoon. They will need to learn both simplified and traditional characters in order to get around in both cities. Today's Chinese-language teachers, therefore, should be able to know how to teach both systems effectively.

Additionally, many Chinese-language teachers need to increase their English proficiency and cross-cultural communication skills in order to pass state-required tests and to effectively communicate with their students, parents, and their colleagues.

PROFESSIONAL DEVELOPMENT: PRESENT CONDITIONS AND DIFFICULTIES

Lack of Teacher Education Program

As discussed earlier, many universities in California have been approved by the California Commission of Teacher Credentialing to offer a Chinese teaching credential. However, with insufficient state requirements, most of the Chinese credential programs do not even offer a Chinese pedagogy course. As mentioned earlier, this phenomenon is mainly due to the lack of sufficient state regulations and the lack of faculty capable of offering the appropriate courses. In other words, we need to develop more masters and doctoral programs in the field of Chinese-language education to ensure the full availability of professional development programs for people who would like to pursue a career in teaching Chinese.

Lack of Credential Candidates

Due to the lack of faculty members in the field of professional development, universities that can offer Chinese teaching credentials do not actively recruit Chinese credential candidates. Many Chinese-language teachers who are interested in getting a credential are often scared away by the various tests required before entering a credential program. They also hesitate to enter a credential program because of the heavy course load and the lack of courses related to teaching Chinese.

Insufficient Regulations for Teacher Licensing

As discussed before, insufficient regulations for teacher licensing lead to improper training of Chinese credential candidates. Many teachers cannot perform effectively in the classroom after receiving their teaching credential in Chinese.

College Board and Teacher Licensing Board

With the advent of AP Chinese, many Chinese-language teachers are seriously thinking about getting the state teaching license. With more schools planning to start Chinese programs, it will be a long time before we can see improvement with the teacher shortage. Based on the federal No Child Left Behind law, all teachers must be certified by the state to teach the subject he/she teaches. With insufficient certified teachers, how can schools begin their Chinese program? How can schools extend their Chinese programs to AP level? These are the challenges faced by all schools.

Insufficient Funding for Research and Development

To ensure the quality of Chinese-language education, many fundamental issues need to be addressed using scientific research data. Topics such as traditional and simplified character recognition and reading comprehension, teaching and learning the four tones and their changes in speech, as well as the differences in pronunciation and meaning of vocabulary, idioms, and overall language use are just a few of the issues that influence the curriculum, pedagogy, and quality of the professional development program for Chinese-language teachers.

Currently, the lack of U.S. research and development funding for research and development in the field of Chinese-language education endangers both the quality and quantity of the professional development program. If more funding is not provided, teacher shortages will continue and the teaching competence of those being trained will remain unsatisfactory. There is an urgent need to prepare teacher trainers so that teacher licensing programs for Chinese-language teachers can be properly staffed.

PROFESSIONAL DEVELOPMENT PROGRAMS OFFERED BY CALIFORNIA STATE UNIVERSITY, EAST BAY

Currently, California State University, East Bay (CSUEB), is the only university in the nation that offers both credential (licensing) and certificate (nonlicensing) programs for Chinese-language teachers.

The nonlicensing certificate program totally focuses on teaching Chinese. Two of the five required courses are Chinese pedagogy with a total of six quarter units or sixty hours of instruction on teaching approaches to Chinese as a heritage or foreign language. Besides the two Chinese pedagogy courses, the other three required courses are Chinese linguistics (five units), cross-cultural communication (two units), and teaching approaches to second language acquisition (three units). Classes are offered on the weekends so people from all walks of life can explore the field of Chinese-language education after their regular work. A student must satisfactorily complete a total of sixteen quarter units or 160 hours of instruction before receiving a teaching Chinese certificate.

The credential program leading to the state teacher license focuses on state required courses. A student must satisfactorily complete fifteen required courses (thirty-seven quarter credits or 370 instructional hours), plus three quarters or two semesters of student teaching. At the time of this writing, only one out of the four pedagogy courses focuses on teaching Chinese (two quarter units or twenty hours of instruction). Although far from being ideal, the CSUEB credential program for Chinese teacher candidates is considered the best at this time because other Chinese credential programs offered by other higher education institutions do not offer any Chinese pedagogy course.

A student admitted into the credential program without completing the certificate program would most likely suffer from lack of competence in teaching Chinese.

CONCLUSION: NEEDS AND PERSPECTIVES

To improve Chinese-language education in general, we not only need to offer more professional development programs leading to the state teaching license, we also need to offer more programs to produce faculty members and teacher trainers for higher education institutions. There is an urgent need to improve the state teacher licensing regulations. Research and experiments in teaching Chinese methodology will need to be designed to enhance the quality of Chinese-language education. Finally, and most importantly, funding for program development and program improvement as well as scholarships for students in professional development programs should be provided to ensure the quality and continuation of the Chinese-language programs from kindergarten to college.

An Overview of the Chinese Language Schools in San Francisco

(Original English title: The Status of Chinese Language Schools in San Francisco)

三藩市華文學校當前的一般狀況

Catherine Leung

梁劉潔鑾

一、學校分佈

三藩市 (舊金山) 位於美國加州的西岸, 面積約四十七平方英里, 約有七十四萬市民, 華人約有十五萬, 華文學校學生人數超過六千人, 約佔華人百分之四左右。

華文教育在三藩市已有超過百年歷史, 由初期創設私塾及專館授課至目前全市共有各類教授華文華語的學校約三十所, 其中南僑學校、中華中學校、金巴崙華文學校、聖瑪利中文學校及協和學校都有近百年的歷史, 是傳統的僑校; 其次有華大三藩市中文學校、青華園國際學校、信義中文學校、潮州中山華文學校 (即潮州會館中文學校)、建國學校、中美國際學校、三藩市華藝文教中心、潮州會館中文學校、金山聖寺中文學校、小星星中文學校、聖安中文學校、頌恩華語學校、聖莫尼卡學校、金門中文學校、育良小學、大覺蓮社中文學校、兆祥中文學校、者佛臣中文學校等。

歷史悠久的傳統的僑校大多數集中在華埠 (Chinatown), 設備完善, 有自已的校舍。其餘日落區 (Sunset) 及烈治文區 (Richmond) 都有不少的華文華語學校。這些學校都是由熱心華文教育的社區團體、地緣團體或宗教團體主辦的。還有一些是由華人家長及英文學校家長會組織的華文學校, 或家庭補習班。雖然辦學團體不一樣, 但大家都有一個共同的目標, 就是要向在海外的華人進行華語及中華文化的教育, 華文教育就是中華民族語言和中華優秀傳統文化的教育。

二、學校體制 學生人數

三藩市華文學校在體制上可分為兩類, 一類是每天英文學校放學後都上課, 每日上課二小時, 名為週日班 (weekday class) 有些學校稱為課後班。另一類是只在星期六或星期日上課, 分上午班、中午班或下午班, 各上課三小時, 名為週末班 (weekend class), 由於星期日上課的班稱為週末班不太適合, 因此有些學校就直接稱為星期六班及星期日班。規模比較大的華文學校, 都設有週日班及週末班, 但亦有只開辦週日班或週末班的。週日班的學生大多是住在華埠或住在學校附近, 否則很難天天準時上課; 週末班的學生大多是住得比較遠, 或是英文學校功課多, 不能每天放學後都到華文學校上課, 因此選讀週末班。跟據不完全統計, 三藩市華文學校學生約有六千人, 而週末班的學生比週日班的學生多五倍以上。由於週日班及週末班上課時間有很大差別, 週日班每週上課十小時, 而週末班則每週只上課三個小時, 因此學生程度亦有差別, 教學內容及課程設計亦不能完全相同。

三、課程設置 教學內容

三藩市的華文學校在課程設計上比較注重華語聽、講、讀、寫的學習, 教學內容包括朗讀課文、默寫生詞、背書、書法、造句、作文等。有些學校更加入歷史、尺牘、翻譯、歌詠、舞蹈及電腦中文輸入法, 或使用電腦軟體學習中文, 務求使教學內容更為豐富。在課程設計上, 週末班因為上課時間短, 則只能注重語文上的學習, 而週日班因為上課時間長, 在課程設計上比較容易處理, 可加入其他課程, 提高學生對學習中文的興趣。

教材方面都是來自兩岸三地 (中國大陸、香港、臺灣), 十多年前, 大多數華文學校都是採用來自臺灣的《華語》《常識》《尺牘》等, 教授注音符號及繁體字。有些學校採用香港出版的教科書, 也有採用中國大陸出版的教科書，亦有些學校是自編教材的，或自編部份教材。近年來部分學校為了配合美國大學課程，與主流教育互相銜接，為了適應社會需求，有些學校已改用漢語教學，教授漢語拼音及普通話，甚至教授簡體字。約十年前，暨南大學華文學院為海外華人子弟學習中文編寫了一套《中文》教材，全套教材共四十八冊，其中課本十二冊，練習冊二十四冊。三藩市有部份華文學校已開始選用該套教材。

　　目前三藩市的華文學校所用的教材及學習工具，繁體字或簡體字，注音符號或漢語拼音，粵語(廣州話)或國語(普通話)，都是各式其適，因材施教。

四、融入主流

三藩市的華文教育，經過多年的努力，終於在一九九三年五月得到了學區的認可。凡就讀於獲學區認可的華文學校學生通過校區每年舉辦的測試，合格同學可取得十個學分。兩年便可取得二十個學分。該二十個學分可移至該生原讀高中的成績單上，成為升讀加州大學必須的外語教育學分。學區認可法例的實施，把此地的華文教育從法律上肯定下來，把華文教育融入主流社會，與教育主流接軌，這是值得興奮的，這也是美國華文教育發展的必由之路。

二零零三年美國國會參議院通過170號決議案，大學委員會宣佈籌畫中文和中國文化進階先修課程和考試，簡稱AP中文 (AP為高中的大學先修課程)，將中文與法文、德文、西班牙文同列為可供高中生選擇的外語課程，從而使中文正式進入美國國民教育系統。AP中文能幫助學生進入理想大學，提高高中平均成績 (GPA) 及整體教學水平。

五、結論

在今年三藩市華文學校聯合會尊孔敬師大會上，鄭觀志會長在致詞中表示為了適應時勢的發展，我們華文學校都應該全面開設普通話和漢語拼音課程，華文字體要教繁識簡，使學生能學以致用，藉以提高學生的閱讀能力和表達能力。在教學內容上給了我們很明確的指示。

　　華文教育在教學主旨今後更應以語言及文化並重，加強文化課程教學，開設才藝課程，使文化才藝課程配合語言課程，把中國歷史、文化編入教學課程，安排學生參加文化之旅，鼓勵中文教師參加各種師資培訓活動。共同努力，為華文教育創造更美好的明天。

More Than Ninety Years of Bay Area History
Group Homes for Chinese Children

(Original Title: China America, A Radiant Light: A Combined 93-Year History
of Orphanages for Chinese Children in the Bay Area)

Phillip Chan, Lynette Choy Uyeda Gin, Richard Mar, and Nona Mock Wyman

LYNETTE CHOY UYEDA GIN, MODERATOR

Lifelong friendships and a few marriages resulted from connections made through two group homes for Chinese children in the Bay Area, Chung Mei and Ming Quong. Many interrelationships are still being discovered. Contrary to public perception of the era, these group homes for Chinese youth served as a safe haven and were not intended for "bad, incorrigible, or delinquent" juvenile offenders. They are a little-known piece of California's Chinese American history. This panel consisted of a fifteen-minute video presentation followed by four panelists who shared their experiences growing up in the group homes.

BRIEF HISTORICAL BACKGROUND

Chung Mei Home for Chinese Boys
Berkeley, 1923 • El Cerrito, 1934

Dr. Charles R. Shepherd was a Cantonese-speaking Baptist minister from England. After years of missionary work in China, Shepherd was sent as a missionary to San Francisco. Chinese boys at that time were barred from mixing with white boys at existing orphanages such as Boys Town. Shepherd secured funding from the American Baptist Home Mission Society, the Bay Cities Baptists Union, and the Bay Area's Chinese Baptists and Chinese business and community leaders, to found the Chung Mei Home for Chinese Boys in Berkeley, California, in 1923. In 1934, Chung Mei was moved to El Cerrito, California, to accommodate the growing number of boys who needed a safe haven from the streets of San Francisco Chinatown. The new building was able to house up to one hundred boys. In Shepherd's book, *The Story of Chung Mei*, he describes racism only as a "difficulty" he encountered while looking for a house to care for Chinese boys. From 1923 until its close in 1954, more than eight hundred Chinese boys aged five to eighteen passed through Chung Mei Home.

The former Chung Mei Home in El Cerrito, California, still exists. The property and building are currently owned and operated by "Windrush School," a private elementary school for students, K–8. It is located at the original site: 1800 Elm Street (at Hill Street) in El Cerrito.

Ming Quong Home for Chinese Girls
Mission Home (Cameron House), Original Site
Sunshine Cottage and Tooker Home, 1915
Mills College Site, 1925
Loma Alta Blvd., Los Gatos, 1934
51 9th Street, Oakland, 1936

Donaldina Cameron, San Francisco's legendary "Angry Angel," was a Presbyterian missionary. The Mission Home, located at 920 Sacramento Street in San Francisco, still exists today as a community resource center. It was renamed "Cameron House" in honor of Donaldina Cameron.

In the early 1900s, the trafficking of young Chinese females was rampant. Girls as young as six years old were "bought and sold" as housemaids, or sex slaves, and for other purposes of exploitation by unscrupulous Chinese. Girls lucky enough to be rescued by Cameron were housed at the present site of Cameron House—then known as the Mission Home. Toddlers and very young girls were moved to Tooker Cottage in Menlo Park. The original Ming Quong Home for Chinese Girls was designed by famed architect Julia Morgan in the style of Chinese homes. It was opened in 1925, on the grounds of what is now part of Mills College in Oakland. In 1936, this property became part of Mills College in exchange for two other facilities—the former Spreckels (Sugar) Estate for preschool to thirteen-year-old children, and in Oakland near Lake Merritt on 9th Street. The Oakland facility was torn down and is the site of a BART facility today.

PANELISTS

Lynette Choy Uyeda Gin, Ming Quong Alumna

In 1942, Lynette Gin was brought to Ming Quong, Los Gatos, at the age of four by her mother, a Cantonese opera performer. She stayed at Los Gatos until 1947 when her mother brought her to live in San Francisco Chinatown in Ross Alley. Lynette returned to the home in 1949, this time to Oakland Ming Quong after her mother decided to return to the stage and traveled. Her teen years were spent in other group homes and three foster homes. Lynette relocated to Los Angeles with her family and graduated high school there. She also married and raised four sons. In 1984, she opened her public relations consulting firm, which she operated for twenty years. In 2000, Lynette retired and remarried to Henry "Mousie" Gin, a former Chung Mei "boy," and consequently returned to the Bay Area. Their blended family consists of eleven children, seventeen grandchildren, and three great-grandchildren. They reside in Belmont. Lynette is the writer and director of the 2003 video documentary about the Chung Mei and Ming Quong homes.

Phillip Chan, Chung Mei Alumnus

Phillip Chan was born in Oakpark, a suburb of Chicago. In 1946, he and his brother were placed at the Chung Mei Home by their parents when they divorced. At that time, Phillip was twelve years old and his brother Paul was seven. Phillip lived at Chung Mei Home until he was seventeen and graduated from El Cerrito High School in 1952. He was employed as a sales representative in food service for Sysco Food until he retired in 1995. Phillip spends his time as a volunteer for the senior center, Travelers Aid at the San Francisco Airport, and doing video productions for not-for-profit organizations. He is the editor and producer of the video presentation. He and his wife Lynn reside in Millbrae.

Richard Mar, Chung Mei Alumnus

Born in San Francisco, Richard Mar has lived in the Bay Area for over thirty years. At the age of eleven, his grandmother placed him at Chung Mei where he lived from 1948 to 1953. At sixteen, he moved back to San Francisco and graduated from Polytechnic High School. Richard graduated from San Francisco State University, University of Hawaii, and the American Institute of International Management in Glendale, Arizona. He has been retired for ten years from the mortgage business. He is a Distinguished Toastmaster in the Daly City Toastmasters and a member of the High Spirits Toastmasters Club in Belmont. His volunteer work includes Self-Help for the Elderly in San Mateo. Richard resides in Foster City and provided the voice narration for the video documentary.

Nona Mock Wyman, Ming Quong Alumna

Nona Mock Wyman was the youngest resident when she went to Ming Quong, Los Gatos, at age three. She lived at Los Gatos and Oakland from 1935 to 1948. Ming Quong was the only home Nona knew as a child. She is the author of *Chopstick Childhood,* a first-person documentary of her childhood memories living at Ming Quong. She has given many readings to groups interested in the history of Chinese children who grew up in the environment of group homes. Nona resides in Walnut Creek where she has owned a gift shop named "Ming Quong" for the last thirty-six years. Her second book, in progress, will feature the women of Ming Quong and their stories.

CONFERENCE SESSIONS, SUPPORTERS, AND PARTICIPANTS

CONFERENCE SESSIONS

1A   FRIDAY, 8:30-9:45   GARDEN A
"Changing Education and Community Outreach in San Francisco's Sunset District"

— Sunset Neighborhood Beacon Center panel

The Sunset Neighborhood Beacon Center is an example of an organization located outside of Chinatown that caters to a wide population of Chinese Americans. The Beacon Center provides a variety of services to the Sunset community, such as after school programs, computer classes, and youth outreach. This panel will focus on the educational and community services offered by the Sunset Neighborhood Beacon Center, Francis Scott Key Elementary School, and the After School Program at Sunset Elementary School.

Moderator: Theresa J. Mah

Panelists: Alice Tam, Sean Yeung

1B   FRIDAY, 8:30-9:45   GARDEN B
Sweet Cakes, Long Journey: The Chinatowns of Portland, Oregon

by Marie Rose Wong

See New Book Talks

Moderator: Donald Chan

1C   FRIDAY, 8:30-9:45   SPRING A
"Rediscovering the Bay Area's Chinese Heritage, Part 1: The Intersections of Buildings, Landscapes, and Family Histories"

This panel explores ways we can learn from and promote conservation of cultural resources related to California's Chinese heritage. While past discrimination downplayed these histories, multi-year research and discoveries-in-progress show there is still much we can recover. We will also discuss legal frameworks on which we can draw in protecting historic buildings and sites.

Moderator: Leigh Jin

Presenters:

Kevin Frederick, *"Rediscovering Alameda's Railroad Avenue Chinatown: The History of 2320 Lincoln Avenue"*

    This presentation discusses Frederick's architectural and archival research into Alameda's Chinatown. Gim's Kitchen, located at 2320 and 2322 Lincoln Avenue, was built in the 1860s and is the oldest documented commercial building still standing in Alameda. The building also had direct ties to the Transcontinental Railroad, which stimulated the early building boom in Alameda, including Alameda's Chinatown.

Anthea Hartig, *"Tracing the Legacy of Asian Americans in the Frontier West: A Commitment to Preserving Historic Buildings and Landscapes That Reflect Our Diverse Heritage"*

    Since 1971, the National Trust's Western Office has been encouraging grassroots efforts to protect the historic buildings, sites, and communities associated with the many cultures that call the West their home. In 2001, the Western Office launched "The Mosaic of Western Heritage," a commitment to use its programs and activities to promote awareness of the contributions made to the West by diverse populations and to increase public support for preservation of Western heritage.

Jeffrey A. Ow, *"The Space-making Possibilities of Chinese American Family History: An Alameda Case Study"*

    Using the 2004 movement to save Gim's Kitchen in Alameda, Ow discusses how Chinese Americans in the San Francisco Bay Area affect preservation at the citywide scale through research, maintenance, and dissemination of their family history.

William Wong, "Oakland's Chinese Pioneers: A Forgotten Generation"

    The pre-World War II generation of Oakland Chinese represents an unsung link between the 1882 generations and the post-World War II generations. Wong will show some Oakland Chinese in their 80s and 90s, and narrate their stories, which are testimony to survival skills and cultural adaptability.

See conference papers and summaries

1D   FRIDAY, 8:30-9:45   SPRING B/C
"100 Years of Protest"

Moderator: Russell Jeung

Presenters:

Jane Leung Larson, *"The 1905 Anti-American Boycott as a Transnational Chinese Movement"*

    China's first nationwide mass movement, the 1905 anti-American boycott protesting the US exclusion policy, was transnational, linking Chinese in China with their counterparts all over the world. The papers of Tom Leung, a Los Angeles leader of the Chinese Empire Reform Association, provide evidence of these links and their political significance.

See conference papers and summaries

Jean Pfaelzer, *"Driven Out: Roundups and Resistance of the Chinese in Rural California"*

    This paper stems from Pfaelzer's forthcoming book and describes the expulsions of Chinese people from over 100 rural towns, from Southern California to the Washington Territory. It exposes and analyzes the purges, the failed purges, and the many successful efforts of Chinese resistance—legal, militant, legislative, and passive. The paper will place these expulsions in a global context of migration, trade, and expansion.

See conference papers and summaries

Phil Ting, *"Asian American Community Building to Fight the Racial Scapegoating of Wen Ho Lee"*

    In 1999, Dr. Wen Ho Lee was terminated from his job as a physicist in Los Alamos National Laboratories because of allegations that he was a spy. US District Judge James Parker apologized to Lee in 2000 and said the Departments of Energy and Justice "have embarrassed our entire nation and each of us who is a citizen of it." This presentation will discuss and analyze how the Asian American community protested the government's espionage case against Lee.

Andy Wang, *"Tracking Baodiao in Asia/America: Diaspora, Sovereignty, and Cold War Imperialism"*

    This paper tracks the Chinese diasporic movement to protect Diaoyutai at the edges of Asia and America in the 1970s. It seeks to reconceptualize the ethnicized notion of Asian America and to offer a narrative of transpacific cultural politics by locating diasporic identifications and the demands for sovereignty at the center of Asian American subjectivity formation.

1F   FRIDAY, 8:30-9:45   IMPERIAL A
High School Conference Orientation

— Sponsored by SFSU President's Office

Greetings: CHSA & SFSU (AAS, Associated Students Inc., Asian Student Union)

Guest Speaker: Eric Mar

1G   FRIDAY, 8:30-9:45   SAKURA A
Look Forward and Carry on the Past

— NAATA documentary presentation

See Documentaries

Presenter: Pamela Matsuoka

1H   FRIDAY, 8:30-9:45   SAKURA B
"Diasporic Poetics: Old and New Homes in Literature"

Moderator: Dorothy Wang

Presenters:

Patricia Chu, *"Where I Have Never Been: Diasporic Narratives of 'Return' by Later Generations"*

    This paper draws upon diaspora theory (Tu Wei-ming, Aihwa Ong) and personal narratives of first-time "return" to Chinese ancestral homelands by Chinese diasporic offspring (Denise Chong, Josephine Khu, and others) to explore how diaspora theories may be transformed when compared with personal accounts, and how Asian American models need to reconsider transnational travel and subjectivity.

Te-hsing Shan, *"Branching Out: Chinese American Literary Studies in Taiwan"*
> This paper addresses another direction of "branching out," namely, the spread of Chinese American literary studies from the United States to Taiwan. By tracing the historical development of this particular branch of American literary studies in Taiwan, this paper tries both to highlight some trends and characteristics of this development in the past 15 years and to offer a critical reflection upon them.

See conference papers and summaries

Steven G. Yao, *"The Changing Face of Chinese American Poetry"*
> This paper outlines the historical poetics of Chinese American verse from the early 20th century to the present. It also interrogates the cultural politics of different formal and rhetorical strategies used by Chinese American poets.

Da Zheng, *"Motherland and Chinese Diaspora"*
> This paper discusses *China Revisited*, a posthumously published volume by travel writer Chiang Yee, that records his trip to China in 1975. Placing the book in its historical context, the paper examines how the sensitivity of a diasporic Chinese and yearning for home(-land) play an important role in this passionate presentation of his motherland.

See conference papers and summaries

1I   FRIDAY, 8:30-9:45   SAKURA C
"Expanding Primary Sources for Chinese American Historical Research at the National Archives Pacific Region-San Francisco, 1975-2005"
— NARA panel
Chair: Daniel Nealand
Presenters:

Erika Lee, *"Documenting Exclusion: The INS Records at the National Archives"*
> This paper discusses the rich and largely unused source material on Chinese Americans located at the National Archives in San Bruno. From arrival records with interrogations and medical examinations to court transcripts and expulsion hearings, these records have been rightly described as the "silver lining" of the Chinese Exclusion laws, as they document the Chinese immigration experience in greater detail than any other source available.

Daniel Nealand, *"Overview and Examples of NARA San Francisco Historical Resources Then and Now, 1975-2005"*
> This presentation chronicles exponential expansion of relevant NARA-San Francisco archival holdings, research opportunities and finding aids from 1975's *Chinese Studies in Federal Records* through acquisition of major Angel Island holdings, and now, a 2004 publication noting archival records of myriad Federal agencies relating to Chinese American history. Exciting audiovisual examples include historic 14th Amendment court cases, family photographs, maps, and INS documents.

See conference papers and summaries

Brian Yee, *"The 13,000 Mile Effect of the National Archives (on Chinese American Youth)"*
> This is the story of research "brought to life" by a student's participation in the "In Search of Roots" Program sponsored by the Chinese Culture Foundation, CHSA, and the Overseas Chinese Affairs Office of Guangdong Province. Archival journeys in search of genealogical documents led to a journey of reunion with relatives in the ancestral home village. Slides portraying research and home village visits are included.

1J   FRIDAY, 8:30-9:45   KYOTO
"Race and Language in Public Education"
—Chinese for Affirmative Action panel
For over two decades, the San Francisco Unified School District has had to fulfill the obligations of two consent decrees. While *Lau* provides bilingual and bicultural instruction for immigrant students, *NAACP* requires school desegregation and educational equity.

Panelists will discuss the advocacy efforts in support of both cases and the District's attempt to balance the decrees.
Moderator: Christina Mei-Yue Wong
Panelists: Laureen Chew, Sandra Fewer

2A   FRIDAY, 10:00-11:15   GARDEN B
"Garment Worker Advocacy and Organizing in the 21st Century"
— Chinese for Affirmative Action panel
CAA, Chinese Progressive Association, the Asian Law Caucus, and a number of organizations are working to organize and advocate on behalf of displaced garment workers. This panel offers a historical perspective on garment work in the immigrant and Chinese American communities, and focuses on current issues and advocacy responses to displaced garment workers.
Moderator: Luna Yasui
Panelists: Joannie Chang, Kimi Lee, Stella Ng, Alex Tom

2B   FRIDAY, 10:00-11:15   GARDEN A
Doctor Mom Chung of the Fair-haired Bastards by Judy Tzu-Chun Wu
See New Book Talks
Moderator: Madeline Y. Hsu

2C   FRIDAY, 10:00-11:15   SPRING A
"Rediscovering the Bay Area's Chinese Heritage, Part 2: Opportunities and Challenges in Using Archaeology to Recover Lost Histories"
This panel explores ways we can learn from and promote conservation of cultural resources related to California's Chinese heritage. While past discrimination downplayed these histories, multi-year research and discoveries-in-progress show there is still much we can recover. We will also discuss legal frameworks on which we can draw in protecting historic buildings and sites.
Moderator: L. Ling-chi Wang
Presenters:

Kelly Fong, *"Return of the 'Heathen Chinee': Stereotypes in Chinese American Archaeology"*
> Archaeology may be the only objective data source countering the biased documentary record. Archaeologists in practice, however, must recognize stereotype's pervasiveness embedded in Euro-American society and permeating archaeology. Before archaeology can reach its objective potential, archaeologists must acknowledge stereotypes, abandon an acculturation/assimilation focus, and incorporate "emic" perspectives in archaeological analyses.

See conference papers and summaries

Anna Naruta, *"Rediscovering Oakland's San Pablo Avenue Chinatown"*
> Despite state law protecting archaeological resources, a redevelopment planned for the location of one of Oakland's earliest Chinatowns taught community members they had to struggle to get the developer to meet legal obligations. This presentation reports how community members worked to positively influence the excavation's scope and execution, and to seek appropriate commemoration of the rediscovered history.

See conference papers and summaries

Annita Waghorn, *"Lives Uncovered: The Cultural Landscape of Chinese Laundry Workers in Stockton, California"*
> The controversy over Chinese immigration was the subject of innumerable newspaper articles, cartoons, and official reports during the 19th century. Obscured by stereotypes and invective, the stories of individual immigrants and their daily lives have often been lost. Archaeology can help recover the links to individual immigrants by investigating the places in which they lived and worked, and adding texture to the bare details available in official records. This paper discusses the archaeological investigations of a laundry operated by Chinese immigrants in Stockton, California and its forty-year history.

2D   FRIDAY, 10:00-11:15   SPRING B/C
"Youth Empowerment: Employing Opportunities"
— CYC panel
Today, 20% of San Francisco are Chinese and Chinese youth make up 29.1% of the youth population in the city. The Mayor's Youth Employment and Education Program (MYEEP) is one of CYC's successful programs. It has a clientele of 95% Chinese immigrant youth. This youth panel will discuss the history of the program, one major success story, best practices, and how this program has impacted them in San Francisco.
Moderator: Michelle C. Wu
Panelists: Polly Fung, David Lin, Anna Liu, Jeffrey Ng
See conference papers and summaries

2G   FRIDAY, 10:00-11:15   SAKURA A
Island Mountain Days: Discovering Nevada's Chinese Miners
See Documentaries
Presenter: Sue Fawn Chung

2H   FRIDAY, 10:00-11:15   SAKURA B
"The Banyan Connection: SFSU and CHSA's Chinese American Migration History Tour"
— SFSU & CHSA panel
The Chinese American Migration History Tour is a collaborative travel program between SFSU's Asian American Studies Department and CHSA. It began as an AAS student travel program in the summer of 2000. It has since evolved into a multi-generational program with participants from across the United States and most recently from Australia. It is a unique migration history tour of the Cantonese emigration areas in Southern China, studying Chinese American ancestral origins in the Pearl River Delta region and how the Chinese American experience has impacted families and villages in the region.
Moderator: Jeannie Woo
Panelists: Brenda Eng, Dorothy Chinn Eng, Jennifer Lau, Victor Lim, William Lowe, Raymond N. Poon, Adolphus Wong

2I   FRIDAY, 10:00-11:15   SAKURA C
"Finding Family Connections"
Moderator: Allyson Tintiangco-Cubales
Presenters:
Colleen Fong, *"Establishing and Maintaining Chinese American Families in the Shadow of Exclusion: The Gin Chow and Jin Fong Families of Santa Barbara County"*
    This presentation is based on a larger paper that examines rural Chinese immigrant family formation and life during Exclusion (c. 1900), specifically the lives of two laborers who eventually became land-owning farmers, the mission inmates they married (one of whom was US-born and biracial), and their children.

Emma Woo Louie, *"Similarities in Given Names of Chinese and Anglo-Saxon Origins"*
    History, language, and social attitudes are some of the information encoded in our names. The diversity of American surnames spelled according to different Chinese dialects and spelling methods is a veritable record of changes that have taken place in Chinese America in the past 50 years. This diversity in surname spelling reveals Chinese Americans are a heterogeneous ethnic group who, although they do not share the same collective memories of life in America, have much in common in their observance of Chinese naming practices.
See conference papers and summaries

Lucky Owyang, *"The Owyang, Law, Sin-Suen Family Presence in the Sacramento River Delta"*
    For almost a decade, Owyang has been actively engaged in his Owyang, Law, and Sin-Suen family genealogy and history. He has discovered over 2,300 family members dating back centuries into southern China.

Henry Tom, *"The Changing Face of Chinese America: Reflections of Chinese American Genealogy"*
    Tom discusses his experience in Chinese American genealogy with various types/ content of information and research methods, with a focus on geographic resources.

2J   FRIDAY, 10:00-11:15   KYOTO
"Asian Pacific Islander Youth Leadership Development Program"
— CYC panel
CYC's API Youth Leadership Development Program provides opportunities for young people to learn about needs assessment, community development, advocacy, and organizing, and to develop leadership skills to empower themselves and their communities. The program incorporates a youth development approach that promotes lifelong learning and self-advocacy skills. Panel participants will discuss the need for a program that teaches these skills, especially in the southeast sector of San Francisco.
Moderator: Hubert V. Yee
Panelists: Lucinda Huang, Jiyang Liu, Calvin Jia Xing Ruan, Wai Kit Tam
See conference papers and summaries

3A   FRIDAY, 1:45-3:00   GARDEN A
"Rediscovering the Bay Area's Chinese Heritage, Part 3: Heritage Sites and Legal Protections"
This panel explores ways we can learn from and promote conservation of cultural resources related to California's Chinese heritage. While past discrimination downplayed these histories, multi-year research and discoveries-in-progress show there is still much we can recover. We will also discuss legal frameworks on which we can draw in protecting historic buildings and sites.
Moderator: Galin Luk
Presenters:
Susan Brandt-Hawley, *"Legal Protections for Community Resources: The California Environmental Quality Act"*
    The California Environmental Quality Act established legal protections for cultural resources, including significant historic buildings. This presentation will focus on CEQA obligations and preservation opportunities and tools.

Bryn Anderson Williams, *"Archaeology and San Jose's Market Street Chinatown"*
    In 1985, archaeologists working for the redevelopment agency of San Jose excavated portions of the Market Street Chinatown in downtown San Jose. This paper chronicles the archaeological project that grew out of that excavation, detailing how archaeological evidence can offer a unique perspective into the past.

3B   FRIDAY, 1:45-3:00   GARDEN B
Impossible Subjects: Illegal Aliens and the Making of Modern America
by Mae M. Ngai
See New Book Talks
Moderator: Robert A. Fung

3C   FRIDAY, 1:45-3:00   SPRING A
"Current Status of and Opportunities for Chinese American Literary Writings in the Chinese Language"
— Chinese language panel sponsored by the Lawrence Choy Lowe Memorial Fund and Poon Foundation
See Chinese Language Track
Chair: Maurice Chuck
Panelists: Frank Cheng, Maurice Chuck, Ray Lau, Ziyi Liu, Hong Lu, Sihong Zhao, Zong Ying

3D   FRIDAY, 1:45-3:00   SPRING B/C
"Unsung Opera"
— Kearny Street Workshop panel
This panel will present a personal view on the significance of Chinese opera to the lives of immigrants and their American-born offspring. Inspired by his father's connection to the opera, photographer Robert Hsiang explores the story of immigrants from China whose memories of the motherland were embodied in the art form.
Moderator: Ly Nguyen
Panelists: Nancy Hom, Bob Hsiang, Genny Lim

3G   FRIDAY, 1:45-3:00   SAKURA A

Chinese Couplets: "El Barrio Chino" and "My Mother's Names"
by Felicia Lowe
See Sneak Peeks
Moderator: Willard Chin

3H   FRIDAY, 1:45-3:00   SAKURA B

"Chinese Crossing Borders: A Roundtable Comparing Chinese in Canada and the United States"
— Chinese Canadian Historical Society of British Columbia panel
This discussion focuses on how local histories and the work of historical societies can intersect with global Chinese diasporas, addressing the challenges of Vancouver and the People's Republic of China, and how old and new migrations are both parallel to and distinct from San Francisco and Los Angeles.
See conference papers and summaries
Facilitator: Henry Yu
Presenters:

Imogene Lim, *"Chinatowns and Chinese Canadian History"*
Past and present Chinatowns in British Columbia are discussed in relation to Chinese Canadian history. The manner in which this history is remembered and presented are also examined, especially with respect to the founding of the Chinese Canadian Historical Society of British Columbia.

Edgar Wickberg, *"Founding a Chinese Historical Society in Canada: Challenges and Lessons from the United States"*
This paper discusses the goals and formative processes of the Chinese Canadian Historical Society, developed between 2003 and 2005. These were shaped by taking the Chinese Historical Society of America as both a model and a caution. Other shaping forces were the timing of CCHS establishment and the differences in history, demography, and organization between Canada and the United States.
See conference papers and summaries

Larry Wong, *"Comparing Chinese Exclusion and the Veterans Who Overcame It"*
The 1923 Immigration Act was the accumulation of efforts to discourage Chinese from entering Canada. The Chinese Exclusion Act devastated the Chinese communities and when Canada entered the war, some 600 Chinese volunteered to serve their country. Their actions helped to repeal the Act and changed the social landscape of the Chinese community forever.
See conference papers and summaries

3I   FRIDAY, 1:45-3:00   SAKURA C

"China City, Los Angeles"
Los Angeles chose Chinatown for its new Union Station site in the 1930s. Two groups competed to build their model. One was "China City." Harry Chandler of *Los Angeles Times* with Christine Sterling opted for a slice of Pearl Buck's hidden life and culture of old China, ancient narrow alleyways, exotic music, and a charming Chinese theater. Just a few blocks away, the former Chinatown merchants joint ventured a "New Chinatown" enterprise, beckoning tourists to a refreshing Jasmine cup of tea at the attractive and inviting restaurant, and luring spectators to chomp the lavish and super China bean sprout burger. Both venues opened in 1939. See and hear about the "China City" images of 100-plus stores and tourist romantic spots, and learn about its fascinating history, story, and people.
Moderator: Paul Louie
Panelists: Suellen Cheng, Paul Louie, Ruby Ling Louie

3J   FRIDAY, 1:45-3:00   KYOTO

Reception for CSU Chancellor Charles B. Reed.
All conference attendees welcome.
Co-hosts: SFSU Chinese American Faculty and Staff Association and Office of International Programs

3K   FRIDAY, 1:45-3:00   PEACE PLAZA

"Not Who You Think I Am: Forging Past, Present, and Future"
— High School Program sponsored by SFSU President's Office
See High School Program
Introduction: Leonard Shek
Youth Speaks Poets/Performers: Nico Cary, Michelle Lee, Adriel Luis

4A   FRIDAY, 3:15-4:30   GARDEN A

"The Mental and Physical Health of Chinese America"
Moderator: Galin Luk
Presenters:

Alvin Alvarez & David Woo, *"Dealing with Racism: Psychological Perspectives on Chinese Americans' Experiences"*
This is an exploratory study examining the psychological impact of racism on Chinese Americans in the Bay Area. Specifically, the presentation will address the types of racism that Chinese Americans encounter, as well as the manner in which individuals react to and cope with racism.

Kent J. Woo, *"The Chinese Health Agenda—Proposed Strategies for Improving Chinese American Community Health and Wellness"*
This presentation will be an overview of NICOS Chinese Health Coalition's "Chinese Community Health Summit," including summaries of primary and secondary research findings illustrating the community's unique demographic and health characteristics. Key issues will be presented as well as strategies proposed to address them.
See conference papers and summaries

4B   FRIDAY, 3:15-4:30   GARDEN B

Yee-Hah!: Remembrance and Longing by Albert Hoy Yee
See New Book Talks
Moderator: Yanchun Zhang

4C   FRIDAY, 3:15-4:30   SPRING A

"Chinese American Political Identities"
— Bilingual panel sponsored by the Lawrence Choy Lowe Memorial Fund and Poon Foundation
See Chinese Language Track
Moderator: Madeline Y. Hsu
Presenters:

Peter Kwong, *"Changing Geographic and Economic Mobility of Chinese Americans: What Does That Mean to the Civil Rights Agenda and How Does It Affect US/China Relations?"* (English)
Systematic analysis of Chinese American community (as part of Asian American Studies) is a product of the Civil Rights movement of the 1960s. The community, however, has changed dramatically since that time. What was once largely a remarkably uniform urban working-class population of limited size grew rapidly to encompass immigrants of diverse origins and unprecedented social and transnational mobility. The high degree of demographic and economic changes that the community experienced is a result that went hand in hand with America's transition from a cold war industrial superpower to an empire with global reach. How do these developments affect the Civil Rights agenda? Can the outdated debates over race and assimilation be modified to accommodate the multiple ways Chinese Americans have adopted to adjust to this country? What impact does the changing dynamics between the United States and China have on the Chinese American community?

Pei-te Lien, *"Homeland Origins and Political Identities among Chinese Americans"* (English)
How has Taiwan's political change towards democracy impacted the political participation of Chinese Americans originated from Taiwan? This paper compares the content and style of homeland politics practiced by Chinese immigrants from Taiwan both before and after the liberalization and democratization of the island of Taiwan.
See conference papers and summaries

L. Ling-chi Wang, *"Race, Space, and Class in Chinese America: Toward a Civil Rights Agenda"*
> Paper synopsis not available at press time.

Yinglong Zhang, *"On Chinese American Post-war Political Activities"* (Chinese)
> Paper synopsis not available at press time.
See conference papers and summaries

4D   FRIDAY, 3:15-4:30   SPRING B/C
"The Chinese Historical and Cultural Project"
— Chinese Historical and Cultural Project panel
The Chinese Historical and Cultural Project of Santa Clara County began by replicating the original temple of San Jose Chinatown as a historical museum. CHCP now holds a Chinese Summer Festival at the site, has developed an educational curriculum, and provides a traveling exhibit. Other outreach includes scholarships, sponsorships of artists, performers, authors, and film festivals. Nearing its 20th anniversary, CHCP stays committed to its mission of educating, promoting, and preserving the history and culture of Chinese Americans.
Moderator: William G. Roop
Panelists: Rodney Lum, Gerrye Wong
See conference papers and summaries

4F   FRIDAY, 3:15-4:30   IMPERIAL A
"APA Politics: New Trends, New Voices"
This roundtable focuses on the growing influence of asian and pacific islanders as candidates and elected officials. APIs are 4.7% Of the US population in 2000, yet there were only 310 elected officials from all levels in 2001, which is one-tenth of 1% of all elected officials in the country. However, in the past 10 years, there has been a noticeable growth in the number and positions held by APIs. While there has not been a US Senator from the mainland since S.I. Hayakawa in the 1970s, APIs have been elected to Congress, Governor, and as state and local representatives in diverse locations in the country. This panel will explore the process of how APIs are getting elected, what role does the API community play in their election, and what are their experiences once they are elected to office. The panelists will also explore how does API electoral politics compare in Hawai'i and the mainland.
Moderator: Sue Lee
Panelists:
Judy Chu — On being and becoming a mayor and assemblymember
Kris Wang — On being and becoming a council member
Kim Geron & James Lai, *"Pathways to Political Incorporation for APAs in Urban and Suburban Contexts"*

4G   FRIDAY, 3:15-4:30   SAKURA A
The Chinese in Hollywood Project by Arthur Dong
See Sneak Peeks
Introduction: Robert A. Corrigan
Moderator: Jenny Lau

4H   FRIDAY, 3:15-4:30   SAKURA B
"East Wind Magazine: Henry S. Louie, The Man and His Dream"
East Wind Magazine was the first publication written in English to cover the issues of the Chinese American youth during the years from 1944 to 1948. This was the dream of Henry S. Louie who grew up in Cleveland, Ohio. It was his hope that the magazine would be a vehicle for the Chinese American youth all over the United States to express, exchange, and communicate their thoughts and concerns. Despite a changing Chinese America, some of the same issues continue to exist for the youth of today. Henry and his dream will be presented by a panel of former associates who helped to make the publication possible.
Moderator: Sylvia Joe Louie
Panelists: Paul Louie, Sylvia Joe Louie, Mamie Moy, Wood Moy

4I   FRIDAY, 3:15-4:30   SAKURA C
"A New Elite: Professional and Intellectual Immigrants"
Moderator: Robert A. Fung
Presenters:
Wei Li, *"The Rise of New 'Creative' Chinese Immigrants"*
> The purpose of this paper is to outline the geographic and social impacts of "creative" immigrants in the United States, with particular attention to how they transform America's suburbs in high-tech regions. The paper compares and contrasts the roles of highly skilled Chinese (including Hong Kong and Taiwan) and Asian Indian immigrants.

5A   SATURDAY, 8:30-10:00   GARDEN A
"Reassessing Chinese American and Australian History with the Help of Archaeologists"
Chair: Sue Fawn Chung
Presenters:
Jessica Axsom, *"The Chinese Six Companies in Virginia City"*
> This paper focuses on the excavation of a Chinese Six Companies mercantile in Virginia City, Nevada to gain a greater understanding of the urban Chinese community within Nevada from the late 1800s. This is done by looking at the amount of assimilation evident with the urban Chinese community in comparison to rural Chinese communities. In addition, there is an interest in the business relationship and artifact exchange between the Euro-American community and the Chinese American community in the Virginia City area.

Sue Fawn Chung, *"History and Archaeology: A Better Understanding of the Chinese American Past"*
> The advent of the Civil Rights movement brought an interest in the diversity of cultures that constitute the United States. Long forgotten Chinese American archaeological sites were uncovered and revealed a history of Chinese Americans not written down in places like a predominately Chinese mining community in Island Mountain, Nevada that thrived from 1873 to 1917, and Chinese lumbering camps in the Sierra Nevada in the late 19th century.

Kelly Dixon and Carrie E. Smith, *"Life along Daggett Creek: Chinese Woodchoppers in the Lake Tahoe Basin"*
> The 1859 Comstock silver strike was centered in Virginia City, Nevada. Lake Tahoe's timber was essential to Comstock's success. The graveyards of Tahoe's forest lie deep in the mine tunnels. Chinese labor fueled this industry. Chinese "woodchoppers" worked in the region beginning 1867. A series of archaeological sites represent their lives.

Barry John McGowan, *"Adaptation and Organization: The History and Heritage of the Chinese in Western New South Wales, Australia"*
> McGowan discusses the extent and significance of Chinese involvement in agriculture and pastoralism in western New South Wales, Australia. Themes include migration patterns, labor organization, contractual arrangements, remuneration and working conditions, environmental impact, technological adaptation, material evidence, and race relationships. Some comparisons with California are also included.
See conference papers and summaries

5B   SATURDAY, 8:30-10:00   GARDEN B
Faithful Generations: Race and New Asian American Churches by Russell Jeung
See New Book Talks
Moderator: Ben Kobashigawa

5C   SATURDAY, 8:30-10:00   SPRING A
"Preserving the Past: New Chinese American Museums"
Representatives from four new Chinese American museums will present and discuss the trials and tribulations of establishing a Chinese American museum. See also Index of Caucus Participants for museum description.
Moderator: Anna Naruta
Panelists:
Auburn Joss House Museum (Lucky Owyang)
Chinese American Museum (Sonia Mak and Pauline Wong)
Chinese-American Museum of Chicago (Chuimei Ho)
Chinese American Museum of Northern California (Brian L. Tom)

5D   SATURDAY, 8:30-10:00   SPRING B/C
"Mandarin for Everyone"
— Chinese American International School panel
With the rise of China in every area from business to politics, the interest in Mandarin education in the United States is greater than ever. At the forefront is Chinese American International School in San Francisco. Founded in 1981, CAIS was the nation's first preK-8 bilingual Mandarin-English immersion school and remains the top institution of its kind. A panel of teachers, students, parents, and alumni will share the secrets of CAIS's success and explain why everyone should learn Mandarin.
Moderator: Joyce M. Chan
Panelists: Nai-Fang Chang, Kimberly Conley, Andrew W. Corcoran, Sherrie Yao, James Young

5E   SATURDAY, 8:30-10:00   OSAKA
Portraits of Pride by Chinese Historical Society of Southern California
See New Book Talks
Moderator: Eugene Moy
Panelists: William F. Chew, Joyce Mar, Wing Mar

5G   SATURDAY, 8:30-10:00   SAKURA A
Courage and Contributions: The Chinese in Ventura County - Ventura County Chinese American Historical Society documentary presentation
See Documentaries
Introduction: Kenneth Louie
Panelists: Linda Bentz, George Sandoval, Angela Soo Hoo, George Yu

5H   SATURDAY, 8:30-10:00   SAKURA B
"Reflecting on *Roots*: The Impact of the *In Search of Roots* Program"
— Chinese Culture Center & CHSA panel
The "In Search of Roots" Program, now in its 14th year, educates young Chinese Americans on their heritage and family history in the United States and in China through seminars, research sessions, and a pilgrimage to ancestral villages in Guangdong, China. This panel, composed of Roots alumni, will explore the development and the successes of the program.
Moderator: Harry Mok
Panelists: Lauren May Choi-Dea, Calvin B. Fung, Matthew Harrison, Alice Kwong, Dickson Lam, Jeremy Jhen Yu Lee, Denise Leo, Evan Leong, Marisa Louie, Nguyen Louie, Monica "Wayie" Ly, April M. Yee, Brian Yee

5I   SATURDAY, 8:30-10:00   SAKURA C
"Chinese Americans in Contemporary Hawai'i"
Chair/Discussant: Franklin Ng
Presenters:
Anthony Chang, *"The Little Chinatown That Could"*
    The Chinese had a significant influence on the development of contemporary Hawaiian culture. Hawai'i, in turn, nurtured its evolving Chinese community, producing individuals who have transformed their world. Examining Dr. Sun Yat Sen and other Chinese in Hawai'i, this presentation will view a heritage that has opened new paths around the world.

Diane Letoto, *"Sandalwood Sojourns: Constructing Cultural Identity through Dance"*
    The development of Chinese in Hawai'i occurred when second and third generation Chinese Americans began searching for their "cultural roots." With lack of resources and no dance teachers, pioneers of Chinese dance in Hawai'i were dependent upon visiting artists to provide dance lessons or constructed dance based upon Chinese opera movements. This paper examines the development of Chinese dance in Hawai'i and some of the transformations that are currently taking place with changes in the political economy.

Jinzhao Li, *"Constructing Chinese America through Beauty Pageants in Hawai'i"*
    This paper examines the representation of Chinese Americans in Hawai'i through the longest running Chinese American beauty pageant—the Narcissus Queen Pageant. It demonstrates the changing meaning of Chineseness, Americanness, and Chinese American femininity in contemporary Hawai'i. This complicates the representation of Chinese America in the continental United States.

Roger Liu, *"Ethnic Chinese in Hawai'i and the U.S. Congress Akaka Bill"*
    Liu will present the consequences and effects on the state of Hawai'i regarding the passage of the Akaka Bill by US Congress.

Leonard Kwai Ming Wong, *"Hawai'i Chinese: The Americanization Movement"*
    In the early 1900s, a new wave of immigrants to America was perceived as intruding upon the lifestyles and values of earlier arrivals. There were substantial efforts to "Americanize" the newcomers. At that time, American-born Chinese in Hawai'i had difficulty being accepted in mainstream society, despite being citizens and educated in Western institutions. To achieve social progress, there arose among them a movement to "Americanize" new Chinese arrivals.

5J   SATURDAY, 8:30-10:00   KYOTO
"Black, White, and Yellow: Crossing the Color Lines"
Moderator: Gregory Mark
Presenters:
John Jung, *"Forming a Chinese Identity When Everyone Else Is Either Black or White"*
    What was it like growing up in the only Chinese family in a Georgia town before the Civil Rights movement? How did Jung's parents shape his Chinese identity that both buffered and exacerbated prejudices from blacks and whites alike? Upon moving to San Francisco at age 15, Jung had to learn what it meant to be Chinese all over again.
See conference papers and summaries

Shanshan Lan, *"Beyond Black and White: Chinese Americans in Multiracial Chicago"*
    Based on ethnographic fieldwork in Chicago's Chinatown and Bridgeport communities, this paper examines how working-class Chinese Americans, who share common social spaces with African Americans in inner city Chicago, tend to have a different understanding of racial difference than middle-class Chinese Americans living in the suburbs.
See conference papers and summaries

Wendy Marie Thompson, *"Black Chinese: Historical Intersections, Hybridity, and the Creation of Home"*
    This paper explores the subjects of mixed race African American Chinese bodies and the everyday encounters among Chinese and African Americans between the late 1800s and the Second World War in an effort to create a discourse on racial hybridity that moves beyond current narratives of African American and Chinese racial conflict.
See conference papers and summaries

6A   SATURDAY, 10:15-11:45   GARDEN A
"Remembering Angel Island: New Research and Preservation Efforts"
— Angel Island Immigration Station Foundation panel
The Angel Island Immigration Station Foundation preserves the Immigration Station, a National Historic Landmark, as a place that honors the inspiring story and rich cultural

heritage of Pacific Coast immigrants and their descendants. This panel will explore new research and projects around the Immigration Station that expand and enrich our understanding of the Chinese immigrants and their experiences on Angel Island.

Moderator: Erika Gee

Presenters:

Charles Egan, *"And the Walls Do Talk: Understanding Immigrants Through the Barracks' Inscriptions"*

A small project team has recently undertaken a survey of the visible inscriptions in the detainee barracks at Angel Island Immigration Station. These include not only the well-known Chinese poems, but also many other messages in Chinese and other languages. Egan will share preliminary results of the research efforts.

Erika Gee, *"Sharing the Angel Island Story: Current Efforts in Site Preservation and Educational Outreach"*

AIISF has been the tireless advocate for the preservation of the poetry and remaining structures on the former detention site, and for the creation of a world-class visitor and genealogical research center. This presentation will highlight the current multi-phase restoration efforts, outreach to schools, teachers, and community members, and the Angel Island Oral History Project, a partnership with the Pacific Regional Humanities Center based out of UC Davis.

Wan Liu, *"The Sustaining Sense of Cultural Community"*

The poems written by the Chinese immigrants who were detained on Angel Island emanate collectively a sense of cultural community. Defined by these poets' expressions of shared feelings, mutual encouragement, and linkage to a common cultural heritage, this sense of cultural community arguably served as an important source of inspiration and support for the immigrants in detainment.

6B   SATURDAY, 10:15-11:45   GARDEN B

Americans First: Chinese Americans and the Second World War

by K. Scott Wong

See New Book Talks

Moderator: Gregory Mark

6C   SATURDAY, 10:15-11:45   SPRING A

"Regional Histories from America and Australia"

Moderator: William G. Roop

Presenters:

Kathie Hoxsie, *"An Overview of Some 21st Century Legacies of Infrastructure Chinese Built in the Mid to Late 1800s in California and Nevada"*

In the mid to late 1800s, Chinese laborers were vital to the construction of numerous railroads, ditches, tunnels, flumes, bridges, dams, and other infrastructure in the American West. Hoxsie's research, conducted since 1998, highlights at least seven sites in California and Nevada where the skill of the Chinese still stands and/or remains in use today. Hoxsie will explain how and why the Chinese were hired, what exactly they built 140 years ago, and what, if anything, communities have done to honor these Chinese.

Murray Lee, *"A Snapshot of the Asian Community in 1930 San Diego"*

Data from the US census of 1930 and city directories were used to locate and identify all the Asians in an eight-block area of downtown San Diego's Asian community. The data allows one to virtually enter the homes of all the people living in the area and to record their names, family relationships, dates of birth, language spoken, date of entry (if an immigrant), occupations, etc. From this data, a map of each block was created locating all the Asians and their businesses.

See conference papers and summaries

Gene Moy, *"Notes on Chicago Chinatown, 1880-1930"*

Using a number of different techniques, the beginnings of the early Chicago Chinese community are reconstructed as it grew from a dozen laundrymen to the bustling Chinatown at its present location.

John Muir, *"A Shrimp Junk for San Francisco Bay: The Building of the* Grace Quan*"*

On October 25, 2003, a crew of staff and volunteers from San Francisco Maritime National Historical Park, in cooperation with China Camp State Park, launched a 43-foot long replica of a San Francisco Bay shrimp junk. These extraordinary vessels were built at the site of the many Chinese shrimp fishing camps that dotted the Bay Area between 1860 and 1910. Muir will discuss the research that supported the design of the *Grace Quan*, and will also share the saga of the boat's construction and first year of sailing.

Raymond N. Poon, *"The Chinese Downunder–A Brief Overview of the Early Chinese Immigrants in Australia"*

This talk will cover a brief overview of the history of Colonial Australia, the Chinese who were employed as indentured labourers and gold seekers to the "New Gold Mountain," and the experiences they encountered.

6D   SATURDAY, 10:15-11:45   SPRING B/C

"Queer Chinese Hapa People and Marriage Rights: Intersections between Same Sex Marriage and Interracial Marriage"

For queer Chinese Americans of mixed heritage, the social and legal conflicts over their right to marry whomever they love reflect their parents' struggle to love and marry interracially. Comparisons of the current struggle over gay marriage with the fight for the right to marry interracially reveal important intersections between social and legal processes of constructing race and sexuality. If we look at race as being "queer" when it is not "pure," then what can we understand about state mechanisms and legal structures designed to control "transgressive" sexualities—those that cross race borders or subvert gender roles or gender boundaries?

Chair: Wei Ming Dariotis

Presenters:

Wei Ming Dariotis, *"My Race, Too, Is Queer: Chinese Hapa People Fight Anti-Miscegenation and Anti-Gay Marriage"*

Dariotis explores the use of arguments about anti-miscegenation by marriage equality (gay marriage rights) activists (like Willy Wilkinson) and artists (like Stuart Gaffney). Through the lens of the legal history surrounding the anti-miscegenation/interracial marriage debate, Dariotis examines the construction of mixed race as a kind of "queer" identity.

See conference papers and summaries

Stuart Gaffney, *"Marriage Rights in the Media"*

Media-making sets the stage for intersecting interracial and same-sex marriage rights in Gaffney's family. Films that Gaffney have directed on marriage themes (from his grandfather's second wife in China to his parents' right to marry interracially) contrast with his experience as the subject of media coverage around his own right to marry his partner of 18 years.

See conference papers and summaries

Willy Wilkinson, *"Double Hapa-ness: Hapa and Trans Perspectives on Same-Sex Marriage"*

Paper synopsis not available at press time.

6E   SATURDAY, 10:15-11:45   OSAKA

"What Is Chinese American Art?"

— CHSA panel

This panel is in conjunction with an exhibition currently held at the CHSA Museum. It addresses the question, "What is Chinese American art," that came about in relation to CHSA's exhibition of C.C. Wang's work. Is Wang, who was a naturalized US citizen living and working New York for many decades, a Chinese American artist or is he a Chinese artist living in America? That is the question.

Moderator: Irene Poon Andersen

Panelists: Mark Johnson, Ch'ingche Lo, Jade Snow Wong

See conference papers and summaries

6G   FRIDAY, 10:15-11:45   SAKURA A
Sam Fow Stories—Memories from Marysville's Chinatown
— Yuba Historical Society documentary presentation
See Documentaries
Moderator: Daniel Barth
Panelists: Doreen Foo Croft, Frank Kim, Jack Kim, Bing Ong

6H   SATURDAY, 10:15-11:45   SAKURA B
"The Emergence of Chinese American Women"
— Square and Circle Club panel
Photos and press clippings depict the 80-year history of the Square and Circle Club, the
oldest Chinese American women's community service organization in America. Its history
is essentially that of Chinese American women's growing independence from stereotypical
roles and emergence into community leadership. Panelists are Chinese American women
who will discuss their successful careers in non-traditional fields.
Moderator: Alice Lowe
Panelists: Loni Ding, Jennie Chin Hansen, Daphne Kwok, Doreen Yang
See conference papers and summaries

6I   SATURDAY, 10:15-11:45   SAKURA C
*Becoming Chinese American: A History of Communities and
Institutions* by Him Mark Lai and *Him Mark Lai: The People's Historian* by Evan Leong
See New Book Talks and Documentaries
Moderator: Eric Mar

6J   SATURDAY, 10:15-11:45   KYOTO
"Sight and Sound: Chinese in American Culture"
Moderator: Daniel Gonzales
Presenters:
Darren Lee Brown, *"Yellow Fever: Asiaphilia and the Maintenance of Orientalism in
Contemporary Popular Music"*
> This paper explores how Asians, through Western lens, have been presented as
> a homogenous and Orientalized other. Particular emphasis will focus on artists
> who utilize Asian aesthetics including music scales (both "learned" or sampled),
> culturally "authentic" motifs, and images appropriated from Asia via popular culture.
> Genre-wise, the paper discusses these phenomena as they occur in a variety of music
> such as jazz, pop, new wave, hip-hop, and R&B.

Di Yin Lu, *"Racialized Images in 1920s and 1930s San Francisco: The Paintings of Eva Fong
Chan"*
> Eva Fong Chan is a Chinese American painter whose career flourished until the
> 1940s. Chan studied painting in San Francisco and exhibited in local institutions
> such as the San Francisco Art Association at the Palace of Fine Arts. Though briefly
> affiliated with a modern art group, Chan's painting style maintained a realistic
> approach that eloquently projects the privileges and constraints of a Chinese
> American, upwardly mobile, middle-class individual in the early 20th century. The
> choices and experiences that Chan's paintings portray give us a unique insight into
> the racial and ethnic discourses concerning Asian Americans and Asian immigrants in
> early 20th century San Francisco.
See conference papers and summaries

Krystyn Moon, *"Looking at Acrobats: Chinese Performers and Globalization, 1850s-1930s"*
> This paper addresses the global implications of Chinese acrobats and their
> performances from the 1850s through the 1930s. These performers traveled
> throughout the world, often for years at a time, to entertain non-Chinese audiences.
> There were, however, limits to the admiration of Chinese acrobats, and they often
> saw different responses from non-Chinese on and off the stage.

7A   SATURDAY, 1:45-3:15   GARDEN A
"Silver Bay Chinese Christian Youth Conference"
The 1943 California Tahoe Chinese Christian Youth Conference voted to send four
delegates to explore and develop a weeklong coed summer program in the East Coast. The

first conference started at Silver Bay, New York in 1944. It drew youth from the East and
Midwest, and continued for 20 years, up to the early 1960s. Three of the original team
will tell the story of this surprising activity, its development during the World War II years,
and the significance it has for the emerging second generation.
Moderator: James Louie
Panelists: George Kan, Paul Louie, Edward Leong Way

7B   SATURDAY, 1:45-3:15   GARDEN B
*Yellowface: Creating the Chinese in American Popular Music and
Performance, 1850s-1920s* by Krystyn Moon
See New Book Talks
Moderator: Gregory Mark

7C   SATURDAY, 1:45-3:15   SPRING A
"Teaching the Chinese Language in America" — Chinese language panel
sponsored by the Lawrence Choy Lowe Memorial Fund and Poon Foundation
See Chinese Language Track
Moderator: Marlon K. Hom
Presenters:
Stella Yu-Mei Kwoh, *"Mainstreaming and Professionalizing Chinese Language Education: A
New Mission for a New Century"*
> This paper discusses the 21st century's trends of development in Chinese language
> education in the United States. Following the availability of SATII-Chinese and AP-
> Chinese tests, Chinese language education has gradually been mainstreamed into
> public and private schools. Various models of Chinese language education have been
> developed. Kwoh reviews today's models of Chinese language education and offers
> some suggestions for reform. She also discusses the basic curriculum and needs of
> a professional development program for Chinese language teachers as well as the
> requirements for Mandarin Single Subject Credential in California.
See conference papers and summaries

Catherine Leung, *"The Status of Chinese Language Schools in San Francisco"*
> Leung will discuss the situation and status of San Francisco's Chinese language
> schools, its structure, demographics, and curriculum.
See conference papers and summaries

Puichee Leung, *"Teaching Huayu Chinese versus Teaching Guoyu, Putonghua, or Hanyu"*
> Today's Chinese language education is unlike that of the past. The Chinese language-
> learning target audience are children of the Chinese living in America or Chinese
> Americans. Huayu is not guoyu, putonghua, or hanyu. Huayu is the language spoken
> by the Chinese Americans. Proper huayu is not Cantonese, Hakka (Kejia), or any
> other Chinese dialect, and should use putonghua as its foundation.
See conference papers and summaries

7D   SATURDAY, 1:45-3:15   SPRING B/C
"Mirrors and Windows: Chinese American Filmmakers"
The filmmakers in this roundtable discuss the ways in which their work reflects and
interprets the concerns of the changing Chinese American community, including constantly
shifting definitions of culture and identity, the Chinese diaspora, representations of Asian
Americans in popular culture, and the ways in which film can be used as a means of
social change. Panelists reflect several different aspects of the Chinese American media
arts community—new immigrants, American-born Chinese, established filmmakers, and
emerging artists, working in a variety of genres and techniques. Each filmmaker will
screen a brief sample of their current work and discuss its relationship to themes and
issues in the Chinese American community at large.
Chair: Valerie Soe
Panelists: Curtis Choy, Felicia Lowe, Simon Mah, Valerie Soe
See conference papers and summaries

7E   SATURDAY, 1:45-3:15   OSAKA
"Religious Practices in Chinese American Communities"
Religious practices in Chinese American communities are very diverse. From the Daoist
rituals and the Bomb Day celebration in Marysville, California to a comparison between

contemporary late 19th century Daoist temples in Shanghai and California to death ceremonies then and now, this panel explores some interesting facets of Chinese American culture.

Chair/Discussant: Sue Fawn Chung
Presenters:

Paul G. Chace, *"Bomb Day Festivals at the Bok Kai Temple in Marysville: Changes and Transformations since the 1880s"*

> Marysville's Bomb Day Festival, a transplanted Chinese village rite and a "birthday party" for the town's patron, has evolved as the community's principal festival, a celebration of civic harmony. It includes parades, banquets, entertainment, and "lucky bomb" competitions. Interpretive restraint is fundamental for support and participation in this multi-ethnic California community.

Roberta S. Greenwood, *"A Change in Direction: Bringing the Ancestors Home"*

> In the early years of immigration, remains of the dead were systematically gathered and shipped to China for burial in the homeland. Because of the time and expense of travel to China for traditional observances, families now permanently established here are bringing the ancestors to the United States so that proper respects can be paid.

See conference papers and summaries

Joan Mann, *"Two Daoist Temples: The Baiyunquan (White Cloud Temple) in Shanghai and the Bok Kai Temple in Marysville, 1880s until Present"*

> In the late 1880s, the Baiyunguan in Shanghai and the Bok Kai Temple in Marysville, California were built and both Daoist temples still have a following. The religious life of the people in both places is tightly woven into the history, economics, language, and cultural fabric. However, both have experienced major problems as the communities around the temples have changed. This paper looks at the similarities and differences in the physical layout, iconography, practices, beliefs, and activities of both temples.

See conference papers and summaries

7G   SATURDAY, 1:45-3:15   SAKURA A
American Knees by Eric Byler
See Sneak Peeks
Moderator: Wei Ming Dariotis

7H   SATURDAY, 1:45-3:15   SAKURA B
"The Alien Files or 'A' Files: The Missing Link"

This panel will showcase a new, as yet barely explored "source frontier" in American immigration, ethnic, and family historical research: the huge US government investigative case files group known as "Alien Registration" or "A" Files. They contain informational and evidentiary documents vital for Chinese American family historians, essential as well for understanding such subjects as American immigration policy/practices and the Chinese diaspora, and of great interest for many other social science areas.

See conference papers and summaries
Moderator: Florence Tu
Presenters:

Jennie F. Lew, *"The ULTIMATE A-File of 'Native Hawaiian Born' Sun Yat Sen!"*

> Paper synopsis not available at press time.

Jeanie W. Chooey Low, *"Access Techniques"*

> This paper examines access techniques to the restricted Alien Registration or "A" Files. Each case file documents an individual's immigration and naturalization history, in some cases, spanning a period of 30 or more years. The case files contain photographs, immigration interviews, and subsequent investigations. At present, these files require a Freedom of Information/Privacy Form.

Daniel Nealand, *"Archival Appraisal Considerations"*

> This presentation highlights recent and breaking developments in response to Chinese American and other research community efforts to bring older "A" Files into the National Archives, finally open for historical public research (though still subject to FOIA exemptions). Discussion includes progress by NARA's "Personal Data Records Appraisal Task Force" and concerns about where prospective new National Archives "A" Files collections might be located.

7I   SATURDAY, 1:45-3:15   SAKURA C
"Culture, Generation, and Class: Current Research on the Health of Chinese Americans"

This panel discusses the Chinese American experience of health and illness from multiple categories, including that of reproductive and sexual health, health care access, cancer, and chronic illnesses. In addition, the panel explores how different generations and cultural perspectives influence concepts of health for Chinese Americans.

Moderator: Grace Yoo
Presenters:

Christine Kwan, *"Accommodating Care of Type 2 Diabetes for the Chinese American Family"*

> The aim is to highlight culturally-unique responses to Type 2 diabetes among new Chinese immigrant families. Narrative group interviews with 16 families yielded three cultural considerations in diabetes management: (1) conceptualizations of illness and its management, (2) the meaning of food, and (3) effects of the disease on family dynamics.

See conference papers and summaries

Amy Lam, *"Young Chinese Americans and Reproductive and Sexual Health"*

> There is limited knowledge about the sexual and reproductive health needs of Chinese American young people. This presentation examines the sexual and reproductive health attitudes and behaviors of Chinese Americans and contrasts them to those of white Americans. Specifically, Lam discusses factors that put individuals at risk for STDS and unintended pregnancy.

Judy N. Lam, *"Chinese and Smoking: A Biopsychosocial Framework to Understand the Current State of Research and Effectiveness of Interventions"*

> As the leading killer of America, tobacco is responsible for more adult deaths than AIDS, legal drugs, illegal drugs, road accidents, murder, and suicide combined (WHO, 2001). The vast majority of smokers recognize that smoking is hazardous to their physiological health. It has been argued that what leads people to engage in such a dangerous habit, however, are the perceived psychological and social benefits. Although there has been little consideration of how emotions and culture influence smoking behaviors, research in cultural psychology has shown that the norms that govern the nature of relationships differ greatly across cultures such as individualistic as compared with collectivistic ones. This paper suggests that it would be beneficial to use the biopsychosocial framework to integrate psychological and cultural influences into smoking prevention and intervention programs.

Evaon C. Wong-Kim, *"Chinese Women, Immigration, and Breast Cancer"*

> This study examines Chinese women and their risk for developing breast cancer. Attitude towards breast cancer screening, treatment, and prognosis among Chinese immigrant women are addressed. Issues relating to cancer survivorship, quality of life, and supportive services after a breast cancer diagnosis are also discussed.

See conference papers and summaries

Joshua Yang, *"Increasing Chinese Immigrant Access to Care: The Development and Role of Ethnic-Specific Health Care Organizations"*

> The current paper describes the role and development of ethnic-specific health care systems in the service of immigrant ethnic groups. Using the Chinese community of San Francisco as a case study, a four-stage model is presented as a framework to increase access to quality health care for marginalized ethnic groups.

7J   SATURDAY, 1:45-3:15   KYOTO
"Masks of Democracy: The Politics of Racism in Political Cartoons"
— CHSA & Manilatown Heritage Center panel

Using examples of political cartoons from the private collections of Philip Choy and Abe Ignacio, "Masks of Democracy" unveils the deceit of our Nation's foreign and domestic politics in the Pacific. This panel is presented in conjunction with two exhibitions currently held at the CHSA Museum and the Manilatown Heritage Center (see p.   ). The panel is also dedicated in memory of Helen Toribio (Asian American Studies lecturer at SFSU and City College of San Francisco; active member of the Filipino American National

Historical Society, East Bay Chapter and the Filipino American Coalition for Environmental Solutions).
Moderator: Benito M. Vergara, Jr.
Presenters:
Philip P. Choy, *"Pandering to Sinophobia: The Chinese Question in Political Cartoons"*
In the second half of the 19th century, one major controversy occupying the nation's politics was to close the door to the coming of the Chinese to America while insisting that China keep her door opened for Americans. The hysterical desire to prohibit Chinese immigration was known as the "Chinese Question" while the obsession for dominance over China was known as the "Open Door." For decades, the press exploited the issue, using the medium of political cartoons, unmercifully demonizing the Chinese.

Jorge Emmanuel, *"The Debate on Manifest Destiny, Imperialism, and the Annexation of the Philippines through Political Cartoons (1898-1906)"*
Political cartoons from popular US magazines and newspapers from 1898 to 1905 are full of racist stereotypical depictions and promote the concept of Manifest Destiny. These cartoons provide a valuable perspective on the decision to annex the Philippines in 1898, imperialism, the forgotten US-Philippine War, and opposition to the war by the Anti-Imperialist League.

8A   SATURDAY, 3:30-5:00   GARDEN A
The China Mystique: Pearl S. Buck, Anna May Wong, Mayling Soong and the Transformation of American Orientalism by Karen Leong
See New Book Talks
Moderator: Harvey Dong

8B   SATURDAY, 3:30-5:00   GARDEN B
The Chinatown Trunk Murder Mystery by Mary Lui
See New Book Talks
Moderator: Paul Fong

8C   SATURDAY, 3:30-5:00   SPRING A
"Chinese American Mass Media" — Chinese language panel sponsored by the Lawrence Choy Lowe Memorial Fund and Poon Foundation
See Chinese Language Track
Moderator: Marlon K. Hom
Presenters:
Joseph Leung
Leung will focus on the *Sing Tao Daily News* in relation to the globalization of Chinese language newspapers.
See conference papers and summaries

Gordon Lew
Lew will discuss the challenges of publishing a paper in English for the Chinese American community.

Franklin Wu
Wu will present "A History of the Development of Chinese Language Television in Northern California."
See conference papers and summaries

8D   SATURDAY, 3:30-5:00   SPRING B/C
"Mixed Media: Discussions with Multi-racial Chinese American Filmmakers"
Three Chinese American filmmakers of mixed descent discuss the place of multiracial filmmakers within Chinese American cinema, and their work in relationship to both mainstream Hollywood and community-based representations of Chinese Americans. They tackle such issues as, "What makes a film or video Chinese American, and who defines when and where that label can be applied?" "Do these filmmakers see their work as Chinese American or Hapa or both?" "What role does a director or actor's phenotype

play in deciding which work is labeled Chinese American?" By addressing these and other issues, the panelists provide an insightful look not only into the experiences of multiracial Chinese American filmmakers but also into the more general state of Chinese American film- and video-making today.
Moderator: Wei Ming Dariotis
Panelists:
Eric Byler, *American Knees*
Byler presents the making of *American Knees.* See also Sneak Peeks (Session 7G), p. 16

Kip Fulbeck, *"Self-Definition: Images and Statements from the Upcoming book: Part Asian, 100% Hapa"*
This presentation features photographic portraits of multiracial Asian Americans of all ages, including their handwritten responses to the question, "What are you?"

William Gow, *"More to the Chinese Side: Ruminations of a 5th Generation Chinese American Documentarian"*
Gow discusses his personal identity as a 5th generation Chinese American of mixed descent and the way in which his work as a community-based media artist attempts to challenge mainstream representations of Chinese Americans. Gow emphasizes the importance of community-based media and its democratizing potential.
See conference papers and summaries

8E   SATURDAY, 3:30-5:00   OSAKA
"Chinese American Lawyers and the Political World"
Even the top law graduate could never anticipate the twists and turns of getting a seat in elected office. Learn from those who have first-hand experience in the political trenches. Find out how being a Chinese American impacts the image of a candidate and the special outreach efforts necessary to engage different Chinese American voter groups.
Chair: Julie Soo
Panelists: John Chiang, Otto Lee, Russ Lowe, Lillian Sing

8F   SATURDAY, 3:30-5:30   IMPERIAL A
Chinese American Historical Society, Museum, and Organization Caucus
See Special Sessions
Moderators: Lorraine Dong & Jeannie Woo
Representatives:
Angel Island Immigration Station Foundation (Erika Gee & Daphne Kwok)
Chicago Chinese American Historical Society (Gene Moy)
Chinatown Historical Society of Honolulu (Anthony Chang)
Chinese American Council of Sacramento (Douglas Yee)
Chinese American Museum (Suellen Cheng)
Chinese-American Museum of Chicago (Chuimei Ho)
Chinese American Museum of Northern California (Brian L. Tom)
Chinese Australian Historical Society (Raymond N. Poon)
Chinese Canadian Historical Society of British Columbia (Larry Wong)
Chinese Historical and Cultural Project (Rodney Lum & Gerrye Wong)
Chinese Historical Society of America (Philip P. Choy & Sue Lee)
Chinese Historical Society of New England (Stefanie Fan)
Chinese Historical Society of Southern California (Wing Mar)
Hawaii Chinese Center (Roger Liu)
Museum of Chinese in the Americas (Cynthia Ai-fen Lee)
San Diego Chinese Historical Society and Museum (Murray Lee)
Ventura County Chinese American Historical Society (Linda Bentz & George Yu)
Yuba Historical Society (Daniel Barth)

8G   SATURDAY, 3:30-5:00   SAKURA A
What's Wrong with Frank Chin? by Curtis Choy
See Documentaries
Moderator: Jeffery P. Chan

8H   SATURDAY, 3:30-5:00   SAKURA B
"Agents of Socialization?"
Moderator: Eric Mar
Presenters:
Jin Feng, *"Exile Between Two Continents: Ettie Chin's War Experience in China (1937-1944)"*

> The writings of Ettie Len-toy Chin (b. 1913), a second-generation Chinese American who taught at Ginling College (1915-1952), an all-women's missionary institution then in exile in Chengdu, China because of the Sino-Japanese War (1937-1945), illustrate the formation of Chinese American identity from the unique angle of her experience in wartime China.

See conference papers and summaries

Jeff Staley, *"Contested Childhoods: The Pacific Society for the Suppression of Vice vs. the WHMS Methodist Oriental Home, 1900-1903"*

> In December 1900, Deaconess Margarita Lake rescued two young Chinese girls in San Francisco Chinatown. This precipitated a three-year battle in the courts for possession of the children. Utilizing recently discovered unpublished documents, this presentation sheds new light on the painful, complicated relationship between Caucasian and Chinese communities.

See conference papers and summaries

Andrew Theodore Urban, *"Rooted in the Americanization Zeal: The SF International Institute, Race, and Settlement Work, 1918-1939"*

> This paper examines how official and social definitions of race informed the settlement work of the San Francisco International Institute. In particular, it explores the Institute's "Americanization" work in relation to the fact that the foreign-born Chinese of San Francisco were barred from becoming legal citizens.

See conference papers and summaries

Nga-Wing Anjela Wong, *"The Role of Urban Community Centers in the Lives of Chinese American Youth"*

> This small-scale qualitative study examines the role of a community-based youth center in the social and educational adjustments of youth from working-class Chinese immigrant families. This study demonstrates that community-based youth centers provide Chinese American middle school students in urban settings with social and emotional support.

8I   SATURDAY, 3:30-5:00   SAKURA C
"Chinese Immigration Law Enforcement"
This panel examines Chinese immigration law enforcement at various sites and times in the United States, drawing on the panelists' original historical research.
Moderator: Charles McClain
Presenters:
Robert Barde, *"Detention at Angel Island: First Empirical Evidence"*

> Who was detained at Angel Island? For how long? Newly-discovered data from the Pacific Mail Steamship Company provide the first factual basis for answering these questions. The surprising results include great variation in the probability and length of detention, which depended on passengers' origin and their "exempt" status under the Exclusion laws.

See conference papers and summaries

Todd M. Stevens, *"Chinese Immigration Law Enforcement"*

> Stevens' research on the legal consciousness of the Chinese American community in the Pacific Northwest reveals that continued residence and expulsion was the chief concern from the 1890s through the first decade of the 20th century. His work focuses on a certain type of legal issue: civil suits for damages brought by Chinese labor contractors against the US immigration service when incarceration of Chinese living in the United States prevented the fulfillment of labor contracts. The enforcement of the Geary Act attempted to criminalize Chinese work and life in the Pacific Northwest by limiting the mobility of Chinese manual laborers who worked in rural logging, canning, and railroad camps. Because the immigration officials

sought to disrupt the operation of an economic system delivering cheap labor to the hinterlands, instead of the residence or practices of Chinese Americans, Chinese merchants were able to recast an immigration dispute as a property rights issue.

John Hayakawa Torok, *"The Arthur Lem Case: A New York Chinese Immigration Fraud Prosecution"*

> This paper about a Chinese interpreter named Arthur Lem draws on a chapter from Torok's dissertation, "The Legal History of McCarthyism and New York Chinatown." It builds on original research in court records, a Freedom of Information Act request to the INS, and secondary sources.

9A   SUNDAY, 10:00-11:30   GARDEN A
"Chinese Global Nomads: Chinese American Tertiary Migration"
Not every Chinese American has ancestors coming to the United States from China. Many people left China to live in another country before settling in the United States. Four panelists will share their family's tertiary migration history. Continents and countries where their families have lived include Africa, Argentina, Bolivia, Brazil, Canada, Japan, Laos, and Thailand.
Moderator: Minh-Hoa Ta
Panelists: Christopher Hsu, Merit H. Ma, Sandra Sengdara Siharath, Wei Wang

9C   SUNDAY, 10:00-11:30   SPRING A
"Treasures in the CHSSC Archives" — Chinese Historical Society of Southern California panel
The Chinese Historical Society of Southern California has assembled numerous treasures in its recently renovated archive facility, now open to scholars at its headquarters in Los Angeles: (1) historic document collections and (2) archaeological site materials. Significant and potentially new interpretive issues will be highlighted.
Moderator: Lorraine Dong
Panelists: Paul G. Chace, Gilbert Hom, Laura Ng

9D   SUNDAY, 10:00-11:30   SPRING B/C
"Accessing Culturally Competent Health Care in the 21st Century"
— Chinese Community Health Care Association and Chinese Community Health Plan panel
This panel provides an overview of NICOS's 2004 Community Health Study as well as introduces an integrated system of delivering culturally competent health care involving the Chinese Hospital (established 1899), the Chinese Community Health Care Association (established 1982), the Chinese Community Health Plan (established 1985), and the Chinese Community Health Resource Center (established 1989).
Moderator: Edward A. Chow
Panelists: L. Eric Leung, Richard Loos, Angela Sun, Brenda Yee
See conference papers and summaries

9E   SUNDAY, 10:00-11:30   OSAKA
"History, Memory, and Social Activism of the Chinese Community in Boston—Projects and Perspectives from the Chinese Historical Society of New England"
— Chinese Historical Society of New England panel
Chair/Moderator: Wing-kai To
Presenters:
Carmen Chan, "The Chinatown Mural—A Symbol of Community Activism"

> For 15 years (1987-2002), the Chinatown mural, "Community and Unity" graced the walls of the former home of the Boston Chinatown Neighborhood Center (BCNC). It depicted the history of Asian Americans in Boston. In 1993, when the adjacent New England Medical Center proposed to build an 11-storey garage on the parcel of land where BCNC rested, the local community mobilized a major protest to preserve the building for community use. In 2002, the mural was torn down with the building to make way for the Metropolitan, a mixed-use development that included housing, commercial use, and BCNC's new community center. As part of a grassroots fundraising campaign, BCNC created a replica of the mural in the lobby of its new center to recognize the history and victory of community activism.

Deborah Dong, *"The Mount Hope Cemetery Project: Building Boston's Chinese Immigrant Memorial"*

Many of New England's first Chinese immigrants, part of the so-called "bachelor society," are buried in Boston's Mount Hope Cemetery. Without local descendants to tend to their graves, their burial grounds eventually fell into disrepair. In 1992, the Chinese Historical Society of New England was founded to restore these burial grounds and to build a proper memorial there to honor all Chinese immigrants. Facing numerous challenges and roadblocks over the years, CHSNE spearheaded a project to coordinate the local community, private sector, and city government, and ultimately raised over $300,000 for the Boston Mount Hope Cemetery Chinese Immigrant Memorial, which is now scheduled for construction in late 2005.

Shauna Lo, *"Change and Continuity: Boston's Chinese American Community at the Turn of the 21st Century"*

Although Chinatown remains the heart of the Boston area's Chinese American community, the Chinese population over the last 15 years has become more geographically dispersed. The fastest growing communities are north and south of Boston in the cities of Malden and Quincy. In some ways, the community has remained remarkably stable and in others, physical and demographic changes have significantly altered the face of the Chinese community.
See conference papers and summaries

Wing-kai To, *"Perspectives on the History of Boston's Chinatown, 1870s to 1980s"*

By focusing on different perspectives of Chinese diasporas, local community building, and Asian American identities, this paper highlights the origins of immigration and settlement, the growth of family and community organizations, and the struggles to combat institutional and environmental racism in Boston's Chinatown from the 1870s to the 1980s. Based on a combination of written and photographic sources collected by the Chinese Historical Society of New England, as well as limited publications on Chinatown's history, this paper demonstrates that the Chinese community acted as agents rather than victims in improving their livelihoods and constructing their identities.

9G   SUNDAY, 10:00-11:30   SAKURA A
Oral History Workshop conducted by Judy Yung
This workshop is intended to provide the nuts and bolts of conducting an oral history interview with Chinese Americans about their life story, family history, or a specific research topic. Drawing from 30 years of experience as a practitioner and teacher of oral history, Yung will cover a range of methodological and ethical issues involved in doing effective oral history.
Limited to 15 participants; please register at Registration Desk.
Introduction: Russell Jeung
See conference papers and summaries

9H   SUNDAY, 10:00-11:30   SAKURA B
"China America, A Radiant Light: A Combined 93-Year History of Orphanages for Chinese Children in the Bay Area"
A 15-minute video presentation will be followed by a four-person panel telling about their experiences growing up in the only group homes or orphanages for Chinese children in the

United States. The two homes highlighted are the Ming Quong Home for Chinese Girls and the Chung Mei Home for Chinese Boys that existed in the San Francisco Bay Area during the 1920s and 1930s.
Chair: Lynette Choy Uyeda Gin
Panelists: Phillip Chan, Lynette Choy Uyeda Gin, Richard Mar, Nona Mock Wyman
See conference papers and summaries

9I   SUNDAY, 10:00-11:30   SAKURA C
"Assimilation and Repression in Cold War America"
This panel explores themes of assimilation and repression among Chinese Americans during the Cold War through legal history, oral history, and other methods.
Moderator: Him Mark Lai
Presenters:
Frederick Hom Dow, *"Harry Hom Dow: Pioneering Massachusetts Lawyer"*

Harry Hom Dow was born in Hudson, Massachusetts in 1904. He served as a Chinese interpreter with the Immigration Services for a number of years, as well as working in the family laundry business. In 1929, he became the first Chinese American to be admitted to the Massachusetts Bar. He then began an immigration law practice with offices in New York City and Boston. In the wake of anti-communist hysteria and McCarthyism, Dow was targeted in 1956 by the US Justice Department for indictment by a Grand Jury for his immigration work. While successful in beating a federal indictment, prosecutors and federal agencies were effective in blackballing the attorney from immigration law practice.

Robin Li, *"Foreign Aid: Cold War America's 'Useful' Chinese"*

During the mid-century period, Chinese people in America experienced changes in legal and social status. While racial prejudice continued to play a role in the lives of Chinese people who desired to belong to America, US government programs that relied upon Chinese inhabitants as cultural informants indicate a simultaneous, if complicated, desire to have (some) Chinese belong.

John Hayakawa Torok, *"Ideological Prosecution: The China Daily News Case"*

In the Cold War, federal policymakers racially associated Chinese American community members with Communist China. This paper, drawn from Torok's dissertation, "The Legal History of McCarthyism and New York Chinatown," discusses the ideological criminal prosecution of a Chinese-language daily newspaper. The McCarthy era's legal regulation of Chinese America may be characterized as a domestic counterpart to the foreign policy strategy of containment.

Chiou-ling Yeh, *"Making Multicultural America: Cold War Politics, Ethnic Celebrations, and Chinese America"*

Most scholars have assumed that multiculturalism emerged in the 1960s, a product of the Civil Rights movement. This paper contends that Chinese American leaders in San Francisco used Cold War politics to stage a Chinese New Year celebration and to reposition themselves in mid-20th century American race relations, thereby contributing to the rise of multiculturalism in the 1950s.

SPECIAL EVENTS AND HIGHLIGHTS

KICK-OFF/PRE-REGISTRATION RECEPTION
OCTOBER 6 (Thursday), **5:00-7:00 P.M.**

CHSA Museum and Learning Center and the Manilatown Heritage Center *(corner of Kearny and Jackson Streets)*
Co-hosted by CHSA and San Francisco State University's College of Ethnic Studies and Asian American Studies Department

OPENING LUNCHEON
"TOWN AND GOWN: A MUTUAL COMMITMENT"
OCTOBER 7 (Friday), **11:30-1:30 P.M.**

Imperial Room, Radisson Miyako Hotel
OPENING ACT: Leung's White Crane Lion & Dragon Dance School
KEYNOTE SPEAKERS:
CSU Chancellor Charles B. Reed and Mr. Henry Der
Introductions by Dr. Robert A. Corrigan and
Dr. Rolland C. Lowe

RECEPTION FOR CSU CHANCELLOR CHARLES B. REED
OCTOBER 7 (Friday), **1:45-3:00 P.M.**

Kyoto Room, Radisson Miyako Hotel
Co-hosted by the Chinese American Faculty and Staff Association and the Office of International Programs at San Francisco State University

CONFERENCE BANQUET AND BIRTHDAY CELEBRATION FOR PHILIP P. CHOY AND HIM MARK LAI
"MAKING HISTORY"
OCTOBER 7 (Friday), **7:00 P.M.**

Empress of China Restaurant, 838 Grant Avenue,
San Francisco Chinatown
OPENING ACT: Yellow River Drummers
KEYNOTE SPEAKER:
Gary Locke, former Governor of the State of Washington
Introduction by Assemblymember Judy Chu
BIRTHDAY EMCEE: Dr. Marlon K. Hom

CHSA PANELS HELD IN CONJUNCTION WITH CHSA EXHIBITS

"Remembering C.C. Wang"
Frank H. Yick Gallery
August 18 to December 19, 2005

As the second anniversary of his passing approaches, the Chinese Historical Society of America presents the first exhibition commemorating the vision of Wang Chi-ch'ien. C.C. Wang, a dedicated scholar of Chinese painting, was a celebrated teacher and a deeply respected connoisseur and collector. As an artist, Wang broadened the international audience for Chinese painting and its rich history, and made invaluable contributions to American appreciation of traditional ink painting. His intellectual and technical innovations merged the traditions of Chinese painting with the explorations of modern art in America like none before him.
Curated by Adam Mikos, the exhibition features works from private and public collection, and is funded by Grants for the Arts.

CONFERENCE PANEL (SESSION 6E):
"WHAT IS CHINESE AMERICAN ART?"
Moderator: Irene Poon Andersen
Panelists: Mark Johnson, Ch'ingche Lo, Jade Snow Wong

"Pandering to Sinophobia: The Chinese Question in Political Cartoons"
Philip P. Choy Gallery
August 30, 2005 to January 15, 2006

"Pandering to Sinophobia: The Chinese Question in Political Cartoons" presents a collection of 19th century political cartoons found in popular press and regional newspapers. The exhibition chronicles mounting national conflicts between politics, labor, and immigration that led to anti-Chinese violence and legislation. Published in such popular media as *Harper's Weekly*, *Leslie Illustrated*, San Francisco's *Wasp*, and New York's *Puck*, these cartoons had a great influence on public opinion—particularly for Americans who had little exposure to actual Chinese communities in the United States.
This exhibition is curated by Philip P. Choy with political cartoons from his private collection and is funded by Grants for the Arts.

CONFERENCE PANEL (SESSION 7J):
"MASKS OF DEMOCRACY: THE POLITICS OF RACISM IN POLITICAL CARTOONS"
Moderator: Benito M. Vergara, Jr.
Panelists: Philip P. Choy, Jorge Emmanuel
This panel is cosponsored by CHSA and the Manilatown Heritage Center. Abe Ignacio's private collection of political cartoons is also currently exhibited at MHC.

COMMUNITY PANELS

Angel Island Immigration Station Foundation (6A)
天使島移民拘留所紀念基金會

CYC (formerly Chinatown Youth Center, now Community Youth Center) (2D, 2J)
社區青年中心

Chinese American International School (5D)
中美國際學校

Chinese Community Health Care Association (9D)
華美醫師協會

Chinese Community Health Plan (9D)
華人保健計劃

Chinese Culture Center (5H)
舊金山中國文化中心

Chinese for Affirmative Action (1J, 2A)
華人權益促進會

Kearny Street Workshop (3D)

Manilatown Heritage Center (7J)

National Archives and Records Administration, Pacific Region (1I)

National Asian American Telecommunications Association (1G)

Square and Circle Club (6H)
方圓社

Sunset Neighborhood Beacon Center (1A)
日落區培根中心

HIGH SCHOOL PROGRAM
October 7, 2005 (Friday)

Sponsored by
San Francisco State University, President's Office,
Dr. Robert A. Corrigan

Session 1F   8:30-9:45 A.M.
Imperial A
High School Conference Orientation
Greetings: CHSA and SFSU (Asian American Studies
Department, Associated Students Inc., and Asian Student
Union)
Guest Speaker: Eric Mar, Esq., President of San Francisco
Board of Education and Lecturer of Asian American Studies
at SFSU

Session 2   10:00-11:15 A.M.
Attend various conference panels

OPENING LUNCHEON   11:30 A.M. - 1:30 P.M.
Imperial Room
Opening Act: Leung's White Crane Lion & Dragon Dance
School
KEYNOTE SPEAKERS: Henry Der and CSU Chancellor
Charles B. Reed

Session 3K   1:45-3:00 P.M.
Peace Plaza
"Not Who You Think I Am: Forging Past, Present, and
Future"

What does it mean to be Chinese American? Asian-
American? Asian/American? AsianAmerican? Or an
American Asian? How do you hold the past and future in
a single clasp? Is it possible to stay true to your culture in a
new country? These are some of the questions we will explore
in this discussion and writing-based workshop. Prepare to
educate. Prepare to enlighten. Prepare to be proud. Youth
Speaks Poet Mentors will perform poems to illustrate their
own experiences, their own truths, and do a writing workshop
encouraging students to think critically about themselves and
their own history.

Introduction: Leonard Shek, *CHSA Program Coordinator*

Youth Speaks Poets/Performers:

Nico Cary has been opening the eyes of
audiences ever since his high school days and as
a UC Berkeley student, continues to paint the
Bay Area with his detailed passion for literature
and politics. He has been a finalist in the Bay
Area Teen Poetry Slam Championships for
three consecutive years and is a member of the
2005 UC Berkeley Slam Team.

Michelle Lee is a performance artist
and an arts educator for Youth Speaks,
working in public schools throughout the
Bay Area. She has performed with Jigsaw
Collective and Proletariat Bronze, and was
part of the 2004 National Champion UC
Berkeley Collegiate Team.

Adriel Luis has collected 21 years
worth of stories as a Chinese American
uprooted from the Toi San tribe. He
has been a Bay Area Teen Poetry Slam
finalist for two consecutive years and
is the 2004 San Francisco Poetry Slam
Champion.

Session 4G   3:15-4:30 P.M.   **Sakura A**
SNEAK PEEK: *"The Chinese in Hollywood Project"* by SFSU
Alumnus Arthur Dong

Introduction: SFSU President Robert A. Corrigan
Moderator: Jenny Lau, *Assistant Professor of Cinema, San
Francisco State University*

High school gifts generously provided by CHSA, the CSU
Chancellor's Office, and SFSU's Associated Students Inc.,
Student Outreach Services, and President's Office.

CHINESE LANGUAGE TRACK 華語討論組

以下小組蒙蔡滄溟紀念基金會及潘氏教育基金會
資助, 歡迎各界人士參加。

> The following panels were sponsored by the Lawrence Choy Lowe Memorial Fund and the Poon Foundation. They were open to the public.

OCTOBER 7 (Friday), 1:45–3:00 P.M. (3C)
CHINESE LANGUAGE PANEL 華語討論組

"The Current Status of and Opportunities for Chinese American Literary Writings in the Chinese Language"
美國華文文學的現象與出路

An introduction to Chinese American literary writings in the Chinese language, from works written by 19th century Chinese laborers to those written by 21st century Chinese students and immigrants in the United States.
簡介美國華文文學幾個歷史時期, 從十九世紀契約華工的華文文學, 到二十一世紀的留學生文學及草根文群的移民文學。

Chair 主持:
Maurice Chuck, publisher, *Literati Magazine*
黃運基,《美華文學》雜誌社長

Panelists 組員:
Frank Cheng, Associate Editor, *Literati Magazine*
程寶林,《美華文學》雜誌副主編

Ray Lau, President, Chinese Literature and Art Association in America
劉荒田, 美國華文文藝界協會會長

Ziyi Liu, Editor-in-Chief, *Literati Magazine*
劉子毅,《美華文學》雜誌主編

OCTOBER 7 (Friday), 3:15–4:30 P.M. (4C)
BILINGUAL PANEL 雙語討論組

"Chinese American Political Identities"
美國華人政治認同

Moderator 主持:
Madeline Y. Hsu, PhD, Associate Professor of Asian American Studies, San Francisco State University
徐元音, 舊金山州立大學亞裔學系副教授

Panelists 組員:
Peter Kwong, PhD, Professor of Asian American Studies, Hunter College and Professor of Sociology, Graduate Center, City University of New York
鄺治中, 紐約市立大學韓特爾學院亞裔學系教授兼研究院中心社會學系教授
PAPER: "Changing Geographic and Economic Mobility of Chinese Americans: What Does That Mean to the Civil Rights Agenda and How Does It Affect US-China Relations?" *(English)*
美國華人的地域與經濟變遷對本土民權運動及中美關係的作用(英語)

Pei-te Lien, PhD, Associate Professor of Political Science and Ethnic Studies, University of Utah
連培德, 猶他州大學族裔研究系及政治系副教授
PAPER: "Taiwanese Americans and the 'New' Homeland Politics in Chinese America" *(English)*
美國臺灣人在美'新'家鄉政治活動(英語)

L. Ling-chi Wang, Professor of Ethnic Studies, University of California at Berkeley
王靈智, 加州大學族裔研究系教授
PAPER: "Race, Space, and Class in Chinese America: Toward a Civil Rights Agenda" *(English)*
美國華人對民權運動中的種族, 時空, 及階級的觀念(英語)

Zhang Yinglong, PhD, Professor, Institute of Overseas Chinese Studies, Ji'nan University, Guangzhou, People's Republic of China
張應龍, 中國廣州暨南大學華僑華人研究所教授
PAPER: "On Chinese American Post-war Political Activities" *(Chinese)*
戰後美國華人參政活動的若干問題(華語)

OCTOBER 8 (Saturday), **1:45–3:15 P.M.** (7C)
CHINESE LANGUAGE PANEL 華語討論組

"Teaching the Chinese Language in America"
美國華語教育

Moderator 主持:
Marlon K. Hom, PhD, Professor of Asian American Studies,
San Francisco State University and Resident Director,
California State University International Programs in Beijing
譚雅倫, 舊金山州立大學亞裔學系教授兼加州州立大學國
際計劃駐北京大學主任

Panelists 組員:

Stella Yu-Mei Kwoh, EdD, Director, Teaching Chinese
as a Heritage/Other Language Program, California State
University, East Bay
郭譽玫, 加州東灣州立大學華文師資培育班主任

PAPER: "Mainstreaming and Professionalizing Chinese
Language Education: A New Mission for a New Century"
華文教育主流化, 華文師資專業化的探討: 新世紀的新使
命

Catherine Leung, Principal, Nam Kue School
梁劉潔鑾, 南僑學校校長

TOPIC: The status of Chinese language schools in San
Francisco
舊金山華人社區華文學校當前的一般狀況

Puichee Leung, Vice Principal, Cumberland Chinese *High
School*
梁培熾, 金巴崙華文中學副校長, 舊金山州立大學亞裔學系
兼職教授

TOPIC: Teaching Huayu Chinese versus teaching guoyu,
putonghua, or Hanyu
華文學校的華語教育與正名

OCTOBER 8 (Saturday), **3:30–5:00 P.M.** (8C)
CHINESE LANGUAGE PANEL 華語討論組

"Chinese American Mass Media"
美華大眾傳媒

Moderator 主持:
Marlon K. Hom, PhD, Professor of Asian American Studies,
San Francisco State University and Resident Director,
California State University International Programs in Beijing
譚雅倫, 舊金山州立大學亞裔學系教授兼加州州立大學國
際計劃駐北京大學主任

Panelists 組員:

Joseph Leung, Chief Editor, *Sing Tao Daily News*, Western
Edition
梁建鋒,《星島日報》美西版總編輯

TOPIC: Sing Tao Daily News and the overall development of
Chinese language newspapers in the United States
從《星島日報》看美國華人華文報業的發展

Gordon Lew, retired journalist, instructor and chair,
City College of San Francisco, Chinese Studies Department
劉池光, 退休報人及教育家

TOPIC: The challenges of publishing a paper in English for
the Chinese American community
在美國華人社區辦英文報紙的困難及挑戰

Franklin Wu, President, Envision Productions, Inc.
吳育庭, 海華傳播公司董事長

PAPER: "The Historical Development of Chinese Language
Television in Northern California"
北加州華語電視發展史

NEW BOOK TALKS

CHSA and AAS are proud to present 11 new books on Chinese America that were published in 2004 and 2005. Meet and hear the authors who will also be available for book-signing at their respective sessions.

Americans First: Chinese American and the Second World War
by **K. Scott Wong**
Harvard University Press, 2005
Moderator: Gregory Mark
Session 6B
Saturday, 10:15-11:45   **Garden B**

SYNOPSIS: This book examines the identity formation of the generation of Chinese Americans born around 1920 and who came of age during the Second World War. It looks at how the war affected Chinese Americans both here on the mainland and in Hawai'i, and offers the first in-depth study of the Chinese American presence in the military during that war.

AUTHOR: K. Scott Wong is a Professor of History at Williams College where he teaches a variety of courses in Asian American history, comparative immigration history, the history of the American West, and American Studies. He is the author of a number of articles and is co-editor with Sucheng Chan of *Claiming America: Constructing Chinese American Identities during the Exclusion Era* (Temple University Press, 1998).

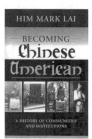

Becoming Chinese American: A History of Communities and Institutions
by **Him Mark Lai**
AltaMira Press, 2004
Moderator: Eric Mar
A special combined session with Evan Leong's documentary entitled *Him Mark Lai: The People's Historian*
Session 6I
Saturday, 10:15-11:45   **Sakura C**

SYNOPSIS: *Becoming Chinese American* discusses the historical and cultural development of Chinese American life in the past century. Representing a singular breadth of knowledge about the Chinese American past, the volume begins with a historical overview of Chinese migration to the United States, followed by a critical discussion of the development of key community institutions.

AUTHOR: Him Mark Lai has researched Chinese American history, written key articles and books, and co-taught with Philip P. Choy the first college-level course on Chinese American history. Active in community cultural activities, Lai produced a weekly hour-long community-based Cantonese language radio program and was coordinator of the Chinese Culture Foundation's "In Search of Roots" program. He was featured in the *Chronicle of Higher*

Education as "the scholar who legitimized the study of Chinese America."

The China Mystique: Pearl S. Buck, Anna May Wong, Mayling Soong and the Transformation of American Orientalism
by **Karen J. Leong**
University of California Press, 2005
Moderator: Harvey Dong
Session 8A   Saturday, 3:30-5:00
Garden A

SYNPOSIS: *The China Mystique* explores how Pearl S. Buck, Anna May Wong, and Mayling Soong Chiang experienced and ultimately embodied American orientalism toward China during the 1930s and 40s. As celebrities popularly associated with China, each woman negotiated what it meant to be Chinese American against the backdrop of the United States' shifting international relations with China, changing roles of women, and the growth of consumer culture.

AUTHOR: Karen J. Leong is an associate professor in Women's Studies and an affiliate faculty member of Asian Pacific Studies, African and African American Studies, and History, at Arizona State University. Her scholarship focuses on the relationships between gender, race, and nationality as articulated in United States popular culture and diplomacy. She is the author of *The China Mystique: Pearl S. Buck, Anna May Wong, Mayling Soong and the Transformation of American Orientalism* (University of California Press, 2005) and co-coordinator of the Japanese Americans in Arizona oral history project. She is currently writing a book-length manuscript about Asian American masculinity and Hollywood.

Chinatown Trunk Mystery: Murder, Miscegenation, and other Dangerous Encounters in Turn-of-the-Century New York City
by **Mary Ting Yi Lui**
Princeton University Press, 2005
Moderator: Paul Fong
Session 8B
Saturday, 3:30-5:00   **Garden B**

SYNOPSIS: *The Chinatown Trunk Mystery* offers a fascinating snapshot of social and sexual relations between Chinese and non-Chinese populations in turn-of-the-century New York City through the lens of the unsolved murder of Elsie Sigel whose corpse was found inside a trunk in the midtown apartment of Leon Ling.

AUTHOR: Mary Ting Yi Lui was first introduced to Chinese American history while working as the curator of the Museum of Chinese in the Americas, formerly known as the New York Chinatown History Project. Her research for the museum's first permanent exhibit, "Remembering New York Chinatown," led her to the unsolved 1909 Elsie Sigel murder case which formed the basis of her book. In 1992, she left the museum to pursue her PhD in American history and Asian American Studies at Cornell University. She is an Assistant Professor of American Studies and History at Yale University. Her research interests include late-nineteenth and early twentieth-century Asian American, immigration, urban, and women's history.

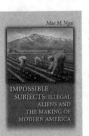

Faithful Generations: Race & New Asian American Churches
by **Russell Jeung**
Rutgers University Press, 2005
Moderator: Ben Kobashigawa
Session 5B
Saturday, 8:30-10:00   **Garden B**

SYNOPSIS: Religion—both personal faith and institutional congregations—shapes the lives of Chinese Americans in diverse ways. This book examines the role of religion in constructing Chinese American identity throughout our history.

AUTHOR: Russell Jeung teaches Asian American Studies at San Francisco State University. He attends New Hope Covenant Church in Oakland, California, where he lives with his wife, Joan, and his baby, Matthew.

Impossible Subjects: Illegal Aliens and the Making of Modern America
by **Mae M. Ngai**
Princeton University Press, 2004
Moderator: Robert A. Fung
Session 3B
Friday, 1:45-3:00   **Garden B**

SYNOPSIS: This book traces the origins of the "illegal alien" in American law and society, explaining why and how illegal migration became the central problem in US immigration policy and the twentieth century. It includes case studies of Filipinos, Mexicans, Japanese, and Chinese who comprised, variously, illegal aliens, alien citizens, colonial subjects, and imported contract workers.

AUTHOR: Mae M. Ngai is Associate Professor of History at the University of Chicago. She earned her PhD from Columbia University in 1998. Her research and teaching focus on twentieth century US history, with emphasis on immigration and ethnicity (Asian American and comparative), politics and law, and labor. *Impossible Subjects*, won the 2005 Frederick Jackson Turner Prize from the Organization of American Historians, the 2004 Littleton-Griswold Prize from the American Historical Association, and the 2004 Theodore Salutous Book Prize from the Immigration and Ethnic History Society. She is now writing a multigenerational biography of the Tape family.

Doctor Mom Chung of the Fair-Haired Bastards
by **Judy Tzu-Chun Wu**
University of California Press, 2005
Moderator: Madeline Y. Hsu
Session 2B
Friday, 10:00-11:15   **Garden B**

SYNOPSIS: Dr. Margaret Chung (1889-1959) was the first-known American-born Chinese female physician. She established one of the first western medical clinics in San Francisco's Chinatown in the 1920s and became a behind-the-scenes political broker during World War II. Through her contacts with white American soldiers, movie stars, and politicians, Chung recruited pilots for the Flying Tigers and lobbied for the creation of WAVES, the US women's naval reserve. This is the first book-length biography of Dr. Margaret Chung. It explores her professional, political as well as transgressive personal life, focusing on her strategies for traversing racial, gender, and sexual boundaries of American society from the late Victorian era through the early Cold War period.

AUTHOR: Judy Tzu-Chun Wu is an Associate Professor of History at Ohio State University. During the 2005-06 academic year, she is Visiting Associate Professor at the University of Chicago's Center for the Study of Race, Politics, and Culture. She teaches courses in Asian American History, Women's History, American History, Immigration History, the US West, and the 1960s. Currently entitled "Radical Orientalism: Asia, Asian America, and American Social Movements," her new book project examines the influence of Asian culture and politics on American forms of radicalism during the mid-1950s through the 1970s.

Portraits of Pride
by **Chinese Historical Society of Southern California**
CHSSC, 2005
Moderator: Eugene Moy
Session 5E
Saturday, 8:30-10:00   **Osaka**

SYNOPSIS: *Portraits of Pride* documents the dramatic life stories of 38 Chinese Americans of World War II and the prior era. Their accomplishments and contributions in science, technology, medicine, and education are largely unknown. Their collective stories in this first of a series of books will present a picture of America in the early 1900s, when the great majority of Chinese Americans were challenged to rise above obstacles in most professions and businesses.

AUTHOR: The Chinese Historical Society of Southern California was created to discover and recognize our pioneers and their history. It aims to increase awareness of Chinese American heritage through public programs, education, and research. Since 1975, its mission has been to bring together people with a mutual interest in the important history and historical role of Chinese and Chinese Americans in Southern California, to pursue, preserve and communicate knowledge of this history, and to promote the heritage of the Chinese and Chinese American community in support of a better appreciation of our rich, multicultural society.

Nameless Builders of the Transcontinental by **William F. Chew**
Trafford Publishing (Victoria, BC), 2004

SYNOPSIS: *Nameless Builders of the Transcontinental* reveals for the first time the individual names of 1,500 Chinese workers of the Central Pacific Railroad Company as they appear on the payroll sheets of the Central Pacific. These are the names of gang bosses who collected pay for crews averaging 28 workers each. This book refutes previously published dates of Chinese employment in the railroad company. It also identifies the first Chinese workers, describes major accomplishments despite grueling and primitive working conditions, and provides a calculated total number of fatalities suffered during construction.

AUTHOR: William F. Chew, past Vice President of the Chinese Historical Society of Southern California and a retired aerospace engineer, was inspired to write this book after volunteering as a history researcher for the Golden Spike National Historic Site. As a descendent of a "coolie" worker of the Central Pacific, he is dedicated to increasing public awareness and appreciation of this monumental construction project built in the 1860s by Chinese pioneers.

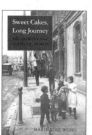

Sweet Cakes, Long Journey: The Chinatowns of Portland, Oregon
by **Marie Rose Wong**
University of Washington Press, 2004
Moderator: Donald Chan
Session 1B
Friday, 8:30-9:45   **Garden B**

SYNOPSIS: *Sweet Cakes, Long Journey* chronicles the social and urban history of Portland, Oregon's first Chinese community. At its height in 1908, Portland had a Chinese vegetable gardening community and an urban Chinatown that partially occupied as many as 70 city blocks, making it the largest Chinatown in terms of geographic coverage.

AUTHOR: Marie Rose Wong is an Associate Professor and Director of the Bachelor of Public Affairs Program at Seattle University. She teaches courses in Urban Studies that include Asian American Community Development, American Housing Design and the Sustainable Community, and Exploring the American City. She is on the Board of Directors

of Interim Community Development Association in the Chinatown/International District and with Historic Seattle. She is currently working on a book about the history of single room occupancy hotels and Asian American community development in Seattle's Chinatown/International District.

Yeee-Hah!: Remembrance and Longing
by **Albert Hoy Yee**
Bookman Publishing, 2005
Moderator: Yanchun Zhang
Session 4B
Friday, 3:15-4:30   **Garden B**

SYNOPSIS: *Yeee-Hah!* analyses definitive issues, such as the Chinese and Jews (two distinct peoples yet similar), the Asian Stereotype (origins, psychological intricacies), and the Pentagon's heroizing metamorphosis of Wernher von Braun and other Nazis while vilifying America's lead rocket scientist, Hsue-shen Tsien of Caltech, who eventually developed China's ICBMs in revenge, and much more.

AUTHOR: Albert Hoy Yee earned degrees from UC Berkeley, San Francisco State and Stanford universities, and completed a post-doctoral fellowship at the University of Oregon in advanced psychology in 1967. After three years of Army service in Korea and Japan, he worked 40 years as an educator, mostly as professor and academic dean in the United States and East Asia before retiring. Elected a Fellow of the American Psychological Association and other societies, he has published many works. This is his 11th book.

Yellowface: Creating the Chinese in American Popular Music and Performance, 1850s-1920s
by **Krystyn R. Moon**
Rutgers University Press, 2005
Moderator: Gregory Mark
Session 7B
Saturday, 1:45-3:15   **Garden B**

SYNOPSIS: *Yellowface* explores the contributions of writers, performers, and songwriters in order to demonstrate how music and performance has played an important role in constructing Chinese and Chinese American stereotypes. The book also looks at Chinese and Chinese American musicians and performers who appeared in a variety of theatrical venues where they displayed their cultural heritage and contested anti-Chinese attitudes.

AUTHOR: Krystyn Moon is an Assistant Professor at Georgia State University in Atlanta, where she teaches US cultural and Asian American history. Her research focuses on the history of Asian Americans in American popular music and performance, which has led to her recently published book, *Yellowface.*

DOCUMENTARIES

Courage and Contributions: The Chinese in Ventura County–63 minutes
Sponsored by the Ventura County Chinese American Historical Society
Introduction: Kenneth Louie
Panelists: Linda Bentz, George Sandoval, Angela Soo Hoo, George Yu
Session 5G
Saturday, 8:30-10:00   Sakura A

SYNOPSIS: This film illustrates the lives of Chinese pioneers who came to Ventura County beginning in 1865. Featured in the documentary are the contributions of Chinese agricultural workers, the Chinese Fire Company, and the history of William Soo Hoo, the first Chinese mayor elected in the state of California. Produced in 2003 by George Sandoval of WestEnd Production, this documentary opened to critical acclaim from both the academic and local community. A teacher's guide accompanies the documentary, copies of which will be donated for use in the Ventura County public school system. The film is available in public libraries and the Ventura County Museum of History and Art.

SPONSOR: The Ventura County Chinese American Historical Society was founded in December 2000 by the Ventura County Chinese American Association. Its mission is to perform original research, preserve, publish, and teach the history and experiences of Chinese Americans in Ventura County. Since 2001, the Historical Society has assisted the Ventura City Council in the construction and funding of the first memorial dedicated to the legacy of the Chinese pioneers in Ventura County. The Historical Society is working on oral histories for a book entitled "The Chinese in Ventura County."

Him Mark Lai: The People's Historian–27 minutes
Presented by Evan J. Leong
Moderator: Eric Mar
A special combined session with Him Mark Lai's New Book Talk, *Becoming Chinese American: A History of Communities and Institutions*
Session 6I
Saturday, 10:15-11:45   Sakura C

SYNOPSIS: *Him Mark Lai: The People's Historian* is a personal journey into the world of Him Mark Lai. This project's goal is not only to pay tribute to an extremely accomplished Chinese American scholar, but rather to preserve the persona and philosophical passion of the man behind the work that will last forever. The documentary will follow his life passion as it has developed throughout his life and explore the fundamental principles that govern his work and philosophy.

FILMMAKER: Evan J. Leong is a 6th generation Chinese American native of San Francisco, California. He graduated from the University of California, Los Angeles, with a BA in Asian American Studies. His first introduction to filmmaking was through the EthnoCommunications program at UCLA. His shorts and documentaries have screened at several Asian American festivals. He was Filmmaker of the Month for the National Asian American Telecommunications Association (NAATA) in 2002. He has worked at Green Pastures Youth Center, an alternative high school in Koreatown, founding and teaching the Future Filmmakers Program.

Island Mountain Days: Discovering Nevada's Chinese Miners–60 minutes
Produced by KLVX-Channel 10-Las Vegas
Moderator: Sue Fawn Chung
Session 2G
Friday, 10:00-11:15   Sakura A

SYNOPSIS: Against the backdrop of virulent anti-Chinese movements, the small mining community of Island Mountain, in northeastern Nevada, developed from 1873 to 1917. About 75-80% of the town's population were Chinese who interacted in positive ways with European Americans and Native Americans. Emanuel Penrod founded the town and Ng Hong Lem ("China Lem") owned the merchandising store that served the residents in the region as well as travelers going between Boise, Idaho and Carlin or Elko, Nevada—major train stations. Photographs of the town were taken in 1903 by Hilda Matthey, a German immigrant from Iowa.

EXECUTIVE PRODUCER: Sue Fawn Chung is an Associate Professor of History at the University of Nevada, Las Vegas, a member of the Board of Advisors and Diversity Council of the National Trust for Historic Preservation, and a member of the Board of Museums and History for the State of Nevada. This year she received the Las Vegas Asian Chamber of Commerce "Outstanding Educator's Award" and the Las Vegas Summerlin Lion's Club "Outstanding Educator's Award."

Look Forward and Carry on the Past: Stories from Philadelphia's Chinatown–27 minutes
Sponsored by **NAATA** *(National Asian American Telecommunications Association)*
Moderator: Pamela Matsuoka
Session 1G   **Friday, 8:30-9:45**   Sakura A

SYNOPSIS: Directed by Debbie Wei, Barry Dornfeld, and Debora Kodish, this video program looks at Philadelphia's Chinatown, its culture and complexity of issues as a part of the greater urban community. It focuses on the role of folk arts and cultural expression in its struggle to survive. It also takes a look at the community's effort to prevent a stadium from being built in the neighborhood. *Look Forward and Carry on the Past* is produced by the Philadelphia Folklore Project and Asian Americans United.

SPONSOR: NAATA was founded in 1980 by Asian American film, video, and radio producers and community activists to counter the scarcity of images of Asians in film and television, to correct the often distorted portrayals of them in the mainstream media, and to create opportunities for the full participation of Asian American producers in the public media. Once an association of groups around the country, NAATA is now a nationally recognized arts and cultural institution based in San Francisco, California. NAATA's mission is to present stories that convey the richness and diversity of the Asian American experience to the broadest audience possible. They fund, produce, distribute and exhibit Asian American films, videos, and new media. Pamela Matsuoka has been NAATA's Distribution Director since 1994.

Sam Fow Stories: Memories from Marysville's Chinatown
−75 minutes
Sponsored by the Yuba Historical Society
Moderator: Daniel Barth
Panelists: Bing Ong, Frank Kim, Jack Kim, Doreen Foo Croft

Session 6G
Saturday, 10:15-11:45   **Sakura A**

SYNOPSIS: Former residents of a rural Sacramento Valley community tell stories of growing up in their "wide-open" neighborhood during the 1920s, 30s, and 40s. Topics include inter-ethnic relationships, poverty, close-knit family ties, brothels, gambling halls, paper sons, school, dating, religion, and a Chinese American festival.

SPONSOR: The Yuba Historical Society exists to advance historical education, preservation, and development in and around Yuba County California. The Society works to preserve the community's Chinese heritage by assisting the restoration of Marysville's Chinese Temple and by producing a documentary film preserving stories from Marysville's unique Chinese heritage.

What's Wrong with Frank Chin?
−97 minutes
Moderator: Jeffery Paul Chan
Session 8G
Saturday, 3:30-5:00   **Sakura A**

SYNOPSIS: The ayatollah of modern Asian Americanism takes on the meaning of "Chinese," selling out, Christianity, and more in this examination of thirty years of controversy and verbal mayhem. *What's Wrong with Frank Chin?* breaks out beyond the confines of one man's personal details and explores the larger implications of the literary, ideological, and cultural changes in Asian America. (Best Documentary Feature, 2005 SFASSFF)

PRODUCER/DIRECTOR: Curtis Choy is the producer/director/ editor and everything else of *What's Wrong with Frank Chin?* He made his first sync-sound film while still in high school, and has been an independent producer and film worker since the early 70s. He has contributed to numerous independent and PBS documentaries, commercials, and feature films as a production sound mixer. In 1977, he was a producer of "Screaming Yellow Hordes," the very first Asian American Film Festival ever, which was held in Chinatown, San Francisco. His works as a sound mixer can be heard in *Chan Is Missing, The Joy Luck Club, Better Luck Tomorrow,* and Academy Award-winning *Breathing Lessons.* His work as a producer/director include *Manilatown Lives!, The Year of the Ox, Making Up, Dupont Guy: The Schiz of Grant Avenue,* and *The Fall of the I-Hotel.* He is a Rockefeller Foundation Media Fellow, and has received the James D. Phelan Art Award in Filmmaking.

SNEAK PEEKS

CHSA and AAS are proud to present the following three sneak peeks. Be the first to hear and see segments from these upcoming new works presented by the filmmakers themselves.

American Knees
Presented by Eric Byler
Moderator: Wei Ming Dariotis
Session 7G
Saturday, 1:45-3:15   **Sakura A**

SYNOPSIS: Long after their breakup, Chinese American Raymond Ding (Chris Tashima) and Amerasian Aurora Crane (Allison Sie) struggle to let go. Torn apart by mismatched ideals, meddling friends, and the complexities of racial identities, they find other suitable mates but cannot stay away from each other. The film is based on the novel of the same name by Shawn Wong. It also features actors Joan Chen ("Betty Nguyen"), Kelly Hu ("Brenda

Nishitani"), Ben Shenkman ("Steve"), and Michael Paul Chan ("Jimmy Chan").

WRITER/DIRECTOR: Bi-racial writer/director Eric Byler grew up in Hawaii, Virginia, and California before graduating from Wesleyan University in Connecticut. Byler was nominated for a 2003 Independent Spirit Award for his first feature, *Charlotte Sometimes* (2003), which also earned nominations for producer Marc Ambrose and actress Jacqueline Kim. His senior thesis film *Kenji's Faith* (1995) premiered at the Sundance Film Festival and went on to win six festival awards, as well as a nomination at the Student Academy Awards sponsored by the Academy of Motion Picture Arts and Sciences. Current projects include "American Knees," "Kealoha: The Beloved," and Showtime's new series, *Infidelity*.

Chinese Couplet: "El Barrio Chino" and "My Mother's Names"
Presented by Felicia Lowe
Moderator: Willard Chin
Session 3G
Friday, 1:45-3:00   **Sakura A**

SYNOPSIS: *El Barrio Chino* is a story about the power of truth and reconciliation, and its impact on four generations in three countries: China, Cuba, and America. It is the journey of a Chinese American woman trying to unravel the mystery surrounding her grandfather who went to Cuba in 1920, leaving behind his pregnant wife. It is about Lowe's mother, who was born in his absence and who met him for the first time when she was 15 years old. *My Mother's Names* explores the impact of Lowe's grandfather's absence on the people he left behind. The grandmother, essentially, became a single mother with two young daughters to support in Doo Tao Village. In war-torn China, she managed to get her daughters out of the country. Buying a paper name was one route, and that became her second name. She would have four others in her lifetime and the social and political context of those name changes will be at the heart of this piece.

PRODUCER/DIRECTOR: Felicia Lowe is a veteran independent television producer, director, and writer with more than 30 years of production experience. Lowe has taught film production and scriptwriting at San Francisco State University and Stanford University, and is a longstanding member of the board of the Angel Island Immigration Station Foundation. Lowe received an Emmy for Best Cultural Documentary for *Chinatown*, an hour-long piece on the history of one of San Francisco's oldest neighborhoods. Other works include *Carved in Silence* which reveals the experiences of Chinese immigrants detained on Angel Island Immigration Station, and *China: Land of My Father* which documents Lowe's journey to China to meet her paternal grandfather for the first time. Her works have been broadcast on PBS and abroad, and shown in film festivals, museums, and classrooms across the

country. Her latest project-in-progress is *Chinese Couplet*, which was inspired by the discovery that her maternal grandfather lived and worked in Cuba from 1920-1935.

The Chinese in Hollywood Project (working title)
Presented by Arthur Dong
Introduction: Robert A. Corrigan
Moderator: Jenny Lau
Session 4G
Friday, 3:15-4:30   Sakura A

SYNOPSIS: This latest documentary from the producer of *Forbidden City, U.S.A.*, and *Sewing Woman*, traces the cultural and social history of the Chinese in American Hollywood feature films, from the early 1900s to present day. Interviews combined with film clips show how Hollywood included and represented the Chinese to detail a neglected but fascinating chapter of movie history.

PRODUCER/DIRECTOR: Oscar-nominated and three-time Sundance award-winning filmmaker Arthur Dong produced the seminal Chinese American documentaries, *Forbidden City, USA* and *Sewing Woman*. During the past twenty years, Dong's work has received over 80 American and international film awards, including the Peabody Award, and has been supported by fellowships from the National Endowment for Arts and both the Guggenheim and Rockefeller Foundations. Recognition for his contributions to the Asian American community include: the Community Visibility Award from the Asian Pacific Gays and Friends, the James Wong Howe Media Award from the Association of Asian Pacific Artists, the Steve Tatsukawa Award from Visual Communications, the Asian American Media Award from Asian CineVision, and the Historian Award from the Chinese Historical Society of America. A graduate of the Film Department at San Francisco State University and the American Film Institute's Center for Advanced Film and Television Studies, Dong currently serves on the Board of Governors at the Academy of Motion Picture Arts and Sciences and represents the Documentary Branch.

Chinese American Historical Society, Museum, and Organization Caucus

Lorraine Dong, PhD and Jeannie Woo, Moderators

A total of eighteen Chinese American historical societies, museums, and history organizations attended the caucus. Agenda items included issues concerning historical preservation, fundraising, grant writing, and how to make the town and gown connection. Two letters were presented for caucus deliberation and signing. (These letters were mailed to boards of the organizations weeks in advance before the conference.) After some sharing of concerns, representatives from twelve of the organizations signed the joint letter to preserve the Alien Files; it was addressed to US Archivist Allen Weinstein of the National Archives and Records Administration. Representatives from only three organizations signed the joint letter to Roger I. Payne of the US Board of Geographic Names to remove the name of "Chinaman's Arch" in Utah and to replace it with "Chinese Arch." CHSA was responsible for mailing these letters.

The idea of developing an umbrella structure for all the organizations was discussed. Twelve representatives signed up to be part of a "cyberspace" committee to continue the discussion. CHSA Executive Director Sue Lee would initiate the first email. This committee was to determine also which organization would host the next Chinese American Studies conference. At the time, there were four possibilities: Chicago, Los Angeles, New York, and Vancouver.

CAUCUS PARTICIPANTS

Angel Island Immigration Station Foundation (1976)
天使島移民拘留所紀念基金會

Angel Island Immigration Station Foundation (AIISF) was founded by community members and descendants of detainees who were committed to preserving the deteriorating immigration station barracks. AIISF is leading the effort to preserve, restore, and interpret the Angel Island Immigration Station, a National Historic landmark, and is promoting educational activities for a greater understanding of Pacific Coast immigration and its role in shaping America's past, present, and future.

Chicago Chinese American Historical Society (2004)
芝城華人歷史學會

The Chicago Chinese American Historical Society is an organization devoted solely to the study and teaching of Chinese American community history in Chicago and the Midwest.

Chinatown Historical Society of Honolulu (1991)

The Chinatown Historical Society of Honolulu acquires, records, and distributes information about Honolulu's Chinatown. Its primary activity is a weekly walking tour under license with the Chinese Chamber of Commerce and customized tours by arrangement. The Society also publishes articles, makes oral presentations, and is the exclusive distributors of a DVD entitled *Hawaii's Chinatown*.

Chinese American Council of Sacramento (1988)
華美協進會

The Chinese American Council of Sacramento (CACS) was founded in 1988 by a group of prominent Chinese American community activists. The organization was spearheaded by famous restauranteur Frank Fat. CACS was to be a voice for the Chinese in Sacramento regarding social, cultural, and political issues. It was one of the first organizations of its kind in the Capital. Today, CACS is also heavily involved in historical preservation and charities for underprivileged children.

Chinese American Museum (1986) 華美博物館

The mission of the Chinese American Museum (CAM) is to foster a deeper understanding and appreciation of America's diverse heritage by researching, preserving, and sharing the history, rich cultural legacy, and continuing contributions of Chinese Americans. CAM is located in the historic Garnier Building at the El Pueblo de Los Angeles Historical Monument in downtown Los Angeles. Through exhibitions, educational programs, public programs, and publications, the Museum illuminates the challenges and achievements of Chinese Americans, from the earliest pioneers to the newest immigrants.

Chinese-American Museum of Chicago (2002)
華埠博物館基金會

A non-profit organization founded in February 2002, the Chinatown Museum Foundation's mission is to establish and maintain a museum in Chicago's Chinatown for the purpose of promoting exhibitions, education, and research related to Chinese America culture and history in the Midwestern United States. The Foundation's museum, the Chinese-America Museum of Chicago, recently opened to the public on May 21, 2005. It is an all-volunteer based organization.

Chinese American Museum of Northern California (2005)

The Chinese American Museum of Northern California is a new museum that will be opening on Bomb Day (the second day of the second lunar month) in 2006. It is located in Marysville, the third most important Chinatown in early California history. Marysville is the only Chinatown in Northern California that has survived from the Gold Rush era; it has an active Chinese temple, three Chinese associations, the oldest Chinese festival in America, and soon a Chinese American museum. The museum will have research facilities and focus on the history of small town Chinatowns. It will be located in the heart of Marysville Chinatown on the corner of 1st and C Streets in a Gold Rush building built in 1858.

Chinese-Australian Historical Association Inc. (2002)

The Organization is located in Brisbane, Queensland and is one of several Chinese Historical Societies in Australia. All the Societies are State based and generally have similar aims and objectives in fostering and promoting an interest in documenting the history of the Chinese in Australia. Our mission is "To promote and foster and interest and awareness of the history, heritage, and culture of the Chinese in Queensland."

Chinese Canadian Historical Society of British Columbia (2004) 加華歷史協會

A broadly-based membership society with educational goals, the Chinese Canadian Historical Society of British Columbia's main objective is to bring out the untold history of ethnic Chinese within the history of British Columbia through document preservation, research, family and oral history promotion, public education programs, an active website, and other initiatives.

Chinese Historical and Cultural Project of Santa Clara County (1987) 中華歷史文物協會

The Chinese Historical and Cultural Project (CHCP) of Santa Clara County began by replicating the original temple of San Jose Chinatown as a historical museum. CHCP now holds a Chinese Summer Festival at the site, has developed an educational curriculum, and provides a traveling exhibit. Other outreach includes scholarships and sponsorships of artists, performers, authors, and film festivals. Nearing its 20th anniversary, CHCP stays committed to its mission of educating, promoting, and preserving the history and culture of Chinese Americans.

Chinese Historical Society of America (1963)
美國華人歷史學會

Founded in 1963, the Chinese Historical Society of America (CHSA) is the oldest and largest organization in the country dedicated to the documentation, study, and preservation of Chinese American history and culture. CHSA operates a Museum and Learning Center located in the landmark Julia Morgan-designed Chinatown YWCA building. Through exhibitions, publications, collections, and public programming, CHSA promotes the contributions of Chinese Americans and preserves the legacy of Chinese America.

Chinese Historical Society of New England (1992)
紐英崙華人歷史學會

The Chinese Historical Society of New England (CHSNE) is a non-profit organization established in 1992 to document, preserve, and promote the history and legacy of Chinese immigration in New England. Projects and activities include oral histories, collection and preservation of historical artifacts, developing an interactive archive, restoration of Mt. Hope Chinese Burial Grounds, and Chinese historic tours.

Chinese Historical Society of Southern California (1975)
南加州華人歷史學會

The Chinese Historical Society of Southern California (CHSSC) brings people together to plan and implement programs to pursue, preserve, and communicate the important history and historical role of Chinese and Chinese Americans in Southern California.

Hawaii Chinese History Center (1970)

The Hawaii Chinese History Center chronicles the life and times of Hawai'i's elder Chinese residents. The Center has published books and recorded the story of these elders. Their current projects include a film for public television about the Chinese community on the island of Hawai'i and another major film on the exodus of foreign residents from Shanghai in the early 1900s.

Museum of Chinese in the Americas (1980)
美洲華人博物館

The Museum of Chinese in the Americas (MoCA) is the first full-time, professionally staffed museum dedicated to reclaiming, preserving, and interpreting the history and culture of the Chinese and their descendants in the Western Hemisphere. Through an ongoing and historical dialogue that shapes MoCA's collections, programs, and exhibitions, people of all backgrounds are able to explore the diversity and complexity of our history and culture, while gaining unique access to the images, papers, oral histories, and artifacts which document the story.

San Diego Chinese Historical Society and Museum (1986)
聖地牙哥中華歷史博物館協會
The San Diego Chinese Historical Museum was a long-time goal of the Chinese Historical Society of San Diego and Baja California. After the old Chinese Mission was moved and renovated, the Museum was dedicated in January of 1996 on a site in historic Chinatown. The Museum and its garden became a cultural and historic center of the Asian Pacific Historic District of San Diego. In May of 2000, the Historical Society Board and Museum Trustees merged, and the new entity became the San Diego Chinese Historical Society and Museum. The ground floor of a new condo across the street was purchased and by October 2004 a new museum extension was opened.

Ventura County Chinese American Historical Society (2000)
加州范杜拉郡華美歷史學會
The Ventura County Chinese American Historical Society was founded under the auspices of the Ventura County Chinese American Association. The Society's mission is to perform original research, preserve, publish, and teach the history and experiences of the Chinese Americans in Ventura County. It also coordinates with city, county, and state government offices and officials in matters relating to the preservation, communication, and recognition of the Chinese American heritage.

Yuba Historical Society (1997)
The Yuba Historical Society exists to advance historical education, preservation, and development in and around Yuba County, California. The Society works to preserve the community's Chinese heritage by assisting in the restoration of Marysville's Chinese Temple and by producing a documentary film that preserves stories from Marysville's unique Chinese heritage.

Lead Sponsors

Chinese Historical Society of America

Established in 1963, the Chinese Historical Society of America is the oldest and largest not-for-profit organization dedicated to fostering an understanding of the Chinese experience in the United States through research, documentation, interpretation, and education. CHSA produces original programs, events, and publications on Chinese American history, including the annual journal, *Chinese America: History and Perspectives*.

The CHSA Museum and Learning Center is located at 965 Clay Street in the historic landmark Julia Morgan Chinatown YWCA building. The museum celebrates the contributions made by Chinese Americans through artifacts, photographs, and immigration documents tracing the history of the Chinese in America.

Mission Statement
- Establish, maintain, and operate a scientific, literary, and educational organization;
- Study, record, acquire, and preserve all suitable artifacts and such cultural items as manuscripts, books, and works of art or their facsimiles which have bearing on the history of the Chinese living in the United States of America;
- Establish a headquarter to enable the display of such items as are acquired;
- Issue publicity and papers pertaining to the findings of the Society; and
- Promote the contributions the Chinese have made to the United States of America.

Asian American Studies Department
College of Ethnic Studies
San Francisco State University

Asian American Studies (AAS) Department, the largest of four departments in the College of Ethnic Studies at San Francisco State University, was established in Fall 1969 as a result of the 1968 Third World Student Strike. The Department currently consists of the following Asian American ethnic units: Chinese, Filipino, Japanese, Korean, Vietnamese, and Asian of Mixed Heritage. It is a full service academic unit that offers a comprehensive program of study on the Asian American experience with a commitment to serving the University, its students, and the Asian American communities. In 1994, the Department was recognized as an "exemplary" program by the Asian Pacific American Education Advisory Committee of the CSU Chancellor's Office.

At present, Asian American Studies Department offers 50 sections of classes taught by a faculty of 25-30 to approximately 2,000 students each semester. Students may take AAS courses for a baccalaureate major, which was established in 1997. A master's degree program was approved by the California State University Chancellor's Office in 1999, and began its first semester in the fall of 2000.

SPONSORS, DONORS, SUPPORTERS, AND VOLUNTEERS

CYPRESS SPONSORS

California State University, Chancellor's Office,
Dr. Charles B. Reed
San Francisco State University, President's Office,
Dr. Robert A. Corrigan
Him Mark and Laura Lai
Lawrence Choy Lowe Memorial Fund
Kou Ping and Connie Young Yu

SANDALWOOD SPONSORS

Paul and Emma Woo Louie
New York Life Insurance Company
PG&E (Pacific Gas & Electric Company)
Poon Foundation
San Francisco State University,
College of Ethnic Studies, Dean's Office,
Dr. Kenneth P. Monteiro

BAMBOO SPONSORS

Ernest Chann
Henry Chin Family
Chao Suet Foundation
Chinese Community Health Care Association
Chinese Community Health Plan
Philip P. and Sarah Choy
East West Bank
United Commercial Bank
Edward Leong Way, PhD

BANQUET LONGEVITY SPONSORS

Stan and Irene Poon Andersen
Burr, Pilger & Mayer, LLP
CST Associates, LLC
Bruce Chin
Philip P. and Sarah Choy
Gee Family Foundation
Thomas Hart, Shorenstein Company
Sue Lee and Noel Chun
Rolland C. Lowe, MD and Kathy Lowe
Lawrence and Gorretti Lui, Cresleigh Management Inc.
Ezra Mersey, Jackson Pacific Ventures
James Nunemacher, Vanguard Properties
Poon Foundation
Jane K. Quon, Edward L. Quon, and Pearl Lee Quong
San Francisco State University, Asian American Studies
Department
Fred Synder, David Allen Trust
Annie Soo
Sterling Bank
Tom Do Hing Foundation
Ann Leong Williams

BIRTHDAY DONORS IN HONOR OF PHILIP P. CHOY AND HIM MARK LAI

Ruth Chan
Thomas and Dorothy Chin
Daisy and Edmund Chong
Lily Chow
Ida Chow
George and Claire Fung
Albert and Edith Gong
Rosalynde Jan
Virginia and Catherine Jeong
Calvin and Helen Lang
Willard and Ida Lee
Karen Lew and David Furmston
Eva Lowe
Alan and Annamarie Louie
Hazel Louie
Benton and Betty Ng
Clifford and Shirley Poon, for Cathay Club
Blossom Strong
Annie Soo
Dai Sue and Victoria Low
Anna Wong
Doris Wong
Bea and Chaney Wong
Puanani Woo
Blossom and Arthur Yim

ADDITIONAL DONORS

Eileen Boussina
Nersi Boussina
Donald Chan
Jeffery Paul Chan
Joyce M. Chan
Ruth Chan
Bruce Chin
Florence Chin
Thomas and Dorothy Chin

Willard Chin
Ida Chow
Arthur Chung
Wei Ming Dariotis, PhD
Lorraine Dong, PhD
George and Claire Fung
Robert A. Fung, Esq.
Forrest Gok
Daniel P. Gonzales, JD
Marlon K. Hom, PhD
Madeline Y. Hsu, PhD
Virginia Jeong
Russell Jeung, PhD
Calvin and Helen Lang
James Yuan Li
Jeanine Lim and Greg Chan
Alexander Lock
Kenneth Louie, CPA
Galin Luk, Esq. and Jinny Kim
Eric Mar, Esq.
Benton and Betty Ng
Jadine Nielsen
Eugene Olivo
Dick G. Quock
Leslie Tang-Schilling
David Twoy
Bea and Chaney Wong
Elizabeth Wong
Germaine Wong
Harry N. Woo
Jeannie Woo
Puanani Woo
Godfrey Lim Yan
Arthur and Shirley Yick

IN-KIND DONORS OF GOODS AND SERVICES
Irene Poon Andersen
CYC
Cala Foods (Hyde/California)
Chinese Performing Arts Foundation (David Lei)
Foods Co
Hing Lung Company
The Kroger Company
Man-U Imports (Frank Jang)
Pasta Pomodoro (Post St.)
Rainbow Grocery
Safeway (Bay, LaPlaya, Taraval, Webster)
San Francisco State University
    Art Department
    Asian American Studies Department
    Associated Students Inc.
    College of Creative Arts
    College of Ethnic Studies
    Instructionally Related Activities Fund
    (Associated Students Inc.)
    Office of Public Affairs and Publications
    Student Outreach Services
Sugar Bowl Bakery
University of California at Berkeley,
    Asian American Studies Program
Yee's Restaurant

CONFERENCE VOLUNTEERS
Irene Poon Andersen
Christopher Banez
Joyce M. Chan
Doni Cho
Sarah Choy
Burke Fong
Amy Hanamoto
Laureen D. Hom
Laura Lai
Karen Lam
Janice Lau
Warren Lee
Shirley Lee Poo
Dorothy Leong
Karenina Lien
Sylvia Louie
Tony Luong
Mamie Moy
Maybelle Ng
Franklin Ng
Florence Owyang
Allyn Quan
Ruth Stevenson
Suzanna Szeto
Richard Tom
Anna Wong
Doris Wong
Jessie Yip
and
the 70+ students from SFSU's Asian American Studies classes
under the leadership of **Lori Koizumi** and **Patrick Toy**

INDEX OF CONFERENCE PARTICIPANTS

Lee, Michelle – Youth Speaks 3K

Lee, Murray K. 李國光 – Curator, San Diego Chinese Historical Society and Museum 6C, 8F

Lee, Otto 李州曉, JD – Sunnyvale City Councilmember; Managing Attorney, Intellectual Property Law Group LLP 8E

Lee, Sue 李閏屏 – Executive Director, Chinese Historical Society of America; President, San Francisco City Planning Commission 4F, 8F

Leo, Denise 廖詠儀 – Graduate Student, San Francisco State University, Dept. of Counseling; Coach, George Washington High School, San Francisco 5H

Leong, Evan J. 梁志輝 – Filmmaker 5H, 6I

Leong, Karen J. 梁春蘭, PhD – Associate Professor of Women's Studies and Affiliate Faculty Member of Asian Pacific American Studies, African and African American Studies, and History, Arizona State University 8A

Letoto, Diane – Graduate Student, University of Hawaii, Political Science Dept. 5I

Leung, Catherine 梁劉潔鑾 – Principal, Nam Kue School, San Francisco 7C

Leung, Joseph 梁建鋒 – Chief Editor, *Sing Tao Daily News*, Western Edition 8C

Leung, L. Eric 梁禮崇, MD – President, Chinese Community Health Care Association 9D

Leung, Puichee 梁培熾 – Vice Principal, Cumberland Chinese High School, San Francisco; Adjunct Professor, San Francisco State University, Asian American Studies Dept. 7C

Lew, Gordon 劉池光 – Retired Journalist; Instructor and Chair, City College of San Francisco, Chinese Studies Dept. 8C

Lew, Jennie F. 劉慧儀 – Producer/Director 7H

Li, Jinzhao 李今朝 – Visiting Assistant Professor, Oberlin College, Sociology and Comparative American Studies 5I

Li, Robin 李悅彬 – Graduate Student, University of Michigan, American Culture Program 9I

Li, Wei 李唯, PhD – Associate Professor of Asian Pacific American Studies and Affiliate Faculty Member of Geography, School of Justice and Social Inquiry, Center for Asian Studies, and Women' Studies, Arizona State University 4I

Lien, Pei-te 連培德, PhD – Associate Professor, University of Utah, Political Science and Ethnic Studies Program 4C

Lim, Genny 林小琴 – Poet-Vocalist, Performer, Director, Playwright, Educator; New College of California Faculty Member 3D

Lim, Imogene 林慕珍 – Anthropologist, Malaspina University College, British Columbia, Canada, Dept. of Anthropology; Chinese Canadian Historical Society of British Columbia 3H

Lim, Victor Wai Ho 林偉浩 – Student, University of California, Berkeley, Asian American Studies and Asian Studies 2H

Lin, David 林承龍 – Student, George Washington High School, San Francisco 2D

Liu, Anna 廖免詩 – Student, Lowell High School, San Francisco 2D

Liu, Jiyang 劉吉洋 – Student, Phillip and Sala Burton Academic High School 2J

Liu, Roger K.S. 廖劍生 – President, Hawaii Chinese History Center 5I, 8F

Liu, Wan 劉碗, PhD – Assistant Professor, Stanford University, Dept. of Asian Languages 6A

Liu, Ziyi 劉子毅 – Editor-in-Chief, *Literati Magazine* 3C

Lo, Ch'ingche 羅青哲 – Artist, Poet; Professor, Fu Jen University, Taiwan, Dept. of Chinese 6E

Lo, Shauna 羅薾 – Assistant Director, Institute for Asian American Studies, University of Massachusetts, Boston; Board Member, Chinese Historical Society of New England 9E

Locke, Gary 駱家輝 – Former Governor of the State of Washington; Partner, Davis Wright Tremaine LLP; Conference Banquet Keynote Speaker

Loos, Richard – CEO, Chinese Community Health Plan 9D

Louie, Emma Woo 胡友愛 – Independent Researcher 2I

Louie, James 雷純泉 – Silver Bay Conference Alumnus 7A

Louie, Kenneth 雷波濤, CPA – Board Member, Chinese Historical Society of America 5G

Louie, Marisa 雷妙玲 – Exhibitions Coordinator, Chinese Historical Society of America 5H

Louie, Nguyen 雷女英 – In Search of Roots Alumna 5H

Louie, Paul 雷純岡 – Former Board Secretary, Chinese Historical Society of America; Co-founder, Chinese Historical Society of Southern California 3I, 4H, 7A

Louie, Ruby Ling 雷林娥柳, PhD – Librarian; Chinese Historical Society of Southern California; Founding President, Friends of the Chinatown Library, Los Angeles 3I

Louie, Sylvia Joe 雷周蘇菲 – Retired Elementary School Teacher 4H

Low, Jeanie W. Chooey 黃育貞 – Author and Independent Researcher 7H

Lowe, Alice 楊阮福瓊 – Co-chair, Square and Circle Club History Committee 6H

Lowe, Felicia 劉詠嫦 – Producer/Director, Lowedown Productions 3G, 7D

Lowe, Russ 劉紹漢 – Office Director, Office of US Senator Dianne Feinstein 8E

Lowe, William 王達雄 – 2H

Lu, Di Yin 陸蒂因 – Independent Researcher; Market Research Specialist, Oracle Corporation 6J

Lu Hong 呂紅 – Chinese Literature and Art Association in America 3C

Lui, Mary Ting Yi 雷婷儀, PhD – Assistant Professor, Yale University, American Studies Program 8B

Luis, Adriel – Youth Speaks 3K

Luk Galin 陸嘉賢, Esq. – Associate Litigation Attorney, Cox, Wootton, Griffin, Hansen and Poulos, LLP; Board Member, Chinese Historical Society of America 3A, 4A

Lum, Rodney M., OD – President, Chinese Historical and Cultural Project of Santa Clara County 4D, 8F

Ly, Monica "Wayie" 李慧儀 – Teacher 5H

Ma, Merit H. 馬希雯 – 9A

Mah, Simon – Filmmaker, D24 Films 7D

Mah, Theresa J. 馬靜儀, PhD – Assistant Professor, Bowling Green State University, Dept. of Ethnic Studies 1A

Mak, Sonia 麥莊雅 – Assistant Curator, Chinese American Museum, Los Angeles 5C

Mann, Joan L. 馬玉 – Graduate Student, University of Nevada, Las Vegas 7E

Mar, Eric 馬兆光, Esq. – President, San Francisco Board of Education; Lecturer, San Francisco State University, Asian American Studies Dept. 1F, 6I, 8H

Mar, Joyce 韋重生 – Independent Researcher, Editor, Writer 5E

Mar, Richard – Retiree; Chung Mei/Ming Quong Alumnus 9H

Mar, Wing 馬榮賢, MD – Retired Physician; Board Member, Chinese Historical Society of Southern California 5E, 8F

Mark, Gregory 余競存, PhD – Chair, California State University, Sacramento, Dept. of Ethnic Studies 5J, 6B, 7B

Matsuoka, Pamela – Distribution Director, National Asian American Telecommunications Association (NAATA) 1G

McClain, Charles J., Jr., PhD, JD – Vice Chair, Jurisprudence and Social Policy Program, University of California, Berkeley School of Law 8I

McGowan, Barry, PhD – Visiting Fellow, Australian National University, School of Archaeology and Anthropology; Researcher, Australian Dictionary of Biography 5A

Mok, Harry 莫卓基 – News Producer, ContraCostaTimes.com; Contributing Editor, *Hyphen Magazine* 5H

Moon, Krystyn Rozalia, PhD – Assistant Professor, Georgia State University, Dept. of History 6J, 7B

Moy, Eugene 梅元宇 – Chinese Historical Society of Southern California 5E

Moy, Gene 梅忠毅 – President, Chicago Chinese American Historical Society 6C, 8F

Moy, Mamie 雷美美 – Editorial Staff, *East Wind Magazine* 4H

Moy, Wood 梅錦活 – Editorial Staff, *East Wind Magazine* 4H

Muir, John – Curator, San Francisco Maritime National Historical Park 6C

Naruta, Anna 安娜.納魯塔 – Graduate Student, University of California, Berkeley, Historical Archaeology; Board Member, Chinese Historical Society of America 2C, 5C, 6I

Nealand, Daniel – Regional Archives Director, National Archives and Records Administration-Pacific Region 1I, 7H

Ng, Franklin 吳兆麟, PhD – Professor, Dept. of Anthropology and Coordinator, Asian American Studies Program, California State University, Fresno 5I

Ng, Jeffrey 伍世昌 – Student, Abraham Lincoln High School, San Francisco 2D

Ng, Laura 伍穎華 – Student, University of California, San Diego, Anthropology Dept. 9C

Ng, Stella 吳秀雯 – Employment Advocate, Center for Asian American Advocacy, Chinese for Affirmative Action 2A

Ngai, Mae M. 艾明如, PhD – Associate Professor, University of Chicago, Dept. of History 3B

Nguyen, Ly – Executive Director, Kearny Street Workshop 3D

Ong, Bing – 6G

Ow, Jeffrey A. 李偉賢 – Graduate Student, University of California, Berkeley, Dept. of Ethnic Studies; Instructor, City College of San Francisco, Asian American Studies 1C

Owyang, Lucky 歐陽華勝 – Independent Researcher 2I, 5C

Pfaelzer, Jean, PhD – Professor, University of Delaware, Dept. of English 1D

Poon, Raymond N. – President, Chinese-Australian Historical Association, Inc. 2H, 6C, 8F

Reed, Charles B. 葦察理, EdD – Chancellor, California State University; Conference Luncheon Keynote Speaker

Roop, William G. – Consulting Archaeologist, Archaeological Resource Service; Board Member, Chinese Historical Society of America 4D, 6C

Ruan, Calvin Jia Xing 阮家興 – Student, Phillip and Sala Burton Academic High School 2J

Sandoval, George J. – President, West End Productions 5G

Shan, Te-hsing 單德興, PhD – Research Fellow, Institute of European and American Studies, Academia Sinica, Taiwan; Fulbright Visiting Scholar, University of California, Berkeley, Dept. of Ethnic Studies 1H

Shek, Leonard 石樹勳 – Program Coordinator, Chinese Historical Society of America 3K

Siharath, Sandra Sengdara 洗凱欣 – IT Consultant, Mayor's Office of Neighbor Services (MONS) 9A

Sing, Lillian 郭麗蓮 – Retired, San Francisco Superior Court Judge 8E

Smith, Carrie E. – District Archaeologist, Truckee Ranger District, Tahoe National Forest 5A

Soe, Valerie, MFA – Writer, Videomaker; Lecturer, San Francisco State University, Asian American Studies Dept. 7D

Soo, Julie 蘇榮麗 – Staff Counsel, California Department of Insurance; Former Board Member, Chinese Historical Society of America 8E

Soo Hoo, Angela 司徒林慕韶 – Ventura County Chinese American Historical Society 5G

Staley, Jeffrey Lloyd , PhD – Visiting Assistant Professor of Religion, Pacific Lutheran University; Adjunct Professor of Religion, Seattle University 8H

Stevens, Todd M. 石濤, PhD – Consultant, Boston Consulting Group, Los Angeles 8I

Sun, Angela 孫傑, MPH – Director, Chinese Community Health Resource Center 9D

Ta, Minh-Hoa 謝明華, EdD – Director, Asian Pacific American Student Success Center, City College of San Francisco; Assistant Professor, San Francisco State University, Asian American Studies Dept. 9A

Tam, Alice 譚寶儀 – After School Program Coordinator, Sunset Elementary School 1A

Tam, Wai Kit 譚偉傑 – Student, Phillip and Sala Burton Academic High School 2J

Thompson, Wendy Marie – Graduate Student, University of Maryland, Dept. of American Studies; Writer, Filmmaker 5J

Ting, Phil 丁右立 – City and County of San Francisco Assessor-Recorder 1D

Tintiangco-Cubales, Allyson, PhD – Assistant Professor, San Francisco State University, Asian American Studies Dept. 2I

To, Wing-kai 杜榮桂, PhD – Associate Professor of History and Coordinator of Asian Studies Program, Bridgewater State College; Board Member, Chinese Historical Society of New England 9E

Tom, Alex – Campaign Director, Chinese Progressive Association 2A

Tom, Brian L. 譚百樂 – Director, The Chinese American Museum of Northern California 5C, 8F

Tom, Henry 譚德欽 – Consultant, United Nations; Retired US Government Geographer 2I

Torok, John Hayakawa – Graduate Student, University of California, Berkeley, Ethnic Studies 8I, 9I

Tu, Florence 杜堅白 – Administrative Assistant to the Dean, College of Behavioral and Social Sciences, San Francisco State University; SFSU Chinese American Faculty and Staff Association 7H

Urban, Andrew Theodore 本安油 – Graduate Student, University of Minnesota, History Dept. 8H

Vergara, Benito M., Jr., PhD – Assistant Professor, San Francisco State University, Asian American Studies and Anthropology Depts. 7J

Waghorn, Annita – Staff Archaeologist, Sonoma State University, Anthropological Studies Center 2C

Wang, Andy 王智明 – Graduate Student, University of California, Santa Cruz, Dept. of Literature 1D

Wang, Dorothy 王梡– Assistant Professor, Northwestern University, Dept. of English 1H

Wang, Kris 胡宜蘭 – City of Cupertino Council Member 4F

Wang, L. Ling-chi 王靈智 – Professor, University of California, Berkeley, Asian American Studies 2C, 4C

Wang, Wei 王偉 – Student, San Francisco State University 9A

Way, Edward Leong 梁棟林, PhD – Professor Emeritus of Pharmacology, Toxicology, and Pharmaceutical Chemistry, University of California, San Francisco 7A

Wickberg, Edgar 魏安國, PhD – Professor Emeritus of Modern Chinese History, University of British Columbia; Founding President, Chinese Canadian Historical Society of British Columbia 3H

Wilkinson, Willy, MPH – Writer; Public Health Consultant; Health Care Access Project Manager, Transgender Law Center 6D

Williams, Bryn Anderson – Graduate Student, Stanford University, Dept. of Cultural and Social Anthropology 3A

Wong, Adolphus 黃乾坤, MD – Retired Anesthesiologist 2H

Wong, Christina Mei-Yue 黃美瑜 – Policy Advocate, Chinese for Affirmative Action, Center for Asian American Advocacy 1J

Wong, Gerrye 黃瓊香 – Co-founder, Chinese Historical and Cultural Project of Santa Clara County; Chinese Historical Society of America Advisory Board 4D, 8F

Wong, Jade Snow 黃玉雪 – Ceramic Artist, Writer 6E

Wong, K. Scott 黃玉智, PhD – Professor, Williams College, Dept. of History 6B

Wong, Larry 王容倫 – President, Chinese Canadian Historical Society of British Columbia; Curator, Chinese Canadian Military Museum 3H, 8F

Wong, Leonard Kwai Ming 黃貴明 – 5I

Wong, Marie Rose 黃玫瑰, PhD – Associate Professor & Director, Bachelor of Public Affairs Program, Institute of Public Service, Seattle University 1B

Wong, Nga-Wing Anjela 黃雅穎 – Graduate Student, University of Wisconsin-Madison, Dept. of Educational Policy Studies 8H

Wong, Pauline 黃寶蓮 – Museum Educator, Chinese American Museum, Los Angeles; Graduate Student, University of California, Los Angeles, Graduate School of Education and Information Studies 5C

Wong, William 朱華強 – Author, Writer, Independent Social Historian 1C

Wong-Kim, Evaon C. 金王竹蘭, MSW, MPH, PhD – Associate Professor, California State University, East Bay, Dept. of Social Work 7I

Woo, David 胡健倫 – Academic Advisor and Internship Coordinator, Student Support Services, San Francisco State University 4A

Woo, Jeannie 胡美容 – Graduate Student, University of California, Davis, Cultural Studies Program; Lecturer, San Francisco State University, Asian American Studies Dept.; Former Board Secretary, Chinese Historical Society of America 2H, 8F

Woo, Kent J. 胡國立, MSW – Executive Director, NICOS Chinese Health Coalition 4A

Wu, Franklin 吳育庭 – President, Envision Productions, Inc. 8C

Wu, Judy Tzu-Chun 吳宇君, PhD – Associate Professor, Ohio State University, History Dept.; Visiting Associate Professor, University of Chicago, Center for the Study of Race, Politics, and Culture (2005-06) 2B

Wu, Michelle C. 伍超薇– Project Manager, Mayor's Youth Employment and Education Program, Employment Component, CYC 2D

Wyman, Nona Mock 莫金顏 – Chung Mei/Ming Quong Alumna 9H

Yang, Doreen 陳淑嫻 – President, Square and Circle Club 6H

Yang, Joshua 楊旭, PhD – Project Director, University of California, Los Angeles, Center for Health Policy Research 7I

Yao, Sherrie 伍湘仁 – Chinese American International School Parent 5D

Yao, Steven G. 姚錚, PhD – Assistant Professor, Hamilton College, Dept. of English 1H

Yasui, Luna M. 安井瑠奈 – Policy Director, Chinese for Affirmative Action, Center for Asian American Advocacy 2A

Yee, Albert Hoy 余永豈, EdD – Author; Retired Professor 4B

Yee, April M. 余美思 – In Search of Roots Alumna 5H

Yee, Brenda 余金玲, RN, MS – CEO, Chinese Hospital 9D

Yee, Brian 趙庇如 – Graduate Student, University of San Francisco 1I, 5H

Yee, Douglas 余維堂 – President, Chinese American Council of Sacramento 8F

Yee, Hubert V. 余文山 – Graduate Student, San Francisco State University, Asian American Studies Dept.; Project Coordinator, Community Youth Center (CYC) 2J

Yeh, Chiou-Ling 葉秋伶, PhD – Assistant Professor, San Diego State University, Dept. of History 9I

Yeung, Sean 楊文光, MSW – Director, After School Programs, Sunset Beacon Neighborhood Center 1A

Yoo, Grace, PhD – Associate Professor, San Francisco State University, Asian American Studies Dept. 7I

Young, James 楊思德 – Student, San Francisco University High School; Chinese American International School Alumnus 5D

Yu, George 余志誠, MD – Founder and Chair, Ventura County Chinese American Historical Society 5G, 8F

Yu, Henry 余全毅, PhD – Associate Professor, Depts. of History, University of California, Los Angeles and University of British Columbia 3H

Yung, Judy 譚碧芳, PhD – Professor Emerita, University of California, Santa Cruz; Former Board Member, Chinese Historical Society of America 9G

Zhang, Yanchun 張硯春, PhD – Assistant Professor, San Francisco State University, Department of Economics; SFSU Chinese American Faculty and Staff Association 4B

Zhang, Yinglong 張應龍, PhD – Professor, Institute of Overseas Chinese Studies, Ji'nan University, China 4C

Zhao, Sihong 招思虹 – Chinese Literature and Art Association in America 3C

Zheng, Da 鄭達, PhD – Associate Professor, Suffolk University, English Dept. 1H

Zong Ying 宗鷹 – Writer 3C

*The banyan tree is one of nature's
most noble and respected creations.
For the Chinese, the banyan tree
is the core of the village,
representing family, home,
community, and communication.
It was under this banner that we
gathered for the 2005 Chinese
American Studies Conference.*

Guidelines for Manuscript Submission

Chinese America: History and Perspectives is published annually by the Chinese Historical Society of America (CHSA).

The journal invites original contributions on all aspects of Chinese American history and culture. Manuscripts should not exceed five thousand words in length (excluding endnotes) and should follow the format outlined in The Chicago Manual of Style. A CHSA style sheet will be sent upon request. Authors shall forward six copies of initial submittals of manuscripts to be considered for publication. When manuscripts are accepted, authors shall send in two hard copies of the final revised version together with a diskette containing an IBM PC- or Macintosh-compatible file of the manuscript input by a commercial word-processing program (Microsoft Word, WordPerfect, Wordstar). Authors will each be sent a copyedited manuscript for revisions or approval before publication. Upon publication, contributors will receive two complimentary copies of the journal.

Please send manuscripts to:

CHSA H&P Journal
Chinese Historical Society of America
965 Clay Street
San Francisco, CA 94108

Chinese Historical Society of America

Established January 5, 1963

965 Clay St. • San Francisco, CA 94108 • (415) 391-1188

MEMBERSHIP FORM

Please print.

❏ Check here if you added extended address information on back.

NAME _____

ADDRESS _____ CITY_____

STATE _____ ZIP_____ COUNTRY _____

PHONE NUMBER_____

❏ Renewal Membership   ❏ New Membership

CHSA is a not-for-profit organization as described in Section 501(c)(3) of the Internal Service Code (Federal Tax ID 94-6122446). Membership and donations are **tax-deductible** to the full extent allowed by law. Membership expires December 31. Persons who join after September 30 are automatically members until December 31 of the *following* year. Please make checks payable to CHSA and send with this form to the above address.

❏ Regular (*individual*) . . . .$50   ❏ Institution (*group*) $100

❏ Senior (*age 60+*) . . . .$30   ❏ Contributing $100

❏ Student (*now enrolled*) . . . .$30   ❏ Sponsor $250

❏ Family . . . .$60   ❏ Patron $500

❏ International (*outside USA*) . . . . .$60   ❏ President's Circle . . . . . .over $1000

❏ Donation . . . . $ _____

❏ I want to help with (*please circle*): Docents • Programs • Field Trips • Publications • Inventory • Special Events • Office Help •

Other (*please specify*) _____

❏ I want to give (*please circle*): a gift membership to • a donation in memory of • a donation in honor of:

NAME _____

ADDRESS _____ CITY_____

STATE _____ ZIP_____ COUNTRY _____

CHSA will send a card to the honored or remembered or his/her family informing them of your gift.